Outline of Equity and Trusts

To my Father
Captain William Brookes Evans

TAWEL HUN, BREUDDWYDION MELYS

PAN DDAW'R CYNLLYN MAITH I BEN

Outline of Equity and Trusts

Third Edition

Michael Evans

BA (Hons), LLM (Syd), LLM (Hons) (Cantab)

Barrister of the Supreme Court of New South Wales and of the High Court of Australia

Senior Lecturer, Faculty of Law and Legal Practice, University of Technology, Sydney

Butterworths

Sydney — Adelaide — Brisbane — Canberra
Melbourne — Perth
1996

AUSTRALIA	BUTTERWORTHS 271-273 Lane Cove Road, North Ryde 2113
	111 Gawler Place, Adelaide 5000
	King George Tower, 71 Adelaide Street, Brisbane 4000
	53-55 Northbourne Avenue, Canberra 2601
	461 Bourke Street, Melbourne 3000
	178 St Georges Terrace, Perth 6000
	On the Internet at: www.butterworths.com.au
CANADA	BUTTERWORTHS CANADA LTD Toronto and Vancouver
IRELAND	BUTTERWORTH (IRELAND) LTD Dublin
FRANCE	EDITIONS DU JURIS-CLASSEUR Paris
HONG KONG	BUTTERWORTHS ASIA
MALAYSIA	MALAYAN LAW JOURNAL SDN BHD Kuala Lumpur
NEW ZEALAND	BUTTERWORTHS OF NEW ZEALAND LTD Wellington and Auckland
SINGAPORE	BUTTERWORTHS ASIA Singapore
SOUTH AFRICA	BUTTERWORTH PUBLISHERS (PTY) LTD Durban
UNITED KINGDOM	BUTTERWORTH & CO (PUBLISHERS) LTD London and Edinburgh
USA	MICHIE Charlottesville, Virginia

National Library of Australia Cataloguing-in-Publication entry

Evans, Michael.
  Outline of equity and trusts.

  3rd ed.
  Includes index.
  ISBN 0 409 31138 3 (pbk.).

  1. Equity — Australia. 2. Trusts and trustees — Australia. I. Title.

346.94004

Foreword to the First Edition

This magistral work demonstrates two points. First, it shows the inestimable benefit of presenting Equity to students as an identifiable body of law unified by principle to complement the common law. Secondly, it shows that when so presented, the range and depth of equitable doctrine displays as its underlying concept an ethical quality which ensures its enduring relevance.

For me, the strength of this treatise lies in the author's vigorous insistence that rules and remedies in their contemporary form be justified by tracing them back to their conceptual foundations derived from the grounds for intervention applied by the Chancellors. It is stimulating to find in the text a number of occasions where the author, not satisfied with the provenance suggested by others for some rule or line of authority, argues in a principled manner his own explanation. It is similarly refreshing to find the author prepared to voice a commonsense dissatisfaction with the present state of authority on several topics and to propound forthrightly and constructively his own view.

The second half of this century has seen a resurgence in Equity which continues apace. This has involved the re-working of established rules to adapt them to novel social and commercial conditions. This process has produced quite profound analysis and refinement of fundamental equitable doctrine, notably in the High Court of Australia in such decisions as *Commercial Bank of Australia Ltd v Amadio* (1983) 151 CLR 447 and *Muschinski v Dodds* (1985) 160 CLR 583. These developments in turn lead to the need in teaching the law for a treatment of the subject capturing the essence of its various aspects without the wealth of discursive detail provided for equity practitioners in the classic texts of *Equity Doctrines & Remedies* by Messrs Meagher, Gummow and Lehane and *Jacobs' Law of Trusts* by Meagher and Gummow, or the abundance of quotation offered by that veritable goldmine, *Cases and Materials on Equity and Trusts* by Heydon, Gummow and Austin. Mr Evans succeeds admirably, satisfying this need with a text which will surely whet the appetite of every serious reader.

J B Kearney
Judges' Chambers
Supreme Court, Sydney

Contents

Preface to the Third Edition

In the preface to the first and second editions of this book I wrote that Equity and Trusts is a necessarily large subject, and difficult in parts for the novice. That still remains the case. But it is also the case that a mastery of this subject still marks a significant stage in the progression from student to practitioner. It is hoped that this new edition will make that progress easier, and perhaps even enjoyable, by providing a concise but comprehensive discussion of the principles of Equity and Trusts.

Equity is, of course, more than just a component in the education of the lawyer. It is a body of principles which impose justice and fairness within a larger legal framework in which those fundamental notions can easily be lost. That is not to say that equity is simply concerned to relieve against unfairness at large. It relies on principle and precedent and the availability of equitable relief in any given case depends upon the subtlety of its doctrines and, to some extent, the skill of the practitioner arguing for an 'equitable' solution. As Deane J said in the landmark case of *Muschinski v Dodds* (1985) 160 CLR 583 at 616, having rejected the proposition that equity amounts to a judicial licence to do what is 'fair' in the circumstances of any case, 'that is not to say that general notions of fairness and justice have become irrelevant to the content and application of equity. They remain relevant to the traditional equitable notion of unconscionable conduct which persists as an operative component of some fundamental rules or principles of modern equity'. The law student concerned with some perceived detachment between so-called black letter law and basic concepts of justice should study the doctrines of equity closely. He or she will find a system which provides remedies for those who suffer from sharp practice, which helps the weak when oppressed by the strong and which insists on each case being considered on its merits, with due regard for questions of conscience and good faith.

Deane J's reference to unconscionable conduct in *Muschinski v Dodds* also states the major theme in the development of modern equity in Australia. With that decision and a number since, particularly *Waltons Stores (Interstate) Ltd v Maher* (1988) 164 CLR 387 (in the field of estoppel) and *Stern v Macarthur* (1985) 165 CLR 489 (in the law of forfeiture), the High Court has demonstrated a willingness to recognise unconscionable conduct as a touchstone of equitable principle, and as a broad foundation justifying equitable intervention in a wide range of cases. At the same time, in a line of cases which have now culminated in *David Securities Pty Ltd v Commonwealth Bank* (1992) 109 ALR 57, the High Court has identified restitution or unjust enrichment as the principle underlying a range of common law doctrines, particularly those previously described as quasi-contract and mistake. The working out of these seemingly parallel notions, unconscionable retention of benefit in equity and unjust enrichment in the common law, provide the challenge for lawyers coming into practice in the last years of this century.

In some areas of equity there have been significant changes since the second edition. The law of estoppel has developed since *Waltons v Maher* with the doctrine established by the High Court with that case finding wider application in cases such as *W v G* (SC(NSW), Hodgson J, 2 February 1996, unreported). The law as it concerns trusts for illegal purposes has been reworked by the High Court in *Nelson v Nelson* (1995) 132 ALR 133. In other sections the changes have been more in the nature of elaboration and clarification, building on the leading cases handed down by the High Court in the late 1980s.

Butterworths have been kind enough to allow me more space in this third edition and, consistent with Parkinson's second law, the work has happily expanded to fill the space available.

I must give special thanks to my Commissioning Editor, Penelope Brandon for her professionalism and patience. I must also thank Sophie Timmins for her work in completing the manuscript, and, particularly, for her work in updating the Index.

As with the second edition I have endeavoured to avoid giving offence to those who might see in my grammar a preference for one gender over the other two. The problem still lies in pronouns. In the indeterminate third person singular it is difficult to avoid using 'he' in the subjective, 'him' in the objective, and 'his' in the possessive. The alternatives are not entirely satisfactory. 'They', 'them' and 'theirs' defies the laws of mathematics as much as grammar. 'He or she', 'him or her' and 'his or hers' provide an option, but they also lengthen sentences. In some cases 'it' is an appropriate alternative, and has been used, especially when talking about trustees in the third person singular, as many are corporations and inevitably neuter. Some sentences have been recast in a neutral or passive form to avoid the difficulty, but not every passage was susceptible to that solution. I have avoided the temptation to write passages in French to escape criticism.

I have stated the law as it was available to me on 14 August 1996.

Michael Evans
Windeyer Chambers
Sydney

Abbreviations

MG&L	RP Meagher, WMC Gummow & JRF Lehane, *Equity: Doctrines and Remedies*, 3rd ed, Butterworths, Sydney, 1992.
Jacobs'	RP Meagher & WMC Gummow, *Jacobs' Law of Trusts in Australia*, 5th ed, Butterworths, Sydney, 1986.
Ford & Lee	HAJ Ford & WA Lee, *Principles of the Law of Trusts*, 2nd ed, Law Book Co, Sydney, 1989.
HG&A	JD Heydon, WMC Gummow & RP Austin, *Equity & Trusts: Cases and Materials*, 4th ed, Butterworths, 1993.
Pettit	PH Pettit, *Equity and the Law of Trusts*, 6th ed, Butterworths, London, 1984.
Goff & Jones	Sir R Goff and G Jones, *The Law of Restitution*, 3rd ed, Butterworths, London, 1990.

Table of Cases

Table of Statutes

Chapter One

The Nature of Equity

1–1 The History of Equity

[1.1] Medieval origins. Equity can be described as that body of law developed by the Court of Chancery prior to 1873.[1] Of course, equity has been modified and expanded since 1873 by courts exercising an equitable jurisdiction and any such description of equity must take note of those developments. This description suggests that equity can be reduced to a set of numbered rules. The principles of equity can be presented in that way, and to some extent, this book ventures such an attempt. But equity is better understood as a jurisdiction, rather than just a body of rules. When seen as a jurisdiction, equity operates as a forum in which certain types of claims will be heard and certain forms of relief granted. In hearing those claims and deciding whether to award any such relief a court of equity will be guided by the principles discussed below. Many of those principles give the court some discretion in deciding whether to grant the relief sought or otherwise to apply some given rule. In such cases much will rest on the facts and merits of the case in question. Cases will often turn on questions such as whether someone has acted in good conscience, or in good faith (and they are not the same thing). That will depend upon the facts as proven and, to some extent, upon the skill with which the argument is put. That again will often turn on the depth of understanding possessed by the advocate of the principles which operate in the case, their origin, meaning and scope.

[1.2] To understand modern equity properly it is necessary to have some grasp of the history of the Court of Chancery prior to 1873 and of the origins of its equitable jurisdiction. The common law system emerged in the twelfth century with the King's judges hearing particular cases brought before them by special writs — a process which was refined in the thirteenth and fourteenth centuries. The common law, however, was necessarily limited by its insistence that matters coming before the King's justices should fall into one of the recognised forms of action. Even for cases which could be fitted into one of those recognised claims the inflexible procedures surrounding the common law writs made justice an elusive goal. The form of action prescribed every aspect of the case, from originating process to procedure to final relief. For those excluded from the common law, or simply disappointed or frustrated by it, the obvious avenue was to petition the King to provide justice. Such petitions became increasingly popular as the common law procedures settled into a rigid form. At first these petitions, or bills, were dealt with by the King's council but in the fourteenth century a practice developed of delegating such matters to the Chancellor and petitions came to be addressed to the Chancellor directly. The Chancellor was keeper

---

1. MG&L, para [101].

of the Great Seal, which was used to authenticate royal documents. He was also head of the Chancery, the King's secretariat, the office responsible for issuing royal writs. The Chancellor was thus associated closely with both the council and the common law judges as well as the issuing of legal process. Most medieval chancellors were also bishops or archbishops, although not necessarily without legal experience — many were graduates in civil and canon law and some had practised as advocates before entering the church.[2] With such a combination of political, clerical and sometimes legal experience the medieval chancellors were well placed to determine claims brought on legal or moral grounds. In exercising this delegated power to respond to petitions on behalf of the King and council the Chancellor was not conducting a court, even though, like other royal officials, he did have power to hear common law cases concerning officials in his own department. In dealing with these applications for extraordinary justice the Chancellor was performing an executive rather than a judicial function. Often the response would be a direction that the petitioner should pursue the claim at common law. If the claim for special consideration was justified the Chancellor could use his power to issue writs to fashion some appropriate relief. In time that practice was standardised by issuing a writ of subpoena requiring the defendant, under threat of punishment, to appear to answer the petition. There was nothing exclusively equitable about the Chancellor's early jurisdiction. In addition to his inherent jurisdiction over actions brought by or against Chancery officials, the Chancellor had jurisdiction over certain writs and claims affecting the King's interests: cases involving royal grants, or inquisitions concerning the Crown's property rights, such as an inquiry as to the status of lands held by a tenant in chief, and the identification of the heir of that tenant on the death of the tenant. But these matters were never a very important part of the business of Chancery.[3] These proceedings, and any records of them, were in Latin and this jurisdiction was known as the 'Latin' side of Chancery. In some common law actions the Chancellor's aid was sought where the law was not at fault but was unenforceable because the case concerned some baron or other figure powerful enough to ignore the normal processes of the common law. Until the emergence of Star Chamber in the late fifteenth century control of these overmighty subjects was a matter for the Chancellor as the King's chief minister.

[1.3] The equitable side of the Chancellor's jurisdiction arose from the delegation of petitions to the King's council, known as the 'English' side of Chancery because the proceedings were conducted in the vernacular. It is from the 'English' side of Chancery that the modern jurisdiction in equity emerged. In the late middle ages and since, it has consisted of a range of measures which can be seen as correcting defects in the law, providing remedies such as injunction and specific performance unavailable at law, recognising and enforcing contracts also unenforceable at law and preventing the enforcement of strict legal rights where it would be unconscionable to insist on those rights because of some act of fraud, forgery or duress. That part of the equitable jurisdiction has been labelled as the 'auxiliary' jurisdiction, in the sense that equity can be seen to be 'helping' the common law. Beyond those auxiliary matters, Chancery also developed an exclusive jurisdiction over uses and trusts, which were unknown in the common law, by enforcing the duty of the feoffee to uses, or trustee, to hold his legal title for the benefit or use of the *cestui que use*, or beneficiary, to use the modern terms loosely. In doing so Chancery did not deny the legal title of the feoffee; it simply enforced its authority over the conscience of the feoffee requiring him to exercise

---

2. JH Baker, *An Introduction to English Legal History*, 3rd ed, Butterworths, London, 1990, p 114.
3. WS Holdsworth, *A History of English Law*, vol 1, 7th ed, Methuen, London, 1956, pp 452–3.

his rights as titleholder for the benefit of the *cestui que use*. The popularity of uses in the fifteenth century ensured a rapid growth in the work of Chancery and this jurisdiction over uses and trusts was from the first and thereafter the most important branch of the business of equity.[4] In those matters equity was seen to be exercising its 'exclusive' jurisdiction, that is, those matters which were exclusively equitable. There is also a third area of equitable jurisdiction sometimes referred to, the 'concurrent' jurisdiction — such matters as fraud, misrepresentation and estoppel which are recognised in both equity and the common law. The term 'concurrent' can be misleading. In some of these areas, as is best shown in the law of estoppel, the equitable principles have developed beyond those available at common law.

Definition under the Tudors and Stuarts: 1485–1714

[1.4] In this period the procedures of the Court of Chancery were improved and regularised under people like Nicholas Bacon, Lord Keeper of the Great Seal from 1558 to 1579, Thomas Egerton, Lord Ellesmere, Chancellor from 1596 to 1617, and Lord Nottingham, Chancellor from 1672 to 1683, described as the father of modern equity. By the end of Nottingham's term a coherent body of equitable principles quite intelligible to the modern practitioner had emerged. Early in the sixteenth century Christopher St Germain, in his *Dialogue between a Doctor and Student*, advanced the cause of equity and established a rational basis for the jurisdiction exercised by the Court of Chancery over men's consciences. St Germain asserted that laws needed to be ruled by equity and provided an explanation of that word which has stood the test of time. As any general rule of law could not take into account every possible circumstance,

> Thus in some cases it is good and even necessary to leave the words of the law and to follow what reason and justice requires and to that intent equity is ordained, that is to say to temper and mitigate the rigour of the law.[5]

St Germain's treatise was, in some respects, a reaction to the arbitrary conduct of Cardinal Wolsey, Chancellor from 1515 to 1529. Wolsey was untrained in the law and took delight in promoting his untutored common sense ahead of the arguments of the lawyers appearing before him. Wolsey was succeeded by Sir Thomas More (1529–1533), a trained common lawyer. Thereafter, apart from Bishop Williams who held the seal briefly after the fall of Sir Francis Bacon in 1621, Chancellors were always chosen from the ranks of trained lawyers.

[1.5] The dispute between common law and Chancery — 1613–16. Early in the seventeenth century St Germain's view of the relationship between law and equity was challenged by Sir Edward Coke, then Chief Justice of the Court of King's Bench. Coke asserted the supremacy of the common law over equity and took to releasing people imprisoned for contempt of Chancery decrees by resort to the writ of *habeas corpus*. This led to a clash with Lord Ellesmere in *The Earl of Oxford's* case (1615) 1 Chan Rep 1. The dispute was settled in favour of Chancery by King James I. It was established that Chancery could set aside judgments at common law where they were against conscience so that when equity and the law came into conflict, equity would

---

4. JH Baker, *op cit*, p 120; ME Avery, 'History of the Equitable Jurisdiction of the Chancery before 1460' (1969) 42 BIHR 129–44; 'An Evaluation of the Court of Chancery under the Lancastrian Kings' (1970) 86 LQR 84–97.

5. TFT Plucknett & JL Barton (eds), *St Germain's Doctor and Student*, vol 91, Selden Society, London, 1974, p 97.

prevail.[6] That rule remains operative as the failsafe mechanism governing relations between the common law and equity today. In *The Earl of Oxford's* case, Lord Ellesmere expressed his views on Chancery, the Chancellor and the role of equity:

> The cause why there is a chancery is, for that men's actions are so divers and infinite, that it is impossible to make any general law which may aptly meet with every particular act, and not fail in the circumstances. The office of Chancellor is to correct men's consciences for frauds, breach of trusts, wrongs and oppressions, of what nature soever they be, and to soften and mollify the extremity of the law ...

That seemingly unlimited power drew criticism for its uncertainty and the apparently arbitrary nature of the Chancellor's jurisdiction. The most famous being John Selden's aphorism written later that century:

> Equity is a roguish thing: for law we have a measure, know what to trust to; equity is according to the conscience of him that is chancellor, and as that is larger or narrower, so is equity. 'Tis all one as if they should make the standard for the measure we call a foot, a chancellor's foot; what an uncertain measure would this be? One chancellor has a long foot, another a short foot, a third an indifferent foot: 'tis the same thing in a chancellor's conscience.[7]

But even at the time it was made, Selden's jibe was inaccurate. During the seventeenth century Chancery developed an increasing regard for precedent and, in 1672 in *Cook v Fountain* 3 Swanst 600; 26 ER 984, Lord Nottingham soundly refuted any idea that the conscience which guided equity was some arbitrary measure:

> With such a conscience as is only *naturalis et interna*, this court has nothing to do; the conscience by which I am to proceed is merely *civilis et politica*, and tied to certain measures; and it is infinitely better for the public that a trust, security, or agreement, which is wholly secret, should miscarry, than that men should lose their estates by the mere fancy and imagination of a chancellor. The rule *nullus recedat a cancellaria sine remedio* (no one should leave Chancery without a remedy), was never meant of the English proceedings, but only of original writs, when the case would bear one ...

The emergence of the modern equitable jurisdiction — 1714–1873

[1.6] In the century and a half after Lord Nottingham the rules of equity were fashioned into a definite system and, particularly under Lord Eldon (Chancellor 1801–06; 1807–27), settled into a rigid form bound as fast by precedent as the common law. In the process the content of modern equity was settled. The matters falling within the jurisdiction of Chancery included:

1. Property: particularly trusts, married women's property, the equitable rules governing mortgages, priorities, marshalling, vendor's lien and equitable waste.

2. Contracts: through the remedies of specific performance and injunction which were unavailable at common law, and by doctrines such as fraud, undue influence, penalties and forfeiture, accident, misrepresentation and mistake which provided some relief against the rigour of the common law.

---

6. JH Baker, 'The Common Lawyers and Chancery 1616' (1969) 4 Ir Jurist 368–92; JP Dawson, 'Coke and Ellesmere Disinterred: The Attack on Chancery in 1616' (1941) 36 Illinois Law Rev 127–52.

7. *Table Talk*, quoted in MB Evans & R Ian Jack (eds), *Sources of English Legal and Constitutional History*, Butterworths, Sydney, 1984, pp 223–4.

3. Deceased Estates: by the doctrines of satisfaction, ademption, performance, hotchpot, and others which assisted in the proper administration of estates.

4. Procedure: by the doctrines of set-off and account and by the power to order discovery and interrogatories to assist litigants both at common law and equity.

5. Guardianship and Lunacy: under which Chancery provided for the care and management of the person and property of people lacking legal capacity.

6. Commercial Matters: the doctrines of fiduciary duties, subrogation and contribution provided a means of ensuring honesty and equity in business affairs.

Chancery also exercised a jurisdiction in areas other than equity, of which the most significant was bankruptcy. The separate administration of law and equity created a procedural nightmare for anyone contemplating litigation and the crowding of the work of Chancery with these other matters did nothing to lighten the workload of the court in which the Chancellor remained the only judge until the appointment of a Vice Chancellor in 1813. Despite the separation of the administration of the two jurisdictions, and the concomitant rule that Chancery lacked the power to decide legal rights, titles and interests, equity, at every point, presupposed the existence of the common law. Even in its exclusive jurisdiction the law of trusts was hinged upon the common law title of the trustee.

[1.7] The reception of equity in Australia. In New South Wales, s 9 of the Charter of Justice, Letters Patent issued under authority conferred by 4 Geo IV c 96, invested the Supreme Court with the jurisdiction exercised by the Lord Chancellor in England, a grant of power continued by the Australian Courts Act 1828, 9 Geo IV c 83, s 11. Ironically, that legislation allowed the administration of common law and equity by the one court some years before a judicature system was introduced in England, although the lack of a common procedure prevented this early arrangement from operating as a proper judicature system.[8] In 1840 that arrangement was undone by the Administration of Justice Act (NSW), 4 Vict No 22, which provided for the appointment of a judge to hear equity matters separately from the other business of the court. Thereafter, until the Supreme Court Act 1970 (NSW), the equity jurisdiction of the Supreme Court of New South Wales was administered separately from the common law under the one nominated judge. A similar separation applied in the other States which, with the notable exception of South Australia, followed the English model, including many of the piecemeal attempts at reform in the mother country, before the introduction of a judicature system in Queensland in 1876, Western Australia in 1880, Victoria in 1883 and Tasmania in 1932. South Australia actually anticipated reforms in England in the boldly conceived Supreme Court Procedure Act 1853 (SA) while adopting later reforms of the equity jurisdiction in the Equity Act 1866 (SA). In 1878 South Australia adopted the English judicature legislation, particularly ss 24 and 25 of the Act of 1873.[9]

---

8. MG&L, para [131].

9. For a detailed discussion of the reception of equity in Australia, particularly the pre-Judicature developments, see MG&L, paras [123]–[139].

1–2 The Relationship between Law and Equity Prior to the Judicature Acts

[1.8] Even though Judicature Acts have now unified the administration of law and equity throughout Australia the two bodies of law remain separate. To obtain a proper understanding of the nature of modern equity it is essential to comprehend the relationship between equity and the law before their administration was united under the one court. There were a number of major features of that relationship.

[1.9] Common law courts would not recognise equitable rights, titles and interests. Thus, at common law, the trustee, and not the beneficiary was regarded as the 'owner' of trust property. This meant, for instance, that no action could be brought at common law for breach of a purely equitable obligation. In *Castlereagh Motels v Davies-Roe* (1967) 67 SR (NSW) 279, for example, a company's claim for damages against a director for breach of fiduciary duty was rejected. Asprey and Jacobs JJ, saying at 285–6, that the principles which governed the duties of directors as fiduciaries had not become, in some manner transposed into the common law so that there was an action at common law for their breach. The courts of equity having developed the principles of fiduciary duties enforced those principles by their own remedies. Those remedies would today include a claim for restitution or equitable compensation for any loss suffered by the company as result of such a breach. There were exceptions to this rule. The common law recognised the validity of devises by will of equitable interests; in *Pawlett v A-G* (1667) Hard 465; 145 ER 550, a devise of an equity of redemption was upheld. The common law also recognised equitable claims in interpleader cases, so that equitable interests in moneys paid into court were recognised at common law: *Gourlay v Lindsay* (1879) 2 SCR (NSW) 278. In garnishee proceedings, where a garnishee was ordered against, say, moneys in a bank account, the common law would respect a trust of those moneys: *MG Charley Pty Ltd v FH Wells Pty Ltd* [1963] NSWR 22. In contracts for the sale of land the common law held a purchaser to be entitled to insist on a conveyance of the equitable as well as the legal title. In contract cases the common law would sometimes take into account the interests of a third party, in whose favour the second party held the benefit of contract on trust, when assessing damages at law: *Robertson v Wait* (1853) 8 Exch 299; 155 ER 1360. In some circumstances courts of common law have recognised trusts, particularly where leases were held on trust (see for example, *May v Taylor* (1843) 6 Man & G 261; 134 ER 891), and decrees in Chancery have for a long time been allowed as a set-off in actions at law. Common law courts also recognised equitable rights, titles and interests where they were the subject matter of a claim in tort or contract, such as breach of a contract to sell some equitable interest. There were other breaches in the wall,[10] but none of any great effect and the disadvantages flowing from the separate administration of common law and equity far outweighed these slim concessions.

[1.10] Equity had no power to decide disputed legal rights and titles. A plaintiff seeking an equitable remedy to enforce a legal right would not be able to do so unless the common law right was admitted. In New South Wales, s 4 of the Equity Act 1880 (later s 8 Equity Act 1901), adopting s 61 of the English Court of Chancery Procedure Act 1852, gave the Supreme Court in its equitable jurisdiction power to determine incidental questions of law arising in suits for equitable relief.

---

10. *Ibid*, para [141].

[1.11] Equity had no power to award damages. The Court of Chancery had power to award monetary remedies by way of restitutionary relief but not damages as they were known at law. In England a power to award damages in lieu of or in addition to the remedies of injunction and specific performance was conferred on Chancery by Lord Cairns' Act in 1858 which was adopted in New South Wales as s 32 of the Equity Act 1880 (s 9 of the Equity Act 1901).[11] This right to award damages was not unlimited. Some entitlement to one of the two equitable remedies had to be shown before damages could be awarded. It was ultimately held that a claim for injunction or specific performance which could be justified on the original pleadings was sufficient, even though the claim might be defeated by some subsequent intervening factor: *Goldsborough Mort v Quinn* (1910) 11 CLR 674, per Isaacs J. However, a plaintiff whose own conduct led to the refusal of specific performance would also lose the right to damages in lieu. A purchaser of rural land who failed in a claim for specific performance on discretionary grounds because he was not willing to pay the full amount of the purchase price, claiming he was entitled to a deduction in the circumstances for the cost of agistment of his stock, was held not to be entitled to damages in lieu of specific performance: *King v Poggioli* (1923) 32 CLR 222. This provision has been carried over into the judicature system and the distinction between damages under Lord Cairns' Act and damages at common law remains a matter of some controversy. At the same time there has been considerable growth in equity's jurisdiction to award monetary relief by way of restitution or equitable compensation: see Chapter 25.

[1.12] The common law courts lacked power to give interlocutory relief. Chancery had inherent power to order discovery, interrogatories, to award interim injunctions and to appoint receivers. The common law courts lacked these powers, although a power to order discovery and interrogatories was conferred on the common law courts in England by ss 50 and 51 of the Common Law Procedure Act 1854. The discovery power was adopted in New South Wales as ss 23–24 of the Common Law Procedure Act 1857. Apart from those limited reforms, litigants at common law had to resort to equity if they wanted any such interim relief.

[1.13] The courts of common law had no power to award specific performance, or injunctions. The common law courts could only award damages. They had no power to award any remedy which might require the supervision of the court. The only exceptions to this were, first, a power to award injunctions in addition to damages given to the common law courts by ss 48-51 of the Common Law Procedure Act (Imp) 1854, as adopted in New South Wales by the Common Law Procedure Act 1857, ss 44–47 which was necessarily limited by the precondition of damages; and secondly, a limited power to award injunctions in commercial causes given in 1965 to

---

11. This statutory power has been re-enacted in most other States and remains part of the modern armoury of the equitable jurisdiction: Supreme Court Act 1935 (SA), s 30; Supreme Court Act 1986 (Vic), s 38; Supreme Court Act 1935 (WA), s 25; and Supreme Court Civil Procedure Act 1932 (Tas), s 11. It was re-enacted as Supreme Court Act 1970 (NSW), s 68 with the introduction of a judicature system in New South Wales. Lord Cairns' Act has not been specifically re-enacted in Queensland, the Australian Capital Territory and the Northern Territory. In those jurisdictions the power to award damages in lieu of, or in addition to, equitable relief comes, indirectly, from legislative provisions giving the Supreme Court power to give such relief as ought to have been given by the court in its equitable jurisdiction prior to the introduction of the judicature system. As that jurisdiction included power under Lord Cairns' Act, the power to award damages in that manner must be preserved along with all other relief available in equity: see Supreme Court Act 1933 (ACT), s 26; Supreme Court Act 1989 (NT), s 62; Judicature Act 1876 (Qld), s 4(1).

the common law side of the Supreme Court by s 7B of the Commercial Causes Act 1903 (NSW).

[1.14] The common law courts lacked power to make declarations. Chancery had an inherent power to make declarations when giving other relief but it was not until Sir George Turner's Act 1850, s 35, that a specific power to make declarations, provided the parties agreed to state a case, was conferred on Chancery. That power was clarified in 1852 by a provision which allowed Chancery to make declarations whether other relief was granted or not.[12] This power was read down to apply only to cases where other relief could have been granted: *Rooke v Lord Kensington* (1856) 2 K & J 753; 69 ER 986 (see Chapter 24).

[1.15] No power existed to transfer cases from one jurisdiction to the other. Under the old system, with equity and the common law administered in different courts, there was a very real risk of commencing proceedings in the wrong court, particularly in cases concerning mistake or breach of contract. It was not until 1854 in England and 1857 in New South Wales that a power to recognise equitable defences was conferred on the courts of common law.[13] But the courts of common law had no power to impose conditional relief. They could only find for or against a party. As a result the right to raise equitable defences at law was restricted to cases in which a court of equity would have granted an absolute, perpetual and unconditional injunction on the pleading raised: *Mines Royal Societies v Magnay* (1854) 10 Ex 489; 156 ER 531. As most injunctions awarded by Chancery were conditional the benefit of this reform was quite limited: see *Carter v Smith* (1952) 52 SR (NSW) 290. Other jurisdictions resolved this continuing procedural dilemma by enacting judicature legislation. New South Wales clung to the ancient system and sought to alleviate it by passing legislation which allowed for the transfer of cases from common law to equity where the judge at common law was of the opinion that the matter pleaded would not produce an absolute, perpetual and unconditional injunction. This produced some ludicrous results.[14] There was no complementary power to transfer cases from equity to the common law where it became clear that equity could not deal with the matter. New South Wales attempted a further patch up piece of reform in 1957 by adding s 8A to the Equity Act 1901.[15] Under s 8A the court, in its equity jurisdiction, was required to transfer a suit to common law when it appeared at any stage of the proceedings that the court had no jurisdiction and that the appropriate remedy lay in the common law. There was some judicial confusion about what was meant by 'no jurisdiction',[16] while the logical conclusion of 'any stage of the proceedings' remained unexplored until 1970 when the Supreme Court Act came to the rescue introducing a judicature system to New South Wales.

1–3 The Judicature System

[1.16] The English Judicature Acts of 1873 and 1875. While law and equity were administered by separate courts the only way to resolve conflicts between the two, as

---

12. 15 & 16 Vict c 86 (Imp), s 50, which was adopted in New South Wales as Equity Act 1880, s 50, and re-enacted as Equity Act 1901, s 10.
13. Common Law Procedure Act (Imp) 1854, ss 83–86; Common Law Procedure Act (NSW) 1857, ss 48–51, re-enacted as the Common Law Procedure Act (NSW) 1899, ss 95–98.
14. MG&L, para [152].
15. By the Supreme Court Procedure Act 1957 (NSW).
16. MG&L, para [153].

in a case where a defendant at common law had a good equitable defence to the claim but could not raise it in common law proceedings, was the common injunction which stopped the proceedings at common law. That clumsy mechanism was replaced in the Judicature Act (Imp) 1873 by s 25(11) which provided that where there was any conflict between the rules of equity and those of the common law, equity would prevail.[17] Under the judicature system the administration of these two bodies of law was brought under control of the one court, obviating any need for a multiplicity of actions on the one cause, let alone an injunction issued by one court to restrain proceedings in another. It is crucial to remember that it is only the administration of these principles which is fused, not the principles themselves. The main features of a judicature system, as re-enacted in the various Australian jurisdictions,[18] are:

1. All branches of the court have power to administer equitable remedies.

2. Equitable defences can be pleaded in all branches of the court and the appropriate relief given.

3. All branches of the court must recognize equitable rights, titles and interests.

4. All branches of the court have a general power to determine legal rights and titles.

5. The common injunction is abolished.

[1.17] Fusion fallacies. The unification of the administration of common law and equity caused some judicial confusion, particularly in the early days of the judicature system in England, resulting in a number of decisions where the judgment proceeded on the erroneous assumption that the Judicature Acts had united the common law and equity into the one bundle of principles from which desired pieces could be picked out like rags at a jumble sale. In *Redgrave v Hurd* (1881) 20 Ch D 1, Sir George Jessel MR suggested that the difference between equity and the common law had disappeared with the passing of the Judicature Acts and that damages might thus be obtainable for innocent misrepresentation which had previously been recognised in equity only as a ground for rescission. More recently damages have been awarded for breach of confidence, a purely equitable obligation, without any reference to Lord Cairns' Act as the basis for the award, nor any suggestion that the remedy was actually a matter of restitution, both of which would have satisfied established principle: *Seager v Copydex* [1967] 2 All ER 415; [1967] RPC 349.[19] The maxim that equity will not assist a volunteer has, in one narrow line of cases, been carried across to the common law to frustrate an action brought by a party entitled to the benefit of a covenant executed under seal which, for over five hundred years, had provided a perfectly good action for damages at common law: *Re Pryce* [1917] 1 Ch 234.

---

17. Supreme Court Act 1933 (ACT), ss 256–33; Law Reform (Law and Equity) Act 1972 (NSW), ss 5–7 (formerly embodied in Supreme Court Act 1970 (NSW), s 64 but re-enacted in separate legislation to make it clear that the principle applied to all proceedings in New South Wales and not just proceedings in the Supreme Court); Supreme Court Act 1979 (NT), ss 61–68; Judicature Act 1876 (Qld), ss 4–5; Supreme Court Act 1935 (SA), ss 20–28; Supreme Court Civil Procedure Act 1932 (Tas), ss 10–11; Supreme Court Act 1958 (Vic); Supreme Court Act 1935 (WA), ss 24–25)

18. Now Supreme Court Act 1933 (ACT), s 33; Law Reform (Law and Equity) Act 1972 (NSW), s 5; Supreme Court Act 1979 (NT), s 61; Judicature Act 1876 (Qld), ss 4, 5; Supreme Court Act 1935 (SA), s 28; Supreme Court Civil Procedure Act 1932 (Tas), ss 10, 11; Supreme Court Act 1958 (Vic), s 62; Supreme Court Act 1935 (WA), ss 24, 25.

19. This practice has continued in breach of confidence cases and is now generally regarded as a matter of equitable compensation rather than a fusion fallacy (see Chapter 25).

The trustee of a marriage settlement[20] approached the court for directions as to whether he ought to sue another party to the deed of settlement for breach of its provisions, specifically, that the party had failed to convey certain after acquired property to the trustee. Eve J held that the trustee 'ought not to sue' as the beneficiaries under the deed, by then the wife's next of kin, were volunteers, and equity would not assist a volunteer. His Lordship also added his view that, 'nor could damages be awarded either in this court or, I apprehend, at common law where since the Judicature Act the same defences would be available to the defendant as would be raised in an action brought in this court for specific performance or damages'.

The survival of the action for damages for breach of covenant at common law testifies to the magnitude of the error in this judgment. If it were correct, apart from a number of odd results, it would be possible to plead the equitable defence of hardship at common law in, say, an action for money had and received, with absurd consequences. With the legal recognition, albeit only by statute, of the rights of married women to own property in their own name, the marriage settlement has passed into history along with the breech loading musket and ignorance of penicillin. The varied fortunes of the law of trusts may produce some new species of arrangements in which covenants to settle after acquired property in favour of future beneficiaries are a central feature. For the moment, the issues which arose in *Re Pryce* and cases of its ilk are unlikely to trouble modern courts of equity.

[1.18] Perhaps the most famous fusion fallacy is that perpetrated by Sir George Jessel MR in *Walsh v Lonsdale* (1882) 21 Ch D 9.

A mill, or factory, was leased for seven years under a written agreement, but no deed of lease under seal was executed as required by s 3 of the Real Property Act (Imp) 1845 and thus the lease was void at law. At law the tenant was merely a tenant from year to year, one year's rent having been paid in advance. Traditionally, equity would have awarded specific performance of the agreement to grant a lease. The Master of the Rolls held that a tenant holding under an agreement to grant a lease of which specific performance would have been decreed stood in the same position as to liability as if the lease had been executed, saying, 'He is not, since the Judicature Act, a tenant from year to year, he holds under the agreement and every branch of the court must give him the same rights ... There are not two estates as there were formerly, one estate at common law ... and an estate in equity under the agreement. There is only one court and equity rules prevail in it'.

If that judgment were taken literally then all distinctions between equitable and common law interests would vanish. The continued existence of trusts shows that has not happened. It is also incorrect to talk of the rules of equity prevailing. The rules of equity only 'prevail' when there is a conflict between the two; it does not apply to the relationship between equity and the common law generally. It is also wrong to talk of a party as having the benefits of a decree of specific performance before the remedy has been awarded. Decrees of specific performance are not automatic. They are discretionary and there are many factors, not the least of which is the conduct of the party seeking relief, which must be taken into account before a court will decree specific performance. Despite these obvious flaws, and considerable criticism since, *Walsh v Lonsdale* has survived and has been accepted as authority for the rule that a written lease not in proper form will, pending a decree of specific per-

---

20. That is, a trust established on the marriage of a woman from a wealthy family whereby property was settled on trust for the woman for life and thereafter for her children or heirs. The woman, and usually her husband to be, were parties to the deed, as were other members of her family. The deed usually contained a covenant to settle property acquired thereafter on the trustees.

formance requiring the lessor to execute the proper form, give rise to an equitable relationship of landlord and tenant between the parties under which the former could, if necessary, be restrained by injunction from acting on the footing that the latter was merely a tenant-at-will or a tenant from year to year: *Progressive Mailing House Pty Ltd v Tabali Pty Ltd* (1985) 157 CLR 17, per Mason J at 26; and the equitable estate thus recognised endures until the contract upon which it is founded is avoided or dissolved: *Cricklewood Property & Investment Trust Ltd v Leighton's Investment Trust Ltd* [1945] AC 221, per Lord Wright at 240. Other obligations arising under the written lease will not, necessarily, be enforceable under the *Walsh v Lonsdale* principle.

> In *Chan v Cresdon* (1989) 168 CLR 242; 89 ALR 522, an agreement for lease was executed under which the respondent agreed to lease certain land in Queensland for five years to Sarcourt Pty Ltd. A form of lease was annexed and a lease in registrable form was simultaneously executed, but not registered under the Real Property Act 1861 (Qld). After default by Sarcourt, the lessor sought to recover from the appellants as guarantors under the unregistered lease. Under s 43 of the Act the lease was not effectual to pass any estate or interest until registration. The High Court, by a majority, held that the appellants were not liable under the guarantee. What they had guaranteed was the 'obligations of Sarcourt Pty Ltd under this lease'. Even if it were assumed that specific performance of the agreement for lease would be granted, that would not have been enough to establish liability on the part of the appellants as guarantors. Only a lease at law would have satisfied that description for the purposes of the guarantee. Mason CJ, Brennan, Deane & McHugh JJ, having discussed *Walsh v Lonsdale* and the cases which had dealt with it since, said, at 252: 'these authorities establish two propositions: first, the court's willingness to treat the agreement as a lease in equity, on the footing that equity regards as done that which ought to be done and equity looks to the intent rather than the form, rests upon the specific enforceability of the agreement; secondly, an agreement for a lease will be treated by a court administering equity as an equitable lease for the term agreed upon and, as between the parties, as the equivalent of a lease at law, though the lessee does not have a lease at law in the sense of having a legal interest in the term'. However, their Honours were of the view that even if it could be assumed that specific performance would be awarded in favour of the respondent, that was not enough, in their opinion, to make the appellants liable as guarantors. Because the liability of a guarantor was, 'At law, as in equity ... *strictissimi juris*, [so] ambiguous contractual provisions should be construed in favour of the surety': *Ankar Pty Ltd v National Westminster Finance (Australia) Ltd* (1987) 162 CLR 549; 70 ALR 641, the requirement that the Chans guaranteed payment of rent 'under this lease' meant just that, and no more. Only a lease at law would meet that description.

1–4   The Maxims of Equity

[1.19] As the principles of equity evolved, a set of maxims, generalisations expressing a sort of collected wisdom of equity, gathered as a guide to courts exercising an equitable jurisdiction. Many of them are of historical curiosity now and most are honoured more in the breach than in the observance but they still serve a useful purpose as an explanation of the nature of equity and some of the broad concepts which have influenced the growth of modern equity.

[1.20] Equity will not suffer a wrong without a remedy. There are many examples of remedies developed by equity in cases where the common law did not provide relief. But this maxim cannot be regarded as accurate today. Equity is capable of adapting in a changing world, as has been shown in the law of estoppel and constructive trusts in recent years. But it is one thing to refine existing principles and quite another to invent new ones. This maxim is primarily a matter of historical interest. It is not a licence for judicial legislation.

[1.21] Equity follows the law. Equity has always recognised legal rights, titles and interests and has developed its own doctrines and estates by analogy with those of the common law. Equity does not, however, follow the law in all things as many of its remedies are designed to correct defects in the law. In *Delehunt v Carmody* (1986) 161 CLR 464, the High Court applied this maxim in holding that equity followed the law in its present form. Thus when a man and a woman agreed to purchase a property in their two names, but the house was registered in the man's name only, equity presumed that they held as tenants in common, following Conveyancing Act 1919 (NSW), s 26, and not the old common law rule which presumed a joint tenancy.

[1.22] When the equities are equal, the first in time prevails. This rule, subject to a number of exceptions, governs the law of equitable priorities which is covered in Chapter 2.

[1.23] He who seeks equity must do equity. Anyone seeking equitable relief must do so on terms that he or she fulfils his or her own legal and equitable obligations. For instance, a beneficiary seeking to recover trust property must be prepared to meet the trustee's reasonable expenses. Equity could insist on this rule as it had the power to impose conditions when granting relief. However, any condition imposed on this basis must be capable of enforcement by the court at the suit of the defendant if need be: *Hanson v Keating* (1844) 4 Hare 1; 67 ER 537 at 539. There are numerous examples of this doctrine. A mortgagor, for instance, cannot restrain a mortgagee from proceeding with a wrongful sale without first paying to the mortgagee or into court all moneys presently owing under the mortgage: *Inglis v Commonwealth Trading Bank* [1972] ALR 591. This maxim cannot be implied to impose conditions on a plaintiff where those conditions, such as repayment of moneys borrowed, would in effect circumvent the policy of legislation declaring some contract unenforceable. This maxim will not apply where a plaintiff seeks declaratory relief only. The source of the court's power to grant that relief is statutory rather than part of its inherent jurisdiction: *Chapman v Michaelson* [1908] 2 Ch 612 at 620–1, per Eve J; [1909] 1 Ch 238 (CA). However, where a plaintiff seeks ancillary equitable relief in addition to a declaration, such as delivery up and cancellation of documents, the granting of that further relief can be made conditional, for instance, upon repayment of any moneys owing to the defendant: *Automobile & General Finance Co Ltd v Hoskins Investments Ltd* (1934) 34 SR (NSW) 375.

In *Mayfair Trading Company Pty Ltd v Dreyer* (1958) 101 CLR 428, the plaintiff sought a declaration that a certain money-lending contract under which he had borrowed moneys was unenforceable, and in addition, sought ancillary relief by way of an injunction and an order for delivery up. The High Court held that the money-lending contract was unenforceable by virtue of Moneylenders Act 1912–48 (WA), s 9, and that the borrower was entitled to the relief sought without being obliged to comply with any condition or terms requiring repayment of the money still outstanding on the loan.

In *Nottingham Permanent Building Society v Thurstan* [1903] AC 6 (HL); [1902] 1 Ch 1 (CA); [1901] 1 Ch 88, a building society advanced moneys to a woman who was under the age of 21 at the time. Of the moneys advanced, £250 was provided toward the purchase price of a certain parcel of land with further advances which were to be paid for the completion of building work on the land. The advances were secured by a mortgage. After completion of the purchase and after the society had made further advances to cover the cost of building work, the society learned that the woman was a minor. The society then discontinued its advances and took possession of the property. At the time the society took possession it was owed £1070 which included the £250 advanced on the purchase of the land. After attaining her majority, the woman took proceedings against the society claiming a declaration that the mortgage was void as against her and seeking delivery up of the mortgage deed and possession of the property, relying on s 1 of the Infants Relief Act (Imp) 1874 which provided that contracts entered into by infants for the repayment of money lent were absolutely void. On appeal, the Society was held to be entitled to a lien over the property and the title deeds to the property but only to the extent of the moneys advanced for completion of the purchase, the £250. The mortgage and thus the contract for repayment of the other moneys advanced was void. In response to an argument by the Society that Mrs Thurstan should 'do equity' by repaying the further moneys advanced under the mortgage, at least to the extent to which the land had benefited by the expenditure of those further advances, Romer LJ said, at [1902] 1 Ch 13, '... The short answer is, that a Court of equity cannot say that it is equitable for a person to pay any moneys in respect of a transaction which, as against that person, the Legislature has declared to be void'.

[1.24] He who comes to equity must do so with clean hands. This is similar in many ways to the previous maxim. Under it, equity examines the conduct, in the transaction or arrangement which is the subject of the suit, of the party seeking relief. Should a petitioner be guilty of some impropriety, in the legal not the moral sense, in some matter pertinent to the suit, then equity may refuse the decree sought. In *Hewson v Sydney Stock Exchange* [1968] 2 NSWR 224, an injunction was refused on this ground. The injunction had been sought against the Stock Exchange by one of its members on the basis of an alleged promise by the Exchange not to take proceedings against him for his discreditable conduct. The man had made false statements to representatives of the Stock Exchange about the state of his trust account and scrip position and had also failed to make adequate disclosure of other breaches of fiduciary duty and of irregular office procedures involving inappropriate mingling of his affairs with those of his clients.

In *Official Trustee in Bankruptcy v Tooheys Ltd* (1993) 29 NSWLR 641, Tooheys Ltd had granted a lease of the Speers Point Hotel to a Mr and Mrs Williams. In the process the incoming tenants agreed to purchase the hotel business from Tooheys at a price of $400,000 of which $344,000 represented payment for goodwill. Tooheys later introduced a policy whereby they would not give outgoing tenants any compensation for loss of goodwill on the surrender of a lease. Upon the failure of their business Mr and Mrs Williams left the hotel without any ejectment proceedings being taken against them. Other tenants of Tooheys in other hotels successfully resisted the claims that they should depart without compensation for loss of goodwill (see, for example, *Bonds Brewing (NSW) Pty Limited v Reffell Party Ice Supplies Pty Ltd* (Waddell CJ in Eq, 17 August 1987, unreported). The Official Trustee in Bankruptcy, on behalf of the Williams, later brought proceedings against Tooheys seeking compensation for this loss of goodwill. At first instance Bryson J held that, but for the point discussed below, Tooheys would have been treated as a constructive trustee of the Williams' interest in the goodwill and thus would be estopped from denying an obligation to compensate them for its loss. The defence raised by Tooheys was that at the time the Williams took up the lease they misrepresented to Tooheys their financial arrangements, in particular, the extent of the finance which they required for the purchase. Tooheys were told that the Williams were borrowing $130,000 whereas, in fact, they were borrowing more than three times that amount. Tooheys had a policy of not approving a transfer in such circumstances. Bryson J held that as a consequence of that fraudulent misrepresentation, the Williams were not entitled to the relief claimed in the proceedings. Bryson J dismissed a claim by the Williams both on the principles applicable to the law of estoppel and also on the basis that they had not come to equity with clean hands. The Court of Appeal,

Gleeson CJ, Meagher and Sheller JJA upheld that decision. Gleeson CJ stated, at 650, that: '[T]he unmeritorious conduct which debars relief is not "general depravity"; it must be conduct which has an immediate and necessary relation to the equity suited for'. On that test, his Honour thought the case was one in which the relationship between the false representation and the equity sued upon was sufficiently close to establish the defence. There was a clear and close connection between the misrepresentations made to Tooheys and Tooheys' willingness to participate in the transaction out of which the alleged estoppel arose.

This maxim will not be applied in some cases, such as suits for purely statutory remedies, including declarations, suits for cancellation and delivery up, and cases where to refuse relief would lead to a multiplicity of actions. The defence of 'unclean hands' is not an absolute bar to relief. The court will take into account the whole of the circumstances of the case before deciding whether to allow a defendant to succeed on this defence. In *Marshall Futures Pty Ltd v Marshall* [1992] 1 NZLR 316, a company alleged to have committed breaches of trust in conducting a futures broking business brought proceedings against some of its former directors alleging knowing receipt of trust moneys and knowing participation in breaches of trust. The court, per Tipping J, at 331, refused an application by one director to strike out the pleadings on the ground that the company, as trustee, was guilty of breaches of trust and thus could not come to court with clean hands.

[1.25] Equity assists the diligent and not the tardy. Delay in itself is not a bar to relief in equity but undue delay or acquiescence can prejudice a claim (see Chapter 21).

[1.26] Equity is equality. Generally speaking, equity looks to an equal distribution of profits and losses proportionate to the claims or liabilities in question. Where the court has to administer a trust under which the trustee holds a power of appointment, subject to the terms of the trust, the court will generally look to distribute the property subject to the power equally among the range of objects of the power. However, as it is no longer necessary for that range of objects to be described with sufficient certainty that a complete list could be made of them, this rule does not carry the same force as it once did (see **[12.21]–[12.30]**).

[1.27] Equity looks to the intent rather than the form. Sometimes expressed as 'equity looks to the substance and not the form', this maxim underlies the equitable doctrine of rectification and can also be seen in other areas where equity will look at the substance of some contract or other document, rather than its strict wording. This maxim applies generally in the operation of equitable doctrines: *Muschinski v Dodds* (1985) 160 CLR 583 at 613, per Deane J.

[1.28] Equity regards as done that which ought to be done. Where a person is under a legal obligation to carry out some task, particularly the duty of an executor to convert property from unauthorised into authorised investments, equity will, for certain purposes, regard the obligation as having been carried out (see **[18.31]–[18.33]**). The maxim is limited in its operation to situations in which what ought to be done can be done.

[1.29] Equity imputes an intention to fulfil an obligation. This is of limited application.

[1.30] Equity will not assist a volunteer. Under this maxim equity will not assist a party who has not provided consideration in a transaction. However, there is a major exception to this rule — the assistance provided by equity for beneficiaries of trusts who are usually volunteers. This and the concomitant maxim, that equity will not perfect an imperfect gift, are dealt with in more detail in the discussion of equitable assignments in Chapter 3. These two maxims were the subject of specific comment in the joint judgment of Mason CJ and McHugh J in *Corin v Patton* (1990) 169 CLR 540 at 557:

> Of course it would be a mistake to set too much store by the maxim (that equity will not assist a volunteer). Like other maxims of equity, it is not a specific rule or principle of law. It is a summary statement of a broad theme which underlies equitable concepts and principles. Its precise scope is necessarily ill-defined and somewhat uncertain. It is subject to certain clearly established exceptions such as the rule in *Strong v Bird* (1874) LR 18 Eq 315 and the doctrine of equitable estoppel, where an equity arises in favour of an intended donee from the conduct of the donor after the making of the voluntary promise by the donor: see *Olsson v Dyson* (1969) 120 CLR at 378–9.

[1.31] Equity acts in personam. This maxim has its origin in the theory that equity did not make orders affecting the property of litigants but rather that it made orders effective against the conscience of the party concerned. Chancery enforced its orders by taking action against the person of any defendant who disobeyed one of its decrees, usually by imprisoning the delinquent for contempt. In private international law equity could make orders which had the effect of dealing with property outside the jurisdiction by making orders against the person of a defendant present in the jurisdiction: *Penn v Lord Baltimore* (1750) 1 Ves Sen 444; 27 ER 1132; *Potter v Broken Hill Pty Ltd* (1905) 3 CLR 479. Equity will enforce a charge arising under a contract made within the jurisdiction where that charge is over foreign land by the exercise of its power to enforce obligations in personam: *Duder v Amsterdamsch Trustees Kantoor* [1902] 2 Ch 132. Equity will also grant an injunction to restrain a party within the jurisdiction from prosecuting proceedings in foreign jurisdiction where the circumstances justify such an order. Such anti-suit injunctions, while an extraordinary remedy, are granted in the exceptional cases available where the court is satisfied that proceedings in the foreign jurisdiction were commenced for some improper motive, or were, in effect, vexatious, oppressive or constituted harrassment of a party in the jurisdiction: *CSR Ltd v New Zealand Insurance Co Ltd* (1994) 36 NSWLR 138; *National Mutual Holdings Pty Ltd v Sentry Corp* (1989) 87 ALR 539; *Re Simomath Pty Ltd (No 3)* (1991) 25 NSWLR 25; *Société Nationale Industrielle Aérospatiale v Lee Kui Jack* [1987] 1 AC 871; *Morguard Investments Ltd v De Savoye* (1990) 76 DLR (4th) 256. This maxim, like several others, can no longer be regarded as literally true. Courts have long since ceased to regard rights in equity as purely personal. A beneficiary of a trust has a direct proprietary interest in the assets of the trust, rather than simply a personal right against the trustee. The precise nature of the beneficiary's rights will depend upon the terms of the trust and not some abstract maxim. If it is a trust arising from a deceased estate the question may turn on whether the estate has been fully administered.

In *Baker v Archer-Shee* [1927] AC 844, the appellant was assessed for tax for income received by his wife from certain stocks in American companies held on trust by trustees in New York as income 'arising from foreign securities stocks and shares'. It was argued that the wife had no proprietary interest in the shares as her rights were restricted to a personal right exercisable against the trustees in New York. The House of Lords rejected that submission and held that Lady Archer-Shee did have a proprietary interest in the income produced from the stocks and that it fell within the expression in the taxing statute.

[1.32] Sometimes, usually in the context of revenue statutes which determine liability to some tax or duty on the basis of the locality of some right or interest in property, it is crucial to determine where a particular person's rights are at a given time. That can depend upon whether they are rights *in rem* or *in personam* at that time. The classic illustration of this occurred in *Commissioner for Stamp Duties (Qld) v Livingston* [1965] AC 694; (1960) 107 CLR 411 (see **[2.10]**). In *New Zealand Insurance Co Ltd v Commissioner for Probate Duties (Vic)* [1973] VR 659, the Full Court of the Supreme Court of Victoria had to consider the liability to probate duty of the estate of a beneficiary of a trust. The assets of the trust were situated in Victoria while the trustees resided in New Zealand. The court held that the deceased had both a proprietary interest in each asset of the trust estate as well as a personal right against the trustees. While the 'interest' of the deceased was susceptible to both descriptions, the decision that the deceased had two types of property, each situated in a different place, is difficult to sustain as a matter of logic. For example, if the Victorian legislation had levied duty on the value of assets of the estate of a person dying domiciled in Victoria, wherever those assets might be situated, a beneficiary in such a trust would be liable for double duty — on the value of a right *in rem* in Victoria, and on the value of the seemingly separate right *in personam* in New Zealand. Meagher, Gummow and Lehane argue that the judgments in *Livingston's* case require the court, when considering the question of the locality of assets for the purpose of determining liability to tax or duty, to select one place with which those rights have the most substantial connection.[21] In the case of a deceased estate still in the course of administration, a residuary beneficiary cannot be described as 'presently entitled' to the income, or the capital for that matter, of the trust estate for the purpose of assessing income tax: *FCT v Whiting* (1943) 68 CLR 199. The same principle would apply to the rights of a beneficiary of a discretionary trust pending the exercise by the trustees of the discretion to distribute the capital and income in selected proportions among the beneficiaries or objects of the trust.

---

21. MG&L, para [423].

Chapter Two

Equitable Rights, Titles and Interests

2-1 The Nature of Equitable Interests

[2.1] The types of estates and interests recognised by modern courts of equity vary greatly in their nature and content. There are the obvious proprietary interests such as that of a beneficiary in the assets of a trust or of a partner in the assets of a partnership, as well as a variety of security interests including equitable mortgages and charges. Those interests can be described as proprietary because they give the holder rights which can be exercised directly against the property which is the subject of the interest. Beyond those interests are others which confer on the holder a right to obtain certain remedies but which do not extend to specific rights of property, although proprietary rights may come into existence upon the exercise of the original right. These lesser rights, or equities as they can be called, include such things as the right of a party to the benefits of an estoppel: whereby a second party, usually the titleholder to the property in question, is prevented from denying the interest claimed in that property by the first (see Chapter 4); or the equity of a mortgagor to set aside an improper sale by a mortgagee.

[2.2] If these interests are to be seen in hierarchical terms, which is not necessarily helpful, the lower ranks consist of personal equities: rights exercisable only by a particular person. For example, the right to rescind a contract for innocent misrepresentation is only available to the party to whom the original misrepresentation was made: *Gross v Lewis Hillman Ltd* [1970] Ch 445. This raises one question which must be considered when assessing the components of any equitable interest — that of assignability or devisability — whether the person entitled to the equity can transfer it to anyone else. Labels may be convenient at times, but attempts to categorise these various equitable interests under simple headings can be misleading. They are not susceptible to any precise definition and are likely to cause confusion if used as expressions of absolute meaning in any analysis of some equitable problem. If treated as generic rather than specific labels can be regarded as the tags on a bag which demand further enquiry as to the true contents of the bag — what rights it really carries before any conclusions can be drawn as to the equitable interest involved.

[2.3] The identification of any particular equitable right will often depend upon the remedy to which it gives access. As Heydon, Gummow and Austin put it:

> Equitable estates and interests are rooted in the remedies by which they are protected;
> the strength or resilience of one equitable right as compared with another will be deter-

17

mined by the availability of equitable remedies to those asserting a claim to the subject matter.[1]

The fact that some equitable remedy is available to protect a particular right or interest does not mean that the right or interest is also equitable. Equitable remedies are applied in support of legal rights but that does not translate the right protected into a creature of equity. It remains a legal right. In *Colbeam Palmer v Stock Affiliates Pty Ltd* (1968) 122 CLR 25, Windeyer J noted the protection given by courts of equity to common law trade marks — trade marks acquired by use and reputation — and noted that there was some circularity in saying that the protection given by Chancery for such trade marks made them a form of property — and then saying that the intervention of equity was based on the protection of some equitable property interest. Equitable rights, titles and interests have not been neatly categorised by the courts into a coherent and cohesive system. The case by case method of considering issues in equity does not lend itself to the production of comprehensive statements about the range and nature of rights and titles recognised in equity. Courts of equity tend not to state principles in hard and fast terms — so as to avoid the possibility that the strict letter of equitable principle might later be used to cloak some fraud. At the same time equity is not concerned with the recognition and enforcement of rights in order to satisfy subjective or idiosyncratic notions of justice or fairness: *Legione v Hately* (1983) 152 CLR 406 at 431, per Mason and Deane JJ; and *Muschinski v Dodds* (1985) 160 CLR 583 at 615, per Deane J.

[2.4] In the process some rules have developed, not all of which can be easily characterised as logical. In *Gross v Lewis Hillman Ltd* [1970] Ch 445, it was held that the right to rescind a contract for the sale of land for misrepresentation did not run with the land and while a subsequent purchaser may have some action against his vendor, that is, the original representee, that subsequent purchaser had no right to set aside the original contract. That decision has to be contrasted with *Dickinson v Burrell* (1866) LR 1 Eq 337 in which the rights of a defrauded vendor were held to pass to an assignee from the original vendor. In *Gross v Lewis Hillman Ltd*, Cross LJ attempted to explain the difference by saying that the assignee from a defrauded vendor was seeking to recover an equitable interest previously conveyed away while the assignee from a defrauded purchaser sought to throw the property back, not onto his immediate assignor but onto the previous assignor.

[2.5] Despite the confusion in labelling, and the uncertain meaning of some of the terms used, such as 'proprietary', it is important to consider the practical aspects of the questions, 'What "rights" can the claimant exercise over the property?'; 'Does the claimant have a right to have the property transferred into his or her name?'; 'Can he or she assign his or her right or interest to some third party?'; 'If title to the property passes to a third party before any claim is pressed, will the claimant's right be extinguished?'; 'Can the claimant take physical possession of the property?' Is the claimant entitled to receive any income produced by it?'; 'Can the claimant leave it to someone in his or her will?'. If clear answers can be given to these questions the label should not matter.

[2.6] A vendor of real estate is often said to hold the property as 'constructive trustee for the purchaser between contract and conveyance'. That label is misleading as the rights of the purchaser are not identical to those of a beneficiary of a trust. The principal right of a purchaser, after contract and pending conveyance, is to obtain specific

---

1. HG&A, para [303].

performance of the contract, provided the purchaser is not in breach and is otherwise ready, willing and able to perform the bargain. That right could be described as a proprietary right in the subject matter of the contract but, because of the proviso, there is an important step to be taken before the description is accurate. The equity of a purchaser of realty does not extend to many other contracts of sale, only to those where specific performance would be available; that is, where damages at law would be inadequate. This restricts the rule otherwise to contracts dealing with rare or unique chattels. The interest of a purchaser under a contract for the sale of realty is, nonetheless, a vested interest and not a contingent one. The rights of the holder of an option to purchase realty are contingent — the contingency, of course, being the valid exercise of the option.

> In *Goldsborough Mort v Quinn* (1910) 11 CLR 674, the defendant gave the plaintiff an option to purchase 2590 acres of land at a price of £1/10/ - per acre, a total price of £3885. Consideration for the option was five shillings. The defendant sought to repudiate the option before the expiry of the week in which it was to have been open. The plaintiff purported to exercise the option and sought specific performance of the agreement. It was held that the plaintiff was entitled to succeed. Isaacs J said that the option gave the optionee an interest in the land, even though not the same as the interest of a purchaser, it was something real and substantial and beyond the power of the optionor to withdraw.

[2.7] The existence of an entitlement to an injunction, or an order for specific performance against a particular party, will not necessarily give the plaintiff similar rights against a third party assignee from the defaulter. In the early 1960s Lord Denning developed a 'deserted wife's equity' which his Lordship extrapolated from a wife's right to restrain her husband from evicting her from the former matrimonial home a similar right available to the wife against third parties, such as a mortgagee of the property. This odd theory was dismissed by the House of Lords in *National Provincial Bank Ltd v Ainsworth* [1965] AC 1175. At 1253 Lord Wilberforce went to some lengths to explain the error which lay in confusing an equitable personal obligation with an equitable proprietary interest:

> The fact that a contractual right can be specifically performed, or its breach prevented by injunction, does not mean that the right is any the less of a personal character or that the purchaser with notice is bound by it: what is relevant is the nature of the right, not the remedy which exists for its enforcement ...

> In my opinion, this line of argument is but a revival of a fallacy that, because an obligation binds a man's conscience, it therefore becomes binding on the consciences of those who take from him with notice of his obligation.

[2.8] Another area in which a distinction must be drawn between an equitable personal obligation and a proprietary interest is that concerning confidential information. A person who receives, in confidence, information of a confidential nature is not entitled to make unauthorised use of that information (see Chapter 8). Equity polices this rule with the remedies of injunction and, if need be, account. While there has been some judicial confusion on the point, it is clear that information which is the subject of such an obligation of confidence is not property and that equity's intervention stems from the obligation of confidence itself rather than any property rights in the information. Unlike real or personal property, information is not susceptible to a transfer of dominion; it can be 'held' by any number of people at once. So, for instance, the doctrine of bona fide purchaser without notice cannot apply to breaches of confidence: *Wheatley v Bell* [1982] 2 NSWLR 544.

[2.9] These instances underline the importance of identifying the content of any right or interest rather than simply ascribing it a label. Both the deserted wife and the party whose confidence has been abused enjoy the benefit of equitable personal obligations but their rights against third parties are quite different. A person purchasing an interest in the former matrimonial home, even with notice, is in a very different position from a person receiving confidential information, even without notice and for value. A third party who comes to know of the facts after acquiring confidential information cannot make use of it, even if the information was acquired for value and without any knowledge of its confidentiality.

[2.10] The issue of the nature of a particular equitable interests was discussed by in *Livingston v Commissioner of Stamp Duties (Qld)* (1962) 107 CLR 411 (HC); [1965] AC 694 (PC).

> Livingston was the executor of the estate of the widow of the late Hugh Livingston. Hugh Livingston's estate included land in Queensland and was still in the course of administration when Mrs Coulson, as she had by then become, died. She was a beneficiary of one third of the residue of Hugh Livingston's estate. The executors of Mr Livingston's estate all resided in New South Wales. The Succession and Probate Duties Act 1892 (Qld) levied a succession duty on the devolution of interests in real or personal property situated in Queensland to which the deceased was 'beneficially entitled' at the date of his or her death. Mrs Coulson's estate was assessed for this duty to the extent of one third of the land in Queensland and the question arose whether, at the date of her death, Mrs Coulson was 'beneficially entitled' to any real or personal property situated in Queensland.
>
> In the High Court, Dixon CJ held that Mrs Coulson had a beneficial interest in the property in Queensland. In doing so rejected the contrary argument because it rested on the proposition that the beneficial interest in the assets of a deceased estate was not vested in anyone while the estate was being administered. Dixon CJ could not accept the notion that the beneficial interest was nowhere until the administration of the estate was completed. Windeyer J agreed with the Chief Justice's conclusion, although for a more simple reason. In his view, Mrs Coulson had an 'interest' in the property in Queensland at the date of her death.
>
> Fullagar J, with whom Menzies J agreed, stressed that the Act imposed a succession duty, that is, a duty on the property to which a beneficiary succeeds, as opposed to a death duty, a duty on the value of property owned by the deceased at death, and that the Act required that Mrs Coulson's rights under Mr Livingston's will be given some location, even though they could not be said to have any natural situation — a process which was to some degree artificial. Fullagar J conceded that Mrs Coulson had an equitable interest in the mass of assets which formed the estate giving her a right to enforce proper administration. But if that right or interest had to be 'located' somewhere, the appropriate place was where that right would be exercised. He rejected the idea that the rights of a beneficiary in the assets of an unadministered or partially administered estate could be described as proprietary.
>
> Kitto J drew a distinction between the existence of Mrs Coulson's interest in the assets of the estate and the nature of that interest. While her 'interest' or rights extended to all the assets of the estate while the estate was in the course of administration, those rights did not entitle her to any particular asset in specie. She was only entitled to receive a share of whatever turned out to be left when the administration was complete, which may not include any of the present assets or their income. As the law required that some locality be attributed to the interest of such a beneficiary, then that interest in any particular asset of the estate had to be considered as an integral part of the beneficiary's rights with respect to the whole estate, and those rights possessed most substantial connexion with the appropriate forum for enforcing due administration of the estate, that is, New South Wales.

The Privy Council agreed with the majority of the High Court. Viscount Radcliffe, who delivered the advice of the Judicial Committee, rejected the argument that the beneficial interest in the assets of the estate had to be somewhere during the period of administration. That view, he said, was based on a fallacy that for all purposes and at every moment of time the law requires the separate existence of two different kinds of estate or interest in property: the legal and the equitable. There was no need to make that assumption when the whole right of property was in the executor. What was important was that the court would control the executor in the exercise of those rights by employing remedies which did not involve the admission or recognition of equitable rights of property in those assets in favour of any particular person or persons. What Mrs Coulson was entitled to under her husband's will was a chose in action capable of being invoked to ensure proper administration of the estate; and the 'location' of that asset lay where the executors resided: the place that constituted the proper forum for administration of the estate.

[2.11] The question posed in *Livingston's* case was artificial, in that the need to attach a locality to Mrs Coulson's interest in her late husband's estate only arose because of the necessity created by the statute that property subject to Queensland succession duty be located in Queensland. The outcome of *Livingston's* case turned on the fact that the estate of Mr Livingston snr was still in the course of administration. An attempt to argue that *Livingston's* case could support a claim to levy death duty on a fully administered estate where the assets and the beneficiary were both located in the United States and only the trustees of the estate remained in New South Wales was firmly rejected in *Perpetual Trustee Co Ltd v Comm'r Stamp Duties* (*Shallard's* case) [1977] 2 NSWLR 472. Under the Bankruptcy Act 1966 (Cth), s 116, a bankrupt's property divisible among his or her creditors includes all property that has been or is acquired by the bankrupt, or has devolved upon or devolves on him or her, after the commencement of the bankruptcy. The chose in action available to a beneficiary of a deceased estate which is in the course of administration is an asset of the beneficiary available to the beneficiary's creditors in the event that the beneficiary is declared bankrupt: *Official Receiver in Bankruptcy v Schultz* (1990) 170 CLR 306; 96 ALR 327. The nature of any equitable interest will often depend on the context in which it is examined and the particular facts of the case in question:

> In *Re Leigh's Will Trusts* [1970] Ch 277, a widow, who was sole administratrix and beneficiary of her late husband's estate, made a specific bequest of 'All shares which I hold and any other interest or asset which I may have in Sheet Metal Fabricators (Battersea) Ltd'. The husband's estate included 51 shares in that company and a debt due to him from the company. The widow died before the husband's estate was fully administered and the question arose as to whether the bequest was good or whether the shares fell into the residue of her estate. Buckley J held that the bequest was good. While Mrs Leigh had not held any shares in the company at the date of her death she did have an interest in the company both in respect of the shares and the debt sufficient to answer the description in the bequest and to entitle the beneficiary of that bequest to receive so much of the shares and the debt as eventually fell into the possession of her executors.

[2.12] The difficulty which confronted the court in *Livingston's* case arose in part from the variety of meanings which can be given to the word 'interest' and the lack of an adequate variety of synonyms for that work in the English language. Under s 160ZM of the Income Tax Assessment Act 1936 (Cth), as amended, capital gains tax is imposed on the disposal of an 'interest ' in a trust. That section has not yet been subject to judicial scrutiny, but it begs the question of what constitutes an 'interest' in a trust. Presumably 'curiosity' about the trust does not count. But what of the interest of an object or beneficiary of a discretionary trust? Discretionary trusts are discussed in more detail in Chapter 12. In essence, a discretionary trust is one in which the allocation or division of the beneficial interests in the trust property is left to the discretion of the trustee. In other words, the trustee has power to decide how to apportion both the income and the capital of the trust among the beneficiaries. Invariably the discretion or power conferred on the trustee to allocate income, and usually capital too, will include power to give to any one beneficiary to the exclusion of all others, so there is no guarantee that a particular beneficiary will get anything. Prima facie, a beneficiary of a discretionary trust will have no right or entitlement to any part of the property of the trust unless and until the trustee exercises its discretion to allocate some part of the income and/or capital in favour of that beneficiary or object. Subject to any revenue legislation that might place some artificial value on the interest of such a discretionary beneficiary, that 'interest' can have no intrinsic value prior to the exercise of the trustee's power, and amounts to little more than a right to be considered when the trustee does come to exercise the power: *Gartside v IRC* [1968] AC 553 (see Chapter 20). But that does not mean that a beneficiary or object of a discretionary trust cannot be said to have an 'interest' in the property of the trust. The rights of a discretionary beneficiary are analogous to those of Mrs Coulson in *Livingston's* case: a right to enforce due administration — at least in the sense that the beneficiary would have standing to prevent maladministration; a right to require the trustee to exercise its discretion bona fide, a right to obtain information about the trust from the trustee: *Spellson v George* (1987) 11 NSWLR 300; and, of course, a right to take whatever is allocated by the trustees.

[2.13] A parallel to the situation in *Livingston's* case can be seen in the circumstances of a company in liquidation. In *Livingston's* case it was decided that the executor of a deceased estate had power over the assets of the estate, at least during the course of administration, but did not have beneficial ownership of those assets. A company in liquidation retains beneficial ownership of its assets during the course of the liquidation, but has no power or control over them: *Franklin's Selfserve Pty Ltd v FCT* (1970) 125 CLR 52; *Re Transphere Pty Ltd* (1984) 5 NSWLR 309. Like the executor of a deceased estate, the liquidator has power over the company's assets but does not have beneficial ownership.[2]

[2.14] A good example of the ways in which equitable interests can be characterised differently for different purposes can be seen in *Latec Investments Ltd v Hotel Terrigal Pty Ltd* (1965) 113 CLR 265.

> A mortgagee of a hotel property exercised its power of sale after default by the mortgagor and sold the hotel to a wholly owned subsidiary — a sale which was later held to be fraudulent. The subsidiary subsequently gave a floating charge over the hotel to a trustee for debenture holders which had no notice of the wrongful sale. Five years after the wrongful sale the defrauded mortgagor sought to set it aside. By then the subsidiary had defaulted under the floating charge which had thus crystallised and a receiver had been appointed by the trustee for debenture holders. A submission by the mortgagee that the mortgagor had delayed so long in bringing its claim that it was guilty of laches failed and the case became a competition between the defrauded mortgagor and

---

2.   A different point of view prevails in England where it has been held that a winding up order divests the company of beneficial ownership of its assets: *Ayerst v G & K Constructions Ltd* [1976] AC 168, although the assets are not then held on trust for the creditors and shareholders. If this view is correct, and the company proves to be solvent at the end of the liquidation, there would then be a reassignment of the property left over to the company — which is plainly absurd.

the trustee which turned on whether the normal rule, where the equities are equal the first in time prevails, would apply.

The High Court held the later interest prevailed. Kitto J, applying *Phillips v Phillips* (1862) 4 De GF & J 208; 45 ER 1164, said that the trustee had acquired an equitable estate, as distinct from an equity, for value and without notice of the mortgagor's interest and that estate would take priority over the earlier equity even though that equity, when exercised, would give the holder an equitable estate.

Taylor J did not accept that conclusion. Relying on *Stump v Gaby* (1852) 2 De G M & G; 42 ER 1015, he said that a party entitled to have a conveyance of property which was previously his set aside for fraud remained the owner of the property in equity and could devise that interest as an equitable estate. Accordingly, he did not follow the reasoning of Kitto J but held that the holder of the prior equity was estopped by his conduct from disputing the later interest acquired bona fide.

Menzies J sought to reconcile the two lines of authority by pointing out that they concentrated on different things. *Phillips v Phillips* looked at the equity of a defrauded mortgagor as a right which had to be exercised before the equitable estate it gave could be established while *Stump v Gaby* was concerned with the devisability of the interest, which, in that context, emphasised the effect of the exercise of the equity on the position *ab initio* — so that in the event of a successful suit the mortgagor had an equitable interest capable of devise.

[2.15] The equity of a defrauded mortgagor has since been held to prevail over that of the purchaser under a wrongful sale prior to completion, even though the purchaser had no notice of the impropriety at the time of contract. Once apprised of the facts he could not, in conscience, proceed to completion: *Forsyth v Blundell* (1973) 129 CLR 477. *Latec Investments* was concerned with a number of different equitable interests. The equitable interest of a mortgagor, certainly of old system land, is an equity of redemption, the right to demand a reconveyance of the land upon payment of the moneys secured by the mortgage. With Torrens title land that equity is more in the nature of a right to demand a discharge of the mortgage upon payment. The equity of a defrauded vendor, or mortgagor, is a right to set aside the fraudulent conveyance. In the case of the mortgagor, that right, once successfully exercised — and that success is not automatic as it is affected by such things as the conduct of the mortgagor — revives the equity of redemption, and a mortgagor seeking to set a wrongful sale aside can only do so on terms that he pays the outstanding mortgage debt: *Latec Investments* (at 292–3) (which explains the five year delay by Hotel Terrigal Pty Ltd). The equitable rights of the trustee for debenture holders were security rights which differed between the time at which the charge was 'floating' and when it became 'fixed'. A floating charge is a charge over the assets of the chargor from time to time, leaving the chargor free to deal with its assets for the purpose of its business while ever it complies with the terms of the charge. If the chargor defaults, depending upon the terms of the particular charge, then the charge crystallises, fixing the assets of the chargor at the time with an immediate security interest which can be exercised directly against the assets to satisfy the outstanding debt — usually the whole principal and any outstanding interest.

[2.16] Equitable security interests were considered in *Swiss Bank Corp v Lloyds Bank Ltd* [1982] AC 584. A finance trust borrowed £2.1 million from a Swiss bank for the purpose of investing in an Israeli bank. The Bank of England placed certain conditions on the foreign borrowing, including requirements that the title documents be held by an authorised depository, that interest on the loan be paid out of income from the securities and that the proceeds of the securities be the primary source for repayment of the loan. The securities were deposited with the parent company of the finance trust, the Triumph Investment Trust ('Triumph') which was authorised to act as depository by the Bank of England. Triumph later gave a charge over the securities to Lloyds Bank. In the ultimate contest between Lloyds Bank and the Swiss Bank, Lloyds prevailed. The House of Lords held that there was nothing in the original loan agreement which charged the securities with repayment of the loan. While the Bank of England conditions required repayment of the loan from the securities, those conditions could be changed at any time and the finance trust in borrowing the money had only agreed to observe the bank's conditions as they applied from time to time. In the Court of Appeal Buckley LJ discussed equitable mortgages and charges (at 594–5):

> An equitable charge may, it is said, take the form of either an equitable mortgage or of an equitable charge not by way of mortgage. An equitable mortgage is created when the legal owner of property constituting the security enters into some instrument or does some act which, though insufficient to confer a legal estate or title in the subject matter on the mortgagee, nevertheless demonstrates a binding intention to create a security in favour of the mortgagee, or in other words evidences a contract to do so ... An equitable charge which is not an equitable mortgage is said to be created when property is expressly or constructively made liable, or specially appropriated, to the discharge of a debt or some other obligation, and confers on the chargee a right of realisation by judicial process, that is to say, by an appointment of a receiver or an order for sale.

[2.17] Statutory rights in property are not necessarily equitable. Rights to claim an interest in property or to enforce a maintenance agreement under the Family Law Act 1975 (Cth) are inchoate (that is, undeveloped) and have no legal existence until ordered by a court: *Sonenco (No 77) Pty Ltd v Silvia* (1989) 24 FCR 105; 89 ALR 437. Transferable rights such as height allowances under Sydney City building codes, while proprietary in character and capable of being the subject of a decree of specific performance, are neither a legal nor an equitable estate: *Uniting Church in Australia Property Trust (NSW) v Immer (No 145) Pty Ltd* (1991) 24 NSWLR 510.

2-2 Equitable Interests and Torrens Title

[2.18] The essence of the Torrens system of title is the absolute supremacy of the register. It would seem contrary to the spirit and the letter of such legislation to allow equitable interests in Torrens land unless those interests were noted on the register. Yet a trustee holding land under Torrens title would get very short shrift in equity if he or she attempted to deny the interests of beneficiaries simply because they were not registered. Despite the essential importance of the register the courts have allowed for the operation of equitable interests in land held under Torrens system title. In both *Barry v Heider* (1914) 19 CLR 197 and *Breskvar v Wall* (1971) 126 CLR 376 the interest of the registered proprietor who had given a second party a signed memorandum of transfer and either the certificate of title or a means of access to the deed was postponed to that of a third party who took on the faith of the documents held by the second, even though the interest of the third party in each case was not registered and could only be described as equitable.

[2.19] Immediate indefeasibility upon registration as the hallmark of Torrens title was established by the Privy Council in *Frazer v Walker* [1967] AC 569 but two exceptions were allowed in that bulwark protecting registered proprietors:

(a) Any specific statutory provision rendering the registered proprietor open to challenge, such as actual fraud under s 126 of the Real Property Act 1900 (NSW), which had to be fraud by the party registered on the title, not simply on the part of the person through whom that party obtained title. Such innocence will not necessarily defeat the original proprietor if action is taken before the third party obtains registration: *Mayer v Coe* [1968] 2 NSWLR 747, although the actions of the original proprietor might lead to his or her own downfall if they constitute postponing conduct: *Breskvar v Wall* (1971) 126 CLR 376.

(b) Where the proprietor is subject to a personal obligation under which he or she may be bound by some claim in personam founded in law or equity to deal with his or her registered title in some particular manner.

There is obviously some overlap between these two categories and the limitation to claims *in personam* in the second would not, despite the use of that expression, appear to exclude the possibility that such claims might be transmitted or assigned. In *Bahr v Nicolay (No 2)* (1988) 164 CLR 604, the High Court recognised such a claim, *in personam*, arising from an acknowledgement of the appellants', the Bahrs', rights as against the then registered proprietor, Nicolay, in a contract signed by purchasers from Nicolay as confirmed by a letter from those purchasers to the Bahrs after registration. The Bahrs sold a parcel of land over which they held a Crown licence, Lot 340, to Nicolay for $32,000 and took a lease back of the land for three years at an annual rental of $4000. In the contract of sale the Bahrs undertook to complete building work required on the land and thereafter to apply for a Crown grant. They did so and a grant was issued in their favour. They then transferred the land to Nicolay. In the contract for sale to Nicolay the Bahrs also agreed to enter into a contract to repurchase Lot 340 for $45,000 at the expiry of the lease. Before the expiry of the lease Nicolay sold Lot 340 to the Thompsons for $40,000. The contract between Nicolay and the Thompsons included a clause in which the Thompsons acknowledged the agreement between the Bahrs and Nicolay. After becoming registered, the Thompsons wrote to the Bahrs' solicitors noting their acknowledgement of the agreement to re-purchase and saying, providing three months notice of their intention to purchase is given on 1 July 1983 with 10% of the purchase money then we will agree to sign an offer for $45,000. At the expiry of the lease the Bahrs sought to exercise their option to repurchase Lot 340. The Thompsons refused to sell. The Bahrs took proceedings seeking, among other things, specific performance against the Thompsons. The High Court held that the Bahrs were entitled to specific performance against the Thompsons: per Wilson, Brennan and Toohey JJ, because by taking a transfer knowing of Nicolay's obligation to re-sell, and accepting that obligation, the Thompsons became subject to a constructive trust in favour of the original owners; per Mason CJ and Dawson J, because the acknowledgement by the Thompsons of the Bahrs' interest gave rise to an express trust to the effect that the Thompsons took the land subject to the rights created in favour of the Bahrs under the first contract. The issue of the right of a party entitled to a personal equity against another who had obtained a registration of an interest contrary to that of the first was also considered by the New South Wales Court of Appeal in *Mercantile Mutual Life Insurance Co Ltd v Gosper* (1991) 25 NSWLR 32.

Mrs Gosper was the registered proprietor of a property at Neutral Bay. The property was subject to a mortgage securing the sum of $265,000. Mrs Gosper's husband negotiated a further loan of $285,000 with the same mortgagee without his wife's knowledge or consent, and obtained a variation of mortgage to that effect. Mr Gosper forged his wife's signature on the variation which was subsequently registered. The Court held, per Kirby P and Mahoney JA, that Mrs Gosper had a personal equity to have the variation set aside which was not defeated by registration. The personal equity arose from the fact that the mortgagee had produced the certificate of title to the property without Mrs Gosper's consent. Meagher JA dissented, finding no enforceable personal equity in the circumstances, although also making no reference to the issue of production of the certificate of title.

2–3   The Equity of Redemption

[2.20] The modern mortgage can be traced to conditional feoffments effected in medieval England under which land was conveyed from one person to another on condition that if the first person paid the second a certain sum of money on or before a certain day the land would be reconveyed. If the feoffor, the mortgagor, failed to pay by the given day the pledge was dead (hence 'mortgage') and he forfeited the land. From the fifteenth century equity intervened to allow the mortgagor to recover the land on payment of the outstanding moneys even after the due date, recognising the conveyance for what it was, a security transaction and not a true transfer. Corresponding rights were given to the mortgagee to obtain an order for foreclosure, thus shutting out the mortgagor's claim for good, or an order for sale, allowing the property to be sold to recover the debt. The principal right of the mortgagor was essentially a right to redeem the mortgaged property. Before the due date it was a legal right under the contract with the mortgagee and after that date, until any order for foreclosure or sale, it was an equitable right — the equity of redemption — and was recognised as a proprietary right, a right in the property being worth the value of the property less the debt secured on it, which could be assigned or devised. Equity was not concerned with any fetters on that legal right, so long as the legal right to redeem was real and not illusory and provided there was otherwise no question of undue influence or unconscionability. In *Knightsbridge Estates Trust Ltd v Byrne* [1931] 1 Ch 441, the Court of Appeal refused a declaration sought by certain mortgagors that they were entitled to redeem a mortgaged property by paying out the mortgage before the due date despite a covenant postponing the contractual right to redeem until all 80 half-yearly instalments had been paid. Restrictions of that sort on the contractual right to redeem have been removed by the Conveyancing Act 1919 (NSW), s 93, by which a mortgagor is given a statutory right to redeem before the contractual date for redemption upon paying the outstanding principal and interest for the balance of the term of the mortgage. Although s 93 is not concerned with the equitable doctrines of redemption, it may be argued that a contractual term excluding redemption for a very long time might be unconscionable in the circumstances.[3]

[2.21] Equity will look at the substance of transactions and not their form. If a dealing is in truth a mortgage, regardless of any other wording used to describe it, equity will recognise the borrower's equity to redeem upon repayment of the moneys secured. Any stipulation for a collateral advantage which is really a term of the mortgage and which is to endure beyond the repayment of the principal will be a clog on the equity of redemption and will be struck down. On payment of the principal,

---

3. P Butt, *Introduction to Land Law*, Law Book Co, Sydney, 1988, p 399.

interest, and costs, together with anything in the nature of a bonus which has been properly stipulated for, and has become payable, a mortgage contract comes to an end, and the mortgagor is entitled to get the mortgaged property back unaltered, and is thereafter free from the burden imposed by the contract: *Bradley v Carritt* [1903] AC 253. Anything which fetters the mortgagor in the free disposition of his or her property, or the free enjoyment of it, is a clog on the equity of redemption. This principle was applied in *Noakes & Co Ltd v Rice* [1902] AC 24 to release the owner of a pub from a covenant in a mortgage requiring the pub owner, as mortgagor, to buy the mortgagee's beer exclusively. The House of Lords held that upon repayment of the loan the mortgagor was released from all obligations under the mortgage, including the beer covenant.

[2.22] This does not mean that any collateral agreement between the parties to a mortgage cannot endure beyond the term of the mortgage. The question is simply one of whether the stipulation in question is in substance a term of the mortgage or truly a collateral matter.

> In *Kreglinger v New Patagonia Meat & Cold Storage Co Ltd* [1914] AC 25, New Patagonia borrowed £10,000 from the Kreglingers and gave a floating charge over all their property as security. The agreement provided that New Patagonia would not sell sheepskins to anyone but the appellants so long as they were prepared to buy for a period of five years from the date of the agreement. New Patagonia paid out the loan and attempted to sell sheepskins to other buyers. The Kreglingers sought an injunction restraining such sales as being in breach of contract. The House of Lords granted the injunction. Viscount Haldane LC said the question was whether the provision complained of had cut down the right to redeem or whether it was a stipulation for a collateral advantage outside and clear of the mortgage. This raised the further question of whether there was just the one indivisible contract or two separate contracts, even though contained in the one instrument. In this case the restriction on the sale of skins was not in substance a fetter on the equity of redemption but a collateral bargain, and a preliminary and separable condition of the loan.

2–4 Co-ownership in Equity

[2.23] Another illustration of the way in which the equitable interest in land may vary from the legal title can be found in cases of co-ownership. Equity will recognise a beneficial co-ownership in favour of two or more parties notwithstanding that the legal title stands in the name of only one. In the absence of evidence of some contrary intention equity will presume that the beneficial interest is held under a tenancy in common: *Delehunt v Carmody* (1986) 161 CLR 464; *Baumgartner v Baumgartner* (1987) 164 CLR 137 at 149. A contrary intention sufficient to rebut that presumption would usually require proof of an agreement between the parties that they should hold as joint tenants, or, as is more likely and their agreement has been expressed in layman's terms, that on the death of one the whole right of property in the land should pass to the other.

[2.24] Where property is held by two or more persons as joint tenants the joint tenancy may be severed in a number of ways, with the result that the parties will enjoy the equitable title as tenants in common, notwithstanding that they continue to be described as joint tenants at law. The various ways in which a joint tenancy can be severed are described in the judgment of Page Wood VC in *Williams v Hensman* (1861) 1 J & H 546; 70 ER 862, in which his Lordship said, at 1 J & H 557–8; 70 ER 867:

> A joint-tenancy may be severed in three ways: in the first place, an act of any one of the persons interested operating upon his own share may create a severance as to that share. The right of each joint-tenant is a right by survivorship only in the event of no severance having taken place of the share which is claimed under the jus accrescendi. Each one is at liberty to dispose of his own interest in such manner as to sever it from the joint fund — losing, of course, at the same time, his own right of survivorship. Secondly, a joint-tenancy may be severed by mutual agreement. And, in the third place, there may be a severance by any course of dealing sufficient to intimate that the interests of all were mutually treated as constituting a tenancy in common. When the severance depends on an inference of this kind without any express act of severance, it will not suffice to rely on an intention, with respect to the particular share, declared only behind the backs of the other persons interested.

[2.25] In *Corin v Patton* (1990) 169 CLR 540, the High Court was required to consider the question of whether a unilateral declaration of intention or other act inconsistent with the continuation of a joint tenancy may suffice for the purposes of the first method of severance. In that case Mrs Patton, who was a joint registered proprietor of land under Torrens title with her husband, executed a memorandum of transfer of her interest in the land in favour of her brother, who accepted, that is, signed, the transfer as transferee. The transfer was expressed to be in consideration for a deed of trust under which Mr Corin declared that he held the half-interest in the land as tenant in common on trust for Mrs Patton. The certificate of title was held by the State Bank of NSW under an unregistered mortgage. Mrs Patton took no action to procure the production of the certificate of title so as to enable registration of the transfer. Mrs Patton died before the transfer had been registered. The High Court held the execution of the transfer did not sever the joint tenancy because at the time of her death Mrs Patton had not alienated any interest in the land. In answering that question in the negative, Mason CJ and McHugh J adopted the words of Lord Hardwicke LC in *Partriche v Powlet* (1740) 2 Atk 54, at 55; 26 ER 430 at 431:

> This is not a severance; for, first, here is no agreement for this purpose; secondly, if no agreement, then there must be an actual alienation to make it amount to a severance ... the declaration of one of the parties that it should be severed, is not sufficient, unless it amounts to an actual agreement.

In the process their Honours declined to adopt the approach taken by Lord Denning in *Burgess v Rawnsley* [1975] Ch 429 at 439 that it is sufficient if there is a course of dealing in which one party makes clear to the other that he or she desires that their shares should no longer be held jointly but be held in common. In giving their reasons for refusing to follow this course, Mason CJ and McHugh J, at 548, provided a useful statement of the operation of the principles at work in the severance of a joint tenancy:

> First, as the judgment of Sir John Pennycuick makes clear (*Burgess v Rawnsley* [1975] Ch 429 at 447), the decision turned on the construction of s 36(2) of the Law of Property Act 1925 (UK), which permits the severance of a joint tenancy by notice in writing by one joint tenant to the other, rather than on the state of the preexisting law. Secondly, as a matter of history and principle, the severance of a joint tenancy can only be brought about by the destruction of one of the so-called four unities: see Blackstone, *Commentaries on the Law of England* (1778), vol 2, pp 185–6. Unilateral action cannot destroy the unity of time, of possession or of interest unless the unity of title is also destroyed, and it can only destroy the unity of title if the title of the party acting unilat-

erally is transferred or otherwise dealt with or affected in a way which results in a change in the legal or equitable estates in the relevant property. A statement of intention, without more, does not affect the unity of title. Thirdly, if statements of intention were held to effect a severance, uncertainty might follow; it would become more difficult to identify precisely the ownership of interests in land which had been the subject of statements said to amount to declarations of intention. Finally, there would then be no point in maintaining as a separate means of severance the making of a mutual agreement between the joint tenants.

Brennan J agreed with that conclusion, at 565–6, as did Deane J, at 584, and Toohey J, at 591. In the process, Deane J pointed out that Lord Denning's approach in *Burgess v Rawnsley* would not have helped Mr Corin in any event because it was essential in that formulation of the law that the party intending to sever the joint tenancy should communicate his or her intention clearly to the other joint tenant.

2–5 Equitable Priorities

The general rule and the general principle of exception

[2.26] The general rule as to priority amongst competing equitable interests was stated by Kitto J in *Latec Investments v Hotel Terrigal* (1965) 113 CLR 265 at 276:

> If the merits are equal, priority in time of creation is considered to give the better equity. This is the true meaning of the maxim *qui priore est tempore potior est jure.*

An example of the application of this principle can be seen in *Wu v Glaros* (1991) 55 SASR 408 in which a party entitled to the benefit of an agreement for lease, albeit one that required rectification, was in competition with that of a subsequent would-be purchaser pursuant to a sale and purchase agreement for the subject land. In that case the court found that there were no circumstances justifying the postponement of the prior equity and the interest of the party entitled to the benefit of the agreement for lease was upheld. The court also held that the fact that the holder of the subsequent equity acquired it without knowledge of the prior equity was not, of itself, a ground for postponing the prior equity. Where the holder of the subsequent equity acquired that equity with notice of the prior equity, the subsequent interest-holder's claim for priority would necessarily fail unless it could be shown that the holder of the prior equity had caused or contributed to a belief in the mind of the subsequent interest-holder at the time of negotiating or acquiring that equity that the prior equity was no longer in existence.

[2.27] Questions of priority arise where there is competition between two or more parties asserting equitable rights or interests in the same subject matter in circumstances in which the various claims are incompatible. Ordinarily the general rule stated above will apply to give priority to the earlier interest but equity recognises exceptions to that rule. Those exceptions are usually listed under a number of headings although, apart from priorities between competing holders of equitable interests in personalty which seem locked in the firm if somewhat archaic grip of the rule in *Dearle v Hall* (1828) 3 Rus 1; 38 ER 475 (see [2.41]–[2.45]) there is scope for pressing the view that these listed exceptions, other than those created by statute, might now be considered as manifestations of a general principle of exception stated in the joint judgment of Mason and Deane JJ in *Heid v Reliance Finance Corp Pty Ltd* (1983) 57 ALR 683.

Heid agreed to sell certain land to Connell Investments Pty Ltd for $165,000 of which $15,000 was to be paid in cash on completion (and was), $100,000 was to be deposited, at call, with Chancellor Finance Pty Ltd and $50,000 was to be secured by mortgage. The mortgage for $50,000 was signed but never registered and the $100,000 never deposited. Connell and Chancellor were both controlled by the same firm of mortgage brokers. Heid handed over a signed memorandum of transfer, dated 2 June 1977, which acknowledged receipt of $165,000. The conveyancing for both parties was done by an employee of Connell who was described as a solicitor but was not, in fact, qualified. On 10 June Connell gave an unregistered mortgage to Reliance Finance securing an advance of $80,000 plus future advances and the certificate of title and transfer were handed to Reliance. Connell gave a further mortgage to a Mr Alexander and took a further advance from Reliance of $20,000. On 6 June Alexander lodged a caveat and on 23 September Heid lodged one as well. Reliance and Alexander had no notice that Heid had any claim until then. The matter became a question of priority between Heid and Reliance. Gibbs CJ, with whom Wilson J agreed, held that Heid was estopped, on the principle of estoppel by representation, the transfer having operated as a representation that Connell was the proprietor of the land Heid was thus estopped from denying the interest acquired by Reliance. Heid was held to have failed in his duty to those who might subsequently deal with the documents by accepting without enquiry that he was dealing with a solicitor. Gibbs CJ found it unnecessary to decide the point but suggested that such an estoppel would not arise where a person gave such indicia of title to his own solicitor, or even to an independent solicitor acting for both parties, in accordance with the common usage in conveyancing.

Mason and Deane JJ rejected estoppel as the basis for deciding the case and applied a more general and flexible principle that preference be given to the better equity in the circumstances, a matter which would usually be determined by an examination of the conduct of the holder of the earlier interest to determine whether, in all the circumstances, his interest should be postponed — in particular whether that conduct made it reasonably foreseeable that a later equitable interest would be created. Heid's conduct fell into that category.

[2.28] The division within the High Court in *Heid* makes it difficult to extrapolate a principle of general application. However, the rule proposed by Mason and Deane JJ should be preferred. Estoppel by representation seems an inappropriate vehicle for resolving questions of priority. If estoppel by representation is to be applied in the manner adopted by Gibbs CJ then it would seem that a representation is a representation when made through the medium of someone who is not a solicitor but not a representation when made through a solicitor, although that may be less certain where the solicitor acts for both sides.

In *Shropshire Union Railway v R* (1875) LR 7 HL 496, a trustee wrongfully deposited share certificates which he held on trust for the railway company as security for advances made to him personally. The equitable interest of the Railway Company was held to prevail. Lord Cairns rejected, in quite strong terms, an argument that an equitable owner who allowed his trustee to hold the indicia of title was guilty of postponing conduct. To decide otherwise would, in his view, cut down the scope of trusts to the point where they could operate only for the benefit of the legally incapable.

The view of Mason and Deane JJ has received sympathy,[4] and has been followed by Brooking J in *Cash Resources Australia Pty Ltd v BT Securities Ltd* [1990] VR 576.

[2.29] There is support for a general principle governing exceptions to the rule that the first in time should prevail in Sykes, *The Law of Securities*, 3rd ed, PUBLISHER,

---

4. MG&L, para [811].

1978, p 336 and in the judgment of Isaacs J in *Lapin v Abigail* (1930) 44 CLR 166 at 186:

> The principle is that the court seeks, not for the worst, but for the best equity. And the best equity — for there may be several claimants — is that which on the whole is the most meritorious, it may be because the others are by reason of (the conduct of one of the rival claimants or some act or omission on the part of the owner of the earlier title), lessened in relative merit, or because one is, by reason of some additional circumstance, not attributable to any act or omission of the others, rendered in equity more meritorious than all the rest.

[2.30] The recognition of such a rule of general application would avoid some of the apparent contradictions in the listed exceptions as generally stated. The doctrinal basis of the first three exceptions, for example, is a matter of some uncertainty and attempts to explain them by reference to estoppel is not helpful in view of the lack of any direct relationship between the two competing parties in most cases. The New South Wales Court of Appeal dealt with a question of priorities without reference to any of the 10 exceptions in *Silovi Pty Ltd v Barbaro* (1988) 13 NSWLR 466:

> The proprietors of a plant nursery had been granted a lease by the owners of an adjoining block for 10 years over part of that adjoining block. The nursery owners planted Cocos palms and installed irrigation on the leased plot. The lease could not be registered as it breached the Local Government Act 1919 (NSW), s 327AA, which prohibited the disposal of land, including by lease, for more than five years unless the land was a lot or portion shown on a current plan. The adjoining block had never been subdivided. The owners of that block contracted to sell it. After contracts had been exchanged but before completion, the proprietors of the nursery sought and obtained relief on the grounds of equitable estoppel against the owners and the proposed purchasers. The purchasers argued, among other things, that their later equitable interest took priority over the personal equity to seek relief on the basis of estoppel available to the nursery owners because their later interest was, in effect, the better equity. Priestley JA, with whom Hope and McHugh JJA agreed, rejected that submission. The plaintiffs' equity arising from equitable estoppel amounted to a personal licence coupled with an interest in the nature of a profit à prendre, represented by their rights with respect to the Cocos palms. Their rights were more than a mere equity enforceable against the former owner and could therefore prevail against the later equitable interest of the purchasers under the contract.

[2.31] The first exception postpones the prior interest where the holder of the prior interest vests the property in someone else enabling that other person to deal with it as his agent, regardless of any parallel relationship of trust thus created: *Abigail v Lapin* (1934) 51 CLR 58. In that case an absolute transfer was given as security for a debt and a subsequent equitable mortgage created by the transferee was held to prevail over the equity of redemption of the original owners. Lord Wright stated the principle (at 68–9):

> Apart from priority in time, the test for ascertaining which encumbrancer has the better equity must be whether either has been guilty of some act or default which prejudices his claim.

Similarly, in *Breskvar v Wall* (1971) 126 CLR 376, the High Court held that the right of the Breskvars to set aside a conveyance fraudulently given to a second party was postponed to that of the third party to whom the second party had conveyed the land because the Breskvars, by their conduct in giving a signed blank transfer as security, had contributed to the assumption upon which the third party, the holder of the later equity, had acted.

[2.32] The second exception arises where the prior holder vests the property in a trustee for sale who sells to a third party and gives the usual receipt but neglects to obtain the price. Any subsequent purchaser from that third party, without notice of the wrong, will obtain an equitable interest having priority over that of the vendor's lien of the original *cestui que* trust: *Lloyds Bank v Bullock* [1896] 2 Ch 192.

[2.33] The third exception postpones the prior interest where the holder has been guilty of some negligence which has led a subsequent taker to assume the non-existence of the prior equity. If fitted into this scheme of listed exceptions *Heid v Reliance Finance* would come under this heading. Failure to lodge a caveat to protect an equitable mortgage within two days of the agreement to grant the security, at which time the mortgagor entered into a contract to sell the property, was held sufficient to postpone the prior interest in *Butler v Fairclough* (1917) 23 CLR 78; while failure to get in the title deeds when he could have done so was held to postpone the interest of an equitable mortgagee of land under common law title to that of a subsequent encumbrancer in *Farrand v Yorkshire Banking Co* (1888) 40 Ch D 182.

[2.34] The fourth exception covers cases such as *Latec Investments v Hotel Terrigal* in which the holder of the prior interest has a mere equity, albeit one which could flower into a full equitable estate if exercised, while the subsequent holder has an equitable proprietary interest, in the form of a security interest or an equitable estate, which has been acquired for value and without notice of the previous equity.

[2.35] The fifth exception applies where the holder of the earlier interest has waived his priority thereby postponing his interest to that of the subsequent taker.

> In *Fung v Tong* [1918] AC 403 a Chinese resident of Chicago provided the funds for the purchase of a lease of land in Hong Kong in the name of his nephew although no gift was intended. The nephew gave two mortgages on the security of the lease and paid them off before fraudulently giving another mortgage to Fung Ping Shan. The uncle later called for a conveyance of the legal estate, which was effected but the conveyance recited that it was subject to the interest of the mortgagee. It was held that, while the earlier equitable estate would ordinarily have prevailed over that of Fung, the uncle had kept the mortgagee's interest alive by accepting the indenture in that form.

[2.36] The sixth exception gives priority to a later interest where the prior interest is in the form of a charge, that is, a floating charge, which gives the grantor a licence to create further legal or equitable interests in the property in the course of its business until the happening of some agreed event, such as default. Equitable interests created pursuant to such a licence will take priority over that of the grantee's initial charge: *Talyor v Bank of NSW* (1886) 11 App Cas 596.

[2.37] The seventh exception gives priority to the later of two, or more, equitable interests created in sequence if the holder of the later interest can obtain from the holder of the legal title a declaration of trust in his, that is the second party's, favour: *Wilkes v Bodington* (1707) 2 Vern 599; 23 ER 991.

[2.38] The eighth exception postpones the equitable interest of a volunteer where the holder of a later interest has paid value and taken without notice: *Taylor v London and County Banking Co* [1901] 2 Ch 231.

[2.39] The ninth exception arises from the Conveyancing Act 1919 (NSW), s 184G, which provides for priority in order of registration in respect of all instruments other than wills affecting land or interests in land which are made bona fide and for valuable consideration. Registration under this Act is not mandatory but failure to register could lead to postponement of the interest concerned.[5]

[2.40] The tenth exception is created by the Real Property Act 1900 (NSW), s 43A, which provides protection against notice for the purchaser of an interest in Torrens title land between settlement and registration by deeming the interest to be a legal estate so as to provide the same protection as that available to purchasers of old system land upon conveyance, so that the purchaser is thereafter 'entitled to perfect his title by registration': *IAC (Finance) Limited v Courtenay* (1963) 110 CLR 550, per Taylor J at 584; *Meriton Apartments Pty Ltd v McLaurin & Tate* (1976) 133 CLR 671. In that sense the purchaser who has taken a registrable instrument from the registered proprietor on settlement without notice of any prior equitable interest does not achieve priority over any previous equitable interests; he defeats them as a bona fide purchaser of the legal estate would under old system title. As a result the benefits of s 43A do not extend to volunteers. A purchaser who takes a registrable instrument on settlement with notice of some prior equity will not be protected against that notice by s 43A.[6] A volunteer transferee who obtains registration having dealt with the registered proprietor, and who takes without notice and is not guilty of actual fraud, that is, dishonesty as opposed to equitable fraud, will take free from any prior equitable interest by virtue of s 43.

The rule in Dearle v Hall: competing equitable assignees of personalty

[2.41] Priorities between competing equitable assignees of personalty are not determined by the rules outlined above. They are governed by the so-called rule in *Dearle v Hall* (1828) 3 Rus 1; 38 ER 475. That rule gives priority, as between competing equitable assignees of personalty, to the assignee who first gives notice to the trustee or fundholder, provided that assignee took the interest for value and without notice of any earlier assignment:

> Brown was entitled to annual income of £93 pa from the residue of his father's estate. In 1808 he assigned that income as security for a covenant to pay certain moneys to Dearle. In 1809 he assigned the income again as security for an annuity which he had covenanted to pay Shering in consideration of an advance by the latter. Later Brown sold his share of the income to Hall as 'an unencumbered fund'. Neither Dearle nor Shering had given notice to the trustees of the estate. Hall did and was held to have priority. Sir Thomas Plumer MR contrasted Hall's prudence with the negligence of the other two, in effect finding them guilty of postponing conduct. He also made much of the necessity for notice to perfect the title of an assignee of personalty.

[2.42] This decision has been questioned but the rule has survived, even though confined very much within its own limits. In *Ward v Duncombe* [1893] AC 369 it was held to be settled law and applied in a case where notice had been given to only one of two trustees. Lord Macnaghten also held that notice, once given, would not lapse even though the trustees might die or be replaced, despite the fact that they were not

---

5. Formerly the Registration of Deeds Act 1897 (NSW), s 12(1), repealed by Act No 20 of 1984 Schedule III. In other states and territories see Real Property Act, 1925 (ACT), s 48; Real Property Act 1861 (NT), s 56; Property Law Act 1974 (Qld), s 246; Registration of Deeds Act 1897 (Tas), s 9; Property Law Act 1958 (Vic), s 6 and Registration of Deeds Act 1856 (WA), s 3.
6. P Butt, *op cit*, para [2029].

required to keep any register of notified interests. One possible exception to that rule arises where an assignee gives notice to less than all of the trustees and those with notice die or retire without communicating their knowledge to the others and notice of a subsequent assignment is then given to the surviving, ignorant trustees, in which case the later assignment will have priority: *Timson v Ramsbottom* (1837) 2 Keen 35; 48 ER 541.[7] As this rule on notice and priority was interpreted so strictly, the conduct of the parties is irrelevant to the application of the rule, despite Sir Thomas Plumer's discussion of the conduct of the earlier assignees in *Dearle v Hall* itself.

[2.43] Notice need not take any particular form and need not even be in writing: *Lloyd v Banks* (1868) LR 3 Ch App 488, but it must be given when the subject matter of the trust or fund is present property; notice of an assignment of future property has no effect under the rule. Similarly, notice to a prospective trustee has no effect and is not cured by the later appointment of that person as trustee without fresh notice being given: *Re Dallas* [1904] 2 Ch 385.

[2.44] The rule is workable if rigid, a rigidity which operates on both its application and its limitation. In *Ward v Duncombe*, Lord Macnaghten said that it ought not to be extended to a new case. That limitation was accepted and applied strictly by the House of Lords in *BS Lyle v Rosher* [1958] 3 All ER 597 to hold that a charge in favour of a moneylender over certain assets ranked after that of trustees of a settlement which included those assets. The charge had been given by the holders of a power of appointment over the assets. The House of Lords held that the rule in *Dearle v Hall* did not apply because the holders of the power of appointment had no interest in the property.

[2.45] The decision in *BS Lyle v Rosher* has been criticised as a misapplication of the rule in *Dearle v Hall*. The trustees of the settlement, whose interest had been reduced to an equitable title which they held on trust for the beneficiaries of the settlement, should have given notice to Lloyds and, as they did not, the notice later given by the moneylender ought to have given his later interest priority under the rule. The mere fact that they held the property as trustees should not have relieved them from the operation of the rule.[8] *Lyle v Rosher* has also been criticised for undermining the one advantage of the rule in *Dearle v Hall*, its simplicity. No one dealing with a beneficiary could be sure, even by checking with the trustee, that they had priority because there might be some secret sub-trust of which the trustee had no notice which would take priority under the principle adopted in *Lyle v Rosher*.[9]

Priority between a prior legal interest and a later equitable interest

[2.46] There is only a limited number of cases in which a later equitable interest will prevail in such circumstances and all require some conscious act or gross fault on the part of the prior legal holder. Mere carelessness or imprudence will not suffice. Those cases are:

1. Where the legal titleholder creates the later interest through some declaration of trust, agreement or other assurance.

---

7. An exception with the potential for an elaborate puzzle: see MG&L, para [831].
8. MG&L, para [840].
9. MG&L, para [842].

2. Where the legal titleholder fraudulently connives at the creation of the later interest.

3. Where the legal titleholder fails to get in the deeds from the party conveying to him or her, thereby enabling the vendor to represent him or herself as legal owner or authorised agent for the property. Mere carelessness or want of prudence will not satisfy this rule: *Saltoon v Lake* [1978] 1 NSWLR 52. An insurance company which took a mortgage from a senior employer was held not to fail under this rule when the manager dishonestly recovered the deeds and used them to give another mortgage: *Northern Counties Ins Co v Whipp* (1884) 26 Ch D 482.

4. Where the legal owner has given another authority to deal with the property and that authority has been exceeded: *Barry v Heider* (1914) 19 CLR 197.

Priorities between competing corporate charges

[2.47] Questions of priority between corporate charges are governed by the Corporations Law, ss 280, 281 and 282. Under s 280 priority is determined by order of registration unless the holder of the later registered charge can show that its charge was created before the other and that the holder of that other charge had notice of the first created charge at the time of creating of the other charge.

The doctrine of bona fide purchaser of the legal estate for value and without notice

[2.48] This doctrine appears to be straightforward and, as far as the first two elements are concerned it is. The interest acquired must be the legal estate and the acquisition must be for valuable consideration, which must be sufficient rather than adequate. Where the legal title is conveyed to a purchaser who has no notice of any prior equity that purchaser takes free from any such equity. A purchaser who receives notice after payment of the consideration but before conveyance of the title will take free from the prior equity once the legal title is conveyed provided that the purchaser is not thereby involved in a breach of trust under the doctrine of *tabula in naufragio*: *Taylor v Russell* [1892] AC 244. For instance, notice of a mortgagor's equity of redemption received after contract but before conveyance will not defeat the purchaser provided he or she gets the legal estate in. If the purchaser has paid for trust property and receives notice of the interest of the *cestui que trust* prior to conveyance he or she will not be able to complete without participating in a breach of trust unless the sale by the trustee is authorised by the terms of the trust. The notice required under this doctrine may be actual, imputed or constructive.

[2.49] Actual notice means actual knowledge on the part of the person in question. Suggestions made in an overheard conversation some five years before was held not to be enough in *Williamson v Bors* (1900) 21 NSWR 302. However, reasonably precise information, even from a stranger, cannot be safely disregarded: *Lloyd v Banks* (1868) LR 3 Ch App 488. Trustees administering a number of estates have statutory protection against being affected in one trust by facts received in another.[10]

---

10. Trustee Act 1925 (NSW), s 62; Trusts Act 1973 (Qld), s 69; Trustee Act 1936 (SA), s 54A; Trustee Act 1958 (Vic), s 35; and Trustees Act 1962 (WA) s 68.

[2.50] Imputed notice is actual or constructive knowledge received by an agent of the purchaser. A client employing a solicitor is deemed to know any information imparted to the solicitor or which the solicitor ought to have acquired while acting properly in the course of the transaction. A principal is not presumed to have notice of his or her agent's fraud: *Schultz v Corwill Properties Pty Ltd* (1969) 90 WN (Pt 1) (NSW) 529.

[2.51] Constructive notice gives a person notice of all matters which would be discovered by making the searches and enquiries usually made in such a transaction or which would have been discovered upon making the enquiries demanded by some relevant fact of which that person had actual notice and which would have put a reasonable person on enquiry. A person who negligently omits to search the register takes subject to such equities as would have been discovered by such searches; although the Registry of Deeds, unlike the Torrens register, is not considered to give notice to all the world: *Mills v Renwick* (1901) 1 SR (Eq) 173. Notice of a deed is considered notice of its contents if it necessarily affects the title: *Davis v Hutchings* [1907] 1 Ch 356; while recital in a deed of a document constitutes notice of any facts discoverable on inspection of that document: *Flower v Owen* (1898) 19 NSWLR (Eq) 72.[11] A purchaser of land with notice that the land is occupied by a third party is deemed to have knowledge, as between him or herself and the occupant, of the occupant's rights with respect to the land: *Williamson v Bors* (1900) 21 NSWR 302 at 307. The bulk of authority supports the view that the onus of proof rests with the party claiming to be a bona fide purchaser although there is significant case law asserting that that onus is discharged once the purchaser shows the payment of value for the title. The onus shifts to the plaintiff to show notice.[12]

[2.52] Statutory protection against this doctrine is given to purchasers by the Conveyancing Act 1919 (NSW) in a number of different situations the most important of which are:

(a) ss 153–154 provide that a person dealing with an executor making a conveyance for the purposes of administration need not enquire as to authority for the transaction or the conveyor's right to convey.

(b) s 165 provides that failure to search at theAustralian Securities Commission will not fix any purchaser of land with notice of any mortgage or charge.

---

11. But cf *Hudson v Viney* [1921] 1 Ch 98 and *Parker v Judkin* [1931] 1 Ch 475; MG&L, para [856].
12. MG&L, para [860].

Chapter Three

3-1 Introduction

[3.1] An assignment is 'the immediate transfer of an existing proprietary right, vested or contingent, from the assignor to the assignee': *Norman v FCT* (1963) 109 CLR 9 at 26, per Windeyer J. An equitable assignment simply means the recognition in equity of the transfer of property — a recognition that may be granted even though some prescribed method of assignment at law, such as registration, has not been completed. In this sense, a court of equity will overlook a failure to comply with statutory requirements, provided the equitable rules are satisfied. With a gift that will require that the assignee is completely constituted as owner of the property at law, or, short of that, is placed in a position from which the transfer can be completed by the donee without the assistance of the donor or the court. The principles governing the recognition of assignments in equity illustrate the operation of some of the maxims of equity; in particular, that equity regards as done that which ought to be done; that equity will not perfect an imperfect gift; and, that equity will not assist a volunteer. The last two would seem to rule out the recognition in equity of voluntary assignments where the legal forms have not been completed. But equity also looks to the intent rather than the form and a donor who has done all that he or she must do to divest him or herself of certain property will not be able to retract his or her bounty simply because of some deficiency in the legal forms which the donee can complete unaided. There are some exceptions to these maxims, the most notable being the assistance equity will provide to the beneficiary of a trust, even though no consideration has been given for the creation of the trust. Some of the complexity surrounding this area of equity can be explained by the friction generated at points at which these various maxims conflict with one another.

[3.2] In assessing whether any particular transaction will be recognised as an effective assignment in equity it is essential to identify correctly the components of the assignment so that the appropriate rule for the validity of any particular transaction can be properly identified. For example, future property — property not yet in existence, at least not yet in the hands of the assignor — can only be assigned in equity and then only for valuable consideration. If the subject matter of the transfer is incorrectly identified as present property it could be assumed that the assignment is valid in equity, even though voluntary, when, in fact, the absence of consideration would be fatal. Assignments for value are generally treated more kindly than gifts. Equity regards consideration as a panacea for a great many ills while the poor volunteer must be able to cure him or herself. It is important to identify whether the interest allegedly assigned is legal or equitable: the rules which govern the recognition of assignments of the two types of property differ. With legal property, there will usually be some prescribed method of transfer, most often statutory, which can be used as a guide in determining whether the assignor has done all that is necessary to effect the gift.

[3.3] Proper recognition of the form of the assignment, whether it is by way of agreement to assign, direct transfer or some other mechanism which has the effect of an assignment but not the form, such as a declaration of trust, will also be crucial to determine the validity of any given assignment, particularly where it is a gift. The form of the assignment will be determined by the intention of the parties, or, in the case of a gift, by the intention of the donor only. It is important to identify precisely how, and sometimes when, the donor intended the gift to take effect. The intention of the supposed donor is all important in determining, in the first case, whether there was a gift; and, second, the way in which the gift was to take effect: *Smith v Perpetual Trustee Co Ltd* (1910) 11 CLR 148. In that case Higgins J expressed the principle in thsese terms, at 167: 'I do not know how there can be any assignment of property — putting aside an assignment by operation of law ... without the intention of the assignor to assign - to pass the property out of himself into someone else. This is the final question in all such cases — what was the intention of the alleged assignor; and this is mainly a question of fact, to be determined by a review of all the circumstances'. The intention of the donor as to when and how a gift is to be effected will be crucial. Once the intended form of the dealing can be identified it will be possible to consider what test to apply to determine whether the alleged assignment is effective. For example, the voluntary assignment of equitable property by way of direction to a trustee will require the communication of a binding direction to the trustee. An assignment of the same interest by way of declaration of trust, that is, by the creation of a sub-trust, can be effected without any communication to the trustee.

> In *Comptroller of Stamps (Vic) v Howard-Smith* (1936) 54 CLR 614, Howard-Smith wrote to the manager of a trustee company that was both his attorney under a power and the executor and trustee of the will of his late wife, under which Howard-Smith was the sole residuary beneficiary. The letter requested the trustee company, as executor of the will and as Howard-Smith's attorney, to pay out of the residue of the estate, upon issue of probate, either in shares or money at the trustee's discretion, certain sums to certain people as shown in a list appended to the letter, those gifts to be free of gift and stamp duty. The letter also said that if there was insufficient in the residue to make all the payments in full they were to abate proportionately. The question arose later whether that letter constituted an assignment of Howard-Smith's interest in the residue. Dixon J held that the letter was a mere authorisation revocable by the donor and had no dispositive effect until acted upon by the trustee. The contents of the letter displayed an intention on the part of the author that the recipients should take on distribution by the trustee company and not before. In addition, the discretion given to the trustee as to the form of the gift and the provision for proportionate abatement in the event of a shortfall rendered the quantum and nature of the benefit being assigned to each of the listed persons uncertain at the time of the letter.

3-2 Voluntary Assignments of Legal Property

Assignments of property assignable at law

[3.4] This covers most forms of legal property. Only such things as part of a chose in action fall outside this net, although before the creation of a statutory power to assign choses in action at law by the Conveyancing Act 1919 (NSW), s 12, no chose in action could be assigned at law. The enactment of that power highlights the central question in this topic: where there is some method of assigning particular legal property at law, must the legal requirements be satisfied before equity will recognise a voluntary assignment of such property (under the maxims that equity will not assist a volunteer nor perfect an imperfect gift) or will equity recognise such a gift as effective at some point before the legal title passes (under the maxim that equity looks to the intent rather than the form)? That question was addressed shortly after the introduction of a statutory means of assigning choses in action in England in *William Brandt's & Sons v Dunlop Rubber Co* [1905] AC 454.

> Brandt's, a banking firm, had agreed to finance purchases of goods by Kramrisch & Co, a rubber merchant. Kramrisch, in turn, agreed to direct its subsequent purchasers to pay Brandt's directly, rather than paying Kramrisch for the goods. Pending such payments Brandt's were to be entitled to a lien on the goods until the full price was paid. Dunlop purchased goods from Kramrisch, and received notice to pay Brandt's but, by mistake, paid another creditor of Kramrisch instead. Brandt's sued Dunlop for the unpaid debt. The House of Lords held that Brandt's were entitled to recover. Dunlop had received clear notice of the assignment in a letter from Brandt's which they were not entitled to disregard. Lord McNaughten bluntly rejected an argument that the assignment of the debt was ineffective because all the statutory requirements for assignment of a chose in action had not been met, saying, at 461, 'Why that which would have been a good equitable assignment before the statute should now be invalid and inoperative because it fails to come up to the requirements of the statute, I confess I do not understand'. His Lordship also said that the style of language used to effect such an assignment was immaterial providing the meaning was plain.

[3.5] That assignment was, of course, for value, but the same principle could be said to extend to voluntary assignments, subject to the general maxim that equity will not perfect an imperfect gift.[1] The basic rule for the recognition of voluntary assignments of legal property was stated by Turner LJ in *Milroy v Lord* (1862) 4 De GF & J 264; 45 ER 1185.

> Thomas Medley executed a voluntary deed in April 1852 purporting to assign 50 shares in the Bank of Louisiana to Lord to be held on certain trusts for the plaintiffs. At law transfer of the shares could only take place by entry in the books of the bank. That was never done. Medley lived for three years after making the deed, during which time dividends on the shares were received by Lord and remitted to the plaintiffs. Lord also held the share certificates and a power of attorney from Medley empowering him to execute a transfer of the shares. On Medley's death the question arose whether the shares formed part of Medley's estate. It was held that they did.

Turner LJ laid down two rules:

> (a) In order to render a voluntary settlement valid and effectual, the settlor must have done everything which, according to the nature of the property comprised in the settlement, was necessary to be done in order to transfer the property and render the settlement binding upon him; and

> (b) If a settlement is intended to be effected by a particular mode or form (ie, direct assignment, declaration of trust, direction to trustee and so forth), the Court will not give effect to it by applying another form. An imperfect assignment will not, for example, be held to be a declaration of trust.

---

1. *Norman v FCT* (1963) 109 CLR 9 at 26, per Windeyer J.

The first 'leg' of Milroy v Lord

[3.6] The words 'necessary to be done' in the first leg of *Milroy v Lord* raise two questions. The first being whether all the legal steps must be completed where there is a method of assignment available at law; and the second being 'done by whom?'. Both those questions were raised in the High Court in *Anning v Anning* (1907) 4 CLR 1049 but the divergence between the judgments given in that case left the issue in an unsettled state in Australia for over 80 years. William Anning executed a deed of gift purporting to convey all his property to his wife and five children several days before he died. Nothing further was done to assure the property to the donees. The property covered by the deed included book debts and money lying to Anning's credit in three banks. It was held that the deed failed as an assignment of everything except the bank deposits and book debts. Griffith CJ took the view that 'necessary to be done' meant necessary to be done by the donor, in the sense that if anything remained to be done by the donor without which the donee could not establish title to the property, the gift would be imperfect, and in the absence of consideration, the court would not assist the donee as against the donor. But, if all that remained to be done could be done by the donee without the assistance of the donor or the court, the gift would be complete. Isaacs J took the view that if the legal title was assignable at law it had to be assigned at law or otherwise equity would not enforce the gift. If for any reason the transfer of the legal title was incomplete when the law permitted it to be complete, Isaacs J was of the view that equity should regard the gift as imperfect and not enforce it. Higgins J said that the donor must do everything he could do, whether obligatory or not, to pass the title.

[3.7] Higgins J's view was not adopted in later cases and played only a minor role in the confusion that followed. The other two judgments remained the subject of debate for decades. Isaacs J's stipulation that all legal requirements be met, including registration, left no apparent room for the recognition in equity of assignments that were incomplete at law. However, his Honour did not make it clear, when talking of the donee 'enforcing' the gift, whether he contemplated that the court would intervene to frustrate a donee who had the power to complete the gift on his own behalf. Equity may not assist a volunteer but there is no maxim that it will frustrate one who has no need of assistance from the court to 'enforce' his or her rights and seeks merely to 'exercise' rights already available. The debate has remained alive largely because there was no categorical rejection of Isaacs J's view by the High Court until 1990, while support for the view of Sir Samuel Griffith was often equivocal.

[3.8] The greatest controversy over the application of the first rule in *Milroy v Lord* showed itself in the question of voluntary assignments of Torrens title land following the decision of Dixon J in *Brunker v Perpetual Trustee Co Ltd* (1937) 57 CLR 555. On the day before his death, a man executed a memorandum of transfer of Torrens title land in favour of his housekeeper. The man handed the transfer to a law stationer without instructions. After the man's death the stationer gave the transfer to the housekeeper's solicitor, who inserted details of the mortgage and presented the transfer for registration. Dixon J, with whom Rich J agreed, said that a memorandum of transfer of Torrens title land could not confer an equitable estate by way of gift on a donee before registration and that only a purchaser, that is, a person who had given consideration, could obtain an equitable interest prior to registration. In Dixon J's view, with Torrens title land the issue was not whether the donee had equitable title to the property but whether the donee had a right, under the statute, to have the transfer registered. He thought that such a right would arise upon delivery to the transferee of a duly executed memorandum of transfer in registrable form. He said, at 603, that he did not think it essential that the donee should also acquire the duplicate certificate of title in New South Wales because the Registrar General had power to dispense with its production when registering an instrument, under the Real Property Act, ss 35, 37, and 38(1), and to require production of that deed under s 12(1)(a). Sections 35, 37, and 38(1) have since been repealed.

[3.9] Dixon J's judgment in *Brunker* has been the subject of considerable criticism over the years,[2] but was never directly overruled until the decision of the High Court in *Corin v Patton* (1990) 169 CLR 540 (see **[3.12]** below). The major complaint was that the rule in *Milroy v Lord* was not applied, despite the fact that there is no reason for its exclusion from the realm of Torrens title land, where equitable interests have long been held to exist even though not registered: *Barry v Heider* (1914) 19 CLR 197. Dixon J placed heavy reliance on the decision of *Scoones v Galvin* [1934] NZLR 1004, in which it was held that a transfer was not complete in equity unless there had been constructive delivery to the donee of a transfer in registrable form and the duplicate certificate of title, as authority for his own decision even though the New Zealand Supreme Court was obviously talking about equitable title and not some statutory right to be registered.

[3.10] Critics of *Brunker* took encouragement from the judgment of Windeyer J in *Norman's* case, a case involving choses in action, not land, but Windeyer J's words were not limited to any particular species of legal property when he said, at 109 CLR 28–9:

> ... the weight of authority is, I think in favour of the view that in equity there is a valid gift of property transferable at law if the donor, intending to make, there and then, a complete disposition and transfer to the donee, does all that on his part is necessary to give effect to his intention and arms the donee with the means of completing the gift according to the requirements of the law.

That is a neat statement of the view espoused by Griffith CJ in *Anning*, and Sir Owen Dixon, who sat as Chief Justice in *Norman*, said of Windeyer J's judgment, at 16, 'I do not know that there is anything contained in it with which I am disposed to disagree'. Torrens title was not mentioned; but neither was it excluded. However, Windeyer J cited *Brunker* as an authority for his proposition and the confusion remained.

> In *Cope v Keene* (1968) 118 CLR 1, a testator executed a memorandum of transfer in favour of his daughters by his first wife. He instructed his solicitor to take all necessary steps to register the transfer. At the time of the testator's death, the transfer had been delivered to one daughter so that she and another could sign and return it. The purported assignment was challenged by the testator's widow and her daughter. It was held that no completed gift had been made during the testator's lifetime. Kitto J said, at 6–7, that to effect the gift the donor would have had to, at least, deliver the executed transfer to the intended donees and, probably, enable them to produce the duplicate certificate to the Registrar General. Taylor J also stressed that such a delivery of the executed transfer was essential. Both cited *Milroy v Lord* and *Brunker* as authority with Taylor J applying the test laid down by Dixon J in *Brunker* at 12.

[3.11] The question arose again in *Taylor v Deputy FCT* (1969) 123 CLR 206, where Barwick CJ, Taylor and Menzies JJ, in a joint judgment, at 213, cited *Brunker* as

2. L Zines, 'Equitable Assignments: When will Equity Assist a Volunteer?' (1965) 38 ALJ 337; MG&L, paras [624]–[628].

authority alongside the judgment of Griffith CJ in *Anning*, without any distinction being drawn let alone a preference expressed. In the area of assignments of choses in action the courts appeared to retreat even further from the rule stated by Griffith CJ in *Anning*.

[3.12] This line of authority left the law in an unsatisfactory state until the decision of the High Court in *Corin v Patton* (1990) 169 CLR 540.

> Mrs Patton was a joint registered proprietor of land under Torrens title with her husband, the respondent. Mrs Patton was terminally ill and wanted to arrange her affairs so as to sever the joint tenancy. She executed a memorandum of transfer of her interest in the land in favour of her brother Mr Corin, who accepted the transfer as transferee. The transfer was expressed to be in consideration of a deed of trust. Under the deed of trust, Corin declared that he held the half interest in the land as tenant in common on trust for Mrs Patton. The certificate of title was held by the State Bank of NSW under an unregistered mortgage. Mrs Patton took no action to procure the production of the certificate of title to enable the transfer of title and died before the transfer was registered. Her husband sought a declaration that he was entitled to the land as sole proprietor. By a cross-claim Corin sought a declaration that the joint tenancy had been severed and that he held a one half interest as tenant in common. Both at first instance and on appeal it was declared that Mrs Patton had not effectively alienated her interest in the land and Mr Patton was entitled to the land by survivorship. The High Court held the execution of the transfer did not sever the joint tenancy because at the time of her death Mrs Patton had not alienated any interest in the land: per Mason CJ, Deane & McHugh JJ on the ground that she had not done all that was necessary to effect such a transfer because she had not authorised the mortgagee to hand the certificate of title to the transferee; per Brennan J, applying *Brunker*, on the ground that in the absence of the certificate of title or dispensation from production the transfer was not registrable; and, per Toohey J that because no consideration had been given for the transfer there was no transaction for equity to enforce.

[3.13] *Corin v Patton* could have been decided on the question of whether Mrs Patton had severed the joint tenancy alone. It was not strictly necessary to address the question of assignments generally. However, the majority took the opportunity to do so and, in the process, probably laid to rest the longest running sore in Australian equity.[3] Mason CJ and McHugh J recognised the uncertainty arising from the first leg of *Milroy v Lord*. Having discussed the point and its chequered history, their Honours endorsed the test preferred by Griffith CJ giving their own statement of the rule, at 559:

> Accordingly, we conclude it is desirable to state that the principle is that, if an intending donor of property has done everything which it is necessary for him to have done to effect a transfer of legal title, then equity will recognise the gift. So long as the donee has been equipped to achieve the transfer of legal ownership, the gift is complete in equity. 'Necessary' used in this sense means necessary to effect a transfer. From the viewpoint of the intending donor, the question is whether what he has done is sufficient to enable the legal transfer to be effected without further action on his part.

As for the Real Property Act, s 41, which provides that until registration an instrument of transfer shall be ineffectual to pass an estate or interest in the land, Mason CJ and McHugh J held, at 560, that s 41 'does not touch whatever rights are behind' the

---

3. I say 'probably' because it has been suggested that the fact that the statements in *Corin v Patton* on *Milroy v Lord* were *obiter* provides scope for the resurrection of the Dixon test from *Brunker*: MG&L, para [630]. I suppose someone might regenerate the smallpox virus too. Hopefully no judge will be tempted, let alone persuaded to indulge in any such wanton vandalism.

instrument: *Barry v Heider* (1914) 19 CLR 197 at 216, per Isaacs J, and thus does not prevent the passing of an equitable estate to the donee under a completed transaction. In the process their Honours noted, at 559, that the Griffith test 'implicitly recognises that the donee acquires an equitable estate or interest in the subject matter of the gift once the transaction is complete so far as the donor is concerned'.

[3.14] Deane J came to a conclusion similar to that of Mason CJ and McHugh J. He said that Dixon J's test, 'should be accepted not as establishing a new kind of statutory right but as identifying the test for determining whether the stage has been reached when a gift of Real Property Act land under an unregistered memorandum of transfer is complete and effective in equity'. His Honour then described that test as a twofold one:

> It is whether the donor has done all that is necessary to place the vesting of the legal title within the control of the donee and beyond the recall or intervention of the donor. Once that stage is reached and the gift is complete and effective in equity, the equitable interest in the land vests in the donee and, that being so, the donor is bound in conscience to hold the property as trustee for the donee pending the vesting of the legal title.

[3.15] Brennan J was not willing to disturb what he described as the orthodox view founded on the judgment of Dixon J in *Brunker*, which denies the existence of an equitable estate or interest in the time between delivery of an executed memorandum of transfer and registration. His Honour thought that a statutory right to registration could arise (at least) on delivery of a registrable transfer. That right, unlike a purchaser's contractual right, was confined by s 41 and gave rise to no equitable estate or proprietary interest.

[3.16] Toohey J considered that the issue in the case was not whether Mr Corin could enforce the transfer against Mrs Patton, but whether the transfer defeated Mr Patton's right to be registered as sole proprietor of the land. That question was decided, in his view, by the fact that the transfer had not been registered at the time of Mrs Patton's death, and that there was no transaction which equity would enforce. In an apparent endorsement of the Dixon test from *Brunker*, Toohey J agreed with the conclusion reached by the Court of Appeal that Corin did not have an unqualified right to have the transfer registered. Corin's right was qualified, in his view, by the fact that Mrs Patton could have recalled the transfer or taken steps, by caveat or injunction, to prevent its registration. Mrs Patton's failure to call on the bank to produce the certificate of title for registration of the transfer to Mr Corin was not, he thought, of great moment. She would not have been expected to do so until a date had been fixed for registration of the transfer and, as joint tenants are not issued with separate certificates of title, there was no certificate representing her interest in the land.

[3.17] Toohey J did not express disapproval of the test laid down by Dixon J in *Brunker*. He also made no comment on the issue of the correctness or otherwise of the divergent views expressed in *Anning*. That is largely because he did not see *Milroy v Lord* as crucial to the decision in *Corin v Patton*. However, in view of his conclusion, at 592–3, that Corin's claim failed because he had not become registered and that 'There was no transaction which equity would enforce; there was a transaction that had not been consummated', it would seem that the question of whether there was an effective assignment in equity was relevant to what he saw as the 'real point' in the case. Toohey J's reference to the transaction as one which equity would not 'enforce' is confusing; recognition is all that is needed. The real question is whether equity will recognise an assignment as effective, not whether it will enforce it.

[3.18] If Toohey J's view were the view of the court then *Brunker* would still be good law, as would the Griffith test in *Anning*, and the confusion redolent in decisions like *Cope v Keene*, *Olsson v Dyson* and *Taylor v Deputy FCT* would still prevail. The majority, Mason CJ and McHugh J and Deane J, has held that *Brunker*, insofar as it stands as authority for the proposition that a voluntary assignment of Torrens title land will only be effective when the donee acquires some statutory right to registration, is no longer good law in Australia. After a long period of uncertainty, the Griffith test in *Anning* has captured the field and the test for the recognition in equity of voluntary assignments of legal property assignable at law is as stated by the majority in *Corin v Patton*.

[3.19] Some questions may remain open after *Corin v Patton*. The first is whether an executed memorandum of transfer, otherwise registrable, can be registered after the death of the transferor without further endorsement or approval by the executor of the estate of that proprietor. Brennan J thought, at 566, that the weight of authority supported the view that such a transfer could be registered after the death of the transferor, although, he noted that Kitto J (with whom McTiernan J agreed) thought otherwise in *Cope v Keene* (1968) 118 CLR 1 at 7. Toohey J thought, at 591, the issue was concluded in favour of the registrability of the transfer after the death of the transferor. That must be the better view, although the Kitto view from *Cope v Keene* cannot be taken to have been dismissed. If Brennan and Toohey JJ are wrong, no one could safely accept a signed transfer on settlement of a conveyance without proof that the proprietor was still alive.

[3.20] The second question asks whether it is necessary, in New South Wales at least, for the donor to deliver the certificate of title to the donee, or otherwise make the title deed available for registration of the transfer to the donee. Section 96(2) of the Conveyancing Act 1919 (NSW) provides that 'a mortgagor shall be entitled to have the relevant certificate of title ... lodged at the office of the Registrar-General to allow ... the registration of any authorised dealing by the mortgagor with the land'. Mortgagor' is defined to include a person deriving title to the equity of redemption under the original mortgagor, or entitled to redeem a mortgage. Mason CJ and McHugh J, at 561, with whom Deane J, at 583, agreed, took the view that s 96 did not help Mr Corin because he was not a person entitled to redeem the mortgage until there had been a transfer of Mrs Patton's interest, which does rather beg the question. Mason CJ and McHugh J, at 560, dealt with the question of production of the certificate of title generally saying that it can scarcely be said that the donor has done everything necessary to be done by him if he has retained the certificate of title, by virtue of the possession of which the gift might well be thwarted. Brennan J, at 566–7, agreed with the majority on the effect of s 96. None of the judges expressed a view on whether a donee in possession of an executed memorandum of transfer in registrable form could claim the benefit of s 96 and obtain possession of the certificate of title, where it was held by a mortgagee, by the simple expedient of paying out the mortgage.

[3.21] The operation of the rule in *Milroy v Lord* was also considered before *Corin v Patton* in *Noonan v Martin* (1987) 10 NSWLR 402:

> An elderly widow gave her grandson several signed withdrawal slips for an Access account with the ANZ Bank in her name. He visited her frequently and she had made advances of money to him in the past. She died on 8 May 1985. At that time she had a

credit balance in the Access account of $87,130.84. On the day of the widow's death, but after she had died, the grandson completed a withdrawal slip, for the sum of $87,130.00, dating it 21 April 1985, and sent his wife with it to the bank where she withdrew the amount and deposited it into an account in the names of herself and her husband. The executors of the widow's estate took proceedings against the grandson and his wife seeking a declaration that the $87,130.00 formed part of the widow's estate. Bryson J held that it did and that a signed withdrawal slip, being merely an authority to withdraw moneys from an account, did not effect an assignment of the moneys in the account. Furthermore, any authority conferred by possession of the signed withdrawal slip was revoked on the death of the account holder. The moneys in the account constituted a debt owed to the customer by the bank and could only be assigned at law under s 12 of the Conveyancing Act 1919 (NSW).

In many respects the decision in *Noonan v Martin* was fairly straightforward. There could have been no other outcome. The case did give Bryson J the opportunity to comment on some aspects of the law of equitable assignments that are worth noting. Having cited *Milroy v Lord* (1862) 4 De G & F & J 264; 45 ER 1185, Bryson J emphasised the last words of Turner LJ's classic test, 'and render the settlement binding upon him'. Having placed stress on those words, Bryson J then said, at 410:

> The words to which I have added emphasis show that it is not enough that a settlor should put a donee in a position to carry registration through, so that the donee has for example the opportunity to complete blank forms in authorised ways or in ways suggested by the nature of the forms, obtain necessary approvals, present them to the registration officer and actually see the process of registration through. It is also necessary that for some legal reason the settlor should be prevented from interrupting and should have no right to interrupt that process.

[3.22] *Noonan v Martin* was, of course, decided before *Corin v Patton*. Bryson J was thus bound, at least to some extent, by *Brunker's* case. His Honour referred to the test laid down by that case as 'an application of and not a gloss on the passage in *Milroy v Lord* to which I earlier gave emphasis'. The issue then became, in Bryson J's view, a question of whether the donee had obtained the property in the memorandum of transfer itself (considered as a piece of paper) and was in a position to have it registered while the donor had no right to prevent its registration so that the gift was, as Deane J put it, 'beyond the recall or intervention of the donor' (see **[3.14]**). That view certainly reflects the approach taken in *Cope v Keene* (1968) 118 CLR 1, in which possession of the memorandum of transfer for a limited purpose, ie, to sign and return it, did not 'arm the donee with the means of completing the gift'. Accordingly, when considering whether the test as stated by the majority in *Corin v Patton* has been satisfied it will be necessary to consider whether the donee has been given property in, rather than mere possession of, the memorandum of transfer and any necessary title documents considered as pieces of paper.[4] The relevant question then is, 'can the donor recall the transaction'?

[3.23] The test stated by the majority in *Corin v Patton* was the test for the recognition in equity of assignments of all legal property, not merely interests in Torrens title land. Indeed, if anything, *Corin v Patton* marked the clear extension of the general test

---

4. Bryson J's decision has been the subject of criticism on this point. But, if one accepts the proviso that the assignor render the settlement binding on him or herself as meaning no more than that it be beyond his or her recall, in the sense that he or she has relinquished possession of all necessary documents and that no actions remain to be performed, and no documents are still held by agents of the assignor who could then revoke the authority to complete the transaction, it is no more than a proper clarification of *Milroy v Lord*.

laid down in *Milroy v Lord*, as interpreted by the majority of the High Court, to Torrens title land in addition to all other legal property assignable at law, which was clearly the domain of *Milroy v Lord* before *Corin v Patton*. In that respect any statements in the judgments in *Grey v Australian Motorists & General Insurance Co Pty Ltd* [1976] NSWLR 669 which suggest that an assignment of legal property cannot be complete in equity until all the legal requirements, including registration if applicable, are met must be considered as no longer correct.

The second 'leg' of Milroy v Lord

[3.24] Under this rule, if an assignment is intended to be effected by some particular form, that is, by direct assignment, declaration of trust, direction to trustee and so forth, the court will not give effect to it by treating it as another form. A purported direct transfer which fails as a transfer cannot be saved by being treated as a declaration of trust. This rule has caused far less controversy. The only question that has been asked concerns the position of the assignor between the time at which the assignment is recognised in equity and its completion at law. While it would be incorrect to treat a failed transfer as a declaration of trust, that does not mean that after an effective transfer in equity the legal titleholder cannot be said to hold the property as trustee for the assignee pending final transfer of the legal title. Inevitably, where one person holds the legal title to something and the equitable interest has passed to someone else, the legal titleholder can be said to hold as trustee for the beneficial owner.

In *Re Rose; Rose v IRC* [1952] Ch 499, the question arose after the death of Mr Rose whether certain shares had formed part of his estate at a given date before his death for the purposes of assessing notional death duty. Rose had executed transfers of the shares and handed them, with the appropriate certificates, to the transferees or their agents. They were registered three months later. The crucial date was ten days after the delivery of the transfers and scrip. It was held that on executing the transfers and handing them over with the scrip Rose had done all in his power to divest himself of his right, title and interest in the shares and that the mere fact that the transaction was intended to take effect as a transfer did not mean that it could not operate as a trust for a limited period and for the limited purpose of giving effect to the transfer in the meantime.

That decision is consistent with *Milroy v Lord* and confirmed an earlier decision coincidentally named *Re Rose* [1949] Ch 78 in which an approach akin to that of Griffith CJ in *Anning* was applied to a similar assignment of shares. Applying the words of Windeyer J from *Norman*, the donee had been clearly 'armed' with the means of completing the gift at law on the relevant date.

Assignments of property not assignable at law

[3.25] Before the introduction of a statutory means of assigning choses in action at law those interests could only be assigned in equity. That restriction has now been lifted but the statutory method of assignment only applies to an assignment of a complete chose. Part of a chose in action still cannot be assigned at law: *Williams v Atlantic Assurance Co* [1933] 1 KB 81; *Re Steel Wing* [1921] 1 Ch 349; except in jurisdictions where there has been statutory relief from this rule: Property Law Act 1969 (WA), s 20(3). The old equitable test still applies to the assignment of part of a chose in action as shown by *Shepherd v FCT* (1965) 113 CLR 385. That test required the donor to do every act to be done by him or her to complete the title of his or her donee, even though the title could never be complete at law: *Fortescue v Barnett* (1834) 3 My & K 36; 40 ER 14. Despite its illogicality, and the fact that the test for the assignment of equitable property would have been preferable, this rule was upheld by the Court of Appeal in *Re Patrick; Bills v Tatham* [1891] 1 Ch 82. This rule, and its application to a voluntary assignment of part of a debt was upheld by Windeyer J in *Norman's* case, at 31–4, and affirmed by the High Court in *Shepherd* in which Kitto J said, at 397, that such an assignment would be sufficient if there was:

> ... a manifestation by the assignor of an intention to transfer the chose in action to the assignees in a manner binding upon himself, as distinguished from an intention merely to give a revocable mandate while retaining ownership of the chose in action.

3–3 Voluntary Assignments of Equitable Property

[3.26] Equitable property means property recognised only in, or rights only enforceable in equity, such as the interest of a beneficiary under a trust, the rights of a partner in the assets of a partnership or any other equitable chose in action, that is, a 'thing' provable in an action in equity. The effectiveness of any purported assignment of such equitable property requires consideration of two different questions. First, the assignment must satisfy the general law test for the validity of assignments appropriate for assignments in that particular form, whether the assignment is in the form of a direct assignment, a declaration of trust, direction to the trustee or whatever. Second, even if the assignment satisfies the general law test it may fail if it is not in writing when it is required to be by the Statute of Frauds, the Conveyancing Act 1919 (NSW), s 23C, or its equivalent in other States.[5] Those two questions are dealt with together as the validity of any assignment of equitable property is inevitably scrutinised under both heads. Where equitable property is assigned for value different considerations will apply in determining its effectiveness. As with legal property, the payment of consideration can cure many formal defects, including the absence of writing, where writing is otherwise required. On the other hand, a voluntary assignment of equitable property must satisfy the necessary formal requirements before it can be recognised.

[3.27] The first 'leg' of *Milroy v Lord* applies to voluntary assignments of equitable property just as it does to assignments of legal property. However, the requirements for an assignment of equitable property will usually be different from those for legal property so that what is 'necessary to be done' will also differ. To paraphrase the test laid down by Mason CJ and McHugh J in *Corin v Patton* (1990) 169 CLR 540 at 559 (see **[3.13]** above): if an intending donor of equitable property has done everything which it is necessary for him to do to effect a transfer of the equitable title, then equity will recognise the gift. From the viewpoint of the intending donor, the question is whether what he or she has done is sufficient to enable the equitable transfer to take effect without further action on his or her part. That will usually mean satisfying the formal requirements of the general law test for assignments in the chosen

---

5. Property Law Act 1974 (Qld), ss 5 & 9; Law of Property Act 1936 (SA), s 29; Conveyancing and Law of Property Act 1884 (Tas), s 60 (2); Property Law Act 1958 (Vic), s 53; Property Law Act 1969 (WA), s 34.

form as well as any statutory requirement of writing, to the extent that any steps are required of the donor.

[3.28] Identification of the form of the dealing is obviously crucial in this scheme because that form will determine the test to be applied to establish the validity of any voluntary assignment of equitable property. The second 'leg' of *Milroy v Lord* also applies to these dealings, in that if they fail to satisfy the requirements set for dealings in their particular form they will not be saved by being deemed to take effect as some other form: an ineffective direction to a trustee will not be deemed to be a declaration of trust, and vice versa. The form of the dealing is determined by the intention of the donor in the circumstances of the transaction: *Smith v Perpetual Trustee Co Ltd* (1910) 11 CLR 148 at 163. As well as ascertaining the form in which the dealing is intended to take effect it is also important to ascertain the intention of the donor to determine whether the assignment is to be immediately binding, in other words, whether the donor intends to part with dominion over the property then and there, or whether it is designed to come about later, such as on the happening of some given event, through the exercise of a revocable mandate, as illustrated by *Comptroller of Stamps (Vic) v Howard-Smith* (1936) 54 CLR 614 (see **[3.3]** above). In that case Dixon J stated his view on the recognition of the form of a purported equitable assignment, at 621–3:

> A voluntary disposition of an equitable interest may take one of at least three forms. It may consist of an expression or indication of intention on the part of the donor that he shall hold the equitable interest vested in him upon trust for the persons intended to benefit. In that case he retains the title to the equitable interest, but constitutes himself trustee, and, by his declaration imposes upon himself an obligation to hold it for the benefit of others, namely, the donees.
>
> In the second place, the disposition may consist of a sufficient expression of an immediate intention to make over to the persons intended to benefit the equitable interest vested in the donor, or some lesser interest carved out of it. In that case communication to the trustee or person in whom the legal title to the property is vested is not required in order effectually to assign the equitable property. Notice to the trustee may be important to bind him to respect the assignment and in order to preserve priorities. But it is not a condition precedent to the operation of the expression of intention as an assignment. Nor does it appear necessary that the intention to pass the equitable property shall be communicated to the assignee. What is necessary is that there shall be an expression of intention then and there to set over the equitable interest, and, perhaps, it should be communicated to someone who does not receive the communication under confidence or in the capacity only of an agent for the donor.
>
> In the third place, the intending donor for whom property is held upon trust may give to his trustee a direction requiring him thenceforth to hold the property upon trust for the intended donee.
>
> ... a voluntary disposition of an equitable interest may (also) be effected by the communication to the trustee of a direction, intended to be binding on him, thenceforward to hold the trust property upon trust for the donee (provided the beneficiary giving the direction is *sui juris* and entitled to an equitable interest corresponding to the full legal interest in property vested in his trustee). But it must be a direction, and not a mere authority revocable until acted upon. Such an authority is not in itself an assignment. It may, it is true, result in a transfer of an equitable interest. For the trustee acting upon it may make an effectual appropriation of the trust property to the new beneficiary, or may acknowledge to him that he holds the trust property thenceforward on his behalf. If the authority contemplates or allows such a method of imparting an equitable interest to the donee, the action of the trustee may be effectual to bring about the result. But, in such a case, it is not the donor's expression of intention which per se

constitutes the assignment. It is the dealing with the trust property under his authorisation.

That analysis of the methods by which equitable property might be assigned is echoed in the judgment of Romer LJ in *Timpson's Executors v Yerbury* [1936] 1 KB 645 at 664:

> Now the equitable interest in property in the hands of a trustee can be disposed of by the person entitled to it in favour of a third party in any one of four different ways. The person entitled to it (1) can assign it to the third party directly; (2) can direct the trustees to hold the property in trust for the third party ... (3) can contract for valuable consideration to assign the equitable interest to him; or (4) can declare himself to be a trustee for him of such interest.

In addition to those four methods equitable property can also be assigned by way of release, in the sense that a beneficiary of a trust can release the trustee from his or her obligations as trustee, thereby enabling the trustee to enjoy complete beneficial ownership of the trust property. While expressed as a release such a transaction has the effect of transferring the equitable interest in the property from the beneficiary to the trustee.

The requirement of writing

[3.29] The necessity for writing to effect an assignment of equitable property arises from the Conveyancing Act 1919 (NSW), s 23C and its equivalents in other States.[6] Section 23C provides:

> **23C(1)** Subject to the provisions of this Act with respect to the creation of interests in land by parol—
>
> (a) no interest in land can be created or disposed of except by writing signed by the person creating or conveying the same, or by his agent thereunto lawfully authorised in writing, or by will, or by operation of law;
>
> (b) a declaration of trust respecting any land or any interest therein must be manifested and proved by some writing signed by some person who is able to declare such trust or by his will;
>
> (c) a disposition of an equitable interest or trust subsisting at the time of the disposition, must be in writing signed by the person disposing of the same or by his will, or by his agent thereunto lawfully authorised in writing.
>
> (2) This section does not affect the creation or operation of resulting implied or constructive trusts.

Under s 23C, writing is clearly required for the disposition or creation of equitable interests in land, except where they arise by operation of law under the principles of resulting or implied trusts (see Chapter 16) or of constructive trusts: see Chapter 17. In other words, any transfer or other disposition of an equitable interest in land must be in writing. The creation of an equitable interest in land suggests a declaration of trust or other act giving rise to an new equitable interest in land. Any purported disposition which does not comply with s 23C(1) is void. This applies equally to dispositions of subsisting equitable interests in real property and personalty: *PT Ltd v Maradona Pty Ltd* (1992) 27 NSWLR 241. As 'a disposition of an equitable interest ... subsisting at the time' such an assignment 'must be in writing signed by the (assignee) ... (etc)'. Failure to comply with s 23C(1)(c) would render the purported assignment

---

6. See note 5 above.

void. Declarations of trust 'respecting any land or any interest therein' need only be manifested and proved by some writing in accordance with s 23C(1)(b). In other words, such a declaration can be satisfied by later writing and is not necessarily void if not expressed in writing at the time of the alleged declaration. This appears to suggest some inconsistency between s 23C(1)(a) and s 23C(1)(b) as to the requirements for the validity of declarations of trust relating to land or any interest in land which lead to the creation of an equitable interest in land. Under s 23C(1)(a), no equitable interest in land can be created by a declaration of trust unless the declaration is in writing. Under s 23C(1)(b), such a declaration may be validated by later writing manifesting and proving the declaration. As s 23C(1)(b) expressly deals with declarations of trust regarding land, it would appear to operate as a qualifier on s 23C(1)(a), requiring that it not be construed as applying strictly to declarations of trust. Dispositions of equitable interests in personalty must also be in writing by virtue of s 23C(1)(c). There is a view to the contrary, that is, to the effect that s 23C applies only to assurances of land or interests in land, but, apart from anything else, the fact that s 23C(1)(c) would be unnecessary if that was so — the ground being entirely covered by paras (a) and (b) — appears to defeat that argument — unless para (a) was confined to dealings with legal interests in land only, a view which appears to defy language, law and logic. In *Adamson v Hayes* (1973) 130 CLR 276 at 292, Menzies J was prepared to give para (a), or its Western Australian equivalent, such a restricted definition. However, Walsh J, at 297, and Gibbs J, at 302–4, were of a different view and that seems to be the view preferred by the commentators. Considering the distinction employed by the legislature between a 'disposition' of an interest and the 'creation' of an interest, it appears to be strongly arguable that s 23C does not require writing for a declaration of trust of personalty by a person who is at the time of the declaration the absolute owner of the personalty. Such a declaration would lead to the 'creation' of an equitable interest in the personalty, there being no such separate interest before. While the definition of 'disposition' in the Conveyancing Act (NSW), s 7 includes 'declaration of trust', the only 'disposition' of an equitable interest in personalty required to be in writing by s 23C is a disposition of a 'subsisting' equitable interest. Accordingly, it must be the case that an oral declaration of trust in personalty, such as, say, shares in a company, must be effective because it leads to the 'creation' of an equitable interest and cannot be characterised as a disposition of a subsisting equitable interest.

In *Hunter v Moss* [1994] 3 All ER 215, the plaintiff claimed that the defendant had made an oral declaration of trust in his favour of 5 per cent of the shares in a certain company. The case turned on the question of whether there was sufficient certainty of description of the subject matter of the trust, and not whether writing was needed for its creation. At first instance the judge found for the plaintiff and upheld the trust. The Court of Appeal dismissed an appeal against that decision. *Milroy v Lord* was referred to in the judgment of Dillon LJ, with whom Mann and Hirst LJJ agreed, at 219–20. In doing 'all that necessary to be done' to effect a settlement of these shares by declaration of trust it was not considered necessary to express the declaration in writing.

In *Secretary Department of Social Security v James* (1990) 95 ALR 615, a woman purchased a home unit in order to provide accommodation for her 35 year old invalid daughter and her granddaughter at a nominal rent. While she purchased the unit in her own name her evidence was that she regarded the unit as her daughters and that she retained it in her own name for her daughter's protection and under her will the unit would go to her daughter alone. The Department of Social Security included the value of the unit as part of the value of the woman's property for the purpose of s 8 of the Social Security Act 1947 (Cth). The Administrative Appeals Tribunal found as a fact that the respondent had declared an intention to hold the unit on trust for her daughter and granddaughter at the time it was purchased. Lee J, on appeal to the Federal Court, held that the material before the Tribunal permitted it to come to that conclusion even though the evidence raised competing inferences. In construing s 34(1)(b) of the Property Law Act 1969 (WA) Lee J said the sub-section may be satisfied by a combination of documents capable of being read together and that any informal writing may stand as existence of trust including correspondence from third parties, a telegram, an affidavit, or answer to interrogatories. He further held that the date of creation of the writing is not material. It may come into existence at any time after the declaration of the trust. While Lee J accepted the finding of the Tribunal as to the declaration of the trust he considered that it had erred in law in finding that s 34(1)(b) was satisfied, in that there was no writing sufficient to evidence the trust. However, he returned the matter to the Tribunal for further hearing and said it would be appropriate for the Tribunal to receive such further evidence as it saw fit. One can assume that the lawyers for the woman read that message loud and clear.

This decision was affirmed by Kearney J in *Hagan v Waterhouse* (1991) 34 NSWLR 308 at 385–6. The requirements of s 23C(1)(b) would be satisfied where a trustee acknowledged a subsisting trust over land in letters. Those letters would constitute sufficient written proof of the trust to enable its enforcement: *Hagan v Waterhouse*, at 386.

Dealings in the form of direct assignments

[3.30] The general law rule here was stated by Windeyer J in *Norman's* case,

> ... except that writing is required by s 9 of the Statute of Frauds, no formality is necessary beyond a clear expression of an intention to make an immediate disposition.

[3.31] If the interest being assigned is an equitable chose in action it would, prima facie, also have to comply with the Conveyancing Act 1919 (NSW), s 12, dealing with assignments of choses in action, as well. Section 12 provides:

> Any absolute assignment in writing under the hand of the assignor ... of any debt or other legal chose in action, of which express notice in writing has been given to the debtor, trustee, or other person from whom the assignor would have been entitled to receive or claim such debt or chose in action, shall be, and be deemed to be effectual in law ... to pass and transfer the legal right to such debt or chose in action from the date of such notice ...

The expression 'legal chose in action' in that section was said to cover to equitable choses as well in *FCT v Everett* (1979) 143 CLR 440 at 447, per Barwick CJ, Stephen, Mason and Wilson JJ. An assignment of an equitable chose would not need to comply strictly with s 12. That section provides a method whereby equitable choses in action may be assigned, but it is not mandatory for the effective assignment of equitable interests in equity, as it is for the valid assignment of legal choses at law. There always was a mechanism in equity for the assignment of choses in action. Section 12 provides the only method of assignment of such interests at law.[7] To hold that compliance with s 12 was mandatory for the assignment of equitable choses in action would overturn the long established rule that notice to the trustee or fundholder is not necessary to effect such an assignment: *Comptroller of Stamps v Howard-Smith*, per Dixon J at 622; although failure to give such notice may affect the priority of the assignee: *Ward v Duncombe* [1893] AC 369 at 392, per Lord McNaughten. Similarly,

---

7. MG&L, paras [604]–[608]; HG&A, paras [726]–[727]. Of course, a purported assignment of a legal chose may be effective in equity even though all the legal requirements under s 12 especially notice, have not been met.

notice to the assignee does not appear to be essential: *Howard-Smith*, per Dixon J at 622; although Lord Wright MR took a different view in *Timpson's Executors v Yerbury* [1936] 1 KB 645 at 658. In Australia, failure to communicate to the assignee would go to the question of the intention of the assignor, rather than to validity alone.

Dealings in the form of declarations of trust

[3.32] This, of course, involves the creation of a sub-trust, as the interest held in the first place is equitable. There has been some debate as to the effect of such a declaration upon the assignor. Clearly, if he imposes active duties on himself then he will 'remain in the picture': *Re Lashmar* [1891] 1 Ch 258. However, if the declaration of trust is expressed as an absolute declaration, the position of the assignor is less certain. In England it has been held that the whole equitable interest thereby passes to the assignee and the assignor disappears from the scene: *Grey v IRC* [1958] Ch 690 at 715; while in Australia the assignor remains beneficiary under the first trust and is under an obligation to hold those rights for the benefit of the assignee: *Comptroller of Stamps v Howard-Smith*, per Dixon J, at 621–2. Unless the assignment is actually in the form of a direction to the trustee to hold the property on trust for some new beneficiary, as was the case in *Grey v IRC*, the Australian view would seem the more logical of the two interpretations. The litmus test would be any attempt by the beneficiary of the sub-trust to enforce the duties of the head trustee. Subject to some special circumstances, such as a separate acknowledgement by the head trustee of duties owed to the sub-beneficiary, any proceedings taken by the sub-beneficiary would have to include the sub-trustee, the beneficiary under the head trust. At the outset those proceedings might take the form of an application for a mandatory injunction against the sub-trustee seeking orders compelling him or her to enforce his or her rights against the head trustee.

[3.33] The general law test for the validity of assignments in this form is similar to that which applies to declarations of trust of legal property: the assignor must indicate an intention to immediately and thenceforth hold the property on trust for the intended beneficiary. Specific words need not be used provided the intention is clear: *Richards v Delbridge* (1874) LR 18 Eq 11; nor is it essential for the declaration to be communicated to the assignee: *Standing v Bowring* (1885) 31 Ch D 282.

[3.34] Fitting these declarations of a sub-trust into one of the pigeon-holes of s 23C is not so simple, a difficulty caused in part by the apparent overlap between the provisions of that section. If the subject matter of the original trust included land or an interest in land s 23C(1)(b) would apply to any declaration of a sub-trust, as would s 23C(1)(a) because the declaration would create an interest in land — and could be said to dispose of one as well. A declaration of sub-trust would also effect the disposition of a subsisting equitable interest, and thus s 23C(1)(c) would require writing even if the original trust included no land. However, if the assignor does not 'disappear from the picture' then it could be said that he had not disposed of his interest and it is arguable that writing may not be required for a declaration of a sub-trust of personalty — an argument complicated by the inclusion of 'declaration of trust' in the definition of 'disposition' in s 7 of the Act. As a declaration of trust of a legal interest in personalty need not be in writing and can be inferred from conduct: *Paul v Constance* [1977] 1 All ER 195, it could seem unduly restrictive to apply a different rule to declarations of trust in equitable interests in personalty. Notwithstanding all that, and particularly in view of the inclusion of the words 'declaration of trust' in the definition of the word 'Disposition' in s 7 of the Conveyancing Act, the better view must be that a voluntary declaration of trust of a subsisting equitable interest, whether in realty or personalty or a mixture of both must be in writing by virtue of s 23C(1)(c). If consideration is provided, or other factors come into play that might give rise to a resulting or constructive trust, and thus bring the transaction under the umbrella of s 23C(2), writing may not be necessary.

Dealings in the form of directions to the trustee

[3.35] To deal with the equitable estate. The general law test for assignments in this form was set by Dixon J in *Howard-Smith*, at 622: provided the beneficiary is *sui juris* and entitled to a beneficial interest corresponding to the full legal interest, he or she may impose a new object on the trustee, by a voluntary disposition which may be effected by the communication to the trustee of a direction, intended to be binding on him, thenceforward to hold the trust property upon trust for the donee. But it must be a direction, and not a mere authority revocable until acted upon. Such an authority is not in itself an assignment, although it may result in the transfer of an equitable interest. If the direction does not amount to an immediate and irrevocable assignment, and it is not acted on prior to the death of the assignor, the authority will be revoked by death: *Parker & Parker v Ledsham* [1988] WAR 32. Assignments in the form of directions to the trustee to deal with the equitable estate, if intended to take effect immediately, must be in writing:

> In *Grey v IRC* [1960] AC 1, a Mr Hunter transferred shares to certain nominees and later gave them an oral direction to hold the shares thereafter on trust, in a number of parcels, for his present and future grandchildren with the intent that he be excluded from all rights or benefit to or in the shares. Declarations of trust were subsequently executed acknowledging the new trusts. The declarations were assessed for stamp duty as voluntary dispositions. The trustees appealed against that assessment arguing that Hunter's interest had been disposed of by the oral direction and the written declarations simply noted trusts to which the shares were already subject. It was held that Hunter's oral direction was a 'disposition of a subsisting equitable interest and thus ineffective without writing'. Thus, the later declaration did effect the disposition of the beneficial interest in the shares and was liable to the duty.

[3.36] *Grey's* case may have settled the need for writing in assignments in this form but it left some confusion over the mechanics of such a transaction. Different views were expressed on that issue. Upjohn J, at first instance, [1958] Ch 375, Lord Evershed MR, in the Court of Appeal [1958] Ch 609, and Lord Radcliffe, in the House of Lords, all expressed the view that such an assignment operated by way of trust and not by way of assignment. Ormerod LJ, in the Court of Appeal, said that following such a direction the equitable interest of the donor ceased to exist and a new interest sprang up in the donee. The first three, at least, are at odds with Dixon J in *Howard-Smith* who was of the view that such a direction operated by substituting new objects for old. In that sense these assignments are clearly different from declarations of sub-trusts where the donor remains in the picture. In an assignment by way of direction to the trustee to deal with the equitable estate, the assignor does disappear from the picture, at least to the extent of the interest assigned. The proposition that an assignment in this form operates by way of trust seems perverse and unnecessary. It carries with it the notion that the assignor, in some way, holds an interest on trust for the assignee at some moment before the instruction takes effect. That is nonsense. If the assignor has the right to instruct the trustee to hold the property in favour of new objects he or she does not need to declare him or herself trustee of the equitable interest in favour of those objects first. All the assignee needs to do is instruct the trustee in the appropriate terms. But the assignor must do that. In the case of an assignment in the form of a declaration of trust, that is, a sub-trust, the assignor does not need to communicate with the trustee at all. He or she simply has to make a sufficiently binding declaration of trust.

[3.37] To deal with the legal estate. The law on this topic turns on the crucial, if curious, case of *Vandervell v IRC* [1967] 2 AC 291 in which the question arose whether such an assignment had to be in writing to satisfy the Law of Property Act 1925 (UK), s 53(1)(c), the English equivalent of the Conveyancing Act 1919 (NSW), s 23C(1)(c).

> On 14 November 1958 the National Provincial Bank was registered as the owner of a parcel of 100,000 shares in a private company, Vandervell Products Ltd, which shares the bank held on trust for Mr Vandervell. The shares held rights to dividend but no voting rights and were pregnant with dividend. Vandervell, through an advisor, directed the bank to transfer the shares to the Royal College of Surgeons. The bank executed a deed of transfer of the shares in blank and handed the deed to Vandervell's solicitor who handed it on to the College of Surgeons, together with a further deed giving a trustee company associated with Vandervell an option to purchase the shares back for £5,000. The College of Surgeons executed both deeds and returned them to Vandervell's advisors who registered the transfer of shares in the books of Vandervell Products Ltd. Over the next two years dividends totalling £250,000 were declared and paid to the College. At the end of those two years trustees for Vandervell exercised the option to repurchase the shares for £5000. Vandervell was assessed for surtax on the dividends and submitted that it was income from property of which he had absolutely divested himself. The revenue argued, inter alia, that because there was no written disposition of Vandervell's equitable interest there had been no effective assignment of the beneficial interest in the shares. The House of Lords held that s 53(1)(c) did not apply to this assignment. Lord Reid, at 307, simply said that the argument of the Revenue Commissioners that Vandervell had not divested himself of his equitable interest in the shares because of s 53C(1)(c) was unsound, without giving reasons. Lord Donovan, at 317, seemed to be of the view that a transfer of the legal estate executed by a trustee under direction from a beneficiary who intended thereby to transfer his beneficial interest as well effected a disposition of the whole legal and beneficial interest. In such a case, in his Lordship's view, there was no room for the operation of s 53C(1)(c).

> Lord Upjohn, with whom Lord Pearce agreed, said, at 311, that the section had been invoked in *Grey* and *Oughtred v IRC* [1960] AC 206 (see **[3.53]**) because there the beneficial owner was dealing only with the equitable estate. That was understandable, in his Lordship's view because, 'the object of the section, as well as the object of the old Statute of Frauds, is to prevent hidden oral transactions in equitable interests in fraud of those truly entitled, making it difficult if not impossible to ascertain who are in truth his beneficiaries. But where the beneficial owner owns the whole beneficial estate and is in a position to give directions to his bare trustee with regard to the legal as well as the equitable estate there can be no possible ground for invoking the section where the beneficial owner wants to deal with the legal estate as well as the equitable estate'. Lord Wilberforce, at 330, said that Vandervell had done everything in his power to transfer the legal interest, with an intention to give to the College and that, thus, no separate transfer of the equitable interest was ever needed. The assignment took effect, in his Lordship's view, on this basis:

>> [Mr Vandervell's solicitor having received from the bank a blank transfer of the shares, executed by the bank, and the share certificate] … at this stage the appellant (Vandervell) was the absolute master of the shares and only needed to insert his name as transferee and to register it to become the full legal owner. He was also the owner in equity … [the solicitor, on behalf of Vandervell, handed the transfer to the college which, in due course, obtained registration of the shares.] The case should

then be regarded as one in which the appellant himself has, with the intention to make a gift, put the college in a position to become the legal owner of the shares, which the college in fact became. If the appellant had died before the college had obtained registration, it is clear on the principle of *Re Rose* [1952] Ch 99 ... that the gift would have been complete, on the basis that he had done everything in his power to transfer the legal interest ... No separate transfer, therefore, of the equitable interest ever came or needed to be made and there is no room for the operation of the subsection. What the position would have been had there simply been an oral direction to the legal owner (viz the bank) to transfer the shares to the college, followed by such a transfer, but without any document in writing signed by Mr Vandervell as equitable owner, is not a matter which calls for consideration here.

Lord Upjohn seemed to give an answer to that question, at 311, where he said, '... If the intention of the beneficial owner in directing the trustee to transfer the legal estate to X is that X should be the beneficial owner I can see no reason for any further document or further words in the document assigning the legal estate also expressly transferring the beneficial interest; the greater includes the less. X may be wise to secure some evidence that the beneficial owner intended him to take the beneficial interest in case his beneficial title is challenged at a later date but it certainly cannot, in my opinion, be a statutory requirement that to effect its passing there must be some writing under s 53C(1)(c)'.

[3.38] The result in *Vandervell* may seem satisfactory on the facts, although Mr Vandervell was still found liable to surtax because of the option vested in the trustee company. The judgments in the case are, however, notable for their lack of proper analysis of the mechanics of the assignment. At no stage do they give any explanation of how, let alone when, the beneficial interest in the shares passed from Vandervell. Lord Upjohn's comment that the section was intended to prevent hidden oral transactions in fraud of those truly entitled must be doubted as a matter of logic as well as legal history. There appears to be a clear difference of opinion between Lord Upjohn and Lord Wilberforce on the question of whether a mere oral direction to a trustee followed by a transfer of the legal title by the trustee would be enough. Lord Wilberforce appeared to take the view that, in the circumstances, Vandervell had obtained control of the legal title, even though he did not actually become the legal owner, and that the case was more one of an assignment of the legal title of an absolute owner, in which case the rule in *Milroy v Lord* applied, rather than one concerning an assignment of an equitable interest only. Lord Wilberforce's doubt that a simple oral direction followed by a transfer by the trustee would suffice did not seem to be shared by the other law lords. The majority view would seem to be that of Lords Upjohn, Pearce and Donovan (and presumably Lord Reid). If the decision in *Vandervell* is correct, particularly on Lord Upjohn's reasoning that the purpose of the section is to prevent dispositions of beneficial interests hidden from trustees, then *Grey's* case must have been wrongly decided — the trustees there were clearly aware of the identity of their new beneficiaries, Mr Hunter had told them, so writing should not have been necessary. In *Vandervell*, Lord Wilberforce suggested, at 330, that the assignment was effective at some point before the registration of the shares in the name of the College on the principle in *Re Rose*, but, with respect, that can only apply to an assignment of the legal title by an absolute owner, not a trustee. The bank could not give what it did not have and all it had was a bare legal title. It must follow, the transaction being voluntary, that the assignor, Vandervell, could have revoked it at any time before it was complete at law.[8] That must have been the case even after the College

---

8. MG&L, paras [726]–[729].

had been handed the deed of transfer. It was not armed with the means of completing the gift because it was always intended that the transfer be returned to Vandervell's solicitor. Even after registration of the shares in the name of the College it was open to Vandervell to advise them that they held the shares as trustees. What could they have done in that event? They could not point to any assignment of Vandervell's beneficial interest and they were certainly not bona fide purchasers of the legal estate without notice of Vandervell's equitable interest. The bank did not become absolute owner of the shares in some way before their registration in the name of the College. As the legal title, therefore, had to vest in the assignee before the assignment was complete, equitable title could only pass by way of a release by the assignor at or after that time. In that case, it is arguable that Vandervell cannot be good law in New South Wales where 'release' is included in the definition of 'disposition' in s 7 of the Conveyancing Act.

[3.39] Doubt must also be expressed whether *Vandervell* would apply to a similar dealing with real property. In *DKLR Holding Co (No 2) P/L v Comm'r of Stamp Duties (NSW)* (1982) 56 ALJR 287, one company executed a memorandum of transfer of Torrens title land in favour of another for nominal consideration, intending to pass only bare legal title, the other having already executed a declaration of trust in favour of the first. It was held that the transfer carried with it the entire property in the land, not merely a bare legal title, even though it was immediately impressed with the trust previously declared. It should be noted, however, that *DKLR* was concerned with a transfer by an absolute owner, and not a trustee acting on the instructions of his beneficiary.

Dealings in the form of a release

[3.40] In the context of assignments of equitable interests this means the release of a trustee from his or her obligations to deal with the trust property for the benefit of the *cestui que trust*, leaving the trustee free to treat the property as his or her own. As 'release' is included in the definition of 'disposition' in the Conveyancing Act it seems reasonable to expect that s 23C requires dealings in this form to be in writing. However, there is other authority, albeit severely weakened by time. In *Crichton v Crichton* (1930) 43 CLR 536, Dixon J upheld an oral release by the beneficiary of a legal chose in action in favour of the trustee. The general law rule was clearly stated, at 563:

> When an intended donee is already constituted as the legal proprietor of the subject matter of the intended gift and the intending donor has only an equitable interest to give, he can do no more than form a definite intention of presently bestowing upon or releasing to the donee the equitable interest and explicitly communicate that intention to him.

That case was decided on the wording of the Trusts Act 1915 (Vic), s 73, and not the Property Law Act 1958 (Vic), s 53(1)(c), the equivalent of s 23C, as the facts occurred before the introduction of the later Act, which Dixon J acknowledged, at 562, as using language of perhaps more general operation.

Dealings in the form of a disclaimer

[3.41] A disclaimer takes place when a donee repudiates a gift. There is authority that writing is not necessary for such an assignment because a disclaimer operates by way of avoidance not disposition: *Re Paradise Motor Co* [1968] 2 All ER 625. That decision has been criticised for failing to address properly the question of how a disclaimer operates.[9] In any event, 'disclaimer' is included in the definition of 'disposition' in s 7 of the Conveyancing Act and it is difficult to envisage *Re Paradise Motor Co* being applied in New South Wales.

Dealings in the form of nomination

[3.42] In *Re Danish Bacon Co Ltd Staff Pension Fund* [1971] 1 All ER 486, Megarry J held that s 53(1)(c) did not apply to the nomination of a recipient of pension benefits, when they became payable, as it was not a disposition of a subsisting equitable interest. That decision is probably correct on the facts of that case but, where the act of 'nomination' constitutes an exercise of a general power of appointment writing may be required by s 23C. In some respects the law regards a general power of appointment as tantamount to beneficial ownership so that the 'nomination' of someone other than the holder of the power would constitute a disposition of a subsisting equitable interest.

3-4   The Rule in Strong v Byrd

[3.43] There are three major exceptions to the maxim that equity will not perfect an imperfect gift:[10] the doctrine of equitable estoppel (see Chapter 4), *donationes mortis causa* (see **3-5** below) and the rule in *Strong v Byrd* (1874) LR 18 Eq 315. Under that rule, where a donor attempts to make a present gift of legal property which is imperfect as a gift and the donee is later named as executor, or as one of the executors, in the will of the donor, and the donor maintained the intention to make the gift until death, then equity will regard the gift as having been completed on the death of the donor. It is doubtful whether the rule extends to interests in land: *Cope v Keene* (1968) 118 CLR 1; except perhaps in systems where the land passes to the executor by statute: *Re Mulholland* (1916) 33 WN (NSW) 89.[11] The basis for the rule rests in the coincidence between the donor's intention to make a gift and his choice of the donee as executor; an administrator could not claim the benefit of the rule: *Re Gonin* [1977] 2 All ER 720. On one line of authority it is sufficient that the donee be named as executor in the donor's will: *Re Applebee* [1891] 3 Ch 422; on another the gift will only be complete when the donee obtains a grant of probate: *Re Hince* [1946] SASR 323. Property affected by this rule remains available as part of the donor's estate for the purposes of the Family Provision Act 1982 (NSW).

3-5   Donationes Mortis Causa

[3.44] Where a person, in contemplation of death, makes a gift of property conditional upon his or her death, in the sense that it can be retrieved if the donor recovers from illness or other peril, and delivers the property which is the subject of the gift, or its indicia of title to the donee prior to death, then the gift will be completed by the

---

9. MG&L, paras [749]-[750].
10. Although the foundation case was concerned with equity's acceptance of the common rule concerning releases of debts: see MG&L, para [2908].
11. MG&L, para [2906].

death of the donor subject to the odd rule that the property will be available to satisfy the deceased's creditors if there is a shortfall in the rest of the estate: *Smith v Casen* (1718) 1 P Wms 406. This rule is one of historical anomaly and is viewed strictly by the courts, as deathbed donations can easily be fabricated. In *Duffield v Elwes* (1827) 1 Bligh (NS) 497; 4 ER 959; [1824–34] All ER 247, Lord Eldon said of the doctrine:

> Improvements in the law, or some things which have been considered improvements, have been lately proposed, and if, amongst those things called improvements, this *dona-tio mortis causa* was struck out of our law altogether, it would be quite as well, but, that not being so, we must examine into the subject of it.

The doctrine is not exclusively a matter of equity although equity will lend its assistance where there has been an effective donation but the legal title remains in the name of the donor, by compelling the legal personal representative of the deceased donor to hold the property on trust for the donee: *Duffield v Elwes* (1827) 1 Bligh (NS) 497 at 534; 4 ER 959 at 972; [1824–34] All ER 247 at 257–8. The trust then imposed is a constructive trust arising after death to give effect to the incomplete donation: *Sen v Headley* [1991] 2 All ER 636 at 647. There are three elements which must be satisfied to establish a valid *donatio, Sen v Headley,* [1991] 2 All ER 636 at 639, per Nourse LJ:

1. The gift must be made in contemplation, although not necessarily in expectation, of impending death;

2. The gift must be made on condition that it is to be absolute and perfected only on the donor's death, being revocable until then;

3. There must be a delivery of the subject matter of the gift, or the essential indicia of title to that subject matter amounting to a parting with dominion over, and not mere physical possession of the subject matter of the gift.

[3.45] Traditionally, real property has not been considered capable of being the subject of *donationes mortis causa* in Australia: *Watts v Public Trustee* (1949) 50 SR (NSW) 130; *Bayliss v Public Trustee* (1988) 12 NSWLR 540, nor in Canada: *Re Sorenson and Sorenson* (1977) 90 DLR (3d) 26. In the case of Torrens title land it is difficult to see how a gift of the certificate of title alone could act as a *donatio* in view of the decision of the High Court in *Corin v Patton* (1990)169 CLR 540 (see **[3.13]**–**[3.20]**). However, the view that the principle of *donatio mortis causa* does not extend to land relies on dicta by Lord Eldon in *Duffield v Elwes* (1827) 1 Bligh (NS) 497 at 534; 4 ER 959 at 972; [1824–34] All ER 247 and the absence of any clear English authority for or against that view. A different opinion now prevails in England where the Court of Appeal held in *Sen v Headley* [1991] 2 All ER 636 that there could be a *donatio mortis causa* of land, in that case by constructive delivery of the title deeds to unregistered land.

> In *Sen v Headley,* a man in hospital and dying of cancer told a woman he had known for years, and lived with for part of that time, that his house and contents were to be hers if he died. He told her that the deeds were in a steel box in the house to which she had the keys. She also had keys to the house. He died three days later, intestate. She opened the box and took possession of the deeds. The woman later took proceedings against the man's estate claiming that she was entitled to the house on the basis that the deceased had given it to her under a valid *donatio mortis causa.* The house stood on unregistered freehold land. At first instance Mummery J rejected her claim on the grounds that *donatio mortis causa* did not apply to a gift of land by delivery of title deeds. The Court of Appeal, in a judgment delivered by Nourse LJ, overturned that decision and held that *donatio mortis causa* could apply to gifts of land by delivery of title deeds. His Lordship cited *Duffield v Elwes* in which Lord Eldon had upheld a *donatio* of moneys secured by a bond and moneys secured by mortgage, effected by delivery of the

bond and mortgage deeds to the intended donee. Lord Eldon drew a distinction between the absolute estate in fee in the land, of which parol evidence of a conveyance could not be admitted because of the Statute of Frauds: *Richard v Syms* (1740) Barn Ch 90; 27 ER 567; and the mortgagee's conditional estate in the land securing payment of a debt. Lord Eldon held that the valid *donatio* gave rise to a trust by operation of law, outside the Statute of Frauds. Nourse LJ noted that trusts arising by operation of law now embraced those produced by the doctrine of proprietary estoppel and the constructive trust found in domestic property cases. In the absence of any specific authority to the contrary, or any sound reason for not doing so, his Lordship considered it appropriate to recognise a *donatio* of land saying, at 647, 'Let it be agreed that the doctrine is anomalous. Anomolies do not justify anomalous exceptions. If due account is taken of the present state of the law in regard to mortgages and choses in action, it is apparent that to make a distinction in the case of land to make just such an exception'.

[3.46] Leave to appeal to the House of Lords was refused Mr Headley and *Sen v Headley* must be recognised as a conclusive statement of the law on this point in England. In *Bayliss v Public Trustee* (1988) 12 NSWLR 540, Needham J noted that there was then no clear English authority on the point and concluded that, 'English law has not allowed *donatio mortis causa* of real property' even though he could not identify the reason why it had not done so. Having come to that conclusion Needham J found it impossible to extend the doctrine and held that there was no justification for the extension of the anomalous principle of *donatio mortis causa* beyond the scope allowed to it by 'adjudged cases and authorities'. Now that English law has recognised a *donatio mortis causa* of real property, it would seem, on the logic employed in *Bayliss*, that Australian courts would have to do likewise, unless they can come up with a new reason for not extending the doctrine to gifts of land. The old reason — that English courts have never done it — has gone.

[3.47] *Donationes mortis causa* are excluded from the normal principles of undue influence applicable to other gifts *inter vivos*: *Rushford v Hunchuk* (1970) 16 DLR (2d) 731 at 735. In New South Wales, property subject to such a donation may be deemed to be part of the deceased's estate under the Family Provision Act (NSW) 1982.

3–6 Assignments for Value

[3.48] An assignment for valuable consideration of property capable of being assigned, whether legal or equitable, will effect a transfer of that property in equity when the consideration is paid or executed notwithstanding any failure to comply with statutory or other formal requirements for such an assignment: *Holroyd v Marshall* (1862) 10 HLC 191; 11 ER 999; *Tailby v Official Receiver* (1888) 13 App Cas 523. While a contract remains executory, that is, simply an exchange of mutual promises, the position of the assignee is not as solid. It is common in the cases to find the interest of the assignee at the point of contract, but before consideration has been provided, described as an 'equitable interest' with the vendor holding the property as 'constructive' trustee for the assignee pending completion of the contract: *Paine v Meller* (1801) 6 Ves 349; *Shaw v Foster* (1872) LR 5 HL 321 at 338, per Lord Cairns; although Sir George Jessel MR in *Lysaght v Edwards* (1876) 2 Ch D 499 at 507, held that this constructive trust only arose when the title was made out by the vendor, or accepted by the purchaser, and that a trust *sub modo* existed prior to that and after contract. Neither description is particularly helpful. While it may be appropriate to say that the purchaser has some 'interest', even an 'equity' in the subject property upon contract, his or her rights remain conditional unless and until the consideration is provided. In the meantime the vendor cannot be said to hold the property under any fiduciary obligation. The 'interest' of the purchaser in the property must be measured against his or her right, if any, to obtain a decree of specific performance. That will depend upon whether the contract is one of which specific performance can be decreed, that is, not a contract for which damages would be an adequate remedy for any breach, and upon the willingness and ability of the purchaser to perform his or her part of the bargain by executing the consideration required by the contract. To say the vendor holds as 'constructive trustee' for the purchaser upon contract pending completion is something of an abuse of that expression. Despite the opinions expressed in the older authorities mentioned above, the only clear point at which such a constructive trust could be said to arise is on payment of the purchase price: *Chang v Registrar of Titles* (1976) 137 CLR 177 at 184, per Mason J. Once the consideration has been paid or provided equity will regard the assignment as complete by virtue of the maxim that equity regards as done that which ought to be done.[12] While equity will not uphold an assignment of a bare right of action, it will recognise an assignment of a present chose in action or of future property, such as the proceeds anticipated from the prosecution of some chose in action, that is, the money to which a party was or might become entitled from certain proceedings for slander: *Glegg v Bromley* [1912] 3 KB 474.

Assignments of legal property for valuable consideration

[3.49] Where one person agrees to assign legal property to another in return for valuable consideration, the vendor will be a constructive trustee of the property in the eyes of equity at least as early as the moment at which the consideration is paid or executed, and perhaps earlier. This rule applies notwithstanding a failure to comply with any statutory requirement that the agreement concerned be in writing or some other particular form where strict observance of the statute would allow it to be used as an instrument of fraud. Section 54A of the Conveyancing Act 1919 (NSW), for example, requires that agreements for the sale of land, or any interest in land, be in writing.

> In *Last v Rosenfeld* [1972] 2 NSWLR 923, two couples jointly owned some land. One couple transferred their interest to the other for the price they had paid for their share, $8,500, with a proviso, which was not put in writing, that if the second couple did not occupy the house on the land within 12 months they would transfer it back to the first two at that same price. The second couple did not occupy the house and, in fact, sold it on to third parties. Hope J held that the plaintiffs, the first couple, were entitled to one half of the cash received by the defendants on this sale and to a half interest in the mortgage which the defendants received back from the third party purchasers subject to the payment by the plaintiffs of $8,500. In doing so his Honour found that this case fell within the principle espoused in *Rochefoucauld v Boustead* [1897] 1 Ch 196 that it would be fraud, in the sense referred to above, for a person to whom land is conveyed as trustee, and who knows it is so conveyed, to deny the trust and claim the land for himself. That would apply whether the beneficial interest claimed was absolute or of some more limited nature.

This should not be taken to mean that any parol agreement for the sale of land will be upheld in equity. Unless equitable fraud can be established, s 54A will render any such agreement unenforceable. However, if a party to such a parol agreement can

---

12. MG&L, para [609].

be shown to have received the benefit available under the contract then it will be equitable fraud for that party to deny the corresponding burden attached to that benefit. In *Last v Rosenfeld*, the transfer by the plaintiffs to the defendants of their half-share for the original price, rather than the current market value, contradicted any suggestion that the plaintiffs were simply trying to enforce a parol agreement.

[3.50] In *Last v Rosenfeld*, Hope J followed *Bannister v Bannister* [1948] 2 All ER 133 in which the English Court of Appeal had recognised the interest of a woman who sold her cottage to a developer on the understanding that she would be allowed to continue living in it. Once the purchase was completed the developer took proceedings for recovery of possession of land and argued that the woman's claim for a right of residence was unenforceable because it was not in writing. The Court of Appeal held that it was equitable fraud for the developer to insist on the absolute character of the conveyance. These principles have been applied to enforce trusts arising from the unwritten (and sometimes unspoken) agreement or common intention of parties living in a domestic situation in *Allen v Snyder* [1977] 2 NSWLR 685, subject to the proviso that the party claiming the interest must have contributed as contemplated. Glass JA held there that the trusts so created were express rather than constructive which could lead one to ask, what's in a name?

Assignments of equitable property for valuable consideration

[3.51] A contract for valuable consideration to assign an equitable interest will give rise to a constructive trust of the interest being assigned, provided the contract is specifically enforceable. It is possible, certainly in Australia, to have a trust of an equitable interest in which case the 'trustee' retains title to the equitable interest but is under an obligation to hold it for the benefit of others: *Comptroller of Stamps (Victoria) v Howard-Smith* (1936) 54 CLR 614 at 621–2, per Dixon J. Prior to the payment of the purchase price, the trust, if it has arisen before then, must be defeasible as the vendor cannot necessarily be compelled to complete the assignment. That proposition is complicated by the Conveyancing Act 1919 (NSW), s 23C.[13]

[3.52] Prima facie an agreement to assign an equitable interest constitutes a disposition of a subsisting equitable interest and must, therefore, be in writing. That was certainly the view of the High Court in *Adamson v Hayes* (1973) 130 CLR 276, which involved an oral agreement dealing with equitable interests in mineral claims in Western Australia.

> Three farmers, Adamson, Hayes and Freebairn pegged out a number of claims on behalf of themselves and others. The latter two wanted to exploit the claims while Adamson wished to sell his interest. It was agreed between the three to pool their various claims in proportions which gave Adamson 56 per cent while the other two held the balance of 44 per cent. In addition Adamson gave the others an option to acquire his interests in certain circumstances. The two nominated a purchaser but Adamson refused to convey. Hayes and Freebairn sought specific performance or, in the alternative, damages. Adamson argued that the agreement, as it was not in writing, was unenforceable. It was held that the mineral claims were 'land' by virtue of s 7 of the Mining Act 1904–71 (WA) and that the agreement was unenforceable for want of writing because of the provisions of s 34(1) of the Property Law Act 1969 (WA), which is identical to s 23C(1) of the New South Wales Act. Menzies J said, at 292–3, that either the

---

13. See para [3.29] above and, in other States is: Property Law Act 1974 (Qld), ss 5 & 9; Law of Property Act 1936 (SA), s 29; Conveyancing and Law of Property Act 1884 (Tas), s 60; Property Law Act 1958 (Vic), s 53; Property Law Act 1969 (WA), s 34.

pooling arrangement involved the substitution of new trusts for old and, thus, s 34(1)(b) applied or, as the transaction concerned the disposition of equitable interests in land, s 34(1)(c) applied to strike the transaction down. In doing so he said that s 34(1)(c) was limited to the disposition of equitable interests in land. Walsh J also held that this transaction was unenforceable but said, at 297, that s 34(1)(a) applied to equitable interests in land. Gibbs J agreed with that view and specifically stated, at 302, that s 34(1)(c) was not confined to dispositions of equitable interests in land, adopting the English decisions of *Grey v IRC* [1960] AC 1; *Oughtred v IRC* [1960] AC 206 and *Vandervell v IRC* [1967] 2 AC 291 in which the equivalent provision to s 34(1)(c) had been held to apply to dispositions of equitable interests in shares. Stephen J agreed with the latter two, holding that either s 34(1)(a) or s 34(1)(b) applied to render this transaction unenforceable.

[3.53] The agreement in *Adamson v Hayes* had not progressed beyond an exchange of promises so that it was not open to Hayes and Freebairn to argue that Adamson held his share as constructive trustee for them. Section 23C(2) allows scope for such an argument, by specifically excepting resulting and constructive trusts from the operation of sub-section (1). Under s 23C(2) proof of the existence of a constructive trust would seem to negate the necessity for writing otherwise required by s 23C(1), although there is authority which would suggest otherwise.

In *Oughtred v IRC* [1960] AC 206, a parcel of 200,000 shares was held by trustees in favour of Mrs Oughtred for life with remainder to her son, Peter. Mrs Oughtred also owned another 72,700 shares in her own name. On 18 June 1956 the mother and son agreed, orally, that on 26 June Mrs Oughtred would transfer her 72,700 shares to Peter and that he would make her absolute beneficial owner of the 200,000 shares. Accordingly, on 26 June three documents were executed:

(a) A Deed of Release of Peter's interest in remainder in the 200,000 shares;

(b) A transfer from Mrs Oughtred to Peter's nominees of the 72,700 shares;

(c) A transfer from the trustees to Mrs Oughtred of the 200,000 shares.

The last of these documents was charged with ad valorem stamp duty as a conveyance or transfer on sale within the meaning of that expression in the Finance Act 1894 (UK). The IRC claimed that the agreement of 18 June was ineffective for want of writing because of s 53(1)(c) of the Law of Property Act 1925 (UK), the equivalent of s 23C(1)(c), and that the transfer on 26 June disposed of Peter's equitable interest in remainder.

It was held, by Upjohn J at first instance, [1958] 1 Ch 383, that the agreement of 18 June gave rise to a constructive trust in Mrs Oughtred's favour of Peter's interest in remainder in the 200,000 shares and that nothing remained to be transferred later.

That decision was overturned by the Court of Appeal, [1958] 1 Ch 678, on the ground that the later assurance constituted the completion of the oral bargain and thus fell within the meaning of 'conveyance or transfer upon sale'. However, the court also indicated that it did not accept Upjohn J's view that Peter's interest had passed to Mrs Oughtred before 26 June.

The House of Lords upheld the decision of the Court of Appeal by a majority of 3 to 2. Lord Radcliffe agreed with Upjohn J and held that Peter became a trustee *sub modo* of his interest in favour of his mother on 18 June as the subject matter of the agreement was property of which specific performance would normally be decreed and thus s 53(1) was overridden by s 53(2). Upon the transfer to Peter of Mrs Oughtred's 72,700 shares on 26 June she became effective owner of all outstanding equitable interests in the 200,000 shares. No more needed to be done to confirm her rights. The transfer to her from the trustees was merely the winding up of the trust, which Mrs Oughtred need not have done. Lord Cohen also in the minority, said that the transfer from the trustees to Mrs Oughtred could not have conveyed the equitable interest to her as the trustees had no such interest to convey. His Lordship speculated that there might have been no document transferring the equitable interest and held that Mrs Oughtred's absolute entitlement to the 200,000 shares arose not because of any transfer but because Peter, having become a constructive trustee of his interest in favour of his mother, could not dispute her title once his nominees had received the 72,700 shares on 26 June.

Lord Denning, in the majority, held the transfer to be a transfer or conveyance on sale, as a transfer authorised by Peter which led to Mrs Oughtred acquiring the reversionary interest as effectively as if Peter had conveyed it directly to her. That might have been enough but Lord Denning also said that he did not think the oral agreement was effective to transfer Peter's interest because s 53(1) clearly made writing necessary to effect a transfer and s 53(2) did not do away with that necessity.

Lord Jenkins, with whom Lord Keith concurred without comment, found it unnecessary to decide the true meaning of s 53(1), let alone the effect upon it of s 53(2). In his view, the mere existence of a constructive trust in favour of a purchaser under a contract prior to completion had never prevented a subsequent transfer, in performance of the contract, from constituting a conveyance or transfer on sale for the purposes of stamp duty.

[3.54] *Oughtred's* case is clearly unsatisfactory as a discussion of the issues surrounding s 23C and its effect on agreements to assign equitable interests for valuable consideration. If it purports to stand as authority for the proposition that the requirement of writing under s 23C(1) overrides the exception of resulting and constructive trusts allowed by s 23C(2), then it is simply wrong as a matter of principle. Of the members of the House of Lords who actually addressed that question, there was a majority of 2 to 1 in favour of the view that a constructive trust arising under such an agreement would obviate the need for writing in compliance with s 23C(1), although there was some divergence of opinion as to when that trust arose and as to its nature. Lord Radcliffe seemed prepared to recognise the trust as early as the agreement of 18 June while Lord Cohen concentrated on the point at which the consideration was executed on the part of the assignee, in other words, when the 72,700 shares were transferred by Mrs Oughtred to Peter's nominees. Lord Denning's view that the rule set by s 53(1) governs the exception contained in s 53(2) is contrary to the rules of statutory interpretation and cannot stand as a matter of law or logic. Curious though the idea might be, we cannot presume that our laws were written by Lewis Carroll. The facts of *Oughtred* are also unsatisfactory in that the document which lay at the heart of the dispute, the transfer from the trustees to Mrs Oughtred, need never have been executed. The deed of release of the son's interest might still have been assessed for duty. That could have produced a more useful discussion of the issue. But the release could only have conveyed the bare legal title of the trustee, an interest of nominal value only. The issues which arose in *Oughtred's* case were artificial in many respects. They were the product of an assessment under a taxing statute which imposed stamp duty on documents effecting the transfer of valuable property. Oughtred was not a dispute between assignor and assignee as to who had true title. In such a case the issue would not turn on the meaning of s 23C and the need or otherwise for writing. The crucial question would be determined by the doctrine of part performance or the principles of equitable estoppel.

3–7 Assignments of Future Property

[3.55] Neither the common law nor equity will recognise any purported voluntary disposition of property not presently held but which will be or may be acquired by the assignor in the future. However, equity will recognise an assignment of such 'future property' provided it is made for value. Any such bargain will be construed as an agreement to assign the thing when it is acquired: *Norman v FCT* (1963) 109 CLR 9 at 24, per Windeyer J. As Deane J, then in the Federal Court, put it in *FCT v Everett* (1978) 38 FLR 26 at 50; 21 ALR 625 at 643–4:

> ... a purported assignment of a mere expectancy (in the sense of the chance of becoming entitled under the will or intestacy of a person who is still living) or of property to be acquired in the future, is inoperative as an assignment, and has no effect unless made for valuable consideration. If there be consideration, it will operate as an agreement to assign the property when acquired, or to hold it in trust (the latter if the whole of the consideration has been satisfied) and this agreement will be binding on the parties as from its date and binding on the property in equity (although not at common law), if and when it is acquired by the assignor, if it is of such a nature and so described as to be capable of being identified. In the interval between the making of the agreement and the acquisition of the property by the assignor, the interest of the assignee is not contractual merely, but he has, as between himself and the assignor, a prospective interest in the property to be acquired which has some of the incidents of a proprietary right.

[3.56] That principle is straightforward enough but there are four areas of difficulty in applying it. The first concerns the distinction between present and future property, particularly between present rights which produce some benefit in the future and that future benefit. The second question deals with the basis of this principle and whether such agreements are specifically enforceable per se or whether specific performance is only available if the subject matter of the agreement is property which would normally attract that remedy. The third is connected with the second and concerns the issue whether these rules apply to contracts for the sale of goods or whether the Sales of Goods Acts of the various States codify the law governing such agreements. The fourth examines the nature of the assignee's rights before the acquisition of the property by the assignor, especially in cases involving the bankruptcy of the assignor.

Distinction between present and future property

[3.57] Some things are clearly future property — an interest under the will of a person still living: *Re Lind* [1915] 2 Ch 345; damages which might be recovered in pending litigation: *Glegg v Bromley* [1912] 3 KB 474; future book debts: *Tailby v Official Receiver* (1888)13 App Cas 523; royalties yet to be earned on some literary or artistic work: *Re Trytel* [1952] 2 TLR 32; and such things as copyright in songs not yet written, freight not yet earned, rent to be paid under a lease, and interest to be paid under a mortgage. The last two indicate the major source of difficulty in this area of definition as each represents the product of some present right.

> In *Norman v FCT* (1963) 109 CLR 9, a taxpayer by a deed purported to assign to his wife certain moneys which otherwise would have been receivable by him. The items of income covered by the deed included 'all his right title and interest in and to certain interest to accrue due on a loan repayable by the borrower at will' and 'all his right title and interest in and to all the ... dividends' which might be declared on certain shares in public companies. It was held that both the interest under the loan and the dividends were expectancies or possibilities which could not be assigned without consideration. Windeyer J dissented on the finding as to the interest holding that the assignment was of a present right to be paid interest at a future date.

In *Shepherd v FCT* (1965) 113 CLR 385, Mr Shepherd held a patent for certain castors and had granted a licence for their manufacture in return for the payment of royalties of 5 per cent of the gross sale price of the castors. In 1957 he purported to assign by deed poll, 'absolutely and unconditionally', to certain assignees, all his 'right, title and interest in and to an amount equal to ninety per centum of the income which may accrue during a period of three years ...' from royalties payable under the licence agreement. He was assessed for tax on the amount he had purported to assign. The High Court, Barwick CJ and Kitto J, with Owen J dissenting, held that the deed constituted an assignment of 90 per cent of Shepherd's present rights and was therefore an effective assignment. Kitto J drew an analogy between the existing contractual right to receive royalties: the tree, and the fruit: the payments which might accrue to Shepherd under the contract. His Honour distinguished *Norman's* case on the ground that the loan there could have been repaid at any time making the right to receive interest an expectancy whereas, in Shepherd, even though the manufacturer might not sell or even produce any castors the contractual relationship, and thus the right to receive any royalties earned, would endure for the three years covered by the deed poll.

[3.58] Considering the results of these two cases, the issue may simply turn on the drafting of any document in question, although the wording of the assignments in *Shepherd* and *Norman* was very similar. Kitto J distinguished the situation in *Norman's* case from that in *Shepherd's*, pointing out that, in *Norman*, the contractual relationship of borrower and lender could be terminated at any time during the relevant year by the borrower, thus making it an expectancy. In *Shepherd*, on the other hand, the contractual licence to manufacture castors would continue for three years, whether any castors were produced or not. With respect, that enquiry seems misconceived and the reasoning of Windeyer J in *Norman* must be preferred as a matter of logic as much as of law. The fact that a present right might be terminated at any time does not make it any less a present right. By the same token, the possibility that a present right might not produce any 'fruit' does not make it an expectancy either. If A gives a lottery ticket to B it is not an assignment of an expectancy, and thus void if not made for value, just because the ticket might not win. As Barwick CJ said in *Shepherd,* at 393, 'That a promise may not be fruitful does not make it incapable of assignment'. The fact that a present right might prove barren should not alter its character as a present right while, at the same time, the fact that potential income, or some other property not yet acquired by the assignor, is certain to come into his or her hands should not alter its character as future property pending its receipt.

This sort of reasoning was employed by Hardie Boys J in *Williams v IRC* [1965] NZLR 395 in which a taxpayer attempted to assign the first £500 of the net income of a trust which conducted a grazing business for his benefit. His Honour held that the first £500 was a mere expectancy as the trust might earn income and it might not. In *McLeay v IRC* (1963) 9 AITR 265, a purported voluntary disposition of all the interest due under a mortgage, even though that mortgage was repayable at any time after a certain date, was found to be valid. McCarthy J held that a mortgagee's right to receive interest under a mortgage was a present chose in action, even though the interest was repayable at some time in the future. These two cases are often presented as examples of the difficulties that exist in distinguishing between present and future property. However, the degree of uncertainty which surrounds the probable acquisition of some property or income by the assignor cannot decide whether it is an expectancy or not, just as the degree of probability that some present right will bear fruit is also not the appropriate test to determine whether the interest concerned is present or future property. The possibility that a present right might be terminated at any time does not magically convert it into future property. The prospect of such a sudden end may affect the value of the interest, but it cannot convert a present right into after acquired property.

The basis for the enforcement of assignments of future property

[3.59] This debate has centred on the decision of the House of Lords in *Holroyd v Marshall* (1862) 10 HLC 191; 11 ER 999, and, in particular whether Lord Westbury's judgment in that case restricted the recognition of agreements to assign future property to contracts involving property which would ordinarily attract the remedy of specific performance; or whether equity lent its aid to all contracts to assign future property.

> In *Holroyd v Marshall*, a Mr Taylor, by what was in effect a security contract, sold 'all machinery, implements, and things, which, during the continuance of this security, shall be placed in or about' his factory to the appellants on terms allowing Taylor to re-purchase the equipment for £5,000. The equipment was transferred to trustees to hold it on trust for Taylor absolutely if he should pay £5,000 to the appellants and otherwise on trust for sale with the proceeds to be applied in payment of the debt owed to the appellants. Taylor acquired more machinery but did nothing further to assign it to the appellants. Subsequently a dispute arose between the appellants and certain judgment creditors of Taylor who had sought to levy execution against the additional machinery.
>
> The House of Lords held that the additional machinery was the property of the appellants whose interest prevailed over that of the judgment creditors. Lord Westbury LC stated the rule that 'if a vendor or mortgagor agrees to sell or mortgage property, real or personal, of which he is not possessed at the time, and he receives consideration for the contract, and afterwards becomes possessed of property answering the description in the contract, there is no doubt that a Court of Equity would compel him to perform the contract, and that the contract would, in equity, transfer the beneficial interest to the mortgagee or purchaser immediately on the property being acquired. This, of course, assumes that the supposed contract is one of that class of which a Court of Equity would decree specific performance'.

[3.60] That statement of principle is quite apt except for the troublesome reference to the necessity for the contract to be one of which equity would decree specific performance. Taken strictly that proviso could exclude all contracts in which damages would be an appropriate remedy for any failure to perform. If Lord Westbury intended that interpretation he did not apply it in *Holroyd v Marshall* where damages would obviously have been appropriate in a contract for the sale of factory machinery. Those doubts were laid to rest by the House of Lords in *Tailby v Official Receiver* (1888) 13 App Cas 523. *Tailby* involved a purported assignment of, among other things, 'all the book debts due and owing or which may during the continuance of this security become due and owing to the said mortgagor'. It was held that that assignment was effective to pass title in equity of a book debt which became due to the mortgagor after the date of the mortgage and that the principle in *Holroyd v Marshall* was satisfied if property came into the hands of the assignor which could be identified as fitting the description in the agreement to assign it. This doctrine was further explained in *Palette Shoes Pty Ltd v Krohn* (1937) 58 CLR 1 at 27, by Dixon J:

> As the subject to be made over does not exist, the matter primarily rests in contract. Because value has been given on the one side, the conscience of the other party is bound when the subject comes into existence, that is when, as is generally the case, the legal property vests in him. Because his conscience is bound in respect of the subject property, equity fastens upon the property itself and makes him trustee of the legal rights of ownership for the assignee.

[3.61] In this sense, the rule in *Holroyd v Marshall* lies in the exclusive jurisdiction of equity. There is no equivalent doctrine at common law; you cannot assign what you do not have. Specific performance lies in the auxiliary jurisdiction of equity and is invoked where the common law remedy for breach of contract is inadequate. The result is that an agreement to assign property already in the hands of the assignor will not confer any rights to that property on the assignee, even after the assignee has paid or provided the consideration stipulated for, unless that property falls within that category of special items, such as land, shares in a company and rare or unique chattels, which equity regards as irreplaceable by an order for damages. By contrast the assignee under an agreement to assign property not presently held by the assignor will be entitled to specific performance of the agreement once property identifiable as the subject matter of the contract is acquired by the assignor, provided, of course, that consideration has been executed on the part of the assignee: *Re Lind* [1915] 2 Ch 345; *Palette Shoes Pty Ltd (in liq) v Krohn* (1937) 58 CLR l; *Re Puntoriero* (1991) 104 ALR 522. The promise binds the property itself from the moment the contract becomes capable of being performed, in accordance with the maxim that equity regards as done that which ought to be done. So once the property is acquired by the assignor, he or she then immediately holds it on trust for the assignee: *Booth v FCT* (1987) 76 ALR 375.

Future property and contracts for the sale of goods

[3.62] Where the subject matter of a contract to assign future property is a chattel, or chattels, there is considerable debate whether the rule in *Holroyd v Marshall* applies.[14] English authorities favour the view that the Sales of Goods Acts codify the law on such agreements, which are known as sales by description within that code, leaving no room for the operation of any equitable principles.

In *Re Wait* [1927] 1 Ch 606, Wait had bought 1000 tons of Western White Wheat ex MV Challenger. Before the wheat was shipped, he sold 500 tons of it, described as 'part of a parcel bought ... under a contract dated November 20', to a sub-purchaser. Wait sent an invoice to the sub-purchaser and was paid for all except freight. Before the cargo of wheat arrived Wait was declared bankrupt. The sub-purchaser sought specific performance of the contract or, alternatively, a lien over the 1000 tons to secure his claim for 500. The Court of Appeal held that the purchaser was not entitled to specific performance as the wheat was not 'specific or ascertained' as required by s 52 of the Sale of Goods Act 1893 (UK) — which confers a jurisdiction to grant specific performance — and that the Sales of Goods Act constituted a complete and exclusive statement of the legal relations both in law and equity as between buyer and seller.

[3.63] Under the Sale of Goods Act 1923 (NSW), s 23, property in goods sold by description will not pass, unless a contrary intention appears, until the chattel, having been acquired by the seller, is unconditionally appropriated to the contract. There is no direct equivalent in the Sale of Goods Act 1923 (NSW) to s 52 of the UK legislation, although s 56 of the New South Wales Act provides that nothing in the Act shall affect any remedy in equity of the buyer or the seller in respect of any breach of a contract of sale or any breach of warranty and thus there is scope to argue that *Re Wait* does not represent the law in New South Wales. Apart from the question of whether the description of the wheat sold by Wait satisfied the particular wording of s 52 of the UK Act, the very fact that equitable remedies are preserved, one way or

---

14. MG&L, paras [666]–[682].

another, in the various Acts would seem to deny that the Sale of Goods Acts were intended to codify the law on the subject to the exclusion of equitable principles. Yet *Re Wait* was followed in Victoria in *King v Greig* [1931] VLR 413, a case involving the purported assignment of part of the timber standing on a particular property.

[3.64] Both *Re Wait* and *King v Greig* involved contracts to assign an unascertained part of some greater whole — who could say which grains of wheat or pieces of timber were the subject matter of the agreement? The principles laid down in *Re Wait* have, nonetheless, been taken to encompass all contracts for the sale of future goods, despite comments to the contrary by Lord Westbury in *Holroyd v Marshall*.[15] Lord Cranworth suggested a contrary approach in *Hoare v Dresser* (1859) 7 HLC; 11 ER 116 saying, *obiter*, that equity would operate to assign property if it could be identified and, if it formed part of a larger but still identifiable mass, then equity would give the buyer a lien over the larger amount to satisfy his claim for the smaller. Lord Cranworth's view can be supported as a matter of logic but not, on the present state of the authorities, as a matter of law. The judgment in *Re Wait* was approved of by the High Court in *Akron Tyre Co v Kittson* (1951) 82 CLR 477, although the proposition that the Sale of Goods Acts codify the law relating to the sale of chattels did not receive the same blessing. In *Hewett v Court* (1983) 149 CLR 639, in which a purchaser of a prefabricated house was found to have an equitable lien over the partly completed structure on the basis of the payment of the deposit and certain instalments of the price, both Gibbs CJ, at 647, and Deane J, at 667, appeared to regard this question as open, although it was not necessary to decide the issue as all members of the court took the view that the contract was one for work done and materials supplied and not one for the sale of goods.

In *Electrical Enterprises Retail Pty Ltd v Rodgers* (1989) 15 NSWLR 473, Kearney J declined to follow the English decision, saying that s 56 of the New South Wales Act seemed to deny that that Act was intended to codify the law on the subject to the exclusion of equitable principles. His Honour concluded, at 493, that equitable principles, not having been clearly excluded by the Act, are applicable in appropriate cases to contracts for the sale of goods. The extent of the operation of those principles must remain a moot point. Kearney J felt constrained by the decision of the High Court in *Hewitt v Court* (1983) 149 CLR 639 to hold that a vendor's lien would only be available in respect of contracts capable of specific performance — the goods in dispute in *Electrical Enterprises v Rodgers* consisted of electrical and video equipment. His Honour was prepared to grant a lien under the Sale of Goods Act but not an equitable lien.

[3.65] Equity has intervened in contracts for the sale of goods in other circumstances. In a number of recent cases the previously held view that the equitable remedy of rescission on the ground of innocent misrepresentation did not apply to contracts for the sale of goods has been rejected: *Graham v Freer* (1980) 35 SASR 424; even where the contract has been executed: *Leason Pty Ltd v Princes Farm Pty Ltd* [1983] 2 NSWLR 381; although Wood J, unfortunately, refused to follow *Leason* in *Vimig Pty Ltd v Contract Tooling Pty Ltd* (1987) 9 NSWLR 731. In the process, the Sale

---

15. A contract for the sale of goods, as, for example, of 500 chests of tea was not a contract which would be specifically performed, because it did not relate to any chests of tea in particular, but a contract to sell the 500 chests of a particular kind of tea which is now in my warehouse in Gloucester, was a contract relating to specific property and would be specifically performed: at 10 HLC 209; see MG&L, para [676].

of Goods Act 1923 (NSW), s 4(2),[16] which provides, among other things, that the rules of the common law, except where they are inconsistent with the Act, continue to apply to contracts for the sale of goods, was held to include the principles of equity within the expression 'the rules of the common law'. Rescission raises different issues from the matters considered in *Re Wait*. This line of cases, and Kearney J's decision in *Electrical Enterprises v Rodgers*, indicates a greater willingness on the part of the courts to recognise equitable rights in contracts for the sale of goods. That equitable intervention will not extend to the remedy of an equitable lien unless it can be shown that the contract would be specifically performable.[17]

The nature of the assignee's right

[3.66] With the notable exception of contracts for the sale of goods, the rights of an assignee under a contract to assign future property once the property is acquired by the assignor are clearly established. The nature of the assignee's rights before the property is acquired are not so clear. In most cases it would not matter; the question would simply not arise. However, if the assignor, having assigned the expectancy for value, is declared bankrupt and is subsequently discharged from that bankruptcy, the question will arise as to whether the discharge frees the assignor from the obligations cast on him or her under the assignment. Section 153(1) of the Bankruptcy Act 1966 (Cth) provides that a discharge from bankruptcy operates to release the bankrupt from all debts, including secured debts, provable in the bankruptcy, although secured creditors can still enforce their security and apply the proceeds towards that part of their debt not proved in the bankruptcy. Under the Bankruptcy Act, s 82, all debts and liabilities of the bankrupt, present and future, certain or contingent, are provable in his or her bankruptcy. In *Collyer v Isaacs* (1881) 19 Ch D 342, Sir George Jessel MR held that an agreement to assign future property created contractual rights which were provable in bankruptcy and that a discharge from bankruptcy discharged the bankrupt not only from his principal liability to pay the debt but also from his ancillary liability to give security for it on after acquired chattels. His Lordship left open two exceptions: (a) marriage settlements which contained covenants to settle after acquired property which were held to survive a bankruptcy in *Re Reis* (1904) 2 KB 769; and (b) definite contracts to settle specific property not in existence at the time of the contract (despite the apparent contradiction of the general rule stated in the case).

[3.67] The second of those exceptions provided an avenue whereby *Collyer v Isaacs* could be effectively by-passed. Sir George Jessel's proviso was taken up by the Court of Appeal in *Re Lind* [1915] 2 Ch 345.

Lind had an expectancy, an interest in his mother's estate upon her death. She had not made a will and Lind would have been entitled to a share in her intestacy. Lind assigned that expectancy to a man by the name of Arnold as security for a loan and later made a similar assignment, subject to the interest of Arnold, to Norwich Union. Lind then became bankrupt and was subsequently discharged. Neither assignee proved in his bankruptcy. After his discharge Lind assigned the expectancy to the plaintiff for value.

16. Sale of Goods Act 1895–1972 (SA), s 59(2).
17. One instance of equitable intervention in contracts for the sale of goods can be seen in the ancient remedy of stoppage *in transitu* available to a vendor where the goods sold are in transit, in the hands of a third party carrier. This remedy is not available where there has been actual or constructive delivery to the purchaser: *Schotsmans v Lancashire and Yorkshire Railway Co* (1867) LR 2 Ch App 332. The fact that damages might be an adequate remedy would not appear to be a bar to this relief.

On Lind's mother's death competition arose between the plaintiff and the two assignees. It was held that Arnold and the Norwich Union retained their rights in priority to the plaintiff. Their rights were more than rights in contract, an agreement to charge future property created an immediate equitable charge upon the property coming into existence independently of any contract.

The Court of Appeal sought to distinguish *Collyer v Isaacs* but the general view is that the decision in *Re Lind* effectively changed the law on this subject and that the later case should be taken as authority on the point. It has been accepted as such in Australia by Dixon J in *Palette Shoes v Krohn* (1937) 58 CLR 1. This line of authority was applied in *Re Puntoriero* (1991) 104 ALR 523. An assignment for value of the proceeds of sale of future produce of a potato farm, up to $200,000, made in August 1988 by a husband and wife, who executed a deed under the Bankruptcy Act, Pt X, in March 1989, was held not to constitute a preference under Bankruptcy Act, s 122. Einfield J held that the produce and its proceeds were held on trust for the assignees once they were received by the assignors so that 'until the $200,000 was paid, the Puntorieros divest themselves, and have nothing more to do with the ownership, of the potatoes or their proceeds ... including throughout the whole process leading to their sale'.

3–8   The Doctrine of Part Performance

[3.68] In some circumstances equity will enforce, by way of a decree of specific performance, parol agreements to assign property which would otherwise be required to be evidenced by writing, under the doctrine of part performance. This doctrine is not confined to contracts concerning land: *JC Williamson Ltd v Lukey and Mulholland* (1931) 45 CLR 282, but is restricted to contracts which are specifically enforceable, so that contracts for personal services are excluded: *Britain v Rossiter* (1879) 11 QBD 123. There is an argument that the doctrine applies to all cases in which equity would have entertained a suit for relief, whether by way of specific performance or some other equitable remedy, if the alleged contract had been in writing.[18] In *JC Williamson v Lukey and Mulholland*, the High Court discussed the application of the doctrine to injunction cases, although only Evatt J, at 308ff, expressly ruled on the point, holding that part performance should not be extended beyond suits for specific performance. It has been argued that it is difficult to see any justification for the proposition that it would only be fraud to rely on the statute to prevent enforcement of the whole of the contract and not to allow it to be used where it is invoked to prevent enforcement of some particular provision, such as a negative stipulation which is sought to be enforced by injunction.[19] Logic, if not necessarily the weight of authority, seems to support that latter view. In practice it is unlikely that the question would fall neatly into the law of part performance. The rapidly developing principles of equitable estoppel would be likely to play the major role in deciding any such case.

[3.69] The basis of the doctrine of part performance was stated in *Caton v Caton* (1865) LR 1 Ch App 137. A man and his fiancee agreed to dispense with the formalities of a marriage settlement in return for the man's assurance that he would provide for the woman in his will. On the husband's death it was found he had made a later

---

18. R Barber, 'The Operation of the Doctrine of Part Performance, in particular to Actions for Damages' (1973) 1 Uni of Qld LJ 79 at 88–90.
19. MG&L, para [2044].

will excluding his wife. She sought to enforce the pre-marital agreement, relying on the doctrine of part performance. Lord Cranworth LC held that when one of two contracting parties has been induced, or allowed by the other, to alter his or her position on the faith of the contract, as for instance by taking possession of land, and expending money in building or other like acts, that it would be a fraud in the other party to set up the legal invalidity of the contract on the faith of which he or she induced, or allowed, the person contracting with him or her to act, or expend his or her money. Having said that, his Lordship held that the rule did not apply to these facts as the preparation of his first will by the husband did not cause the woman to alter her position and the will was, necessarily, revocable at any time by the man. The test for the application of the doctrine of part performance was laid down in *Maddison v Alderson* (1883) 8 App Cas 467.

> The appellant had lived for many years as housekeeper in the service of Thomas Alderson, who died in 1877. In return for her unpaid services, Alderson had promised to leave her a life estate in Moulton Manor Farm. He included that gift in a will which he signed in 1874 and which later failed for want of proper attestation. After Alderson's death the appellant took possession of the title deeds to the farm. Alderson's heir sought to recover the deeds. In her defence the appellant claimed that she was entitled to the benefit she would have received under the will because of the parol agreement between herself and the deceased. The House of Lords, led by Lord Selborne LC, held that the agreement was one on which the appellant might have been entitled to relief but for the Statute of Frauds, there being no written memorandum of it, and that the acts of the appellant were not sufficient to invoke the doctrine of part performance which required that the acts relied upon as part performance be unequivocally, and in their own nature, referable to some such agreement as that alleged. The defendant would then be 'charged' upon the equities resulting from the acts done in execution of the contract and not upon the contract itself. Mere continuance in Alderson's service, though without payment of wages, was not of itself evidence of a new contract, much less one concerning land.

[3.70] That statement of the rule in *Maddison v Alderson* was followed by the High Court in *McBride v Sandiland* (1918) 25 CLR 69, in which Isaacs and Rich JJ, in a joint judgment, at 78, confirmed that 'some such agreement as that alleged' meant some contract of the general nature of that alleged. *McBride v Sandiland* has since been followed in *Cooney v Burns* (1922) 30 CLR 216, and in *Regent v Millett* (1976) 50 ALJR 799. The latter case was applied in *Watson v Delaney* (1991) 22 NSWLR 358 as authority for the principle stated in *Maddison v Alderson* to give effect to an oral grant of a tenancy for life. The acts of part performance, which were held to be sufficient, included going into possession, paying rent, and effecting substantial capital repairs on the premises. The doctrine is not a rule of evidence through which the court can find proof of a contract otherwise required to be in writing; it is a rule of substantive law concerned with the question of whether the acts of part performance relied upon by the plaintiff give rise to an equity entitling him or her to specific performance. The acts of part performance are not manifestations of the alleged agreement which satisfy some spirit of the legislation requiring that the agreement not be secret. In many cases, of which *Caton v Caton* is a good example, the fact of the agreement was clearly accepted by the court but the circumstances were not such as to make it inequitable for the defendant to rely on the statute.

[3.71] The requirement that the acts be 'referable' to some such agreement as that alleged was put in some doubt, at least in England, by the House of Lords in *Steadman v Steadman* [1976] AC 536, in which their Lordships, or at least four of them, seemed prepared to accept acts which proved the existence of some contract and were 'consistent' with the one alleged. The alleged contract was a purported settlement of divorce proceedings including an agreement to transfer the matrimonial home in consideration of a payment of £1600. The wife later contended that the agreement was unenforceable because there was no written memorandum of it. The agreement was held to be enforceable against her. The husband's acts in paying part of the moneys as agreed and announcing the settlement in court were held to be sufficient acts of part performance as they were done in reliance on a contract: per Lord Reid, at 541–2, proved the existence of some contract and were not inconsistent with the contract alleged: per Viscount Dilhorne, at 553, and, were more likely than not acts in performance of some contract to which the defendant was a party: per Lord Simon, at 562. Lord Salmon agreed with the conclusions of the majority although he essentially recited Lord Selborne's rule while also holding that a payment of money could be an act of part performance. Their Lordships confirmed that the doctrine operated to enforce the equities arising in the circumstances, and thus that it was not a mere rule of evidence, but also relied heavily on a passage from *Fry on Specific Performance*, 216th ed, 1921, 278, para 582, talking of acts which prove the existence of some contract and were consistent with the contract alleged.

[3.72] While much of the reasoning in *Steadman v Steadman* is convoluted, and it is difficult to isolate any concise majority rule, there appears to be enough in the judgments of Lords Simon and Reid and Viscount Dilhorne to say that the doctrine will be satisfied by acts which are referable to some contract, rather than to the agreement relied on and no other, per Lord O'Hagan in *Maddison v Alderson*, at 485, or referable to some agreement of the type alleged, the rule applied in Australia in *McBride v Sandiland*. That appears to be a radical extension of this doctrine, and has been described as a 'remarkable decision' by Mason J.[20] Despite that there are some who argue that this development may not be so unfortunate. If the essence of the doctrine is that the Statute of Frauds should not be used as an instrument of fraud, and that the defendant should not take advantage of the plaintiff by unconscionably relying on the strict terms of the statute, then it would be proper to seek some uniformity among the various doctrines, such as those of constructive trusts, equitable estoppel and resulting trusts, which are concerned with such equities.[21] That approach would be in keeping with the general emphasis in equity on the conscience and conduct of the defendant rather than the strict legal position of the plaintiff, and the maxim that equity looks to the intent rather than the form.

The prospects for improvement in the law of part performance may have already been overtaken by other developments. Any material alteration in the position of the plaintiff which would have been characterised as an act of part performance in the past is more likely now to be presented as an act to the plaintiff's detriment grounding an action based on equitable estoppel.[22] *Steadman v Steadman* was referred to by Gibbs CJ in *Regent v Millett*, but his Honour found it unnecessary to consider the questions raised by the English case and it cannot be taken to have altered the law of part performance in Australia. Viscount Dilhorne's view in *Steadman v Steadman* as to whether the court should look at the alleged contract first, and then see whether there have been acts of part performance which point unequivocally to it was

---

20. 'Declarations, Injunctions and Constructive Trusts; Divergent Developments in England and Australia' (1980) 11 Uni of Qld LJ 121 at 131.
21. HG&A, paras [3821]–[3825].
22. *Waltons Stores (Interstate) Ltd v Maher* (1988) 164 CLR 387; *Commonwealth v Verwayen* (1990) 170 CLR 394.

referred to by Clarke JA in *Watson v Delaney* (1991) 22 NSWLR 358 at 362–3. The alternate approach, as put by Fullagar J in *Thwaites v Ryan* [1984] VR 65 at 77, requires the court to look at the acts of performance first and then proceed to the nature of the contract implied by those acts. In the event, Clarke JA did not consider it necessary to decide the question as there were sufficient acts of part performance in that case. Meagher JA, with whom Mahoney JA agreed, made no mention of *Steadman v Steadman* and applied the 'unequivocally referable' test, endorsing the established line of authority in Australia.

[3.73] There is some dispute as to whether the acts of part performance need to be acts done in execution of the contract or whether the doctrine is satisfied by acts authorised or allowed by the contract or even by acts neither required nor authorised by the contract but which are simply done in reliance upon it.

In *Cooney v Burns* (1922) 30 CLR 216, the defendant agreed to sell the plaintiff a lease of a hotel together with furniture in the hotel and later pleaded the Statute of Frauds when the plaintiff sought to compel him to complete the agreement. The plaintiff had taken an inventory of the furniture; his solicitor had received the defendant's lease and he had incurred expense in connection with the assignment and his application for transfer of the hotel licence. The High Court held that these acts, being only acts ancillary to the contract and not acts done in pursuance of the contract, did not constitute sufficient acts of part performance.[23]

A different approach was taken in an earlier case, an appeal to the Privy Council from South Australia, in *White v Neaylon* (1886) 11 LR App Cas 171 .

Two brothers carried on a land development business, acquiring Crown Land and selling it off. As part of that business a grant of a parcel of Crown land was obtained in the name of Thomas Neaylon. Thomas later sold it on to the appellant who took it with notice of the claims of the other brother John Neaylon. Those claims arose from a dispute within the partnership which had been settled on the basis that John took that parcel in lieu of his other claims. John had taken possession of the land and done certain work on it, sinking wells, building a stockyard, a stone house and a hut. It was held that, as those things were beyond the scope of the partnership business, they must, therefore, refer not to the partnership title but to the ownership of John and thus gave rise to an equity enforceable against Thomas and any purchaser from him with notice.

[3.74] This issue was raised in the New South Wales Court of Appeal in *Millett v Regent* [1975] 1 NSWLR 62. Glass JA, at 69ff, found that acts done in consequence of an unwritten agreement, but not in execution of it, were excluded from consideration but was not certain that acts done in execution were confined to acts required by the contract and did not extend to acts authorised by it. Hutley JA, at 66, was prepared to go further and held that acts done in reliance on a contract, if they unequivocally pointed to a contract, even though neither expressly required or authorised by it, should satisfy the doctrine. That view has since received support elsewhere, but was not considered when the case went on appeal to the High Court where Gibbs CJ, who gave the judgment of the court, found that there had been a giving and taking of possession of land which he described as 'an act of part performance par excellence'.[24]

---

23. Compare the approach taken on somewhat similar facts in *Waltons Stores (Interstate) Ltd v Maher* (1988) 164 CLR 387.
24. MG&L, para [2037].

3-9 Property Which Cannot be Assigned

Personal contracts

[3.75] There are certain types of property, generally the benefit of particular contracts, which cannot be assigned in law or equity. These include the right to receive payment by a holder of public office and other contracts where the benefits provided are peculiar to the party entitled to or providing them, such as contracts for personal services: *Nokes v Doncaster Amalgamated Collieries Ltd* [1940] AC 1014. Similarly, a contract for insurance of a motor vehicle cannot be assigned as it is dependent on the insurance record of the insured: *Peters v General Accident and Life Assurance Co* [1937] 4 All ER 628. It may be a term of the particular contract that benefits provided by it may not be assigned and such a term may be express or implied.

Bare rights to sue

[3.76] To supply a plaintiff or defendant with financial assistance for proceedings in court constitutes the common law wrong of maintenance while a further agreement to divide the proceeds compounds the offence into champerty. Legal aid is exempt from this rule. As a result a person cannot agree to sell a bare right to sue although an assignment of the proceeds of litigation does not offend the rule: *Glegg v Bromley* [1912] 3 KB 474. That does not prevent the operation of the principle of subrogation under which an insurer is able to sue in the name of the insured after paying out the damages covered by the policy: see Chapter 9. In *Trendtex Trading Corp v Credit Suisse* [1980] 3 All ER 721; [1981] 3 WLR 766, the House of Lords re-affirmed the rule that such an assignment may only occur where the assignee has acquired a property right to which the cause of action was incidental and, in the process, rejected a view that a cause of action could be assigned where it arose out of a right which was in itself assignable.

[3.77] These principles are restricted to actions for breach of contract and would not extend to a right to sue for unliquidated damages for such a breach. Bare rights to sue in tort, and similar rights to sue in equity: *Prosser v Edmonds* (1835)1 Y & C Ex 481; 160 ER 196, remain unassignable.

Chapter Four

4-1   The Varieties of Estoppel

[4.1] Estoppel occurs when a person who is entitled at law to the benefit of some right or rights is prevented, or estopped, by law from insisting upon that right or those rights. An estoppel may arise to prevent insistence on strict rights under a contract; it may preclude a party from pleading certain facts in litigation; it may prevent the bringing of some claim or cause of action entirely. It may operate to restrain a titleholder from asserting rights over property, or at least from denying a claim to an interest in that property by someone else. In equity, estoppel is now seen as a source of substantive rights. Estoppels can arise from a range of different sources and can operate in a variety of circumstances. Most commonly, an estoppel will arise where a party possessing certain legal rights makes a representation or causes a representation to be made, that those rights will not be enforced or will be granted to the representee, or by some other conduct, including acquiescence, causes another party to assume that those strict legal rights will not be enforced. If the second party acts on the faith of the representation made or the assumption fostered by the first, and would suffer some detriment if the first party is allowed to resile from the representation or assumption, estoppel will operate to prevent the first party from insisting on his or her strict legal rights. This is something of a generalisation to give the flavour of estoppel. It will not apply, for instance, to estoppel by judgment and the closely related concept of issue estoppel.

[4.2] Since 1988 there has been explosive growth in this area of the law and it is fair to say that the developments triggered in that time, particularly by the decision of the High Court in *Waltons Stores (Interstate) Ltd v Maher* (1988) 164 CLR 387; 76 ALR 513, have not yet been fully worked through. While the final details of the law of estoppel in Australia remain to be settled, the general shape of the modern doctrine can be ascertained. The trend appears to be toward doctrinal unity, although it ought not to be assumed that that process will be completed, nor that it is necessary or desirable. The major feature of that trend so far is the emergence of the doctrine of equitable estoppel, a seeming marriage of the earlier concepts of promissory and proprietary estoppel. Unification of equitable and common law estoppel has not been achieved: *Lorimer v State Bank of New South Wales* (CA(NSW), Kirby P, 5 July 1991, unreported); although some members of the High Court have been converted to this idea, first mooted by Deane J in *Waltons Stores (Interstate) Ltd v Maher*, at 446–53, a view repeated in *Foran v Wight* (1989) 168 CLR 385 at 431–7 and in *Commonwealth v Verwayen* (1990) 170 CLR 394 at 434–6. Mason CJ accepted Deane J's case for unification in *Foran v Wight*, at 411–12, and *Verwayen*, at 413. Gaudron J appeared to join this group in *Verwayen*, at 458–9. Other members of the court have expressed their continuing preference for the maintenance of the distinction between equitable and common law estoppel: *Commonwealth v Verwayen*, per Brennan J, at 428–9; per Dawson J, at 453–6; and per McHugh J, at 499–502.

[4.3] The principal distinction between equitable estoppel and common law estoppel is that an estoppel by representation at common law can only arise from a representation as to an existing fact: *Jorden v Money* (1854) 5 HLC 185; 10 ER 868; 23 LJ Ch 865, while equitable estoppel will apply where the representation, or assumption on which the plaintiff operates, includes matters of future intention or conduct. There are other differences. Common law estoppel remains essentially a rule of evidence and pleading available principally as a defence available to the representee against a claim by the representor seeking to enforce strict rights. Equitable estoppel can be used as a cause of action: a 'sword' as well as a defence, a 'shield'. At common law a party seeking to rely on estoppel must plead the cause of action arising from the representation, that is, breach of contract where the representation was that there was a contract. If the defendant, the representor, purports to deny those facts, the plaintiff can then plead the estoppel by way of reply.[1] The relief available for such a claim would, of course, be confined to that appropriate to the common law cause of action originally pleaded. There would be no special remedy fashioned to satisfy the estoppel. Where estoppel is pleaded as a defence at common law the relief available to the party relying on the estoppel is also quite narrow. The court is restricted to orders, in effect, requiring the representor to make good the representation, usually by denying that party any opportunity to present a case on the basis that the facts are other than as represented. In equity, the court may fashion an appropriate remedy on the basis of the minimum equity required to do justice between the parties.[2] The bottom line in equitable estoppel is the prevention of unconscionable insistence on strict rights.

Unconscionability is a foreign concept in the common law and it is questionable how such a notion could be incorporated into any common law doctrine. The question of whether these two concepts of estoppel remain separate has not been finally resolved. It remains to be seen which of the two views on the matter will prevail, and what the practical consequences of either might be. It also remains to be seen whether the trend toward doctrinal unity will extend to what might be called the estoppels of record, commonly labelled estoppel by judgment and estoppel by deed. In practical terms the continuing distinction seems to do little harm. Any set of facts which might give rise to a claim based on common law estoppel will also found a claim in equitable estoppel which shares a concurrent jurisdiction with the law in matters arising from representations of fact. The views espoused by Deane J in favour of one doctrine have won some converts although it is not clear what benefits, if any, would flow from unification of the law of estoppel by conduct. By the same token there appears to be no particular reason for such a marriage. The retirement of Mason CJ and the appointment of Deane J as Governor-General will remove the two most powerful advocates of the unification of common law and equitable estoppel from the High Court. In their absence it must be open to doubt that the cause of unification will be pressed with any great force.

[4.4] Another trend in recent years has been the development of estoppel as a cause of action rather than merely a defence; a 'sword' as well as a 'shield'. That was always the case with the equitable doctrine of proprietary estoppel but not so with promis-

---

1. A Leopold, 'The Elements of Estoppel' (1991) Building & Construction Law 248 at 253.
2. *Crabb v Arun District Council* [1976] 1 Ch 179 at 199, per Scarman LJ; *Waltons Stores (Interstate) Pty Ltd v Maher* (1988) 164 CLR 387 at 404, per Mason CJ and Wilson J.

sory estoppel until *Waltons*. Common law estoppel has been regarded traditionally as a rule of evidence, a defensive mechanism precluding a party from denying or otherwise traversing certain facts pleaded by his or her opponent. Estoppel is not available as a cause of action, a 'sword', at common law. However, as noted, a claim can be pleaded at common law on the cause of action said to arise from the assumed facts (see **[4.3]**). The estoppels by record also operate as defences; although it is difficult to see how they could be employed otherwise.

[4.5] One difficulty which afflicts this area of the law is that of categorisation and labelling. The common law estoppel, estoppel in pais (that is, 'on the country'), embraces ordinary common law estoppel as well as estoppel by representation and estoppel by convention, although the distinctions between these variants is not always clearly drawn. Throughout his judgments in *Waltons, Foran v Wight*, and *Verwayen*, Deane J consistently refers to common law estoppel as estoppel by conduct. Despite the apparent unification of promissory and proprietary estoppel under the doctrine of equitable estoppel it is quite common to see writers and judges talking about promissory estoppel, leaving one with the impression that they may regard that estoppel as a continuing doctrine separate from the new equitable estoppel, or that the equitable estoppel which emerged from *Waltons* was simply an extension of promissory estoppel, and did not incorporate proprietary estoppel. Some writers also refer to 'conventional estoppel', by which they probably mean 'estoppel by convention', which is a form of common law estoppel, although the concept of estoppel by convention could embrace estoppel by deed as well. Experienced practitioners may not be fazed by this endless variety of different labels. But those using them should spare a thought for students who can find the concepts in the law of estoppel difficult enough without being baffled by the names from the outset.

The categories of estoppel

[4.6] Estoppel occurs under a number of different guises, some equitable and some of the common law, variously labelled as estoppel of one type or another. In brief those various types and their usual labels are:

(a) *Estoppel by deed* — whereby a party to a deed is prevented, as between the parties to the deed, from denying any allegation of fact made in it, particularly those facts recited in the deed as the basis upon which the parties have agreed to the terms of the deed.

(b) *Estoppel by judgment* — which prevents any party to litigation from denying in any subsequent litigation between him or herself and any other party to the original case anything decided as between the parties by judgment in that first matter. This encompasses both *res judicata* and issue estoppel. Under *res judicata* a party to prior litigation in which final judgment has been given is estopped from taking proceedings against the other party to that litigation on the cause or causes of action which were the subject of those proceedings, or any other cause of action arising from the facts which were the subject of the earlier case which might reasonably have been available on the facts: *Port of Melbourne Authority v Anshun Pty Ltd* (1981) 147 CLR 589. Issue estoppel prevents a party raising issues of fact or law necessarily determined as between the parties by some judgment, decree or order in earlier proceedings.[3]

---

3. *Blair v Curran* (1939) 62 CLR 464 at 532.

(c) *Estoppel in pais* — which embraces both common law estoppel and estoppel by representation as well as estoppel by convention, although that third category can be seen as simply a variant of the first:

    (i) *common law estoppel* precludes a person from denying an assumption which has formed the conventional basis of a relationship between him or herself and another, or which he has adopted against another by the assertion of some right based on it: *Legione v Hately* (1983) 152 CLR 406 at 430, per Mason and Deane JJ. It is based on the acts of the party against whom it is asserted, rather than on representations made by that party. While similar to estoppel by convention, this common law estoppel is not necessarily mutual.

    (ii) *estoppel by representation* under which a person who, by a representation of fact, has led another to alter his or her position, is prevented from denying that the fact is other than as represented. This estoppel is said to have emerged later than common law estoppel, having its origins in equity.[4] It was not firmly established in the common law until *Pickard v Sears* (1837) 6 Ad & E 469; 112 ER 179. On the existing state of the law, an estoppel by representation at common law can only arise from a representation as to an existing fact: *Jorden v Money* (1854) 5 HLC 185–10 ER 868; 23 LJ Ch 865. This estoppel can arise against government bodies when they are operating in what might be described as their 'private' or commercial capacities. But it cannot be raised so as to hinder the exercise of a ministerial or public discretion: *Minister for Immigration and Ethnic Affairs v Kurtovic* (1990) 21 FCR 193; *A-G (NSW) v Quin* (1990) 170 CLR 1 at 17–19, per Mason CJ: 'I am unable to perceive how a representation made or an impression created by the Executive can preclude the Crown or the Executive from adopting a new policy'; *Haoucher v Minister for Immigration and Ethnic Affairs* (1990) 169 CLR 648 at 678–9, per McHugh J.

    (iii) *estoppel by convention* under which parties are estopped, as between themselves, from denying the truth of assumptions adopted by them as the conventional basis of their dealings. It is not founded on any representation of fact made by one and acted on by the other but on the basis of an agreed or assumed state of facts: *Con-Stan Industries of Australia Pty Ltd v Norwich Winterhur Insurance (Australia) Ltd* (1986) 160 CLR 226 at 244. Estoppel by convention is, by its nature, mutual: *Hawker Pacific Pty Ltd v Helicopter Charter Pty Ltd* (1991) 22 NSWLR 298 at 308, per Handley JA, a proposition underlined by the judgment of the majority of the New South Wales Court of Appeal in *Corumo Holdings Pty Ltd v Itoh Ltd* (1991) 24 NSWLR 370 at 402–3, per Meagher JA.

(d) *Proprietary estoppel* — a form of estoppel recognised in equity under which a person is estopped from insisting on some proprietary right having encouraged another to act to his or her detriment by some representation of benefit, or having acquiesced in such action, aware of the mistaken belief under which the second party was operating. This encompasses estoppel by encouragement, being the active, positive form of proprietary estoppel, and estoppel by acquiescence, the passive form.

(e) *Promissory estoppel* — sometimes called *High Trees* estoppel after the case seen as the foundation of the modern rule.[5] Promissory estoppel operates where a

---

4. MG&L, para [1703].
5. *Central London Properly Trust Ltd v High Trees House Ltd* [1947] 1 KB 130.

party to some pre-existing legal relationship gives some assurance or makes some representation that rights available under that relationship will be enforced, thereby causing the other party to act in reliance on that assurance. In such a case the first party will be estopped from reverting to his or her original position at will.

(f) *Equitable estoppel* — the estoppel applied by the High Court in *Waltons v Maher*, perhaps best summarised by Priestley JA in *Austotel Pty Ltd v Franklins Selfserve Stores Pty Ltd* (1989) 16 NSWLR 582 at 612, 'For equitable estoppel to operate there must be the creation or encouragement by the defendant in the plaintiff of an assumption that a contract will come into existence or a promise be performed or an interest granted to the plaintiff by the defendant, and reliance on that by the plaintiff, in circumstances where departure from the assumption by the defendant would be unconscionable'.

Estoppel by deed and estoppel by judgment are doctrines of the common law. Neither has yet been nominated as a candidate for Deane J's concept of an all embracing estoppel by conduct. Further discussion of them here is not warranted in view of the dictates of space and subject matter.

4-2 Estoppel in Pais

[4.7] Estoppel in pais was discussed in detail by Sir Owen Dixon in two decisions: *Thompson v Palmer* (1933) 49 CLR 507 at 547 and *Grundt v Great Boulder Pty Gold Mines Ltd* (1937) 59 CLR 641 at 674–6. It is founded on the principle that the law should not permit an unjust departure by a party from an assumption of fact which that first party has caused another party to adopt or accept for the purpose of their legal relations. A party seeking to rely on this estoppel must show that he or she has acted or abstained from acting upon the assumed state of affairs and that he or she would suffer a detriment if the first party was allowed to set up contrary rights inconsistent with the assumption. Before a party can be estopped under this doctrine it must be shown that that party played such a part in the adoption of the assumption by the other party that it would be unfair or unjust if he or she was left free to ignore it. That 'part' may be played in a number of different ways:

1. The assumption may form the conventional basis upon which the parties entered into contractual or mutual relations; that is, a bailee will be precluded from denying his bailor's title to the goods bailed.

2. The party estopped may have exercised rights against the other which would only exist if the assumption was correct; an insurer who had retained possession of the salvage was estopped from denying that the insured had made a valid claim: *Yorkshire Insurance v Craine* [1922] 2 AC 541.

3. Knowing the mistake under which the other was labouring, one refrained from correcting the other when it was the first party's duty to do so. In *Waltons Stores (Interstate) Ltd v Maher* (1986) 5 NSWLR 407, in the New South Wales Court of Appeal, which treated the case as one involving common law estoppel on the basis that the representation was one of existing fact (that is, that a valid lease had come into existence), the appellant was held to be estopped from denying that a lease had been concluded when it knew that the respondents had proceeded with demolition and construction work on the site to be leased on the

assumption that the lease had been finalised and failed to inform them that it had decided not to proceed with the lease.

4. The imprudence of the party said to be estopped, where care was required of that party, was a proximate cause of the other party adopting and acting upon the assumption.

5. One directly made representations upon which the other party founded the assumption.

[4.8] In *Grundt*, Dixon J did not say that the representation leading to the assumption under which the parties operated had to be one of fact. He said, at 676:

> Belief in the correctness of the facts or state of affairs assumed is not always necessary. Parties may adopt as the conventional basis of a transaction between them an assumption which they know to be contrary to the actual state of affairs.

Dixon J made no distinction between the operation of estoppel in equity and at law, and appeared to speak on the footing of a general doctrine of estoppel by conduct (or 'estoppel in pais') spanning both jurisdictions.[6] He did not expressly confine the estoppel he described to one arising from representations, or assumptions, as to existing facts. Both *Thompson v Palmer* and *Grundt v Great Boulder* were cases involving assumptions as to existing facts, and neither judgment challenges *Jorden v Money* expressly. While not a challenge to the principle in *Jorden v Money* (1854) 5 HLC 184; 10 ER 868, these comments have been taken as evidence of a broad view of that deceptively simple term 'a representation of fact': *Legione v Hately* (1983) 152 CLR 406 at 432, per Mason and Deane JJ. In the Court of Appeal decision in *Waltons v Maher*, Priestley JA set out what he considered to be the four elements of the test for the application of this estoppel in pais:

1. Did the plaintiff adopt a mistaken assumption of fact which the defendant had caused them both to adopt or accept for the purpose of their legal relations?

2. Would departure by the defendant from that assumption operate to the plaintiff's detriment?

3. Did the defendant know of the mistake laboured under by the plaintiff?

4. Did the defendant refrain from correcting the plaintiff when it was the defendant's duty to do so?

4–3 Estoppel by Representation

[4.9] During the first half of the nineteenth century the Court of Chancery developed a broad jurisdiction in estoppel designed to prevent people from resiling from representations solemnly made. The representations enforced in this way did not have to be supported by consideration and could be representations of fact or of intention and did not need to be made fraudulently. The relief given usually required the representor to make good the representation: *Burrowes v Lock* (1805) 10 Ves 470; [1803–13] All ER Rep 477. In *Loffus v Maw* (1862) 3 Giff 592; 66 ER 544, a testator induced his niece to act as his housekeeper on the faith of a representation, which proved untrue, that certain properties would be left to her in his will. The niece was able to secure a decree that the properties were held on trust for her. In *Hammersley v*

---

6. MG&L, para [1705].

De Biel (1845) 12 Cl & Fin 45; 8 ER 1312, a father's estate was held liable to pay £10,000 where the father had induced a suitor to marry his daughter on the faith of a representation that such a sum was to be settled upon her and her future children by the father's will.

[4.10] The growth of estoppel by representation threatened the jurisdiction of the common law in contract, which was concurrently settling the modern doctrine of consideration, by enforcing unsupported but solemnly given promises. A series of decisions from the middle of the nineteenth century set limits on estoppel by representation which have kept it within narrow bounds since. The first of those restrictions confined it to representations of fact only, and not of intention.

In *Jorden v Money* (1854) 5 HLC 184; 10 ER 868, Mrs Jorden was entitled to enforce a bond against Mr Money but assured him she would never do so. Relying on that assurance, Money married. Mrs Jorden later obtained a judgment at law on the bond. Money sought an injunction to restrain her from enforcing the judgment. It was held by the House of Lords, reversing the decision of Sir John Romilly MR, that the doctrine that a person who makes a false representation to another which causes the other to act on the faith of the representation will not afterwards be able to resile from the truth of the representation only applied to representations of fact and not to statements of intention by the first party. According to the majority of the House this limitation applied to estoppel by representation in both law and equity.

[4.11] Some years later, in *Maddison v Alderson* (1883) 8 App Cas 467, acts done in reliance upon oral promises, forming part of an agreement rendered unenforceable by the Statute of Frauds, were dealt with under the doctrine of part performance and could only be enforced, and then only within a contractual framework, by a decree of specific performance, provided they were unequivocally referable to some such contract as that alleged. Common law estoppel was also inhibited by *Derry v Peek* (1889) 14 App Cas 337 which restricted the tort of false representations, or common law fraud, to those made knowingly, or without belief in their truth, or without caring whether they were true or false. Finally, in *Low v Bouverie* [1891] 3 Ch 82, the jurisdiction of equity to order compensation for some unfulfilled representation was restricted to cases of fraud. Bowen LJ also held that estoppel was only a rule of evidence and could not be used to ground a cause of action, a net from which Lord Haldane later rescued representations made by fiduciaries to their principals: *Nocton v Lord Ashburton* [1914] AC 932 at 950. On the common law side actionable representations remained within their late Victorian cage until prised out by *Hedley Byrne & Co Ltd v Heller & Partners Ltd* [1964] AC 465 which made some negligent misrepresentations actionable, and then only as the basis for a claim for damages.

[4.12] Shorn of its early nineteenth century grandeur, and before its more recent renovation, estoppel by representation could be said to arise against a person responsible for a representation of fact, whether made by words or conduct, innocently or fraudulently, in circumstances where a reasonable person would regard him or herself as invited to act upon it and where the representation has been material in inducing another to alter his or her position so that it would be to his or her detriment if the representation was not adhered to: *Franklin v Manufacturers Mutual Ins Ltd* (1936) 36 SR (NSW) 76 at 82, per Jordan CJ. Until the current upheaval in the law of estoppel, the elements of estoppel by representation were those stated by Sir Frederick Jordan. In that form it acted as a rule of evidence and could only be used by the party entitled to it as a defence in proceedings brought by the representor seeking to enforce strict legal rights.

[4.13] The elements of estoppel by representation outlined by Sir Frederick Jordan in *Franklin v Manufacturers Mutual* have been subjected to judicial scrutiny recently. In *Foran v Wight* (1989) 168 CLR 385 at 435, Deane J rejected the distinction between representations of fact and representations of law as illusory.[7] In *Waltons v Maher* Mason CJ and Wilson J noted, at 399, the repeated acceptance of *Jorden v Money* over the years as authority for the narrow compass of common law estoppel, and said that it would be necessary to reverse that decision if common law estoppel were to be held to arise on an assumption as to future events. No argument along those lines was put in that case and the matter was left there. The tone of the judgment suggests an invitation to counsel in future cases to argue that *Jorden v Money* ought to be over-turned. The ammunition for such an argument can be found in Meagher, Gummow and Lehane's analysis of that odd case: see RP Meagher, WMC Gummow and JRF Lehane, *Equity: Doctrines & Remedies*, 3rd ed, Butterworths, Sydney, 1992, para [1707].

4–4 Proprietary Estoppel

[4.14] Alongside the jurisdiction it shared with the common law governing estoppel by representation, equity also developed a jurisdiction to prevent a person from insisting upon strict legal rights to property, usually land, in circumstances in which the person concerned had either encouraged another to act to his or her detriment on the faith of a belief that no such contrary right existed, or that such a right would not be enforced, or where that first person had acquiesced with knowledge in the actions of the other. This estoppel, known most commonly as proprietary estoppel because it usually leads to a proprietary remedy, is different from estoppel by representation in a number of ways, although the distinction between the two was not always clearly drawn. The equity which arises in favour of the plaintiff in these cases generally results in the extinction, qualification or suspension of the rights of the legal titleholder, rather than a requirement to make good some representation made by that titleholder. Proprietary estoppel also does not necessarily rely on any expectation created or encouraged by the defendant. Acquiescence with knowledge in the plaintiff's mistaken belief will also satisfy the doctrine. Furthermore, proprietary estoppel is not just a rule of evidence. It can be used as a cause of action — it is both a sword and a shield. Proprietary estoppel, always only a creature of equity, was also not confined to representations or assumptions as to existing facts.

[4.15] The doctrine of proprietary estoppel can be traced to two decisions each of which suggests a different basis for the estoppel. Both ground the relief awarded upon the fraud of the defendant, and in both the subject matter of any orders given is property of the defendant, rather than the falsity of some representation made by the defendant and the subject matter of that false representation.

> In *Dillwyn v Llewelyn* (1862) 4 De G F & J 517; 45 ER 1285, a father put his son in possession of some land and signed an instrument of conveyance which proved to be ineffective. The son occupied the land and built a house on it, all with the knowledge and approval of the father. On the father's death, the son obtained a declaration that he was equitable owner of the land. Lord Westbury LC stated the rule that if A puts B in possession of land and tells him that he may build a house on it and B, on the strength of

---

7. An approach much strengthened by the High Court's rejection of the old distinction between mistakes of law and mistakes of fact in *David Securities v Commonwealth Bank* (1992) 109 ALR 57.

that promise, with the knowledge of A, expends money in building a house then B will acquire a right to compel A to complete the contract and perfect the imperfect donation.

[4.16] It is not surprising that resort was had to the analogy of contract to explain this rule: see *NSW Trotting Club v Glebe Municipal Council* (1937) 37 SR (NSW) 288 at 308, even though the reference to the transaction as a donation in the same sentence plainly shows the contradiction inherent in the analogy. The second line of authority places much stronger reliance on equitable fraud arising in circumstances where B improves the land of A, under a belief that he has some right to that land, and A, knowing of B's mistaken assumption and of his work on the land, stands by and allows B to proceed with the improvements.

In *Ramsden v Dyson* (1866) LR 1 HL 129, the plaintiffs sought to defeat proceedings against them in ejectment on the ground that the land in question was not subject to a customary lease terminable at will but to a lease for sixty years. It was held that the circumstances of the case did not show anything more than a tenancy from year to year but, in the process the principle to be applied in these cases was stated by Lord Cranworth at 140–1: 'If a stranger begins to build on my land supposing it to be his own, and I, perceiving his mistake, abstain from setting him right, and leave him to persevere in his error, a court of equity will not allow me afterwards to assert my title to the land on which he had expended money on the supposition that the land was his own'. And by Lord Kingsdown at 170: 'If a man, under a verbal agreement with a landlord for a certain interest in land, or, what amounts to the same thing, under an expectation created or encouraged by the landlord, that he shall have a certain interest, takes possession of such land, with the consent of the landlord, and upon the faith of such promise or expectation, with the knowledge of the landlord, and without objection by him, lays out money upon the land, a court of equity will compel the landlord to give effect to such promise or expectation '.

[4.17] Despite the similarity between these statements of principle and estoppel by representation before *Jorden v Money*, this later estoppel, sometimes known as estoppel by acquiescence, survived both the restrictions imposed on estoppel by representation as well as the attempts of some to explain it away as a matter of contract. It was subsequently applied by the Privy Council in *Plimmer v Mayor of Wellington* (1884) 9 App Cas 699 to allow compensation to a man who had built a jetty on public land, with the permission and encouragement of the government at the time, when the government later sought to resume the jetty.

[4.18] The decision in *Plimmer* can be seen as working toward the union of the two strands of authority, at least in the area of the relief given, although it left two questions in doubt: whether the doctrine was simply based on the implication of a contract from the facts; and whether the relief was granted on the ground of the false expectation created in the plaintiff or because of the inequitable conduct of the defendant in insisting on its strict legal rights. Had proprietary estoppel been restricted to one concerned with granting expectations fostered by implied contracts it may have developed into little more than a doctrine of equitable quasi-contract. That did not happen and the subsequent history of proprietary estoppel saw it expand to become a powerful weapon in equity's arsenal. That expansion did not take place without some confusion as to the fundamental basis of the doctrine and whether it consisted of one rule or two.

[4.19] In *Willmott v Barber* (1880) 15 Ch D 96, Fry J set out five probanda often since quoted as stating the elements of this estoppel:

1. The plaintiff must have made a mistake as to his or her legal rights; and

2. The plaintiff must have expended money or done some other act on the faith of that mistaken belief; and

3. The defendant must know of his or her own legal right which is inconsistent with that claimed by the plaintiff; and

4. The defendant must also know of the plaintiff's mistaken belief; and

5. The defendant must have encouraged the plaintiff in his or her expenditure or other actions either directly or by abstaining from asserting his or her own rights.

Those elements appear to cover cases of both encouragement and acquiescence, but in many cases of encouragement, such as those in which there has been an imperfect gift, the issue will have nothing to with the defendant's knowledge of the plaintiff's mistaken belief and his own inconsistent right. The question will be whether the defendant can resile from the expectation fostered by the statements made and other conduct and which have led to the action taken by the plaintiff. If it is reasonable to expect that a normal person would respond to the act of encouragement it should not matter whether the encouraging party also knew that the plaintiff was responding. In *Olsson v Dyson* (1969) 120 CLR 365 there was an imperfect gift of a debt. Kitto J said, at 376, of such cases that, while there was no equity to perfect an imperfect gift:

> ... some subsequent conduct of the intending donor, encouraging the intended donee to act to his own prejudice on the footing that the property or some interest in it has become his, may make it unconscionable for the donor to withhold the property or interest from the donee, and equity may on that ground hold the donee entitled to the property.

That suggests some additional act on the part of the donor to encourage the donee to act to his or her detriment on the faith of the gift or, at least, knowing acquiescence in such an act. But the act of donation itself should constitute the necessary encouragement to satisfy the test provided the donee acts on the faith of it and it is reasonable in the circumstances to expect him or her to do so. Kitto J's extra requirement can only be seen as an example of equity's reluctance to lend its assistance to complete imperfect gifts.[8]

[4.20] Proprietary estoppel is founded upon equity's jurisdiction to prevent unconscionable insistence upon strict rights by the legal titleholder rather than the enforcement of some expectation created in the claimant. In *Shaw v Applegate* [1977] 1 WLR 970 at 978, Buckley LJ, when talking of the five probanda in *Willmott v Barber* said:

> I do not ... think ... that it is essential to find all five tests set out by Fry J literally applicable and satisfied in any particular case. The real test ... must be whether upon the facts of the particular case the situation has become such that it would be dishonest or unconscionable for the plaintiff, or the person having the right sought to be enforced, to continue to seek to enforce it.

[4.21] It has been suggested that in Australia where A encourages B in a mistaken belief A must also be aware of his or her own right inconsistent with that of B.[9] That

---

8. PD Finn, 'Equitable Estoppel in PD Finn (ed), *Essays in Equity*, Law Book Co, Sydney, 1985, pp 59–94 at p 82.

9. MG&L, para [1717]; *Svenson v Payne* (1945) 71 CLR 531 (although this is clearly a case of estoppel by acquiescence).

would seem inconsistent with a general jurisdiction to prevent unconscientious insistence upon strict rights, as in the case where A purports to assign some interest to B and both operate under the assumption that the assignment is effective and B alters his position, particularly where A has been the author of the common misapprehension. In England such conduct has been upheld as grounds for estoppel in *Inwards v Baker* [1965] 2 QB 29, where a father encouraged his son to build on land owned by the father. After the father's death, trustees of the father's estate were estopped from denying the interest of the son which was held to be a right to remain in occupation of the land so long as he desired it for his home. More precision was employed in applying the same principle in *Taylors Fashions Ltd v Liverpool Victoria Trustees Co Ltd* [1982] 1 QB 133 to prevent a landlord from denying the validity of an option, which both the landlord and the tenant had believed to be valid, after the tenant had effected improvements to the property. Oliver J held that it was not necessary to satisfy the five probanda of *Willmott v Barber* in order to establish proprietary estoppel. Those five elements might be the test where there has been silent acquiescence but not where there has been encouragement, particularly where that has fostered an expectation in the minds of both parties.

[4.22] Proprietary estoppel was applied by the Privy Council in an appeal from Western Australia in *Cameron v Murdoch* (1986) 63 ALR 575 in which two brothers, who had continued their father's farming business in partnership after the father's death, allowed a third brother to build a home and to farm certain lands on the property. There had been a representation made to the third brother that he would, in some way, be enabled to acquire those lands, and as he had acted, by improving the land, and abstained from acting, in not establishing himself and his family on some other property on the faith of that representation, and as his estate would suffer detriment if denied the right to purchase the lands at a discount, it was held that his estate was entitled to an equity which could most appropriately be satisfied by allowing the estate to purchase the lands at a discount of one third. Proprietary estoppel, arising from encouragement rather than acquiescence, was also applied in Queensland in *Riches v Hogben* [1986] 1 Qd R 315 to prevent an elderly woman from denying her 64 year old son a proprietary interest in a house she had purchased in Brisbane in her name. The son had migrated from England with his family on the basis of an assurance by the mother that she would purchase a house in his name if he came out to look after her. Within a week of the son and his family moving in, the mother asked them to leave following a disagreement.[10]

[4.23] The authority commonly cited in support of the proposition that it would be essential for the party insisting on his or her rights to have known of them at the time of the acquiescence or encouragement in the expenditure by the other is *Svenson v Payne* (1945) 71 CLR 531. In that case a lessee, having expended considerable money on the property, sought to defend an action for cancellation of the lease by the remainderman on the grounds of estoppel. The lease had been granted by the life tenant of the property, who was also trustee of the estate in favour of himself and the remainderman. The term of the lease exceeded the time for such grants allowed by the will. The High Court applied *Ramsden v Dyson* and held that the lessee was not

---

10. This decision has been criticised for taking too wide a view of the ambit of the doctrine of proprietary estoppel, particularly as it is not clear what 'strict legal rights' the mother was insisting on. The question was made much easier by the fact that the mother actually purchased a house. Had she not done so, would the court have intervened to tell her how to spend her money? KG Nicholson, 'Riches v Hogben: Part Performance and the Doctrines of Equitable and Proprietary Estoppel' 60 ALJ 345 at 318.

entitled to the benefit of estoppel because the remainderman had not known of her inconsistent right at the time the lessee acted to his detriment, in the sense that she had not known she could exercise her rights against the lessee while the life tenant was alive, and also, because the trustee's lack of power was discoverable by searches. *Svenson v Payne* was clearly a case of acquiescence and not encouragement. It should not be a bar to the acceptance in Australia of the rule in *Taylors Fashions*.[11] It might have been very different if the life tenant, that is, the party who had encouraged the lessee in the belief that the lease was valid, was the one seeking to have it avoided, although the lessee's failure to search might still have defeated his hopes.

[4.24] The relief awarded in cases of proprietary estoppel has been described as the minimum equity required to do justice: *Crabb v Arun District Council* [1976] 1 Ch 179 at 199, per Scarman LJ. This has often been held to require fulfilment of the expectation created in the 'encouragement' cases, while in the 'acquiescence' cases the concern has generally been to prevent A from enjoying the benefit conferred on him or her by B, or to compensate B for any exertions, sometimes by charging the property of A. As a principle concerned to prevent unconscionable insistence upon strict rights, relief will generally take the form of some qualification, suspension or extinguishment of the rights of A unless that has become impossible, in which case compensation for the detriment may be awarded. In extreme cases the court may go further. In *Pascoe v Turner* [1979] 1 WLR 431, the English Court of Appeal held that the minimum equity required to do justice was to compel the man to execute a conveyance of the fee simple in the house to a woman with whom he had lived for some time and who had arranged her affairs on the faith of certain assurances made by the man. In coming to that decision the court took into account the need to provide the woman with quiet enjoyment and security of tenure and the ruthlessness shown by the conduct of the man during the proceedings.

> In *Jackson v Crosby* (1979) 21 SASR 280, a man was awarded effectively half the unencumbered, improved value of a block of land on which he had built a house. The land was owned by a woman with whom he had been living and was intended to be their home. The court considered half the value of the house and land, that is, about $19,000, more appropriate in the circumstances than the value of the man's labour, that is, about $12,000.

4–5 Promissory Estoppel

[4.25] The modern foundation of this doctrine lies in the decision of Denning J in *Central London Property Trust Ltd v High Trees House Ltd* [1947] 1 KB 130. Its adoption in Australia was sanctioned by the High Court in *Legione v Hately* (1983) 152 CLR 406. Under this doctrine, as originally formulated, where parties to some subsisting legal relationship which might arise from contract, statute or some fiduciary obligation, enter into some course of negotiation or other conduct whereby one gives the other an assurance that strict legal rights will not be enforced, and the other acts on that assurance, the first party will be estopped from reverting to the original position, at least not without adequate notice provided such a resumption is still possible, where the second party has placed him or herself in a position in which he or she will suffer material disadvantage should departure be allowed from the assurances given. The

---

11. MG&L, para [1720], still say that *Svenson v Payne* stands as authority for the proposition that knowledge is required in Australia.

isolated development of promissory estoppel in Australia has now been overtaken by the development of the doctrine of equitable estoppel by the High Court in *Waltons Stores (Interstate) Ltd v Maher* (1988) 164 CLR 387; 76 ALR 513.

4–6 Equitable Estoppel

[4.26] The two strands of estoppel in equity, proprietary estoppel and promissory estoppel, have now been joined under the one doctrine of equitable estoppel. Some details of this new doctrine remain to be settled. The principal source of authority on the point, and the case which established the principle, is the decision of the High Court in *Waltons Stores (Interstate) Ltd v Maher* (1988) 164 CLR 387; 76 ALR 513:

> Waltons Stores negotiated with the Mahers about the granting of a lease in favour of Waltons over land owned by the Mahers in Nowra. Waltons intended to use the site for a department store which would necessitate demolition of the building on the site and the construction of new premises. The new store needed to be ready for occupation in February 1984. On 7 November 1983 the Mahers' solicitors told Waltons' solicitors of the 'need to conclude the agreement within the next day or two' in order to complete the building in time. On the same day, Waltons' solicitors sent lease documents incorporating amendments discussed by 'phone to the Mahers' solicitors. The covering letter said that specific instructions had not yet been received from Waltons on each amendment. On 11 November the Mahers' solicitors forwarded 'by way of exchange' completed lease documents to Waltons' solicitors. The Mahers proceeded with the demolition. It was found that Waltons became aware of this, at least from 10 December. Neither Waltons nor their solicitors communicated with the Mahers until 19 January 1984 when Waltons' solicitors wrote to the Mahers' solicitors advising that Waltons did not intend to proceed with the matter. The new building was then 40 per cent complete. The High Court held that Waltons was estopped from resiling from its implied promises that the contract of lease would be exchanged and that a lease would thereby come into existence. Mason CJ and Wilson J considered that the evidence was insufficient to sustain a finding that the Mahers believed that contracts had been exchanged or that a binding contract had come into existence. That meant that Waltons' silence after 11 November could not constitute a representation of an existing fact and that, therefore, the Mahers could not rely on common law estoppel. Their Honours said that promissory estoppel extends to the enforcement of voluntary promises made outside any contractual framework on the footing that a departure from the basic assumptions underlying the transactions between the parties must be unconscionable. In that sense, promissory estoppel shared a common thread with proprietary estoppel, namely that equity will come to the relief of a plaintiff who has acted to his detriment on the basis of a basic assumption in circumstances where it would be unconscionable for the other party to the transaction to ignore the assumption. Their Honours underlined their view, at 405, that equitable estoppel has its basis in unconscionable conduct rather than the making good of representations. While, on the facts, it would not have been unconscionable for Waltons to have refused to exchange contracts in November it was unconscionable of them not to have communicated that intention to the Mahers within a reasonable time after receiving the counterpart deed and certainly after 10 December when they knew the demolition was proceeding.

> Brennan J considered equitable estoppel to be binding in conscience on the party estopped and thought it better described as an equity created by estoppel. His Honour saw little purpose in dividing those cases into categories of promissory and proprietary estoppel. In his view it is better to consider those as instances in which such an equity has been held to arise. The object of the equity is not to compel the estopped party to fulfil the assumption or expectation created or encouraged by his words or conduct; it

is to avoid the detriment which will be suffered by the other party, who has thereby been induced to act or abstain from acting, if that assumption or expectation goes unfulfilled. To establish equitable estoppel Brennan J said, at 164 CLR 428–9; 76 ALR 542, that the plaintiff must prove that:

1. He assumed a particular legal relationship existed, or would come to exist, between himself and the defendant;
2. The defendant induced the plaintiff to adopt that assumption or expectation;
3. The plaintiff acted or abstained from acting on the faith of the assumption or expectation;
4. The defendant knew of the plaintiff's action, or intended the plaintiff to act in such a way;
5. The plaintiff's action or inaction will cause him or her to suffer detriment if the assumption or expectation is not fulfilled;
6. The defendant has failed to act to avoid the detriment by fulfilling the expectation or otherwise.

Deane J said that Waltons' conscious policy of silence and going slow on the deal gave rise to an assumption on the part of the Mahers that a binding agreement existed sufficient to found an estoppel on the principles stated by Dixon J in *Thompson v Palmer* (1933) 49 CLR 507 and *Grundt v Grundt Boulder Pty Gold Mines Ltd* (1937) 59 CLR 641. In addition, Deane J thought, that as there had been doctrinal unity between equity and the common law on estoppel by conduct prior to the Judicature Acts (in that both required an assumption or representation as to an existing fact, and not some representation as to future conduct), the extension of estoppel by conduct by the principles of promissory estoppel now should not be seen as purely a development of equitable principle. Estoppel by conduct must now be seen as applying to preclude departure from a represented or assumed state of future affairs in at least some categories of case.

Gaudron J accepted that equitable estoppel encompassed both proprietary and promissory estoppel, but was not prepared to accept the concept of unification of estoppel at law and equity. However, Her Honour considered that the relevant assumption was that an exchange of contracts had taken place, that is, an assumption as to an existing fact, and dealt with the case as one of common law estoppel.

The major difficulty with *Waltons v Maher* is the apparent divergence between the views expressed on the bench. All were agreed on the final result and there was near consensus as to the emergence of a new doctrine of equitable estoppel embracing proprietary and promissory estoppel; the one dissentient being Deane J who wanted to go further and include both the equitable estoppels and estoppel in pais under the one heading of estoppel by conduct. Despite the slight divergence in opinion in the High Court the better statement of principle appears to that applied by Mason CJ and Wilson J, at 404–5, that equity will come to the relief of a plaintiff who has acted to his detriment on the basis of a basic assumption in relation to which the other party to the transaction has played such a part in the adoption of the assumption that it would be unconscionable of that other party to ignore the assumption. In that sense, equitable estoppel is based on relief against unconscionable conduct, rather than the making good of representations. Brennan J's approach is not at odds with this view. Brennan J placed emphasis on the detriment which the plaintiff would suffer if the expectation or assumption remained unfulfilled. The extent of the detriment which the plaintiff has suffered, or might suffer, is obviously relevant to establishing one element of the cause of action in the first place; and second, as a factor in determining whether it is unconscionable in the circumstances for the defendant to insist on its strict rights. The detriment which the plaintiff would otherwise have to bear will also be relevant in determining the appropriate relief.

[4.27] The High Court had another opportunity to consider the doctrine of equitable estoppel in *Foran v Wight* (1989) 168 CLR 385. The vendors under a contract for the sale of land gave notice to the purchasers shortly before the date due for settlement that they would not be able to complete. Time was of the essence. The date passed and two days later the purchasers purported to rescind the contract and demanded repayment of their deposit. It was later shown that the purchasers could not have completed on the due date. The High Court held that the purchasers' notice of rescission was valid and that they were entitled to return of the deposit. Deane and Dawson JJ came to that conclusion on the ground that the vendors were estopped from demanding performance by the purchasers by their own statement that they would not be able to complete. Dawson J did not consider it necessary to apply the estoppel found in *Waltons v Maher* saying instead that 'the principles of promissory estoppel as they were accepted in *Legione v Hateley*' were sufficient for the purpose. Deane J pressed again the argument he had raised in *Waltons v Maher* for a unified doctrine of estoppel by conduct. In the circumstances he thought the purchasers would suffer real detriment if the vendors were allowed to insist on their strict rights. By accepting the notice given by the vendors, the purchasers had lost the benefit of a real chance that they would have tendered performance within the time fixed by the contract and thereby avoided any need to establish what might have happened but for the vendors' intimation. Other members of the court decided the matter on other grounds, Mason CJ dissenting from the majority said, at 411, that in view of the acceptance of promissory estoppel by the High Court, a representation or a mistaken assumption as to future conduct should, in appropriate circumstances, create a common law estoppel as well an equitable estoppel. However, he concluded that no such estoppel could operate on the facts before him because, in his view, the necessary element of reliance was missing. Brennan and Gaudron JJ did not consider it necessary to address the question of estoppel.

[4.28] Estoppel was again considered by the High Court in *Commonwealth of Australia v Verwayen* (1990) 170 CLR 394; 95 ALR 321:

> Verwayen was a member of the crew of *HMAS Voyager* when that ship was sunk in a collision with *HMAS Melbourne* off Jervis Bay on the night of 10 February 1964 during naval exercises. In 1984 he commenced proceedings against the Commonwealth seeking damages for injuries sustained in the collision which he alleged had been caused by the negligence of the officers and crew of one or both ships. At the time proceedings were commenced and for some considerable time thereafter, the Commonwealth stated that it would not plead any defence based on the Statute of Limitations, nor would it contest liability on the ground that the *Voyager* was engaged in a combat situation at the time of the collision, so that the only issues to be tried would whether the injuries sustained by the plaintiff had resulted from the sinking of the *Voyager* and the appropriate measure of damages. In November 1985 that policy was changed and in 1986 the Commonwealth sought and obtained leave to amend its defence to contest liability, on the basis that it did not owe a duty of care, and that the claim was statute barred. The respondent delivered a reply which asserted, among other things, that the Commonwealth was estopped from relying on either defence. The High Court held, by a majority, that the Commonwealth could not change its position and that it could not introduce either defence: Deane and Dawson JJ on the ground that the Commonwealth was estopped; Toohey and Gaudron JJ on the ground that the Commonwealth had waived its right to rely on either defence. Mason CJ, Brennan and McHugh JJ dissented.

Mason CJ, having discussed the various strands of estoppel, concluded, at 413:

[It] should be accepted that there is but one doctrine of estoppel, which provides that a court of common law or equity may do what is required, but not more, to prevent a person who has relied upon an assumption as to a present, past or future state of affairs (including a legal state of affairs), which assumption the party estopped has induced him to hold, from suffering detriment in reliance upon the assumption as a result of the denial of its correctness. A central element of that doctrine is that there must be a proportionality between the remedy and the detriment which is its purpose to avoid ... The assumption may be one as to a legal as well as to a factual state of affairs.

Brennan J, at 422, stated what he considered to be the law of estoppel in pais and of equitable estoppel. Estoppel in pais, in his view, precludes a party who, by representation, has induced another to adopt or accept the fact and thereby to act to the other party's detriment from asserting a right inconsistent with the fact on which the other party has acted. Equitable estoppel precludes a person who, by a promise, has induced another party to rely on the promise and thereby to act to his detriment from resiling from the promise without avoiding the detriment.

Deane J, at 444–6, set out the elements of a doctrine of estoppel by conduct, the central element of which was that the law would not permit an unconscionable departure by one party from an assumption adopted by the other party as the basis of some act or omission which would operate to that other party's detriment if the assumption be not adhered to. The first party must have played such a part in the adoption of, or persistence in, the assumption that he would be guilty of unjust and oppressive conduct if he were allowed to depart from it. The party seeking to rely on the assumption must have relied on it in the course of action or inaction, and that conduct must have involved some action to his or her detriment, or be such that he or she would suffer detriment if the first party were allowed to escape from the assumption. The assumption may be of fact or law, and may be either present or future.

Dawson J, at 454, was of the view that while estoppel at common law and equity may have had common origins, that was where the similarity stops. The vastly expanded role of estoppel in equity, and the discretionary nature of the relief it can offer, appear to draw a clear distinction between the two doctrines. In *Verwayen*, however, he thought it unnecessary to go beyond promissory estoppel, relying on *Legione v Hateley*. In this case the pre-existing legal relationship was that of parties to litigation. In that relationship the Commonwealth had a right to bar the action. By its conduct it caused the appellant to assume that it would not exercise that right, and, in the circumstances, departure by the appellant would be unconscionable and would operate to the detriment of the appellant.

McHugh J, at 499, acknowledged that common law and equity enjoyed a concurrent jurisdiction in estoppel by representation concerning a past or present fact. However, common law estoppel did not extend, in his view, to representations or assumptions concerning the future:

The equitable doctrines of estoppel create rights. They give rise to equities which are enforceable against the party estopped. The equitable doctrines result in new rights between the parties when it is unconscionable for a party to insist on his or her strict legal rights if that party has induced the other party to assume that a different legal relationship exists or will exist between them, if he or she knew that the other party would act or refrain from acting on that assumption and if, as a result, the other party will suffer detriment unless the assumption is maintained.

Gaudron J, at 487, while coming to her decision on other grounds, noted her agreement with Mason CJ that the substantive doctrine of estoppel permits a court to do what is necessary to avoid detriment, and that does not necessarily mean making good the assumption.

Toohey J based his decision on waiver and did not address the law of estoppel.

Verwayen is an odd case. It is seen as an endorsement of the principle of equitable estoppel, in the sense that it followed *Waltons v Maher* and, subject to the continuation of the debate about the possible unification of equitable and common law estoppel, there was no retreat from the bold step taken in the earlier case. The fact is, however, none of the judges sitting on *Verwayen* decided the case in favour of the appellant on the principles of equitable estoppel. Of the two who relied on estoppel, Deane J and Dawson J, the former sought to argue for the unified estoppel by conduct, rather than the purely equitable estoppel found in the majority judgments in *Waltons v Maher*, while Dawson J relied on promissory estoppel, and saw no need to go further for authority. At the end of the day the High Court refused to let the Commonwealth get away with a miserable and shabby decision.

[4.29] In *Lorimer v State Bank of NSW* (CA(NSW), 5 July 1991, unreported), Kirby P expressed a preference for what he described as 'the single substantive doctrine espoused by Deane J and more lately embraced by other members of the High Court'. This preference was based on a view that the doctrine is conceptually simpler and easier of practical application. In *Lorimer* a farmer sought to prevent the bank from enforcing its security on the ground, among other things, that it was estopped because of representations made, or assumptions fostered, that certain facilities would be made available to him when, in fact they were not. The Court of Appeal held that the case in estoppel was not made out.

[4.30] The principles of equitable estoppel were discussed and applied by the Full Court of the Federal Court in *S&E Promotions Pty Ltd v Tobin Bros Pty Ltd* (1994) 122 ALR 637. S&E was the holder of a Crown lease in the Australian Capital Territory. Tobin Bros held a sub-lease for five years which was due to expire on 30 June 1991. The lease included an option to renew for a further three year provided notice of intention to exercise the option was given by 31 March 1991. In 1988, S&E entered into discussions with Tobin Bros about a proposal to redevelop the property in conjunction with another party, McGrath who purchased a share of the Crown lease from S&E. In the course of these discussions it was agreed that Tobin Bros would be granted a new lease for a three year period, commencing on 1 July 1988. In return for that agreement Tobin Bros commenced paying a higher rent from 1 July 1988. The new sub-lease was to include eight three-year options to renew. Correspondence ensued between solicitors for the parties with proposed forms of lease with suggested amendments passing back and forth. In the course of this correspondence the date for exercise of the option under the original lease, which was also the date for exercise of the first of the options under the proposed new lease, 31 March 1991, passed without Tobin Bros giving notice of intention to exercise either option. The new sub-lease was executed on 10 May 1991, although it referred to a lease commencing on 1 July 1988. On 31 January 1992, Tobin Bros was served with a Notice of Termination relying on the expiry of the first three year term of the new sub-lease and Tobin Bros' failure to exercise the option to renew within the time required. At first instance, in the Supreme Court of the Australian Capital Territory, Gallop J held S&E and its partner to be estopped from asserting any right to terminate the lease. Applying equitable estoppel Gallop J set out the following criteria:

1. Tobin Bros believed it would have a lease from 1 July 1988 to 30 June 1994 with options thereafter;

2. S&E and McGrath induced Tobin Bros to adopt that assumption by acceptance of a higher rate of rent, by offering to sell McGrath's share of the land and by requesting amendments to the proposed sub-lease on 25 March 1991 without setting any time limit on acceptance of those amendments;

3. Tobin Bros acted in reliance on the assumption;

4. S&E promotions and McGrath knew or intended that Tobin Bros would act in that way;

5. Tobin Bros' inaction on the basis of the assumption would operate to its detriment if the assumption was not fulfilled;

6. S&E and McGrath had failed to act to avoid the detriment.

The Full Court, Neaves, Gummow and Higgins JJ, dismissed the appeal holding that in March 1991 S&E and McGrath as sub-lessors came under a duty to inform Tobin Brothers that the assumption that it was unnecessary to exercise any option under the proposed new sub-lease was wrong. The Full Court effectively endorsed Gallop J's analysis of the case making slight amendments to the final orders. In discussing the elements of equitable estoppel the Full Court noted the comment of Gaudron J in *Waltons* (at 164 CLR 462; 76 ALR 567), that in some cases it might not be necessary to show that the defendant had actual knowledge or a belief that the plaintiff had acted in reliance where the actions, or the imprudence of the defendant was a 'proximate cause of the other party's adopting and acting upon the faith of the assumption' then the justice of an estoppel would be made out. As far as reliance was concerned their Honours cited with approval the comment by Handley JA in *Austral Standard Cables Pty Ltd v Walker Nominees Pty Ltd* (1992) 26 NSWLR 524 at 540 that it would be sufficient for the representee to establish that reliance caused it to lose a real chance of avoiding the detriment.

[4.31] The utility of equitable estoppel is demonstrated by the judgment of Hodgson J in *W v G* (SC(NSW), 2 February 1995, unreported). The plaintiff and the defendant lived together in a lesbian relationship for eight years from 1986, although with some periods of separation. During the course of the relationship the plaintiff had two children, each having been conceived by artificial insemination with sperm provided by a male acquaintance. The defendant participated in the first insemination and agreed to and supported the plaintiff in the second. The defendant also, by her words and actions, conveyed to the plaintiff that she would act with the plaintiff as a parent of the children and would assist in and contribute to the raising of the children. After the breakdown of the relationship between the pair, the defendant denied any responsibility for the cost of bringing up the children. Hodgson J found that the elements of equitable estoppel were satisfied. The defendant had created or encouraged the adoption of an assumption by the plaintiff that a promise would be performed: that the defendant would act with the plaintiff as a parent to the children. The plaintiff acted in reliance on that promise in having the two children. The plaintiff thereby incurred detriment in that she was faced with the expensive and onerous task of raising two children. In the circumstances, his Honour thought it unconscionable of the defendant to refuse to make any contribution toward the cost of the children. He ordered the defendant to pay half the cost of raising the children by way of lump sum maintenance in a sum consistent with the approach taken by the Family Court in providing such relief.

4–7 Conclusions: the Current State of the Law

[4.32] While the processes of change unleashed in the law of estoppel seem likely to keep this debate alive, there are some points which can be identified as stating the law of estoppel in equity at the moment:

1. Common law estoppel in pais and equitable estoppel share the same rationale, as expressed by Dixon J in *Thompson*, at 547, the object of the estoppel being to prevent an unjust departure by one person from an assumption adopted by another as the basis of some act or omission which, unless the assumption is adhered to, would operate to that other's detriment. Whether a departure by a party from the assumption should be considered unjust and inadmissible depends on the part taken by the first party in occasioning its adoption by the other party.

2. Common law estoppel in pais requires proof of some representation, or an assumption fostered by the defendant, as to an existing fact. Equitable estoppel shares this jurisdiction with estoppel in pais; it can also arise from a representation as to an existing fact. Equitable estoppel can also arise from assumptions as to future conduct: see *Waltons v Maher,* at 398–9, 415 and 459.

3. Estoppel in pais remains essentially a rule of evidence, although it can be used as a 'sword' where the assumed facts provide the basis for a recognised cause of action. The aggrieved party can then sue on that cause of action. The estoppel will operate to preclude the defendant from denying the assumed facts in its defence. Equitable estoppel, on the other hand, is a source of substantive rights and may be pleaded as a cause of action in its own right.

4. The remedy available at common law for estoppel in pais is less flexible than that which equity can give in a case of equitable estoppel. The only remedy which the common law can give is to hold the party estopped to the assumed state of affairs: per Dawson J in *Verwayen,* at 454.

5. Equitable estoppel creates an equity in the party who can successfully assert it. The remedy granted will be that necessary to prevent detriment resulting from the unconscionable conduct of the other party: *Silovi Pty Ltd v Barbaro* (1988) 13 NSWLR 466 at 472, approved by McHugh J in *Verwayen,* at 501. The appropriate relief has also been described as 'the minimum equity to do justice to the plaintiff': *Crabb v Arun District Court* [1976] Ch 179 at 193–4; *Waltons v Maher,* at 404, per Mason CJ and Wilson J.

6. While both estoppels can be said to stem from the same base, as outlined in 1 above, the essential feature of the modern doctrine of equitable estoppel is its operation as a principle designed to prevent unconscionable conduct, or the unconscionable insistence on strict rights. Estoppel in pais also operates to prevent 'unjust' conduct, and perhaps that can be taken to be synonymous with 'unconscionable conduct'. But it may not be enough to simply establish that similarity. The equitable doctrine operates to prevent unconscionable conduct by fashioning appropriate remedies to achieve that object. The common law can only prevent a party from pleading that a certain state of affairs is not true. Unless developments in the concurrent jurisdiction of common law are to proceed on some revolutionary course, it is difficult to see how the common law could suddenly acquire the arsenal of remedies available to equity to impose

appropriate relief in cases of estoppel. Devices such as liens, charges, injunctions, not to mention the general power to impose conditions on its remedies, are simply not available at common law.

7. The elements of the cause of action available under the principle of equitable estoppel remain to some extent in a state of uncertainty. The principle stated by Mason CJ and Wilson J in *Waltons v Maher* appears to be slightly different to that proposed by Brennan J. The distinction between the two is more a matter of emphasis than substance. The Mason–Wilson view sees estoppel in equity as a doctrine principally intended to prevent unconscionable conduct. On the Brennan view, equitable estoppel arises mainly to prevent the detriment which would otherwise be suffered by the plaintiff if the assumption or expectation were not adhered to. The Brennan view has some support,[12] although In *S&E Promotions Pty Ltd v Tobin Bros Pty Ltd* (1994) 122 ALR 637 at 653, the Full Court of the Federal Court noted this view, effectively, as a useful checklist against which any claim could be measured. Detriment is relevant in the Mason–Wilson approach as an element to be considered in determining whether it is against conscience for the defendant to insist on his strict rights. McHugh J appears to support the notion that unconscionability must be the touchstone. While Mason CJ has been converted to the cause of unification of equitable and common law estoppel, it does not appear that, in doing so, he changed his view on the central role of unconscionability in the law of estoppel. In *Verwayen*, at 413, in giving his reasons for doing away with the distinction between estoppel at law and in equity, he says, 'It would be wholly inequitable and unjust to insist upon a disproportionate making good of the relevant assumption'. If anything, it appears that Mason CJ supports unification because he considers that it would produce uniform results consistent with conscience.

8. On the current state of the authorities, the elements of equitable estoppel appear to be:

   (a) One party must adopt an assumption that a certain state of affairs exists or will come into existence; that state of affairs can be legal or factual, present or future. It is submitted that this assumption must be reasonably clear or certain. In *Legione v Hateley* (1983) 152 CLR 406 at 435–6, Mason and Deane JJ stated that it has long been recognised that a representation must be clear before it can found an estoppel in pais,[13] and that the same principle must apply to promissory estoppel. That principle must extend to equitable estoppel. However, that does not mean that all the terms of any proposed transaction must be set in concrete. In *Austotel Pty Ltd v Franklin's Self Serve Stores Pty Ltd* (1989) 16 NSWLR 582 at 604, Priestley JA noted the distinction between cases like *Waltons v Maher* where all the terms of the proposed contract had been agreed and cases like *Plimmer v City of Wellington* (1884) LR 9 AppCas 699 where, as he put it:

   > ... a plaintiff, despite being unable to point to some agreement which, although unenforceable, contains precise terms describing what he expected from the defendant, has nevertheless been held to be entitled to equitable relief which may be of a proprietary kind.[14]

   (b) That party acts or refrains from acting on the faith of that assumption in

12. MG&L, para [1710].
13. Citing *Low Bouverie* [1891] 3 Ch 82 at 106, 113; *Newbon v City Mutual Life Assurance Society Ltd* (1935) 52 CLR 723 at 738; *Woodhouse AC Israel Cocoa Ltd SA v Nigerian Produce Marketing Co Ltd* [1972] AC at 755–6, 768, 771.

such a way that he or she would suffer detriment if the assumption was denied.

(c) A second party, who possesses some legal rights which might act as a bar to the fulfilment of the assumption, has played a role in the adoption by the first of the relevant assumption, either actively, by encouraging the first party in adopting that belief, or passively, by acquiescing with knowledge in the first party's actions on the faith of the assumption.

(d) It is not essential that the second party be aware of its legal rights which run contrary to the assumption held by the first: *Linter Group v Goldberg* (1992) 7 ACSR 580 at 613.

(e) In all the circumstances it would be unconscionable for the second party to insist on his or her strict legal rights and deny the assumption.

(f) If all those elements are satisfied an equity arises in favour of the first party which can be satisfied by the imposition of relief affording the minimum equity required to do justice to the first party in the circumstances, which may not mean giving effect to the assumption in its entirety.

[4.33] On present numbers, unification of common law and equitable estoppel does not appear certain to succeed. On the recent High Court bench, Mason CJ, Deane and Gaudron JJ favoured unification, while Brennan, Dawson and McHugh JJ were against it. Toohey J has not expressed a view, although it could be said that he declined to take the opportunity provided by *Verwayen*. The departure of Mason CJ and Deane J to retirement and Vice-Regal office respectively appears to shift the balance in favour of the retention of equitable estoppel as a separate doctrine although the addition of Kirby J seems to restore one vote for unification. As there is a concurrent jurisdiction between equitable estoppel and estoppel in pais in the field of representations of fact, there seems little need for unification. If unification is what is really meant. In view of Mason CJ's comments in *Verwayen* quoted above, unification may really mean abolition of common law estoppel, at least in the area of estoppel by conduct, his Honour's view really only leaving room for the operation of equitable estoppel. If Deane J means what he says about estoppel by conduct, as he describes it, not being available as a cause of action, it may be that his theory of unification only brings common law estoppel and promissory estoppel together. Proprietary estoppel would remain free to act as a 'sword' as it always has done. The alternative would be quite perverse. While some may see Deane J's proposal as a desirable reform and advocate the cause of unification, it may be better to pause and consider the need, if any, for such a change, and the benefits, if any, which might then flow. If the rule in *Jorden v Money* were overturned, and common law estoppel freed from the shackles of representations of existing facts, much of what is sought to be achieved by unification would be satisfied. Equitable estoppel could continue to operate on the 'equities' of any given case without any need to cart the cumbersome and curious baggage of common law estoppel along with it. It is also difficult to see how the toothpaste of estoppel as a cause of action might be put back into the tube. The labelling and categorisation of estoppel is not so precise that a judge at first instance could dismiss a claim pleaded on estoppel simply because, if it were to happen, a majority of the High Court adopted Deane J's formulation of estoppel by conduct. *Waltons v Maher* could be taken to have expanded the law of proprietary estoppel as much as promissory estoppel, and the sword would still be available.

---

14. While Priestley JA was in the minority in *Austotel v Franklins*, the majority, Kirby P and Rogers A-JA did not disagree with Priestley JA's statement of principle. This view was followed by Wilcox J in *Lyndel Nominees Pty Ltd v Mobil Oil Australia Limited* (FCA, 22 May 1996, unreported).

Chapter Five

5-1 Fiduciary Duties

[5.1] Fiduciary duties are the obligations of trust and confidence which equity imposes on a person in circumstances where that person, the fiduciary, is bound to act for the benefit of another, the principal. In such a case the fiduciary cannot allow any personal interest to conflict with his or her duty to the principal. This is inevitably circular. A fiduciary must not allow personal interest to conflict with duty. A person under an obligation to place duty to another ahead of personal interest is a fiduciary. Fiduciary obligations can be mutual as in the case of a partnership. Both the relationship and the duty owed are described as fiduciary. While the term 'fiduciary' carries a general connotation of the nature of the duty owed, equity imports fiduciary duties into a wide variety of relationships, and the duties arising from those relationships are not always identical. In that sense, while it may be helpful to identify a relationship as one giving rise to obligations of a fiduciary nature, that alone is not enough. The precise scope of the obligations must also be defined. It is also important to distinguish, in any given relationship, between obligations arising from the relationship which are fiduciary in character and others which are not. In broad terms a fiduciary relationship has been said to arise where:

> ... one party reposes confidence in another who is expected to act in the interests of the first party rather than in his own interests.[1]

A fiduciary has also been said to be:

> ... simply, someone who undertakes to act for or on behalf of another in some particular matter or matters. That undertaking may be of a general character. It may be specific and limited.[2]

A common theme in fiduciary relationships is the representative role of the fiduciary. As Mason J put it in *Hospital Products Ltd v United States Surgical Corp* (1984) 156 CLR 41 at 97:

> The critical feature of these relationships is that the fiduciary undertakes or agrees to act for or on behalf of or in the interests of another person in the exercise of a power or discretion which will affect the interests of that other in a legal or practical sense. The relationship between the parties is therefore one which gives the fiduciary a special opportunity to exercise the power or discretion to the detriment of that other person who is accordingly vulnerable to abuse by the fiduciary of his position. The essence of the fiduciary relationship can thus be seen in the power the fiduciary holds

---

1. HG&A, para [1101], p 181.
2. PD Finn, *Fiduciary Obligations*, Law Book Company, Sydney, 1977, p 201.

to influence the affairs of the principal for good or ill and the trust which the principal places in the fiduciary to use that power for the principal's benefit.

It is not necessary that parties to a fiduciary relationship also have some other concluded legal relationship. A fiduciary relationship can arise and fiduciary duties can exist between parties who have not reached and who may never reach agreement upon the consensual terms which are to govern the arrangement between them: *United Dominions Corp Ltd v Brian Pty Ltd* (1985) 157 CLR 1 at 11–12.

[5.2] The nature and extent of the duty undertaken by the fiduciary will be a question of fact in each case: *Hospital Products Ltd v United States Surgical Corp* (1984) 156 CLR 41 at 69, per Gibbs CJ. But one element will always be found in any relationship properly described as fiduciary: equity will not allow a person owing fiduciary duties to enter into any engagement in which the fiduciary has, or could have, a personal interest conflicting with that of the principal: *Aberdeen Railway Co v Blaikie Bros* (1854) 1 Macq 461 at 471; [1843–60] All ER Rep 249 at 252, per Lord Cranworth LC; nor will it allow the fiduciary to retain any benefit or gain obtained or received by reason of his fiduciary position or through some opportunity or knowledge resulting from it: *Chan v Zacharia* (1984) 154 CLR 178 at 198–9, per Deane J. Such a relationship can vary from that between:

> ... myself [and] an errand boy who is bound to bring me back my change up to the most intimate and confidential relations which can possibly exist between one party and another where the one is wholly in the hands of the other because of his infinite trust in him: *Re Coomber; Coomber v Coomber* [1911] 1 Ch 723 at 728–9, per Fletcher-Moulton LJ.

Fiduciary relationships cannot be readily simplified. As La Forest J put it in *Lac Minerals Ltd v International Corona Resources Ltd* (1989) 61 DLR (4th) 14 at 26:

> There are few legal concepts more frequently invoked but less conceptually certain than that of the fiduciary relationship. In specific circumstances and in special relation-ships, courts have no difficulty in imposing fiduciary obligations, but at a more funda-mental level, the principles on which that obligation is based is [sic] unclear.

One should thus be wary of verbal formulae and concentrate on the precise terms, actual or implied, of the relationship in question and the obligations which necessarily flow from them. Fletcher-Moulton LJ's errand boy, for example, is only required to bring back the object of the errand and any change. If, say, he was sent to buy a cup of coffee, there would be no breach if, at the same time, he bought coffee for others or for himself, provided he did not use his principal's money. On the other hand, a solicitor advising one group interested in taking over a company could not advise any other party interested in acquiring an interest in the target company, nor could the solicitor buy shares in that company for him or herself, not at least without the informed consent of the client.

5–2 The Fiduciary Relationship

[5.3] Much ink has been spilt, and much wasted, in attempting to state clearly a single principled basis for the recognition of a fiduciary relationship in any given set of facts. The courts have not been precise in stating the circumstances in which one per-son will be found to owe fiduciary duties to another and have preferred to deal with the matter on a case-by-case basis: *Hospital Products Ltd v United States Surgical Corp*

(1984) 156 CLR 41, per Gibbs CJ, at 69; Mason J, at 96. The debate is usually between the 'entrustment' theory, which has it that a fiduciary relationship will arise whenever one party reposes particular trust and confidence in another, viewing the matter from the perspective of the supposed principal in the relationship, and the 'undertaking' theory, which concentrates on the undertaking given by the supposed fiduciary to act on behalf of the supposed principal. Yet neither theory provides an adequate answer and examples can be found which contradict both: one places trust in one's doctor, and, perhaps, in the police, or the government, but that does not mean that the relationship can be characterised as fiduciary. The fact that one person undertakes to act on behalf of another will not be decisive unless the circumstances are such that the 'representative' is bound to place the interests of the principal first and is not free to have regard to its own interests, as was the case in *Hospital Products Ltd v United States Surgical Corp* (1984) 156 CLR 41 where the High Court ultimately found that the relationship in that case, one of manufacturer and distributor, gave *Hospital Products* scope to look after its own interests, if need be in advance of those of USSC. The search for a single formula may be more than fruitless, it could be detrimental. In raising a spectre suggesting that any relationship can be examined to see whether it can fit some imaginary mould marked 'fiduciary' we create a tantalising prospect which some judges may find irresistible. In *Catt v Marac Australia Ltd* (1987) 9 NSWLR 639, Rogers J found that lenders owed fiduciary duties to their borrowers. In *Reading v A-G* [1949] 2 KB 232 (CA); [1951] AC 507 (HL), the English Court of Appeal and the House of Lords held that a sergeant in the British Army in Egypt during World War II owed fiduciary duties to the Crown for the manner in which he carried out his duties while in uniform.[3]

If any relationship can be labelled fiduciary the word will lose its meaning, and our legal system will be the poorer for it. Perhaps the better view, or at least the common sense view, must be that there are certain relationships which the law regards as fiduciary. Beyond those recognised categories fiduciary duties may be found in relationships not normally considered to be fiduciary if the circumstances warrant such a finding. The *Hospital Products* case provides a good example of this. Both at first instance, [1982] 2 NSWLR 766, and in the Court of Appeal, [1983] 2 NSWLR 157, it was found that the contract between Hospital Products and USSC contained an implied term that the distributor would not do any act inimical to the market for USSC products in Australia and that, on that basis, Hospital Products was a fiduciary to USSC in respect of the market for USSC products in Australia. In the High Court, the majority rejected the implied term and the finding of a fiduciary relationship fell away with it. Recognition of a relationship as fiduciary, whether because it falls within one of the recognised categories, or outside that list because of the special circumstances of the relationship, is only part of the process. It will be necessary to identify the scope of the relationship in order to determine whether the matter in issue between the parties falls within the fiduciary's duties or not.

---

3. One can only assume their Lordships had not read advance copies of Spike Milligan's memoirs. One night in 1940, while on sentry duty at Eastbourne, Spike (aka Gunner Milligan) reported a German invasion, just to relieve the boredom. He has never been asked to account for the seventeen shillings and sixpence it cost to mobilise the British army to meet the reported threat.

The element of vulnerability

[5.4] The list of relationships in which fiduciary duties are normally implied is similar to that of the relationships in which the presumption of undue influence will arise, but the two doctrines are quite different. Some relationships, such as that between parent and child, give rise to the presumption of undue influence but not to any fiduciary duty. Similarly, while an agent will usually owe fiduciary duties to a principal in respect of the matters in which he or she is engaged as agent, any transfer from principal to agent will not necessarily give rise to a presumption that it was a product of undue influence unless it could be shown that some special trust had been placed in the agent in the circumstances: *McKenzie v McDonald* [1927] VLR 134. It has been said that the essential feature of a fiduciary relationship is the vulnerability of the principal in the hands of the fiduciary. This was the view taken by the majority, although a bare majority, of the Supreme Court of Canada in *Lac Minerals Ltd v International Corona Resources Ltd* (1989) 6I DLR (4th) 14. The proposition that 'vulnerability' can act as a litmus test for the identification of fiduciary obligations is attractive for its simplicity as much as for any other reason. But the essential question must always be whether the alleged fiduciary is obliged to place the interests of the principal first and to avoid any situation of conflict between personal interest and duty. That begs another question: why is the 'fiduciary' obliged to place the interests of the 'principal' ahead of the fiduciary's own interests? A bailee having possession and control over the bailor's goods will be in a position to harm the bailor so that it might be said that the bailor was in a position of vulnerability vis-à-vis the bailee. A patient will be 'vulnerable' to his or her doctor, but that does not make the relationship fiduciary. This illustrates the difficulty with the vulnerability analysis. At first instance, in *United States Surgical Corporation v Hospital Products Ltd* [1982] 2 NSWLR 766, McLelland J suggested that the reason for the principle concerning conflict between duty and interest lay in 'the special degree of vulnerability of those whose interests are entrusted to another'. The Court of Appeal took a different view, [1983] 2 NSWLR 157, saying:

> But we doubt that this can be so. There are many examples of legal relationships not regarded as fiduciary in which such a power may be found ... It seems to us that it is always necessary first to find [the fiduciary's] undertaking to act for or on behalf of [the principal].

This must be correct. Any party to a contract may detrimentally affect the interests of the other party by breaking the contract, but that does not convert the common law duty to comply with the terms of the contract into a fiduciary obligation. Merely undertaking to act for another will not give rise to a duty where the agent, expressly or by implication, reserves the right to pursue his or her own interests in the same matter or matters. The same proposition can apply where parties to a joint venture expressly or by implication reserve the right to act in their own interests in some matters connected with the venture: *Noranda Australia Ltd v Lachlan Resources NL* (1988) 14 NSWLR 1.

The scope of the fiduciary relationship

[5.5] The existence of a relationship which fits into one of the recognised categories, or indeed of a special relationship identifiable as one giving rise to obligations of trust and confidence, will not automatically establish that for all things and for all purposes the alleged fiduciary is bound to place the interests of the principal first. It is essential to determine the scope of any fiduciary duties within the general framework of the relationship.

In *NZ Netherlands Society 'Oranje' v Kuys* [1973] 2 All ER 1222 in 1966, the respondent, who had been a member of a society for Dutch people in New Zealand, purchased a Dutch newspaper, which he called 'The Windmill Post'. In January 1967 a new Dutch society (NZNS) was incorporated. It was agreed to produce a newspaper called 'The Windmill Post' which would be Kuys' property, while NZNS had the right to publish the society's news in it. The society guaranteed to purchase copies of issues of the newspaper, at 1s per copy, for each of the society's 2000 members for six months. Kuys was also the unpaid secretary of NZNS and a member of the committee. In June the parties fell out and the society made plans to publish a rival newspaper under the same name. Kuys obtained an injunction restraining them from using the name. NZNS claimed that Kuys had acquired the newspaper and his attendant rights by virtue of his relationship with the society and thus could not retain ownership of the newspaper without accountability to the society. The Privy Council said that a person may be in a fiduciary position quoad, that is, to the extent of, one part of his activities and not quoad another part, and that, while Kuys' position as an officer of the society cast duties upon him not to profit from his position of trust, no part of his activities relating to the operation of the Windmill Post placed him in a fiduciary position in relation to the society . That finding was based on the fact that the society's only commitment to the paper was to purchase 2000 copies at 1s each for six months while Kuys had to cover all outgoings and expenses from his own pocket and could not ask the society to cover any losses.

5-3   The Recognised Categories

Solicitor and client

[5.6] This is a relationship in which fiduciary duties will be implied but, as with all other such relationships, it is important to state clearly the scope of the solicitor's duty before forming any view on whether it has been breached. The mere fact that the parties are solicitor and client in respect of, for instance, the conveyance of the client's house, does not mean that they will still be regarded as solicitor and client in some other transaction. The relationship of solicitor and client imposes fiduciary duties on the solicitor in dealings with or for the client, but that should not extend to third parties.

In *Boardman v Phipps* [1967] 2 AC 46, the respondent, one of the residuary beneficiaries of the estate of the late CW Phipps, took proceedings against Boardman and Tom Phipps, another beneficiary, seeking orders that they held a parcel of about 22,000 shares in Lester & Harris Limited (L&H) as constructive trustees for the estate and that they were liable to account for profits made from those shares. Boardman had acted as solicitor to the trustees of the estate which held 8,000 of the 30,000 issued shares in L&H. On behalf of the trust, Boardman and Tom Phipps attended the Annual General Meeting of L&H to attempt to have Tom elected to the board. That attempt failed but Boardman formed the view that the shares in L&H were considerably undervalued and could be enhanced if the company were reorganised. Boardman and Tom Phipps then decided to acquire the outstanding shares in the company. Two of the three trustees, an accountant, and the testator's daughter, were informed of that proposal and approved. The third trustee, the testator's widow, was senile and was not consulted. It was not open to the trust to invest further in L&H as such shares were not an authorised investment. Court approval could have been sought but would not necessarily have been given while the investment was at all speculative. The initial take-over offer was only partially successful. Boardman then put proposals to the directors for a division of the assets of the company. In doing so he claimed to be representing the trust and, in the process, learnt considerably more about the financial position of L&H. Those negotiations failed but Boardman and Tom Phipps decided to make another takeover offer for the balance of the shares. Before this further offer was put, Boardman wrote to the beneficiaries telling them what he was doing and asking for their consent, which was given. The takeover offer was made and succeeded. Once a controlling interest had been acquired, assets of the company were liquidated and cap-ital dividends of £5 17s 6d were paid out on each share after which the shares were still worth £2. The House of Lords, per Lords Hodson, Guest and Cohen, held that Boardman and Tom Phipps had placed themselves in a special position, which was fiduciary in character, in negotiating with the directors of L&H and out of that special position they had obtained an opportunity make a profit and knowledge that there was a profit to be made. That profit was made and they were liable accordingly. While the two had acted honestly, and thus were allowed expenses on what was described as a liberal scale, they were both fiduciaries; Boardman because of his position as solicitor to the trust and his action in that capacity on behalf of the trust in negotiations with the company, and Phipps as agent for the trust and because he did not seek to be treated in a different way from Boardman. Boardman's breach of duty arose from the possibility of a conflict of interest as he could have been asked to advise on whether the trust should seek leave of the court to acquire further shares. Because the two had received the opportunity to profit while acting in a fiduciary capacity they could only escape liability for their actions through the informed consent of their principals. Approval by two out of three trustees was ineffective. The letter sent by Boardman to the beneficiaries was held to contain insufficient detail to constitute adequate disclo-sure. It was immaterial that neither the trust nor the beneficiaries could have taken advantage of the information about L&H. Lord Hodson, at 107; and Lord Guest, at 115, expressed the view that confidential information could be the property of a trust. Viscount Dilhorne, in dissent, agreed that the appellants' relationship with the trust was fiduciary but took the view that because the information they acquired was not property of the trust and because the trust did not contemplate purchasing further shares at any stage, no conflict between duty and interest arose when the appellants acquired shares in their own names. Lord Upjohn, also in dissent, took the view that Boardman and Tom Phipps were not under any fiduciary obligation to the trust in their actions with respect to L&H. Their agency was limited to seeking the election of Tom Phipps to the board of L&H. When that attempt failed, the agency was termi-nated. He also strongly rejected the proposition that information could be property: at 127–8.

[5.7] *Boardman v Phipps* is a very useful decision; it is extreme in some respects; and it is also a very troublesome decision. It is useful because it is complex and raises just about every issue relevant to any discussion of fiduciary duties; it is extreme, in that it charts the boundaries of many of the questions it raises. The case is clearly correct as a statement of principle, as recently endorsed by the High Court in *Warman Interna-tional Ltd v Dwyer* (1995) 128 ALR 201 at 209. But it is the manner in which those principles were applied which smack of injustice. The judgments of the majority are found wanting when examined for any precise analysis of the source or the scope of the fiduciary obligation which their Lordships so readily and heavily cast upon Boardman and Tom Phipps. The only judgment which attempted any careful consid-eration of the scope of Boardman's obligation was that of Lord Upjohn. The source of Boardman's duty, in the eyes of the majority, lay in his position as a solicitor, even though it was conceded that there was no such position as 'solicitor to the trust', and despite the fact that most of Boardman's activities clearly fell outside the scope of the work normally done by a solicitor for a client. The suggestion that Boardman had 'trust property', in the form of confidential information in his possession lacks any merit as information cannot be property in any strict sense. Boardman did hold himself out as a representative of the trust in conducting his investigations into the company, but that alone would not make him a fiduciary, nor would it prove that there was any conflict between his interests and those of the trust. It could be said that Boardman's interests were more in concert with those of the trust than in conflict. The takeover offer was made by Boardman and Tom Phipps as principals, not agents, and it is difficult to see any conflict between their duty and their interest in doing so. The possibility that Boardman might be instructed to advise the trust on a possible acquisition has been described as 'remote',[4] and, of course, he could have declined to act. Tom Phipps did not seek to separate his case from that of Boardman. Had he done so, their Lordships might have had to think the matter through more carefully. Tom Phipps does not fit into any recognised fiduciary category. He could be said to have been acting as agent for the trust, or more correctly the trustees. But that agency only extended as far as the attempt to have him elected to the Board of L&H. Those criticisms really go to the application of the principles to the facts of the case, not to the principles themselves, which have been accepted as the law in Australia: *Queensland Mines Ltd v Hudson* (1978) 52 ALJR 399 and *Consul Development Pty Ltd v DPC Estates Pty Ltd* (1975) 132 CLR 373.[5] Where a party acquires a property in some representative capacity, or otherwise in circumstances where the party acquiring the property cannot, in conscience, deny an interest claimed in it by another, equity will, properly, deem the property to be been acquired for the plaintiff or true purchaser.

> In *Walker v Webb* (1845) Res & Eq Jud NSW SC, the defendant assigned a crown lease to the plaintiff. The lease carried with it a right to apply for a grant of freehold from the Crown. Fraudulently representing himself to still be the person entitled to apply, the defendant applied for and obtained a grant of freehold on the land. The court declared that he held the land in trust for the plaintiff. While the defendant did not in fact hold himself out as applying for the grant on behalf of the plaintiff, that was the only basis upon which he could properly obtain a grant. Accordingly, as against the plaintiff, he could not deny that he had obtained the grant on the plaintiff's behalf.

Director and company

[5.8] This is one of the most easily recognisable fiduciary relationships but, again, a director does not owe a duty to the company in everything he or she does. The nature of this duty was stated in the High Court by Dixon J in *Mills v Mills* (1938) 60 CLR 150 at 188:

> Directors of a company are fiduciary agents, and a power conferred upon them cannot be exercised in order to obtain some private advantage or for any purpose foreign to the power. It is only one aspect of the general doctrine expressed by Lord Northington in *Aleyn v Belchier* (1758) 1 Eden 132 at 138; 28 ER 634 at 637: 'No point is better established than that, a person having a power, must execute it bona fide for the end designed, otherwise it is corrupt and void'.

A director will not necessarily be involved with the management of the company's business. When a director is involved in management, it should be possible to identify matters which fall within the scope of his or her duties and matters which do not: *Bell v Lever Brothers* [1932] AC 161; *P&O Steam Navigation Co v Johnson* (1938) 60 CLR

---

4. MG&L, para [513].
5. Except, of course, for the erroneous notion that confidential information can be trust property.

189. It is also possible to be a director or agent of more than one company and a sensible approach must be taken to resolving any competition between a person's various duties: see *BLB Corporation of Australia v Jacobsen* (1974) 48 ALJR 372. The fiduciary obligations imposed on directors extend to promoters of companies: *Tracy v Mandalay Pty Ltd* (1952) 88 CLR 215. Directors do not owe a fiduciary duty to individual shareholders: *Percival v Wright* [1902] 2 Ch 421 at 425–6. However, once a director is found to have breached his or her duty, the courts will show little mercy.

> In *Regal (Hastings) Ltd v Gulliver* [1967] 2 AC 134, the directors of Regal (Hastings) Ltd (Regal) in 1935, formed a subsidiary, Hastings Amalgamated Cinemas Ltd (HAC), with the intention of using HAC as the vehicle to acquire two cinemas. The issued capital of HAC was £5,000 representing the 2000 shares at £1 each issued to Regal and 3000 shares which were purchased by the five directors and their solicitor, each effectively taking up 500 shares at £1 each, so that HAC would have enough to purchase the cinemas. HAC acquired the cinemas and two weeks later the company was sold producing a profit of £21 6s 6d per share. Regal, under its new management, took proceedings against the ex-directors seeking an account of the profits they had made on the sale of their shares in HAC. The House of Lords held that the ex-directors were liable to Regal for these profits on the ground that they had obtained their shares by reason of their position as directors of Regal and in the course of their office as directors. At the time of the decision by the directors to take up shares in HAC, Regal had received an offer of £92,500 for its original cinema and the two new cinemas. Viscount Sankey, at 381, stated the rule in these terms: 'No one who has duties of a fiduciary nature to perform is allowed to enter into engagements in which he has or can have a personal interest conflicting with the interests of those whom he is bound to protect. If he holds any property so acquired as trustee he is bound to account to his *cestui que trust*'. Lord Russell set out his version of the rule, at 144, having considered the judgment of Lord Greene MR in the Court of Appeal in which the learned Master of the Rolls had said that once it was found that the directors had acted bona fide the case had failed: '... with all respect I think there is a misapprehension here. The rule of equity which insists on those, who by use of a fiduciary position make a profit, being liable to account for that profit, in no way depends on fraud, or absence of bona fides; or upon such questions or considerations as to whether the profit would or should otherwise have gone to the plaintiff, or whether the profiteer was under a duty to obtain the source of the profit for the plaintiff, or whether he took a risk or acted as he did for the benefit of the plaintiff, or whether the plaintiff has in fact been damaged or benefited by his action. The liability arises from the mere fact of a profit having, in the stated circumstances, been made. The profiteer, however honest and well intended, cannot escape the risk of being called upon to account'.

[5.9] While it is correct to say that a director cannot appropriate to him or herself an opportunity for benefit or profit which arises by virtue of his or her position as a director, the decision in *Regal (Hastings)*, like that in *Boardman v Phipps*, is a bit harsh. Had the supposedly delinquent directors remained in control of Regal, the question would never have arisen. HAC could have been sold, or simply operated the cinemas at a profit, and Regal and the directors would have pocketed their respective shares of the profit without being called upon to account. That does not mean they would not have been in breach of their duties as directors, it is not simply a matter of not getting caught. But, had Regal acquired the cinemas in its own name, with money provided by the directors in the form of subscriptions for shares in Regal, their conduct would be hard to question. Regal would have acquired all the benefits of the transaction while the directors would have benefitted indirectly through the enhancement of the value of their shares in Regal and from dividends. It is also unlikely that the directors would have been held liable had they had loaned the money to HAC and received a commercial rate of interest in return. The profit to be made from the sale of Regal's business was known at the time the directors decided to put their money into HAC. Had the investment been more speculative, the position could have been different. Had HAC been sold at a loss, for instance, the directors would not have had a corresponding claim against Regal for an indemnity for their losses. Where directors lay out their own money as risk capital in a venture in which, otherwise, the company might be exposed to undue risk, but where both could make a good profit if the venture succeeds the question of 'opportunity for profit' and conflict of interest is less clear. The decision in *Regal (Hastings) Ltd v Gulliver* has recently been referred to with approval in a joint judgment of the High Court in *Warman International Ltd v Dwyer* (1995) 128 ALR 201 at 209.

[5.10] The strict approach taken by the House of Lords in *Regal (Hastings)* was not followed by the Supreme Court of Canada in *Peso Silver Mines Ltd (NPL) v Cropper* (1966) 58 DLR (2d) 1. There a director of a mining company was held not to have breached his fiduciary duty by taking up some mineral claims which were offered to him after the company had rejected them, after a bona fide consideration of the matter by the Board of Directors. Those facts were almost identical to a hypothetical situation put up by Lord Greene MR in the Court of Appeal in *Regal (Hastings)*, and in respect of which the learned Master of the Rolls said there was 'no particle of authority cited' for the proposition that the company should be entitled to claim any profit on the investment.[6] Cartwright J, for the court, expressed approval of the point made by Lord Greene MR. The decision in *Peso Silver Mines Ltd (NPL) v Cropper* was followed in *Canadian Aero Services Ltd v O'Malley* (1973) 40 DLR (3rd) 371. In that case Laskin J said, at 390, in his opinion it was a mistake to seek to encase the principle stated and applied in *Peso Silver Mines* as adopted from *Regal (Hastings)*, in a straightjacket of special knowledge acquired while acting as directors or senior officers. Rather, as he put it, at 391:

> The general standards of loyalty, good faith and avoidance of a conflict of duty and self-interest to which the conduct of a director or senior officer must conform, must be tested in each case by many factors which it would be reckless to attempt to enumerate exhaustively. Among them are the factor of position or office held, the nature of the corporate opportunity, its ripeness, its specificness and the director's or manager's relation to it, the amount of knowledge possessed, the circumstances in which it was obtained and whether it was special or, indeed, even private and factors of time relating to whether the director's duty had been terminated by retirement, resignation or discharge.

The fiduciary obligations of a director do not fall away simply because a person has ceased to hold office as a director, nor does it matter that the opportunity was not available to the company: *Industrial Development Consultants Ltd v Cooley* [1972] 1 WLR 443. The narrowness of the test in *Regal (Hastings)* has been criticised elsewhere with the suggestion that the better test would be the 'line of business' test proposed by Professor Austin: that a director may not take up an opportunity for profit if it is within the scope of the business which the company carries on or plans to carry on.[7] There is some merit in that proposition but the directors of Regal (Hastings) would have been caught by it. The trouble with expounding a general test to cover these

---

6. The Court of Appeal decision in *Regal (Hastings)* is unreported but this passage appears in 58 DLR (2d) at 9. The same hypothetical was not discussed in the House of Lords except by Lord Russell who, at 391, said that it bore little resemblance to the facts of the case in *Regal*.
7. MG&L, para [520]; RP Austin, 'Fiduciary Accountability for Business Opportunities' in PD Finn (ed), *Equity and Commercial Relationships*, Law Book Company, Sydney, 1987.

cases is that the terms used inevitably require value judgments when applied to a given set of facts. It is not enough to show that a director has made a profit through some opportunity which he or she came across through a position as a director. It must be an opportunity which, in the ordinary course of events, the director ought to put to the company or cause the company to take up, in other words an opportunity within the company's 'line of business'. If the opportunity is a new 'line of business' but one the company could pursue just as easily as the director, and the prospects of success are good, then the director should offer it to the company first. If the director conceals it from the company so that he or she can get to it first, the 'line of business' defence would seem a bit lame. The manner in which the opportunity is pursued must also be taken into account. If the director puts his or her own funds at risk in a speculative venture, and the venture succeeds, it would be a bit rough to say that the director had breached his or her duty. Had he or she put the shareholders' funds at risk and lost the director could be condemned on other grounds. In *Queensland Mines Ltd v Hudson* (1978) 18 ALR 1, the Privy Council held a director not to be in breach of duty where he took up an opportunity which had previously put to the company and rejected by it and where the company had assented to him taking up the venture.

[5.11] While *Queensland Mines v Hudson* and *Peso Silver Mines Ltd (NPL) v Cropper* provide some comfort to the honest company director, it remains the law that good faith alone is not a sufficient defence. While that is in accord with the finest traditions of equity, and only appropriate in view of the strictness of equity's policy on fiduciary duties generally, it also casts strict duties on the court. If a court is to hold an honest director, or any other honest fiduciary for that matter, liable for breach of duty, particularly on the ground that the fiduciary has appropriated an opportunity which in conscience was that of his or her principal, the court must analyse the facts closely, taking into account the matters posed by Laskin J in *Canadian Aero Services Ltd v O'Malley* and must satisfy itself that the matters complained of fall within the scope of the fiduciary's duty and that the conduct of the fiduciary constituted a breach of duty. No one should have their life and fortune ruined by the sloppy reasoning so prevalent in the majority decisions in *Boardman v Phipps*, nor by the the attitudes of commercial puritanism which pervade the judgments in *Regal (Hastings)*.

Trustee and beneficiary

[5.12] This is the classic source of fiduciary obligation. But even in this relationship the fiduciary obligations cast on the trustee will be limited to matters pertinent to the trust. Within that field, however, the duty of the trustee is very strict and, at least in some circumstances, such as the renewal of a lease previously held on trust in the name of the trustee, stricter than that of other fiduciaries: *Chan v Zacharia* (1984) 154 CLR 178 at 201, per Deane J.

Partners

[5.13] Partners owe fiduciary obligations to one another in relation to the conduct of the business of the partnership and in respect of the assets of the partnership, although the exact subject matter of their mutual obligations will be determined by the venture or undertaking for which the partnership exists, as shown by any written agreement and the course of dealing actually pursued by the firm: *Birtchnell v Equity Trustees, Executors and Agency Co Ltd* (1929) 42 CLR 384 at 407–8, per Dixon J. Those obligations endure beyond any formal dissolution of the partnership to cover any matters involved in its winding up: *Chan v Zacharia* (1984) 154 CLR 178, although, where the partnership is dissolved by the death of one of the partners the continuing partners do not become trustees for the estate of that former partner of such part of the profits of the business as are attributable to the use of the deceased's share of the original partnership assets. The relationship between the continuing partners and the estate of their former partner is more in the nature of that between debtor and creditor: *Cameron v Murdoch* (1986) 63 ALR 575. The fiduciary obligations which do exist between partners apply, by analogy, to relations between prospective joint venturers: *United Dominions Corp Ltd v Brian Pty Ltd* (1985) 157 CLR 1; *Lac Minerals Ltd v International Corona Resources Ltd, supra; Ravinder Rohini Pty Ltd v Krizaic* (1991) 105 ALR 593; and to other relationships as well, including, in some circumstances, a de facto husband and wife: *Muschinski v Dodds* (1985) 160 CLR 583 at 614–15, per Deane J.

> In *United Dominions Corp Ltd v Brian Pty Ltd*, Brian Pty Ltd (Brian) and Security Projects Ltd (SPL) were joint venturers in several land development projects which were largely financed by borrowings from United Dominions Corp (UDC). The development realised a substantial profit but UDC claimed that it was entitled to retain all the proceeds of sale from land developed by the venture because of a 'collateralisation clause' in a mortgage given to it by SPL before the joint venture agreement was concluded. The collateralisation clause purported to charge the joint venture land with repayment of all amounts advanced from time to time by UDC to SPL, whether advanced solely to SPL or to SPL jointly with some other party. Brian argued that the clause was in breach of the fiduciary duty owed by UDC under the joint venture The mortgage was executed on 23 October 1973 and the joint venture on 23 July 1974. The High Court, per Mason and Deane JJ, with whom Gibbs CJ and Dawson J agreed, held that, as the arrangements between the prospective joint venturers had passed beyond the stage of mere negotiation at the time the mortgage was executed, the participants in the joint venture were under fiduciary obligations to one another at that time, and, in particular, that each party was under a fiduciary duty to refrain from pursuing, obtaining or retaining any collateral advantage in relation to the proposed project without the knowledge and informed assent of the other participants. By combining to apply the joint venture land to the mortgage UDC and SPL had obtained for themselves such a collateral advantage. By doing so without the knowledge or consent of Brian they had breached their fiduciary duty.

The principle that fiduciary obligations may exist between prospective joint venturers has been held to apply to relationships between prospective partners involved in negotiations for a partnership: *Edmiston v AGT (Qld) Pty Ltd* [1988] 2 Qd R 1.

Broker and client

[5.14] While a stockbroker is not trustee to his or her client, the relationship between the two is of a fiduciary character and money placed in the stockbroker's hands by the client for investment, and money coming into his or her hands as the proceeds of the client's securities may be followed, that is, traced.[8] The relationship of broker and client is largely governed by statute and the rules of the stock exchange. A broker is not permitted to compete with clients by trading in the market: *Hewson v Sydney Stock Exchange Ltd* [1968] 2 NSWR 224; 87 WN (NSW) Pt 1 422; but that was put as a matter of commercial morality and the professional standards of brokers rather than one of a fiduciary obligation owed to the client. While it is correct to describe the rela-

---

8. *Halsbury's, Laws of England*, 3rd ed, vol 36, p 514.

tionship of broker and client as fiduciary, not every aspect of their dealings will fall under that label.

In *Daly v Sydney Stock Exchange Ltd* (1986) 160 CLR 371, a doctor, wishing to invest some money on the stock exchange, sought advice from a firm of stock brokers, Patrick Partners. Despite its good reputation, that firm was in a precarious financial position. An employee of the firm told Dr Daly that it was not a good time to purchase shares and suggested that the money be placed on deposit with the firm until the time was right to buy. Daly placed two parcels of money with the firm, in April and June 1975, as loans at a high rate of interest at 90 days' call. He later assigned his interest in those funds to his wife. In July 1975 Patrick Partners ceased trading. A claim against the stock exchange fidelity fund failed. Under s 97 of the Securities Industry Act 1975 (NSW) that fund was only available where money which had been entrusted to a broking firm in the course of its business of dealing in securities was lost through some defalcation or fraudulent misuse of the money by a partner or employee. It was argued that Patrick Partners owed a fiduciary duty to Dr Daly which they had breached by failing to advise him of their financial difficulties when borrowing money from him. The High Court held that even though the relationship between Patrick Partners and Dr Daly, as a relationship between stock broker and client, was fiduciary, their relationship as far as the money was concerned was that of debtor and creditor. The money advanced to the firm had not been 'entrusted' to it. It was the firm's money, to use as it wished and its failure to repay the advance was not a defalcation. Gibbs CJ acknowledged that normally the relationship between stockbroker and client was fiduciary but said that that alone was not enough to hold that any money received by the firm thereafter on behalf of the client was impressed with a constructive trust.

5–4 Other Relationships

Commercial transactions

[5.15] Where the parties have dealt at arm's length, as principal and principal, in a commercial transaction where no special trust or reliance has been placed by one in the other, no fiduciary relationship will be implied. Courts have generally been reluctant to impose fiduciary duties upon parties to a commercial arrangement.[9] That does not mean that fiduciary obligations cannot arise in commercial relationships.[10] Joint venturers will owe fiduciary obligations to one another. Agents will owe fiduciary duties to their principals. The fiduciary element in those relationships will not lose any force because the parties are involved in some commercial arrangement. But courts have normally been reluctant to find fiduciary relationships in a commercial setting.

In *Keith Henry & Co Pty Ltd v Stuart Walker & Co Pty Ltd* (1958) 100 CLR 342, the appellant (KH) obtained a licence for the importation of hog casings from Ireland. KH offered the casings to the respondent (SW) who agreed to take them. KH then made its import licence available to SW for the purpose of obtaining a letter of credit and to clear the goods through customs. The goods were invoiced to SW and KH was later paid a commission by the Irish supplier. In 1955 there was a change in the policy of granting import licences under which future licences were to be granted on the basis of goods imported in the fifteen months prior to March 1955. Both KH and SW

---

9. JRF Lehane, 'Fiduciaries in a Commercial Context' in PD Finn (ed), *Essays in Equity*, Law Book Co, Sydney, 1985, pp 95–109.
10. MG&L, para [504].

applied for licences on the basis of the casings imported under the previous licence. A licence was awarded to SW because it had been the importer of the goods brought in under KH's licence. KH brought proceedings seeking a declaration that SW held its import quota upon trust for KH and that SW was liable to account for profits from the use of that licence. The High Court held that there was no room for the application of the rule that a fiduciary must not use his position to make a gain for himself. The relationship between the parties was that of business firms engaged in ordinary commercial transactions dealing at arm's length. Similarly, there was no ground for saying that the advantage enjoyed by SW had been gained by any misuse of its position vis-à-vis KH.

Notwithstanding the obvious common sense of the proposition that parties to a commercial transaction will not normally owe fiduciary obligations to one another courts have been willing to stretch the meaning of the word 'fiduciary' in some odd decisions. In *Catt v Marac Australia Ltd* (1987) 9 NSWLR 639, Rogers J held that the sponsors or instigators of arrangements whereby syndicates of investors acquired aeroplanes owed fiduciary obligations to the investors and that the financiers involved in the scheme owed fiduciary duties to the investors as well. In *Hill v Rose* [1990] VR 129, Tadgell J held that a company and its controllers owed fiduciary obligations to an investor in the company's business, which duty they breached by failing to provide adequate information about the affairs of the company. This line of authority seems a bit perverse and has been questioned.[11] One is left to wonder how it came about that the 'fiduciaries' in each case lost the right to have regard for their own interests; how it was that they came to be acting for or on behalf of the investors, and why the law of contract, misrepresentation and even negligent misstatement was inappropriate or insufficient.[12] A mortgagee is not a trustee of its power of sale for the mortgagor. In conducting a sale the mortgagee is bound to exercise the power of sale in good faith and is not entitled to sacrifice the interest of the mortgagor in the surplus of the proceeds of sale but it is also entitled to have regard for its own interests: *Commercial and General Acceptance Ltd v Nixon* (1981) 152 CLR 491, per Gibbs CJ, at 494; per Mason J, at 502; and per Aickin J, at 515.

[5.16] In any relationship said to be 'fiduciary', the fiduciary obligations will usually form part of a raft of mutual rights and duties between the parties stemming from a variety of sources, including contract, tort and statute. The terms of the arrangement or contract between the parties will often provide the source of fiduciary obligation — as will be the case if the contract requires one to act for the sole benefit of the other in circumstances of trust and confidence. The terms of the contract between the parties may also contradict any suggestion of fiduciary duty:

> In *Hospital Products Ltd v United States Surgical Corp* (1984) 156 CLR 41, the respondent (USSC) manufactured surgical stapling devices and disposable loading units. In late 1978 it made an agreement with Blackman, who had previously been one of its dealers in America, to appoint him as its exclusive Australian distributor. Blackman set up Hospital Products International Pty Ltd (HPI) which was later substituted for Black-

---

11. MG&L, para [503].
12. In *Catt v Marac*, Rogers J used the analogy of the fiduciary duty owed by a promoter to the company being formed, at 9 NSWLR 653, citing *Erlanger v New Sombrero Phosphate Co* (1878) 3 App Cas 1218 at 1236, per Lord Cairns. In the case of the financier this seemed to arise from its additional role as purchaser of the aircraft from the British manufacturer and vendor to the syndicate at a profit and that it dealt with the syndicate through an agent who was to receive a commission. If lending money at interest, buying and selling at a profit, and agents taking a commission become grounds for finding fiduciary duties, and also constitute breaches of those duties, all commercial relationships would be fiduciary and all benefits obtained in commercial dealings would be improper.

man as distributor. HPI acted as exclusive distributor for USSC from April to December 1979. Shortly after Christmas that year HPI, through Blackman, advised USSC that it was terminating the distributorship. During all of this Blackman set about manufacturing surgical staples based directly on the US product by reverse engineering and sold them, together with repackaged USSC demonstration models, as HPI's own products. In that marketing process customers of USSC staples were advised that stocks of the US product were short and the HPI staples were offered as a substitute. In June 1981 the business and assets of Blackman and HPI were acquired by the appellant, HPL. USSC sued HPL, Blackman and related companies, seeking an account of profits from the sale of the stapling units and orders that the business of HPI and other assets were held on constructive trust for USSC. At first instance USSC was awarded an account of profits for the sale of stapling units from December 1979 to November 1980. On appeal the Court of Appeal held that USSC was entitled to a constructive trust over all the assets of HPI, an order which bound HPL as well. That decision was based on a finding that it was a term of the contract between USSC and Blackman that the latter would not do anything inimical to the interests of USSC in the Australian market and, thus, that Blackman, and through him HPI and HPL, owed duties of a fiduciary nature to USSC in respect of the distribution and sale of USSC products in Australia. The High Court upheld an appeal, the majority taking the view that the arrangement between Blackman, and his companies, and USSC was not one which gave rise to fiduciary obligations. Gibbs CJ (with whom Wilson and Dawson JJ agreed) held that while there was an implied term in the contract between USSC and HPI that the latter would use its 'best efforts' to promote the sale of USSC products in Australia, there was no scope to imply a further term that HPI would not, during the distributorship, do anything to damage or destroy USSC's market in Australia. In those circumstances the relationship between USSC and HPI was not a fiduciary one because:

(a) the arrangement was a commercial one entered into by the parties at arm's length and on an equal footing; and,

(b) as it was intended that both USSC and HPI would profit from the distributorship arrangement it could not be said that HPI was under an obligation not to profit from its position.

Accordingly the only relief available to USSC was damages for breach of contract. Mason J agreed with the majority on the question of terms to be implied in the contract, and that there was thus no comprehensive fiduciary relationship; but he also said, at 100, that because USSC had entrusted HPI with exclusive responsibility for marketing USSC's products in Australia and the manner in which those products were to be promoted in that market, HPI owed a limited fiduciary duty in respect of USSC's product goodwill which placed HPI under a duty not to make a profit or take a benefit by virtue of its position as a fiduciary without the informed consent of USSC; further, within the ambit of that fiduciary responsibility, it should not act in a way in which there was a possibility of conflict between its own interests and those of USSC. By manufacturing copies of USSC's products and by promoting its products in the way it did, HPI had breached that duty.

Deane J agreed with the majority in finding that the distributorship arrangement between USSC and HPI did not give rise to a fiduciary relationship either in broad terms or in a narrower sense in respect of USSC's local product goodwill. He thought, however, that HPI could still have been held liable as constructive trustee of the profits of its Australian business on the ground that it was inequitable to retain a benefit acquired in breach of its legal obligations. But, as that matter had not been raised in argument, and the majority were against any finding of a constructive trust, he put the suggestion aside.

[5.17] *Hospital Products* has been criticised for not advancing the search for principle in these cases and for possibly retarding the developments achieved by the decision of the New South Wales Court of Appeal.[13] It is certainly true that the Court of Appeal's decision is consistent with the more active role taken by equity in the last two decades while that of the High Court appears to give judicial licence for a rather cynical act of commercial piracy. But the interpretation placed on the contract between Blackman and USSC by the majority of the High Court gave them little choice and provided some assistance to those attempting to settle the grounds upon which fiduciary obligations can be implied in commercial transactions. The crucial element in the eyes of the majority in *Hospital Products* was the freedom which the distributorship agreement gave to HPL to have regard to its own interests, so that it was not duty bound to place those of USSC first. In strict terms that is a reasonable view, and could even be regarded as helpful to those examining the theory of fiduciary obligations, but one is still left feeling that, unlike the unfortunate Boardman, Mr Blackman got off rather lightly.

[5.18] The question of fiduciary duties in a commercial context was also discussed in *Moorgate Tobacco Co Ltd v Philip Morris Ltd (No 2)* (1984) 156 CLR 414. Deane J, with whom the rest of the High Court agreed, rejected the submission that fiduciary obligations arose out of licence agreements for the marketing of cigarettes. He found that the rights and obligations of the parties were defined by the agreements and that neither party was under a general obligation to avoid any conflict between its own interests and those of the other nor to prefer the interests of that other party, nor the joint interest to its own. He also found that, apart from the general relationship between the parties, there was no particular matter in which one had undertaken to act on behalf of the other which could give rise to fiduciary duties in respect of that particular matter.

Receipt of a sum of money

[5.19] Most of the traditional relationships in which fiduciary duties have been implied have involved some contractual or otherwise consensual framework in which the fiduciary duties form part of the overall terms of the relationship. There are some cases, however, in which the mere receipt of a sum of money, either paid under a mistake of fact, or paid under certain conditions, has been held to give rise to obligations of a fiduciary nature to repay the money or apply it in accordance with the conditions under which it was paid. In *Sinclair v Brougham* [1914] AC 398 (see summary at **[20.11]**), a building society which had run a banking business without authority was held to be bound to repay money held on behalf of *intra vires* investors (in the building society) and *ultra vires* depositors (in the banking business) on an equal basis *parri passu*. Lord Parker held that the relationship between the lender and the directors or agents of a corporation which borrowed outside its powers was a fiduciary relationship and the money in their hands was treated as trust money. Lord Parker's opinion has been most generally accepted as the ratio of *Sinclair v Brougham*, even though the majority did not endorse his view on the fiduciary relationship between the directors and the unauthorised depositors. His judgment was followed on this point by the Court of Appeal in *Re Diplock 's Estate* [1948] 1 Ch 465 at 532, although the finding that a fiduciary relationship arose between the directors and the *ultra vires* depositors has been described as 'a surprising discovery' on the grounds that the money had not passed through the directors' hands and that, as the directors did not owe in a fiduciary duties to their shareholders, it was difficult to see how they could owe such duties

---

13. JRF Lehane, *op cit*, p 102.

to *ultra vires* depositors.[14] It has been held that payment of a sum of money into the wrong hands, by bank error, was sufficient to give rise to fiduciary obligations and that it did not necessarily require a consensual transaction: *Chase Manhattan Bank NA v Israel-British Bank (London) Ltd* [1979] 3 All ER 1025, per Goulding J, applying *Sinclair v Brougham*.

Employee and employer

[5.20] Employees are often described as owing fiduciary duties to their employers but like so many generalisations in this area that statement must be heavily qualified by the proviso that the facts of any case be examined closely. In some cases the terms of the contract of employment will create such duties. In *DPC Estates Pty Ltd v Grey and Consul Development Pty Ltd* [1974] 1 NSWLR 443, the first defendant was employed by the plaintiff, a property investment company, as manager under a service agreement which required him to devote himself exclusively to the business of the plaintiff and related companies, not to divulge to any other person any information concerning that business and not to be concerned with the business of real estate, except as manager of the plaintiff and related companies, without the consent of the managing director. Grey's duties involved investigating prospective properties for investment. He entered into an arrangement with a third party, unbeknown to the managing director of the plaintiff, under which certain properties were purchased by the third party on terms that the profit from the sale of those properties would be shared between the third party and Grey. The claim that Grey owed a fiduciary duty to the plaintiff company was not contested on the pleadings and the Court of Appeal accepted that as an accurate statement of the position.

In *Hivac Ltd v Park Royal Scientific Instruments Ltd* [1946] Ch 169, the English Court of Appeal granted injunctions restraining skilled manual workers employed by one manufacturer of valves for hearing aids from working for a rival manufacturer in their spare time. Lord Greene MR talked of an employee's duty of fidelity, rather than using the word fiduciary. His Lordship saw two competing principles at work: one being the right of a worker, particularly a manual worker, to make use of his leisure for profit; and the other being his duty not to do anything which would inflict harm on his employer's business. These principles can extend to a person working for a nominee company which has a consultancy arrangement with the de facto employer. The question is whether the person concerned is obliged to act for the principal: *Avtex Airservices Pty Ltd v Bartsch* (1992) 107 ALR 539. Where an employee has the responsibility for managing some part of his or her employer's business, or has the conduct of negotiations for the acquisition of further business on behalf of the employer, he or she would be in breach of his duty if he or she appropriated the contract or the benefit of the business for him or herself.

In *Industrial Development Consultants Ltd v Cooley* [1972] 1 WLR 443, Cooley was employed as managing director of the plaintiff company and, in that capacity, entered into negotiations with the Gas Board with the aim of securing contracts for the design and construction of new gas depots for the Board. The Gas Board indicated to Cooley that they would be prepared to give him the work in a private capacity. Cooley obtained a release from his service contract by falsely representing himself to be in poor health and then set up his own company which duly won the Gas Board contract. Roskill J held that Cooley had breached his fiduciary duty to pass on to his employer the information he had received about the contracts, as it was of concern to Industrial Develop-

---

14. Goff & Jones, pp 70–1.

ments, and, because he had allowed his personal interest to conflict with that duty he was accountable and held the Gas Board contract as constructive trustee for the plaintiff, even though it was very unlikely it would have been awarded the contract in its own right.

An employee who is privy to trade secrets of his or her employer will be in breach of the duty of confidence if he or she discloses confidential information during the course of employment to some interested third party. The duty of confidence extends beyond the term of employment in the case of information which properly fits the description 'confidential' but there seems to be a lesser category of information which the employee can be restrained from disclosing to another during the course of employment, but not after leaving that job; not because of the confidentiality of the information but because it would be in breach of his contract of employment to divulge it to a third party: *Printers & Finishers v Holloway* [1965] RPC 239. The obligation imposed on the recipient of confidential information is slightly different from that of a fiduciary. The confidant cannot make unauthorised use of the information. The fiduciary must not place his or her own interests ahead of, or in conflict with, those of his or her principal. There is obviously some common ground between the two. But an employee bound by the duty of confidence is not necessarily a fiduciary as well. An employee also enjoys certain protections under the law. There is the right to work: *Buckley v Tutty* (1971) 125 CLR 353, and the right to make use of knowledge and skills acquired during the course of a working life: *Herbert Morris Ltd v Saxelby* [1916] AC 688.

[5.21] This category also encompasses what might be called the inventor or designer cases in which employees have been held to be constructive trustees for their employers of inventions which fall within the scope of their duties as employees to design. In *British Reinforced Concrete v Lind* (1917) 86 LJ Ch 486, the employee was employed to design gallery headings for coal mines. He produced a design containing four important elements but omitted a fifth crucial piece in each. He later patented the missing element and was held to be a constructive trustee of the patent for his employer. In *Sterling Engineering Co v Patchett* [1955] 1 All ER 369, Lord Simonds expressed the principle in these terms:

> ... where an employee in the course of his employment, that is, in his employer's time and with his materials, makes an invention which it falls within his duty to make ... he holds his interest in the invention and in any resulting patent as trustee for his employer.

The same principle would apply to any creative contract, such as one for songwriting, and, by analogy to many fields of employment such as business attracted or work performed by an employed solicitor.

Agent and principal

[5.22] While not all agents are fiduciaries they do hold a representative position which will, in most cases, cast fiduciary duties on them in the conduct of affairs on behalf of their principals. In any case in which an agent enters into some transaction with his or her principal, particularly one in which the agent purchases property from the principal, very strict duties will be imposed on the agent to ensure the propriety of the transaction.

In *Haywood v Roadknight* [1927] VLR 512, a farmer purchased some land for his son at a price of £28 per acre. The purchase price was payable over three years. The son proved unable to meet the payments and assigned the land to his father. The father, on the advice of his solicitor, employed a land agent to sell the land before the vendors exercised their power of sale. The land failed to sell at auction and the farmer gave the agent an option to purchase it himself for £29 per acre. The agent subsequently exercised the option and, within the year sold the land for £90 per acre. The rise in value was caused by the purchase of land in the vicinity by the Ford Motor Co as a site for an assembly plant. The farmer sought to set the sale to the agent aside. He acknowledged that he had heard rumours about the possibility of Ford buying land in the area. Dixon AJ, in a decision affirmed by the Full Court, held that the agent was in breach of the fiduciary duty cast upon him by his role in the sale and was liable to account to the farmer for the profits he had made. The agency gave him knowledge of the plaintiff's difficulties and of the value of the property. He had failed to make proper disclosure and had manifestly failed to give the plaintiff the benefit of his expert opinion and advice. The solicitor was also held to be in breach of his fiduciary duty for failing to disclose that he also acted for the agent.

Banker and customer

[5.23] Normally the relationship between banker and customer will be that of debtor and creditor and not subject to fiduciary duties. The notion that a bank may owe fiduciary duties to its customer is not novel. In most instances where a bank acts as financier it will have an obvious personal interest to pursue. If a fiduciary relationship is alleged it will be necessary to show that special circumstances exist which demonstrate that the bank has assumed a fiduciary responsibility towards the customer. This will be easier to show where there has been a long history of dealings between the two and the customer can be shown to have placed some special reliance on the bank manager: *Hayward v Bank of Nova Scotia* (1984) 45 OR (2d) 542; or where the bank has placed itself in a particular position of conflict of interest without advising the customer of that fact and has played an active role in inducing the customer to follow a particular course of action: *McBean v Bank of Nova Scotia* (1981) 15 BLR 296. Where a bank takes on the role of investment advisor to its customer the relationship becomes much more than that of debtor and creditor.

In *Commonwealth Bank v Smith* (1991) 102 ALR 453, long term customers of the local branch of the appellant bank sought the assistance of the bank in buying the licensed leasehold of a hotel. The bank gave assistance by urging the Smiths to buy the lease of a certain hotel, saying it was a 'good buy'. The bank manager told the Smiths that he was in a position of conflict of interest, because the bank also acted for the vendor, and that would affect the information he could provide to them. He did not suggest that they obtain independent financial advice and actually discouraged them from seeing an accountant or a hotel broker. The bank did not disclose to the Smiths a mortgagee valuation which was significantly lower than the price the Smiths were to pay. The bank also acted for the vendor company, whose account with the bank was overdrawn. The bank was held to owe fiduciary duties to the Smiths, principally because the bank acted as their financial adviser and that the crucial incident in that relationship was the conflicting interests between the two sets of customers. The information provided to the Smiths by the bank was held not to be sufficient to amount to fully informed consent and the bank was held to be liable to compensate the Smiths by paying them the difference between what they paid for the lease and what it was actually worth. The Smiths employed an independent solicitor but did not rely on him for financial advice.

Other and special relationships

[5.24] There is no rule which sets any limit on the relationships in which fiduciary obligations can be owed by one party to another. Outside the established categories it is less likely that any special trust or confidence will be placed by one person in another such as to give rise to fiduciary duties but, if the facts establish such a reliance by one upon the other, it is no defence to argue that the case does not fall into a recognised field. In *Mabo v Queensland* (1992) 175 CLR 1; 107 ALR 1, Toohey J was prepared to find that the Crown, at least in right of Queensland, owed fiduciary duties to the native landholders of the Torres Strait. He based that finding , in part, on a decision of the Supreme Court of Canada in *Guerin v The Queen* [1984] 2 SCR 335; (1984) 13 DLR (4th) 321, and, in part, on the vulnerability of the native people to the Crown in light of the power of the Crown to alienate land otherwise subject to native title. In *Guerin v The Queen*, Dickson J, with whom Beetz, Chouinard and Lamer JJ concurred, expressed the principle upon which he relied, at SCR 376; DLR 334:

> The fiduciary relationship between the Crown and the Indians has its roots in the concept of aboriginal, native or Indian title. The fact that Indian Bands have a certain interest in lands does not, however, in itself give rise to a fiduciary relationship between the Indians and the Crown. The conclusion that the Crown is a fiduciary depends upon the proposition that the Indian interest in the land is inalienable except upon surrender to the Crown.

While the *Mabo* case was put, in part, on the basis of fiduciary obligation only, Toohey J addressed the point in his judgment. The proposition that the Crown owes fiduciary duties, at least to some of its subjects, has not met with judicial approval in other circumstances. In *Tito v Waddell (No2)* [1977] 3 All ER 129, Megarry V-C dismissed a claim that the Crown, in right of the United Kingdom, owed fiduciary obligations to the Banaban Community of Ocean Island in respect of the depredation of that island by the mining of super phosphate because the obligation owed by the Crown to the Banabans was a governmental obligation or 'trust in the higher sense' and was not justiciable in the courts; it was not a 'true trust' in the conventional sense but a trust in the sense in which the welfare of the community is entrusted to government and the organs of the state. Nor was the Crown subject to any other fiduciary obligations in respect of the Banabans because of the transactions and arrangements between them. Megarry V-C found that the Crown was never constituted an agent for the Banabans or any of them. In coming to that view, Megarry V-C echoed the words of Lord Selborne LC in *Kinloch v Secretary of State for India* (1882) 7 App Cas 619, that the Crown and officers discharging duties or functions on behalf of the Crown are engaged in work in the nature of a 'higher' trust unlike other trusts of the 'lower' kind which are justiciable in Courts of Equity. Toohey J dismissed both those judgments as being decisions which turned upon the construction particular instruments. But that cannot be an acceptable basis for dismissing the views expressed by their Lordships. If the Crown is truly bound by fiduciary duties when exercising its powers to alienate otherwise native lands then it could not have regard to its own interests in doing so. On that basis the Crown could not, for example, take land for the purpose of, say, building a lighthouse to guide shipping in the Torres Strait without the informed consent of the native titleholders or for the purpose of building a military base for national defence. The problems with Toohey J's analysis of the matter is that it rests very heavily on the concept of vulnerability discussed above. The analysis of the legal relationship between the Crown and native titleholders expressed in the other majority judgments in the High Court must be considered preferable to this fiduciary approach.

5–5 Breach of Duty: 'Conflict of Interest' and 'Improper Gain'

[5.25] The doctrine in *Keech v Sandford* (1726) Sel Cas T King 61; 25 ER 223, imposes a rigorous duty upon fiduciaries to avoid situations of possible conflict between interest and duty by making the fiduciary accountable for any benefit acquired by virtue of his or her position, even though that benefit was not one which was necessarily available to the principal.

Keech v Sandford (1726) Sel Cas T King 61; 25 ER 223 concerned a lease held on trust in which the lessor refused to renew the lease to the trust. The trustee sought and was granted a renewal of the lease in his own name. The trustee was held to hold the new lease upon trust for his beneficiary. Despite the rigour of the rule, Lord Chancellor King said that it was better that the lease be allowed to run out than to allow a trustee to take such a benefit for himself.

[5.26] Once the relationship of fiduciary and principal has been shown to exist the next question to be answered must be whether the fiduciary is in breach of his or her duty. That begs a subsidiary question which has been mentioned — the scope of the duty involved. These two questions have not been analysed with consistent clarity in the judgments which have dealt with these issues. Too often, some 'gain' has been found and then explained in terms of conflict between interest and duty, or some element of personal interest has been held to be constitute a breach of duty without any precise delineation of the extent of that duty. One clear exception to that criticism is the judgment of Deane J in *Chan v Zacharia* (1984) 154 CLR 178 in which his Honour identified two circumstances in which a fiduciary could be in breach of his duty.

Zacharia operated a medical practice in Adelaide at three different locations including one at Mansfield Park where he leased premises from Ajay Investments Pty Ltd (Ajay). In September 1978 Zacharia entered into an agreement with Chan to sell the latter one half of the practice and to thereafter conduct the practice as a partnership. The partnership was determined in May 1981. In January 1979 Ajay gave the doctors a written lease of the Mansfield Park premises for a term of three years with an option to renew the lease for a further two years upon written request being made not less than three months before the expiry of the term, that is, 30 September 1981. The partnership agreement provided for a general account to be taken of the assets of the partnership upon a dissolution. Chan, despite requests from Zacharia and the receiver of the practice to do so, declined to join in any exercise of the option to renew the lease. Instead he sought and obtained a renewal of the lease in his own name from Ajay having offered a premium for the renewed lease. Zacharia sought a declaration that Chan held the new lease as a constructive trustee for the two of them as an asset of the partnership. Deane J, with whom Brennan and Dawson JJ agreed, held that Chan was a constructive trustee for himself and Zacharia of the new lease which was an asset of the partnership. In doing so he said, at 198–9, that the general principle of equity requiring a fiduciary to account for personal benefit or gain embodied two themes: the first appropriated for the principal any benefit or gain obtained or received by the fiduciary in circumstances where there existed a conflict of personal interest and fiduciary duty or a significant possibility of such conflict; the second required the fiduciary to account for any benefit or gain obtained or received by reason of or by use of his fiduciary position or of some opportunity or knowledge resulting from it.

Deane J said that the rule in *Keech v Sandford* applied to this case and said it should not be seen as either a completely independent principle of equity nor as a mere manifestation of the general principle governing the liability of a fiduciary to account for personal benefit or gain.

[5.27] The question also arises, in light of *Regal (Hastings) Ltd v Gulliver* [1967] 2 AC 135, whether a fiduciary who obtains some benefit or gain through his or her fiduciary position is automatically liable to account to the principal for that benefit or whether it must also be shown that the profit or gain was made 'improperly'. On the authority of *Regal (Hastings)* and *Boardman v Phipps* [1967] AC 46, it is not necessary to show lack of good faith, but some fiduciaries, such as solicitors, profit from their office by charging fees and yet do not have to account for those profits. Directors will often be paid fees or a salary. It could be said that in each of those cases there was informed consent on the part of the client, but that is a convoluted way of absolving something that was never wrong in the first place.

5–6   Defences: the Duty of Disclosure and Informed Consent

[5.28] The only way a fiduciary can enter into some engagement involving a potential conflict of interest and duty, or otherwise retain some benefit or gain obtained by virtue of the fiduciary position, is with the informed consent of his or her principal. That casts a duty on the fiduciary to disclose to the principal all information pertinent to the transaction and, if need be, to provide some adequate explanation of that information. A fiduciary's duty to make full disclosure extends to all material information known to the fiduciary, including any information the fiduciary has deliberately refrained from acquiring. The duty of disclosure does not extend to other facts of which the fiduciary is unaware, even though prudent enquiry would reveal their existence. In *BLB Corporation of Australia v Jacobsen* (1974) 48 ALJR 372, the director of a company supplying yarn was also manager of Bel-Knit, a customer of the company. He was held not to have breached his duty by allowing Bel-Knit to purchase a large amount of yarn from the defendant on credit at a time when Bel-Knit was insolvent. The accounts of Bel-Knit were not prepared until the end of the year and he had not known of a substantial trading loss incurred at the relevant time. He had advised the company of Bel-Knit's debts and that it was struggling to establish itself in the market. The High Court held that to be a sufficient discharge of his duty. This question was addressed at first instance in *Phipps v Boardman* [1964] 2 All ER 187 at 205, by Wilberforce J who considered the letter sent by Boardman to Anthony Phipps, the plaintiff, detailing the deficiencies of that letter in the following terms:

> In my judgment, the letter of March 10 fell far short of what was required. In the first place, it gave no idea of the lengthy and protracted struggle — with the directors to get the fullest possible information about the company and its assets ...
>
> Secondly, it wholly failed to make available or to indicate the existence of the mass of knowledge which Mr Boardman had accumulated ...
>
> Thirdly, the letter (did not say) that Mr Boardman and Mr Tom Phipps were not committed to the purchase until after they had satisfied themselves on the spot as to the value of the Australian subsidiary, thus reducing appreciably the risk element. Fourthly, the letter did not mention that Mr Boardman had been in touch with a finance house which was willing to provide the whole of the finance on terms which would strictly limit the risk to the purchasers, while leaving them with the greater part of any profit.

Having said that, Wilberforce J then said of Boardman:

I acquit Mr Boardman entirely of any intention to deceive or suppress material information; but I think, having himself lived with this situation for eighteen months or so and become soaked in its details, he failed to appreciate the degree of explanation and the quantity of supporting documents which would be needed to enable someone coming fresh to it (as did Anthony Phipps) to appraise it, or even to see that this was a matter which required careful consideration and expert advice.

[5.29] There have been some suggestions that disclosure will not be necessary where the information which would otherwise have been provided would not have affected the result: *Walden Properties Ltd v Beaver Properties Ltd* [1973] 2 NSWLR 815 at 847, per Hutley JA, although that is a very fine line to tread and seems somewhat inconsistent with the stringency of the rule rendering a fiduciary accountable for a benefit which would not have been available to the principal in any case: cf *Gemstone Corporation v Grasso* (see **[5.33]**).

[5.30] It is no defence to show that the fiduciary has acted honestly or with good faith in the transaction. The clearest authority for that is *Boardman v Phipps* [1967] 2 AC 46 in which their Lordships were anxious to stress Boardman's integrity.[15] That sentiment was echoed by the High Court in *Warman International Ltd v Dwyer* (1995) 128 ALR 201 at 209.

5–7   Remedies for Breach of Fiduciary Duty

[5.31] In general terms a fiduciary will be held to be accountable for any benefit or gain acquired through breach of his or her duty but the nature of the remedy awarded will vary according to the circumstances of the case. In some cases it will be appropriate to decree that the delinquent fiduciary holds his or her ill-gotten gains on constructive trust for the principal. This remedy was applied by Kearney J in *Timber Engineering Co Pty Ltd v Anderson* [1980] 2 NSWLR 488 against two officers of a company who had set up another business in competition to that of their employer. A constructive trust may be imposed where the fiduciary has acted dishonestly, as in *Timber Engineering*, or honestly, as in *Boardman v Phipps*, provided a breach of duty can be shown. The remedy of constructive trust is discretionary and *Timber Engineering*, because of the extreme nature of its facts, must be regarded as something of a high water mark in these cases. Courts may award lesser relief, such as an account of profits covering a certain period. That was the approach taken by McClelland J at first instance in *Hospital Products* and by Mason J in the same case in the High Court, his Honour preferring an account of profits to a constructive trust because of the narrower scope of the appellant's fiduciary obligation in his judgment and because he felt some allowance should be made for the appellant's diligence in building up the Australian business. A distinction must be drawn between cases in which a specific asset is acquired and cases in which a business is acquired and operated; for example, see *Re Jarvis (dec'd)* [1958] 1 WLR 815 at 821, per Upjohn J, cited with approval by the High Court in *Warman International Ltd v Dwyer* (1995) 128 ALR 201 at 211:

> In the case of a business it may well be inappropriate and inequitable to compel an errant fiduciary to account for the whole of the profit of his conduct of the business or his exploitation of the principal's goodwill over an indefinite period of time. In such a case, it may well be appropriate to allow the fiduciary a proportion of the profits,

---

15. At 104, 105 and 112.

depending upon the particular circumstances. That may well be the case when it appears that a significant proportion of an increase in profits has been generated by the skill, efforts, property and resources of the fiduciary, the capital which he has introduced and the risks he has taken, so long as they are not risks to which the principal's property has been exposed.

The mere fact that a fiduciary has made a profit or acquired some benefit will not necessarily render the fiduciary liable to account. It may be that, as Deane J put it in *Chan v Zacharia* (1984) 154 CLR at 204–5; 53 ALR at 438:

> ... the liability to account for a personal benefit or gain obtained or received by use of or by reason of fiduciary position, opportunity or knowledge will not arise in circumstances where it would be unconscientious to assert it or in which, for example, there is no possible conflict between personal interest and fiduciary duty and it is plainly in the interests of the person to whom the fiduciary duty is owed that the fiduciary obtain for himself rights or benefits.

Ordinarily a fiduciary will be ordered to render an account of the profits made within the scope and ambit of his or her duty. Of course, if the loss suffered by the plaintiff exceeds the profits made by the fiduciary, the plaintiff may elect to have a compensatory remedy against the fiduciary. That election will bind the plaintiff: *Kendall v Masters* (1860) 2 De G F & J 200; 45 ER 598.

[5.32] Damages or equitable compensation can also be awarded for breach of fiduciary obligations as they were in *Mordecai v Mordecai* (1988) 12 NSWLR 58 (see **[25.3]**) and *Commonwealth Bank v Smith* (1991) 102 ALR 453 at 478–9. The remedies of equitable compensation and account of profits were discussed at some length by the High Court, in a joint judgment by Mason CJ, Brennan, Deane, Dawson and Gaudron JJ in *Warman International Ltd v Dwyer* (1995) 128 ALR 201 (see **[25.5]**).

Dwyer was general manager of the Queensland branch of Warman International Ltd (Warman). Warman's business included an agency for distribution of gearboxes and other products manufactured in Italy by the Bonfiglioli group. By 1986 Dwyer was dissatisfied with Warman's conduct of the agency. Their policies had resulted in a diminution of Dwyer's status and, potentially, his salary. Bonfiglioli wanted to set up a joint venture, preferably with Warman, for the assembly of Bonfiglioli products in Australia. Warman's Sydney management, Dwyer's superiors, made it clear that Warman would not be interested in participating in such a venture. Dwyer entered into secret negotiations with Bonfiglioli and subsequently arranged for two companies to be formed; one (BTA) in which Dwyer and his wife and Bonfiglioli interests held shares, and another (ETA) which was was wholly owned by Dwyer and his wife.

In June 1988 Bonfiglioli terminated its agency with Warman as from 26 August 1988. On 30 June 1988 Dwyer left Warman. On 12 June 1988 a subsidiary of Bonfiglioli and BTA entered into a joint venture agreement with Dwyer and his wife, which provided for the assembly and distribution of Bonfiglioli gearboxes in Australia. ETA distributed some Bonfiglioli products and a range of complementary products in conjunction with the joint venture. BTA took over the agency business in Australia which included the assembly and distribution of the gearboxes. The businesses were successful with net profits (before tax) of $1.6 million over the four years preceding the trial. Warman commenced proceedings against Dwyer and the corporate respondents on 25 October 1988, seeking relief including an account of profits. At all levels Dwyer was found to have breached his fiduciary duty to Warman. The differences of judicial opinion lay in the matter of the appropriate relief. The trial judge found that Warman was entitled to 'equitable damages' for 'the loss of Warman's chance of retaining the agencies business' even though the agencies were likely to be lost. Dwyer was found to have breached his fiduciary duty to his employer, Warman, by appropriating, effectively, the agency business previously run by Warman. The trial judge held that Warman was entitled to 'equitable damages' or, in the alternative, to an accounts of profits for four years' profits plus payment of a purchase price for goodwill at the end of that period. The Court of Appeal upheld the finding of breach of fiduciary duty but, by a majority, held that Warman was not entitled to an account of profits but only to its losses flowing from the breach of duty. The High Court preferred the trial judge's view that an account of profits was the appropriate remedy but said that the order requiring accounts for four years' profits plus payment of a purchase price for goodwill at the end of that period went beyond what was equitable in the circumstances. The appropriate period was two years. On that basis, the High Court ordered the respondents to account on the basis of the approach less favourable to them; they had to account for the entirety of the net profits of the businesses before tax over the first two years of their operation, that is, from 12 September 1988, less an appropriate allowance for expenses, skill, expertise, effort and resources contributed by them. In that respect Warman was put to its election as to whether it would seek to retain the order for equitable compensation made in the Court of Appeal or whether it would accept the order for account of profits allowed by the High Court.

[5.33] A fiduciary in breach may be ordered to pay equitable compensation by way of restitution to the principal where the principal has suffered a loss as a result of the fiduciary's breach, even though the fiduciary has not received any corresponding profit or gain. In such a case notions of causation relevant in questions of tortious liability will not be available to reduce or negate the liability of the fiduciary.

In *Gemstone Corporation of Australia Ltd v Grasso* (1994) 13 ACSR 695, the appellant company (Gemstone) was converted from a private to a public listed company. With the float, each of the directors was issued with 500,000 ordinary shares of 50 cents each partly paid to one cent per share. The directors were allowed to take their partly paid shares in the name of a nominee. Grasso took his 500,000 shares in the name of a $2 company under his control (Star). Star had no assets beyond the money nominally paid for its two issued shares. The prospectus issued with the float referred to the partly paid shares issued to the directors as evidence that the directors were 'standing behind the company with uncalled capital, as further evidence of faith that the directors were wholly committed'. In the event, the company suffered losses and the partly paid shares were called. Star did not pay — it had no means of doing so. The Full Court held Grasso liable finding that he had breached his fiduciary duty by substituting an ephemeral nominee, Star, for himself on the issue of the partly paid shares, without making proper disclosure to the Board and was liable to make good the loss which flowed from that breach. The Full Court held that accountability for breach of fiduciary duty arose immediately upon breach, that is, immediately the fiduciary enters into an engagement in which there is the possibility of a conflict of interest. In such a case proof of subsequent causative consequences of the transaction is not a pre-condition to a cause of action. The court said that there are real differences between liability for damages in tort and the award of compensation for breach of fiduciary duty in equity. In equity it is irrelevant speculation to enquire into what might have been the outcome had there been appropriate disclosure of the true situation when the issue of the partly paid shares was mooted.

The Full Court declined to follow the view expressed in the New South Wales Court of Appeal in *Walden Properties Ltd v Beaver Properties Pty Ltd* [1973] 2 NSWLR 815 at 846–7, per Hutley JA, that a fiduciary may escape liability if he or she can show that the information obtained, though not disclosed to the principal, would not have affected the principal's decision. In coming to their decision the court applied the principles stated by the High Court in *Furs Ltd v Tomkies* (1936) 54 CLR 583 at 592, per Rich, Dixon and Evatt JJ, that, 'except under the authority of a provision in the articles of association, no director shall obtain for himself a profit by means of a transaction in which he is concerned on behalf of the company unless all the material facts are disclosed to the shareholders and by resolution a general meeting approves of his doing so, or all the shareholders acquiesce'.

5-8 Secret Commissions and Equitable Debt

[5.34] An employee who receives a secret commission or 'kickback' from a third party in return for carrying out his or her job in a certain way will be liable in equity to the employer. However, the cases in which such liability has been found have held the employee liable in debt for the amount of the secret commission, rather than as constructive trustee of the ill-gotten gain. Taking the secret commission is clearly a breach of the employee's duty of fidelity and, depending upon the nature of the work performed by the employee, may also be a breach of fiduciary duty. This approach was taken in *Metropolitan Bank v Heiron* (1880) 5 Ex D 319, in which a director of a bank accepted a payment from a debtor to the bank in return for using his influence to secure an arrangement between the bank and the debtor which was favourable to the debtor. The same principle was also applied in *Boston Deep Sea Fishing and Ice Co v Ansell* (1888) 39 Ch D 389, in which the managing director of the plaintiff received secret commissions from people and companies dealing with the plaintiff, and in *Lister v Stubbs* (1890) 45 Ch D 1, where kickbacks were paid by suppliers of materials used in the plaintiff's business to the employee responsible for ordering those materials. In all three cases the English Court of Appeal took the view that, while all these employers were entitled to be paid the bribe received by the employee, their rights were those of a debtor against a creditor, not of a *cestui que trust*, as the money was never 'money of the company'. This line of authority has been strongly criticised,[16] and described as anomalous and not to be extended beyond its own facts by the New South Wales Court of Appeal in *DPC Estates Pty Ltd v Grey* [1974] 1 NSWLR 443, but survives to bedevil this area of the law. The principle in *Lister v Stubbs* appears to rest on the erroneous notion that a constructive trust is only available where assets of the principal can be traced into the hands of the delinquent fiduciary or some third party. That proposition is contrary to the preferred view in Australia as stated in the judgment of Gummow J in *Re Stephenson Nominees* (1987) 76 ALR 485 at 502 and 503 that the constructive trust may be imposed as a cautionary or deterrent remedy even where there has been no unjust enrichment of the defendant at the expense of the plaintiff and no assets of the plaintiff can be traced into the defendant's hands.

[5.35] It has been argued that, at its highest, *Lister v Stubbs* is authority for the proposition that an agent is, before decree, not a trustee of any illicit profits but that, upon proof of the relevant facts, the court will declare him to be a trustee but not retrospectively.[17] That proposition is difficult to sustain. A thief, for instance, has been held to be a constructive trustee of his loot: *Black v Freedman* (1910) 12 CLR 105, and so, one would think, would an embezzler, or a blackmailer and, if so, why not the recipient of a bribe or secret commission which might also be a criminal act? In view of the general recognition of the constructive trust as a remedy to prevent unconscionable conduct, particularly unconscionable retention of a benefit acquired at the expense of the plaintiff: *Muschinski v Dodds* (1985) 160 CLR 583, and the prevailing

---

16. MG&L, paras [538]–[587]; and JRF Lehane, 'Fiduciaries in a Commercial Context', *op cit*, p 107.
17. *Jacobs'*, para [1323], p 299.

view of constructive trusts as a cautionary or deterrent remedy as expressed by Gummow J in *Re Stephenson Nominees*, it is difficult to envisage circumstances in which *Lister v Stubbs* would not be followed. The dishonest employee might have other problems with the law apart from paying his or her ill-gotten gains over to his or her principal — he or she and any accomplices may be guilty of a criminal offence punishable by imprisonment.[18] In *Daly v Sydney Stock Exchange Ltd* (1986) 160 CLR 371 at 379, Gibbs CJ, with whom the rest of the Court substantially agreed, said of *Lister v Stubbs*, 'The decision in that case has been criticised as unjust, but the reasons of Lindley LJ appear to me to be impeccable when applied to the case in which the person claiming the money has simply made an outright loan to the defendant'. *Lister v Stubbs* has also been accepted by the New Zealand Court of Appeal in *A-G (Hong Kong) v Reid* [1992] 2 NZLR 385 at 392, although that view was expressed on the basis that the validity of *Lister v Stubbs* in New Zealand law was a matter for the Privy Council not the New Zealand Court of Appeal.

[5.36] One other case involving the receipt of secret commissions which has been the subject of some controversy is *Reading v A-G* [1951] AC 507.

Reading was a sergeant in the British Army in Egypt during the war and lent his assistance, by shepherding trucks through police checkpoints under the protection of his uniform, to smugglers of illicit spirits. He received bribes of £20,000 for his efforts. He was court-martialled and sentenced and some of his profits were confiscated. After his release he sought to recover the money which had been seized. The House of Lords held that the Crown was entitled to retain the money as it represented profit made by Reading in breach of his fiduciary duty, and that it was had and received to the use of the Crown. In the Court of Appeal [1949] 2 KB 232, in a judgment approved of by the House of Lords, Asquith LJ held that a person wearing the Crown's uniform was under a fiduciary duty to use it for his master's benefit, a duty which Reading had breached. His Lordship also adopted the *Lister v Stubbs* approach to hold that an employee receiving a secret profit was liable to the extent of the secret profit.

Finn has criticised the finding of a fiduciary relationship in *Reading's* case on the ground that the duties of someone holding such a public office would be better regulated by some distinct body of public law.[19] Meagher, Gummow and Lehane see no discomfort in fitting Sgt Reading as a fiduciary.[20] Considering some of the things which the Crown asks of its employees in uniform from time to time one must be wary of attaching the adjective 'fiduciary' too readily to their duties. That said, the law of fiduciary duties is not an inappropriate weapon to employ against black marketeers, particularly in time of war when opportunities for such activities are rife.[21] Of course, by retaining Sgt Reading's booty the English Government was simply profiting from a fraud perpetrated on the Government of Egypt. These principles do not extend to commissions paid in a commercial context where the parties concerned have dealt at arm's length. In *Jirna Ltd v Mister Donut of Canada Ltd* (1973) 40 DLR (3d) 303, the plaintiff held a franchise to sell donuts [sic] and American style coffee pursuant to an agreement which required it to purchase its supplies from nominated distributors. It failed in an attempt to recover secret rebates paid by those suppliers to the franchisor.

---

18. Section 249D of the Crimes Act 1900 (NSW) as added by the Crimes (Secret Commissions) Amendment Act 1987.

19. Finn, *op cit*, p 215.

20. See MG&L, para [524].

21. Sgt Reading would also be caught by s 249D of the Crimes Act 1900 (NSW) as added by the Crimes (Secret Commissions) Amendment Act 1987 which includes employees of the Crown in its definition of agents.

Chapter Six

Unconscionable Transactions

6-1 Introduction

[6.1] Equity will not set aside a contract, let alone re-write one, simply because it shows some rough edges. It will only intervene to set aside a concluded transaction where it is against conscience for one party to hold the other to the arrangement. This will usually mean that one party has been guilty of some fraud, in the equitable sense of the word. It is not enough to argue that a contract is 'unfair'. It is necessary to show that equitable intervention is justified on some recognised ground. Equity is not so concerned with the terms of the contract. If two parties, dealing at arm's length and acting properly towards one another, make a contract which is heavily weighted in favour of one as against the other, equity will not be concerned. But where one party obtains the agreement of another to a bargain by taking advantage of some situation of superiority or dominance in circumstances where equity considers it unconscionable to obtain the contract in that way, equity will intervene. It is not enough, however, merely to demonstrate a position of superiority. This is the case particularly in commercial transactions where it is appropriate and legitimate for one party in a position of superiority to take advantage of that superiority. The matters discussed below have been grouped under the heading of unconscionable transactions because they all have, to a large extent, a common thread: one party to the transaction has taken advantage of some inappropriate means to obtain the assent of the other to a bargain, or otherwise to obtain some benefit at the other's expense, and insists on holding the other party to the bargain in circumstances where equity may consider it against conscience to do so.

6-2 Fraud in Equity

[6.2] Fraud in equity embraces a wider concept of fraud than that recognised by the common law. Common law fraud requires proof of conscious dishonesty, that is, that some false representation has been made knowingly in the knowledge that it was untrue or, at least, with reckless indifference to its truth or falsehood: *Derry v Peek* (1889) 14 App Cas 337. This element of knowledge restricted the common law action of deceit to a narrow field and placed a heavy onus on a plaintiff seeking to avoid a contract for fraud at common law. In *Derry v Peek*, a false representation in a prospectus that the company had Board of Trade consent to propel their tramway carriages by steam or mechanical power was held not to be sufficient to render the company liable in deceit because it was not found to have been made with conscious dishonesty. In cases of actual fraud, that is, conscious dishonesty, the Courts of Chancery and of Common Law exercised a concurrent jurisdiction from the earliest times as outlined by Lord Haldane in *Nocton v Ashburton* [1914] AC 932:

> Nocton, a solicitor, advised his client, Lord Ashburton, to release part of the land subject to a mortgage in Lord Ashburton's favour to assist a building development on the site. The release of that mortgage also had the effect of promoting a second mortgage in favour of Nocton on the same property. Upon default Lord Ashburton's remaining security proved insufficient. He took proceedings against Nocton but he failed at first instance because of the Statute of Limitations and because failed to prove 'actual fraud' as required by *Derry v Peek*. On appeal it was held that Nocton had breached his fiduciary duty to Lord Ashburton and was liable to indemnify him for the loss. Lord Haldane rejected an argument that *Derry v Peek* governed the meaning of fraud in equity, saying that while Chancery exercised a concurrent jurisdiction in cases of actual fraud it also had an exclusive jurisdiction in cases not necessarily involving intentional fraud. Fraud when used in this wider sense meant not moral fraud in the ordinary sense, but a breach of the sort of obligation which is enforced by a court of equity. No actual intention to cheat need be proven. It was sufficient if a man misconceived the extent of an obligation imposed on him by a court of equity, the fault being that he violated, however innocently, an obligation which he must be taken by the court to have known. Such conduct has in that sense always been called fraudulent in equity, even in such a case as a technical fraud on a power.

[6.3] Equity traditionally provided relief by way of rescission in cases where a contract was induced by innocent misrepresentation. In the early days of the judicature system there was some confusion over the relationship between the various forms of relief available at law and in equity and suggestions arose that damages might be available for innocent misrepresentation. The common law has since developed the doctrine of negligent misstatement to overcome some of these problems. The introduction of statutory relief for misleading and deceptive conduct, at least in trade and commerce, by s 52 of the Trade Practices Act 1974 (Cth) and corresponding Fair Trading legislation in various states has opened up a vast new field of litigation in misrepresentations beyond the scope of this book. Equity, however, retains the power to set aside transactions procured by fraud, even though the fraud involved may be only fraud in the equitable sense:

> In *Vadasz v Pioneer Concrete (SA) Pty Ltd* (1995) 130 ALR 570, Vadasz sought to set aside a guarantee he had entered into guaranteeing the debts owed by Vadipile Drilling Pty Ltd to Pioneer Concrete. Vadipile purchased concrete products from Pioneer. The guarantee was set aside, but only as it applied to past debts. Vadesz claimed that officers of Pioneer had told him that the guarantee only related to the Vadipile's future indebtedness. The trial judge accepted that and found that Vadasz was entitled to rescind the guarantee only to the extent that it related to the past indebtedness of the company. Vadasz was entitled to rescission irrespective of whether the misrepresentation was fraudulent, negligence or innocent. That decision was accepted by the Full Court and left undisturbed by the High Court. The High Court held further that unconscionability provided a justification for setting aside a transaction in its entirety so as to prevent one party obtaining an unwarranted benefit at the expense of the other. Vadasz was seeking the assistance of a Court of Equity and must therefore do equity. The court had to look at what was practically just for both parties, not only the appellant. To enforce the guarantee to the extent of future indebtedness would be to do no more than hold Vadesz to what he was prepared to undertake independent of any misrepresentation.

[6.4] The operation of the principle of equitable fraud stated by Lord Haldane in *Nocton v Lord Ashburton* can be seen in *Keech v Sandford* (1726) Sel Cas T King 61; 25 ER

223 and *Boardman v Phipps* [1967] 2 AC 46 (see [5.6]). A technical fraud on a power is another good example. Various powers may be conferred on fiduciaries, usually such things as powers of investment held by trustees, or powers of appointment — powers to 'appoint' or nominate the recipients of some settlement or other fund. A trustee exercising such a power who makes an investment which is unauthorised, or 'appoints' property to some object outside the authorised range of objects, will be in breach and liable to indemnify the trust, notwithstanding that he or she acted honestly and even sought legal advice.[1] Equitable fraud in this sense, however, does not apply generally to all transactions and all relationships. A party claiming under this doctrine must first show a pre-existing relationship such as that of fiduciary and principal giving rise to equitable obligations. Apart from that a plaintiff must show some special circumstances which would attract the intervention of a Court of Equity.

6-3 Pressure as Fraud

[6.5] Equity will intervene in transactions brought about by the improper use of a position of advantage under the doctrine of undue influence but other forms of pressure will also be regarded as unconscionable depending upon the circumstances of the case. In *Williams v Bayley* (1866) 1 LR (HL) 200, an agreement by a father to settle debts incurred by his son was held to be unenforceable because the father had been told by the manager of the creditor bank that if he did not enter into the arrangement his son would face criminal prosecution. In *Barton v Armstrong* (1973) 47 ALJR 781, an agreement under which one director and major shareholder in a company was bought out by another was set aside. The departing member had made serious threats, including death threats to the other director to pressure him into the agreement. The Privy Council held that it did not matter that the agreement might have been entered into if the threats had not been made provided that they were a 'reason' for the decision to enter into it. In life, and particularly in commerce, various pressures are applied to achieve commercial goals all the time. Even though that pressure may be irresistible it is not unlawful, nor will it constitute equitable fraud. It is only when the pressure is in some way illegitimate or constitutes taking some improper advantage that relief can be obtained on these grounds.

[6.6] Where a party's consent is obtained to some transaction or dealing by exercise of pressure which the law regards as illegitimate the consent will be treated in law as revocable unless approbated either expressly or by implication after the illegitimate pressure has ceased to operate on the mind of the plaintiff: *Universal Tankships Inc of Monrovia v International Transport Workers Federation* [1983] 1 AC 366 at 384, per Lord Diplock; *Crescendo Management Pty Ltd v Westpac* (1988) 19 NSWLR 40. It is not necessary to show that the pressure or duress exercised amounted to a compulsion of the will of the victim. The fact that the victim chooses to submit to the demand or the pressure rather than take an alternative course of action will not preclude the right to relief. The proper approach is to ask whether any applied pressure induced the victim to enter into the contract and then to ask whether that pressure went beyond what the law would accept as legitimate: *Crescendo Management Pty Ltd v Westpac* (1988) 19 NSWLR 40 at 46, per McHugh JA. In *Hawker Pacific Pty Ltd v Helicopter Charter Pty Ltd*

---

1. Subject, of course, to the statutory power given to the court by s 85 of the Trustee Act 1925 (NSW), and similar legislation in other States, to relieve a trustee who has acted honestly and reasonably and who ought fairly to be excused from any personal liability, either in whole or in part.

(1991) 22 NSWLR 298 at 301–2, Priestly JA, with whom Clark and Handley JJA agreed on this point, accepted that 'compulsion' in this context included every species of duress or analogous conduct whether actual or threatened by or on behalf of the defendant applied to the person or the property or any right of the person under coercion. In *Hawker Pacific*, the court found that there was vitiating duress. The plaintiff was entitled to take its helicopter away from the defendant's premises but was not permitted to do so unless it signed a particular agreement. In the circumstances the defendant knew that the plaintiff had an urgent need for the helicopter and had no practical choice but to sign the agreement. This question was again considered by the Court of Appeal in *Equiticorp Finance Ltd v Bank of NZ* (1993) 32 NSWLR 50.

> Under pressure from BNZ, a creditor of companies in the Equiticorp group, the chairman, chief executive and major shareholder of that group applied the liquidity reserves of three companies within the group towards the discharge of a debt of a wholly owned subsidiary of another company within the group. Equiticorp later sought to set the transaction aside on a number of grounds including that of economic duress or undue pressure. At first instance ((1992) 29 NSWLR 260) Giles J said, at 297:
>
> > ... having reviewed the authorities on the point ... a consistent theme in the cases is that commercial pressure even to the point where the party the subject of the pressure is left with little choice but to act as he did, is not of itself sufficient. Where the conduct of the alleged oppressor is the threat of unlawful action (including ... breach of contract) illegitimacy may be readily found, but where that is not so it must be determined whether as well as finding pressure bringing practical absence of choice, the pressure should be characterised as illegitimate. Even if the adjective "unconscionable" be invoked, that requires close regard to the facts and the making of a judgment as to unconscionability or other reason to categorise the pressure as illegitimate.
>
> Under the relevant loan agreement, dated 21 July 1987, repayment of the debt was not due for a year, that is, 21 July 1988. By a supplementary agreement dated 13 January 1988, BNZ was entitled to repayment in full on 30 June 1988. In the circumstances, Giles J found it was as important to Equiticorp to maintain its credibility in the marketplace by retaining the support of its principal banker as it was to BNZ to recover the money and, accordingly, BNZ's demand for payment prior to 28 July 1988 did not constitute undue pressure. In the Court of Appeal, Kirby P, at 106, and Clark and Cripps JJA, at 149–51, upheld Giles J's analysis of the principles of commercial pressure and their application in this case.

The English Court of Appeal has held that a threat to withdraw credit terms as to obtain payment of a debt which was disputed did not amount to undue pressure: *CTN Cash and Carry Ltd v Gallaher Ltd* [1994] All ER 714.

[6.7] The measure of damages for fraud at common law, or deceit as it is most commonly called, is the loss or expenditure incurred by the plaintiff as a consequence of the inducement less the corresponding advantage in money or money's worth gained by the plaintiff from the transaction. The plaintiff cannot recover the entire price he or she has paid unless the thing proves wholly worthless. If the thing has any appreciable value the damages must be reduced *pro tanto*: *Toteff v Antonas* (1952) 87 CLR 647 at 650–1, per Dixon J; *Gould v Vaggelas* (1985) 157 CLR 215. Chancery, even in cases of actual fraud in which it exercised a concurrent jurisdiction with the common law, provided more elastic remedies. By operating *in personam*, as a court of conscience, it could make orders imposing conditions on the defendant which were not available at common law.[2] Accordingly, a court of equity can grant relief for fraud which is not

---

2. *Nocton v Lord Ashburton* [1914] AC 932 at 951–2.

available at common law. It can award full compensation to the plaintiff on terms, such as that on satisfaction of the judgment, the defendant will succeed to any unrealised benefits which accrued to the plaintiff under the transaction which would or might reduce the plaintiff's loss: *Demetrios v Gikas Dry-cleaning Industries Pty Ltd* (1991) 22 NSWLR 561 at 573. Equity can also declare and enforce rescission where such relief would not have been available at common law: *Munchies Management Pty Ltd v Belperio* (1988) 84 ALR 700 at 607–711; *Demetrios v Gikas, supra,* at 573.

6–4   The Equity to Set Aside a Judgment Obtained by Fraud

[6.8] Where a party to proceedings obtains a judgment, but that judgment is obtained by fraud, an action lies in equity to set aside the judgment wrongfully obtained on the grounds of that fraud: *Jonesco v Beard* [1930] AC 298. This jurisdiction illustrates a point of friction between two broad principles. The first is the public interest in the finality of litigation and the second that the court will not tolerate a miscarriage of justice nor allow its procedures to be used to work a fraud. This jurisdiction is of ancient origin and is based on the fact that the court will not tolerate a miscarriage of justice where fraud is proved: *Hillman v Hillman* [1977] 2 NSWLR 739 at 744. Fraud, as Lord Buckmaster put it in *Jonesco v Beard,* at 301–2, is an 'insidious disease, and if clearly proved to have been used so that it might deceive the court, it spreads and infects the whole body of the judgment'. The issue of fraud in proceedings is not the same as that of the introduction of fresh evidence on an appeal: *McCann v Parsons* (1954) 93 CLR 418 at 425–8.[3] Proceedings of this nature in equity are separate proceedings commenced afresh and are concerned solely with the issue of whether the judgment ought to be set aside on the grounds of the alleged fraud. A similar action lies to set aside orders made by consent where that consent has been obtained by fraud: *Spies v Commonwealth Bank* (1991) 24 NSWLR 691. The party bringing the action on grounds of fraud, as in all actions based on fraud, must give particulars in the pleadings of the fraud and the allegations must be established by the strict proof which such a charge requires: *Jonesco v Beard, supra,* at 301; *McHarg v Woods Radio Pty Ltd* [1948] VLR 496 at 497; *Wentworth v Rogers (No 5)* (1986) 6 NSWLR 534 at 538, per Kirby P.

---

3. See *McDonald v McDonald* (1965) 113 CLR 529 at 533, per Barwick CJ: 'fresh evidence, though it suggests fraud, surprise, or subornation of witnesses must fully satisfy all the criteria laid down with respect to fresh evidence warranting a new trial though it may be, that, in some cases, the tendency of the evidence to show fraud may make it more likely to be conclusive ... But fresh evidence does not satisfy all these requirements so that a new trial could not be ordered on the basis of the discovery of fresh evidence (that is, on appeal,) but does tend to establish the verdict was obtained by fraud or surprise or that there has been subornation of witnesses, the court may grant a new trial upon a motion therefore, though a separate proceeding is clearly the preferable course, if the court itself, on a trial of such issues, finds the fact of the fraud, the surprise or subornation of witnesses, as the case may be to be proved to its reasonable satisfaction'. His Honour went on to say that the question of whether the court would make such an order will depend on the court's view as to whether or not such an order is in the interests of justice, either particularly in relation to the parties or generally in relation to the administration of justice. The normal test for the grant of a new trial on the basis of fresh evidence is that stated by the High Court in *Greater Wollongong City Council v Cowan* (1959) 93 CLR 435 at 444, that is, it must be reasonably clear that if the evidence had been available at the first trial and had been adduced an opposite result would have been produced. Any evidence so present must be 'fresh' in the sense that it could not have been presented at the original proceedings.

In order to set a judgment aside on these grounds the party seeking relief must show that the facts on which the claim is based are newly discovered facts; that the facts are material such as to make it reasonably probable that the claim will succeed; that they go beyond mere allegations of perjury on the part of witnesses at the trial, and that the opposing party who took advantage of the judgment is shown, by evidence, to have been responsible for the fraud in such a way as to render it inequitable that that party should retain the benefit of the judgment: *Wentworth v Rogers (No 5)*, *supra*. Mere suspicion of fraud, raised by fresh facts later discovered, will not be sufficient to secure relief: *Birch v Birch* [1902] P 130 at 136, 139; *McHarg v Woods Radio Pty Ltd*, *supra*, at 498; *Ronald v Harper* [1913] VLR 311 at 318. Proof of perjury alone will not normally suffice to provide relief under this doctrine, although in exceptional cases it may be enough to establish fraud: *Cabassi v Vila* (1940) 64 CLR 130 at 147–8; *Wentworth v Rogers (No 5)*, *supra*, at 539. In *Australasian Meat Industry Employees' Union v Mudginberri Station Pty Ltd* (1986) 12 FCR 14 at 19, Morling J distinguished *Jonesco v Beard* and *Hip Foong Hong v H Neotia & Co* [1918] AC 888, saying *Jonesco* like *Hip Foong Hong*, was a case in which the fraud, if established, would have effected the credibility of the whole of the successful party's case. In *AMEIU v Mudginberri*, the alleged fraud related to the evidence of one witness. Rejection of that evidence, in Morling J's view, would not cause any change to be made in the orders made in the (original) injunction proceedings. The desirability of there being an end to litigation gave rise to powerful considerations of public policy against setting aside orders made in contested litigation where such orders would have been made in any event because of other uncontradicted evidence which supported the making of those orders.

[6.9] It is not clear from these authorities that the fraud which must be proved in order to set a judgment aside is fraud of the common law variety involving conscious dishonesty, in which case it would be invoked in equity's concurrent jurisdiction in such matters, or whether it is sufficient to show conduct which falls within the wider definition of fraud recognised in equity. In *Flower v Lloyd* (1877) 6 Ch Div 297 at 302, James LJ, having stated the principle that such proceedings must be brought by separate action and not by way of rehearing of the original case, by way of illustration said that the positive issue to be tried would concern a party who obtained the judgment or decree by fraud in the sense of bribing a witness, bribing a solicitor or counsel for the other party or committing some fraud or other of that kind. Helsham CJ in Eq in *Hillman v Hillman* cited *Daniell's Chancery Practice*, 5th ed, p 1471:

> ... it is a general rule, that whenever a party, by fraud, accident, or mistake, or otherwise, has obtained an advantage in proceedings in a court of ordinary jurisdiction, which must necessarily make that court an instrument of injustice, a Court of Equity will interfere to prevent a manifest wrong, by restraining the party whose conscience is thus bound, from using the advantage he has there gained.

It is not clear, for instance, whether a failure to comply with the rules of the court as to, for instance, discovery, might constitute fraud in the proceedings. Even though not a matter of 'fraud', such conduct will provide grounds for setting aside a judgment if it can be shown that the proceedings have not been properly conducted: *Commonwealth Bank of Australia v Quade* (1991) 102 ALR 487. In *Quade's* case, the High Court expressed approval of the principles stated by Burchett J in the Full Court of the Federal Court (*Quade v Commonwealth Bank* (1991) 99 ALR 567 at 578), 'that a party should not be permitted to mock the orders of the court, which would surely be mocked if the opponent could be deprived permanently of a fair prospect of success by a party's failure to comply with the obligation so important in the conduct of litigation as an order for discovery'. While the High Court considered it neither practicable nor desirable to state a general rule to be mechanically applied in such cases, it did say that is was not necessary that the court be persuaded in such a case that it is 'almost certain' or 'reasonably clear' that an opposite result would have been produced if proper discovery had been given, only that it must appear that there is at least a real possibility that a different result would have been obtained. *Quade* was not conducted as a case resting on the equity to set aside a judgment obtained by fraud but rather as an appeal on fresh evidence. However, where a party to litigation deliberately conceals documents otherwise discoverable which are material to the case and adverse to that party's case, then an action in fraud on the grounds discussed above could be made out. If no positive proof of an intention to deceive can be shown, but no adequate explanation is forthcoming for the failure to give discovery of relevant material which could not have been overlooked by mere inadvertence, the onus must rest on the party who has failed to give adequate discovery to provide a sufficient explanation. In that latter example the ground for setting aside the initial verdict would be based on the proposition that the prior proceedings had not been conducted properly and that in the interests of justice a new trial should be ordered rather than on the equity to set aside for fraud, although if there is a conscious concealment of documents it could rest on both grounds.

6–5   Mistake

Recovery of money paid under mistake

[6.10] Equity has a jurisdiction to recover moneys paid, or assets transferred, by a fiduciary under some mistake of law or fact, entitling the fiduciary to deduct any such overpayments from subsequent distributions to the beneficiary concerned. There is said to be no general equitable jurisdiction for the recovery of mistaken payments: *Rogers v Ingham* (1876) 3 Ch D 351 at 356. But, in *Chase Manhattan Bank NA v Israel-British Bank (London) Ltd* [1979] 3 All ER 1025, Goulding J, relying on *Sinclair v Brougham* [1914] AC 398, held that receipt of a sum of money paid by mistake gave rise to a fiduciary duty owed by the recipient to the true owner of the money obliging the recipient to respect the continuing proprietary interest of the true owner. Goulding J's reasoning has been criticised for applying a principle found only in cases in which there was a pre-existing fiduciary obligation.[4] *Sinclair v Brougham* is not the most reliable foundation on which to build an argument in view of the dubious logic employed by the House of Lords in that case.[5] Despite those criticisms, the proposition that a recipient of money paid by mistake, once aware of the mistaken payment and of the identity of the true owner of the money, is under a fiduciary obligation to refund the money, or at least hold it for the true owner, seems to be consistent with the general doctrines of equity.

[6.11] At common law, money paid under a mistake could be recovered as money had and received provided the mistake was one of fact, and not of law: *Bilbie v Lumley* (1802) 2 East 469; 102 ER 448. The same limitation applied in equity except where a fiduciary made a payment under a mistake of law. A trustee in bankruptcy, or other officer of the court, who receives a mistaken payment will be obliged to make restitution, even though the mistake might be one of law: *Ex parte James* (1874) LR 9 Ch

---

4. MG&L, para [1402].
5. See [5.19].

609, and a similar obligation now rests upon an officer of a common law court: *Re Carnac* (1885)16 QBD 308, although there is doubt whether this exception extends to solicitors, who are officers of the court, in respect of moneys received by them on their own account or on behalf of clients.[6] The limitation of the right to recover money paid under mistake to mistakes of fact and not law, other than the equitable exceptions, was justified by Lord Ellenborough in *Bilbie v Lumley* by the rule that ignorance of the law is no excuse. This distinction was unfortunate and its rationale dubious. In many cases it is difficult to say whether the mistake is one of law or fact, particularly where it concerns some fact which, if true, establishes liability. Other than payments made in settlement of an honest claim there seems no good reason why payments made under a mistake of law should not be recoverable.[7] This distinction was rejected in Canada by Dickson J in a dissenting judgment in *Electric Commission of Nepean v Ontario Hydro* (1982) 132 DLR (3d) 193 at 201–15, in which he said, at 209:

> Once a doctrine of restitution or unjust enrichment is recognized, the distinction as to mistake of law and mistake of fact becomes simply meaningless.

That view was subsequently adopted by the rest of the Supreme Court of Canada in *Air Canada v British Columbia* (1989) 59 DLR (4th) 161 at 190–4 in which the court held that *Bilbie v Lumley* no longer represented the law in that country. Mistake of law is thus no longer available as a defence to an action for recovery of money paid under mistake in Canada, except in an action for recovery for taxes paid under a mistake by a taxpayer under a mistake as to liability. The authority of *Bilbie v Lumley* has also been rejected in Australia by the High Court:

> In *David Securities Pty Ltd v Commonwealth Bank of Australia* (1992) 109 ALR 57, the appellants had suffered losses through a foreign currency loan transaction arranged for them by the respondent bank. They sought to recover from the bank moneys paid under the loan contract pursuant to a 'grossing-up' clause, whereby the borrower from a foreign sourced lender was required to pay additional amounts to cover withholding tax so that the net amount received by the lender by way of interest was not reduced. At first instance Hill J held that these moneys were paid under a mistake of law, that is, that withholding tax was payable on such moneys and were thus not recoverable. The Full Court of the Federal Court, while noting criticism of the distinction between mistakes of law and fact in such cases, upheld that decision. In the High Court, in a joint judgment, Mason CJ, Deane, Toohey, Gaudron and McHugh JJ, discussed the history of the doctrine of mistake of law, and the academic and judicial criticism of it in recent years, quoting with approval the comment of Dickson J in *Ontario Hydro, supra*. Their Honours then concluded that the rule precluding recovery of moneys paid under a mistake of law should be held not to form part of the law in Australia. The basis for recovery of moneys paid under mistake of law lay, in their view, in unjust enrichment. The unjustness of the enrichment arose not from subjective evaluation of what is fair or unconscionable, but upon the existence of some qualifying or vitiating factor, such as mistake, duress or illegality. In coming to that decision, the majority rejected the propositions that the mistake concerned should be as to the payor's legal liability to make the payment, and that the mistake should be fundamental. Because the right to recover moneys paid under a mistake of law was founded on the unjust enrichment of the defendant they considered it inappropriate to concentrate on the nature of the mistake made by the plaintiff. What was more important was the nature of the enrichment of the defendant and whether the defendant was entitled to retain the moneys paid. Dawson J agreed with the majority on the general principle. He thought that a defence

---

6. MG&L, para [1405].
7. See Goff & Jones, p 119 ff.

of voluntary payment could be maintained where the payment was made, not because of a mistaken belief in the law, but because the contract provided that it should be made. Brennan J agreed with the majority and was prepared to apply the principle to cases involving payments made in satisfaction of an honest claim, so-called 'voluntary' payments, although it is not precisely clear from the majority judgment that such payments would be irrecoverable. All members of the court underlined their acceptance of the defence of change of position, as adopted in *ANZ v Westpac*.

This decision effectively abolishes the distinction between mistake of fact and mistake of law as a basis to found an action for recovery of moneys had and received. It builds on the High Court's development of the principle of unjust enrichment, at least in certain recognised categories, in decisions such as *Pavey and Matthews v Paul* (1987) 69 ALR 577 and *ANZ Banking Group Ltd v Westpac Banking Corporation* (1988) 164 CLR 662. In the latter case, the High Court held that the common law action to recover money paid under a mistake of fact should now be recognised as lying not in implied contract, but in restitution or unjust enrichment.[8] The approach taken by the High Court, at least the view apparently taken by the majority, accords with that of Goff & Jones: that the principle in *Bilbie v Lumley* should only preclude recovery of money paid in settlement of an honest claim. Any other claim for money paid under a mistake of law should be recoverable if it would have been recovered if the mistake had been one of fact.[9] These decisions have changed the focus of a court's inquiry from whether the mistake operating on the payer's mind at the time of the payment was one of law or fact to whether it is unjust in the circumstances for the payee to retain the money, or all of it. A payment to a taxing authority in compromise of some claim would fall under Goff & Jones' suggested exception of compromise of an honest claim where the taxpayer otherwise has access to review processes by way of objection and appeal to challenge a tax assessment. Sauce for the goose in such a case is also sauce for the gander. In *Chamberlain v Deputy Commissioner of Taxation* (1988) 164 CLR 502, the Deputy Commissioner was held bound by a judgment entered by consent against a taxpayer for a sum of $25,000 when the actual tax said to be owing was $255,000. The relevant principle applied by the court was that of *res judicata*, but it is otherwise consistent with the principle proposed by Goff & Jones. It remains to be seen whether Brennan J's view that even money paid in compromise of an honest claim may be recoverable if the compromise is affected or vitiated by mistake will be taken any further. If the emphasis is really on whether it is unjust for the defendant to retain the payment or other benefit, rather than whether the plaintiff made the payment by mistake, it seems logical not to exclude such cases, although the defendant would be unlikely to succeed in most instances. On the other side of the coin, a too generous approach could make the valid receipt of any payment uncertain.

Rectification

[6.12] Equity has a jurisdiction to rectify documents marred by some mistake: see Chapter 26.

---

8.   164 CLR 662 at 673.
9.   Goff & Jones, at 119; *Hydro-Electric Commission of the Township of Nepean v Ontario Hydro* (1982) 132 DLR (3d) 193 at 206–7, per Dickson J, in dissent.

Hardship and specific performance

[6.13] In some circumstances a defendant acting under some mistaken belief will be allowed to raise the hardship he or she would otherwise suffer as a defence to an action of specific performance. This assumes a mistake for which the plaintiff was not responsible. The grounds upon which the court will deny specific performance in such a case are quite narrow. In *Slee v Warke* (1952) 86 CLR 271, the High Court adopted the rule laid down by James LJ in *Tamplin v James* (1879) 15 Ch D 215 at 221 that the hardship must amount to an injustice inflicted upon the defendant if he or she is held to the bargain, and that it is unreasonable to hold him or her to it. Any such decision in favour of a defendant would still leave the plaintiff with rights at common law, or, possibly, to damages in equity under Lord Cairns' Act or equitable compensation: see **[22.10]**

Rescission for mistake in equity

[6.14] Where a contract is vitiated by some mistake, that is to say where one or more of the parties is mistaken as to some fact crucial to the contract, the contract will be held to be void *ab initio* at common law because the parties lacked the necessary intention to make the contract. Obviously there is no room for equitable intervention where a contract is void at common law but there is some authority to support the view that rescission in equity for mistake should be available where the mistake is serious but not sufficient to render the contract void at law. The scope of this doctrine of mistake in equity is a matter of some debate; a debate which is not helped by the uncertain state of the common law. Mistake affecting the validity of contracts at law have traditionally been characterised as unilateral, mutual and common.

[6.15] **Unilateral mistake.** This occurs when one party to a contract is mistaken as to some matter fundamental to the contract, usually the identity of a party, a term of the contract or the nature of the document signed and the other party knows or ought to be aware of that mistake. In such a case there will not be sufficient consensus to create a contract and equity will have no role to play. Where there is a unilateral mistake as to some point which is not sufficiently fundamental to avoid the contract equity may order rectification although only in exceptional cases.[10]

[6.16] **Mutual mistake.** This occurs when the parties are at cross-purposes with each labouring under a misapprehension as to the intentions of the other. For example, A offers to sell his car to B and B accepts thinking that A means his Mercedes when in fact A was referring to his Volvo. In those circumstances despite the apparent lack of any common understanding, the contract is not automatically void at common law. An objective test is applied to determine whether a reasonable person would infer a contract from the facts. In *Goldsborough Mort & Co Ltd v Quinn* (1910) 11 CLR 674, the High Court applied that test in holding that an option granted by the defendant for the sale of land held under crown lease was for a price inclusive of the cost of converting the land to freehold. Generally speaking, unless fraud or misrepresentation can be shown, equity will not intervene to rescind a contract affected by mutual mistake.

> In *Riverlate Properties v Paul* [1975] Ch 133, the parties executed a lease under which the lessor was responsible for the cost of all repairs. The lessor had intended that the lessee should contribute to these expenses and sought rectification, or, in the alternative,

---

10. MG&L, para [2615].

rescission of the lease. The Court of Appeal held that rescission was not available. The defendant had obtained a leasehold interest on certain terms free from any knowledge of the lessor's mistake. Without any other wrongdoing his conscience was clear and there were no grounds for equity to disrupt the transaction. In their Lordships' view rescission would only be available in such a case where it could be shown that the lessee was guilty of some sharp practice. That might be shown, in their view, if the lessee, knowing of the lessor's mistake, was lying low and saying nothing, like the Tar Baby in Uncle Remus.

In *Taylor v Johnson* (1983) 151 CLR 422, a vendor sought rescission of a contract for the sale of two pieces of land, each of about five acres, on the ground that the purchase price stipulated in the contract was $15,000 while she had believed that the price was to be $15,000 per acre. The High Court held in her favour because the purchasers seemed to be aware of her mistaken belief. Mason CJ, Murphy and Deane JJ said, at 432, that rescission for mistake would be available where a party entered into a written contract under a serious mistake about a fundamental term and the other party was aware of circumstances indicating that the first party was entering the contract under some serious mistake or misapprehension and deliberately sought to ensure that the first party did not learn of the mistake.

[6.17] The decision in *Taylor v Johnson* has been criticised for failing to distinguish between misrepresentations for which the defendant is responsible, which may produce a mistaken belief, and other mistakes for which the defendant is not to blame. It is argued that it is appropriate to say that someone cannot, in conscience, hold another to a contract induced by a misrepresentation for which the first is responsible but quite different to say the same where a party tries to hold another to a contract entered into on the strength of some mistaken belief for which the first party was not responsible but which he or she could have discovered.[11] While it might be true to say that the first case outlined above clearly involves equitable fraud it would be wrong to suggest that equity would be indifferent to the second scenario. If one party takes advantage of some mistaken belief held by the other where the first party knew about that mistaken belief and did nothing to correct it a court of equity could find the conduct of the first party unconscionable. Is the conduct of the Tar Baby lying low and saying nothing while knowing that the other party is acting to his or her detriment under some false impression any less unconscionable because the Tar Baby is not responsible for the other's mistake? Perhaps, but the question has to be whether it is unconscionable in the circumstances for one to gain and keep an advantage from the other's mistake. The cause of that mistake will just be one of the factors, admittedly an important one, to be taken into account when answering that question.

[6.18] **Common mistake.** This occurs when both parties are under the same mistaken belief; that is, that the plaintiff's horse which he or she has agreed to sell still exists when, in fact, it has been killed. At common law a common mistake will not render a contract void unless it involves a matter so fundamental to the contract that both parties regard it as a condition precedent to the existence of a binding contract. Under that rule the contract given in the example would be void: a common mistake as to the existence of the subject matter being sufficiently fundamental to void the contract. Similarly, a sale, or lease of property to a person who already owns it will be a nullity: *Bingham v Bingham* (1748) 1 Ves Sen 126; 27 ER 1105. However, a mistake as

---

11. MG&L, para [1410].

to the quality, nature or value of the subject matter of the contract will not be sufficient.

[6.19] A shared, but mistaken belief as to the subject matter of a contract will not automatically render it void at law.

In *Bell v Lever Brothers Limited* [1932] AC 161, the appellant had been appointed managing director of the Nigerian subsidiary of the respondent on a five year contract After three years Bell was made redundant and Lever Brothers agreed to pay him £30,000 for the early termination of his contract. The company later became aware that Bell had committed breaches of duty by trading on his own account and that he would have thus been liable to dismissal without compensation. They sued Bell seeking damages for losses caused by his misconduct and repayment of the £30,000 as money paid under a mistake of fact, that is, that they were obliged to make the payment. The majority of the House of Lords upheld Bell's appeal on the ground that the mistake was not sufficiently fundamental. The company had got what it wanted, a termination of Bell's contract. The fact that they could have got that result by some other means was regarded as immaterial. The mistake was treated as common, because the jury found that Bell's mind was not directed to his acts of misconduct at the time, rather than mutual or unilateral which both appear more appropriate. It was also regarded as a mistake of fact when it could have been considered one of law.

Bell v Lever Brothers left some questions unanswered as to the nature of the mistake required to render a contract void at law and as to the rights of the parties to a contract vitiated by a fundamental mistake of this kind. Those questions were, in part, resolved in Australia in *McRae v Commonwealth Disposals Commission* (1951) 84 CLR 377.

The Commission advertised for tenders for the disposal of a tanker wrecked on a reef. McRae's tender of £285 was accepted and he spent considerably more fitting out a salvage expedition. In fact neither the reef nor the wreck of the tanker existed. McRae sought to recover his expenses, including the cost of the expedition. The Commission argued that the contract had been rendered void by the mistake and that only the tender fee was recoverable. The High Court, per Dixon and Fullagar JJ, held that this was not a case of common mistake as McRae had relied on the Commission's assurance that the tanker existed. Therefore, the contract was still on foot and, as the Commission had contracted that there was a tanker, they were liable for damages for breach. Their Honours also expressed the view that if the contract had been voided by a common mistake, the respondent would have been estopped from relying on that mistake as a defence because the mistake had been induced by the fault of its own servants.

[6.20] A mistake as to the nature, quality or value of the subject matter of the contract will not render it void, as was shown in *Leaf v International Galleries* [1950] 2 KB 86 where the plaintiff purchased a painting titled 'Salisbury Cathedral' which both parties mistakenly believed to be by Constable. The mistake went to the quality of the subject matter and the contract was therefore not voided by the error. Also, because the mistake was not discovered for five years, the right to reject the goods after delivery was lost through lapse of time as was any claim for rescission on the ground of innocent misrepresentation.

[6.21] On those authorities, at least in Australia, the common law appears to deal adequately with common mistake but, in England, apart from some lingering confusion caused by *Bell v Lever Brothers*,[12] there is also a thin strand of authority in favour of the view that a contract subject to a common mistake but not void at law may still be rescinded in equity where the mistake is not in any way the fault of the plaintiff, where it would be unconscionable to allow the defendant to benefit from the mistake and the rights of third parties will not be affected: *Solle v Butcher* [1950] 1 KB 671, per Lord Denning. That decision has been criticised as lacking authoritative foundation, except for the odd case of *Cooper v Phibbs* (1867) LR 2 (HL) 149 in which a man was allowed to have a lease of a fishery set aside, on certain terms. He had taken the lease from his cousin, believing she was the owner of the fishery when, in fact, his uncle, the previous owner, had left it to him.[13]

[6.22] The extent and indeed the very existence, of any separate doctrine of rescission for common mistake in equity is a matter of some doubt. *Cooper v Phibbs* is authority for saying that some such rule exists, but does little to reveal the content of that rule and its distinction, if any, from the common law. Some say that an independent doctrine of mistake in equity is desirable because it would allow rescission for mistakes not sufficiently fundamental to render a contract void at law but still critical enough for the court to consider it against conscience for the bargain to be upheld.[14] The court would also have the flexibility to impose conditions on any relief granted, as it did in *Grist v Bailey* [1967] Ch 532 in which a house was sold, 'subject to the existing tenancy', which both parties mistakenly thought was a protected tenancy. The contract was thus not void at law, but Goff J held that it could be set aside in equity on terms that the vendor entered into a fresh contract at a proper vacant possession price. Others would deny any general equitable jurisdiction in this area, restricting the operation of equity to intervention after a conveyance of land in which there has been a total, or practically total, failure of consideration as in *Svanosio v McNamara* (1956) 96 CLR 186, or to compromises where there has been a common error as to the substance of the claim concerned and, otherwise, in its auxiliary role, where a contract is ineffective at law, to decree consequential relief such as delivery up and cancellation of documents.[15]

[6.23] These two views represent the present divergence in the law on this question between England and Australia; the Australian view being that there could be no right of rescission for mistake without evidence of equitable fraud by the party seeking to maintain the contract.[16] Where both parties are genuinely mistaken, pre-existing fraud will be difficult to prove unless some constructive fraud can be established, as it was in *Taylor v Johnson*. That would still leave cases like *Grist v Bailey* out in the cold. The risk of a too liberal interpretation is that the claim of mistake could be fraudulently raised by a party who has some other reason to be unhappy with the bargain. Any need for resolution of these questions has been overtaken by developments in the law of estoppel in equity and by the growing statutory jurisdiction in misleading and deceptive conduct. A party who acts to his or her detriment under some mistaken assumption is much more likely to obtain relief under the law of estoppel these days than under the technical and complex law of mistake. A case like *McRae v Com-*

---

12. MG&L, para [1410]
13. See also *Magee v Pennine Insurance Co Ltd* [1969] 2 QB 507; *Associated Japanese Pank (International) Ltd v Credit Che Nord SA* [1988] 3 All ER 902; MG&L, paras [1412]–[1416].
14. MG&L, paras [1420]–[1424].
15. Goff & Jones, pp 183–90.
16. MG&L, para [1426].

monwealth Disposals Commission would be more likely to be dealt with under the law of misleading and deceptive conduct although a case could also be made out on those facts on estoppel in support of a claim for equitable compensation.

6-6 Misrepresentation

[6.24] At common law, until the emergence of the doctrine of negligent misstatement, misrepresentation was only a ground for relief where the misrepresentation had been made fraudulently, that is, with conscious dishonesty. Equity, on the other hand, traditionally granted rescission of a contract where one party had been induced to enter into it by a representation made by the other and the representation proved to be false, even though made innocently. Equity regarded it as against conscience for one person to hold another to a bargain induced by a falsehood for which the first party was responsible.

> In *Redgrave v Hurd* (1881) 20 Ch D 1, a solicitor's practice was advertised for sale. The sale included the solicitor's residence. The vendor made an oral representation that the practice brought in £300 per year and showed the purchaser papers which indicated receipts of not quite £200 per year. No reference to the income of the practice was included in the contract. The business was, in fact, worthless and the purchaser refused to complete. The vendor sought specific performance to which the purchaser replied with a claim for rescission and damages for his expenses. Sir George Jessel MR refused damages as knowledge of the falsity had not been pleaded but granted rescission as, in equity, a man is not be allowed to benefit from a statement which he now admits to be false nor can the author of the falsehood say in his defence that the other party could have discovered the truth if he had used due diligence.

[6.25] It is not sufficient to simply show that some misrepresentation was made in negotiations leading up to the contract. The party seeking rescission must show that he or she was influenced by the misrepresentation and that it was one of the reasons, even though it need not be the major cause, for entry into the contract. That rule applies even though the plaintiff has exercised his or her own judgement: *Sagar v Closer Settlement Ltd* (1929) 29 SR (NSW) 199. Inducement may be inferred from entry into the contract: *Simons v Zartom Investments Pty Ltd* [1975] 2 NSWLR 30; and may be found even though the purchaser carried out his or her own inspection of the property, provided it can shown that the misrepresentation disturbed the purchaser's mind and acted as an inducement to enter into the contract: *Wilcher v Steain* [1962] NSWR 1136. If the purchaser had already decided to act before the representation was made, rescission would still be available provided that it has the effect of inducing the purchaser to continue with the decision: *Australian Steel and Mining Corp Pty Ltd v Corben* [1974] 2 NSWLR 202. Where the representation is ambiguous the purchaser will have to show that he or she interpreted it in the sense that was false: *Smith v Chadwick* (1884) 9 App Cas 187.

[6.26] There is some authority for the view that rescission was only available in equity for misrepresentations so serious as to suggest a complete difference in the subject matter of the contract: *Kennedy v Panama Royal Mail Co* (1867) LR 2 QB 580; *Hynes v Byrne* (1899) 9 QLJ 154; *Watt v Westhoven* [1933] VLR 458; and *Seddon v NE Salt Co Ltd* [1905] 1 Ch 326. This proposition has been strongly challenged as contrary to the fundamental principle underlying this doctrine in equity.[17] The idea of total fail-

---

17. MG&L, para [1307].

ure of consideration is a common law notion going to reality of consent on the part of the purchaser — who simply did not get what he or she paid for. Equity is not concerned with the reality of the plaintiff's consent but with the conscience of the defendant, the party responsible for the misrepresentation: *Wilson v Brisbane City Council* [1931] St R Qd 360. The latter view was accepted in New South Wales in *Simons v Zartom Investments Pty Ltd* [1975] 2 NSWLR 30.

Misrepresentation and contracts for the sale of goods

[6.27] In New Zealand and Victoria contracts for the sale of goods have been held to fall outside the general rule allowing rescission for innocent misrepresentation: *Riddiford v Warren* (1901) 20 NZLR 572; *Watt v Westhoven* [1933] VLR 458. There were two grounds for this. It was said that equity did not interfere in contracts for the sale of goods, which was only true in part. Equity would not normally award specific performance of a contract for the sale of chattels as damages would be an adequate remedy. But that was not the case where the contract was for the sale of some rare or unique chattel, or where damages would otherwise be inadequate: *Aristoc Industries Pty Ltd v RA Wenham (Builders) Pty Ltd* [1965] NSWR 581 at 588, per Jacobs J. The second ground held that the counterpart to s 4(2) of the Sale of Goods Act 1923 (NSW), which preserves 'rules of the common law, except where they are inconsistent with the Act' excluded the rules of equity except for the provision made for equitable remedies in s 56. That view has since been rejected, at least in South Australia and New South Wales: *Graham v Freer* (1980) 35 SASR 424 and *Leason Pty Ltd v Princes Farm Pty Ltd* [1983] 2 NSWLR 381. In *Graham v Freer* and *Leason*, s 4(2)[18] was held to include the principles of equity within the expression 'the rules of the common law'. In *Leason*, rescission was even allowed after the contract had been executed. Wood J has since refused to follow *Leason* in *Vimig Pty Ltd v Contract Tooling Pty Ltd* (1987) 9 NSWLR 731 and the jurisdiction of equity to rescind a contract for sale of goods on these grounds must be considered somewhat unsettled in New South Wales at present.

Representations and contractual terms

[6.28] It has been held in England that rescission will not be available where the misrepresentation has been made a term of the contract, because the wronged party would be entitled to relief at common law for breach: *Pennsylvania Shipping Co v Compagnie Nationale de Navigation* [1936] 2 All ER 1167. But that view has been rejected in New South Wales: *Kramer v McMahon* [1970] 1 NSWR 194; and in Victoria: *Academy of Health and Fitness Pty Ltd v Power* [1973] VR 254. This distinction between misrepresentations which become warranties in a contract and others which become conditions has been criticised as lacking in foundation as it assumes that the common law right to treat a breach of a contractual condition as a repudiation is equivalent to the equitable right of rescission whereas they are different things — the one discharging a party from the obligation to perform any further, and entitling that party to damages for the breach at the same time, while rescission seeks to restore the parties to their original positions.[19]

---

18. Sale of Goods Act 1895 [1972] (SA), s 59(2).
19. MG&L, para [1315]–[1317].

Rescission of a completed contract

[6.29] Rescission on the ground of innocent misrepresentation is not available where a contract has been completed by conveyance.

> In *Seddon v NE Salt Co Ltd* [1905] 1 Ch 326, rescission of a contract to purchase shares was refused. The net trading loss of the company had been stated to be much less than it actually was. Fraud was not alleged. Joyce J thought there was no misrepresentation and that the representation as to losses had not induced the plaintiff to enter into the contract. In doing so he said that while equity would not compel a person to complete an executory contract affected by misrepresentation, it would only set aside an executed contract in cases of actual fraud.

[6.30] There is no sound reason for this distinction, although equity may refuse to assist a purchaser who delays unduly in seeking to set a transaction aside. Equity may also decline to exercise this jurisdiction where the misrepresentation was made innocently and the vendor has changed his or her position after completion of the contract but before receiving notice of any claim by the purchaser. The view expressed by Joyce J has been the subject of considerable criticism,[20] and has not been followed in cases involving allotments of shares: *Grogan v 'The Astor' Ltd* (1925) 25 SR (NSW) 409; entry into a partnership: *Senanayake v Cheng* [1966] AC 63; and the bailment of goods under a hire purchase agreement: *Mihaljevic v Eiffel Tower Motors Pty Ltd* [1973] VR 545. It was applied, however, by the High Court in *Svanosio v McNamara* (1956) 96 CLR 186 in a case involving a conveyance of land. Dixon CJ and Fullagar J held that a conveyance of land would only be set aside where there had been fraud or something amounting to a total failure of consideration. It is unlikely that rescission for innocent misrepresentation would be available after registration under Torrens system title but the story might be different prior to registration, or at least completion in view of the operation of s 43A of the Real Property Act 1900 (NSW) and its equivalents.

Misrepresentation legislation

[6.31] The Trade Practices Act 1974 (Cth), s 52 prohibits misleading or deceptive conduct by corporations during the course of their business and provides relief in the form of injunctions under s 80 and damages under s 82 where the standard set by s 52 is breached. The right to recover damages includes cases of loss arising from an innocent misrepresentation which has induced a party to enter into a contract, even though that misrepresentation has not become a term of the contract: *Brown v Jam Factory Pty Ltd* (1981) 35 ALR 79; *Mister Figgins Pty Ltd v Centrepoint Freehold Pty Ltd* (1981) 36 ALR 23. The damages recoverable are those actually lost and not merely those reasonably in the contemplation of the parties: *Yorke v Ross Lucas Pty Ltd* (1982) 45 ALR 299. Section 87 also gives the court a much wider power to set aside or vary a contract induced by a representation in breach of s 52 than that possessed by a court of equity in rescinding a contract, although the section is predicated on the concept of the loss or damage suffered by one party, which is not a necessary element in the purely equitable claim. Similar and complementary fair trading legislation has also been enacted by most States.

---

20. See Fair Trading Act 1987 (NSW), s 42; Fair Trading Act 1989 (Qld), s 38; Fair Trading Act 1987 (SA), s 56; Fair Trading Act 1985 (Vic), s 11; Fair Trading Act 1987 (WA), s 10.

[6.32] The Contracts Review Act 1980 (NSW), s 9 empowers the court to take into account a wide range of matters when considering whether a contract is unjust. Misrepresentation is not specifically listed but could be relevant in such matters as the extent to which the contract was capable of being understood by any of the parties and the advice or explanation given as to its terms. If a contract is found to be unjust in the circumstances, the court has wide powers to provide appropriate relief, including setting the contract aside or varying it. This Act is, however, restricted to contracts not entered into in the course of trade, business or commerce, unlike those covered by s 52 of the Trade Practices Act (see **[6.46]–[6.51]**).

[6.33] The Misrepresentation Act 1971–72 (SA), s 6 allows rescission for misrepresentation even though the misrepresentation has become a term of the contract, and despite the completion of the contract by performance, conveyance or the registration of any transfer pursuant to the completion of the contract. That right can be barred by the intervention of the rights of some innocent third party. Section 7(1) creates a right to receive damages where damages would have been recoverable had the misrepresentation been made fraudulently. Section 7(2) makes it a defence to a claim under s 7(1) that the defendant had reasonable grounds to believe that the representation was true or could not have reasonably been expected to know that the representation was untrue. Section 7(3) gives the court power to award damages in lieu of rescission in any case in which a party has established a right to the latter remedy.

6–7 Undue Influence

[6.34] Where one person is in a position of influence over another, equity will presume that any transfer from the subordinate to the dominant party has been brought about by the exercise of undue influence by the latter and will strike the transaction down unless the dominant party can show that it was a product of the free and independent will of the other. This doctrine rests on two bases: the first, which is peculiar to undue influence, is that equity seeks to prevent relationships which give rise to influence from being abused as a matter of public policy; the second, which is common to other doctrines dealt with in this chapter, is that no person should be allowed to retain a profit arising from his or her own fraud. In *Allcard v Skinner* (1887) 36 Ch D 145, Cotton LJ attributed these two principles to the two different types of cases which arise in this area. The first involved cases where the relationship between the donor and donee was sufficient to raise a presumption that the donee possessed influence over the donor and the second occurred where the court was satisfied that the gift resulted from influence expressly used by the donee for the purpose. The doctrine of undue influence is thus an example of a particular application of the equitable concept of fraud. Historically it also provided some relief from the inadequacies of the common law principle of duress under which a contract could only be avoided if it was induced by some physical threat to the person of the plaintiff. While the exercise of influence held by the stronger party in some relationship giving rise to influence can be characterised as unconscionable conduct, and there is a close relation between the equitable principles relating to undue influence and those relating to unconscionable dealing generally, the two doctrines are distinct as Deane J put it in *Commercial Bank of Australia Ltd v Amadio* (1983) 151 CLR 447 at 474:

Undue influence, (like) common law duress, looks to the quality of the consent or assent of the weaker party (see *Union Bank of Australia Ltd v Whitelore* [1906] VLR 711 at 720; *Watkins v Coombes* (1922) 30 CLR 180 at 193–4; *Morrison v Coast Finance Ltd* (1965) 55 DLR (2d) 710 at 713). Unconscionable dealing looks to the conduct of the stronger party in attempting to enforce, or retain the benefit of, a dealing with a person under a special disability in circumstances where it is not consistent with equity or good conscience that he should do so.

As Mason J put it in the same case, at 461, having noted the resemblance between unconscionable conduct and the doctrine of undue influence:

> ... there is a difference between the two. In the latter [undue influence] the will of the innocent party is not independent and voluntary because it is overborne. In the former the will of the innocent party, even if independent, and voluntary, is the result of the disadvantageous position in which he is placed and of the other party unconscientiously taking advantage of that position.

Presumptive relationships

[6.35] In some relationships equity presumes that one party has influence over the other. In such a case the onus is cast upon the dominant party to justify the dealing in question. In other cases influence must first be proved by the party seeking to set the transaction aside. The relationships in which influence is presumed include:

- *Parent over child* — this applies to anyone in a position of parental authority over another and thus includes guardians. Parental influence is presumed to continue until the emancipation of the child which is not presumed from the attainment of any age, nor from evidence of independence and capability on the part of the child if the child remains obedient to the parent's wishes: *West v Public Trustee* [1942] SASR 109. The onus of establishing emancipation rests on the parent: *Lamotte v Lamotte* (1942) 42 SR (NSW) 99 at 102–3, per Roper J.

  In *Bullock v Lloyds Bank Ltd* [1955] 1 Ch 317, in June 1940, shortly after turning 21, the plaintiff executed a settlement of moneys she had inherited in favour of herself for life with interests in remainder in favour of her father and brother. She received no advice other than that of her father and his solicitor. Nine years later she questioned the deed. It was held that it should be set aside. In doing so the court found that the father had not acted dishonestly but that such a settlement could only be justified if executed under the advice of a competent adviser capable of surveying the whole field who explains to the person making the settlement that she can do exactly as she pleases, including not make the gift. Undue influence was said to arise not only where a person exerted influence to secure a benefit but also where a person of imperfect judgement was placed under the direction of someone possessing greater experience and such a force was inherent in the parent/child relationship.

- *Solicitor and client* — this is not as simple as it seems because the relationship of solicitor and client is not necessarily permanent and will often relate to only one or two matters. It is also a commercial relationship in which the solicitor can expect to receive some financial reward. The relationship of solicitor and client need not be continuous over a period and it may exist even though the client uses another solicitor for other business at that or some other time. Courts will usually scrutinise dealings between solicitor and client closely as there must be entire good faith between the two: *Haywood v Roadknight* [1927] VLR 512.

- *Trustee and beneficiary* — this is always included in any list of presumptive relationships although the presumption is inappropriate in cases where there is no personal relationship between trustee and beneficiary. Where the trustee is one of the major trustee companies, for example, it is unlikely that any personal relationship of influence could be said to exist. Nevertheless, the public policy basis of this doctrine is enough to place the onus on any trustee to justify the propriety of dealings with its beneficiaries and the weight of authority supports the application of the presumption once the relationship of trustee and beneficiary is shown. That does not mean, however, that dealings between trustees and beneficiaries cannot be allowed to stand where they can be shown to have resulted from the exercise of a free and independent will on the part of the beneficiaries: *Whereat v Duff* [1972] 2 NSWLR 147 (CA); (1973) 1 ALR 363 (HC).

- *Man and fiancée* — the presumption does not arise in transactions between husband and wife, largely because that relationship is one in which gifts from one to the other, even of quite substantial pieces of property, are not uncommon: *European Asian Bank of Australia Ltd v Kurland* (1985) 8 NSWLR 192; *Midland Bank v Shepherd* [1988] 3 All ER 17. That does not mean, however, that in particular circumstances, a relationship of control and dominance could not exist giving rise to a presumption of influence by a husband over his wife: *Farmers Co-operative Executors & Trustees Ltd v Perks* (1989) 52 SASR 399. However, the presumption has been held to apply to transactions between couples engaged to be married, at least in respect of gifts from the woman to the man: *Lovesy v Smith* (1879) 15 Ch D 655; *Yerkey v Jones* (1940) 63 CLR 649. In more recent times the ready assumption of such influence has been challenged: *Zamet v Hyman* [1961] 3 All ER 933. While a relationship of husband and wife is not one of influence and there will be no presumption in equity against a transaction in which a wife voluntarily confers a benefit upon her husband, there is, under the principle in *Yerkey v Jones*, a limited principle allowing a wife to claim relief against influence supposedly exerted by her husband. Under that principle if a husband causes his wife to become a guarantor for his debt in circumstances in which, assuming the husband and the wife were the only parties to the transaction, the wife would be able to set aside the transaction as against the husband, the guarantee will be voidable as against the creditor if it could be shown that the creditor relied on the husband to obtain the guarantee from his wife and had no independent grounds for reasonably believing that she fully comprehended the transaction and freely entered into it. While the principle in *Yerkey v Jones* is redolent of an earlier age in which women were regarded as weaker vessels it has been regularly applied in Australian jurisdictions.[21] One exception is now found in New South Wales where the Court of Appeal has held that the presumption no longer applies to the wives in that State: *Teachers Health Investments Pty Ltd v Wynne* (CA(NSW), 16 July 1996, unreported). The notion of any special equity available to wives has been rejected by the House

---

21. In *ANZ Banking Group Ltd v Dunosa Pty Ltd* (SC(Vic), Hassen J, No 4319/92, 22 June 1994, unreported), although *Yerkey v Jones* was distinguished as it was found that the wife freely and voluntarily signed all documents when required. In *ANZ Banking Group Ltd v McGee* (SC (Tas), Cox J, No A53/1994, 7 July 1994, unreported), *Yerkey v Jones* was distinguished on the ground that the wife was shown to have a beneficial interest in the debt and thus have signed the document as principal not only as surety. In *Challenge Bank Ltd v Walters* (SC(WA), Master Ng, No 2525/94, unreported), the wife was found to have waived her right to challenge the security on the ground that she had affirmed the terms of the mortgage in subsequent Family Court proceedings and was thus precluded from raising any equitable defence.

of Lords in *Barclays Bank plc v O'Brien* [1993] 4 All ER 417 at 428. In the process, their Lordships declined to follow the reasoning in *Yerkey v Jones*. In their view there is no need for the use of a special equity in these types of cases. A wife who has been induced to stand as a guarantor for her husband's debts by his undue influence, misrepresentation or some other legal wrong has an equity as against him to set aside that transaction under the ordinary principles of equity. Lord Browne-Wilkinson expressed the view, at 428, that a creditor would be put on inquiry when a wife offers to guarantee her husband's debts by the combination of two factors: (a) the transaction not being to the financial advantage of the wife; and (b) there being a substantial risk in transactions of that kind, that, in procuring the wife to act the husband has committed a legal or equitable wrong that entitles the wife to set aside the transaction. In *Barclays Bank v O'Brien*, the House of Lords found that the bank was under an obligation to warn the wife that she and the matrimonial home were potentially liable for the debts of the company or to recommend that she take legal advice, and that the bank was thereby fixed with constructive notice of the wrongful misrepresentation made by the husband to the wife and she was entitled as against the bank to set aside the legal charge on the matrimonial home securing the husband's liability to the bank. Accordingly, while the principle in *Yerkey v Jones* has been rejected in England, the result, in practical terms, is a regime not markedly different in substance from that prevailing in most States in Australia.

- *Doctor and patient* — this really means the influence of attendants of the sick over those in their care. In *Haskew v Equity Trustees* [1918] VLR 571, it was applied to upset documents executed by a father in favour of a daughter who was looking after him. The father had been so weak that he was completely in the daughter's control.

- *Spiritual advisor and flock* — this is not restricted to ordained ministers of established religions, and seems more likely to apply to fringe faiths. In *Morley v Loughnan* [1893] 1 Ch 736, the presumption was applied in a case in which an epileptic with a large fortune had placed moneys at the disposal of a member of a religious sect who had become his travelling companion. While often listed as one of the presumptive categories this could almost be described as falling outside that list as some evidence would need to be led in advance to establish the relationship.

[6.36] The categories of relationships in which influence will be presumed cannot be considered closed. The growing reliance upon professional advisors in an increasingly complex world offers room for growth. In *Brusewitz v Brown* [1923] NZLR 1106, the presumption was applied in a case in which a man in his sixties suffering from chronic alcoholism transferred his only asset, a mortgage worth £1000, to a regular companion, in return for an annuity of £108 pa, which would have been adequate only if the drunkard had enjoyed a normal expectation of life. Salmond J held that the presumption that the transaction had been procured by the undue influence of the grantee was not restricted to the established categories and that the question in every case was whether the parties had contracted at arm's length and on terms of equality, or, whether there was a relationship of superiority on one side and inferiority on the other containing the opportunity and the temptation for the unconscientious abuse of the power and influence possessed by the superior party sufficient to justify the legal presumption that the transaction was procured in that way.

Non-presumptive relationships

[6.37] In these cases the burden of proof rests on the complaining party at the outset to show the existence of the influence said to have procured the transaction. In *Watkins v Coombes* (1922) 30 CLR 180, a 69 year old woman transferred property to two 'friends' upon whom she had come to rely in return for the promise that they would 'look after her' was able to set the transaction aside. While she was competent to transact business, her mind was completely under the dominion of the defendants during the last years of her life when she was living with them. The defendants had failed to prove that she had been removed from their influence at the time of the transaction or that she had independent advice on the matter.

In *Johnson v Buttress* (1936) 56 CLR 113, a 67 year old man, who was illiterate, of low intelligence, lacking in business experience and habitually reliant on others for advice and assistance, transferred to a relative of his late wife the land on which his house stood shortly after his wife's death. He did not have any independent advice but was known to be appreciative of the kindness shown to him from time to time by the donee. The transfer was signed in the office of the solicitor for the donee. At the suit of the donor's son the High Court set the transfer aside as having been made under the undue influence of the donee. Dixon J, at 134–6, said that the power to practise unconscientious domination over another may arise from an antecedent relationship, or from a particular situation, or in the deliberate contrivance of the party. If one of the latter two, then facts must be proved which show the transaction was the outcome of such an actual influence over the mind of the alienor that it cannot be considered his free act. Where the parties stand in some antecedent relationship, the party in the position of influence cannot maintain beneficial title to property of substantial value made over to him by the other as a gift, unless he satisfies the court that he took no advantage of the donor and that the gift was the independent and well-understood act of a man in a position to exercise free judgement. The doctrine is confined to no fixed category. It applies whenever one party occupies or assumes towards another a position naturally involving an ascendancy or influence over that other, or a dependence or trust on his part.

In *Louth v Diprose* (1992) 175 CLR 621, a man who had purchased a house in the name of and for a woman with whom he was infatuated was able to set aside the transaction and have the house transferred into his name. The man was found to be under a special disability in dealing with the woman. That special disability arose not merely from his infatuation with her. It extended to his 'extraordinary vulnerability in the false atmosphere of crisis' which she was found to have manufactured in which he believed that she was facing eviction from her home and was contemplating suicide unless he provided the money for the purchase of the house in her name. She was aware of that special disability and had manipulated it to her advantage to influence him to make a gift of the money to purchase the house. The transaction was plainly improvident in view of the man's resources and the size and nature of the gift involved. Deane J, with whose reasons Dawson, Gaudron and McHugh JJ agreed, said, at 637, that the adverse circumstances which may constitute a special disability for the purposes of the principle relating to relief against unconscionable dealing may take a wide variety of forms and are not susceptible of being comprehensively catalogued.

Rebutting the presumption

[6.38] In any transaction impeached under this doctrine there are a number of matters on which a defence can be raised to show that the dealing was proper in the circumstances.

- *Adequacy of consideration* — if it can be shown that the transaction was a sale at full value then, generally, no further proof will be required of the propriety of the transfer. In *Watkins v Coombes*, Isaacs J was of the view that such a transaction could still be set aside if the exercise of undue influence can be shown, a view supported by Deane J in *Commercial Bank of Australia v Amadio* (1983) 151 CLR 447 at 475 (see **[6.40]**). In *Wright v Carter* [1903] 1 Ch 27, Vaughan Williams LJ, when expressing the view that independent advice was not always necessary, said, 'it may be that a particular transaction appears to be so manifestly fair that independent advice is not necessary. By contrast gifts are more closely scrutinised to see whether the donor's intention was freely formed'. Adequacy of consideration will not suffice, it is submitted, where the transaction is otherwise improvident, as in the case where a person deprives himself of his only home, or where the value is superficial, as was the case in *Brusewitz v Brown*.

- *Independent advice* — there is no rule of law that where a relationship of influence exists the donor should have independent advice at the time of making the gift in order to rebut the presumption: *Union Fidelity v Trustee Co of Australia Ltd v Gibson* [1971] VR 573 at 577; but, obviously, if a person has been properly advised by someone independent of the grantee and adequately qualified to give the necessary advice then the dealing will be difficult to impeach. While there is no rule requiring independent advice, its presence or absence will be an important factor. The mere fact that independent advice has been given will not, of itself, decide the issue. The nature and quality of that advice can be the crucial matter.

In *Inche Noria v Shaik Allie Bin Omar* [1929] AC 127, a Malay woman, who was of great age and quite illiterate, executed a deed of gift transferring land in Singapore to her nephew, who had the management of all her affairs. She received advice from an independent solicitor before executing the deed. He acted in good faith but was unaware that the property in the gift was practically the whole of the woman's property and did not advise her of other measures by which she could have benefitted the nephew, such as leaving the property to him in her will. The Privy Council, led by Lord Hailsham LC, found that this was not sufficient to rebut the presumption of influence. In doing so they rejected the argument that independent legal advice was the only way in which the presumption could be rebutted. The presumption required the donee to prove that the gift was the result of a free exercise of independent will on the part of the donor. The best way of doing that was to show that the transaction had been previously explained to the donor by some independent and qualified person so completely as to satisfy the court that the donor was acting independently of any influence from the donee and with the full appreciation of what he was doing.

In *Bester v Perpetual Trustee Co Ltd* [1970] 3 NSWR 30, the plaintiff inherited half her late father's estate and, upon her coming of age in 1949, she was advised by her uncle, by the defendant company, which was administering the estate, through its trustee officer, and by a solicitor married to one of her aunts, to make a settlement of her fortune. Arrangements were made for her to see an independent solicitor who read the deed to her and then asked whether she had any questions. She said, 'No'. He then asked if she realised that she would not have access to the capital during her lifetime and she said she did. He gave her no advice on the desirability of the settlement generally nor on the possibility of including a power of revocation in the deed. In 1969 she challenged the settlement on the ground that she had been subjected to undue influence. Street J held that the relationship between the plaintiff and her uncles and the officer of the trustee company was sufficient to show the existence of influence. He also found that the settlement was improvident, as the girl had placed her property beyond recall. He also found that the advice given was inadequate to make available to the plaintiff informed and comprehensive advice of the various alternatives open to her in deciding the form in which she wished to cast her affairs, including the option that she was under no obligation to make any settlement at all. While, to an informed and intelligent listener, advice confined to explaining the deed would enable an intelligent choice to be made, that conclusion could not be drawn in a case such as this where the plaintiff had no business or financial experience.

Undue influence in the execution of a will

[6.39] Undue influence in the execution of a will is quite different from undue influence in transactions *inter vivos*. While in the case of gifts *inter vivos*, influence will be presumed in transactions between parties to certain relationships, no such presumption applies to gifts made by will: *Winter v Crichton* (1991) 23 NSWLR 116 at 121. The deceased cannot take it with him, or herself. Anyone asserting undue influence in the execution of a will carries the onus of proving that a will, apparently regularly executed, was procured by the exercise of undue influence: *Boyse v Rossborough* (1857) 6 HLC 1 at 49; *Parfitt v Lawless* (1872) LR 2 P & D 462 at 469–70; *Craig v Lamoureux* [1920] AC 349 at 356. To unsettle a gift in a will it is necessary to show more than the exercise of influence. The proposition that the testator cannot take it with him, or her, comes into play again. A testamentary gift is unlikely to be found to be improvident from the deceased's point of view. To show undue influence in this context it is necessary to show coercion amounting to pressure on the testator to do something which he or she does not wish or desire to do: *Wingrove v Wingrove* (1885) LR 11 PD 81 at 82–3. Where a person is weak and feeble through age or illness it may not take much pressure to amount to such coercion: *Wingove v Wingrove; Winter v Crichton* (1991) 23 NSWLR 116 at 122. It is also necessary to show more than circumstances from which the inference of an exercise of influence can be drawn. It is not enough to show that a person has the power. The party alleging undue influence must also show that the influence was exercised: *Wingrove v Wingrove, supra,* at 83. It is not enough to show that the circumstances in which the will was executed are consistent with the hypothesis that it was executed under the sway of undue influence. It must be shown that the circumstances are inconsistent with a contrary hypothesis: *Boyse v Rossborough,* above, at 51.

6–8   Unconscionable Bargains

[6.40] Outside the recognised categories listed above there is a broad category in which equity will interfere to set aside a contract where it would be against conscience for the party maintaining the bargain to be allowed to succeed. Equitable intervention to set aside a contract on these grounds may be invoked, 'Whenever one party by reason of some condition or circumstance is placed at a special disadvantage vis-a-vis another and unfair or unconscionable advantage is then taken of the opportunity thereby created'.[22] This jurisdiction does not rest on the unfairness of the con-

---

22. *Commercial Bank of Australia v Amadio* (1983) 151 CLR 447 at 474, per Mason J.

tract itself. It is mainly concerned with the circumstances in which the contract was procured. Inadequacy of consideration and such matters as the relative bargaining power of the parties will obviously be relevant in analysing any transaction, but there must also be conduct which fits the description of 'unconscionable'. Mere inequality of bargaining power will not suffice as proof of special disadvantage, despite Lord Denning's attempt to synthesise the law of unconscionable bargains under that heading in *Lloyds Bank v Bundy* [1975] QB 326 at 339. That overstated simplification has been rejected by both the High Court, in *Commercial Bank of Australia v Amadio*, per Mason J, at 462, and by the House of Lords, in *National Westminster Bank v Morgan* [1985] AC 686 at 708.

[6.41] It is not enough to show merely that one party held some special advantage over the other. The power must, in fact, be exploited by the dominant party. In *Hart v O'Connor* [1985] AC 1001, for example, the Privy Council overruled a decision of the New Zealand Court of Appeal striking down a contract made by a person suffering an intellectual disability as the other party had not been aware of the handicap and had not therefore taken advantage of it. In the absence of direct knowledge of the disadvantage, the test is whether there were such facts known as would raise in the mind of any reasonable person a very real question as to the other party's ability to make a judgement as to what was in his or her own interests.[23] It is the manner in which the bargain is procured, what might be called 'procedural injustice', not its contents, which can be called 'substantive injustice', that attracts equitable intervention, although the disparity in benefits provided by the contract may be so great as to raise a strong inference of procedural unfairness. Adequacy of consideration may be raised as a defence to a claim of unconscionability, but it is not a watertight defence. In *Commercial Bank of Australia v Amadio*, Deane J, with whom Wilson J agreed, said, at 475:

> In most cases where equity courts have granted relief against unconscionable dealing there has been inadequacy of consideration moving from the stronger party. It is not however, essential that that should be so. Notwithstanding that adequate consideration may have moved from the stronger party, a transaction may be unfair, unreasonable and unjust from the viewpoint of the party under the disability. An obvious instance of circumstances in which that may be so is the case where the benefit of the consideration does not move to the party under the disability but moves to some third party involved in the transaction.

Procedural injustice can take on many different forms. In *Wilton v Farnworth* (1948) 76 CLR 646, a Kalgoorlie miner, dull witted, with poor hearing and little education, was persuaded by his stepson to sign away all his interest in the estate of his late wife in favour of the stepson, who had not explained to Farnworth the contents of the documents he was signing, nor their implications. Rich J explained that the decision of the court to set aside the transaction was based on unconscientious dealing, saying, at 655:

> It has always been considered unconscientious to retain the advantage of a voluntary disposition of a large amount of property improvidently made by an alleged donor who did not understand the nature of the transaction and lacked information of material facts such as the nature and extent of the property, particularly if made in favour of a donee possessing greater information who nevertheless withheld the facts.

---

23. *Commercial Bank of Australia v Amadio* (1983) 151 CLR 447 at 462–3, per Mason J and at 474, per Deane J.

Similarly, in *Blomley v Ryan* (1956) 99 CLR 362, a man in his late seventies, lacking in education, and prone to bouts of alcoholism, challenged the enforceability of a contract to sell his grazing property. The contract had been signed the day after a visit to the property by the purchaser and his agent, at a time when the man was engaged in one of his drinking bouts. The visitors brought a bottle of rum with them to the negotiations. The contract price was £25,000, even though the property was really worth over £33,000. The man received no independent advice. McTiernan and Fullagar JJ, with Kitto J dissenting, held that the contract should be set aside. Fullagar J stressed that this was not one of those cases in which a contract could be avoided at common law because a man's mind is so affected by drink, or some natural infirmity, that his mind did not go with his deed. Rather it was one of those cases in which equity looked to the conscience of the party seeking to enforce the bargain. Mere drunkenness afforded no ground for resisting a suit to enforce a contract, but equity would set a contract aside where it was 'disadvantageous' to the party affected and had been obtained by 'drawing him to drink', or by otherwise taking unfair advantage of his condition.

Fullagar J listed some situations giving rise to special disadvantage in which this jurisdiction could be invoked, saying , at 405:

> The matters adversely affecting a party which may induce a court of equity to set aside a transaction include poverty or need of any kind, sickness, age, sex, infirmity of body or mind, drunkenness, illiteracy or lack of education, lack of assistance or explanation where assistance or explanation is necessary. The common characteristic is that they have the effect of placing one party at a disadvantage vis-à-vis the other. It is not essential that a party should suffer loss or detriment by the bargain. But inadequacy of consideration, while never of itself a ground for resisting enforcement, will often be a specially important element in cases of this type.

Kitto J added his own view as to when these rules would apply, at 415:

> ... whenever one party to a transaction is at a special disadvantage in dealing with the other party because of illness, ignorance, inexperience, impaired facilities, financial need or other circumstances which affect his ability to conserve his own interests, and the other party unconscientiously takes advantage of the opportunity thus placed in his hands.

[6.42] Some take the view that this jurisdiction is shrinking as poverty and illiteracy recede.[24] It may be true that those particular problems are not as acute as they once were but, in an increasingly complex and technical society, it would be wrong to assume too readily that circumstances of relative disadvantage will not be recognised by the courts even though the supposedly weaker party possesses some education and is not necessarily poverty stricken. Apart from anything else, the laissez-faire attitudes which characterised equity in the nineteenth century, and even the first half of the twentieth, have been displaced by a greater readiness to intervene in what might otherwise appear to be private arrangements. Statutory expansion of this jurisdiction, at least in the area of consumer transactions, seems sure to keep it in good health (see **[6.47]–[6.52]**). The rule stated by Fullagar J in *Blomley v Ryan* also provides scope for the further judicial development of these principles as was recently shown by the High Court in *Commercial Bank of Australia v Amadio* (1983) 151 CLR 447.

---

24. MG&L, para [1607], although the learned authors now opine that a large immigrant population will help keep it alive. The same authors also refer to this area of the law under the quaint title 'Catching Bargains', which really refers to sales by expectant heirs of their anticipated inheritance. As such people now have access to credit cards, overdrafts, personal loans and other sources of finance, this title does seem a little anachronistic.

Two elderly migrants who had lived in Australia for some time, but whose grasp of English was limited, executed a mortgage in favour of a bank, over land which they owned, to secure an overdraft in favour of a company controlled by their son. The mortgage also contained a personal guarantee. The couple mistakenly believed that their liability was limited to $50,000 when, in fact it was unlimited, and that the mortgage was only for six months, when it was not. The document was signed by the couple in their kitchen in front of a bank officer who had brought the document to them there on the same day that the bank had been told by the son that his parents would give an overdraft. The bank relied on the son's advice that he had explained the transaction to his parents. The mortgage was set aside unconditionally on the ground that the Amadios were in a position of disability in relation to the bank and that their lack of knowledge and understanding of the contents of the mortgage and the circumstances in which the document was signed, particularly the lack of any assistance and advice where assistance and advice were plainly necessary, was sufficient to make it 'unconscientious' of the bank to rely on the guarantee.

Deane J stated the relevant principle, at 474–5:

Unconscionable dealing (unlike undue influence which, like common law duress, looks to the quality of the assent of the weaker party) looks to the conduct of the stronger party in attempting to enforce, or retain the benefit of, a dealing with a person under a special disability in circumstances where it is not consistent with equity or good conscience that he should do so. The adverse circumstances which may constitute a special disability for the purposes of the principles relating to relief against unconscionable dealing may take a wide variety of forms and are not susceptible to being comprehensively catalogued.

Mason J, at 461–3, expressed the principle in these terms:

… 'unconscionable conduct' is usually taken to refer to the class of case in which a party makes unconscientious use of his superior position or bargaining power to the detriment of a party who suffers from some special disability or is placed in some special situation of disadvantage.

Mason J also expressed the view that the situations in which relief will be granted cannot be described definitively and that the situations described by Kitto J and Fullagar J in *Bromley v Ryan* are not exhaustive.

[6.43] Since the decision of the High Court in *Amadio* there has been something of an explosion in cases based on these principles, particularly against banks and other financial institutions seeking to enforce guarantees linked to the debts to many of the small business that have foundered in the sea of recession that swamped Australia in the late 1980s. The cases which have arisen in this swell of litigation have operated as application of the broad principle stated in *Amadio* rather than effecting any change in that principle.

[6.44] There can be no precisely defined limits to the equitable jurisdiction to set transactions aside on the ground of unconscionability. Each case will depend upon its particular facts and the decided authorities can offer little more than general guidelines. In any case in which these questions arise particular attention will be devoted to the circumstances in which any documents were signed and to the events preceding execution. The competency of the claimant in English and his or her capacity to otherwise understand the nature of the transaction will be of great importance. The court will also be concerned about the benefit to be derived from any party entering into these transactions which of necessity means that contracts of guarantee will be scrutinised more closely where the guarantor derives no benefit from the advance or other facility being guaranteed. The information provided by the stronger party to the weaker will also be an important factor. Where the contract is one of guarantee, and the guarantor has no direct involvement with the principal debtor, the information given to the guarantor about the financial position of the principal debtor will obviously bear greatly on any claim that the lender has acted unconscionably towards the guarantor. This doctrine should also be distinguished from undue influence, although there is a strong resemblance. Undue influence is concerned with the dominance of the will of the innocent party by another possessing influence over that party, and thus, like common law duress, is concerned with the reality of the weaker party's consent to the dealing. In unconscionable bargains, the actions of the innocent party may be independent and voluntary, so that there is real consent, but the transaction will be struck down, either in whole or in part depending upon the circumstances, where the dominant party has unconscionably exploited the relative disadvantage of the weaker to obtain that consent. In a relationship in which undue influence can be presumed the onus will rest on the party possessing the influence to show that the transaction was an act of independent free will on the part of the other. If that onus is not discharged it will not be necessary to show, in addition, that there was an inequality of bargaining power or other relative disadvantage. Similarly, in cases dealt with under the general head of unconscionable bargains, it will not be enough merely to show relative disadvantage. It must also be shown that the defendant's superior position was abused; as Mason J put it in *Commercial Bank of Australia v Amadio*, at 463, 'it is necessary for the plaintiff who seeks relief to establish unconscionable conduct, namely that unconscientious advantage has been taken of his disabling condition or circumstances'.

[6.45] Equity's jurisdiction to set aside transactions on the ground of unconscionability is not restricted to what might be described as domestic or consumer credit arrangements. In *Federal Airports Corporation v Makucha Developments Pty Ltd* (1993) 115 ALR 679, Davies J in the Federal Court held that there is a general equitable jurisdiction to relieve against the detriment caused by unconscionable conduct. That case concerned a strip of land owned by the Federal Airports Corporation (FAC) which ran alongside land owned by Makucha. Makucha operated a carpark on its land and access to the carpark was effected by entry across the strip of land owned by the FAC from Qantas Drive, a private road also on land owned by FAC. After disputes over this strip of land an agreement was entered into in March 1993 whereby Makucha was required to give to FAC a performance bond of $50,000 within 14 days of the date of the agreement. At the time the agreement was made, the principal of Makucha was overseas and the agreement was executed by an attorney. On 24 March 1993 FAC served a notice of termination of the agreement on Makucha, relying on the failure to provide the performance bond of $50,000 and the failure of the principal to personally execute the agreement. The agreement was executed by Mr Makucha on 25 March 1993 and the performance bond provided on 26 March 1993. Davies J held that the circumstances were such that it was appropriate for the court to exercise its jurisdiction to relieve against the forfeiture of Makucha's interest in the land affected by the termination of the agreement: the breaches were trivial and were not wilful in the sense of deliberate; there were no adverse consequences for FAC and FAC had not given reasonable notice of this intention to terminate. In the circumstances the loss to Makucha would have been enormous and wholly disproportionate to any injury to FAC. Davies J, however, made it a condition of the relief that Makucha pay FAC's costs of the proceedings and expressed the view that there was now an acceptance of the general principle of equity that a court may relieve against the detriment caused by unconscionable conduct. Davies J referred to *Commercial Bank of Australia Ltd v Amadio* (1983) 151 CLR 447; *Legione v Hatley* (1983) 152 CLR

406; *Ciavarella v Balmer* (1983) 153 CLR 438 and *Waltons Stores (Interstate) Ltd v Maher* (1988) 164 CLR 387. The jurisdiction to relieve against detriment caused by unconscionable conduct arose particularly in the view of Davies J, at 698, when it is associated with fraud, accident, surprise or mistake.

The Contracts Review Act 1980 (NSW)

[6.46] The jurisdiction of equity to intervene in contracts on grounds discussed above has now been supplemented, in New South Wales, by the introduction of this Act. In its preamble it is described as an Act with respect to the judicial review of certain contracts and the grant of relief against harsh, oppressive, unconscionable or unjust contracts. None of that is new. Any court of equity which found a contract to be any of those three things would grant relief to the oppressed party. But the courts have taken a wider view of the effect of this legislation, while being careful to acknowledge that it is not designed to strike down contracts which are simply 'unfair' in the sense that they favour one party, provided there has been no abuse of power or unfair conduct: *West v AGC (Advances) Ltd* (1986) 5 NSWLR 610 at 621–2, per McHugh JA.

[6.47] Exclusion of commercial contracts. Section 6(1) denies relief under the Act to the Crown, any public or local authority and, perhaps most significantly, to corporations, while s 6(2) provides that relief may not be granted under the Act in relation to contracts entered into in the course of, or for the purpose of, a trade, business or profession, other than a farming undertaking, carried on by the person seeking relief. That restriction narrows the field of contracts effected by this legislation quite sharply although the courts have so far taken a liberal approach to the interpretation of those words.[25]

[6.48] Principal relief. Section 7(1) provides, among other things, that where the court finds a contract or a provision in a contract to have been unjust in the circumstances relating to the contract at the time it was made, the court may, if it considers it appropriate to do so, apply certain remedies for the purpose of avoiding the unjust consequences of the contract. Various remedial powers including that of declaring the contract void, or of varying the contract, are set out in s 7 and further ancillary relief, as listed in Sch 1, is made available under s 8.

[6.49] Grounds for relief. Guidance in determining whether a contract, or a provision in a contract, is unjust in the circumstances is given in s 9. In particular, s 9(2) lists matters to which the court shall have regard in making that determination. Those matters are, perhaps, helpful, but they do appear to restate much of the judge-made law in this area, giving the impression that the act does little more than codify the law as it already exists while arming the courts with greater flexibility in the way in which they can fashion their orders. In *West v AGC (Advances) Ltd* (1986) 5 NSWLR 610, all the members of the Court of Appeal took the view that the Act should be interpreted liberally and supported McHugh JA's judgment that the matters listed in s 9(2) do not exhaustively indicate the criteria which can be taken into account in determining whether a contract or any of its provisions is unjust.

In *West v AGC (Advances) Ltd* (1986) 5 NSWLR 610, Mrs West borrowed $68,000 from AGC in 1980 under a deed of loan which was secured by a mortgage over her house. The loan was jointly guaranteed by her husband, by The World of Quiche Pty Ltd

---

25. See *Toscano v Holland Securities Pty Ltd* (1985) 1 NSWLR 145.

(Quiche) and by three directors of that company. Of the $68,000, $30,000 was used to discharge an earlier mortgage to AGC over Mrs West's house, $8,000 was used to pay off a loan to one of the directors, by AGC, and the rest was paid to Quiche as working capital. It had been part of the agreement between Mrs West and the directors of Quiche that they would assume responsibility for the payments due on the mortgage in return for her putting the house up as security. Mrs West was in default under the earlier mortgage at the time. The mortgage payments were not kept up and AGC took proceedings for possession of Mrs West's house. She cross-claimed seeking various orders, including one under the Contracts Review Act that the deed of loan be varied to reduce her liability under it to $30,000 on the ground that the deed of loan was unjust in the circumstances. At first instance, Hodgson J refused to grant that relief, having found on other grounds that Quiche was the principal debtor and that Mrs West's role was that of a guarantor, along with the other four, and that, under the equitable doctrine of contribution, she was only liable for a portion of the total debt. By the time of the appeal the value of that right to contribution had been shown to be somewhat worthless by the actual bankruptcy of two of the directors and the imminent bankruptcy of the third. A winding up order had been made against Quiche before the case was heard by Hodgson J.

Mrs West appealed against the decision to refuse her relief under the Contracts Review Act. McHugh JA, with whom Hope JA agreed, dismissed her appeal. In doing so he held that the definition of 'unjust' in s 4 of the Contracts Review Act was not exhaustive and that the Act was not only concerned with contracts or contractual provisions which were unconscionable, harsh or oppressive in the classical sense and that any contract or provision not excluded from the operation of the Act which the court considered unjust in the circumstances may be the subject of relief under the Act. He added that s 9(2) did not exhaustively state the criteria to be taken into account in determining whether any contract or provision is unjust, particularly in the light of s 9(1) which requires the court to have regard for the public interest. McHugh JA referred to procedural and substantive injustice and said that while the provisions of s 9(2) were principally concerned with procedural injustice the court was entitled to have regard to all the circumstances of the case and to the public interest and that in an appropriate case gross disparity between the price of goods or services and their value may render the contract unjust in the circumstances even though none of the provisions of s 9(2) can be invoked by the applicant. In conclusion he said that the Contracts Review Act is beneficial legislation and must be interpreted liberally but that it also operates within and not outside the domain of the law of contract. While acknowledging the perilous nature of Mrs West's predicament, McHugh JA upheld the decision of Hodgson J that the deed of loan and mortgage were ordinary commercial documents containing no unfair or unjust terms and that AGC was guilty of no unfair conduct towards Mrs West.

[6.50] Kirby P dissented, expressing a view that the contract was unjust in the circumstances. He based that finding on the facts that Mrs West had not received independent advice, even though cautioned against the transaction by her son, an accountant, and by a barrister friend, that she was under pressure having defaulted under her previous mortgage, that the payments on the new loan were beyond her means and that she had played little part in the negotiations leading to the loan. Most of those were facts known to AGC. Kirby P did acknowledge, at 615, that such a wide view of the Act 'would diminish marginally the unobstructed privilege of individual initiative' and 'would add slightly to the costs of such transactions' but considered those matters to be consequences envisaged by the Act. That judgment could be accepted if one ignored the finding of Hodgson J that Quiche was the principal debtor in the transaction and that Mrs West's position was that of a guarantor. She was not ignorant of financial matters, nor of mortgages and their ramifications. She stood to gain a lot from the deal if Quiche had been successful; $30,000 to be exact. Her hopes proved to be ill-founded, but that should not be a ground for injustice alone. If a finance company lends money to a punter who invests the money on a certain horse in a certain race, the loan should not be unenforceable just because the horse loses.

[6.51] The Contracts Review Act came up for consideration before the Court of Appeal again in *Beneficial Finance Corporation Ltd v Karavas* (1991) 23 NSWLR 256. Most of that case turned on the extent to which an appellate court could review findings of fact by a trial judge in a case concerning relief under this act. The decision in *West v AGC (Advances) Ltd* was cited with approval, including by Kirby P, at 267.

> Beneficial Finance made a loan of $564,000 to a company called Socair Pty Ltd (Socair) for the purchase and operating costs of a small airline which was in receivership. The directors of Socair guaranteed the repayment of the loan by 30 July 1988 with the security of nine properties in the Sydney metropolitan area owned by themselves and their parents. Meagher JA noted a number of features of the loan transaction including that the same solicitors had acted for the borrowers and the lenders, which though imprudent had no legal consequence. Socair had also obtained a previous loan from the National Australia Bank of which Beneficial had no knowledge. Socair had obtained independent advice regarding the financial position of the airline and its operations. That information was 'distinctly bullish' and demonstrated that Socair could service the loan and make an income and even if that were not sufficient the securities offered were sufficient to cover the loan. The business failed and Beneficial called in the loan and demands were made on the guarantors and the mortgagors. The mortgagors sought relief on the basis of the equitable doctrine exemplified by *Amadio* and the Contracts Review Act. The *Amadio* defence failed. The trial judge found that Beneficial had in no sense sought to take advantage of a superior bargaining position nor had it sought to gain a benefit for itself. The trial judge did find for the defendants under the Contracts Review Act.

> Meagher JA upheld that decision stating that the principles of law were: there is no duty on a financier to provide either a borrower or a third-party guarantor with any commercial advice, although if such advice is tendered the financier may assume a duty of care; the Contracts Review Act is a remedial piece of legislation and should be interpreted liberally, free from fetters imposed by analogous legal and equitable doctrines; the Act is directed to contracts not transactions; there is jurisdiction under the Act to make orders in favour of a party to a contract who proves that at the date of the contract he suffers from a relevant disability even though the other party to the contract is unaware of that disability although in general this jurisdiction should not be exercised because it would be unjust in most cases to deprive an innocent person of valuable property in such circumstances. Section 9(2)(i) of the Act allows that relief may be granted if a finding is made that a party to a contract did not understand 'the provisions and their effect' of a contract. Meagher JA upheld the finding of the trial judge that the mortgagors had not fully understood the implications of the contract and if they had then they would not have made their properties available.

Trade Practices Act 1974 (Cth), ss 51AA and 51AB

[6.52] These sections were inserted in the Trade Practices Act in 1992 replacing the former s 52A which had been added to the Act in 1986. Section 51AA provides that a corporation must not, in trade or commerce, engage in conduct that is unconscionable within the meaning of the unwritten law, from time to time, of the States and Territories. By s 51AA(2), s 51AA does not apply to conduct that is prohibited under s 51AB. Section 51AB provides:

(1) A corporation shall not, in trade or commerce, in connection with the supply or possible supply of goods or services to a person, engage in conduct that is, in all the circumstances, unconscionable.

Section 51AB(2) then sets out a list of matters, which are described non-exhaustive, which the court may take into account in determining whether a corporation has contravened subsection (1). Those matters are similar to some of those listed in s 9(2) of the Contracts Review Act, and, it is submitted, that the fact that the list is shorter than that in the New South Wales Act does not mean that unconscionability under s 51AB is intended to have a narrower compass than it does under the Contracts Review Act. Section 51AB is, however, directed against unconscionable conduct in the supply of goods or services, and not with unconscionable contracts, placing greater emphasis on procedural injustice and leaving little room for matters of substantive injustice. The relief available under s 51AB is, however, different in nature as the purpose of the section is to provide for relief against unconscionable conduct by appropriate order under s 87(1A), so that neither prosecutions nor any action for damages can be brought for a breach of the section.[26] Section 51AB is also restricted in its operation to consumer transactions. Subsection (5) provides that any reference in the section to the supply of goods or services is a reference to goods or services of a kind ordinarily acquired for personal or domestic or household use or consumption as was outlined in *Atkinson v Hastings Deering (Qld) Pty Ltd* (1985) FCR 331 where the court held that a tractor purchased by the farmer for use on his farm was not a good acquired for personal, domestic or household use. Subsection (6) excludes any reference to the supply or possible supply of goods for the purpose of re-supply or for the purpose of using them up or transforming them in trade or commerce.[27]

[6.53] Section 52AA is directed at unconscionable conduct by corporations in the field of trade and commerce at large while s 51AB deals with the more limited field of unconscionable conduct in relation to the supply of goods and services to consumers. The reference to the 'unwritten law' in s 52AA must mean the judge-made law rather than statute law, and presumably means the law laid down in writing by judges as found in the cases discussed above. It remains to be seen whether this provision widens the scope of the law of unconscionability or not. One must presume that a court, on finding that a corporation had acted unconscionably in some matter concerning trade or commerce, such as *FAC v Makucha Developments Pty Ltd* (1993) 115 ALR 679, would grant appropriate relief, whether such conduct was condemned by the Trade Practices Act or not.

---

26. Sections 79(1) and 82(3).
27. Similar provisions exist in the various State Fair Trading Acts (see n 18): NSW, s 43; Qld, s 39; SA, s 57; Vic, s 11A; WA, s 11.

Chapter Seven

Penalties and Forfeiture

7–1 Penalties

[7.1] A stipulation in a contract which provides for the payment of an agreed sum of money by way of damages in the event of a breach of the contract will be struck down as a penalty, rendering it unenforceable, unless the agreed sum amounts to a genuine pre-estimate of the damages actually flowing from the breach. That does not mean that the plaintiff will be denied any remedy; damages can still be recovered for the actual loss flowing from the breach. The basic principles were stated by Lord Dunedin in *Dunlop Pneumatic Tyre Co Ltd v New Garage & Motor Co Ltd* [1915] AC 79:

> A manufacturer of car tyres sold them on terms whereby the purchasers agreed to sell the tyres at certain listed prices. The agreement provided that £5 damages were payable for each tyre sold under the listed price, an arrangement which the appellant had with all its customers to prevent underselling. The House of Lords held that the £5 payment was a penalty. Lord Dunedin said the difference between a penalty and liquidated damages was that the former was a payment of money stipulated as *in terrorem* of the offender while the latter was a genuinely covenanted pre-estimate of damage. The question is one of construction and a penalty is more likely to be construed if the amount is extravagant and larger than the greatest loss that could conceivably flow from the breach, or if it is a single lump sum payable as compensation on the happening of a number of events, or if the breach constitutes a failure to pay a sum of money and the sum stipulated is greater than the amount originally payable. On the other hand, an agreed damages clause will stand if the consequences of the breach are such as to make a precise preestimate almost impossible.

[7.2] This doctrine has been said to have its origins in equity's jurisdiction to relieve against unconscionable bargains.[1] It can be traced to the relief given by Chancery in the late fifteenth century against penal bonds in covenants, the principal device at

---

1. RP Meagher, 'Penalties in Chattel Leases', in PD Finn (ed), *Essays in Equity*, Law Book Co Ltd, Sydney, 1985, pp 46–58 at p 57. (It has also been variously attributed to the 'absurdity' of requiring payment of a larger sum upon non-payment of a lesser amount: *Wallis v Smith* (1882) 21 Ch D 243 at 256, per Jessel MR; to giving effect to the contract, by awarding the creditor the money secured by the imposition of the penalty: *Peachy v Duke of Somerset* (1724) 1 Stra 447 at 453, per Lord Maccles-field; to the granting of relief against accident, or fraud, or surprise.)

common law for securing contractual performance in the later middle ages.[2] The antiquity of Chancery's disapproval of penalties sets this doctrine apart from the modern law of unconscionable dealings. The law of penalties is not concerned with the circumstances in which a contract was procured and such things as the relative bargaining positions of the parties. It is also not concerned with the propriety or otherwise of sums payable in performance of a contract. It is solely concerned with the question of whether an amount agreed to be paid upon breach of a contract is appropriate as a pre-determined measure of the compensation payable for the breach and not with the conduct of the party seeking to enforce the contract. The jurisdiction to relieve against oppressive contracts was rejected as the basis of the law of penalties by the House of Lords in *Shiloh Spinners Ltd v Harding* [1973] AC 691 at 723, per Lord Wilberforce. The question is essentially one of arithmetic,[3] or mechanics 'no doubt, a reflection of the common law origin of the doctrine of penalties' as Meagher JA put it *PC Developments Pty Ltd v Revell* (1991) 22 NSWLR 615 at 651. In addition, this rule is restricted to contractual penalties; it does not apply to penalties and forfeitures arising by operation of law, nor does it apply to contractual provisions granting indulgences upon certain terms: *IAC (Leasing) Ltd v Humphrey* (1972) 126 CLR 131 at 142–4, per Walsh J. The operation of these principles can be seen in *Wanner v Caruana* [1974] 2 NSWLR 301, in which a provision in a mortgage provided that in the event of default by the debtor, the debtor was to pay the balance of the principal plus interest on the balance of the unexpired term of the mortgage. That provision was struck down as a penalty because it imposed a liability on the debtor to pay interest which was unearned and unaccrued and referable to a period when the principal would have been recovered because of the default. On the other hand it will not be a penalty where a creditor agrees to accept a payment of part of the debt owed in full discharge of the debtor's obligations providing certain other conditions are satisfied, but stipulates that if those other conditions are not satisfied then the full amount of the debt will become payable: *Thompson v Hudson* (1869) LR 4 HL 1, affirmed in *O'Dea v All States Leasing System (WA) Pty Ltd* (1983) 152 CLR 359 at 367; 45 ALR 632.

[7.3] Under the traditional view of the law of penalties, an agreed damages clause will only be struck down as a penalty if it requires payment upon breach of the contract, and not if the payment arises upon some other event: *Export Credit Guarantee Department v Universal Oil Products Company* [1983] 2 All ER 205. This rule has met with some criticism. In the context of hire purchase agreements it puts the hirer who acts properly by electing to terminate the agreement when he or she cannot maintain the payments in a worse position than one who simply stops paying: *Associated Distributors v Hall* [1938] 2 KB 83. The correctness of this rule has been disputed in England:

> In *Bridge v Campbell Discount Co Ltd* [1962] AC 600, a hirer under a hire purchase agreement, after paying the initial deposit of £105 and only one instalment of £10 9s 2d, returned the car and gave notice of termination of the agreement. The purchase price for the car was £482 10s. The agreement provided that, in the event of termination for any reason before the car became the hirer's property, the hirer should pay, by way of

---

2. SFC Milsom, *Historical Foundations of the Common Law,* 2nd ed, London, 1981, pp 250–3; JH Baker, *An Introduction to English Legal History,* 3rd ed, London, 1990, pp 368–71, 'By the end of the fifteenth century, however, the Chancery had adopted the view that to recover more than a creditor had actually lost was unconscionable. If a creditor tried to extract more than the principle debt or actual damages, with reasonable costs, relief was available': *Capell v Scott* (1494) 102 SS 13; EG Henderson, 'Relief from Bonds in the English Chancery Mid Sixteenth Century' 18 AmJLH 298.
3. Or, as put by Lord Davey in *Clydebank Engineering and Shipbuilding Co v Don Jose Ramos Yzquierdo y Castenada* [1905] AC 6 at 15, 'not one of words or of forms of speech, but of substance and of things'.

agreed compensation for depreciation, two thirds of the hire purchase price, with an allowance for his payments up to that time which, in this case, meant payment of a further £206 3s 4d. The Court of Appeal held that the law of penalties could not apply because the hirer was not in breach. He had lawfully terminated the agreement. The House of Lords reversed that decision finding that the hirer was in breach and struck the payment down as a penalty. Lord Radcliffe said the agreed sum was not a proper compensation for depreciation, especially because it anomalously decreased as the vehicle aged, and that its true purpose was to act as a guarantee against the loss of the hiring contract. His Lordship also said that it was not unconscionable for owners to require payment of some agreed damages. In such a contract, to protect themselves against the risk of having to dispose of second-hand goods to make up their true loss but that, 'Unconscionable' must not be taken to be a panacea for adjusting any contract between competent persons when it shows a rough edge to one side or the other … (as) … the courts of equity never undertook to serve as a general adjuster of men's bargains'. Their Lordships found that the hirer was in breach so it was not necessary to decide whether the law of penalties could apply where a contract was terminated otherwise than by breach. Viscount Simonds and Lord Morton thought it could not. Lords Denning, at 631, and Devlin, at 633, thought it could, as otherwise equity would give relief to the man who broke his contract but not to the man who kept it. Lord Radcliffe did not express a view on the question.

The High Court has rejected this rule so that in Australia a sum of agreed damages will be held to be a penalty not only where it is payable in the event of a breach of contract but also where it becomes payable following termination where the right to terminate arises from a breach: *AMEV-UDC Finance Ltd v Austin* (1986) 162 CLR 170 (see **[7.7]**).

[7.4] Agreed damages provisions most commonly occur in rental agreements, usually of the hire purchase or chattel leasing type. The owner or lessor under such contracts will be concerned to ensure a reasonable revenue return from the leased chattel while also protecting its capital investment in what will often be a rapidly depreciating item. Consequently these agreements usually contain some appraisal or residual value, an estimate of the depreciated value of the chattel at the end of the lease. If the agreement runs its full term, the hirer or lessee will usually be given an option to purchase the chattel by paying the agreed residual value at the end of the lease or period of hire. If the chattel is returned to the lessor at the end of the lease it may then be sold or valued and, if the sale price or valuation fall below the residual, the lessee may be liable to compensate the lessor for the difference. If the goods bring in more than the residual value, provision may be made for the difference to be paid to the lessee. These residual value clauses operate where there has been no breach and thus cannot be characterised as penalties in the normal course of events. In each of the scenarios considered above the lease or hire purchase contract will have run its full term without default by the lessee or hirer. Where the lease is terminated before the expiry of the term there will usually be provision for payment of the unpaid rent for the balance of the term of the agreement, in some form or other, and for the repossession of the goods by the lessor. Where future instalments of rent are payable there will normally be some provision for those payments to be discounted to take into account the acceleration of the lessor's profit.

In *IAC (Leasing) Limited v Humphrey* (1972) 126 CLR 131, a lease of a tractor and other equipment required the lessee, upon default, to pay the entire rent, equal to the sum of eighteen monthly instalments of $1,304, subject to an adjustment of rent as provided by cl 4. Clause 4 provided that in the event of the goods being repossessed upon default future instalments of rent would be payable immediately 'rebated to reflect their then value by applying an interest rate of 10% to each instalment over the period by which its payment had been brought forward'. Upon return of the equipment at the end of the term, or at any earlier time, the lessor was to sell it and if it brought in less than the appraisal value then the lessee was obliged to make up the difference. If the equipment sold for more than the appraisal value then the difference was to be set off against outstanding rent over the balance of the term. The lessee defaulted with about two months to go. The lessor claimed outstanding rent of $4,512 and indemnity for a loss of $13,190 on the appraisal value. The lessee argued that both the accelerated rent payments and the indemnity were penalties. The High Court held, per Walsh J, with whom Barwick CJ and McTiernan J agreed, that the provision for payment of future instalments of rent was not a penalty because the lessor's right to repossess the equipment was qualified by the requirement that any 'profit' from its sale after repossession was to be set off against outstanding rent. The indemnity provision which applied upon the return of the goods at the end of the term was not a penalty either because the obligation to pay the indemnity did not arise upon breach.

[7.5] Where a sum of money is presently owing and the creditor grants the debtor an indulgence by agreeing to accept payment by instalments over a period on certain conditions there will be no penalty if the entire sum becomes payable upon breach of a condition, including a failure to pay an instalment on time: *The Protector Loan Co v Grice* (1880) 5 QBD 592. In such cases the full sum owing is a present debt which, because of the indulgence granted by the creditor, is payable in the future, or in a lesser amount. Accordingly, there is no penalty if the full amount becomes payable upon breach of a condition. Similarly, there is no penalty where it is agreed to charge a certain rate of interest on condition that if payment is made punctually the rate will be reduced: *Astley v Weldon* (1801) 2 Bos & Pul 346 at 353; 126 ER 1318 at 1322. There will also not be a penalty when a creditor agrees to accept payment of part of his or her debt in full discharge if certain conditions are met but stipulates that if the conditions are not met he or she will be entitled to recover the original debt: *Thompson v Hudson* (1869) LR 4 HL 1 at 15, 16, 27, 28, 30; *Re Neil; Ex Parte Burden* (1881) 16 ChD 675.[4] A loan agreement which provides that upon default the interest rate is increased from the date of default will not be a penalty, provided the interest rate increase does not act retrospectively: *David Securities Pty Ltd v Commonwealth Bank* (1990) 93 ALR 271. A moratorium deed which effected a compromise of a dispute as to the terms of antecedent debts and accorded benefits to debtors and creditors alike was construed as an indulgence for the payment of a due debt and not a penalty in *Acron Pacific Pty Ltd v Offshore Oil NL* (1985) 157 CLR 514. The rule allowing indulgences has been employed in leases and hire purchase contracts to express the total sum of the instalments as presently due upon signing of the agreement, with a proviso that that full amount will not be payable as long as the instalments are paid as and when they fall due. The courts in recent times have been unwilling to accept such arrangements unless they are genuine and proper in the circumstances.

In *O'Dea v Allstates Leasing System (WA) Pty Ltd* (1983) 152 CLR 359, a lease of a prime mover provided for payment of rent by monthly instalments. It also provided, among other things, that the entire rental was due upon signing the lease; however, if the lessee observed all the covenants and duly paid the instalments, the lessor would refrain from demanding payment of the full amount at once. The lessee defaulted. The vehicle was repossessed and sold for an amount exceeding the appraisal value. There was no obligation under the lease for the lessor to account to the lessee for any such profit. The lessor then sought to recover the balance of unpaid rent. The lessee argued that that was a penalty. The lessor argued that it was not a penalty because it was either an indul-

---

4. Affirmed by the High Court in *O'Dea v All States Leasing System (WA) Pty Ltd* (1983) 152 CLR 359 at 367, per Gibbs CJ; at 380, per Wilson J; and at 386, per Brennan J.

gence, or a sum payable in accordance with the contract, not a sum payable upon breach. The High Court held that the required payment constituted a penalty and not a genuine pre-estimate of the lessor's loss. Because the outstanding balance became payable upon breach by the lessee of his obligations to pay instalments it was not a payment made in performance of the contract. It was also not a case involving an indulgence as there was no presently existing obligation to pay the whole rental at the date of contract. In the circumstances the outstanding balance of the rental could not possibly represent a genuine pre-estimate of the loss.

[7.6] In light of the High Court decisions in *IAC (Leasing) Ltd v Humphrey* and *O'Dea v Allstates Leasing* it would appear that an agreed damages provision which calls for payment of outstanding instalments to compensate the lessor for lost profits, with a rebate to account for the acceleration of that profit, plus an allowance for any excess over the residual value to be set off against the rent owing will not be a penalty.[5] However, in *Citicorp Australia Limited v Hendry* (1985) 4 NSWLR 1, the New South Wales Court of Appeal held that a damages clause of that style in which the lessee was allowed a rebate of 10% pa on the accelerated instalments payable upon breach was a penalty as it did not take proper account of fluctuating interest rates over the period during which the effective interest rate went as high as 24%. The court criticised the narrowness of the law of penalties, particularly that a term found to be a penalty was simply rendered unenforceable, and could not be varied to allow for some proper recompense for the lessor, as commercial dealings could be greatly assisted by proper provision for pre-estimates of loss.

[7.7] In *AMEV-UDC Finance Ltd v Austin* (1986) 162 CLR 170, the High Court expressed a less rigid view of penalties without specifically disapproving of the decision in *Citicorp v Hendry*. The majority confirmed the Court of Appeal's view that the law will not allow a variation of a provision found to be a penalty. The facts in *AMEV-UDC* were unexceptional, the lease agreement being similar to that in *O'Dea*. The lessee was in breach of the contract, being behind on a number of instalments, but had not repudiated the contract. Instead the lessor exercised its option under the contract to terminate the lease. Before the High Court the question of whether the clause in question constituted a penalty was not even argued. The issues raised went solely to the question of the appropriate relief, and, in particular, whether the lessor was restricted to recovering only arrears of rent plus interest on those arrears (the damages flowing from the lessee's breach), or whether it could also recover the losses occasioned by its termination of the agreement, its loss of bargain. Gibbs CJ held that the lessor was only entitled to recover the damages flowing from the breach, that is, the arrears up to the date of termination plus interest, and not any additional damages as those did not result from the lessee's breach but from the lessor's termination of the hiring. Mason and Wilson JJ agreed with that conclusion but also reviewed the doctrine of penalties generally. Some salient points emerged from their Honours' joint judgment:

(a) Where a sum becomes payable upon the happening of some specified event other than a breach of contract it will not be a penalty, because it is not the function of the courts to relieve a party from a contract on the mere ground that it proves to be onerous or imprudent, unless the option to terminate the contract is exercised on the occasion of the hirer's breach of contract, in which case it will be a penalty — the doctrine being concerned with matters of substance

---

5. This was certainly the view taken by Mason and Wilson JJ in *AMEV-UDC Finance Ltd v Austin* (1986) 162 CLR 170 at 194.

rather than form. In such a case the amount of agreed damages will be a penalty unless it is a genuine pre-estimate of damage.

(b) In determining whether a given sum is a penalty the better view is that set by the older cases, such as *Dunlop Pneumatic Tyre*, that is, an agreed sum would be a penalty if it is 'extravagant, exorbitant or unconscionable', rather than merely an amount greater than the damages which could possibly be awarded for the breach in question, 'thereby allowing the parties to a contract greater latitude in determining what their rights and liabilities will be, so that an agreed sum will only be a penalty if it is out of all proportion to the damage likely to be suffered as a result of breach'.

(c) A penalty clause cannot be enforced to the extent to which it is not a penalty because this would involve the court in rewriting the clause so as to enable the plaintiff to recover the loss he had actually sustained by awarding some figure by way of compensation which would be different from the damages he or she could recover at law. The better approach is that outlined in (b): giving the parties greater latitude in framing their contracts; rather than having the courts rewrite them.

(d) The appropriate remedy for a lessor in the position of the lessor in *AMEV-UDC* is a properly drawn indemnity clause. There is no reason to suppose that an indemnity clause would be struck down as a penalty if it gave the lessor, upon termination following the lessee's breach, all unpaid instalments of rent, suitably discounted for early receipt, plus the residual value of the goods adjusted so as to reflect their actual value at the relevant time.

[7.8] Any advantage gained from the greater latitude which the majority in *AMEV-UDC* were prepared to grant to parties in framing agreed damages clauses in leasing agreements of this sort appears to have been neutralised by their decision not to award the lessor any compensation for the loss of its bargain. Instead of giving lessors and hirers more freedom in providing relief within the terms of their contracts, the majority of the High Court have invited them to play a kind of Russian roulette. If a lessee falls behind in his or her payments the lessor is presented with a dilemma. If he or she terminates the lease and calls up the indemnity the lessee may well challenge it. The lessee has little to lose, except costs, and much to gain. If the indemnity clause is struck down as a penalty, the lessee will only be liable for arrears of rent to the date of termination while the lessor is stuck with used goods. It is cold comfort to say that Mason and Wilson JJ have authorised agreed damages clauses which might require payment of a sum exceeding the damages actually incurred. Their Honours were not very specific in saying what would, and what would not, be 'extravagant, exorbitant or unconscionable' in an agreed damages clause. Their failure to comment on the strict approach taken by the New South Wales Court of Appeal in *Citicorp v Hendry*, leaves a question mark over the meaning of 'suitably rebated' in point (d) above.[6] If the lessor wishes to avoid those problems he or she will have to convert the non-payment of rent into a repudiation and sue for damages, making the agreed damages clause, and his or her supposed new found freedom, meaningless. At the same time, the lessee's position is not very comfortable either. The question of whether a sum of agreed damages is 'extravagant, exorbitant or unconscionable' is not easily answered. The question has to be answered in the context of the circumstances prevailing at the time of the contract, rather than those at the time of the

---

6. Although it must be said that lower stable rates of interest prevailing at the time of this edition make it unlikely that the factual scenario in *Citicorp v Hendry* could be repeated.

claim. It is not enough to establish simply that the agreed sum exceeds the damages which could otherwise be recoverable for the particular breach. It becomes a question of degree which must, in the event, depend very much on the attitude of the judge hearing any such case.

[7.9] Deane and Dawson JJ, in two forcefully argued dissenting judgments, criticised the reasoning behind the majority decision in *AMEV-UDC*. Deane J argued that the unenforceability of a penalty should be restricted to the extent to which the amount payable exceeds the damage actually sustained, and that the damage thereby recoverable would include any losses arising upon termination, so that the lessor could recover his actual loss. In the alternative, he thought that losses arising from breach should include any loss suffered as a result of a termination effected in consequence of the breach. Deane J pointed to the absurdity of distinguishing between the losses flowing from the breach and the losses arising upon termination for the purposes of assessing the relief payable to the lessor when no such distinction is drawn when determining whether the indemnity clause could be considered as a penalty, that is, in saying whether it is a sum payable upon breach of the contract or a sum payable in performance of the contract, nor when assessing whether the indemnity constituted a genuine pre-estimate of loss. Dawson J launched a similar attack on the illogicality of reasoning which would allow a lessor to recover his or her losses upon termination under an agreed damages clause which was not a penalty but, if the agreed sum was struck down, would deny him or her the right to recover the actual loss. Unlike Deane J, however, Dawson J preferred to compensate the lessor by treating the loss arising from the termination as damage flowing from the original breach, rather than enforcing the penalty clause in part. While there is some merit in Deane J's proposal that an agreed damages clause which is found to be a penalty should only be unenforceable to the extent that it is a penalty it also gives cause for some concern. The idea of judges rewriting commercial contracts on the run is a bit frightening. It perhaps overstates judicial omniscience. One might ask where such powers will end — judges rewriting the tunes and lyrics in copyright disputes over rock music?

[7.10] The approach of the majority in *AMEV-UDC* was endorsed by the High Court in *Esanda Finance Corporation Ltd v Plessnig* (1989) 166 CLR 131. The issue there concerened the 'recoverable amount' under a contract for the hire of a prime mover. The sum was defined in the contract as being the total rent and all other moneys payable for the period of hire, including the costs of re-possession, storage and sale of the vehicle less: (a) all moneys paid by way of deposit or rental for the goods; (b) the value of the goods (being the wholesale price obtainable for them at the time of re-possession); and (c) a rebate of charges calculated by multiplying the total charges under the contract by the number of months left to run in the contract and dividing that figure by the total number of months in the contract. The court held this agreed sum not to be a penalty. Wilson and Toohey JJ expressed approval of the statement by Dickson J in *Elsley v J G Collins Insurance Agencies Ltd* (1978) 83 DLR (3d) 1:

> ... it is now evident that the power to strike down a penalty clause is a blatant interference with freedom of contract and is designed for the sole purpose of providing relief against oppression for the party having to pay the stipulated sum. It has no place where there is no oppression.

In their opinion an agreed sum could only be characterised as a penalty if it was out of all proportion to damage likely to be suffered as a result of breach: *Robophone Facilities Ltd v Blank* [1966] 1 WLR 1428 at 1447–8; [1966] 3 All ER 128 at 142–3.

[7.11] The decisions in *AMEV-UDC* and *Esanda v Plessnig* have left the law of penalties in something like its early modern state. A contractual provision will be deemed to constitute a penalty when it requires, in the event of breach, or termination following breach, payment by the party in breach of a sum of money calculated in a particular way where the sum, when calculated, not only exceeds the damages ordinarily recoverable for the particular breach but which 'is extravagant and unconscionable in amount in comparison with the greatest loss that could conceivably be proved to have followed from the breach'. The question of whether an amount payable by way of agreed damages is 'extravagant or unconscionable' will be determined in the light of conditions existing at the date of the contract, and not at the date of breach. It cannot be answered simply by looking at events as they have fallen out. The question of the appropriate test was further considered by the New South Wales Court of Appeal in *PC Developments Pty Ltd v Revell* (1991) 22 NSWLR 615:

> A contract for the sale of land gave the purchaser a revocable licence to enter onto the land prior to completion and to carry out work on the land, including demolition and construction of buildings. Another Clause, 34, provided that in the event that the agreement was not completed other than because of default by the vendor, the purchaser could not remove any works from the property nor claim compensation or reimbursement for any such work. The purchaser could also be required by the vendor to reinstate the property at the purchaser's expense. The purchaser failed to complete and the vendor terminated the contract and forfeited the deposit. The vendor then resold the land for $1.29 million. The original purchase price had been $829,000. At first instance, Cohen J refused the purchaser's claim for relief against forfeiture, but held that cl 34 constituted a penalty and awarded the purchaser compensation in the sum of $350,000 for work he had carried out on the land. By a majority, Mahoney and Meagher JJA, Clarke JA dissenting, the Court of Appeal upheld the vendor's appeal against the finding on cl 34. In the view of the majority, the monetary value of the vendor's right to retain any improvements effected by the purchaser, when considered in the light of circumstances at the time of the contract, was not necessarily in excess of the damages recoverable by the vendor for breach. The purchaser might build, or he might not. He might only demolish. The land might increase in value and it might not. The vendor could not know at the date of contract whether cl 34 would provide adequate protection against the losses which might flow if the purchaser failed to complete.
>
> Clarke JA considered that a penal clause may be used as a sword or as a defensive shield. In the latter role a defendant from whom a sum of agreed damages is claimed would argue that the sum in question is a penalty. If that defence is upheld then the term setting the agreed damages is held to be unenforceable. If the claim is for return of money or property retained under some term of a contract then the claim will be, in essence, that the provision under which the property is retained is a penalty. In Clarke JA's view the claimant would have to do more than show that the clause is penal in nature he or she would have to show that it would be unconscionable for the vendors to retain the money or property.

The terms used by Clarke JA, and the second element of the test laid down by Mason and Wilson JJ in *AMEV-UDC*, and followed by Wilson and Toohey JJ in *Esanda v Plessnig*, suggest that the courts are more inclined to consider whether a contractual provision alleged to be a penalty can be justified as a matter of conscience, rather than being considered simply as a question of arithmetic. If that is the case then it suggests a subtle change in the character of this doctrine, a move away from the bluntness of its late medieval common law origins into the mainstream of modern equitable doctrine where unconscionability acts as the main benchmark. This was illustrated by the approach taken by the New South Wales Court of Appeal in *Amev*

Finance Ltd v Artes Studios Thoroughbreds Pty Ltd (1989) 15 NSWLR 564, in which the court preferred the test that contractual terms providing for the payment of an agreed sum and by way of liquidated damages should be struck down as a penalty only if the agreed sum was extravagant in amount or otherwise imposed an unconscionable burden upon the party paying as opposed to a test which would classify an agreed damages sum as a penalty if the sum stipulated was greater than the amount of damages which might flow from the breach of contract in question. In coming to that decision the Court of Appeal also held that the fact that the sum of agreed damages is payable upon the happening of certain events which may in themselves be trifling in terms of the damage they cause is of little relevance where the parties agree that the contract will be terminable upon the happening of certain events, including the breach complained of and the sum of agreed damages is paid to compensate for the early termination of the contract and not merely the particular breach.

7–2 Forfeiture

[7.12] Equity exercises a jurisdiction to grant relief against forfeiture where some right or interest is expressed to be forfeit upon the breach of a covenant or condition where the main object of the forfeiture provision is to secure some stated result and that result can be shown to be obtainable by other means when the matter comes before the court.[7] Where a contract provides for the forfeiture of some proprietary right upon breach, equity will strike it down if that forfeiture constitutes a penalty. The right of a lessee of land to relief against forfeiture has been reinforced by statute in various Australian jurisdictions. Generally these statutory protections against forfeiture operate by restricting the right of a landlord or mortgagee to re-enter or otherwise effect a forfeiture in the event of a breach of covenant by the lessee until the lessor or mortgagee has served notice on the lessee or mortgagor and the latter has failed to remedy the breach.[8] Relief against forfeiture has been allowed against forfeiture of an interest in a Crown lease under the Western Lands Act 1901 (NSW): *Minister for Lands v McPherson* (1991) 22 NSWLR 687. Relief has also been allowed against fortfeiture of a purchaser's interest in land under a terms contract: *Mehmet v Benson* [1964] NSWR 766. A lessee who is in default in payment of rent will be entitled to relief against forfeiture where the full amount due has been tendered: *R v Dale* [1906] VLR 662. Relief against forfeiture for non-payment of rent will only be refused on the ground of breaches of other covenants in the lease in exceptional circumstances, usually on condition that the other breaches be speedily remedied: *Lo Guidice v Biviano (No 2)* [1962] VR 420; *Plait v Ong* [1972] VR 197.[9] But relief against forfeiture is not restricted to interests in land. It applies to purported forfeitures of chattels and other proprietary interests. Relief has been granted to prevent forfeiture of the possessory or proprietary rights of the hirer of goods under contracts for hire: *Esanda Finance Corporation Ltd v Plessnig* (1989) 166 CLR 131 at 151, per Brennan J; and hire-purchase: *Re Vanruyten Radio Supplies Pty Ltd (in liq)* (1938) VLR 209.

---

7. *Shiloh Spinners Ltd v Harding* [1973] AC 691 at 723, per Lord Wilberforce.
8. Landlord and Tenant Act 1949 (ACT), s 63(1)–(2); Conveyancing Act 1919 (NSW), s 129; Tenacy Act 1979 (NT) ss 42, 42A; Property Law Act 1974 (Qld), ss 123–128; Landlord and Tenant Act 1936 (SA), ss 9–12; Conveyancing and Law of Property Act 1884 (Tas), s 15; Law of Property Act 1958 (Vic), s 146; Property Law Act 1969 (WA), s 81(1).
9. Compare *Brice v Slee* (1909) 11 WALR 174.

In *Forestry Commission of NSW v Stefanetto* (1976) 133 CLR 507, the Commission, under a road construction contract, was allowed, in the event of default by the contractor, to complete the works itself and to take possession of any plant on the site for that purpose. The contractor was not entitled to compensation for the use of such plant and, if the ultimate cost of completing the works exceeded the contract price, the Commission could retain the plant as security for the payment of the difference by the contractor. The contractor argued that these provisions constituted a penalty. The High Court, per Barwick CJ and Jacobs J, held that they were not penal because the Commission's primary concern was not damages for breach of contract but completion of the work on time and the provisions were a means to that end. Mason J, in dissent, considered the retention of the plant to be a penalty as there was no obligation cast on the Commission to use the machinery to complete the work and because no compensation was allowed to the contractor for the use of the machinery.

[7.13] A provision which deprives the owner of possession of goods will be a penal forfeiture, just as much as one which purports to deprive him or her of title. With the increasing flexibility shown by the courts in interpreting these principles the reasoning of the majority in *Stefanetto* must be questioned. The result desired by the Commission in that case could have been achieved by the payment of money, for the hire of other equipment, or the employment of another contractor, without disabling the respondent. Considering that, the decision of the High Court does not sit comfortably alongside that of the House of Lords in *Shiloh Spinners Ltd v Harding* [1973] AC 691.

A lessee had assigned its interest in part of the leased premises to a third party upon certain conditions, including obligations as to fencing and continuing support of the premises retained by the principal lessee, who had reserved a right to re-enter upon breach of any of those conditions. An assignee from the third party breached those conditions. The House of Lords upheld the principal lessee's right to re-enter. Lord Wilberforce discussed the doctrine of forfeiture, saying that from the earliest times equity had intervened to relieve against forfeiture of property. Where the object of the insertion of the right to forfeit is essentially to secure the payment of a sum of money, equity has been willing to relieve on terms that the payment is made with interest, and costs, if appropriate. Equity also intervened on traditional grounds of fraud, accident, mistake or surprise. Where the default giving rise to the right to forfeit involved something other than the payment of money, such as breach of a covenant to repair, or some act of waste, the old cases held that equity would not relieve against the forfeiture: *Wadman v Calcroft* (1804) 10 Ves Jun 67, and even that payment of a sum of money, where the right of forfeiture was intended to secure that payment, might not suffice if the receipt, even with interest, had lost some of its usefulness: *Hill v Barclay* (1811) 18 Ves 56, per Lord Eldon LC. Lord Eldon also took the view in *Hill v Barclay* that equity would not relieve against forfeiture where there had been a wilful breach of covenant. Lord Wilberforce said the House was not bound by those old decisions and that courts of equity had the right, in appropriate and limited cases, to relieve against forfeiture for breach of covenant or condition where the primary object of the bargain is to secure a stated result which can effectively be attained when the matter comes before the court, and where the forfeiture provision is added by way of security for the production of that result. Wilful breaches should only be relieved against in exceptional circumstances. In *Shiloh* the nature of the breaches by the respondent, and the circumstances of the case, were such as to deny him relief. Lord Simon was prepared to say that equity has an unlimited and unfettered jurisdiction to relieve against contractual forfeitures and that any restrictions placed on that jurisdiction by the older authorities, including the sanctity of contractual promises, now fell into the category of things to be considered by the court in making its decision, not as absolute bars to relief.

[7.14] Some greater flexibility in the application of these principles was indicated by the High Court in *Legione v Hately* (1983)152 CLR 406 where the question of relief against forfeiture was remitted back to the court below for consideration notwithstanding the High Court's denial of relief to the plaintiffs on grounds of estoppel.

[7.15] *Legione v Hateley* was applied in *Ciavarella v Balmer* (1983) 153 CLR 438, to refuse relief against forfeiture on the application of a purchaser who had defaulted in the payment of an instalment of purchase moneys on the grounds that no exceptional circumstances had been shown. Relief against forfeiture was further considered in *Stern v McArthur* (1985)165 CLR 489; 81 ALR 463:

> The appellants were vendors under a terms contract for the sale of land. The contract price was $5,250 of which $250 was paid as a deposit on exchange with the balance, including interest at 8.5%, payable by monthly instalments of not less than $50.00. In the event of default by the purchasers the deposit would be forfeited and the vendors were to be entitled to terminate the contract and sue for breach or to resell the property to recover the deficiency. The respondents went into possession following exchange and built a house on the land. After approximately eight years they defaulted in their repayments for a period of 11 months. The purchasers offered to make up the arrears by paying the outstanding amount. The vendors, relying on their contractual rights, demanded the whole of the purchase price and served a Notice to Complete. When the contract was not completed the vendors purported to rescind. The purchasers sought relief against forfeiture and specific performance.
>
> The High Court held, by a majority, that relief against forfeiture ought to be granted and decreed specific performance. Deane and Dawson JJ said that relief against forfeiture may involve relief against forfeiture of the deposit or instalments of purchase money or it may mean forfeiture of the purchaser's 'estate' under the contract, the right to specific performance. Applying *Legione v Hateley* (1983) 152 CLR 406, their Honours said that only in exceptional circumstances will orders for relief against forfeiture and specific performance be made at the instance of a purchaser who is in breach of an essential term. Those exceptional circumstances need not involve unconscionable conduct. As they put it, at 526–7: 'The general underlying notion is that which has long been identified as underlying much of equity's traditional jurisdiction to grant relief against unconscientious conduct, namely, that a person should not be permitted to use or insist upon legal rights to take advantage of another's special vulnerability or misadventure for the unjust enrichment of himself'. Deane and Dawson JJ found that the forfeiture provision was intended as security for the payment of a sum of money and, being a vendor finance contract, it was essentially parallel to a purchase by mortgage and therefore the forfeiture provision by way of security for the payment of purchase moneys was a penalty and the equitable interest held by the purchasers was being overturned by the unconscionable enforcement of the appellants' legal rights. They also noted that the purchasers had built a house on the land and occupied it as their home and that the land had increased substantially in value over the original purchase price.
>
> Gaudron J thought the matter was determined in favour of the purchasers by the unconscionable conduct of the vendors. On default, they had a choice as to whether they sued for specific performance, to recover all outstanding purchase moneys, or whether they exercised their rights of forfeiture. They chose the latter course, electing to sell the property and, notwithstanding that the property had substantially increased in value, to retain the deposit and all instalments paid as 'security' for any deficiency which might arise on sale. In view of the consequences for the purchasers in those circumstances, her Honour considered that conduct to be unconscionable.
>
> Mason CJ and Brennan J, in separate dissenting judgments, expressed the view that the vendors' conduct in this case was not unconscionable. The Chief Justice thought that to extend relief against forfeiture to instances in which no exceptional circum-

stances were established would eviscerate unconscionability of its meaning (that is, drain it of its juices). Brennan J gave the warning that unconscionability is not a charter for judicial reformation of contracts. He thought there was nothing in the vendors' conduct which equity would regard as unconscionable except possibly the time allowed in their notice to complete, in view of the circumstances and the history of the transaction at the time the notice was served. However, the case had been conducted on the basis that the contract was validly rescinded and no objection had been taken to the notice itself.

[7.16] Following *Stern v McArthur* it appears that relief against forfeiture may be argued by a party in breach in two situations. The first will occur where the forfeiture provision is inserted to secure the payment of a sum of money or some other stated result which can be achieved without forfeiture. The party in default can then seek relief on the basis of payment of the amount owing plus appropriate compensation, or otherwise performance of the stated result. Similarly, relief may be sought where the consequences of forfeiture far outweigh the loss occasioned by the breach which triggers the forfeiture. In those cases, however, relief will be sought principally on the ground that the forfeiture provision constitutes a penalty. On the reasoning of Gaudron J, the right to relief in those two types of case will depend on a considera-tion of the circumstances at the time the contract was made. The validity of the for-feiture provision will depend on its own terms, rather than the conduct of the party seeking to rely on it. There is, however, another class of case in which the court will be concerned with the conduct of the vendor in trying to enforce a forfeiture in the context of the circumstances at the time of the purported forfeiture. The court will have to decide if it is unconscionable of the vendor to exercise the right of forfeiture in the light of all the circumstances at that time, which will include the true construc-tion of the forfeiture provision but may extend to other matters outside the precise terms of the contract itself. These principles were applied in *Federal Airports Corpora-tion Ltd v Makucha Developments Pty Ltd* (1993) 115 ALR 679 (see **[6.45]**) to allow relief against forfeiture against the Federal Airports Corporation (FAC) where it sought to terminate a licence agreement following failure by the licensee to provide a perform-ance bond and to have the agreement executed by its principal officer. Relief against forfeiture was granted on the grounds that the exercise of the right to terminate under the terms of the contract constituted unconscionable conduct in the circum-stances. Davies J held that the conduct of FAC in purporting to terminate the agree-ment on 24 March for non-payment of the performance bond, which was provided two days later, and for non-execution of the deed by the principal of Makucha Devel-opments, who signed the document the next day, was such that it was appropriate for the court to exercise its jurisdiction to relieve against the forfeiture of Makucha's interest in the land affected by the termination of the agreement. The breaches were trivial and were not wilful in the sense of deliberate; there were no adverse conse-quences for FAC and FAC had not given reasonable notice of its intention to termi-nate. In the circumstances the loss to Makucha would have been enormous and wholly disproportionate to any injury to FAC. Davies J, however, made it a condition of the relief that Makucha pay FAC's costs of the proceedings. On the other hand where a contract is terminated following service of a valid notice to complete and there were no circumstances taking the matter out of the ordinary, relief against for-feiture has been refused: *Ciavarella v Balmer* (1983) 153 CLR 438.

[7.17] The divergence of views on the law of penalties and forfeiture in *PC Develop-ments v Revell*, and the strength of the arguments put by Deane J in the High Court suggest that the law of penalties is not firmly settled yet in Australia. In other areas, particularly estoppel: *Waltons Stores (Interstate) Ltd v Maher* (1988) 164 CLR 387; *Commonwealth v Verwayen* (1990) 170 CLR 394; and constructive trusts: *Muschinski v Dodds* (1985) 160 CLR 583; the High Court is developing a broad doctrine of equitable relief based on unconscionable conduct. A claim brought on what Clarke JA described in *PC Developments* as using a penal clause as a sword could also be argued on the ground of unconscionable retention of benefit, on the authority of *Muschinski v Dodds*. The High Court has also recognised a limited but growing jurisdiction in unjust enrichment, for example, as the underlying basis of the common law action of quantum meruit in *Pavey & Matthews Pty Ltd v Paul* (1987) 162 CLR 221; and recovery of moneys paid under mistake in *ANZ v Westpac* (1988) 164 CLR 662; including mistakes of law: *David Securities Pty Ltd v Commonwealth Bank* (1992) 109 ALR 57. It is not inconceivable that these developments might eventually embrace the law of penalties and free it from its medieval shackles. The judgment of Gaudron J in *Stern v McArthur* may point the way. The correct approach may be, if it is not already, to ask whether a term of a contract is a penalty, or gives rise to a forfeiture, with the real aim of securing payment of money or some other stated result, in the context of the circumstances at the date of contract. If that question is answered in the affirmative, relief will be available on established grounds. Beyond that, however, it may be necessary to ask a further question: is it against conscience for the provison to be enforced? It may be necessary to ask both questions. If this two step approach is employed as the standard method for resolving cases concerning alleged penalties and relief against forfeiture, Deane J's preferred view, that penal clauses should be struck down only to the extent that they are a penalty, may have some room to grow. If the answer to the first question is that an agreed damages clause providing for payment of $X on breach is a penalty, but the answer to the second question is that it is not unconscionable to recover $X – $Y, a court of equity may be able to grant that limited relief. One approach might be to invoke the maxim that he who seeks equity must do equity. A lessee seeking equitable relief against enforcement of a penalty might be required to do equity by agreeing to pay an appropriate sum to compensate the lessor for any losses arising from the lessee's breach.

Relief against forfeiture as against the Crown

[7.18] Relief against forfeiture was only available in England against the Crown by virtue of statute: 21 Jac I Ch 25 s 2 which provided for relief against forfeiture by the Crown for non-payment of rent or non-performance of a service or duty . That statute was held to be in force in the Australian colonies: *Kickham v R* (1882) 8 VLR 1; *R v Dale* (1906) 12 ALR 549. Although in *Kickham v R* argument was submitted that the right to relief against forfeiture rested on the statute but Molsworth J simply said that it has been decided in several cases that have been cited, that the Crown had its tenant stand in the same position as an ordinary landlord and tenant. The statute 21 Jac I Ch 25 s 2 has been repealed in New South Wales,[10] and is not listed as current legislation in Imperial Acts legislation in Victoria,[11] Queensland,[12] and the Australian Capital Territory.[13] It is also not listed or included in the list of Imperial Acts in force in Western Australia and Tasmania. In the circumstances it is arguable that the repeal in New South Wales and the omission of this statute elsewhere has revived the Royal

---

10. Imperial Acts Application Act 1969 (NSW), s 8.
11. The Imperial Act Application Act 1980 (Vic).
12. Imperial Act Application Act 1984 (Qld).
13. Imperial Acts (repealed) Ordinance 1988 (ACT).

Prerogative Immunity in those states and the Australian Capital Territory.[14] Despite these concerns about the availability of a specific statutory right to relief against forfeiture against the Crown it has been held that, at least in the case of Crown leases, that such leases give rise to a contactual relationship of landlord and tenant and that the ordinary necessary incidents of such a contract attach to such leases, in much the same way as if the lessor or the grantor were a subject and not the Crown: *O'Keefe v Williamson* (1910) 11 CLR 171 at 190–3, per Griffith CJ and at 207–9, per Isaacs J; subject only to the possibility that relief against forfeiture will not be available where the right or interest conferred by the Crown arises under a statute which operates as an exhaustive code for the disposal of such Crown Lands, leaving no room for the operation of such equitable doctrines: *Davies v Littlejohn* (1923) 34 CLR 174. In *Minister for Natural Resources v McPherson* (1991) 22 NSWLR 687, relief against forfeiture was granted against the Crown in respect of an interest in a Crown lease created under the Western Lands Act 1901 (NSW) to the extent that such relief was compatible with the provisions of the Act:

> The McPhersons had taken a a transfer of certain land held under a statutory lease under the Western Lands Act 1901 (NSW) from a Mr Gadsby. For various reasons, none the fault of the McPhersons, their transfer remained unregistered and certain charges on the land such as annual rent, interest for late payment and wild dog destruction rates accrued on the property and could not be charged against the McPhersons. This led the Minister to gazette the forfeiture of the lease in the name of Mr Gadsby for non-payment of Crown dues. That forfeiture was notified in the *Gazette* on 14 June 1985. Despite the forfeiture the McPhersons remained on the property and tendered moneys more than sufficient to meet the outstanding Crown dues. That money was tendered on 21 June 1985 but refused. In Febuary 1986 the Western Lands Commission instituted proceedings in the local court to secure possession of the land. The McPhersons responded by taking proceedings in the Supreme Court seeking equitable relief claiming, among other things, relief against forfeiture of their interest in the lease. At first instance Kearney J upheld the claim for relief against forfeiture. The Crown did not seek to rely on any royal perogative immunity but argued instead that the provisions of the Western Lands Act operated to exclude the equitable jurisdiction to grant relief against forfeiture. On that point both Kearney J at first instance and the Court of Appeal, Kirby P, Mahoney and Meagher JJA, found against the Crown, relying on *O'Keefe v Williams*. On the authority of *O'Keefe v Williams* when the Crown grants a lease that lease will carry with it an implied covenant that the lessor will not interfere with the lessee's possession, per Mahoney JA, at 710. Such rights may not be available where the relevant Crown land legislation operates as an exhaustive code for the disposition of Crown lands under that statute: per Mahoney JA, at 711–12, citing *Davies v Littlejohn* (1923) 34 CLR 174.

---

14. *A-G (UK) v De Keyser's Royal Hotel* [1920] AC 508 at 539, 554 and 561 and MG&L, para [1808].

Chapter Eight

Confidential Information

8-1   Introduction

[8.1] A person who receives information of a confidential nature in circumstances of confidence cannot make unauthorised use of that information. Equity will restrain any threatened abuse and otherwise will hold the confidant accountable for any profits acquired by such improper use: *Coco v A N Clark (Engineers) Ltd* [1969] RPC 41. That bald statement is not without difficulty. The plaintiff, the confider, must show that the information was of a confidential nature, and not a matter of common knowledge: *Saltman Engineering Co Ltd v Campbell Engineering Co Ltd* (1948) 65 RPC 203 at 215, per Lord Greene MR. The circumstances in which the information is imparted must be confidential, which can be difficult to determine. The trade secrets of an employer will be protected under this doctrine, but an employee will not be prevented from using skills and knowledge acquired in the course of employment: *Herbert Morris Ltd v Saxelby* [1916] AC 688; *Potters Ballotini Ltd v Weston-Baker Ltd* [1977] RPC 202. The basis of this doctrine, and particularly whether it sounds in contract or falls within the exclusive jurisdiction of equity, or indeed whether it rests on some other foundation, has also been the subject of considerable debate.[1] The use of the information by the confidant must not be authorised under the arrangement with the confider or on any other grounds, a question which has been complicated considerably in recent years by arguments justifying disclosure as being in the public interest.

8-2   Information that is Confidential

[8.2] The title suggests information in the nature of a secret, which is often the case, but the matter is not that simple. The component parts of the information might all be matters within the public domain but the ingenuity or novelty with which they are combined will give the final product the necessary degree of confidentiality, as is often the case with ideas for television and radio programmes for example: *Fraser v Thames Television* [1983] 2 All ER 101. Unlike copyright, the material protected by the equitable action for breach of confidence is the information itself, not its physical manifestation and, unlike patents, it is the quality of confidentiality attaching to the information, rather than its novelty, which brings it within this doctrine. It has been said of the subject matter of this action that it may 'potentially be any fact, idea, invention, device, process, or article that possesses the necessary quality of confi-

---

1. See generally: MG&L, paras [4101]–[4108]; F Gurry, 'Breach of Confidence', in PD Finn (ed), *Essays in Equity*, Sydney, 1985, pp 110–21.

dence or secrecy'.[2] That still begs the question of what is confidential, but, perhaps as is the case with the meaning of the word 'charitable' at law,[3] no absolute test can be settled and the issue will always be one requiring consideration through the medium of analogies drawn from decided authorities and a close analysis of the facts of each case, particularly the nature of the information and its relationship to the business or other activity of the confider. We know, for instance, that information concerning the design and construction of machines for making rubber gloves has been held to be confidential: *Ansell Rubber Co Pty Ltd v Allied Rubber Industries Pty Ltd* [1967] VR 37, as has the design of an invisible carpet grip: *Seager v Copydex Ltd* [1967] 2 All ER 415; [1967] RPC 349, etchings by Queen Victoria: *Prince Albert v Strange* (1849) 18 LJ Ch 209, the personal affairs and private lives of a prominent married couple: *Argyll v Argyll* [1967] 1 Ch 302, the designs of certain styles of brassiere: *Peter Pan Manufacturing Corp v Corsets Silhouette Ltd* [1963] RPC 45; [1964] 1 WLR 96, and the contents of illegally taped telephone conversations: *Francome v Mirror Group Newspapers Ltd* [1984] 2 All ER 408. On the other hand, a solicitor's precedents for unit trust deeds were held not to possess the necessary quality of confidentiality, despite the skill and ingenuity which went into producing them, as much of their contents was common knowledge. In the same case, a tax minimisation scheme based on an 'overseas trust concept' was also rejected as being confidential in nature on similar grounds, although there was also doubt as to whether there had been adequate communication of that idea: *O'Brien v Komesaroff* (1982) 150 CLR 310. The information must also be susceptible to objective and specific description. The court must be able to identify what the defendant is to be restrained from using.[4] The confidentiality of the information may be evanescent, and it may not matter that thousands of other people are also aware of it. In *Exchange Telegraph v Central News* [1897] 2 Ch 48, the plaintiff sold sports results to subscribers and, even though the entire live audience at each event would have known of the result, the plaintiff was held to be entitled to prevent unauthorised resale of the information.

> In *Talbot v General Television Corporation Pty Ltd* [1980] VR 224, the plaintiff, a film producer, developed a concept for a television series titled 'To Make a Million' about the success stories of selected millionaires, with the aim of giving viewers the inspiration to make their own fortunes. He prepared a written submission which was used in negotiations with Channel 9 in December 1976. At the station's request he also prepared a pilot script for the programme and forwarded it to the channel. He received no response from Channel 9 thereafter. In April 1977 he learnt from advertisements run on that channel of a proposed programme produced by a subsidiary of Channel 9 in which millionaires would be interviewed about their success with the question, 'Could you be a millionaire too?' being posed for the viewers. The plaintiff sought to restrain the broadcast of these programmes on the basis that they constituted piracy of his concept. Harris J granted the injunction holding that the plaintiff's concept had been sufficiently developed to be capable of protection as confidential information, that it possessed a quality which removed it from the realm of public knowledge, and that it had been communicated in circumstances importing confidence. On an enquiry as to damages, Marks J awarded damages under s 62(3) of the Supreme Court Act 1958 (Vic), by way of restitution of the value by which the plaintiff's equitable right had been depreciated by the breach of confidence. Apart from reducing the injunction from a perpetual order to one lasting until 31 December 1979, the Full Court dismissed the defendant's appeal.

---

2. WR McComas, MR Davison & DM Gonsh, *The Protection of Trade Secrets — A General Guide*, Butterworths, Sydney, 1981.

3. See Chapter 15.

4. MG&L, para [4111]; *Lawrence David Ltd v Ashton* [1991] 1 All ER 385 esp at 393.

[8.3] Information which was once secret may lose that character, disentitling the plaintiff to relief. In *Commonwealth v Walsh* (1980) 147 CLR 61; 32 ALR 500, a claim for confidentiality in certain government secrets was refused. Documents had been published in a book. Some had already appeared in foreign books, but particularly, 71 copies of the book at issue had been sold before the conclusion of the case, some seemingly to be representatives of foreign countries named in the documents. These issues were highlighted by the 'Spycatcher' litigation, reported at first instance as *A-G (UK) v Heinemann Publishers Australia Pty Ltd* [1987] 8 NSWLR 341.

> In Australia, the United Kingdom Government sought to restrain publication of the memoirs of Peter Wright, a former officer of MI5, recounting some aspects of his career in that service. Powell J found that the officer had received confidential information in circumstances of confidence but that since then much of that information had passed into the public domain, largely through the publication of a number of books obviously based on information received from members or former members of the security services and television interviews with such people, including Mr Wright himself, and that in most cases Her Majesty's Government had prior knowledge of those works and had either not sought to restrain their publication or, in one case, had agreed to publication in an abridged form. Powell J held that the conduct of the plaintiff in that regard constituted acquiescence in the publication and thus a surrender of the claim to confidentiality. His Honour also expressed the view that some of the material covered in Wright's book concerning the penetration of the British security services by the Soviet Union justified publication on the ground of public interest.

The question of confidentiality was not dealt with in the Court of Appeal nor in the High Court in Australia. In the United Kingdom proceedings were taken against *The Guardian* and *The Observer* which sought to publish extracts from the book. The House of Lords ultimately refused to grant an injunction to restrain reporting the contents of the book,[5] largely on the grounds that since the worldwide publication of *Spycatcher* had destroyed any secrecy as to its contents, and copies of it were readily available to anyone who wished to obtain one, continuation of the injunctions was not justified.

[8.4] Government secrets. Governments produce their own confidential information. They also receive and deal with confidential information of others. Governments and their agencies are subject to the same duties of confidence as private individuals in dealing with confidential information supplied to them: *Castrol Australia Pty Ltd v EmTech Associates Pty Ltd* (1988) 33 ALR 31. Their rights to make use of any such information will depend upon the circumstances under which it is provided: *Smith Kline & French Laboratories (Aust) Ltd v Secretary, Department of Community Services and Health* (1991) 99 ALR 679. The government's own confidential information is treated differently from that of private individuals. As McHugh JA put it in *A-G (UK) v Heinemann Publishers Australia Pty Ltd* [1987] 10 NSWLR 86 at 191:

> Private citizens are entitled to protect or further their own interests, no matter how selfish they are in doing so. Consequently, the publication of confidential information which is detrimental to the private interest of a citizen is a legitimate concern to a Court of Equity. But governments act, or at all events are constitutionally required to act, in the public interest. Information is held, received and imparted by governments, their departments and agencies to further the public interest. Public, and not private interest, therefore, must be the criterion by which Equity determines whether it will protect information which a government or a governmental body claims is confidential.

---

5.   *A-G (UK) v Observer Ltd* [1990] 1 AC 109.

protect information which a government or a governmental body claims is confidential.

This view echoes that of Mason J in *Commonwealth v John Fairfax & Sons Ltd* (1980) 147 CLR 39 (see **[8.23]**). The onus of proving that publication would be contrary to the public interest rests with the government.

8–3 Receipt in Confidential Circumstances

[8.5] In many cases the obligation of confidence will arise out of a contract between the parties and the extent of the obligation will then be determined by that agreement although the existence of such an agreement will not necessarily exclude the operation of general equitable principles. Where the obligation arises independently of contract, some other test must be found. In most cases this extra-contractual duty will arise from some special relationship between the parties, such as that between solicitor and client: *Parry Jones v Law Society* [1969] 1 Ch 1, or director and company: *Cranleigh Precision Engineering Ltd v Bryant* [1966] RPC 81, or between an officer of the British Security Service MI5 and Her Majesty's Government where no contract of employment existed and the officer was recruited by an exercise of the royal prerogative: *A-G (UK) v Heinemann Publishers Australia Pty Ltd*, or employer and employee (see **[8.6]**). Aside from the obvious categories, an obligation of confidence may arise simply from the circumstances surrounding the receipt of the information. In such cases the question generally posed is whether the information was disclosed for a limited purpose.[6] The test to be applied in answering that question has sparked some controversy. On one view the test is said to be an objective test, under which the confidant will be found to have received the information for a limited purpose if a reasonable man, standing in the shoes of the recipient, would have realised that the information was being given to him in confidence: *Mense v Milenkovic* [1973] VR 784 at 801, per McInerney J; *Hay Court Tennis Pty Ltd v Seymour* (1980) 53 FLR 240 at 255, per Dunn J; *Castrol Australia Pty Ltd v Emtech Associates Pty Ltd* (1980–81) 33 ALR 31 at 46, per Rath J.

[8.6] The notion of employing the reasonable man to determine such a crucial question is not without its critics. In *Deta Nominees Pty Ltd v Viscount Plastic Products Pty Ltd* [1979] VR 167 at 191, Fullagar J suggested that rather than dragging the reasonable man off the Clapham omnibus and into a court of equity to say whether the information in question was the property of the plaintiff, a better test would be to ask whether an equity lawyer, 'observing the analogies so far drawn from the produce of labour, would in all circumstances recognize the information in question as being the property of the plaintiff'. That suggests an objective test of a different nature. But, as Fullagar J himself then noted, equity acts *in personam* upon the defendant to restrain unconscionable conduct, which usually implies some violation of the plaintiff's property rights or a breach of some contractual or equitable obligation incumbent upon the defendant. The idea of relying on the reasonable man has also been ridiculed on the ground that the standards of conduct expected by equity are quite above those expected of the commonalty of mankind.[7] Of course, this question is not concerned

---

6. Gurry, *op cit*, p 118; *Interfirm Comparison (Australia) Ltd v Law Society of NSW* [1977] RPC 137: *Castrol Australia Pty Ltd v Emtech Associates Pty Ltd* (1980–81) 33 ALR 31 at 46, per Rath J.

7. MG&L, para [4104].

with the standard of the confidant's conduct so much as with the confidant's aware-
ness of his or her position as the recipient of confidential information. The test
clearly must be whether the recipient knew, or ought to have known, that the information was being provided in confidence, and it would be stretching things to
assume that the recipient should have had an equity silk looking over his or her
shoulder. If trustees and, particularly, other fiduciaries can be expected to know their
duties without special assistance, so should confidants. The reasonable man concerned is also not the unsuspecting commuter from Clapham, whose views might be
out of touch in Australia in any case, but the reasonable man in the shoes of the confidant. In the television cases that will usually mean the reasonable programme manager, whose knowledge of industry practice would put him or her above the
commonalty of mankind in that situation. In practice this issue will in most cases not
be crucial as the circumstances will be such as to make it clear that the original communication was confidential. Tests of reasonableness or reasonable foreseeability
have also been employed by equity in other contexts, such as that of equitable priorities,[8] without causing undue harm. The 'limited purpose' test can act as a guide in
determining whether information has been supplied in circumstances of confidence,
but it does not necessarily provide a complete answer.

In *Smith Kline & French Laboratories (Australia) Ltd v Secretary, Department of Community
Services and Health* (1990) 95 ALR 87 (Gummow J); (1991) 99 ALR 679 (Full Court), the
applicant, a pharmaceutical company, supplied information to the respondent over a
number of years in support of applications to import the drug 'cimetidine'. The information included data relating to the chemistry and quality control of cimetidine products marketed as Tagament and Duractin. The department proposed to use the
information for the purpose of evaluating other applications. The applicants sought an
injunction restraining the department on the ground that the information had been
supplied in confidence and that its use in assessing other applications was unauthorised. At first instance Gummow J refused the injunction. That decision was upheld by
the Full Court. The applicant had not made known the limited purpose for which the
information was supplied. The respondent's officers were only aware that the information could not be disclosed to third parties. The extent of an obligation of confidence
is not to be determined solely by the purpose of the confider. It turns on a consideration of all of the circumstances.

[8.7] The relationship of employer and employee may give rise to obligations of confidence; and it may not. While employees owe their employer a general, and somewhat vague, duty of loyalty, any argument that they owe a more specific duty of
confidence must be based on a more precise analysis of the circumstances and must
be balanced against the right of the employee to make use of the skills of the trade or
profession learnt during the course of the employee's working career.[9] The type of
information which an employee may obtain in the course of employment was classified under three categories by Goulding J in *Faccenda Chicken Ltd v Fowler* [1984] ICR
589 at 598–9. The first category covers information which is publicly available or
trivial, which cannot be regarded as confidential. The second concerns information
which the employee must treat as confidential during the course of employment but
which he or she is free to use after termination of the employment. The third concerns trade secrets which the employee cannot use, even after cessation of the
employment. Goulding J noted that information in the second category might be

---

8. See Chapter 2, esp **[2.20]**–**[2.23]** and para **[2.26]**.
9. McComas et al, *op cit*, p 66 *et seq*; *Hivac v Park Royal Scientifc Instruments* [1946] Ch 169; *United Sterling Corp v Felton* [1974] RPC 162.

protected after the period of employment by express agreement restraining the employee from competing, subject to reasonable limits such as time and geography. On appeal, the Court of Appeal rejected Goulding J's gloss on the right to protect information in the second category — saying that only 'trade secrets' could be protected from disclosure by a former employee. The Court of Appeal's decision has since been criticised as 'a serious error' and 'incorrect'.[10] It has also been rejected by the New South Wales Court of Appeal in *Wright v Gasweld Pty Ltd* (1991) 22 NSWLR 325 where the majority preferred the approach of Goulding J.

> Wright was employed by the respondent (Gasweld) from about 1980 to 1988. Most of the goods for Gasweld's business were imported from Taiwan. Gasweld purchased from four particular suppliers in Taiwan, out of approximately 3,000 who produced similar goods. The preferred four suppliers were chosen for their reliability. Until 1985 only Gasweld's managing director dealt directly with the suppliers in Taiwan. In 1985 Wright was sent to Taiwan but before he went he was required to sign a written agreement containing a promise to keep confidential the identity and whereabouts of any supplier used by Gasweld during his employment with the company and thereafter. After leaving Gasweld, Wright set up in competition. Gasweld sought to restrain him from using information about its suppliers. At first instance Hodgson J granted an injunction restraining Wright from using the information for a period of four years from the date of termination of his employment. The clauses of the contract restraining Wright, being unlimited as to time, were void at common law as an unreasonable restraint of trade. To the extent that the agreement was too wide, s 4 of the Restraint of Trade Act 1976 (NSW) was able to sustain it in a modified form. Kirby P and Samuels JA upheld Hodgson J's decision, applying, in effect, Goulding J's qualification to information in category 2, with the contract in this case being read down by the Restraint of Trade Act to a restraint for four years. While the particulars of these suppliers, like the other 3,000 in Taiwan, were a matter of public record, the fact that these four were reliable was not. Information of that type was of commercial value as indicated by Mr Wright himself when questioned about the identity of his customers.

Wright v Gasweld has ensured that sanity will prevail on this point in Australia. The alternative is absurd. If only trade secrets can be protected then would there would be no middle ground for an employee on leaving employment. Everything he or she knew about his or her employer's business could be used immediately in competition with the employer or it could never be used — locked away as if it was the formula for Coca-Cola.

[8.8] Customer lists present a particular problem in claims against former employees for breach of confidence. The risk confronting employers these days is all the greater because of the ease with which computerised lists, and even printed lists, can be copied. The problem, however, is not new.

> In *Robb v Green* [1895] 2 QB 1, an employee surreptitiously copied details of his employer's customers while still in the service of the employer. He planned to use the names in a rival business after leaving employment. He was held to have obtained the information in breach of his contractual and/or equitable obligations to use the information only for the purpose for which it was imparted. He was restrained from using the information and required to pay damages for economic loss arising from its use. The fact that all the names could be obtained from public sources did not prevent the information from being confidential. It required a lot of work to select and list those names from public directories and to identify likely customers for the plaintiff's products.

---

10. R Dean, *The Law of Trade Secrets*, Law Book Co, Sydney, 1990, pp 222 and 386.

An employee cannot escape this obligation simply by memorising the list: *Westminister Chemical NZ Pty Ltd v McKinly and Tasman Machinery & Service Ltd* [1973] 1 NZLR 659 at 666. The major problems confronting an employer in such a situation concern matters of proof. The court may look at a number of customers of the former employer who have been approached by the employee as a percentage of the total of those approached by the employee: *Metrans Pty Ltd v Courtney-Smith* (1983) 8 IR 379; 11 IPR 185.

[8.9] Information obtained by reprehensible means. Someone who obtains information by dishonest, unlawful or surreptitious means cannot be said to have been given information 'in confidence' and yet there can be no good reason why a person in that position should not be treated with at least the same stringency as a consensual recipient of such information. In the United States information obtained by improper means is treated in this way: *El du Pont de Nemours & Co Inc v Rolfe Christopher* 431 F 2d 1012 (1970). In that case the defendant took aerial photographs of the plaintiff's plant during construction. The same approach has been taken in the United Kingdom: *Francome v Mirror Group Newspapers Ltd* [1984] 2 All ER 408, and in Australia: *Franklin v Giddins* [1972] Qd R 72. In the latter case the defendant stole budwood from special nectarines grown by his neighbour and grafted it onto his own trees). In the latter case, Dunn J held the budwood to be a trade secret of the plaintiff and ordered it to be delivered up, along with any trees and fruit propagated from it. In doing so his Honour dealt with a submission that the doctrine of breach of confidence did not apply in such a case:

> I find myself quite unable to accept that a thief who steals a trade secret, knowing it to be a trade secret, with the intention of using it in commercial competition with its owner, to the detriment of the latter, and so uses it, is less unconscionable than a traitorous servant.

[8.10] The springboard doctrine. A person who has received information in confidence will not be allowed to use it as a springboard for activities detrimental to the party who provided the information, even though all other aspects of the product have been published or can be ascertained by actual inspection by any member of the public. Anyone possessing such information is placed at a special disability in the sphere of competition so that he or she cannot gain an unfair start. The basic principle was stated by Roxburgh J in *Terrapin Ltd v Builders Supply Co (Hayes) Ltd* [1967] RPC 375 at 391:

> ... a person who has obtained information in confidence is not allowed to use it as a springboard for activities detrimental to the person who made the confidential communication, and springboard it remains even when all the features have been published or can be ascertained by actual inspection by any member of the public ... The possessor of the confidential information still has a long start over any member of the public ... It is, in my view, inherent in the principle upon which the Saltman case rests that the possessor of such information must be placed under a special disability in the field of competition to ensure that he does not get an unfair start.

The New South Wales Court of Appeal expressed approval of this principle in *USSC v Hospital Products International Pty Ltd* [1983] 2 NSWLR 157 at 228 *et seq*. The court recognised that the 'headstart' gained by abuse of confidence will often be the gain made by the unauthorised user. If the information concerned is the design for some manufactured product it will be considered to be in the public domain once the product is on the market and thus vulnerable to duplication by reverse engineering. That will not mean that a confidant who receives plans for the design of that product under licence from the manufacturer will then be free to build the product on its own account. Subject to any other contractual restrictions, the confidant will be restrained from using the information for such time as it retains its confidentiality. In some cases that will be lost immediately it hits the market, in others a reasonable time for reverse engineering would have to be taken into account.[11] This time frame can be crucial. The manufacturer of a new product knows it may be copied once it is launched. But if the competition takes some time to gear up, the innovator enjoys the benefit of capturing the market lead.

[8.11] Receipt by third parties. The obligation of confidence will apply not only to the original confidant but to any third party to whom the information is conveyed and who knows, or who becomes aware, of the confidentiality of the original communication. That further obligation will arise regardless of whether the third party acquired the information innocently, or for value: *Wheatley v Bell* [1982] 2 NSWLR 544. Third parties who receive confidential information may fall under the so-called second leg of *Barnes v Addy* (1874) 9 Ch App 244 and be held liable to account, as constructive trustees if need be as strangers participating with knowledge in a dishonest and fraudulent design on the part of a trustee or fiduciary. In Australia that principle requires the third party to possess actual knowledge of the dishonesty or of the circumstances surrounding it so that only someone morally obtuse would not realize what was on foot: *Consul Development Pty Ltd v DPC Estates Pty Ltd* (1975) 132 CLR 373. It may be that the third party will not receive notice of the breach of confidence until service of a summons seeking orders restraining him or her from using the information. The question then becomes one of whether there would be any circumstances under which the third party could proceed to use the information. In *Wheatley v Bell*, Helsham J held the defence of bona fide purchaser to be inappropriate in this context but said that a claim of change of position might not be, subject perhaps to an order for monetary restitution in lieu of an injunction, to reward the author or originator for his or her ingenuity.[12] The original confidant would, of course, also remain liable to make restitution to the plaintiff.[13]

8–4 Breach of the Duty

[8.12] Breach of the duty of confidence will generally result from any unauthorised use of the information, even though not necessarily a conscious use: *Talbot v GTV*; *Seager v Copydex*. It is not clear whether the confider must suffer any detriment from such use. In *Coco v Clark*, Megarry J included the requirement of detriment in his statement of the general principle and then questioned whether it was necessary for the plaintiff to show it in order to obtain relief. In *Commonwealth v John Fairfax & Sons Ltd* (1980) 147 CLR 39 at 50–1, Mason J said that detriment was essential but that finding has not escaped criticism.[14] In most cases, of course, the information will be commercially valuable and its misuse will obviously result in detriment. However, this

---

11. Gurry, *op cit*, pp 119–21.
12. A defence strengthened by the further recognition of change of position as a defence to a claim for money paid under mistake: *David Securities Pty Ltd v Commonwealth Bank* (1992) 109 ALR 57.
13. See J Stuckey, 'The Liability of Innocent Third Parties Implicated in Another's Breach of Confidence' (1981) 4 Uni of NSW LJ 73.
14. MG&L, para [4110]. His Honour was dealing with a case concerning government information. It may be that detriment should be an element in proving breach of a government confidence. The embarrassment which a private individual might suffer from a breach of confidence may warrant the protection of equity and may constitute 'detriment' in this context. The same cannot be said of the embarrassment of a government or part of its bureaucracy.

does not cover cases like *Argyll v Argyll* involving personal confidences, where the plaintiff is not motivated by the financial damage which would flow from the breach of confidence but by other concerns. It seems that it is not necessary to show detriment in England: *Nicrotherm Electrical Co Ltd v Percy* [1956] RPC 272 and certainly not in the United States: *Ohio Oil Co v Sharp* (1943) 135 F 2d 303. The House of Lords attempted to reconcile the conflicting views on this point in *A-G (UK) v Observer Ltd* [1990] 1 AC 109, in which Lord Keith, with whom Lord Jauncey agreed, said, at 256, that sufficient detriment could be shown if information given in confidence is disclosed to persons whom the plaintiff would prefer not to know it, even though the disclosure would not be harmful to him in any positive way. Apart from any other considerations, the need to show detriment, if essential, gives the action for breach of confidence the flavour of a cause of action at common law with the necessary element of damage, rather than that of an equitable claim concentrating on the conduct of the defendant.[15] It is not necessary to prove detriment in an action to restrain a breach of fiduciary duty. While duties of confidence and fiduciary duties are not the same, they are not so different that one duty can only be enforced by proving detriment or damage. Of course, if proof of detriment is not held to be an essential element in an actionable breach of confidence the action appears more like one protecting a property right, where violation of the right alone justifies the intervention of the court although Deane J dismissed that as the basis of this action in *Moorgate v Philip Morris (No 2)* (1983–84) 156 CLR 414 at 438.

8–5 The Basis of the Doctrine

[8.13] The source of the court's jurisdiction in matters of confidence has been variously attributed to express contractual terms: *Exchange Telegraph v Gregory* [1896] 1 QB 147, implied contractual terms: *Ansell Rubber v Allied Rubber* [1967] VR 37, tort — in the sense of inducing a breach of contract: *Ansell Rubber*, and in the sense of interference with a right of property: *Lamb v Evans* [1893] 1 Ch 218. This multiplicity of sources is not in itself a problem. Where the express or implied terms of a contract create a duty of confidence a court of equity will enforce that duty in its auxiliary jurisdiction by the remedy of injunction and, if appropriate, may award damages in lieu of or in addition to that equitable remedy. If the matter arises outside contract then it can still be dealt with as a matter of general equitable principles within the exclusive jurisdiction by resort to the remedies of restitution or equitable compensation, including account of profits and constructive trust as well as injunction. This does not mean that there is any strict division based on the source of the obligation of confidence in any given case. As with fiduciary obligations, courts of equity have been prepared to import the general equitable doctrine into any relationship giving rise to a duty of confidence, even though the initial source of that duty might lie in contract.[16] Should the contract fail for any reason equity will not abandon the plaintiff once it shown that information has been imparted on a confidential basis: *Saltman Engineering v Campbell Engineering* (1948) 65 RPC 203.

[8.14] Obligations of confidence can also arise in fiduciary relationships, or relationships which suggest fiduciary obligations. The two duties can exist in the one rela-

---

15. JE Stuckey, 'The Equitable Action for Breach of Confidence: Is Information ever Property?' (1981) 9 Syd LR 402 at 407.
16. *Peter Pan Manufacturing Corp v Corsets Silhouette* [1963] RPC 45; [1964] 1 WLR 96.

tionship, as the House of Lords found, albeit on dubious reasoning, in *Boardman v Phipps* [1967] 2 AC 46 (see **[5.6]**).[17] Duties of confidence and fiduciary duties are not mutually exclusive nor are they synonymous. It is important to analyse the facts of any given ease closely to sort one from the other: see *Lac Minerals Ltd v International Corona Resources Ltd* (1989) 61 DLR (4th) 14. The claim that equity's intervention in these cases is based on the protection of a property right is cause for some concern, not least because of the effect which such a conclusion would have on the position of third parties who acquire the information for value without notice. The view that confidential information is a form of property has received some support: *Deta Nominees Pty Ltd v Viscount Plastic Products Pty Ltd* [1979] VR 167 at 190–1 per Fullagar J. The better view must be that information is not property, although principles drawn from the law of property may be applied in appropriate cases by analogy.

> In *Smith Kline & French v Secretary, Department of Community Services and Health* (1991) 99 ALR 679, a submission was put that the supply of information about a certain drug constituted an 'acquisition of property' under s 51(xxxi) of the Commonwealth Constitution. At first instance, (1990) 95 ALR 87, Gummow J noted that the definition of 'property' under s 51(xxxi) was wide and that the protection afforded by equitable doctrines and remedies gave confidential information a proprietary character. That was not, however, because property is the basis upon which that protection is given, but because of the effect of that protection. The Full Court took the view that the department had not acquired the information.

Indeed, how could information be acquired? Unlike true property rights, dominion over information cannot be passed. The originator can tell the confidant, but the originator will still possess the knowledge. If the confidant wishes to exercise exclusive rights over the information he or she can only seek an undertaking of confidence from the originator.

[8.15] The description of information supplied in confidence as property has been said to stem from a confusion of the nature of the action for breach of confidence and the manner of its exercise.[18] In determining a remedy for misuse of commercially valuable information, courts have equated the information with property and thereby opened the door to the compensatory relief available at common law in cases of misappropriation of property. In the process attention has been drawn away from the duty of confidence imposed on the recipient of the information. While it might be appropriate in some cases for the court to frame its relief by analogy with cases concerning the violation of some property right, that does not mean that the analogy can be treated as the reality and that all the incidents attaching to property can be imported holus-bolus into the doctrines protecting information imparted in confidence. The property analogy stands up when applied to commercially valuable information but falls down badly when applied to personal confidences. Equity protects both, and does so on the same grounds, not because the information is the property of the confider, but because of the duty cast upon the confidant by receipt of the information in circumstances of confidence. The better view seems to be that the fundamental principle in these cases is that confidences will be protected and that the use of property, or some other ground, such as implied contract, as the basis for relief in any given case should be seen simply as a device for implementing the broad policy

---

17. Viscount Dilhorne, at 89–90, said 'that some information and knowledge can be properly regarded as property; Lord Hodson, at 107, expressed dissent from the view 'that information is of its nature something which is not properly to be described as property'; while Lord Guest, at 115, saw 'no reason why information cannot be regarded as trust property.
18. JE Stuckey, 'The Equitable Action for Breach of Confidence', *op cit*, pp 408–9.

which holds confidences 'sacrosanct' (*Norwich Pharmacal Co v Commissioners of Customs and Excise* [1972] RPC 743 at 766, per Lord Denning),[19] and that equity, in fashioning the relief appropriate in any given case may do so by drawing analogies from other doctrines. On the other hand, it has been argued that a property based theory is the only sensible approach to this doctrine because the alternative 'good faith' analysis falls down in cases like *Seager v Copydex* and *Talbot v GTV* where there is no contract and the confidant is found to have acted innocently when using the information.[20] That argument seems to overlook equity's enforcement of strict duties in cases such as fraud on a power by a trustee where an innocent and honest trustee can still be held liable to make restitution to the trust for what is a purely technical breach. It is true that a trustee in such a case would be exercising those powers over trust property but the strict enforcement of his or her duties arises from the nature of those duties rather than any necessary connection with the property rights of the beneficiaries. In Australia at least, this debate appears to have been settled by the decision in *Moorgate v Philip Morris (No 2)* (1983–84) 156 CLR 414 at 438 where Deane J said:

> Like most heads of exclusive jurisdiction, its rational basis does not lie in proprietary right. It lies in the notion of an obligation of conscience arising from the circumstances in or through which the information was communicated or obtained.

8–6 Remedies

[8.16] Injunction. The equitable remedy of injunction, in either its interlocutory or final form, is obviously the appropriate device to restrain apprehended or continuing breaches of confidence.[21]

[8.17] Restitution. Where the confidant, or some third party, has made a profit from unauthorised use of information supplied in confidence, the confider will be entitled to an account of those profits. In the case of an innocent third party, such an account will only apply to profits made after receipt of notice of the breach of confidence: *Butler v Board of Trade* [1971] Ch 680; *G v Day* [1982] 1 NSWLR 24. A plaintiff seeking monetary relief must elect to pursue either an account of profits or damages, the one being restitutionary in nature and the other compensatory; he or she cannot claim both. Apart from account of profits, equity in its exclusive jurisdiction has wide powers to award restitutionary relief in cases involving breaches of equitable obligations, in which case the duty of the defendant will be to restore the plaintiff to the position which he or she would have enjoyed had the breach not taken place: *Re Dawson* [1966] 2 NSWR 211.

In *Peter Pan Manufacturing Corp Ltd v Corsets Silhouette Ltd* [1963] RPC 45; [1964] 1 WLR 96, Peter Pan Manufacturing Corp (PP), an American company, granted a licence to Corsets Silhouette Ltd (CS) to manufacture women's underwear based on PP's designs. PP gave CS complete patterns and other material relating to the design of certain styles of brassieres. PP subsequently, in America, showed one of CS's designers their new designs for long line bras. CS later manufactured two new styles of bra, the U15 and

---

19. Gurry, *op cit*, pp 114–15.
20. M Neave & M Weinberg, 'The Nature and Function of Equities' (Part 11), (1979) Uni Tas LR 115 at 121, 'It is submitted that it would be unprecedented for equity to require a defendant who has acted in good faith to restore lost benefits to a plaintiff unless a property interest of the plaintiff has been infringed'.
21. See Chapter 22.

the U25, which were based in part on the PP designs shown to their designer. PP took proceedings seeking an injunction perpetually restraining CS from making or selling any bra based on its design or merely colourably differing from them. PP also claimed an account of profits on the sale of the U15 and U25. Pennycuick J held that CS had made unauthorised use of confidential information in manufacturing the U15 and U25 and awarded the injunction sought. In addition to that order Pennycuick J also considered that PP was entitled to claim damages for the invasion of their rights which had already occurred, or, alternatively, an account of profits made from the copied bras. That election is taken, by analogy, from the trade mark and patent cases. The profit to be accounted for will be the net profit made by the defendant from the number of items sold. In other words: What has the defendant expended on manufacturing the goods? What price has he received on their sale? And the difference is the profit.

[8.18] Damages. Where the obligation of confidence arises from contract, or when participation in the breach of confidence can be treated as the tort of inducing a breach of contract,[22] damages are obviously an appropriate form of relief. In some cases, however, damages have been awarded for breach of a purely equitable obligation: *Talbot v General Television Corp* [1980] VR 224; *Nicrotherm Electrical Co Ltd v Percy* [1956] RPC 272; and, most notably, *Seager v Copydex* [1967] 2 All ER 415; [1967] RPC 349, an approach which has been criticised for jurisdictional impurity and for failing to recognise the amplitude of restitutionary remedies in the exclusive jurisdiction of equity.[23] Despite that criticism, the practice of awarding damages to remedy breaches of confidence now seems entrenched in England, where the only issue still open to debate is the proper basis for assessing those damages. The present rule is that a successful plaintiff should receive a sum sufficient to place him or her in the position he or she would have been in had he or she not suffered the wrong: *Dowson & Mason Ltd v Potter* [1986] 2 All ER 418. Despite the charge of doctrinal impurity, an award of monetary relief, characterised as 'damages' if need be, will often be the most appropriate remedy in the 'concept' cases like *Talbot v GTV* and *Seager v Copydex*, where the originator of the idea aims to exploit it by selling it outright, rather than by receiving royalties from its employment by others. The inherent power of the courts of equity to award compensation provides an adequate jurisdictional base. In *Concept Television Productions Pty Ltd v ABC* (1988) 12 IPR 129, Gummow J said that he would not accept what was said in *Talbot v GTC* [1980] VR 224 as to the source of jurisdiction towards monetary relief for breach of confidence. Gummow J's preferred approach was an award for equitable compensation in the inherent jurisdiction of equity in accordance with the principles stated in *Re Dawson (dec'd)* [1966] 2 NSWR 211; *Bartlett v Barclays Bank Trust Co Ltd (No 2)* [1980] Ch 543 and *United States Surgical Corporation v Hospital Products International Pty Ltd* [1982] 2 NSWLR 766 at 816. In *Aquaculture Corporation v NZ Mussel Co Ltd* [1990] 3 NZLR 299, the New Zealand Court of Appeal made an award of exemplary damages for breach of confidence. 'Exemplary damages' is a creature of the common law peculiar to and available in certain common law doctrines. It would seem that the New Zealand Court of Appeal erred in principle in finding that such damages were available as a matter of equitable compensation.[24]

[8.19] Delivery up. Equity has a general jurisdiction to order the delivery up and cancellation of documents where a party is entitled to avoid those documents. This remedy has been employed in aid of successful plaintiffs in actions of confidence in

---

22. *Ansell Rubber v Allied Rubber* [1967] VR 37.
23. MG&L, para [4126].
24. MG&L, para [4127] at p 888 and see also Chapter 25 on Damages in Equity Generally.

some circumstances where the remedy has been appropriate, for example, *Ansell Rubber v Allied Rubber* and *Franklin v Giddins*. The order requires the defendant to hand back the documents or chattels which are the subject of the action of breach of confidence. Where a defendant has manufactured articles by misusing confidential information, property in the items so manufactured will not vest in the plaintiff and an alternative form of order will then be available for delivery up to a court officer for destruction or for destruction by the defendant under oath. If the defendant has proved to be unreliable under oath the latter alternative will not be available: *Industrial Furnaces Ltd v Reeves* [1970] RPC 605 at 627.

8-7 Defences

[8.20] Change of position. Where a party receives confidential information innocently, or at least in innocence of the limitations placed on its use, and, believing he or she has the right to use the information, makes some significant investment or otherwise acts to his or her detriment by materially altering his or her circumstances on the understanding that he or she can use the information, that party can plead that change of position as a defence against a confider seeking to assert a right to confidentiality. This defence has been recognised by the High Court in a case of mistaken payment of money: *ANZ Banking Group Ltd v Westpac Banking Corporation* (1988) 164 CLR 662; *David Securities Pty Ltd v Commonwealth Bank* (1992) 109 ALR 57. Some have argued that it provides the best means of balancing the equities between the parties.[25] A change of position by the defendant may still be raised, where such a change forms part of a defence based on laches and acquiescence.[26]

[8.21] Public interest. Courts have recognised that in some circumstances the confidant will be justified in disclosing the information when it is in the public interest. It will obviously be in the public interest to disclose information about criminal activity as 'there is no confidence as to the disclosure of iniquity,'[27] but, beyond that example, the boundaries of this defence have been difficult to draw and cannot be regarded as finally settled. Disclosure of the methods and practices of the Church of Scientology was held to be justified as being in the public interest where those practices were shown to be injurious to health: *Church of Scientology v Kaufman* [1973] RPC 635, or simply dangerous to the public: *Hubbard v Vosper* [1972] 2 QB 84. In *Initial Services Ltd v Putterill* [1968] 1 QB 396, Lord Denning allowed the defence of just cause and excuse where the confidant had revealed to the press that the plaintiff was guilty of misleading advertising by attributing a price increase to the introduction of a new tax when, in fact, the price increase went largely toward improving the profits of the plaintiff. The high water mark was probably reached in *Woodward v Hutchins* [1977] 2 All ER 751 in which the Court of Appeal allowed disclosure of the uglier details of the lives of certain pop stars in a book written by their former manager on the basis that the stars had presented to the public an image of themselves as well-behaved decent citizens and that it was in the public interest that this false image be corrected. The tide has receded since then and courts, particularly in Australia, have required more cogent reasons for allowing a breach of confidence on these grounds.

---

25. Goff & Jones, *Restitution*, p 520.
26. See Chapter 21.
27. *Gartside v Outram* (1857) 26 LJ Ch (NS) 113 at 114.

In *Castrol Australia Pty Ltd v Emtech Associates Pty Ltd* (1980–81) 33 ALR 31, the plaintiff had provided certain documents to the Trade Practices Commission for the purpose of establishing whether some proposed advertisements satisfied Pt V of the Trade Practices Act 1974. The Commission later attempted to prosecute Castrol for other breaches on the basis of information contained in the documents. Castrol sought to restrain the use of the documents in this way on the ground that they had been supplied for a limited purpose. The Commission argued that such use was justified in the public interest. Rath J held that the proposed use was a breach of confidence and that the defence of public interest was not made out as it, at most, extended to disclosure of actual or threatened breaches of security of the law or misdeeds of similar gravity relating to such things as public health. His Honour declined to follow the decision in *Woodward v Hutchins* saying that a just cause for breaking a confidence must be more weighty and precise than a public interest in the truth being told.

[8.22] The retreat from a very broad definition of what may constitute just cause for a breach of confidence in the interests of the public has not been a rout. In *Allied Mills Industries Pty Ltd v Trade Practices Commission* (1981) 34 ALR 105, Sheppard J held that breaches of Pts IV and V of the Trade Practices Act 1974 (Cth) was an iniquity justifying breach of confidence. In *A v Hayden* (1984) 156 CLR 532, the High Court held that an express contractual stipulation for confidentiality would not be enforced where to do so would obstruct the administration of justice, as a matter of public policy. In *Francome v Mirror Newspapers Ltd* [1984] 2 All ER 408, the defendant sought to defend publication of the contents of tapes of illegally recorded telephone conversations on this ground, as they showed that a well-known jockey had participated in wrongful acts. Sir John Donaldson found that the moral imperative to reveal antisocial behaviour did not justify breaking the law prohibiting publication of illegal 'phone taps. His Lordship also stressed that the public interest should be distinguished from the interests of the defendant and that the public interest would be just as well served by providing the information to the police and the jockey club as by publishing it in the *Mirror*. In *Lion Laboratories Ltd v Evans* [1984] 2 All ER 417, a manufacturer of breath test devices used by the police, sought to restrain publication of confidential internal correspondence, leaked by certain former employees, which questioned the accuracy and reliability of the breath testing instruments. The Court of Appeal held that, as the information concerned the reliability of a device used to test for drink-driving offences, and that the liability of a person to disqualification, fine or even imprisonment, depended upon its accuracy, publication was justified in the public interest. The defence of a just excuse or public interest was accepted by the House of Lords in *A-G(UK) v Observer Ltd* [1990] 1 AC 109 at 268–9, 282–3. In *Corrs Pavey Whiting & Byrne v Collector of Customs* (1987) 74 ALR 428, Gummow J expressed doubt about the existence of a 'public interest' defence to breaches of confidence in Australian law (at 445–52), preferring instead to consider such matters under traditional equitable grounds such as unclean hands and the conduct of the plaintiff. Gummow J's challenge to the public interest defence seems quite odd. The old maxims of clean hands, and he who seeks equity must do equity, are far too narrow to provide an effective basis for reviewing the propriety or otherwise of an alleged breach of confidence. The defence of unclean hands is confined to matters arising from the transaction or arrangement which is the subject of the suit (see [1.24]). The defence of public interest in the disclosure of confidential information is clearly wider than that. Despite His Honour's attempt to read down the High Court's decision in *A v Hayden* (at 448) the public interest defence appears settled as a matter of law in Australia.

[8.23] Where the confider is the government, or some government agency, the public interest consideration takes on a different meaning. In *Commonwealth v John Fairfax & Sons Ltd* (1980) 147 CLR 39 at 51, Mason J drew attention to this difference:

> The equitable principle has been fashioned to protect the personal, private and proprietary interests of the citizen, not to protect the very different interests of the executive government. It acts, or is supposed to act, not according to the standards of private interest, but in the public interest. This is not to say that equity will not protect information in the hands of the government, but it is to say that when equity protects government information it will look at the matter through different spectacles. It may be sufficient detriment to the citizen that disclosure of information relating to his affairs will expose his actions to public discussion and criticism. It is unacceptable in our democratic society that there should be a restraint on the publication of information relating to the government when the only vice of that information is that it enables the public to discuss, review and criticize government action.

[8.24] Access to government documents in the normal course of events is governed by the Freedom of Information Act 1982 (Cth). Exemptions from disclosure are granted under s 43 of the Act to trade secrets, information of commercial value which would be reduced in value if disclosed and information which would or could adversely affect someone in the conduct of their business or professional affairs, or which could prejudice the future supply of information to the Commonwealth. Under s 45 protection from disclosure is given to any document which would constitute a breach of confidence. The variation between the wording of that section and the judgment of Mason J has been noted elsewhere.[28]

> In *Corrs Pavey Whiting & Byrne v Collector of Customs* (1987) 74 ALR 428, the Full Court of the Federal Court of Australia, by majority, Sweeney and Jenkinson JJ held that s 45 conferred exempt status on any document containing information received under circumstances imposing an obligation of confidence. Gummow J, in dissent, said that s 45 used 'confidence' in its technical sense so that a document was exempt only if its disclosure would be actionable at general law. This would have the effect of preventing consideration of such matters as public policy in determining whether information received in confidence should, nonetheless, be published. The Privacy Act 1988 (Cth) also imposes obligations of confidence on agencies and officers of the Commonwealth Government (s 89) and confers a statutory cause of action for breach of that obligation regardless of whether relief might be obtainable (s 90).

[8.25] In some circumstances the law compels disclosure of information received in confidence, such as disclosure by a doctor of the identity of a person suspected of dangerous driving, under s 168(2)(b) of the Road Traffic Act 1972 (UK).[29] In New South Wales, the Child Welfare Act 1939 (NSW) requires medical practitioners, and a list of others, to report suspected cases of child sexual abuse.

---

28. MG&L, para [4124]; Kearney, *op cit*, p 71.
29. *Hunter v Mann* [1974] QB 767.

Chapter Nine

9-1 Introduction

[9.1] Subrogation means the transfer of rights from one person to another by operation of law, that is to say without the assent of, or any positive action by, the person from whom the rights have passed. The most common example occurs when an insurer is 'subrogated' to the rights of the insured against a third party upon payment by the insurer to the insured under the contract of insurance. Despite some views to the contrary: Lord Diplock in *Orakpo v Manson Investments Ltd* [1978] AC 95 at 104, subrogation is a creature of equity and not some product of the law of contract. The origin of the principle lies in 'natural justice': per Sir Samuel Romilly in *Craythorne v Swinburne* (1807) 14 Ves Jun 160; 33 ER 482, and, 'is enforced solely for the purpose of accomplishing the ends of substantial justice; and is independent of any contractual relations between the parties': *Memphis and Little Rock Railroad v Dow* (1887) 120 US 287 at 302, per Harlan J. Judges sometimes talk of subrogation allowing one party to 'stand in the shoes' of another: *Re National Permanent Benefit Building Society; Ex parte Williamson* (1869) 5 Ch App 309 at 313, per Giffard LJ. But the shoes are not necessarily those of the second party with whom the subrogated party has some pre-existing relationship. In insurance cases this will be the case: the insurer, A, will stand in the shoes of the insured, B, with power to exercise any rights B might have against C, the third party presumably responsible for the loss suffered by B which gave rise to the claim. In contracts of guarantee or suretyship the guarantor, A, will be subrogated to the rights of the creditor, C, whom he or she has paid out against the debtor, B, upon whose behalf the guarantee was originally given. Similarly, where A pays out a mortgage on behalf of B, the actual mortgagor, A will be subrogated to the rights of C, the discharged mortgagee, against B.

Subrogation inevitably involves a tripartite arrangement.[1] Goff and Jones argue that subrogation must be seen essentially as a remedy, which is fashioned to the facts of the particular case and which is granted to prevent the unjust enrichment of the defendant.[2] As a creature of equity, like constructive trusts and injunctions, it ought to be appropriate to fashion relief by way of subrogation suitable to the facts of the case. If, for example, a plaintiff claims to be subrogated to rights of some security he or she has paid out which is unenforceable by statute, for breach of moneylending or other similar legislation, and is thereby denied access to a secured proprietary claim, that should not prevent a court from allowing subrogation to the discharged

---

1. Goff & Jones, p 525.
2. Goff & Jones, p 526.

creditor's personal claim. The basic principles underlying subrogation were considered by Kearney J in *Cochrane v Cochrane* (1985) 3 NSWLR 403:

> A mother provided in her will for the discharge of a mortgage debt owed to her by her son and daughter in law. The young couple's marriage broke down and the son sought to restrain his wife from registering the discharge of mortgage. As the mortgage had been paid out from the son's share of the estate he claimed to be subrogated to the mother's rights as against his wife, the co-mortgagor. Kearney J held that subrogation was not available in this case because, as a co-mortgagor who had paid out the whole of the debt, the son was entitled to relief under the principles of contribution and that the equity calling for subrogation did not exist between co-mortgagors. In the process his Honour stated what he saw as the fundamental basis of subrogation, at 405: 'The principle is based on equity's concern to prevent one party obtaining an advantage at the expense of another which in the circumstances of the case is unconscionable. Hence, there is a common thread running through the relevant cases to the effect that the conscience of the mortgagor should be affected so as to cause the mortgage to be kept alive'.

[9.2] While there is no general doctrine of unjust enrichment in Australian law: *Muschinski v Dodds* (1985) 160 CLR 583 at 617, per Deane J, unjust enrichment or restitution has been recognised as the fundamental basis of certain common law doctrines: *quantum meruit* in *Pavey & Matthews Pty Ltd v Paul* (1987) 162 CLR 221, and recovery of money paid under mistake in *ANZ Banking Group Ltd v Westpac Banking Corp* (1988) 164 CLR 662; *David Securities Pty Ltd v Commonwealth Bank* (1992) 109 ALR 57. If Kearney J is correct in his view in *Cochrane*, and it is submitted he must be, unconscionable retention of benefit can be seen as the basis for the doctrine of subrogation just as it has been recognised as the foundation of the doctrine of constructive trusts in *Muschinski v Dodds* (1985) 160 CLR 583. Beyond that, unconscionability, or the desire to prevent unconscionable conduct, can be seen as the fundamental basis underlying the doctrines of constructive trusts, subrogation and equitable estoppel: *Waltons Stores (Interstate) Ltd v Maher* (1988) 164 CLR 387. On that analysis, the relevant question must be whether, in the circumstances, it is unconscionable for the defendant to retain the benefit conferred in the circumstances without recognising the subrogated rights of the plaintiff. Within that framework it would also be appropriate to ask, for instance, if the security rights of the discharged creditor to which the plaintiff seeks to be subrogated are barred by statute, whether it is unconscionable for the debtor to deny subrogation of the discharged creditor's personal claim for any moneys owing. So, where driver C is responsible for damage to the car of B, but B is compensated for that loss by insurer A, C could say, in response to a claim by B, that B had been fully compensated for the loss by A. However, if A sues C, either in B's name or directly, A can recover. C would be enriched unjustly if he could plead that A's compensation of B absolved him of liability.

[9.3] If unconscionability, or at least unconscionable retention of benefit, is recognised as the basis for subrogation then the various categories of subrogation must be seen as manifestations of the one underlying principle. In this case an argument must exist, based on the proposition put by Deane J in *Muschinski v Dodds*, at 615, that the constructive trust, as an equitable remedy, is available only when 'warranted by established equitable principles or by the legitimate processes of legal reasoning, by analogy, induction and deduction, from the starting point of a proper understanding of the conceptual foundation of such principles', so the remedial device of subrogation could also be applied by the same methods of reasoning to other cases in which subrogation had not previously been available. If, however, subrogation is not founded on general principles of unconscionability, the question remains as to whether it is a doctrine of general application or whether it is confined to a range of recognised categories. While, at least on the authority of Kearney J in *Cochrane v Cochrane*, the various categories of subrogation can be seen as manifestations of the one basic principle, they are discussed below under their separate headings for convenience of reference and because some of the issues which arise are peculiar to the category in which they occur.

9-2 Volunteers

[9.4] A person who confers some benefit on another and then claims to be subrogated to some rights of or against the party benefited must show that he or she did so under some obligation to the second party. Those who voluntarily or officiously pay the debts or losses of others are not entitled to the benefit of this doctrine. Ordinarily where one person confers some benefit on another, usually by the payment of a sum of money, and thereby discharges an obligation owed by that second person to a third, or an obligation owed by the third person to the second, the person making the payment will not be entitled to exercise any rights which the second party may have held against the third, or which the third may have had against the second. If you pay your friend's debts, you will not be entitled to exercise the rights of the discharged creditors against your friend. Similarly, if you pay for repairing the damage done to your friend's car in a collision, you will not be entitled to sue the other driver for your expenses. In each of those examples the person making the payment or conferring the benefit acts as a volunteer and can be said to have been acting officiously. Where such a payment is made pursuant to some obligation owed by the first person to the second, such as that between guarantor and principal debtor, or insurer and insured, then the doctrine of subrogation will operate to confer on the payor rights otherwise exercisable only by the second or third party, as the case may be.

In *Falcke v Scottish Imperial Insurance Co* (1886) 34 Ch D 234, a man paid outstanding premiums on a policy of life assurance in the belief that he had a valid agreement with the policyholder to purchase the policyholder's equity in the policy. In fact, the agreement was ineffective because consents had not been obtained from the holders of prior encumbrances on the policy. After the death of the policyholder the man was held not to be entitled to a lien over the proceeds of the policy. Cotton LJ expressed the general principle in these terms:

> A man by making a payment in respect of property belonging to another, if he does so without request, is not entitled to any lien or charge on that property for such payment.

[9.5] That principle was affirmed in *Re Cleadon Trust Ltd* [1939] Ch 286. One of two directors of a company paid a debt owed by a subsidiary of that company. The debt had been guaranteed by the parent company. A resolution was later passed at a meeting of the two directors acknowledging an obligation on the part of the company to reimburse the payor. That resolution was held to be invalid because the director who made the payment was disqualified from voting on a contract in which he had an interest and the articles required a quorum of two. When the company was liquidated, the director sought to prove the debt he had paid. The Court of Appeal held that he was not entitled to succeed. His payment of the subsidiary's debt had conferred a benefit on the company, relieving it of a debt which it would have otherwise been liable to pay, but the director could not recover the money from the company because his payment had not been made at the request of, nor had it been acquiesced in or ratified by the company. This rule has been taken to mean that where a person officiously pays the debts of another the first party cannot be subrogated to the creditor's rights against the debtor.

> In *Owen v Tate* [1976] 1 QB 402, the plaintiff lodged a sum of money with a bank and executed a guarantee to secure a debt owed to the bank by the defendants. In return for the provision of that security the bank agreed to release the title deeds of a property owned by a former employee of the plaintiff who had lodged them with the bank as security for the loan to the defendants. The defendants protested at this action but, when pressed for payment by the bank, asked the bank to have recourse to the security provided by the plaintiff. The plaintiff sought reimbursement from the defendants. The Court of Appeal held that he was not entitled to be indemnified by the defendants because he was a volunteer, having assumed the obligation without their knowledge and consent and in the absence of any necessity to do so otherwise.

The decision in *Owen v Tate* has been accepted by some commentators,[3] and challenged by others.[4] The discharge of a debt can only be effected in English law with the consent or subsequent ratification of the debtor. If a stranger makes such a payment and finds that the debtor has refused to adopt it then he or she should be able to recover the money from the creditor on the ground of total failure of consideration: *Walter v James* (1871) LR 6 Ex 124 at 127, per Kelly CB. If the creditor retains the money then, at the least, the payor should be entitled to be subrogated to the rights of the creditor against the debtor. Where a debtor accepts a benefit arising from such a payment, and seeks to retain that benefit without acknowledging any obligation to indemnify the payor, then the latter may have a claim based on unjust enrichment: *Pavey & Matthews Pty Ltd v Paul* (1987) 162 CLR 221. In this context it should be noted that the decision in *Falcke v Scottish Imperial Insurance Co*, above, was cited with approval by the High Court in *Hill v Ziymack* (1908) 7 CLR 352 and applied as authority for the proposition that a person who voluntarily paid out a mortgage over personal property belonging to someone else, under a mistake of fact not caused or contributed to by the true owner, could not claim a lien over the property by virtue of that payment: per Griffiths CJ, at 364.

9-3 Sureties

[9.6] A surety or guarantor who pays out the debt owed by the principal debtor is subrogated to any securities and other rights given by the debtor to the creditor as security for the debt. It is in the nature of a contract of suretyship that the debtor indemnifies the surety for any payments made pursuant to the guarantee. This right of subrogation only arises where the surety has discharged the whole of the debt covered by the securities concerned: *Re Howe* (1871) 6 Ch App 838. Where a payment by a surety has had the effect of discharging some security held by a creditor, the surety will not be subrogated to that security right under the general law: *Copis v Middleton* (1823) 2 LJ (OS) Ch 82. Section 5 of the Mercantile Law Amendment Act 1856 (Imp), as re-enacted in Australian jurisdictions,[5] provides that where a surety pays a

---

3. MG&L, para [921].
4. Goff & Jones, p 530.
5. Usury Bills of Lading and Written Memoranda Act 1902–34 (NSW), s 8A; Mercantile Act 1867 (Qld), s 4; Mercantile Law Act 1935 (SA), s 17; Mercantile Law Act 1935 (Tas), s 13; Supreme Court Act 1958 (Vic), s 72; Act 31 Vic No 8 (WA).

debt he or she will be entitled to have assigned to him or her every security which is held by the creditor in respect of that debt and to stand in the place of the creditor to obtain from any co-surety or co-debtor indemnification for the loss sustained in paying the debt, at least as to a just proportion of the co-ordinate liability. In *D & J Fowler (Australia) Ltd v Bank of New South Wales* [1982] 2 NSWLR 879, the securities covered by that section were held to extend to personal guarantees given by the directors of the debtor company, and by the wives of those directors, to the creditor. That decision has since met with the approval of the Full Court of Queensland in *Maxal Nominees Pty Ltd v Dalgety Ltd* [1985] 1 Qd R 51 and strong criticism in the Privy Council in an appeal from Victoria in *Scholefield Goodman & Sons Ltd v Zyngier* (1985) 63 ALR 43 in which their Lordships doubted that s 8A gave the drawer of certain bills of exchange which had been dishonoured a right of either indemnification or contribution against such personal guarantors, unless those personal guarantors had constituted themselves as co-sureties with the drawer of the bills or indemnified the drawer against any potential liability for the bills (see **[10.7]** and **[10.9]**).

9–4 Insurers

[9.7] An insurer under a contract of indemnity insurance who pays out the insured's claim for the loss concerned will be subrogated to the insured's right to receive and exercise all rights accruing to the insured by virtue of the circumstances of the loss or by which the loss can be recovered or reduced.

> In *Castellain v Preston* (1883) 11 QBD 380, a house was damaged by fire between contract and completion. The vendor was paid for the damage by his insurer and the purchaser, having failed to maintain a claim to an interest in the insurance moneys in reduction of the purchase price, paid the full price to the vendor. The insurer was held to be entitled to recover a sum equal to the full amount of the insurance moneys from the vendor. Brett LJ said, at 388, that an insurer was entitled to 'the advantage of every right of the assured, whether such right consists in contract, fulfilled or unfulfilled, or in remedy for tort capable of being insisted on or already insisted on, or in any other right, whether by way of condition or otherwise, legal or equitable, which can be, or has been exercised or has accrued, and whether such right could or could not be enforced by the insurer in the name of the assured ...' whereby the loss can be, or has been diminished.

But those are rights against a true third party. Where a tenant paid the landlord a proportion of the premiums payable in respect of the insured premises as required by the lease, and the building was destroyed by a fire caused by the tenant's negligence, the insurer was held not to be entitled to recover from the tenant after paying out the full sum insured. The tenant was able to say in its defence, as much against the insurer as against the landlord, that the landlord had been fully indemnified for its loss by insurance to which the tenant had contributed: *Mark Rowlands Ltd v Berni Inns Ltd* [1986] QB 211.

[9.8] When exercising the rights of the insured by way of subrogation an insurer must bring any proceedings in the name of the insured seeking, in effect, an indemnity for the insurance moneys paid out. Where the risk insured against is covered by more than one insurer, and the insurer who has paid out the insured seeks to recover from other insurers, the claim is not one for indemnity but for contribution and must be brought by the insurer in its own name.

In *Sydney Turf Club v Crowley* [1971] 1 NSWLR 724 the Sydney Turf Club (STC) was insured with the Australian Jockey Club (AJC) under the Workers' Compensation Act 1926 (NSW), for liability for injury to a worker, and with the GIO under a public liability policy which excluded liability for injuries to people arising in the course of their employment with STC. A stablehand was injured when riding a pony and leading a racehorse and claimed damages from STC, which then sought indemnity from both insurers. The AJC denied liability while the GIO accepted service of a writ and undertook the defence of the action, eventually paying out $41,255 for the damages awarded against STC. The GIO, in the name of the STC, then sued the AJC, through Crowley, its representative, seeking indemnity. McLelland J held that the stablehand fell within the definition of a worker under s 6(10) of the Workers' Compensation Act, and also the he came within the exclusion in the GIO policy. On appeal, the Court of Appeal held that while the stablehand's claim fell within the workers' compensation policy, it was not excluded by the exception to the public liability policy because the boy was not an employee of the STC. He was therefore covered by both insurances and the claim was for contribution, not indemnity.

Where a party is under-insured, it may retain any moneys received from its insurer as well as any recovered from the third party responsible for the damage up to the point at which it is fully indemnified. Beyond that, the insured will be required to account to the insurer for any excess received: *Baltic Shipping Co v "Merchant"* (1994) 36 NSWLR 361 at 369–70. An insured party who has been partially indemnified and brings a claim against a third party is not free to disregard the interests of its insurer: *Baltic Shipping Co v "Merchant"*, *supra*, at 370; *Smidmore v Australian Gas Light Co* [1981] 2 NSWLR 219.

[9.9] Where an insurer, in enforcing the rights to which it has been subrogated, receives a windfall and recovers more than it has paid out it will not be entitled to keep the profit. In *Yorkshire Insurance Co Ltd v Nisbet Shipping Co Ltd* [1962] 2 QB 330, an insurer paid out the agreed value of a ship which had been lost, £72,000, and then took proceedings against the Canadian Government over the sinking. Eventually Canada paid the sum of C$336,000 which, owing to a devaluation of the pound in the meantime, came to £126,000. Diplock J held that a contract of insurance was a contract of indemnity and of indemnity only and that the insurer's rights were limited to a right to recover what it had paid out. A similar result was obtained in *L Lucas Ltd v Exports Credit Guarantee Dept* [1973] 2 All ER 984. This rule may seem somewhat harsh as an insurer cannot call upon the insured to share any loss arising in the event of a shortfall but, in each case, the restriction on the insurer arose from the contract of insurance, not from the general law. It is clear that parties may limit or vary rights of subrogation by contract and these cases should not be taken as limiting the entitlement of parties in other circumstances to exercise in full any rights to which they are subrogated, and to retain any windfall arising from the exercise of those rights. In Australia, s 67 of the Insurance Contracts Act 1984 (Cth) provides that, unless the contract of insurance expressly allows otherwise, an insurer cannot recover an amount greater than the sum paid to the insured.

9–5 Unpaid Vendor's Lien

[9.10] In some circumstances a party financing a purchaser of real property will be subrogated to the rights of the vendor to exercise a lien over the property sold to enforce payment of moneys outstanding on the loan. Whether such a right arises will depend upon the intentions of the parties, as evidenced by the circumstances of the transaction, as to whether the lender was intended to have security over the property for the loan so that it would be inequitable to deny the claim for security: *Evandale Estates v Kek* [1963] VR 647 at 652, per Hudson J.

In *Nottingham Permanent Building Society v Thurstan* [1903] AC 6, Mrs Thurstan, a married woman then under the age of 21, joined the appellant building society in 1898. In July of that year she applied for loans totalling £1,200 for the purpose of purchasing certain land and completing the construction of six houses which were being built on the land. By one deed, dated 21 July 1898, Mrs Thurstan took a conveyance of the land for a consideration of £393 of which the building society contributed £250. By a deed of 22 July she mortgaged the property to the society as security for advances up to £1,200. Thereafter the society made further advances to her to cover the cost of building work until October 1898 when it learned that she was a minor. The society then discontinued its advances, took possession of the property and expended a further £268 in completing the building work. The society then leased the buildings and collected the rents. At the time the society took possession it was owed £1,070 which included the £250 advanced on the purchase of the land. In April 1899, having attained her majority, Mrs Thurstan commenced proceedings against the society claiming a declaration that the mortgage was void as against her and seeking delivery up of the mortgage deed and possession of the property relying on s1 of the Infants Relief Act 1874 (Imp) which provided that contracts with infants for money lent were absolutely void. In their defence the society claimed a lien or charge over the property and offered to deliver up possession of the property and its title deeds upon payment of the money owing to them. At first instance, [1901] 1 Ch 88, Joyce J held that the purchase and the mortgage formed the one transaction and that the plaintiff could not repudiate one part of the transaction while affirming and taking the benefit of the other part. He held that Mrs Thurstan was not entitled to the property free from the charge in favour of the building society for all the moneys advanced and their costs of the action which he allowed to be added to the security.

On appeal, [1902] 1 Ch 1, Vaughn-Williams LJ held that the purchase of the land and the mortgage were separate transactions. He considered that the £250 advanced for the purchase stood on a different footing from the money advanced for the building, which was simply money lent, for which the society had no security except the mortgage, which, in his view was void as a contract for money lent under the Infants Relief Act 1874 (Imp), s 1. In the transaction of purchase, the society, in his Lordship's view, acted as agents for Mrs Thurstan in paying the purchase money and taking the conveyance. In that case, she could not adopt their actions and claim the title deeds and the conveyance without repaying them the purchase money and that the society was entitled to a lien or charge to that extent, by way of subrogation to the lien of the vendor whom they had paid off. Or, as Romer LJ put it, at [1902] 1 Ch 11–12, '... To the extent to which the money advanced by the defendant society went to complete the purchase by the plaintiff ... the plaintiff cannot affirm the purchase and repudiate the advance. But for the advance the vendor would have had a vendor's lien on the estate purchased for the amount of the purchase-money, and to that extent I think the defendant society can stand in the shoes of the vendor. But beyond this I do not think we can go with the judgment of the Court below ... It is impossible to treat the advances ... made subsequent to the completion of the purchase as forming one transaction with the purchase, and I think these advances cannot be treated as binding the infant'. Cozens-Hardy LJ agreed. The House of Lords affirmed the decision of the Court of Appeal and dismissed the society's appeal with costs, the Earl of Halsbury LC saying, at [1903] AC 8, 'my Lords, in this case I cannot doubt that the judgment of the Court of Appeal was right, and I move your Lordships that the appeal be dismissed with costs'.

In the Court of Appeal, [1902] 1 Ch at 12, Romer LJ considered whether the society might stand in the shoes of the builder paid out with the money advanced. His

Lordship said that the contract between the builder and the infant was not one of loan but a contract for goods supplied, but surmised that would not help the society because the builder was not entitled to any lien or charge to enforce his claim for payment for work done. That is so, but the builder could still on a personal claim for breach of contract or *quantum meruit* for any moneys owing. If the society acted as Mrs Thurstan's agent in paying the vendor, it could also be said to have acted as her agent in paying the builder. As the society's contract of loan was rendered totally void by the Infants Relief Act, it would have been of assistance to the society to be subrogated to the builder's personal claim, even if they could not insist on a lien over the property as security for the moneys thereby owing. However, the Infants Relief Act also voided contracts for goods supplied. The decision in *Thurstan* appears to be consistent with the principle stated in *Evandale Estates* although there seems no good reason for allowing subrogation to the secured claim of a hypothetical unpaid vendor and yet not allowing subrogation to the unsecured rights of a hypothetical unpaid builder.

In *Orakpo v Manson Investments Ltd* [1978] AC 95, the plaintiff borrowed money from a moneylender on seven accounts: five to complete purchases of land and two to pay off existing mortgages. He later sought a declaration that the loans were unenforceable under s 6 of the Moneylenders Act 1927 (UK), which provided that no contract for repayment and no security given by the borrower would be enforceable unless a note or memorandum in writing of the contract, containing all its terms, was made. Such a note was prepared but did not contain one of the terms of the contract. The defendant counterclaimed that it was entitled by way of subrogation to the rights of the discharged mortgagees and the 'unpaid' vendors. The House of Lords held that no right of subrogation arose as such a right could only arise from some common intention of the parties that the moneys would be used to discharge some existing security. Any such common intention would have to be a term of the contract and would have to be included in any note or memorandum of that contract. Lord Diplock expressed the view that a right of subrogation could only arise where the contract expressly provided that the moneys advanced would be used to discharge some existing security, a view which cuts across the language of 'intention' used in this context, and many others. Lord Edmund Davies thought it would be contrary to the intention of the legislature to allow a moneylender in breach of s 6 to recover in spite of the statutory prohibition of a remedy.

[9.11] It is difficult to reconcile *Orakpo* and *Thurstan*. The House of Lords expressed approval of the decision in *Thurstan*, while overruling the Court of Appeal's decision in *Congresbury Motors Ltd v Anglo-Belge Finance Ltd* [1971] Ch 81 in which *Thurstan* had been applied in a case involving the Moneylenders Act. If the distinction lies between contracts rendered void by statute, in which subrogation can be allowed, and contracts merely rendered unenforceable, where it cannot, the result seems illogical. If it is contrary to the intention of the legislature to allow subrogation to a lender under a defective moneylender's contract why is it not also contrary to the intention of the legislature to allow subrogation to someone who has advanced money to a minor? The legislative policy behind moneylending legislation is surely the protection of the weak and inexperienced from the machinations of heartless lenders. It is hard to picture Mr Orakpo as such an innocent. He successfully argued his own case all the way to the House of Lords! It might be reasonable to argue that subrogation should not be allowed, at least to all the rights of a previous mortgagee, where the lender, otherwise denied relief, would thereby be put in a better position than that which it would have enjoyed had it complied with the moneylenders' legislation in the first place. That should not mean that a lender could not be subrogated to the personal claim of a discharged mortgagee. Despite criticism of the decision in *Orakpo* it may well be followed in Australia.

> In *Pavey & Matthews Pty Ltd v Paul* (1987) 162 CLR 221, the High Court upheld a *quantum meruit* claim by a builder for work done and materials supplied under an oral building contract. Section 45 of the Builders Licensing Act 1971 (NSW) rendered such contracts unenforceable without writing. The court held, however, that the builder's claim rested not upon any implied contract (which would have also been unenforceable) but upon restitution based on the unjust enrichment arising from the respondent's acceptance of benefits accruing from the builder's performance of his obligations under the unenforceable contract. While allowing that claim, the High Court distinguished statutory unenforceability, which was limited to the judicial and curial remedies available for the enforcement of a contract, and unenforceability which extended to all remedies which might be available, including those provided by the contract: (1987) 162 CLR 221 at 226, per Mason and Wilson JJ, and at 262, per Deane J. In that case the policy of the legislation would operate as a juristic reason for denying relief under the doctrine of unjust enrichment.

While that might provide cause for denying the lender any remedy under the contract, or subrogation to any secured claim, it should not necessarily preclude a right to be subrogated to a personal claim for the moneys advanced, free of interest unless and until judgment.

9–6 Payment Out of Prior Securities

[9.12] Where a third party pays off a secured creditor, the third party will be regarded in equity as being entitled by virtue of subrogation to exercise the rights of that secured creditor: *Ghana Commercial Bank v Chandiram* [1960] AC 73. This is based on the principle that the party paying out the mortgage intends to keep it alive for his or her benefit. If it can be shown that the party paying out the mortgage actually had no such intention, the presumption will be overturned and subrogation will not be available: *H & S Credits Ltd (in liq); Tucker v Roberts* [1969] QdR 280; *Whitely v Delaney* [1914] AC 132. Subrogation will be available on this basis whether the moneys advanced are paid directly to the outgoing mortgagee or to the mortgagor for the purpose of paying out the mortgage. Where the moneys are advanced by way of loan generally and not for a special purpose, the lender will not be entitled to be subrogated to the rights of any secured creditor paid out with those moneys: *Porter v Associated Securities Ltd* (1976) 1 BPR 97027; *State Bank of NSW v Geeport Developments Pty Ltd* [1991] ACL Rep 185 NSW 17. Subrogation is only available where the whole of the secured debt has been paid off: *Wilkins v Gibson* (1901) 38 SE 374. The question of whether the third party has kept the security alive by paying out the previous secured creditor will largely be a matter of the intention of the party making the payment. If all the lender bargained for was an unsecured loan, and that was what it got, it will not be entitled to seek to improve its position by asking for more: *Paul v Speirway Ltd* [1976] 2 All ER 587.

> In *Rogers v Resi-Statewide Corporation Ltd* (1991) 105 ALR 145, a woman, whose signature had been forged by her husband on a mortgage in favour of the respondent over property in the joint names or the husband and wife, sought a declaration that the mortgage was void. Von Doussa J granted that declaration but ordered the woman, and the Official Trustee on behalf of the then bankrupt husband, to execute a fresh mortgage in favour of the respondent. The money advanced by the respondent had been used to

pay out a prior mortgage to Westpac and the respondent was thereby subrogated to the benefit of the security previously held by Westpac.

Subrogation does not create a fresh right, in this or any other circumstances. The interest to which the payor is subrogated is the pre-existing mortgage interest and not some new equitable right: *State Bank of NSW v Geeport Developments Pty Ltd* [1991] ACL Rep 185 NSW 17.

9–7 Unauthorised and Unenforceable Borrowings

[9.13] In some cases where money was lent to, say, a married woman or an infant, for the supply of 'necessaries', that is, items which the husband or father had a common law duty to supply, equity would allow the lender to be subrogated to the rights of the borrower, that is, the wife or child, against the father or husband to recover the moneys loaned: *Harris v Lee* (1718) 1 P Wms 482; 24 ER 482. The same principle has been applied to assist lenders in cases involving unauthorised borrowings. However, where a lender seeks to be subrogated to the rights of a debtor whose debt has been discharged without the debtor's authority, the lender must show that the money loaned was either under the control of the debtor at some stage or that the payment had been requested or ratified by the debtor. A lender who pays the creditor directly will not necessarily recover: *Re Cleadon Trust Ltd* [1939] Ch 286.

9–8 Executors and Trustees

[9.14] An executor or trustee who is empowered to conduct a business on behalf of the estate or trust will be personally liable for debts incurred in conducting that business but will be entitled to an indemnity for those debts from the estate or trust. Where an executor is empowered to conduct the business for the purposes of realisation of the estate only, this right of indemnity will extend to all the assets of the estate. Where the executor is authorised to conduct the business as a going concern, and not for the purpose of winding it up, the right of indemnity will apply only to assets available for, or acquired in, the course of that business. Creditors of the business will not have direct access to the assets of the trust but will be subrogated to the executor's right of indemnity: *Vacuum Oil Co Pty Ltd v Wiltshire* (1945) 72 CLR 319 (see [19.5]).

In *Re Staff Benefits Pty Ltd* [1979] 1 NSWLR 207, a company which carried on a business as manager of a general investment fund went into liquidation. The company received money from investors pursuant to an agreement entered into between the company and each investor. The company had power to borrow and had done so, receiving money from several depositors. The company was held to be a trustee for the investors, and thus entitled to an indemnity from them for liabilities incurred by it in the administration of the trusts. The moneys owing to the depositors were liabilities incurred by the trustee in administering the trusts and the depositors were entitled to be subrogated to the trustee's remedies against the investors, that is, the beneficiaries, and the trust fund. The investors argued that the company had committed a breach of trust by entering into an arrangement with a consultant. Needham J noted the general principle that a trustee who commits a breach of trust will forfeit the right to indemnity but said that not every breach of trust will debar the trustee from indemnity. The breach must be shown to relate to the subject matter of the indemnity. The employ-ment of a consultant, even if it were a breach, was not a matter which resulted in any damage to the general fund of investors' moneys and the trustee's right to indemnity would not fail for such a breach .

An executor or trustee who is not authorised to conduct a business by the will or trust instrument will not be entitled to any such indemnity and there will be no corre-sponding right of subrogation available to any creditors of the trustee. That position will change if the executor or trustee is given authority by the beneficiaries of the estate to conduct a business: *Vacuum Oil v Wiltshire.*

In *Octavo Investments Pty Ltd v Knight* (1979) 144 CLR 360, Coastline Distributors Pty Ltd (Coastline), which acted as trustee of a trust of which the beneficiaries were five named companies, had made payments of $49,750 to Octavo Investments Pty Ltd (Octavo), by way of repayment of a loan in the six months before a winding up order was made against Coastline. Octavo and Coastline had a common board of directors. The liquidator obtained orders that the payments to Octavo were void as preferences. Octavo appealed on the ground that the money was property held in trust by Coastline and was thus not subject to any bankruptcy. The High Court held that as a trading trustee was personally liable for any debts incurred in carrying on the business, and was entitled to be indemnified for those liabilities from the assets of the trust in prior-ity to the beneficiaries, the rights of creditors to be subrogated to the trustee's indem-nity fell within the definition of 'property' and 'property of a bankrupt' under s 5 of the Bankruptcy Act 1966 (Cth) thus making the money paid to Octavo available to the liq-uidator. For these same reasons the court held that the assets of a trading trust could not be described simply as 'trust property' because the trustee had a right, which could be described as a proprietary right, to be indemnified out of those assets for debts incurred in the business. That right to indemnity gave the trustee a beneficial interest in those assets which took priority over any claim by the beneficiaries (see **[19.5]–[9.7]**).

[9.15] A trustee is also entitled to be indemnified by the beneficiaries for any liability incurred in carrying out the trust: *Hardoon v Belilios* [1901] AC 118 at 124–5, per Lind-ley LJ (see **[19.3]–[9.4]**) subject to any express provision in the trust instrument excluding any such liability on the part of the beneficiaries: *McLean v Burns Philp Trus-tee Co Pty Ltd* (1985) 2 NSWLR 632. In *Countryside (No 3) Pty Ltd v Bayside Brunswick Pty Ltd* (SC(NSW), Brownie J, 20 April, 13 May 1994, unreported), a creditor of the trustee of a unit trust took proceedings against the trustee and the unit holders for damages arising from a breach of contract alleged against the trustee for failure to complete a contract for the purchase of land from the plaintiff. There was no provi-sion in the trust excluding the beneficiaries from any liability to indemnify the trus-tee. By the time the action was commenced the trustee had gone into liquidation and was clearly insolvent. Citing the judgment of O'Bryan J in, *Re Wilson; Kerr v Wilson* [1942] VLR 177, Brownie J held that the plaintiff was entitled to be subrogated to the trustee's right of indemnity against the unit holders and that the plaintiff could exer-cise that right by bringing proceedings directly against the unit holders without first obtaining a hollow judgment against the trustee.

9–9 Employers and Employees

[9.16] Where an employer incurs liability through some wrongful act on the part of an employee, the employer will be entitled at common law to an indemnity from the employee for any loss suffered: *Lister v Romford Ice & Cold Storage Co Ltd* [1957] AC 555. In practice this right is not much used for the sake of harmonious industrial relations. In theory it opens up the possibility that an insurer who has paid out some loss incurred by an employer might seek to recover the sum paid out from the negligent employee by way of subrogation to the rights of the employer. In *Morris v Ford Motor Co Ltd* [1973] 2 All ER 1084, the Court of Appeal, by a majority, rejected such a claim. Lord Denning did so on the basis that subrogation of the insurer to the employer's rights would be 'inequitable' because it would lead to a strike, while James LJ did so on the ground that it was an implied term of the contract of employment that no such action would be taken. This thorny question has been relieved by statute in Australia. Under the Insurance Contracts Act 1984 (Cth), s 65, an insurer will not be subrogated to the rights of the insured against some uninsured third party where the insured might reasonably not be expected to exercise its rights against the third party because of some family or other personal relationship, or because the insured consented to the third party having the use of a motor vehicle. Section 66 of the same Act expressly precludes an insurer from subrogation to any rights of the insured against an employee of the insured except where the loss was caused by the serious or wilful misconduct of the employee: see *Boral Resources (Queensland) Pty Ltd v Pyke* [1992] 2 Qd R 25. In New South Wales the Employee's Liability Act 1991 (NSW), s 3,[6] provides that where an employee commits a tort for which his or her employer is also liable, the employee is not liable to indemnify the employer nor to pay any contribution as a joint tortfeasor or otherwise in respect of that liability. This statutory exclusion from liability does not apply, by virtue of s 5, where the conduct constituting the tort involved serious and wilful misconduct or did not occur in the course or or arise out of employment.

---

6. Which repealed the Employee's Liability (Indemnification of Employer) Act 1982 (NSW) which provided a similar exclusion from liability: see *McGrath v Fairfield Municipal Council* (1985) 59 ALR 18.

Chapter Ten

10–1 The General Principle

[10.1] Contribution is a doctrine of both equity and the common law under which parties who share a co-extensive liability are entitled to seek contribution, each from the other or others, for any payment or other detriment incurred in meeting that liability, so that the burden is shared properly amongst those liable for it. 'Persons who are under co-ordinate liabilities to make good the one loss (that is, sureties liable to make good a failure to pay the one debt) must share the burden pro rata': *Albion Insurance Co Limited v GIO (NSW)* (1969) 121 CLR 342 at 350. In equity, contribution has long been recognised in cases involving those under co-ordinate fiduciary obligations, such as co-trustees and partners. The equitable doctrine has also been enlisted in the aid of people sharing common law obligations. In 1584, in *Offley and Johnson's case* (1584) 2 Leon 166; 74 ER 448, it was held that there was no action at common law for contribution between co-sureties, but by the late 1700s the action was allowed as between indemnity insurers: *Godin v London Assurance Co* (1758) 1 Burr 489; 97 ER 419, and as between sureties: *Toussaint v Martinnant* (1787) 2 TR 100; 100 ER 55. It is an essential feature of a right to contribution available to one of two or more parties subject to co-ordinate liabilities that the right to claim contribution excludes the right to claim complete indemnity. The purpose of the doctrine of contribution, where it applies, is to avoid throwing the whole burden of liability onto one of those liable to the exclusion of others: *Commercial & General Insurance Co Ltd v Government Insurance Office of NSW* (1973) 129 CLR 374 at 380; *Re La Rosa; Norgard v Rodpat Nominees Pty Ltd* (1991) 104 ALR 237 at 244.

[10.2] The origin of the doctrine at common law can be traced to the rules developed in the Admiralty jurisdiction during the time of Lord Mansfield, in cases such as *Godin v London Assurance Co* (1758) 1 Burr 489; 97 ER 419, under which parties to a common maritime venture were required to contribute pro rata to any losses incurred in preserving ship and cargo. It was not a difficult step to extend that principle to co-insurers of the same cargo under the heading of the 'general average'. Where the goods of one were jettisoned or lost in saving the ship and the rest of its cargo, and the peril encountered threatened the goods of all, then the loss was borne by all interests in proportion to the value of the goods saved. Lord Eldon later attributed the development of this jurisdiction in common law to an inferred contract — an implied assumpsit — among those sharing the co-ordinate liability: *Craythorne v Swinburne* (1807) 14 Ves Jun 160.

[10.3] The cases in this area have generally concerned questions of liability between co-sureties or co-insurers but the right to contribution is not limited to those categories. As Goff and Jones have put it, 'Any obligor who owes with another a duty to a third party and is liable with that other to a common demand should be able to claim contribution'.[1] This view of a broader application of the principles of contribution is supported by the majority decision of the High Court in *Muschinski v Dodds* (1985) 160 CLR 583 in which a man was held liable to reimburse his former de facto spouse for her greater share of payments toward the purchase of a house in their joint names as tenants in common in equal shares. Gibbs CJ came to this decision on the ground that, as the parties had contracted jointly and severally to pay the purchase price for the property, the woman was entitled to contribution on the ground that they were joint debtors under the contract. Deane J, with whom Mason J agreed, applied by analogy the principles applicable to the rights and duties of parties to a partnership or joint venture upon the failure of the venture in the absence of express contractual provisions dealing with such circumstances, and in the absence of any attributable blame, under which the partners or joint venturers were entitled to proportionate repayment of their capital contributions to the failed venture. The latter principle was more akin to a duty to account for benefits received through the venture than an obligation to contribute toward a common loss but, that having been said, the principles are essentially the same; Deane J's approach being more concerned with unconscionable retention of benefit while that of Gibbs J could be described as unconscionable refusal to share a common loss. By the same token, where one co-tenant expends money on repairs or improvements to real property jointly owned, that co-tenant will be entitled to an allowance in the nature of contribution from the other, although only in a partition or administration suit, equal to the cost of the improvements or the amount by which the value of the property has been enhanced, whichever is the less, from the other co-owners: *Brickwood v Young* (1905) 2 CLR 387; *Boulter v Boulter* (1898) 19 LR (NSW) 135; *Squire v Rogers* (1979) 27 ALR 330 (see Chapter 17). If one co-owner pays more than his or her fair share of rates the one who has made the payment can recover the excess from the other or others: Local Government Act 1919 (NSW), s 147.

[10.4] The equitable rules concerning contribution differ in some significant respects from contribution at common law:

(a) Equity could join all parties, whether as plaintiffs or defendants, so that a general accounting could be made.

(b) Equity could make allowance for insolvent contributors by leaving them out of consideration.

(c) Unlike the common law, equity could pursue the estate of a deceased contributor.

(d) At common law a contributor could not bring an action until after paying more than his or her fair share. Equity allowed this to be anticipated provided it was imminent and ascertainable.

The introduction of a judicature system resolved these difficulties in favour of employing the equitable approach whenever contribution was called for.

[10.5] The basis of the equitable doctrine of contribution was first clearly stated by Eyre CB in *Dering v The Earl of Winchelsea* (1787) 1 Cox Eq Cas 318; 29 ER 1184, in which his Lordship said that where sureties had a common interest and a common burden, whether from the one or different documents and whether bound jointly or severally or both, they were bound as effectually *quoad* contribution as if they were

---

1. Goff & Jones, p 272.

bound in the one instrument with the only difference being that, if they were bound by different instruments those instruments might fix the sum of their liability thus ascertaining their proportions but, if joined in the same engagement they must contribute equally. The foundation of the doctrine has been described as resting on principles of natural justice independent of any contract between the parties, although, of course, if contribution is provided for in a contract between the parties, or if the right to contribution is modified or excluded by contract, then the terms of the contract will govern the question: *Swain v Wall* (1641) 1 Rep Ch; 21 ER 534; *Windsor Shire Council v Enoggera Divisional Board* [1902] St R Qd 23. Subject to any such variation of the rights of co-obligors by contract, Goff and Jones claim that the right to contribution is based on the principle of unjust enrichment.[2]

> In *Albion Insurance Co Ltd v GIO (NSW)* (1969) 121 CLR 342, Albion had indemnified an employer company under a workers' compensation policy for liability at common law to an employee for injuries sustained by the employee from the use of a motor vehicle in the course of his employment. The GIO was the company's insurer under the Motor Vehicles (Third Party) Insurance Act 1942 (NSW). Albion sought contribution from the GIO. The High Court discussed the doctrine of contribution generally and, per Barwick CJ, McTiernan J and Menzies J, said that the doctrine applied whenever two or more insurers insured against the same risk, even though the insurances were not identical. The test was whether payment by one insurer of the policyholder's claim for indemnity would provide the other insurer with a defence to a like claim — if so, the payment by one was for the benefit of both and the payor would be entitled to contribution. Kitto J expressed the rule in the form of a proposition that a right to contribution exists whenever a loss has occurred against which each of two insurers has contracted to indemnify the one insured, whatever differences there may be in other respects between the policies. This was a case of double insurance of the risk covered and Albion was entitled to contribution.

[10.6] The equitable right to contribution arises when one surety, or other contributor, has paid or been called upon to pay more than his or her proportion of the whole debt guaranteed. The aim is to ensure that all the rights of the contributors *inter se* can be determined in the one action: *Tucker v Bennett* [1927] 2 DLR 42. One or several guarantors who has not paid the whole amount due, nor incurred a judgment in respect of the debt, will not be entitled to declaratory relief against a co-guarantor: *Woolmington v Bronze Lamps Restaurant Pty Ltd* [1984] 2 NSWLR 242. The right to contribution may be varied or extinguished by contract, including a contact between the creditor and a surety: *Ward v National Bank of NZ* (1883) 8 App Cas 755; *Hong Kong Bank of Australia Ltd v Larobi Pty Ltd* (1991) 23 NSWLR 593; or by a contract between the potential contributors: *Windsor Shire Council v Enoggera Divisional Board* [1902] St R Qd 23.

10–2 Co-ordinate Liabilities

[10.7] The essence of the duty to contribute is that the liabilities of the parties be co-ordinate, in other words that there be some obligation which both, or all, share and in respect of which a payment by one will relieve the other, or others, in whole or in part from a liability which they could otherwise be called upon to meet. This is not limited to co-sureties and co-insurers; it can apply to any situation of co-ordinate liability.

---

2. Goff & Jones, p 272.

The liability need not be incurred voluntarily. Contribution will apply, for instance, between parties jointly and severally liable to pay the same tax debt: *Armstrong v Commissioner of Stamp Duties* (1968) 69 SR (NSW) 38; or the same statutory liability to pay, for instance, the debts of a company under Companies (NSW) Code 1981, s 556: *Spika Trading Pty v Harrison* (1990) 19 NSWLR 211.[3] The liability must be co-ordinate. A principal surety cannot demand contribution from a secondary surety: *Craythorne v Swinburne* (1807) 14 Ves Jun 160; 33 ER 482. This would seem to apply to the liabilities of an endorser of a bill of exchange and an acceptor of such a bill, as they are more principal and secondary sureties rather than parties under a co-ordinate liability, so that contribution does not arise as between endorser and acceptor.[4]

In *Scholefield Goodman & Sons Ltd v Zyngier* (1985) 63 ALR 43, the drawer of five bills of exchange claimed contribution from a third party, Mrs Zyngier, after the bills had been dishonoured by the acceptor and the drawer had been called upon to pay the bank which held the bills. Mrs Zyngier had executed a mortgage as security for debts owing to the bank by her or by the acceptor, including any sums owing (primarily or secondarily) in respect of bills of exchange discounted by the bank. The drawer's claim was rejected. The Privy Council held that where a party guarantees a bill of exchange for the benefit of a bank which discounts it then, normally, that surety will not place him or herself on the same level as the drawer of the bill and thus will not be obliged to make contribution to the drawer if the acceptor defaults and the drawer is called upon to pay. In this case the security imposed no liability upon the third party in respect of the bills unless there was default by both the acceptor and the drawer.

[10.8] In giving that opinion their Lordships expressed disapproval of two other decisions of Australian courts: *D & J Fowler (Australia) Ltd v Bank of New South Wales* [1982] 2 NSWLR 879 and *Maxal Nominees Pty Ltd v Dalgety Ltd* [1985] 1 Qd R 51. In the first case the drawer, under a dishonoured bill of exchange, had been allowed to be subrogated not only to certain equitable charges held by the bank over the assets of the acceptor but also to the bank's rights under personal guarantees given to the bank by the directors of the acceptor company and their wives. Their Lordships were of the view that the personal guarantors had not constituted themselves co-sureties with the drawer of the bill nor had they indemnified the drawer. In *Maxal Nominees*, Dalgety Ltd was held to be entitled to contribution from a guarantor after paying out $66,831.77 on certain bills of exchange drawn and indorsed by Dalgety and accepted by an import company which were dishonoured upon presentation following the winding up of that company. Maxal had executed a guarantee in favour of the bank, guaranteeing the indebtedness of the company, including a guarantee of moneys due to the bank in respect of any bill of exchange. The Queensland Full Court distinguished *Maxal* from *Scholefield Goodman*, which had then been before the Victorian Full Court, on the ground that the guarantee in *Scholefield* was confined to the 'ultimate balance due' to the bank and that the guarantor could not have been held liable under that guarantee for a dishonoured bill of exchange as a separate item. The opinion of the Privy Council would seem to be the better view if one considers the rights of the guarantor against any drawer of a bill in the event that the bank claimed on the guarantee first. A guarantor who had paid out the debt would surely be subrogated to any rights exercisable by the bank under the bill of exchange and would thus be entitled to recover in full against the drawer by way of indemnity rather than for some aliquot part of the debt by way of contribution.

---

3. Now the Corporations Law, s 592.
4. MG&L, para [1010].

[10.9] In any given case the question may turn on the construction of the guarantee given by the surety. Subject to that qualification, the principles of contribution are somewhat foreign to the world of bills of exchange where liability is usually primary and sequential, rather than co-ordinate. Once a bill of exchange has been 'accepted' by the party against whom it is drawn the 'acceptor' becomes primarily liable to pay the amount drawn on the bill.[5] The payee can present the bill to the acceptor for payment on maturity. If the payee sells or 'discounts' the bill by indorsing it he or she then becomes primarily liable, as an endorser, to the purchaser. A bill might be discounted several times with successive endorsements. Each endorser is then primarily liable to the next holder of the bill. The ultimate holder can demand payment from the acceptor. If the acceptor defaults the holder can claim against the drawer,[6] or any intermediate endorser. Any endorser required to pay on the bill is entitled to an indemnity from prior endorsers.[7] Where an endorser pays the holder of a bill, the endorser will be entitled to any securities given by the acceptor: *Duncan Fox & Co v North & South Wales Bank* (1880) 6 App Cas 1; *Commissioner of State Savings Bank of Victoria v Patrick Intermarine Acceptance Ltd (in liq)* [1981] 1 NSWLR 175. The distinction between that line of authority and *Scholefield Goodman* must lie in the nature of the guarantee given in each case. In *Patrick Intermarine*, the defendant gave a specific indemnity for any money paid or loss sustained by the bank in respect of a bill. To the extent that *Patrick Intermarine* suggests that endorsers are liable as contributors *inter se*, it must be wrong. Their liability is sequential, not co-ordinate and one of indemnity, not contribution.[8] That appears to the nature of any liability attaching to a bill of exchange. Ultimate liability to the holder or any endorser who has paid out the holder rests on the drawer, who can then claim against the acceptor. If the acceptor's liability on the bill has been guaranteed the drawer could claim against that guarantor, but the claim would be for an indemnity, not for contribution.

In *Street v Retravision (NSW) Pty Ltd* (1995) 135 ALR 168, the applicants guaranteed the debts of Terry's Sound Lounge Pty Ltd (Terry's). Retravision, a creditor of Terry's, subsequently obtained judgments against the applicants on those guarantees in the sum of $2.124 million. The applicants took proceedings against the respondents as the persons responsible for the management of Terry's under Corporations Law, s 592. It was agreed that between 18 June 1992 and 23 June 1993, Terry's incurred debts to Retravision of $2.134 million. It was also agreed that on and from 17 June 1992 there were reasonable grounds to expect that Terry's would not be able to pay all its debts as and when they became due and that throughout the relevant period, Terry's was trading at a loss and was insolvent. Gummow J held that the liabilities of the applicants, the guarantors, and the respondents, those responsible under s 592 for the company's insolvent trading, were not co-ordinate and that no right of contribution arose in favour of the applicants against the respondents. The liability imposed by s 592 was a primary liability while that of guarantors was secondary. Gummow J held that there was no right of indemnity either. The applicants had guaranteed the obligations of Terry's, not those of the respondents under s 592.

The final note in this case seems a bit harsh. The report does not indicate, however, whether an argument was put on behalf of the applicants that, having paid out the debt to Retravision (and it appears from the facts that they had not paid out that debt), could be subrogated to any rights Retravision might have under s 592 against the respondents.

---

5.   DW Greig & NA Cunningham, *Commercial Law*, 3rd ed, Butterworths, 1988, pp 292–3.
6.   *Ng Chee Chong v Austin Taylor & Co Ltd* [1975] 1 LIR 156 at 160.
7.   The Bills of Exchange Act 1909 (Cth), s 62.
8.   See MG&L, para [1010]; Bills of Exchange Act 1909 (Cth), s 62.

10–3 The One Loss

[10.10] The subject matter of the obligation must be the same. Anyone claiming contribution must be able to show that he or she has made a payment or incurred a liability for which the other party also would have been liable. This means not only that the claim must involve the same property but also the same interests in that property. So insurance by a bailee of goods held by it with one insurance company did not entitle that company to contribution from another company which had insured the same goods for the owner: *North British & Mercantile Insurance Co v London, Liverpool & Globe Insurance Co* (1876) 5 Ch D 569. An insurer, Australian Eagle, was held not to be liable to contribute to insurance cover paid by Mutual Acceptance after fire damage to a house. Both companies had insured the house but the Eagle policy, the first taken out, excluded liability if the owner took out another policy, except to the extent of any excess over the sum insured by that policy. The Mutual policy gave cover up to $75,000 and the loss suffered was $47,700. The liability was sequential not concurrent: *Australian Eagle Insurance Co v Mutual Acceptance (Insurance) Pty Ltd* (1983) 3 NSWLR 59.

Policies of insurance must also cover the one peril. In *Harvey Trinder (NSW) Pty Ltd v GIO (NSW)* [1965] NSWR 1095, an employee was injured in a fall from a mobile crane which was not in use at the time. The Full Court held that the workers' compensation insurer could not recover contribution from the third party insurer because the third party policy only applied to liability arising from the use of the crane 'as a mobile crane'. Insurances covering the same risk must also relate to the same time period. Where separate insurers provided worker's compensation coverage to an employer for different periods during which injuries occurred giving rise to concurrent partial incapacities which amounted to total incapacity when the employer was unable to provide suitable work, the injuries not being cumulative, the insurers were held to be liable to contribute equally: *Borg Warner (Aust) Ltd v Switzerland General Insurance Co Ltd* (1989) 16 NSWLR 421. The central point in contribution as between insurers is that the insured should not recover more than a proper indemnity for the one loss: *Albion Insurance Co Ltd v GIO (NSW)* (1969) 121 CLR 342 at 345. As Menzies, Walsh and Mason JJ put it in *Commercial and General Insurance Co Ltd v GIO (NSW)* (1973) 129 CLR 374 at 380:

> ... The doctrine [of contribution] is not concerned with the working out of the rights of insurers and third parties. It is concerned with distributing the indemnity to which the insured is entitled under policies of insurance with two insurers. If the rights of insurers and third parties are involved, a further element is introduced, namely, what is, or could be, the result of the exercise by an insurer of his right of subrogation to the position of the person who has been indemnified

Co-ordinate liabilities of different quantum

[10.11] Often parties can be liable in respect of the same loss and co-ordinately so, as opposed to being liable for distinct portions of the same loss, but liable on different terms for that loss, especially as to the limit of their liability. For example, A, B and C all give guarantees for a loan to D but, in each case, they limit their liability — A to $5,000, B to $3,000 and C to $1,000. In the event of default by D and the guarantees being called up, A, B and C would be required to contribute 5/9, 3/9 and 1/9 respectively, provided that their contribution does not exceed the limit of their respective liabilities: *Re McDonough* (1876)10 Ir Rep Eq 269.

In *GIO (NSW) v Crowley* [1975] 2 NSWLR 78, the GIO had insured the Sydney Turf Club (STC) on a number of counts, including liability for bodily injury arising from negligence in the course of carrying on its business. The cover was limited to $2 million for any one accident. Another insurer covered the STC for liability at common law for injuries sustained by employees in the course of their employment. The maximum under this second policy was $40,000. Following an injury to a stablehand the GIO indemnified the STC in the sum of $43,768 and then sought contribution from the second insurer. The second insurer argued that the proportions of contribution between the insurers should be determined by reference to the total aggregated cover given by both insurers which, in this case, would give a proportion of 1:51. Helsham J said that determining the proportions by reference to the total aggregated cover might be appropriate where the amount of the cover bears some direct relationship to the amount of the loss but that in many cases that would not be so. In this case the relative involvement of the insurers was dealt with on the basis of their actual liability, that is, $43,768 for the GIO and $40,000 for the other insurer with the result that their respective proportions were $22,869 and $20,899.

[10.12] The formula employed in *GIO v Crowley* is not the only possible method of dividing the burden between parties under co-ordinate liabilities of differing limits. There are other possibilities.[9]

In *Cornfoot v Holdenson* [1932] VLR 4, Holdenson had guaranteed a debtor's account with a bank up to £3,000 plus interest while Cornfoot, by a separate and later deed, guaranteed the same account up to £2,000 plus interest. On the insolvency of the debtor the bank called on the two guarantors to discharge a debt of about £3,500. Cornfoot paid his full amount, about £2,300, and Holdenson paid the rest. Holdenson argued that a term of the contract of guarantee between the bank and Cornfoot, which provided that the guarantor would not claim the benefit or seek to require the transfer of any other guarantee or security held or promised to the bank, precluded Cornfoot from seeking contribution. Mann J held that, while such a provision might deny a guarantor access to the bank's rights by way of subrogation, it did not preclude him from seeking contribution from a co-surety. Contribution was ordered in proportions of 2:3.

There will be no right to contribution on this basis where the policies include a specific provision that in the event of double insurance the liability of the insurer will not exceed one-half of the loss: *Panorama Plant Hire v MMI* [1980] 2 NSWLR 618.

Contribution and subrogation

[10.13] These two doctrines are quite different. Subrogation is concerned with the pursuit of a complete indemnity for some loss by resort to the rights of another, which inevitably means taking any legal proceedings in the name of that other party. Contribution involves recovery of a just proportion of some loss from other parties under a co-ordinate liability. A party seeking contribution must take proceedings in its own name. Contribution between co-insurers must be sought in proceedings brought directly by one insurer against the other: *Dawson v Bankers & Traders Insurance Co Ltd* [1957] VR 491. This sounds simple but there can be circumstances which give rise to considerable conceptual difficulties. In *Northern Assurance Co Ltd v Coal Mines Insurance Ltd* [1970] 2 NSWR 223, an employee was injured in a collision involving a

---

9. *Ibid*, para [1018].

car in which he was a passenger. The car was owned by his employer and driven by another employee and the collision resulted from the negligence of that other employee. The third party motor vehicle insurer paid out the claim brought by the injured man and then sought contribution from the workers' compensation insurer. Hope J held that the third party insurer was not entitled to contribution. Both the employer and the negligent employee were covered by the third party policy while the workers' compensation policy only protected the employer, and the employer had a right to recover a full indemnity from the negligent employee. On a working out of the ultimate responsibility to make good the employer's liability, the third party insurer had to bear the entire loss. One can see the logic in that decision but its correctness as a matter of law is open to doubt, particularly in view of the fact that the parties to the proceedings were the insurers, appropriate parties to contribution proceedings, but not to a claim for indemnity. If a claim was to be pressed against the employee supposedly ultimately liable, it would have to be by way of subrogation in the name of the insured and the employee would have to be joined as a defendant.[10]

In *Commercial & General Insurance Co Ltd v GIO (NSW)* (1973) 129 CLR 374, a workman was injured through the negligent operation of a mobile crane on a construction site. The workers' compensation insurer indemnified the employer against a claim brought by the injured man and then sought an indemnity, and, in the alternative, contribution, from the third party insurer on the basis that the third party insurer covered the liability of the employer and of the employee responsible for the accident. The High Court held that, whatever the merits of any claim which the employer might have been able to bring against the negligent employee, or which that employee might then have brought against the third party insurer, this was an action between two insurers for contribution, and that any such right to contribution could never amount to a full indemnity. The only way the appellant's claim could be properly tested would be for the workers' compensation insurer, exercising the rights of the employer by subrogation, to take proceedings against the negligent employee. It would then be up to that employee to make a claim for indemnity against the third party insurer.

[10.14] Doubt has been expressed about whether an action against the negligent employee by the workers' compensation insurer in such a case would necessarily succeed in any event. On the authority of *Sydney Turf Club v Crowley* [1971] 1 NSWLR 724, the obligation of the employee to indemnify his or her employer for such a loss is only secondary and a payment by the insurer could provide a complete defence to any claim against the employee.[11] There is a possibility that a claim for contribution could be made against the negligent employee, on the ground that he or she shares a co-ordinate liability with the two insurers. As the employee could claim an indemnity from the third party insurer in such an event, the true proportions of contribution between the third party and workers' compensation insurers would be 2/3:1/3 respectively.[12] An employee's obligation to indemnify his employer under such circumstances, by virtue of *Lister v Romford Ice & Cold Storage Co Ltd* [1957] AC 555, was held to be excluded in *Morris v Ford Motor Co* [1973] 2 All ER 1084,[13] and has, in any case, been removed by statute in New South Wales and elsewhere.[14] In *McGrath v Fairfield Municipal Council* (1985) 59 ALR 18, this statutory bar was held to exclude a

---

10. *Northern Assurance* took place before the statutory protections available now to employees against being called upon to indemnify their employers for losses negligently caused: see **[9.16]**.
11. MG&L, para [1037].
12. MG&L, para [1038].
13. See **[9.13]**.
14. Employees Liability Act 1991 (NSW), ss 3 and 5 (formerly Employees Liability (Indemnification of Employer) Act 1982 (NSW)); Wrongs Act 1936–72 (SA), s 27c.

claim for contribution by the employer as well as a claim for indemnity. An employer's possible rights against a negligent employee in such a case have also been cut down by s 66 of the Insurance Contracts Act 1984 (Cth) which provides that an employer will not be entitled to be subrogated to the rights of an insured party against its employee where the conduct giving rise to the loss occurred in or arose out of the employment and did not constitute serious or wilful misconduct.

Loss of the right to contribution

[10.15] The right to contribution can be lost where the party obliged to contribute is declared bankrupt and those entitled to claim contribution fail to prove in that person's bankruptcy, that is, fail to lodge a proof of their debt. In *Gye v Davies* (1995) 37 NSWLR 421, two partners, Gye and Perkes, of five who had gone into partnership in 1980 to buy and operate a hotel brought a claim against one of their former partners, Davies, after the collapse of the business. The five partners borrowed money on mortgage from the vendor to finance the scheme. There was default on the mortgage and, in June 1982, the mortgagee obtained a judgment against the partners for $224,240. Gye and Perkes subsequently obtained a judgment against the vendor in deceit of the sum of $214,606 in connection with representations made in the sale of the hotel. Gye and Perkes were later held to be entitled to set-off the moneys owing to them in the claim in deceit against the sum owing under the judgment against the partners under the mortgage. They then sought to claim against Davies for the moneys owing after the set-off. The Court of Appeal held that the former partners were not entitled to contribution from their former partner. Davies had previously entered into a deed of arrangement with his creditors pursuant to Bankruptcy Act 1966 (Cth), Pt X. The claim was held to be barred because the claimants had not proved in bankruptcy. Davies' obligation to contribute to the joint loss was held to be a debt or liability 'present or future, certain or contingent' under Bankruptcy Act 1966 (Cth), s 82.

Chapter Eleven

11-1 Marshalling

[11.1] Where two parties are entitled to security over the one fund or asset of some debtor, with one of those creditors having priority of security over the fund in question, and the creditor with priority also has access to another fund or asset belonging to the same debtor, equity will not allow the single creditor, that is, the one with access to only one fund to be prejudiced in his or her security by the double creditor's decision to proceed against the joint fund or asset first. Equity provides assistance to the single creditor in that situation by allowing access to the balance of the proceeds from the second fund or asset in priority to other unsecured creditors of the same debtor. In other words, equity will not allow the single creditor to be prejudiced by an election on the part of the double creditor to proceed against the jointly secured asset first by allowing the single creditor to marshal against some other asset or fund over which he or she has no actual security. For instance, D, the debtor, owns both Blackacre and Whiteacre. Blackacre is mortgaged to A with a second mortgage to B. Whiteacre is mortgaged only to A. Upon default by D, A has a choice: he can enforce his security by selling either Blackacre or Whiteacre. Assuming neither property will yield enough to satisfy all of A's debt, if he sells Blackacre first the proceeds will be exhausted in paying out part of D's indebtedness to A with nothing left over to satisfy B's second mortgage. B, of course, has no rights against Whiteacre. If A sells Whiteacre first there will be a surplus after Blackacre is sold to pay out B. If A proceeds against Blackacre first the doctrine of marshalling will allow B to exercise A's rights against Whiteacre.

[11.2] The doctrine of marshalling does not restrict the choices of the double creditor, A, in the example above. The double creditor, or double claimant cannot be inhibited in the exercise of its rights to enforce its security and collect the debt.[1] What equity does is to give B priority over general creditors of D in respect of the surplus proceeds from the sale of Whiteacre, the asset subject to only one security. Equity thus allows B to 'marshal' against a fund to which B has no access otherwise by giving him or her a right, in the nature of subrogation, to exercise A's rights against an asset against which A could have proceeded first had he chosen to do so. This is a matter of equity employing its remedies in the administration of estates for the pur-

---

1. *Jenkins v Brahe and Gair* (1902) 27 VLR 643 at 648. But note that this view is not unchallenged — MG&L, para [1102]. There is a suggestion, *obiter*, that the single claimant could restrain the double claimant from resorting to the double fund first in (1885) 30 Ch D 192 at 200, but this has been dismissed as contrary to the great weight of authority: *Mir Bros Projects Pty Ltd v Lyons* [1977] 2 NSWLR 192 at 196.

pose of doing equal justice between all legatees, claimants and creditors. Marshalling is only available in respect of securities given by the same debtor or debtors. It cannot be used to gain access to a security given by another debtor, not even if the other debtor is a wholly owned subsidiary of the first debtor: *Re O'Leary; Ex parte Bayne* (1985) 61 ALR 674.

[11.3] Marshalling does not create rights of property in the alternative fund in favour of the single claimant; nor does it make the double claimant a trustee for the single claimant of the alternative fund:[2]

> In *Commonwealth Bank of Australia v The Colonial Mutual Life Society Ltd* [1970] Tas SR 120, Colonial Mutual (CML) advanced $5,000 to a mortgagor on the security of a first mortgage over land and an assignment of an insurance policy. The Commonwealth Bank advanced $6,000 to the same mortgagor and took a second mortgage over the land. The mortgagor defaulted on both loans and CML exercised its power of sale over the land to recover the moneys due to it. Those funds were recovered in full from the proceeds of the land and CML then reassigned the insurance policy to the mortgagor. There was insufficient money left from the sale of the land to pay out the bank in full. CML was not aware of that fact, although it did know of the second mortgage at the time the insurance policy was reassigned. The bank sought a declaration that the reassignment of the policy was a breach of trust and that it was therefore entitled to damages. Neasey J rejected the bank's claim holding that marshalling did not confer an equitable right of property in the alternative fund or asset on the party entitled to the benefit of the doctrine. All it did, in his Honour's view, was to confer a right on the single claimant, in the nature of a right of subrogation, to stand in the shoes of the double claimant in respect of that other property.

The single claimant cannot force the issue. If, as second mortgagee, a single claimant exercises its power of sale to sell the doubly charged asset, and the debt to the double claimant first mortgagee is thereby paid out, the single claimant second mortgagee cannot press any claim to the other single charged fund. It has not suffered from the election of the double claimant.[3]

[11.4] The *Commonwealth Bank* case was, of course, a contest between the single claimant and the double claimant and not between the single claimant and the debtor or, perhaps more importantly, the unsecured creditors of the debtor. While the doctrine of marshalling might not have rendered the double claimant liable in damages for going against the doubly secured asset first, that does not mean that the single creditor would not have been entitled to the alternative asset, the insurance policy, or the proceeds from that asset in the hands of the debtor, or his trustee in bankruptcy, in priority to other creditors. There is American authority, *Burnham v Citizens' Bank of Emporia* 40 P 912 (1895), in which the Supreme Court of Kansas held that a prior double creditor with notice of the rights of the single creditor was bound to exhaust his or her security on the property not covered by the junior security and to account to the single claimant if he or she released the security on that property. That view is, however, contrary to the principle expressed above, that marshalling is not a doctrine which inhibits the senior creditor's rights in the enforcement of his security.[4] This must mean that marshalling creates no right of action against the double claimant in favour of the single claimant, with the possible exception of a claim for injunctive relief to restrain the double claimant from dealing with the single fund in some man-

---

2. Although, again, this question is not beyond doubt: see MG&L., paras [1104]–[1155].
3. *Bond Securities Pty Ltd v AGC (Advances) Ltd* (Master Windeyer, 31 August 1990, unreported); *Aldrich v Cooper* (1803) 32 ER 382.
4. *Jenkins v Brahe and Gair* (1902) 27 VLR 643; *Mir Bros Projects Pty Ltd v Lyons* [1977] 2 NSWLR 192.

ner which might prejudice the rights of the single claimant to marshal.[5] The single claimant does not need to have notice of the rights of the double claimant to the other, single fund. Notice of prior charges is immaterial to the right to marshal: *Smyth v Toms* [1918] 1 IR 338.

[11.5] The debt secured on the two funds, or assets, by the double claimant must be the same debt, and not separate debts. This limitation seems to apply even where separate debts are later consolidated.[6] The position where securities given by a debtor to a particular creditor are expressed to be collateral to all other securities between those two parties and default under any one mortgage makes every loan immediately repayable is perhaps less certain.

In *Webb v Smith and Goldsmith* (1885) 30 Ch D 192, auctioneers held two sums of money. One was the balance of the purchase money from the auction of a brewery. The other was the proceeds from the sale of furniture belonging to the same customer. The auctioneers had a lien over the brewery proceeds, but not the furniture money, for their charges. If sued by the customer for the furniture money they could have set-off their expenses against any judgment, but they had no rights against that fund otherwise. The plaintiff took an equitable charge for £500 over the brewery proceeds from the vendor of the brewery and gave notice of that charge to the auctioneers. The auctioneers paid the furniture money in full to the customer and took their expenses of £75 out of the brewery money. That left a balance of £82 in the brewery proceeds which they paid to the customer. The plaintiff sued the auctioneers for the brewery moneys arguing that they should have taken their expenses out of the furniture moneys and left the brewery moneys to it. The Court of Appeal dismissed the claim by the plaintiff holding that the doctrine of marshalling only applies where the double claimant has similar rights against the two funds in question. It does not apply where there are different funds against which different rights exist.

[11.6] It was suggested in *Webb v Smith* that the doctrine gives the single claimant a proprietary interest in the alternative fund. To some extent such a description of the single claimant's rights in that fund is justified in the sense that marshalling gives the single claimant priority over other unsecured creditors in respect of that asset and also in that the single claimant will be subrogated to the security rights of the double claimant. However, the matter seems more one of bringing the asset, or its proprietor, within reach of the court. Where the debtor is bankrupt and the single claimant is engaged in a contest with unsecured creditors it is better to look at the single claimant's rights as rights against the asset or fund rather than against the debtor, whose capacity to pay in full is gone. In other cases, the more appropriate course seems to be to ensure that the proper parties are joined, particularly the debtor and/or any party to whom the alternative fund or asset has been transferred. Where that asset or fund has been transferred to a third party who takes without notice of the claim of the single claimant, even though that third party is a volunteer, and even though the interest taken by that third party is a security interest, that is, a second mortgage, the third party will take the asset in preference to the single claimant: *Dolphin v Aylward* (1870) LR 4 H L 486. The priority given to a third party volunteer in such circumstances would also seem to contradict the argument that marshalling gives the single claimant a proprietary interest in the alternative fund. On the other hand, where a third party takes the doubly charged asset with notice of the equity of the single

---

5. MG&L suggest that the single claimant would have standing to seek this relief, at [1106]: see *Deta Nominees Pty Ltd v Viscount Plastic Products* [1979] VR 167 at 192. MG&L also suggest that the single claimant has at least standing to set aside a fraudulent sale by the first mortgagee, at [1105].
6. MG&L, para [1110].

claimant, even though the third party takes for value, the right to marshal will survive: *Cheesebrough v Millard* (1815) 1 Johns Chan 408, although there may be some adjustment or apportionment between the single claimant and the third party.

[11.7] Where there are two single claimants involved, as can be the case where the debtor gives a second mortgage over the alternative fund or asset, both single claimants will face the prospect of recourse to marshalling. Equity's response in such a case is to apply marshalling by apportionment so that the claims of the two single claimants are distributed rateably across the balance of the proceeds of the two assets. So, for instance, assume D owns Blueacre and Redacre and mortgages both to A to secure a loan, and then gives a second mortgage over Blueacre to B, and later a second mortgage over Redacre to C. If D then defaults under the mortgage to A, and A exercises his power of sale over Blueacre to recover his debt in full, leaving no surplus, then B, by the equity to marshal, and C, by his second mortgage, will both have access to Redacre, the proceeds of which will be apportioned rateably between the two, unless, of course, there is some agreement between the two second mortgagees excluding any such apportionment: *Flint v Howard* [1893] 2 Ch 54. There will be no such right to apportionment where one of the second mortgagees has security over both assets: *Mir Bros Projects Pty Ltd v Lyons* [1978] 2 NSWLR 505.

[11.8] The right of a surety to be subrogated to the security or rights of a creditor he or she has paid out is not a matter of marshalling. The single claimant's right to access to the single fund in a marshalling case operates by way of subrogation, but that is where the similarity ends, despite some judicial confusion on the distinction.[7] The surety is limited to access to the securities previously available to the creditor, although it would seem, if the surety has guaranteed a loan by a second mortgagee, and that second mortgagee was entitled to marshal against some other asset, the surety would be subrogated to that right as well. Conversely, where a surety has access to assets against which some other creditor seeks to marshal, it will not be open to the surety to oppose the equity of the other creditor simply because he or she is the guarantor of the debt and not the original debtor. While this seems plain enough, it has not been consistently or logically dealt with by the courts.[8]

[11.9] There is some debate over the basis of the doctrine of marshalling. Meagher, Gummow and Lehane reject Ashburner's suggestion that marshalling grew from the doctrine of consolidation, under which a mortgagee who held several mortgages from the same mortgagor on different properties could insist that the mortgagor redeem all the mortgages if he or she sought to redeem one, because marshalling survived the abolition of consolidation by statute.[9] Instead the learned authors, relying on the language of Lord Eldon in *Aldrich v Cooper* (1803) 8 Ves 382 at 390, as echoed by the High Court in *Miles v Official Receiver* (1963) 109 CLR 501 at 510, argue that marshalling stems from equity's reluctance to allow one creditor, who is over-endowed with security, to exercise its rights so as to prejudice those of another puisne claimant with access to only one fund.[10] That explanation concentrates on the actions of the double claimant who, properly speaking, ought not to be a party to any proceedings by a single claimant seeking to enforce an equity to marshal. A better explanation, and one more consistent with the underlying bases of other doctrines of

---

7. *Heyman v Dubois* (1871) LR 13 Eq 158, see MG&L, para [1131].
8. MG&L, paras [1131]–[1134].
9. Conveyancing Act 1919 (NSW), s 97; Property Law Act 1958 (Vic), s 93; Property Law Act 1969 (WA), s 56; Law of Property Act 1925 (UK), s 93.
10. MG&L, para [1140].

equity, might be that equity, by allowing the single claimant to marshal against some asset over which he or she has no security, would be acting to prevent the unjust enrichment of the unsecured creditors of the debtor at the expense of a creditor who was prudent enough to obtain security, while the others were not. In other words, it would be unjust in the circumstances to allow the unsecured creditors to profit from the caprice of the doubly secured creditor at the expense of the single puisne creditor whose security would otherwise be destroyed.

11–2 Election

[11.10] A person taking a benefit under a deed or will cannot 'elect' to accept only that part of the instrument conferring the benefit and reject the rest; he or she cannot approbate and reprobate. 'Where a deed or will professes to make a general disposition of property for the benefit of a person named in it, such person cannot accept a benefit under the instrument without at the same time conforming to all its provisions, and renouncing every right inconsistent with them': *Codrington v Codrington* (1875) LR 7 HL 854 at 861–2, per Lord Cairns. Election in equity will apply where, for instance, a testator purports to dispose of property he or she does not own while also making a gift to the true owner of that property. If a testator purports to devise Blackacre in his will to Adam, when Blackacre is really the property of Bruce, and also makes a gift of a pecuniary legacy of $50,000 to Bruce, Bruce will have to elect whether to accept the terms of the will or to reject them. If he accepts the will he can receive the legacy of $50,000 but will have to convey Blackacre to Adam. If he elects to keep Blackacre, he cannot get the legacy which will be applied in compensating Adam's disappointment, at least to the value of Blackacre. If Blackacre is worth more than $50,000, Adam will only get the $50,000, while Bruce will get nothing of the legacy but will, of course, keep Blackacre. If Blackacre is worth less than $50,000, Adam will get its value from that amount and the balance will go to Bruce. The last example illustrates the fact that election operates by way of compensation, not forfeiture. In the event that the party put to an election elects to take against the will, and not under it, he or she will not forfeit all benefits under the will, only so much of those benefits as will be necessary to compensate other beneficiaries disappointed by the election.

[11.11] Election requires a gift by will, or deed, of property which is not the testator's or disponor's, and a benefit given under the same instrument to the true owner of that property. The doctrine will not apply where a testator makes a gift in his or her will of property which he or she does own at the time of making the will but which is later transferred to another during his or her lifetime. In that case the gift is adeemed; the will must be read as if there is no intention to make such a gift. In most cases in which the doctrine of election applies, the testator will have made a mistake that he or she has rights over certain property which he or she does not, in fact, possess. Where a testator, or donor, has only a limited interest in the property concerned, and, on the face of the instrument, appears to have attempted an absolute gift of the property, the courts will construe the gift, wherever possible, as one of the disponor's limited interest, thus preventing any need for election. The property purportedly disposed of by the disponor must be capable of alienation by the party called upon to elect. If he or she is not free to transfer the property, there can be no room for the doctrine of election: *Re Chesham* (1886) 31 Ch D 466.

[11.12] Election in equity should be distinguished from election at common law. Election at common law arises where a person is entitled to alternate but inconsistent rights on the same facts and must elect which of those rights he or she will pursue, such as in the case where a party to a contract, when faced with a breach of that contract by the other party, may elect to terminate the contract and sue for damages for the breach or to keep the contract on foot and seek specific performance: *Commonwealth v Verwayen* (1990) 170 CLR 394 at 421, per Brennan J; *Sargent v ASL Developments Pty Ltd* (1979) 141 CLR 634; *Ciavarella v Balmer* (1983) 153 CLR 438.

11-3 Conversion

[11.13] This is a doctrine which used to apply to effect a notional conversion of real property into personal property, and personalty into realty, in certain cases, where different rules governed the succession to real and personal property in intestate estates, on the basis of the maxim that equity regards as done that which ought to be done. In England, before the Law of Property Act 1925, when a person died intestate, their real estate would go to the heir at law while the personalty went to the next of kin. The effect of the doctrine was that money directed to be employed in the purchase of land and land directed to be sold and converted into cash would each be treated as the species of property into which it was intended they be converted; and that the conversion would be deemed to have taken effect in the manner directed whether by will, contract, marriage articles, settlement, or otherwise: *Fletcher v Ashburner* (1799) 1 Bro CC 497; 28 ER 1259.

> In *Sweetapple v Bindon* (1705) 2 Vern 530; 23 ER 947, a testatrix bequeathed £300 to be applied in the purchase of real property for the benefit of her daughter and that daughter's children. The daughter married and had a child but both died before any realty was purchased with the fund. The daughter's widower brought an action claiming to be entitled to the £300 by virtue of the doctrine of curtesy (under which a widower had rights at common law over his wife's realty, but not her personalty). It was held that the money should be treated as realty and the claim was upheld.

[11.14] The abolition of the distinction between realty and personalty for the purposes of succession has rendered this doctrine all but obsolete in its original context but conversion still applies in other circumstances. For instance, where a testator or settlor gives his trustee a direction, which can be express or implied, to purchase or sell realty then the property or fund in question will be treated as if it had actually been converted from the time the instrument comes into effect. The direction must be imperative. There can be no conversion where there is a mere power to sell land. The fact that the sale may be subject to the consent of a third party will not prevent the trust for sale being an immediate trust, the consent being treated as regulating the sale, not preventing it; nor will the existence of a power to postpone the sale prevent conversion taking place: *Duke of Marlborough v A-G* [1945] Ch 145. Thus, where a testator makes separate dispositions of realty and personalty, and is at the time of his or her death entitled to the benefit of a settlement, or a deceased estate, to which the doctrine of conversion applies, that doctrine will determine whether the property or fund in question passes to the testator's devizees or legatees.

[11.15] An order of the court for the sale of realty will effect a conversion from the date of the order, or, in the case of the appointment of trustees for sale under the Conveyancing Act 1919 (NSW), s 66G, from the date of appointment of the trustees.

Entry into a contract for the sale of land will also effect a conversion of that land into personalty in the estate of the vendor should the vendor die before completion: *Re Williamson* (1904) 10 ALR 197. Any specific devise of the land contained in a will made before such a contract will be revoked or adeemed: *Andrew v Andrew* (1856) 4 WR 520. If the will is made after the contract it will be a matter of construction of the will as to whether the devizee is to get the proceeds of sale: *Re Calow* [1928] Ch 710. By the same token, if a testator enters into a contract to purchase land, but dies before the contract is completed, his or her rights under the contract will pass as realty, even if the contract is validly rescinded after the testator's death: *Hudson v Cook* (1872) LR 13 Eq 417. If the transaction in question is only an option to purchase, no conversion will take place unless and until the option is validly exercised: *Re Isaacs* [1894] 3 Ch 506, as conversion is only deemed to take place from the date of the agreement: *Re Marlay, Duke of Rutland v Bury* [1915] 2 Ch 264.

[11.16] Where the purposes for which conversion is directed fail, in whole or in part, for instance, where the object of a trust for conversion predeceases the testator, or where such a gift fails for uncertainty, or breaches the rule against perpetuities,[11] the property will be treated as though no conversion has taken place, even if the property has been actually converted, at least to the extent of the failure of the purpose: *Re Hopkinson* [1922] 1 Ch 65. So that where money is directed to be applied in the purchase of land for the benefit of X and X predeceases the testator, the money designated for the trust will pass as personalty. The only difference between total and partial failure of a trust for conversion is one of form, not of substance. Where there is a total failure of the purposes of a trust for conversion the property will pass as though there never was any trust for conversion and will pass in its original, unconverted state. Where, however, there is only a partial failure of the purposes of a trust for conversion there will be a partial success as well. That will necessitate the conversion of the whole of the property, with the share in that property which is the subject of the partial failure passing in its converted state to the appropriate recipient upon failure of the trust for conversion: *Smith v Claxton* (1820) 4 Madd 484; 65 ER 784. For example, where a testator leaves certain realty on a trust for conversion and directs that the proceeds be held on trust for A and B, while leaving the rest of his estate, as to realty, to X, and as to personalty, to Y, and A predeceases the testator, the trust for conversion will take effect for the benefit of B, and the land will be converted, but half the proceeds will go, as personalty, that is, cash, to X, the devizee. Where the trust for conversion is created by a settlement *inter vivos*, any failure of the objects of conversion will lead to a resulting trust in favour of the settlor. If there is a total failure, the settlor will take the property unconverted. If the failure is only partial, it will revert to the settlor in its converted form: *Merriman v Perpetual Trustee Co Ltd* (1895) 17 LR (NSW) Eq 325.

[11.17] Where conversion has been directed in favour of someone who will take the property as absolute owner, that beneficiary may elect to take the property in its unconverted form, thus effecting a 'reconversion'. In such a case equity treats the notionally converted property as having been restored to its original state.

---

11. An unlikely proposition in New South Wales since the introduction of the Perpetuines Act 1984 which, under s 8(1), allows a wait-and-see period instead of the old common law rule of initial uncertainty.

11–4 Merger

[11.18] This is a doctrine under which some lesser right will be extinguished by operation of law when that lesser right coincides with another greater right to which the lesser is subservient, by merger of the title to both interests. For instance, if a life tenant purchases the reversion in fee simple the life tenancy will be extinguished on the merger of the lesser and greater estates. Similar considerations apply to extinguish an easement where the ownership of both the dominant tenement and the servient tenement are merged. Merger by operation of law cannot apply to Torrens title land: *Shell Company of Australia Ltd v Zanelli* [1973] 1 NSWLR 216. An easement over Torrens title land will not be extinguished unless the register is amended in the appropriate manner. Where a person entitled to the benefit of a charge over land acquires the land the merger will extinguish the charge, unless the parties intend that the charge be kept alive. Where that charge is registered on the title, failure to register a discharge will be evidence of an intention to keep the charge alive.

[11.19] A second form of merger occurs when, upon completion of a contract for the sale of land, the contract is said to merge with the conveyance, thus extinguishing the rights of the parties under the conveyance. Some contractual terms, such as a covenant for vacant possession, will survive conveyance and the question of whether any particular term survives will depend upon the intention of the parties.[12]

11–5 Satisfaction and Ademption

[11.20] Equity will consider an obligation to have been fulfilled in a number of different circumstances. The easiest and most obvious is performance, under which the party under the obligation, the obligor, will do what he or she has agreed to do. Satisfaction occurs where a party already subject to a prior obligation to another makes a gift or confers a benefit on that other party with the intention, actual or presumed, that the gift or benefit should satisfy the prior obligation owed. Ademption is almost the converse of satisfaction, although it has the same effect. It also removes the need to carry out an obligation. A gift or legacy which has been adeemed has been taken away. So, where a testator disposes of the subject matter of a legacy during his or her lifetime, that gift will be adeemed. Ademption can be effected by a gift to the designated legatee.

Satisfaction of a debt by a legacy

[11.21] The most common instance of satisfaction occurs where a debtor leaves a legacy to his creditor, in which case the legacy will be presumed to be given in satisfaction of the debt owed: *Atkinson v Webb* (1704) 2 Vern 478; 23 ER 90. In that case an annuity left in a will was held not to constitute satisfaction of prior obligation arising from a bond because the amount of the annuity was less and not as beneficial as the bond. The debt must be owed at the date of the will. A testator cannot be presumed to intend to satisfy a debt incurred after making his will: *Thomas v Bennet* (1725) 2 P Wms 341; 24 ER 757. The courts have taken a very narrow view of this presumption, which Kindersley VC even described as a 'false principle',[13] and have readily

---

12. MG&L, paras [4010]–[4011].
13. *Hassell v Hawkins* (1859) 4 Drew 468 at 470; 62 ER 180 at 181.

seized upon any difference between the legacy and the debt, or other obligation, as grounds for rebuttal. For instance, satisfaction will not be presumed if the legacy is less than the debt: *Gee v Liddell (No 1)* (1866) 35 Beav 621; 55 ER 1038, nor if the amount of the gift is uncertain, as will be the case with a gift of residue: *Thynne v Earl of Glengall* (1848) 2 HLC 131; 9 ER 1042, or conditional: *Mathews v Mathews* (1755) 2 Ves Sen 635; 28 ER 405, nor if the debt is uncertain, as would be the case where the debt fluctuates between the date of the will and the date of the testator's death: *Webb v Webb* (1900) 2 NSWLR (Eq) 245, nor if the debt is presently payable and the legacy is expressly postponed until some date after the testator's death so that it does not bear interest until that later date: *Clark v Sewell* (1744) 3 Atk 96; 26 ER 858. The presumption will not arise at all where what is given is substantially different from what is owed; so a gift of land will not satisfy a cash debt: *Eastwood v Vinke* (1731) 2 P Wms 613; 24 ER 883. A direction in a will to pay debts will also rebut the presumption: *Re Manners, Public Trustee v Manners* [1949] 2 All ER 201.

In *Royal North Shore Hospital v Crichton-Smith* (1938) 60 CLR 798, a husband entered into a covenant in 1922 to pay an annuity to his wife of £630 by equal quarterly instalments while she remained chaste. By his will, made in 1931, he directed that income from his residuary estate, up to but not exceeding £630 per annum, be paid to his wife by equal quarterly instalments for her life or until she remarried. The testator died in 1937 and it was held that the legacy was in satisfaction of the annuity otherwise payable to the wife and that the wife was therefore put to her election as to which she would take. Dixon J said (at 815), that to come to such a view the court had to be satisfied that the testator intended the gift in the will to substitute for the gift inter vivos.

This could not apply in a case of ademption, as a matter of logic as much as law, where the covenant to pay an annuity was entered into after the making of the will. In that case there would be no possibility that the testator intended the gift in the will to operate in substitution for the *inter vivos* covenant.

Satisfaction of a portions debt

[11.22] When a father, or someone who stands in *loco parentis* to a child,[14] takes an obligation to provide a portion for the child, that is, some permanent and substantial provision for the benefit of the child, usually in the nature of some gift to establish the child in life, and that father figure later makes a will in which a legacy, in the nature of a portion, is bequeathed to the same child, the gift in the will is presumed to have been made in satisfaction of the obligation incurred *inter vivos* to grant a portion to that child. This has also been described as a rule against double portions, the principle being that the father is presumed not to intend to benefit one child twice over at the expense of other children: *Thynne v Earl of Glengall* (1848) 2 HLC 131; 9 ER 1042. This rule only applies to cases where the father has incurred an obligation to pay the portion; it does not apply if the portion has already been paid. If the portion has been paid, a legacy to the lucky child cannot be presumed to be in satisfaction of the same portion: *Taylor v Cartwright* (1872) LR 14 Eq 167. If, on the other hand, the father makes his will first, a legacy to a child contained in that will can be ademed by a subsequent *inter vivos* covenant to provide a portion, whether that portion is actually paid or not: *Hopwood v Hopwood* (1859) 7 HL Cas 728. A presumption of ademption can also arise where a testator, not necessarily a parent, gives a legacy for a particular purpose and later advances money to the legatee for the same or a similar purpose. The debt owed on the advance is ademed by the legacy: *Re Sparrow* [1967] VR 739 at 741.

---

14. In the sense that that person has taken on a father's duty of providing for the child or children.

As this doctrine operates by presuming the intention of the testator, it can be rebutted by evidence of a contrary intention, whether displayed in the will or elsewhere. Such evidence can include parol evidence of statements by the testator contradicting the presumption: *Re Tussaud's Estate* (1878) 9 Ch D 363.

[11.23] The provision made in the will must be *ejusdem generis*, that is, of the same nature, as the portion conferred *inter vivos*. This means both that the property promised *inter vivos* must be of the same general type as that bequeathed or devised, and that the interest of the child in each portion must be the similar. Some English authorities have taken that to mean that a devise of land cannot be presumed to satisfy a covenant to provide money: *Bellasis v Uthwatt* (1737) 1 Atk 426; 26 ER 271. Although the same distinction would not appear to apply in New South Wales: *Lake v Quinton* [1973] 1 NSWLR 111 at 142, per Hutley JA.[15]

[11.24] The so-called rule against double portions, in the cases of both ademption and satisfaction, operates *pro tanto*: *Pym v Lockyer* (1841) 5 My & Cr 29; 41 ER 283; *Thynne v Earl of Glengall* (1848) 2 HLC 131; 9 ER 1042. So, if a father covenants to give his eldest son $10,000 and later makes a will leaving that son a legacy of $6,000 the portion of $10,000 will be satisfied only to the extent of $6,000, and the father's executor will still be obliged to pay the balance of $4,000 due under the covenant.

[11.25] Despite the apparent reasoning behind the rule against double portions, that there should be equality or consistency in treatment of the children of a testator, there is no authority to prevent a stranger, who happens to be the residuary beneficiary, from benefitting by an increase in the residue resulting from the application of this doctrine, unless the testator's children are also listed as residuary beneficiaries. In *Meinertzagen v Walters* (1872) 7 Ch App 670, the court refused to allow a stranger to benefit where the residue was given to the stranger and the testator's children. Thus, where a testator gives each of his two sons, A and B, legacies of $40,000 and gives the residue to someone else, X, and then before his death, gives B $25,000, the legacy to B will be adeemed to the extent of that sum. A will get $40,000 under the will, B will get $15,000; and the residue will be what is left after paying out $55,000 to the two sons under the will, rather than the $80,000 originally designated. If, however, a testator gives his two sons, A and B, legacies of $40,000 each, with the residue given equally to A, B and X, and adeems B's legacy to the extent of $16,000 by an *inter vivos* gift of a portion after making the will, X will not be allowed to benefit by the increase thus effected in the residue under the will. That windfall will be shared equally by A and B. So, assuming after payment of debts and duties there is $134,000 in the estate, A will receive his $40,000 legacy, B will receive the unadeemed share of his, that is $24,000. The balance of $70,000 will be shared out between A, B and X by giving A and B the windfall flowing to the residue from the ademption, the $16,000, so that each gets $8,000 of that, and then dividing the remaining $54,000 equally between the three of them, so that A and B will each get $26,000 of the residue while X gets $18,000. The rule against double portions may also be excluded by evidence of clear intention on the part of the testator or donor. In *Seaborn v Marsden* (1926) 26 SR (NSW) 485, a testator expressly disclaimed any fixed plan on which his estate was to be divided against his children and stated in his will that he intended making further advances to his children *inter vivos* but said that only advances which were entered into the books of account were to be taken in satisfaction of gifts in the will. Upon the testator's death it was shown that some gifts were not noted in the testator's accounts

---

15. MG&L, paras [3116]–[3121].

and thus were held not to be presumed to have been made in satisfaction of gifts in the will.

[11.26] Where a testator covenants to provide the portion before making his will, so that a gift in the will can be presumed to satisfy the promised portion, at least in part, the doctrine of satisfaction will operate by way of election. The legatee will be put to his or her election. If he or she elects to take the legacy in full, he or she will forego any rights under the covenant. No such election arises in a case of ademption. By adeeming the legacy, the testator is presumed to have also removed any possibility of an election on the part of the beneficiary. Ademption also differs from satisfaction in this context where there is a legacy for a particular purpose. While satisfaction, other than satisfaction of a debt by a legacy, can only apply where a father or someone in *loco parentis* incurs an obligation to provide a portion to a child, a legacy to someone other than the testator's child can be adeemed where that legacy is given for a particular purpose and the testator makes a gift *inter vivos* to achieve that same purpose. For example, in *Re Sparrow* [1967] VR 739 a gift to the testator's widow of a share of the income of residue was held to be adeemed by a provision for maintenance in a deed of separation.

11–6 Performance

[11.27] This is a doctrine of limited application, and questionable relevance in Australia.[16] The basic principle is that where someone covenants to do something, and does an act which may be converted into a completion of that promise, equity will presume that he or she meant to complete it. Equity 'proceeds upon the ground that a person is to be presumed to do that which he is bound to do; and that if he has done any thing, that he has done it in pursuance of his obligation': *Tubbs v Broadwood* (1831) 2 Russ & M 487; 39 ER 479. Despite the apparent width of this doctrine it has, in fact, been confined to two particular cases:

(a) Where someone covenants to purchase land and settle it on trust, or to convey and settle land, or to pay trustees money to be applied in the purchase of land to be held on trust, and fails to carry out that covenant, but nevertheless subsequently purchases land, the court will presume that the purchase has been made in performance of the covenant and declare that the land is held on trust: *Lechmere v Lady Lechmere* (1735) Cas t Talb 80; 25 ER 673.

(b) Where a person covenants to make a bequest of money, or to make other arrangements for financial provision from his or her estate, that is, that his or her executors will pay money or a share of his or her personalty to someone else, and the promisor dies intestate, but the promisee is a beneficiary of a share of the deceased's estate on intestacy, that share is presumed to be taken in performance, or part performance, of the covenant: *Blandy v Whitmore* (1715) 1 P Wms 324; 24 ER 408. This presumption of performance can also, it seems, arise from a gift of a legacy to the promisee.[17] Performance in this sense should not be mistaken for satisfaction. In satisfaction what is tendered is substantially equivalent to what was promised, giving the promisee the election of whether to accept it in satisfaction or not. In performance what is done is considered by

---

16. MG&L, para [3301].
17. M Cullity, 'Performance and Satisfaction' (1964) 38 ALJ 147; MG&L, para [3306].

equity as identical to what was promised and thus there is no election: *Goldsmid v Goldsmid* (1818) 1 Swans 211; 36 ER 361.

Chapter Twelve

12-1 The Classification of Trusts

[12.1] A trust exists where the owner of property is obliged to deal with that property for the benefit of some other person or persons, or for some purpose recognised by law. The trust has three necessary elements:

- the trustee, the titleholder, whose title may be legal or equitable, who is under a personal obligation to deal with the property for the benefit of the beneficiary or object of the trust;
- trust property which must be identifiable and capable of being held on trust and which is impressed with the trust so that the beneficiary has rights against the property as well as the trustee; and
- the beneficiary or object sometimes called the *cestui que trust*, a person, or group of persons (*cestuis que trust* in the plural), including children yet unborn, for whose benefit the trustee holds the property.

A trustee can be a beneficiary of the trust of which he or she is trustee provided he or she is not the only one. The object of a trust need not be a human beneficiary. Property can be held on trust for some purpose recognised as charitable at law. Trusts fall into two broad groups, although the second group contains two elements often treated separately:

(1) Express trusts are trusts arising from express declaration, which can be effected by some agreement or common intention held by the parties to the trust. Trusts for charitable purposes are usually express trusts.

(2) Trusts arising by operation of law — which might be either:

   (a) Resulting trusts — which may arise from a failure to dispose of the entire beneficial interest in property under a settlement or other instrument creating a trust, or upon the purchase of property by one person in the name of another where there was no intention to make a gift; or,

   (b) Constructive trusts are trusts imposed by the court irrespective of the intentions of the parties in circumstances where it would be unconscionable for the legal titleholder to deny the beneficial interest claimed by another party.

[12.2] Trusts have their origin in feoffments to uses employed in late medieval England. Under those arrangements a landholder, the feoffor, would convey land to certain trusted agents, the feoffees to uses, who were bound to hold the land for the benefit of (to the use of) whomever the feoffor designated. Usually the feoffor would instruct the feoffees to hold the land to the use of him or herself (that is, the feoffor)

for life and thereafter to those nominated by the feoffor by deed or will. The object or beneficiary of the use was known as the *cestui que use*. Feoffments to uses allowed feudal landholders to make wills of their lands, which previously would simply pass to the heir at law, the eldest son, or the eldest daughter if there were no sons. Uses also made conveyancing easier. Land could be transferred by giving directions to the feoffees to uses, much easier than the cumbersome method of common law livery of seisin. Feoffments to uses allowed landholders to effect settlements of their land which created future interests in the land, something unknown to the common law. Feoffments to uses also enabled landholders to avoid feudal incidents, the costs of holding land by feudal tenure, particularly the most expensive incidents of wardship and marriage which were imposed when a feudal tenant died leaving an infant heir. By 1450 much of the land in England was held in use, that is, subject to feoffments to uses.[1] The courts of common law would not recognise these arrangements. In their eyes, the feoffees to uses held title to the land and the *cestuis que use* had no rights at all. The Court of Chancery recognised uses and enforced the obligations of feoffees to uses in its 'English' jurisdiction by resort to principles which came to be known as equity. Widespread employment of uses had an impact on royal revenues but no monarch was strong enough to challenge this device until Henry VIII, who found himself in need of finance in the 1530s. He attempted to have a bill passed by the parliament abolishing uses but that met with opposition in the Commons. He then arranged a test case, *Re Lord Dacre of the South*[2] in which the judges, intimidated by the King's Secretary, Sir Thomas Cromwell, agreed with the proposition that no will could be made of an interest in land held in use. The Commons then compromised and the result was the Statute of Uses 1535.[3] That statute provided that where one person held, that is, was 'seised' of any lands to the 'use, trust or confidence' of another person in any estate, that thereafter that second person would be deemed to hold an estate at law equal to that previously held for him in use; in other words the statute was said to 'execute the use', converting the previously equitable title of the *cestui que use* into an estate at law. That had the immediate effect that future estates could be created at law, by the simple device of concocting a dummy conveyance to uses. Rather than insert a fictitious and unnecessary feoffee in such conveyances, that is, by making them 'to A to the use of B etc', the use would be expressed as 'to B to the use of B'. Such settlements were accepted as satisfying the statute and were used as the device to create the entailed estates that were such a feature of English life and society over the next three centuries. The Statute of Uses did not 'execute' all uses. In particular, conveyances in which active duties were cast on the feoffee were held not to be caught by the statute.[4] In addition, the device of 'a use upon a use' came to be accepted, certainly by 1635,[5] on the basis that the first use was caught by the statute and converted the title of the object of that use into an estate at law, but not the second use which remained an estate in equity only. So that in a settlement 'to A to the use of B to the use of C', A would drop out of the picture, B would have legal title, and C would be entitled to an interest in equity, by way of a trust. By rolling the first two elements together, 'to A to the use of A to the use of C', or, as it came to be expressed, 'to A unto and to the use of C' the wording for a settlement by way of the

1. ME Avery, 'An evaluation of the effectiveness of the Court of Chancery under the Lancastrian Kings' (1970) 86 LQR 84.
2. *Spelman's Reports*, Selden Society, vol 93, p 228; excerpt in MB Evans & R Ian Jack, *Sources of English Legal & Constitutional History*, Butterworths, 1984, p 201.
3. 27 Hen VIII c 10; see Evans & Jack, *op cit*, p 202.
4. *Hummerston's* case (1575) Dyer 166a; 73 ER 363.
5. *Sambach v Daston* (1635) B & M 126; 21 ER 164.

modern trust came to be recognised, causing Lord Hardwicke LC to comment in 1738 that the statute 'had no other effect than to add at most three words to a conveyance' (his Lordship's mathematics).[6] The passing of the Statute of Uses gave rise to a concern that people could no longer make wills of their land. That led to an uprising in the north known as the Pilgrimage of Grace. Although the pilgrimage was brutally suppressed, a new statute, the Statute of Wills[7] was introduced in 1540 which gave a statutory right to make testamentary gifts of land, subject to a proviso that the crown should enjoy wardship of one third of the lands so devised. The need for such an artificial exception to the operation of the Statute of Uses was reduced with the abolition of feudal tenures in 1645 but by then the die was cast and the modern trust was set to emerge from the exceptions to the statute. Since those days trusts have been employed in the English legal system in various forms and have proved to be legal instruments of great versatility and utility. As Professor Scott has said of them:

> It was chiefly by means of uses and trusts that the feudal system was undermined in England, that the law of conveyancing was revolutionised, that the economic position of married women was ameliorated, that family settlements have been effected, whereby daughters and younger sons have been enabled to participate in the family wealth, that incorporated associations have found a measure of protection, that business enterprises of many kinds have been enabled to accomplish their purposes, that great sums of money have been devoted to charitable enterprises; and by employing the analogy of a trust, the courts have been enabled to give relief against all sorts of fraudulent schemes whereby scoundrels have sought to enrich themselves at the expense of other persons.[8]

Superannuation trusts as a vehicle providing savings and retirement, death and sickness benefits for a growing proportion of the working public, a principled basis for resolving property disputes between de facto spouses and others living in close domestic circumstances and unit trusts providing efficient investment opportunities for a multitude of small investors could be added to that list. Express trusts may be employed for a number of purposes and fitted to different requirements by the use of various forms. In these different guises the powers conferred on the trustee and the nature of the beneficial interests created produce trusts which are usually given labels which indicate the type of trust concerned.

[12.3] Discretionary trusts. These are trusts so called because of the discretions conferred on the trustee in dealing with or distributing the beneficial interests in the trust estate. Those discretions will usually include:

1. A discretion to select from the designated range of objects of the trust those who are to receive benefits and an accompanying power to decide the amount of the benefits to be allocated to the selected objects.

2. That discretion carries with it a corresponding power to decide not to allocate benefits to some objects, or, indeed not to allocate benefits to all but one. This is usually expressed in a positive sense as a power to distribute to any one object to the exclusion of all others.

In addition to those powers there will sometimes be an additional discretion: a power to add to the designated range of objects. As a result no beneficiary has any entitlement to any specific part of the trust property unless and until nominated by

---

6. *Hopkins v Hopkins* (1738) 1 Atk 581 at 591; see JH Baker, *An Introduction to English Legal History*, 3rd ed, Butterworths, London, 1990, p 330.
7. 32 Hen VIII c 1.
8. AW Scott, 'The Trust as an Instrument of Law Reform' (1922) 31 Yale Law Journal 457.

the trustee, and the rights of the beneficiaries are restricted to a right to be considered for nomination by the trustee and to compel proper administration of the trust: *Gartside v IRC* [1968] AC 553. The interest of an object of a discretionary trust is thus not an 'interest in possession' and can best be described as a 'mere expectancy': *Pearson v IRC* [1981] AC 753.

[12.4] The discretion described in point 1 above, to decide the proportions in which the trust fund is allocated, may also be coupled with a power not to distribute at all to the class or range of objects of the power. Where the trustee is obliged to make a distribution the trustee is said to hold under a 'discretionary trust', as opposed to a 'discretionary power', because, despite the width of discretion in exercising the power, the trustee is bound to make a distribution. In such a case, the trustee has a single discretion: a discretion as to the proportions in which the property will be distributed. In the second case, the trustee has a 'discretionary power', meaning that it has power to distribute, but is not bound to do so, and thus has a double discretion: whether to allocate the property in the first place, and then, if it does so, a discretion as to the proportions in which it makes that allocation, again usually including power to give all to one to the exclusion of the others. The 'power' conferred on the trustee in the latter case is a discretionary power, under which the trustee is 'authorised' but not obliged to distribute property among some group or class. This sort of power has been described as a 'mere' or 'bare' power of appointment, as opposed to a power of appointment 'in the nature of a trust', or 'trust power'. Under a trust power the trustee is obliged, or 'directed', to distribute among the designated group. A power of appointment is an authority vested in a person to deal with or dispose of property not his or her own, that is, a power to distribute the property of someone else, usually conferred by will or settlement, or, to put it another way, a power to 'appoint' people or objects as recipients of the bounty: see also [12.21]–[12.34].

[12.5] In the case of a discretionary power there is, arguably, no trust at all because the objects of the power are not beneficiaries in the true sense; the trustee is not bound to hold the property for their benefit; they cannot compel the trustee to make a distribution, and the trustee can, if it so chooses, refrain from conferring any benefits on any of them. To put it another way, for every trust there must be a beneficiary, and as the objects of the power of appointment cannot fulfil that role there is a view that there must be a trust in default of appointment, that is, a trust in favour of some group or class who will take if the trustee elects not to exercise the power to appoint the property in favour of the objects of the discretionary power. The formal structure of a discretionary trust built around a discretionary power would, therefore, be one of a trust apparently in favour of the class of takers in default of appointment whose interests are liable to be defeated by the exercise of the discretionary power in favour of the designated objects in the meantime. This argument that a mere power of appointment can only be validly created by trust where there is an express trust in favour of a definite class of takers in default of appointment was firmly rejected by Windeyer J in *Lutheran Church v Farmers' Cooperative Executors and Trustees Ltd* (1970) 121 CLR 628 at 654–5 on the grounds that there would be a trust in default of appointment by operation of law under the doctrine of resulting trusts (see Chapter 16) in favour of the next of kin of the testator, in the case of a power conferred by will, or the settlor, or the settlor's next of kin in the case of a power created by a settlement *inter vivos*.[9] It is also the case that discretionary powers of the type discussed

---

9. Although that view is not free from challenge: *Re Gulbenkian's Settlement Trusts* [1970] AC 508: see [12.25].

above are commonly found as part of the machinery of the modern discretionary trust. In other words they are conferred on trustees, as part of the standard terms of the deed of trust of discretionary trusts in use throughout Australia and elsewhere.

[12.6] The distinction between discretionary trusts, or trust powers, and discretionary powers, or mere powers, is less crucial in practical terms than it might seem. Even though the holder of a trust power is 'obliged' to exercise the power and appoint the property that obligation, as least so far as the capital of the trust is concerned, is invariably expressed as an obligation to distribute no later than the expiry of a period of time fixed by reference to the Rule against Perpetuities, which might be 80 years or 21 years after the death of the survivor of the immediate members of the royal family living at the date the instrument conferring the power came into effect, depending upon the rule in force in the jurisdiction: see Chapter 14. During that time there is no rule requiring the trustee to exercise the power within a 'reasonable period': *Neill v Public Trustee* [1978] 2 NSWLR 65. The holder of a trust power might be required to distribute the income of the trust every year but the penalty tax payable on undistributed income of a trust places the same obligation on a trustee holding a discretionary power,[10] both in practical terms and in accordance with the trustee's duty to exercise reasonable care in managing the trust.[11]

[12.7] Subject to one case mentioned below, neither the objects of discretionary powers nor the members of a class of beneficiaries of a discretionary trust have any right to demand a distribution in their favour. Both have an 'interest' in the assets of the trust in the sense that they can enforce due administration of the trust. They are entitled to information about the trust: *Spellson v George* (1987) 11 NSWLR 300; *Tierney v King* [1983] 2 Qd R 580. But they cannot require the trustees to give reasons for the exercise of their discretions: *Re Londonderry's Settlement* [1956] Ch 918. Where the class of objects of a discretionary trust is ascertained, that is, they can be identified and listed, and all are of legal age, and unanimous, that class of objects combined can call for a distribution: *Sir Moses Montefiore Jewish Home v Howell & Co (No 7) Pty Ltd* [1894] 2 NSWLR 406.

[12.8] A trustee may be given other discretions, many of them concerned with the management of the trust property such as powers of investment and the like. Those discretions do not, by themselves, attract the label of discretionary trust which implies the discretion to determine the proportions of the beneficial interests in the trust: see *Neill v Public Trustee* [1978] 2 NSWLR 65.

[12.9] Unit trusts. These are trusts in which property is purchased by a 'manager', usually a proprietary company, and vested in a trustee under the terms of a trust deed in which the beneficial interest is divided into a number of units which can be sold or granted as the case may be by the original beneficiary, usually the managing company which established the trust. The manager sells the units to investors. The purchase price of the original units will include the investment in the trust and a service charge or commission for the manager. If further trust property is acquired, further units may be issued. The units entitle the holders to specific shares of the income of the trust and usually to a return of a proportion of the capital investment. The manager will generally undertake to redeem, or repurchase the units on demand, at some price determined by the terms of the trust, making them a marketable investment more flexible than ordinary shares in a company which cannot be repurchased without

---

10. Income Tax Assessment Act 1936 (Cth), s 99A.
11. See Chapter 18.

reducing the capital of the company. A unit in a unit trust is different from a share in a company in other ways. Unlike a shareholder, a unitholder has an equitable interest in the assets of the trust: *Charles v FCT* (1954) 90 CLR 598. Other doctrines of company law, such as fraud on the minority and the right to vote at meetings and elect officers do not apply to unit trusts. Offers of units in a unit trust are covered by those provisions of the Corporations Law which deal with offers to the public to subscribe for interests but, otherwise, unit trusts are not regulated by that legislation.

[12.10] Trading trusts. These are trusts in which the trustee carries on a business for the benefit of the *cestuis que trust*. The trust deed will, of course, provide the trustee with the necessary powers to conduct a business and will usually include wide powers of investment. Trading trusts have been preferred to corporations in recent years, especially for smaller business concerns, as they are not taxed in the same way as companies both for income tax and payroll tax. Unit trusts may be employed as the vehicle for a trading trust. In that capacity they provide a useful device for giving effect to a business partnership. The unitholder's right to redemption of his or her units also provides a neat safeguard against fraud on any minority.

[12.11] Family trusts. As the name suggests, these are trusts for the benefit of a family group in which the trustee will often be one or more of the family members, or a proprietary company in which family members are the shareholders and directors. The trust property will usually be held on discretionary trusts and the principal advantage of the trust will lie in the taxation advantages of splitting the income earned by the trust among the family members. The taxation benefits provided by these trusts have declined in recent years but limited benefits are still available particularly in families in which one spouse does not work and/or there are children over the age of 18 to whom income can be channelled through the trust: see **[12.40]**.

[12.12] Superannuation trusts. These are trusts established for the purpose of providing superannuation benefits, in the form of retirement benefits — either by way of lump sum or pension — and other allowances, including death and disability benefits, to the employees of companies and businesses. As well as enabling workers and employers to provide for their retirement, these trusts are attractive because contributions to them are generally tax deductible and income from the investments of the superannuation fund enjoys favourable treatment under the tax system, provided the fund satisfies the requirements of the Superannuation Industry Supervision Act 1993 (Cth) and related legislation regulating modern superannuation funds. There are two principal types of superannuation funds:

(a) Defined Benefit Schemes in which members are paid a lump sum on retirement, which may be commuted to a pension, where the sum payable is calculated with reference to the length years of service or membership of the scheme, salary at retirement and other factors such as age at retirement. As the name suggests, these schemes provide predetermined levels of benefit. They can be contributory, that is, the members contribute, or non-contributory, that is, the employer makes all the contributions.

(b) Defined Contribution, or Accumulation Schemes in which the level of contributions made by or on behalf of members is set and each member's benefit on retirement is based upon the total contributions made by or for that member plus an appropriate share of total fund earnings attributable to that member's account.

12-2 The Distinction between Trusts and Other Institutions

[12.13] Trusts and fiduciary obligations. A trustee owes fiduciary obligations to his or her *cestui que trust* but not every fiduciary is a trustee. The essential distinction between the position of the trustee and that of other fiduciaries is the trust property. A trustee has title to the trust property which is also impressed with the trust. In other fiduciary relationships there will be no property to which the personal obligation of the trustee and the rights of the beneficiary are attached. A person can be both a trustee and a fiduciary in this sense in respect of the one transaction, as was the case in *Chan v Zacharia* (1984) 154 CLR 178 where the two doctors were held to occupy dual roles with regard to the legal rights, including an option to renew, under a lease formerly held by them as partners. The first was as trustee of those legal rights and the second was in their positions as former partners in which each remained under a fiduciary obligation to assist in the realisation, application and distribution of the partnership property. A fiduciary who benefits improperly from his or her office will, of course, hold any ill-gotten gains on a constructive trust for his or her principal.

[12.14] Trust and agency. A trustee must act in the interests of his or her beneficiaries just as an agent must act in the interests of his or her principal and, like the trustee, the agent will usually be under some fiduciary obligation. But while an agent may sometimes have possession of some of the principal's property, the agent will not have title to that property and will lack a trustee's power to deal with it, particularly to give good title to a bona fide purchaser for value. An agent will also be more subject to the directions of his or her principal in matters concerning the agency while a trustee cannot be governed by the instructions of its beneficiaries in the day to day management of the trust: *Re Brockbank* [1948] Ch 206. An agent who receives money on behalf of his or her principal will not ordinarily be trustee of that money but a solicitor, who is bound to keep such money separate and to account for it, will hold any such money as trustee for the client: *Re Jones, Ex parte Mayne* (1953) 16 ABC 169.

[12.15] Trust and bailment. A bailee has possession of, not property in, the items bailed and thus does not hold them as trustee. A bailment is a contract and a breach of its terms will give rise to remedies at law for breach of contract. The question of whether a particular thing is given to someone as a bailee or upon a trust will depend upon the intentions of the parties, particularly that of the true owner. A bailee will also not be able to give good title to a bona fide purchaser without notice of the title of the bailor.

[12.16] Trust and contract. From the earliest times trusts and contracts have been treated as different things. The enforcement of feoffments to uses in Chancery was not based upon any 'contract' between the feoffor and the feoffee. The common law did not recognise these arrangements and so trusts could not be recognised as contracts at law. The rise of the doctrine of consideration in the sixteenth century ruled out any belated union. There are other differences between the two institutions which separate them in any case. A contract arises from agreement while a trust is created principally by the intention of the settlor. The extent of the liability of a party to a contract for breach is to compensate the other party for loss occasioned by the breach as determined by the common law rules on assessment of damages while that of a trustee involves a duty to restore the trust to the position in which it would have stood but for the breach: *Re Dawson* [1966] 2 NSWR 211. Where the trust is embodied in a deed under seal a beneficiary who is a party to the deed may have rights in covenant for damages against the trustee for any breach of the terms of the deed in addition to any rights of action in equity for breach of trust.[12] Similarly, where a beneficiary is a party to a deed of trust and has made some promise in that deed, that is, under seal, the trustee will be able to seek damages at common law for breach of any such covenant, subject to the odd and unsatisfactory line of authority flowing from *Re Pryce* [1917] 1 Ch 234.[13]

[12.17] Previously it was the law that where A contracts with B to provide a benefit for C, C will acquire no rights at common law nor in equity because he or she is not a party to the contract and thus cannot enforce it: *Wilson v Darling Island Stevedoring and Lighterage Co Ltd* (1956) 91 CLR 43. In the event of a breach by A, B will only be able to recover nominal damages, as he has not lost anything, unless A's promise was to pay B or 'as he directs', in which case B could recover substantial damages: *Cathels v Commissioner of Stamp Duties* [1962] SR (NSW) 455. However, where A transfers money or conveys property to B on terms that the latter will use it for the benefit of C there will be a trust of that money or property in favour of C. C would not be able to sue on the contract but, in the event of a breach by A, B would be able to recover substantial damages on behalf of C. The existence of a trust of the benefit of the promise is determined by the intention of the parties, particularly that of the promisee. On this 'trust' approach it is only where the promisee holds the benefit of the promise on trust for the third party that the promisee can recover substantial damages for breach of the promise, unless, of course, the promisee will suffer actual loss from the promisor's failure to pay the third party — which will be the case if the third party is, say, a creditor of the promisee. In that event the promisee will be able to recover the damages for him or herself rather than just for the third party: *Coulls v Bagot's Executor and Trustee Co Ltd* (1967) 119 CLR 460 at 501, per Windeyer J. The existence of a trust of the benefit of a contract in favour of a third party will still not give the third party any right of action against the promisor — he or she could only sue the promisee seeking either a mandatory injunction requiring the promisee to sue the promisor or equitable compensation for the 'loss' suffered by the trust. These untidy limitations on the law concerning third party contracts have now been broken down to some extent. In *Trident General Insurance Co Ltd v McNiece Bros Pty Ltd* (1988) 62 ALJR 508 the High Court, by a majority, held that a third party not a party to the contract in question, one of workers' compensation insurance, was entitled to recover under the contract as a member of the class of persons intended to benefit from the performance of the contract. This marks a significant departure from the previous reverence for the doctrine of privity which had been a feature of this area of the law. Trident has not led to a flood of actions in contract by third parties and appears likely to be confined to special cases which can fit within its scope. In this context it provides an alternative to the argument that the promisee holds the benefit of the promise on trust for the third party, thus reducing the need for the construction of artificial trusts in contractual situations.

[12.18] **Trust and debt.** A debtor is not normally trustee for his or her creditor. There is not a specified fund held on trust and even in the case of a secured debt the rights of the creditor to the security are very different from those of a beneficiary to the property of a trust. A beneficiary, of legal age and fully entitled, can call for the

---

12. Ford & Lee, p 37.
13. *Jacobs'*, paras [612]–[615].

trustee to transfer the trust property to him or her at any time. A secured creditor may only sell the security to recover the debt in the event of default by the debtor. Similarly, a creditor is restricted to the common law remedy of damages to recover money lent whereas a person who has paid money on trust, say, for instance into a solicitor's trust account, can trace the money into any other property into which it has been converted. The question of whether a trust or a debt is created in any given transaction will depend upon the intention of the parties. It had been thought that the concepts of trust and debt were mutually exclusive but that proposition was rejected by the House of Lords in *Barclays Bank Ltd v Quistclose Investments Ltd* [1970] AC 567: see **[13.4]–[13.7]**.

[12.19] Trust and body corporate. Unlike a body corporate, a trust is not a separate legal entity. Property held in the name of the trustee is beneficially owned by the *cestui que trust*. Property held in the name of a corporation is beneficially owned by the corporation, not its shareholders.

[12.20] Trustee and personal representative. An executor is in a fiduciary relationship with the beneficiaries of a deceased estate and many of the essential elements of a trust are present but the respective powers and duties of executor and trustee differ. The executor's duties are limited to matters necessary for the administration and distribution of the estate. An executor may become a trustee of property in the estate if he or she holds it in his or her name for the beneficiaries after administration of the estate is completed. In that sense he or she could be executor in respect of some parts of the estate and trustee in respect of others. The beneficiaries of a deceased estate do not obtain any equitable interest in the assets of the estate by virtue of the will alone. Their rights initially are restricted to a right to secure proper administration of the estate: *Comm'r of Stamp Duties (Qld) v Livingston* (1960) 107 CLR 411; [1965] AC 694. An executor has wider powers to deal with the assets of the estate than a trustee. An executor, for example, can sell realty for the purposes of administration while a trustee cannot unless expressly authorised by the trust deed.

[12.21] Trusts and powers. A power of appointment is a power to dispose of or distribute the property of some other person.[14] It is not necessary for the holder of such a power to have title to the property subject to the power, nor is the holder necessarily subject to any fiduciary duty in the manner of his or her exercise of the power. The objects of a power of appointment, those in whose favour the power can be exercised, do not necessarily have any beneficial interests in the property subject to the power nor do they necessarily have any right to compel the holder to make an appointment. Those matters spell out the basic differences between trusts and powers of appointment. That simple picture is, however, considerably complicated by the fact that powers of appointment are most commonly conferred, either by settlement *inter vivos* or by will, upon people who are also trustees. As has been mentioned, such powers form the basis of the modern discretionary trust and the power then becomes part of the machinery of the trust, rather than something which can be readily distinguished from it. Powers of appointment come in three different types:

(a) General — a power is to appoint the property to anyone, including the holder of the power him or herself. General powers are thought to be distinguishable from trusts because there are no particular parties in whose interests equity might intervene, the objects of power being the whole of humanity.[15] The fact

---

14. Pettit, p 25.
15. *Jacobs'*, para [247].

that the holder of the power can make an appointment in favour of him or herself would seem to negative any intention on the part of the settlor or testator to create a trust: see **[13.2]**–**[13.3]**. However, the holder of a general power of appointment is not considered to have 'property' in the assets or fund which are the subject of the power: *Hudson v Gray* (1927) 39 CLR 473 at 492, per Isaacs J.

(b) Special — a power to appoint the property to third persons. The objects of such a power must be described with the necessary certainty. Special powers are normally described as powers to appoint among the members of a group or class. But as it is now sufficient if the objects of such a power are described with sufficient certainty that it can be said whether a given individual is, or is not, a member of the range or class of objects, that description may not be particularly apt.

(c) Intermediate or hybrid — these fall between general and special powers of appointment and are usually described as powers to appoint to anyone in the world with the exception of some excluded class or group. The holder of the power must be excluded, either expressly or by necessary implication, which will be the case if the power is conferred on a trustee. If the holder can appoint to him or herself, it must be a general power.

The question of what type of power has been conferred in any given case will often be one of construction of the provisions of the instrument conferring the power. Where a power of appointment is conferred on someone who is also a trustee or otherwise subject to fiduciary obligations, in the absence of any contrary intention expressed or implied in the instrument the trustee or fiduciary will not be entitled to exercise the power for his own benefit. The power will therefore be a special and not a general power. In *Metropolitan Gas Company v FCT* (1932) 47 CLR 621, the Commissioner of Taxation challenged the entitlement of a superannuation fund to tax benefits on the ground that the deed gave the directors of the employer, with the consent of the trustees, wide powers of amendment, including power to determine the disposal of any surplus in the fund on a winding up. The High Court held that the deed was suitable for the purpose, pointing out that the company held its power of amendment subject to fiduciary duties and could not divert to itself benefits secured to members of the fund. That decision did not mean that the company could not amend the deed to provide for the refund of any surplus to itself. In that respect it could be said to have retained a general power of appointment in respect of the surplus. However, the company could not exercise that power to revoke any accrued benefits in favour of members. The general power of appointment did not extend to the whole of the fund. Similarly, in *Re Burton; Wily v Burton* (1994) 126 ALR 557, Davies J held that a power as appointer of a family trust, that is, a power to appoint the trustee including a power to remove and replace the trustee, was not 'property' of a bankrupt under the Bankruptcy Act 1966 (Cth), s 116. The trustee in bankruptcy had argued that as the bankrupt, as 'appointer', could appoint a trustee he could control and thereby obtain a distribution from the family trust in his favour. Davies J rejected that submission saying, at 559:

> This submission equates the power s under the trust with 'property' (as described in s 116(1)(a)) or with a power in over or in respect of property 'as might have been exercised by the bankrupt for his own benefit' (under s 116(1)(b)) ... (noting that even a general power of appointment is not property) ... the power to remove a trustee and to appoint a new trustee is neither a general power of appointment nor a power which may be executed in the interests of the appointer. The interests of persons other than the appointer must be taken into account. The power is a trust or fiduciary power, being a power conferred by a deed of trust, and must be exercised accordingly, in the interests of the beneficiaries.

The same principle must apply to a general power of appointment held by a trustee, provided there is sufficient certainty as to the interntion to actually create a trust.

[12.22] The question of certainty of description of the objects of these powers, and of trusts generally, is discussed in more detail below. In the light of *Re Baden's Deed Trusts; McPhail v Doulton* [1971] AC 424 there are now good grounds for saying that there should only be two classes of powers of appointment: general, in which the holder of the power may appoint to him or herself and/or to others, and special, in which the donee can only appoint to third parties who must be described with adequate certainty, whether by inclusion or exclusion, for the power to be exercised. That apparently sensible approach is hamstrung in New South Wales where the distinction between hybrid and special powers has been maintained, although only where such powers are conferred by will, by preservation of the unfortunate rule that hybrid powers of appointment may not be conferred by will as they infringe a supposed rule against delegation of will-making power: *Tatham v Huxtable* (1950) 81 CLR 639; *Horan v James* [1982] 2 NSWLR 376; although such a power may be validly conferred by will in England: *Re Park* [1932] 1 Ch 580; *Re Abrahams' Will Trusts* [1969] 1 Ch 465, esp at 474 ff (see **[12.31]–[12.34]**).

[12.23] As well as the 'type' of power, it is also important to identify the nature of a power, although this is now less important than it was before *Re Baden's Deed Trusts; McPhail v Doulton*. In this sense a power of appointment might fall into one of two categories:

(a) Mere or bare powers—powers of appointment in which the holder of the power is 'authorised' but not obliged to exercise the power. Usually where such powers are conferred there will be a gift over in default of appointment in favour of some other object or objects, although, as mentioned in **[12.4]**, the presence of such a gift over is not essential to the validity of the power.

(b) Trust powers — powers in the nature of a trust under which the holder of the power is 'directed' or obliged to exercise the power. In such a case there will not be any gift over in default of appointment because there can be no default in appointment; the holder is under a fiduciary obligation to exercise the power.

[12.24] The inclusion of a mere power of appointment in a trust does not convert that power into a trust power. The trustee is still not bound to make any appointment under the power but a trustee who holds such a power will be subject to fiduciary obligations in the manner in which the power is exercised, including any decision not to exercise it. In other words, 'A settlor or testator who entrusts a power to his trustees must be relying on them in their fiduciary capacity so they cannot simply push aside the power and refuse to consider whether it ought in their judgment to be exercised': *Re Gulbenkian's Settlement Trusts* [1970] AC 508 at 518 per Lord Reid.[16] The objects of a mere power have no right to compel the holder of the power to exercise it. They can, however, prevent any improper exercise of the power, such as an appointment in favour of someone outside the designated range of benefit. A major consequence of the inclusion of such powers, both mere and trust, in modern trusts

---

16. In the same case, at 524–5, Lord Upjohn expressed the view that the holders of mere powers, whether trustees or others, could not be controlled in any way in the exercise of their power, including in deciding whether to exercise it at all, apart from the right of the takers in default to restrain any exercise of the power outside the range of designated objects. In *McPhail v Doulton* [1971] AC 424 at 449, Lord Wilberforce disagreed strongly with that proposition; Lord Guest agreed with Lord Upjohn's view, at 445; Lord Hodson did not comment on the point and Lord Reid and Viscount Dilhorne agreed with Lord Wilberforce.

has been that the discussion of the requirements of certainty for the description of the objects of trusts in recent times has revolved around cases concerning powers of appointment.

[12.25] The identification of mere and trust powers is a matter of construction of the instrument creating the power in question. The crucial test is whether the donee or holder of the power is under an obligation to exercise it. If he or she is, it will be a trust power. If the holder of the power can decline to exercise it, the power will be a mere or bare power. The use of imperative language in the deed, where the imperative relates to power to appoint, will indicate a trust power. The presence of a gift over in default of appointment will indicate that the settlor or testator contemplated that the power might not be exercised and that it is thus a mere power; although the absence of such a gift over is not conclusive proof that a trust power has been created. In determining whether a mere or trust power is intended the whole of the instrument must be taken into consideration, not just the provision conferring the power, to ascertain the intention of the settlor or testator: *Horan v Borthwick* (SC(NSW), Helsham CJ in Eq, 12 Dec 1980, unreported).

[12.26] The distinction between mere and trust powers is of less importance than it once was. The requirements of certainty for the description of objects of trust powers used to be more stringent than that required for the objects of mere powers. In the case of trust powers the class of objects had to be 'ascertainable' at the date the instrument came into operation, ie, such that a complete list of those objects could be made at the date of the testator's death, or at the date of execution of a settlement inter vivos: *IRC v Broadway Cottages Trust* [1955] Ch 20. This test has come to be known as 'list certainty', while the test for the description of objects of mere powers is known as 'criterion certainty':

> In *Re Gulbenkian's Settlement Trusts* [1970] AC 508, settlements made by Calouste Gulbenkian provided that the trustees should during the life of his son Nubar 'at their absolute discretion pay all or any part of the income of the fund settled to or apply the same for the maintenance and personal support or benefit of all or any one or more to the exclusion of the other or others of the following persons ... '. The persons designated included 'any person or persons in whose house or apartments or in whose company or under whose care or control or by or with whom the said (Nubar) may from time to time be employed or residing ... '. That class of potential beneficiaries was challenged as lacking sufficient certainty for the trustees to operate the power. The House of Lords held that the clause was sufficiently certain. The test applied was that, provided there was a valid gift over or trust in default of appointment, a mere or bare power of appointment among a class would be valid if it could be said with certainty whether any given individual was or was not a member of the class.

[12.27] The stricter test for trust powers was relieved shortly thereafter by the House of Lords which adopted criterion certainty as the test for certainty of objects of such powers, subject to a qualification that the range of objects should not be so hopelessly wide as to render the trust administratively unworkable.

> In *Re Baden's Deed Trusts; McPhail v Doulton* [1971] AC 424, a fund was settled on trustees to provide retirement and other benefits for the staff, including former staff, of a certain company and their relatives and dependants. Clause 9 of the deed provided that 'The trustees shall apply the net income of the fund in making at their absolute discretion grants to or for the benefit of any of (the staff, or their relatives or dependants etc.) in such amounts at such times and on such conditions (if any) as they think fit ...'. The trustees were not bound to exhaust the income of the fund in any given year. No one was to have any rights to or in the fund except by exercise of the trustees' discre-

tion. The settlor's executors sought a declaration that the trust was void. Their Lordships were in agreement that this was a trust power. While the words of the trust gave certain discretion to the trustees, the trust, when considered as a whole, clearly cast an imperative obligation on the trustees to exercise the power of appointment in favour of the members of the designated range of objects. The language of cl 9 was also clearly imperative. Lord Wilberforce, with whom Lord Reid and Viscount Dilhorne agreed, held that the tests for certainty for the description of objects of mere powers and trust powers were to be assimilated. Accordingly, a trust power will be valid if it can be said with certainty whether a given postulant is or is not a member of the range of objects. In coming to that decision his Lordship noted that there were precedents in which the court, when called upon to administer a trust, had distributed the property in other than equal proportions and said that the court's main role was to give effect to the intention of the settlor which could be done by appointing new trustees or authorising some scheme of distribution. When discussing the application of criterion certainly Lord Wilberforce distinguished linguistic or semantic uncertainty, which would render any settlement void, from evidentiary uncertainty which he said could be resolved by directions. Beyond that he also suggested, at 457, that a trust might fail where the definition of beneficiaries was so hopelessly wide as not to form 'anything like a class' so that the trust was administratively unworkable.

Criterion certainty and administrative workability

[12.28] While the tests for certainty of description of the objects of mere and trust powers were assimilated by *McPhail v Doulton* some differences remain between the two. Lord Wilberforce's qualification, that the description of objects of trust powers should not be so hopelessly wide as not to form 'anything like a class' so that the trust was administratively unworkable, has led to statements that there was an additional 'loose class' requirement to be satisfied for certainty of object in trust powers. In *Blausten v IRC* [1972] Ch 256, Buckley LJ even went so far as to suggest that this so-called requirement applied to mere powers as well. That reasoning was rejected by Templeman J in *Re Manisty's Settlement* [1974] 1 Ch 17. Despite the frequent reference to this proviso as the 'loose class' requirement it should be noted that those were not his Lordship's words. Clearly any interpretation which restored list certainty through some back door would be contrary to the rest of Lord Wilberforce's judgment. Administrative workability, which was the point of concern, is a matter which a court can assess. If the trust could not be practicably administered in its native form then it might be a matter for opinion, advice or directions under the Trustee Act 1925 (NSW), s 63,[17] in which case it could not be said to be unworkable, or it might be irreparable and sufficiently serious to render the trust void. In any case, this requirement might have no practical effect. Lord Wilberforce's judgment was adopted in New South Wales by the Court of Appeal in *Horan v James* [1982] 2 NSWLR 376. That case involved a trust power to appoint to anyone other than the testator's wife and his two sons. The power was struck down for other reasons but was considered sufficiently certain within the terms laid down by Lord Wilberforce. If a trust power to appoint in favour of anyone except A, B and C is administratively workable it is difficult to see how a power could fall foul of this requirement unless it was also void for uncertainty. The approach in *Horan v James* on this question followed that taken in *Re Manisty's Settlement* [1974] 1 Ch 17 and *Re Hay's Settlement Trusts* [1982] 1 WLR 202, although both of those cases involved mere powers.

---

17. Trusts Act 1973–81 (Qld), s 96; Trustees Act 1962–78 (WA), s 92.

[12.29] Some of the questions raised by *McPhail v Doulton* were discussed when the Baden trust was referred back to the courts below for consideration of the question of certainty in the light of the new test.

> In *Re Baden's Deed Trusts (No 2)* [1973] Ch 9, it was claimed that the power failed to satisfy criterion certainty, particularly in respect of the words 'dependants' and 'relatives'. Sachs LJ rejected an argument that the court had to be able to say whether any given postulant was not a member of the class, provided there was sufficient conceptual, or semantic, certainty to be able to say whether a given individual did fall within the description. If someone was not proved to be within the range then he was not in it. His Lordship also said that the need seen by Lord Wilberforce for trustees to be able 'to make such a survey of the range of objects or possible beneficiaries as will enable them to carry out their fiduciary duty' meant that the trustees had to bear in mind the size of the problem before them, rather than recreating an obligation to make an exhaustive list of the potential objects. Megaw LJ thought the test was satisfied if, as regards a substantial number of objects, it could be said with certainty that they fell within the trust, even though for a substantial number of others it would have to be said that it was not proven whether they were in or out. In doing so his Lordship rejected the notion that the test was satisfied if one single person could be shown as a member of the range of benefit. Stamp LJ thought the test was not satisfied unless one could say affirmatively either that a given individual was within the class or that he was outside it. That depended upon the construction placed on the words used. In his Lordship's view 'relatives' was not uncertain if taken to mean nearest blood relations.

[12.30] It is clear that the courts will attempt to give effect to the sensible expectations of the settlor or testator and will only strike a gift down for uncertainty where it is simply not possible to establish any such expectation or to give effect to one. In *Baden (No 2)* notice was taken of the fact that if the expressions 'dependants' and 'relatives' were held to be uncertain, very few trusts could stand. The *Baden* cases concentrated on semantic or linguistic uncertainty, taking the view that evidentiary uncertainty was simply a matter for directions. It has been argued that there could be a case in which the concept, or criterion, was certain but the evidentiary difficulties such that the gift was administratively unworkable in the sense referred to by Lord Wilberforce.[18] So, for instance, a power to appoint in favour of people who attended the 1992 Rugby League Grand Final between St George and Brisbane would be conceptually certain but an administrative impossibility. In this view the test should be one of practicability, or to use Lord Wilberforce's words, administrative workability.

Powers and testamentary dispositions

[12.31] The use of powers of appointments in wills has a long history and can be traced back to feoffments to uses before the Wills Act of 1540. There is no good reason for treating powers created in wills and powers conferred *inter vivos* differently but, at least in Australia, we have been saddled with authorities which do draw this distinction. By applying a supposed rule against delegation of will-making power, which is based on the assumption that the power to make a will is derived solely from statute and must be exercised personally by the testator: *Houston v Burns* [1918] AC 337; *Chichester Diocesan Fund v Simpson* [1944] AC 341; a distinction has been drawn between general and special powers of appointment, which do not infringe this rule and which can be validly created by will, and hybrid powers which do infringe the

---

18. RP Austin, 'Discretionary Trusts: Conceptual Uncertainty and Practical Sense' (1981) 9 Syd LR No 1, pp 58–70.

rule, at least in Australia. Whatever the scope of the operation of this so-called cardinal rule in England, it clearly does not operate to strike down hybrid powers of appointment created by will in that jurisdiction.

> In *Re Park* [1932] 1 Ch 580, a testator gave his residuary estate to trustees to pay income to any person or charitable institution, other than herself, as his sister should direct and after her death on trust as to both capital and income for the Imperial Merchant Service Guild. Clauson J upheld this gift, which was a mere hybrid power, as a valid power and one which was sufficiently certain for the court to enforce, if need be.

The High Court, in a case which did not concern hybrid powers, chose to criticise this line of English authority:

> In *Tatham v Huxtable* (1950) 81 CLR 639, a testator included a provision in his will empowering his executor 'to distribute any balance of my real and personal estate ... to the beneficiaries of this my will and testament ... or to others not otherwise provided for who in my opinion have rendered service meriting consideration by the trustee' ('in my opinion' was taken to mean 'in the opinion of the trustee'). The validity of that clause was challenged and, by a majority, the High Court held it to be invalid. Fullagar J cited the principle prohibiting delegation of testamentary power and said that some powers of appointment would not be valid if contained in a will. His Honour excluded general and special powers from that condemnation. In the case of a special power, however, Fullagar J said unless there was a class designated with certainty, to say that the creation of a power to select beneficiaries amounts to a testamentary disposition of property was not merely to relax the principle (against delegation) to meet an exceptional case but to deny that principle absolutely. In other words he would recognise a special power to appoint in favour of a class designated with certainty as a valid testamentry disposition. Accordingly, he rejected the approach taken in English cases such as In re Park upholding hybrid powers in wills. Kitto J also said that there was a cardinal rule that a man may not delegate his testamentary power and that it was therefore necessary, except in the case of charitable trusts, for the objects to be benefited by the will to be ascertained or ascertainable. He conceded that the creation by will of a general or special power of appointment did not amount to such a delegation, provided that, in the case of a special power, the class or group of objects was described with sufficient certainty. He acknowledged that certainty may be achieved as well by an exclusive as by an inclusive description and held that a testamentary disposition by way of a power of appointment, if it was not to fail under the non-delegation rule, 'must either confer upon the person authorised to make the selection a general power equivalent to ownership or define with certainty a class or group from which the selection is to be made'.

[12.32] The decision in *Tatham v Huxtable* has since been accepted as authority in Australia for the proposition that a hybrid power of appointment in a will is void because of the so-called non-delegation rule. This view has been maintained despite the fact that only Fullagar J specifically condemned hybrid powers, while Kitto J seemed more concerned with the question of certainty of object, and despite the fact also that the power in *Tatham v Huxtable* was a special power and not hybrid; and that it was clearly void for uncertainty. This prevailing view has had unfortunate results.

> In *Lutheran Church v Farmers' Co-operative Executors and Trustees Ltd* (1970) 121 CLR 628, a testatrix, after bequeathing certain legacies, made the following gift: '6. My Trustees have discretionary power to transfer any mortgages and property, and shares in companies invested in my name to the Lutheran Mission (at a stated address) for building homes for Aged Blind Pensioners after all expenses paid ...'. The will contained no other provision. The question arose as to whether that clause created a valid disposition, or constituted a valid charitable trust, or whether it was void for uncertainty.

Bray CJ in the Supreme Court of South Australia held there was no gift because the 'discretionary power to transfer' made no gift to the objects of the power and merely delegated discretionary powers to the testatrix's trustees.

McTiernan and Menzies JJ upheld the decision of Bray CJ, while Barwick CJ and Windeyer J found the gift to be valid. As there was a bench of four the decision appealed against stood, by virtue of s 23 of the Judiciary Act 1903–67 (Cth).

Barwick CJ said the creation by will of a general or special power of appointment constituted a disposition of the property the subject of the power and, unless the power was a trust power, would necessarily involve a discretion whether or not to exercise the power. Provided the subject matter and the appointees were indicated with sufficient certainty the gift would be valid even though it created no beneficial interest in the objects of the power unless and until it was exercised in their favour. Here there was no question of certainty of object. The absence of any specific gift over in default of appointment would not invalidate the power as there would be one by operation of law in the event of non-exercise.

McTiernan and Menzies JJ considered that the use of the words 'discretionary power' negatived the gift and that a mere special power without any gift over in default offended the rule against delegation of will-making power discussed in *Tatham v Huxtable* (1950) 81 CLR 639.

Windeyer J said such a power could be validly created and that the trustees would be under a duty to consider whether to exercise it. If they refused to consider the matter the court could remove them and appoint new trustees. This was also not a case in which a testator had given his executor a power to dispose of the estate in favour of such other people as he chose. His Honour thought the lack of a gift over was not crucial because the next of kin would take in such an event. In discussing the distinction between mere and trust powers Windeyer J said that in the case of the non-exercise of a trust power the beneficiaries would be entitled to the subject property in equal shares.

[12.33] The supposed cardinal rule against delegation of testamentary powers has been widely criticised and its pedigree is, at best, dubious.[19] The two authorities from which this rule is supposedly derived, *Houston v Burns* [1918] AC 337 and *Chichester Diocesan Fund v Simpson* [1944] AC 341, concerned, respectively, gifts to 'charitable or benevolent purposes' and 'charitable or benevolent objects in England', both void for uncertainty of object, as 'benevolent' purposes are not necessarily charitable at law, and neither was concerned with hybrid powers of appointment. Hybrid powers continue to be recognised in England:

In *Re Manisty's Settlement* [1974] Ch 17, a settlor conferred on his trustees a power to apply trust funds for a class made up of his infant children, his future children and remoter issue, and his two brothers and their future issue born before a closing date defined as 79 years from the date of settlement. An 'excepted class', consisting of the settlor, his wife for the time being, and any other person settling property on the trust, was excluded from benefit. The trustees were given power at their absolute discretion to declare that any person, corporation or charity other than a member of the excepted class or a trustee be included in the class of beneficiaries. In 1972 the trustees exercised that power to add the settlor's mother and any widow of the settlor to the class of beneficiaries. A summons was taken out to determine whether the power to add beneficiaries was valid. Templeman J held that it was saying that the principle of non-

19. RA Sundberg, 'The Status and Authority of the decision in *Tatham v Huxtable*' (1974) 48 ALJ 52; IJ Hardingham, 'The Rule against Delegation of Will-making Power' (1974) Melb Univ LR 650; 'Re Manisty's Settlement — The Continuing Saga of Certainty of Object of Discretionary Trusts' (1975) 49 AW 7.

delegation did not apply where a settlor or testator conferred an intermediate (or hybrid) power on his trustees. The power was also not void for uncertainty. His Lordship said that such a power or trust will be valid if it can be said with certainty whether a given individual is or is not a member of the class (of objects). Having regard to the definition of the excepted class, it could be said with certainty in this case whether any given individual is or is not a member of the class. The conduct and duties of trustees and the rights and remedies of any person who wishes the power to be exercised in his favour are the same for both intermediate and special powers. Where a settlor gives his trustees a power which enables them to take into account all contingencies the court will not strike it down unless it is capricious, ie, where the terms of the power negative any sensible consideration of the objects by the trustees. A power will not be uncertain merely because it is wide in ambit.

A perfect opportunity arose in the early 1980s in New South Wales to overcome the confusion. At first instance Helsham J was prepared to get rid of this humbug but, on appeal, the Court of Appeal felt bound by loyalty to follow the High Court. The estate lacked the funds to carry the fight any further and we have been left saddled with a conspicuous anomaly.

In *Horan v James* [1982] 2 NSWLR 376, a testator gave the residue of his estate to his two trustees with power to pay and/or transfer it to whomsoever they selected, with each having power to dispose of half in the event that they could not agree. The testator included a special direction that no benefit should thereby be conferred on his wife as well as an expression of hope and expectation that none of the estate subject to the power should be appointed to his two sons. The next of kin challenged the validity of the power. At first instance, *Horan v Borthwick* (12 December 1980, unreported), Helsham CJ in Eq held the power to be valid. He distinguished *Tatham v Huxtable* on the ground that that case had not actually concerned a hybrid power. Having discussed the supposed principle of non-delegation, he concluded that, assuming such a principle was part of the law, the use of powers of appointment as a means of disposing of property by will did not infringe it. Helsham CJ in Eq considered there were three bases upon which that conclusion rested:

1. The creation of a power of appointment as a means of disposition by a testator is an exercise of testamentary power, and not a delegation of it.

2. Powers of appointment are a conventional form of machinery for the disposition of property and too firmly established as such to be swept away in some oblique fashion.

3. The so-called rule against delegation is no more than a rule of construction and not a distinct rule forbidding delegations by a testator of decisions affecting distribution of his estate.

The Court of Appeal overturned that decision on the basis that the court was obliged to follow the dicta of the High Court in *Tatham v Huxtable* (1950) 81 CLR 639 and *Lutheran Church v Farmers' Co-operative* (1970) 121 CLR 628 which would set aside such powers as delegations of will-making power. Hutley JA noted the dubious foundations of the so-called rule against delegation of testamentary power, foundations he had criticised himself when he was just FC Hutley.[20] In the process the court expressed approval of criterion certainty as the test for certainty of description of the objects of trust powers, and said that this power satisfied that test. Curiously, the Court of Appeal felt no sense of disloyalty in adopting criterion certainty as the test for certainty of description of the objects of a trust power, notwithstanding the absence of any High Court authority in support of any test other than list certainty.

---

20. FC Hutley, 'The Rule Against Delegation of Will-Making Power' (1956–58) Syd LR 93.

[12.34] The decision of the Court of Appeal in *Horan v James* has left the law on this point in a clearly unsatisfactory state. Hybrid powers of appointment remain perfectly good dispositions if made by a settlement *inter vivos* but not, if *Horan v James* is to be accepted, when contained in a will. Accordingly, a settlement in favour of the settlor for life and thereafter for the benefit of such persons as the trustees shall select, with the exception of themselves and perhaps some other small group, will be good, as such settlements have been since the days of feoffments to uses in the fourteenth century. But a trust in a will requiring the executors to appoint in favour of certain persons together with such others as they select with the exception of themselves and some small group, will be bad. Not only that, but such a power will be good if created in a will in England, presumably even though it conferred power over property in New South Wales as well, but not in a will made in Australia. Apart from that, now that the rule for description of objects of trust powers has been assimilated, for all practical purposes it seems, with that for mere powers, so that it is only necessary to be able to say whether a given individual is or is not within the range of benefit, it is much more difficult to distinguish between special and hybrid powers. A trust power to appoint, for example, among young Australian athletes, with the exception of any ever convicted of possession or supply of a narcotic drug, would be difficult to classify as special or hybrid. It might be considered lacking in certainty. But no one with any common sense would have any trouble administering it. The better view must be that the decision of Helsham CJ in Eq in *Horan v Borthwick* was the correct decision in principle and ought to be preferred to the approach taken by the Court of Appeal on the point.

12–3 Trusts and Taxation

[12.35] Trusts are not separate legal entities. Accordingly, trust income is treated as the income of the beneficiaries presently entitled to it. The taxation of trusts, with the exception of capital gains tax, is covered for the most part by Div 6 of the Income Tax Assessment Act 1936 (Cth) (ITAA). Under s 97 beneficiaries not under a legal disability who are presently entitled to a share of the net income of a trust estate are assessed for tax on their share of that income which is then taxed as part of the total taxable income of each individual beneficiary. A beneficiary is only 'presently entitled' to a share in the net income of a trust estate when he or she has a right to demand immediate payment from the trustee: *FCT v Whiting* (1943) 68 CLR 199.

[12.36] The objects of a discretionary trust have no present entitlement to the income of the trust unless and until the trustee exercises its discretion to pay or apply income in their favour. Under ITAA, s 101 the exercise of a discretion to pay or apply income to or for the benefit of a beneficiary will give rise to a present entitlement. Once a trustee makes a determination to apply some part of the trust income to the credit of a beneficiary, even if only by way of a book entry, so that that portion of the income is irrevocably vested in favour of that beneficiary, that beneficiary will then be presently entitled to the income so allocated or 'appointed': *Ward v IRC (NZ)* (1968) 10 AITR 663.

[12.37] Where a beneficiary is under a legal disability, such as infancy, but is otherwise presently entitled to a share in the net income of a trust, the trustee is liable to tax under ITAA, s 98 as if it were income of the beneficiary. If no beneficiary is presently entitled to the income of a trust, so that neither ITAA, s 97 nor s 98 applies, as will be the case where income of a discretionary trust has not been distributed or allocated to any of the objects of the trust, the trustee will be assessed for tax on the net income of the trust estate, under ITAA, s 99 or s 99A. Section 99 applies to trusts arising from death or bankruptcy, damages settlements, lottery wins and such fortuitous events. Section 99A is an anti-avoidance device under which trust income to which no one is presently entitled is taxed, in the hands of the trustee, at the highest marginal rate. Section 99A(2) gives the Commissioner a discretion to tax such undistributed income at the trustee's personal rate rather than the higher rate, having regard to the circumstances set out in s 99A(3), which include matters similar to those appropriate to s 99. Where a trustee pays income on any part of the income of the trust under ss 98, 99 or 99A, no tax will be payable on those moneys when they are later paid to a beneficiary: *Union Fidelity Trustee Co v FCT* (1969) 119 CLR 177.

[12.38] The 'net income' of a trust is defined by ITAA, s 95 as the total assessable income of the trust estate calculated as if the trustee were a taxpayer, except that concessional deductions and deductions under Div 16C may not be taken into account. The 'trust estate' for these purposes means the 'trust property', that is property to which the trustee's personal obligation is annexed: *FCT v Trustees of the Lisa Marie Walsh Trust* (1983) 14 ATR 399; *Stewart Dawson Holdings Pty Ltd v FCT* (1965) 39 ALJR 300. Beneficiaries who have no interest in the capital of the trust, or who are only life tenants, are not entitled to deductions for losses of previous years under ss 80, 80AA and 80AAA. If the allowable deductions available to the trust estate exceed its taxable income a loss will result. Such losses may be carried forward and set off against future income of the trust, but cannot be 'distributed' to the beneficiaries to be set off against any other income they might receive.

[12.39] Where the settlor or other creator of a trust retains effective control over the trust property, as will be the case where the settlor retains a power to revoke a trust, the settlor will be assessed for tax on the trust income under ITAA, s 102. The transfer of property to an established trust will not fall under s 102: *Truesdale v FCT* (1970) 120 CLR 353. For this reason, where a trust is established by the settlement of some moneys forming the initial trust fund it is common to have a third party settlor quite separate from the other parties to the trust and to ensure that the trust contains no machinery whereby it might be revoked or dismantled by the settlor.

[12.40] Trusts can provide advantages to the taxpayer, particularly by allowing income to be split among the members of a family, by such means as a discretionary trust used as a trading trust to carry on a business, thereby sharing the tax burden at lower marginal rates. The attractiveness of this device has waned since the introduction of Div 6AA in 1980, and its further amendment in 1982. Division 6AA imposes tax at penalty rates on the 'eligible taxable income', above a tax free threshold of $416, of 'prescribed persons'. Prescribed persons are children under the age of 18, people in receipt of a handicapped child's pension, and people in full time employment at the end of the tax year or for an aggregate of three months during that year. 'Excepted trust income' is exempt from these provisions. Excepted trust income includes income from employment, income derived from a deceased estate, income from damages awards and settlements and the like.

[12.41] Trusts may have foreign connections. It is a basic principle of our tax laws that only Australian residents or income from Australian sources can be taxed by the Australian government. Section 97 provides that the assessable income of a beneficiary presently entitled to a share of the income of a trust shall include so much of the net income of the trust as is attributable to the period when the beneficiary was a resident and to so much of the income as is derived from Australian sources during the time when the beneficiary was not a resident. Similar provisions apply under ITAA, s 98 to a trustee who is liable to pay tax on behalf of a beneficiary presently entitled but under a legal disability. Income being the net income of a resident trust estate which is not included in the assessable income of a beneficiary under ITAA, ss 97 or 98 is taxed under s 99A(4)–(4C). Section 99D allows a non-resident beneficiary to claim a refund of tax paid under ss 99(2) or (3) and 99(4) or (4A) on income attributable to a period when the beneficiary was not a resident and which is also attributable to sources outside Australia. Section 95(2) defines a 'resident trust estate' as a trust where either the trustee was a resident of Australia or the central management and control of the trust was in Australia at any time during the year of income.

Corporate unit trusts and public trading trusts

[12.42] The introduction of Div 6B, in 1981, and Division 6C, in 1985, created separate regimes for the taxation of corporate unit trusts and public trading trusts, respectively. The trustee of a corporate unit trust is required to pay tax on the net income of the trust at the rate declared by parliament, ie the corporate tax rate, presently 39%, under ITAA, s 102M. Under ITAA, s 102J a corporate unit trust must be both a public unit trust and an 'eligible unit trust'. A unit trust will be an eligible unit trust if property of the trust, at any time in that year of income or the preceding year, was subject to a 'prescribed arrangement'. A 'prescribed arrangement', in relation to a company, is one whereby the trustee of the unit trust carries on a business which had been previously carried on by the company or an associate of the company. Division 6B is thus aimed at companies which change their operations so that their business is carried on by the trustee of a unit trust. A 'public unit trust', under ITAA, s 102G, is a trust whose units are listed on the stock exchange or offered to the public or held by more than 50 people. In any event, if 75 per cent or more of the units are held by 20 persons or less, the trust is not treated as a public unit trust. The trust must also be a 'resident' unit trust, under ITAA, s 102H, in that property of the trust is situated in Australia, or the trustee carries on business in Australia and the central management and control of the trust is situated in Australia or more than 50 per cent of the beneficial interest in the income or property of the trust is held by persons who are resident in Australia.

[12.43] Division 6C deals with the income of public trading trusts. A trust will be a 'trading trust' under ITAA, s 102N if it carries on a trading business or controls another person who carries on such a business. 'Trading business' is defined in ITAA, s 102M as a business that does not consist wholly of eligible investment business. Under the same section 'eligible investment business' means investing in the land for the purpose of deriving income from rent or investing in a range of things including unsecured loans, shares in a company, bonds, debentures or other securities, units in a unit trust, life assurance policies and other financial dealings. Section 102P defines a trust as a public unit trust if at any time during the year of income any of its units were offered on the stock exchange; any of its units were offered to the public; or the units were held by not fewer than 50 persons, except, in the latter case, where 20 or fewer persons hold 75 per cent or more of the beneficial interest in the property or income of the trust. Section 102P(2) includes other unit trusts in this category, particularly unit trusts in which 20 per cent or more of the beneficial interest in the trust is held by exempt entities, being mainly bodies exempt from tax under various paragraphs of ITAA, s 23. Under ITAA, s 102S the trustee of a public trading trust is liable to pay tax on the net income of the trust at the rate determined by parliament which, at present, is the company tax rate.

Capital gains tax and trusts

[12.44] Part IIIA of the ITAA, which became effective on 24 June 1986,[21] imposes tax on the value of capital gains made upon the disposal of assets acquired after 19 September 1985, or deemed to be so made, provided that such a gain is not taxed otherwise under the ITAA,[22] with an allowance for inflation so that only the real gain is taxed. Where a 'capital gain' has been included in the assessable income of a taxpayer after the disposal of an asset under another provision of the ITAA, apart from Pt IIIA, the taxable value of the gain under Pt IIIA is reduced by the amount so included or declared: s 160ZA(4). Trusts other than Unit Trusts are taxed under Div 6 of Pt IIIA, ss 160ZYC–160ZYB, upon any capital gain which accrues to the trust upon the disposal or deemed disposal of an asset of the trust. Bonus units in unit trusts are dealt with under Div 7, ss 160ZYB–160ZYC. Sections 160V(1) (disposals by bare trustees), 160ZM (return of capital on investment in trust), 160ZZPAA (exchange of units in the same unit trust) and s 160ZZT (disposal of shares or other interest in partnership or trust), are also relevant.

[12.45] In essence, Pt IIIA imposes tax on the capital gains of a trust, by deeming those gains to be assessable income, so that they are taxed in the same manner as the income of a trust under Div 6 of Pt III, ss 92–102. Tax on capital gains made by the trust are payable by the beneficiaries where they are presently entitled to the capital gain and not under a legal disability. Where no beneficiary is presently entitled, the trustee will be liable to pay the tax on any capital gain. Where a trust has separate classes of capital and income beneficiaries, the income beneficiaries will be assessed for capital gains tax even though the capital beneficiaries will ultimately receive the capital gain.

[12.46] Capital gains tax is payable on the disposal of assets acquired after 19 September 1985, other than certain listed 'personal-use assets'.[23] An asset of a trust will be deemed to have been disposed of when a beneficiary under the trust becomes absolutely entitled to the asset as against the trustee under ITAA, s 160ZX (1). The expression 'absolutely entitled as against the trustee' is not defined in Pt IIIA, nor anywhere else in the ITAA. The form of words suggests a meaning different from 'presently entitled', so that a right to demand immediate payment or transfer of the asset cannot be taken to be the test to determine whether a beneficiary is absolutely entitled.[24] The expression 'absolutely entitled as against the trustee' occurs in the UK Finance Act and is defined in that Act as applying where a person:[25]

> ... has the exclusive right, subject only to satisfying any outstanding charge, lien or other right of the trustees to resort to the asset for payment of duty, taxes, costs or other outgoings, to direct how that asset shall be dealt with.

---

21. Income Tax Assessment Amendment (Capital Gains) Act 1986, ss 160A–160ZZU.
22. As it may be under ss 26(e) (employment allowances), 47 (distributions by liquidator), 59(2) (disposal of depreciated property), 108 (loans to shareholders), 109 (excessive payments to shareholders and directors), and 177E (stripping of company profits).
23. Section 160B.
24. *FCT v Whiting* (1943) 68 CLR 199.
25. Schedule 19, para 9.

If that approach is applied in Australia, a beneficiary of a partially administered estate, such as Mrs Coulson in *Livingston's* case, could be considered to be 'absolutely entitled' even though his or her rights are perhaps best characterised as rights *in personam* enforceable against the trustee rather than rights in rem enforceable against the assets of the trust,[26] and he or she is not, therefore, 'presently entitled' to any asset of the trust.

[12.47] As a general principle, the objects of a discretionary trust do not have a proprietary interest in the assets of the trust although they do have an 'interest' in those assets in the sense that they have standing to enforce due administration of the trust: *Gartside v IRC* [1968] AC 553; *Re Weirs Settlement Trusts* [1971] Ch 145. In *Leedale v Lewis* [1982] BTC 355, the House of Lords held that discretionary beneficiaries held 'interests' in the assets of the trust for the purposes of UK capital gains tax, even though that ruling meant that the UK resident beneficiaries of the trust were potentially exposed to liability for the whole of the tax payable in respect of the trust assets, the non-resident beneficiaries being beyond the Commissioner's reach. By Ruling IT 2340 the Australian Commissioner has indicated that the assets of a discretionary trust acquired before 19 September 1985 will be deemed to have been acquired by the then beneficiaries of that trust under ITAA, s 160ZZS, thus exempting those beneficiaries from capital gains tax on the 'disposal' of those assets after that date. It also seems likely that a discretionary beneficiary will be deemed to have an 'interest' under ITAA, s 160ZM so that the payment of an amount that is not assessable income to that beneficiary by the trustee will constitute a deemed disposal of that beneficiary's interest under that section. A resolution by the trustee to appoint an asset in favour of a beneficiary will also constitute a deemed disposal of that asset under ITAA, s 160M(3)(a).

Bonus units in unit trusts

[12.48] Under ITAA, s 160ZYC, where a taxpayer, who holds units in a unit trust, and that trust is not a corporate unit trust or public trading trust, is issued with bonus units in the trust, the bonus units will be deemed to have been acquired at the same time as the taxpayer's original units and the amount paid for those original units will be deemed to have been paid as consideration for the bonus units. This means that bonus units issued to a taxpayer in respect of units acquired prior to 20 September 1985 will not be treated as a capital gain, unless, under ITAA, s 160ZYD, the bonus units were issued after 10 December 1986 in return for the payment of money to the trustee in which case the bonus units will be deemed to have been issued at the time at which the liability to pay that consideration arose.

Exchange of units in a unit trust

[12.49] Section 160ZZPAA provides roll-over relief, thereby permitting the deferral of capital gains tax liability, where units in a unit trust are redeemed and replaced by freshly issued units in the same trust and the taxpayer elects to have the units treated as rolled over under ITAA, s 160ZZPAA by submitting the appropriate form on or before the date for lodgment of his or her tax return in that year. Where the original units were acquired before 20 September 1985 the taxpayer will be taken to have acquired the new units before that date.

---

26. *Livingston v Commissioner of Stamp Duties (Qld)* [1965] AC 694.

Return of capital on investment in a trust

[12.50] Section 160ZM applies where a trustee pays an amount to a beneficiary in respect of that beneficiary's interest in the trust which amount is not assessable income. If the beneficiary acquired his or her interest or units in the trust before 20 September 1985, no capital gains tax is payable and ITAA, s 160ZM has no further application to the payment. It has been suggested that this section will not ordinarily apply to the interests of the objects of a discretionary trust who do not have an interest but merely a right to be considered, unless those objects have a default interest in the capital of the trust.[27] It is then suggested that this could be avoided by having tax exempt institutions as the class of takers in default. However, it may not be necessary to complicate the trust with the addition of some such third party organisation. A gift to a class in default comprising the capital beneficiaries, and the income beneficiaries if you like, or the surviors of that class, or their successors, would consitute a sufficiently certain class of the takers in default. However, in view of the approach taken by the Commissioner in Ruling IT 2341, he may seek to apply ITAA, s 160ZM to the disposal of capital of a discretionary trust to the objects of the trust.

27. D Graham Hill, 'Trusts and Partnerships and Capital Gains Tax Taxation of Australia', Intensive Seminar on Capital Gains Tax, Wollongong, November 1986.

Chapter Thirteen

The Creation of Express Trusts

13–1 The Requirements of Certainty

[13.1] An express trust can be created by anyone possessing adequate legal capacity provided the necessary formal requirements are satisfied.[1] In particular those requirements involve the three certainties: certainty of intention to create a trust, certainty of the subject matter of the trust, and certainty as to the object of the trust.

Certainty of intention to create a trust

[13.2] Where a person executes a formal deed of trust it is unlikely that there is any question but that a trust was intended. However, in many other situations, most commonly in cases where a bank account is opened, supposedly 'on trust', the question can arise as to whether a trust was intended. No formal or technical words are required provided that a sufficiently clear intention to create a trust is shown. The creation of a trust of land or some interest in land inter vivos must be manifested and proved by writing,[2] while testamentary trusts must be created by will. In the latter case, courts of equity have had to grapple with wills containing expressions of prayer or entreaty that some property be held for the benefit of someone else without express directions creating a trust. Such 'precatory trusts', from the latin *precari* 'to pray', are less common now that most wills are professionally drawn and most lawyers keep standard precedents on computer. Where a person opens a bank account supposedly as trustee for someone else, the question of whether a trust has actually been created will depend upon the intention of the person opening the account, notwithstanding any words used, if the person intended to operate the account for his or her own benefit, no trust will be created: *Commissioner of Stamp Duties (Qld) v Joliffe* (1920) 28 CLR 178. The matter will turn on the facts of each case: see *Kauter v Hilton* (1953) 90 CLR 86.

[13.3] The effectiveness of any attempt to create a trust will also depend upon the circumstances. A trust purportedly created by a debtor within six months of the presentation of a bankruptcy petition will not be upheld as it would constitute a voidable preference in favour of the beneficiary under the Bankruptcy Act 1966 (Cth), s 122. The receipt of money or other property in the course of a commercial transaction will not, ordinarily, give rise to a trust in favour of the party placing the money or other property. A trust will only arise in such an event where the circumstances are sufficient to cast obligations of a fiduciary nature on the recipient. An agent for sale will not necessarily hold the proceeds of sale on trust for his or her principal. The question of whether a trust arises in such a case will depend upon the intentions of

---

1. *Jacobs'*, paras [401]–[409].
2. Conveyancing Act 1919 (NSW), s 23C(1)(b).

the parties, the nature of the legal obligations imposed on them in the transaction, whether by contract inter se or by statute and, in particular, whether the agent is obliged to keep the principal's money separate, or whether the agent's obligation is simply to account to the principal for the money or other property from general funds.

In *Walker v Corboy* (1990) 19 NSWLR 382, fruit and vegetable growers who sold their produce through Lojon Pty Ltd (Lojon) claimed that moneys representing the proceeds of sale of their produce was held on trust for them by receivers of Lojon's business. Lojon went into liquidation in August 1989. Shortly before that, Westpac, which had an equitable floating charge over the assets of the company, appointed the appellants receivers of Lojon's business. Moneys collected by the receivers from sales of produce were paid, by agreement between the receivers and the growers, into a separate account, which at the date of hearing totalled $326,000. Lojon was a licensed farm produce seller under the Farm Produce Act 1983. That act required the seller to account to growers for produce sold, although it did not stipulate that the growers be paid out of the proceeds of sale of their produce; it would suffice if the seller paid them out of its general funds. All payments made by purchasers were paid into the agent's general account, and all payments to growers were made from that account. The agents made no attempt to separate the proceeds of sale of growers' produce from their other funds, and no attempt was made to separate funds referable to the sale of the produce of one grower from another. The Court of Appeal held that the receivers did not hold the proceeds of sale on trust for the growers; the proper relationship between the parties was that of debtor and creditor. Meagher JA noted that the growers remained owners of the produce until it was sold, but also that the Act did not require the seller to keep the proceeds of sale separate from its general funds. The only protection afforded to growers by the Act was a requirement that they be paid within a specified time regardless of whether the agent had been paid by the purchaser.

A trust will not necessarily arise in every situation in which two or more parties have dealings between themselves which affect property and which give rise to equitable obligations concerning that property. As Gummow J noted in *Re Australian Elizabethan Theatre Trust* (1991) 102 ALR 681 at 694, those dealings will often give rise to equitable obligations falling short of those owed by a trustee to a beneficiary. Such obligations can include equitable charges and liens, similar to those considered in *Perpetual Trustee Co Ltd v Godsall* [1979] 2 NSWLR 785 at 792 and *Muschinski v Dodds* (1985) 160 CLR 583 at 605–6, 624–5 and in *Countess of Bective v FCT* (1932) 47 CLR 417 at 418–19.[3] In that case, Dixon J noted, at 420–1, that an obligation to apply

---

3. Where, by a will or gift inter vivos, moneys are paid to one person with some instruction that that they be paid to another person or for some purpose beneficial to another person, or persons, there are four possible interpretations:

(a)   the 'instruction' is taken as no more than an expression of a wish or expectation, in which case the first recipient takes beneficially: for example, *Lambe v Eames* (1871) LR 6 Ch 597; *Mackett v Mackett* (1872) LR 14 Eq 49;

(b)   the 'instruction' operates as an equitable condition whereby the first person takes beneficially but subject to an equitable obligation to perform the condition to which the gift is subject. If the condition requires the payment of money, the payment must be made whether the property given is adequate for the purpose or not: for example, *Messenger v Andrews* (1828) 4 Russ 478; 38 ER 885;

(c)   the first person takes the gift beneficially, but, particularly where the stated purpose involves the payment of money, the gift is subject to an equitable charge in favour of some other person or persons. This interpretation is common in bequests to parents for the maintenance and benefit of their children. The gift is subject to a charge but the surplus will belong to the parent: see, *Raikes v Ward* (1842) 1 Ha 445 at 450; 66 ER 1106 at 1108; *Re Booth; Booth v Booth* (1894) 2 Ch 282; *Cunningham v Foot* (1878) 3 App Cas 974 esp at 1002;

(d)   the first person acquires no beneficial interest in the subject matter of the gift and whether he or she receives it in the character of a trustee or some lesser category, such as a guardian, the fund is bound by the stated purpose and must be applied for that cause. This has been held to be the case with gifts providing for the maintenance of children: for example, *Re Yates; Yates v Wyatt* (1901) 2 Ch 438; *Re Morgan* (1883) 24 Ch D 114.

money for the maintenance of children, for example, ordinarily will not carry with it the liability which arises from from a trust, and that it is the general rule that guardians of infants and committees of the person of lunatics (now persons appointed to manage the estates of persons lacking capacity) and others entrusted with funds to be expended in the maintenance and support of persons under their care are not liable to account as trustees. They do not have to vouch for items of expenditure and, provided that they meet the obligation imposed on them to provide an appropriate level of maintenance for the person under their care, an account will not be taken. Sometimes, as his Honour noted, the care and maintenance will be provided in a joint household or common establishment. In such circumstances it would be inappropriate to require precise accounting for each item of expenditure. Such a requirement might, in fact, 'defeat the very purpose for which the fund is provided'.

'Quistclose' trusts

[13.4] Money received in the course of a commercial transaction will not, ordinarily, give rise to a trust in favour of the party placing the money. As Bramwell LJ put it in *New Zealand and Australian Land Co v Watson* (1881) 7 QBD 374 at 382:

> Now I do not desire to find fault with the various intricacies and doctrines connected with trusts, but I should be very sorry to see them introduced into commercial transactions, and an agent in a commercial case turned into a trustee with all the troubles that attend that relation.

Bramwell LJ's dictum has been referred to occasionally by later judges but a different approach was taken by Priestley JA in *Walker v Corboy* (at 385):

> It seems to me to be prudent not to approach the question whether equitable doctrines are applicable in a commercial situation with the thought in mind that one should be disinclined to give a positive answer to the question. The question simply is, do the particular circumstances attract equitable rules. There is no reason to regret one answer rather than the other. If there are express agreements between parties to a commercial transaction, or a series of commercial transactions, requiring the application of equitable rules for their working out, then it is difficult to see that commercial life will be any the worse for those rules, which in one very real sense are as much legal rules as are common law rules, being applied.

[13.5] Where one party places money with another, or advances money to that other in a commercial situation, the two will become creditor and debtor rather than beneficiary and trustee, unless the circumstances are sufficient to cast obligations of a fiduciary nature on the recipient: *Barclays Bank Ltd v Quistclose Investments Ltd* [1970] AC 567.

> Rolls Razor Ltd, in serious financial difficulties, sought to borrow further funds. A financier was willing to lend £1 million but only on condition that the company found a sum of £209,719 to pay a dividend which had been declared in July 1964. The company obtained a loan from the respondent for the purpose of paying that dividend and a cheque for the necessary amount was paid into an account opened especially for the purpose. Before the dividend was paid Rolls Razor went into voluntary liquidation. The respondent claimed that the £209,719 was held by that company on trust to pay the dividend and, as the trust had failed, the money should be repaid. The appellant bank claimed the money was available as part of the general funds of the company. Their Lordships decided that the funds were held on a resulting trust for the lender. Lord Wilberforce stated that arrangements of this character, for the payment of a person's debts by a third person, gave rise to a relationship of a fiduciary character in favour, as a primary trust, of the creditors and, secondarily, if the primary trust fails, of

the third person. Once the purpose is carried out the lender has only a remedy in debt. Until then the lender has an equitable right to see that the money is applied for the specified purpose.

[13.6] *Barclays Bank v Quistclose Investments* has been accepted in Australia as authority for the rule that where one party advances money to another with the mutual intention that it should not become part of the assets of the borrower but should be used for some specific purpose, then a trust of the moneys will be implied if the purpose fails: *Australasian Conference Ass'n Ltd v Mainline Constructions Pty Ltd* (1979) 141 CLR 335. The requirement of 'mutual intention' suggests that the principle emanating from *Barclays Bank v Quistclose* must be distinguished from the principle applied in decisions such as *Re Kayford Ltd* [1975] 1 WLR 279. In that case a mail order company set up a trust account into which it deposited customers' payments pending receipt by them of the goods ordered. On winding up it was held that the moneys in that account were held on trust for the customers and did not form part of the general assets of the company. The 'trust' in *Re Kayford* was created unilaterally by the company. It was not a product of mutual intention. Moneys settled on a trust unilaterally created by a company within six months before it went into liquidation would be voidable as a preference (see **[13.3]**),[4] at least to the extent that moneys paid into such an account came from the general funds of the company. Moneys received subsequently, that is, after the creation of the trust, would not form part of the assets of the company if the company did not give a beneficial receipt for them. Mere payment into a specially named account will not be enough, by itself, to show the necessary intention to create a trust. In *Re Fada (Australia) Ltd* [1927] SASR 590, a company paid money received with applications for new shares into an account opened for the purpose styled 'Fada (Australia) Ltd Trust Account'. The company had said in the prospectus that new shares would not be allotted until a certain number had been applied for. If that number was not reached the application moneys were to be refunded. On liquidation it was held that payment into a 'trust account' did not, of itself, create any trust in favour of the applicants. The question of whether a trust is created will turn on the intention of the alleged settlor. In *Re Multi Guarantee Ltd* [1987] BCLC 257, a company which gave guarantees on domestic appliances after the manufacturer's guarantee had expired, in return for the payment of a premium collected by stores selling the appliances, agreed to pay premiums received from one store into a special account from which funds could only be withdrawn with the consent of both parties. The English Court of Appeal held that no trust was created. The guarantee company did not manifest a sufficient intention to create a trust. A trust created by unilateral action in the style of *Re Kayford* must be an express trust which comes into being by virtue of the express declaration of the party setting the moneys aside. That style of trust can be distinguished from a *Quistclose* trust, at least in the sense of the secondary trust in favour of the person providing the money, which is more in the nature of a resulting trust.[5] The primary trust, the trust in favour of the mutually agreed purpose, would be an express trust, although one arising from agreement or common intention rather than unilateral declaration.

[13.7] *Quistclose* trusts have not revolutionised the law of trusts. The proposition that where A pays moneys to B for a specified purpose, and B sets those moneys aside upon receipt, a trust of those moneys for the fulfilment of that purpose is created

---

4. *Jacobs'*, paras [214]–[217].
5. CEF Rickett, 'Different Views on the Scope of the Quistclose Analysis: English and Antipodean Insights' (1991) 106 LQR 608 at 609.

and, failing that, there is, a resulting trust in favour of A, is not a radical departure from established authority. *Barclays Bank v Quistclose Investments* was applied in *Carreras Rothmans Ltd v Freeman Mathews Treasure Ltd (in liq)* [1985] 1 All ER 155 as authority for the principle that a trust arose whenever money was transferred from one person to another for a specific purpose which was made known to that other person. The money was not received by the payee beneficially and the payee was not entitled to use the money for any other purpose. In *Carreras Rothmans* an advertising agency used by a cigarette manufacturer went into liquidation. Prior to that, when the agency was in financial difficulties, it came to an arrangement with the cigarette company client whereby moneys were paid by the client into a special account with the agency's bank for the sole purpose of paying accounts and invoices arising from advertising arranged by the agency for that client. After the agency went into liquidation the liquidator claimed moneys remaining in the special account as an asset of the agency available to pay its general creditors. Applying *Quistclose*, Peter Gibson J held that the moneys were held by the agency on trust. His Lordship stated what he saw as the principle in these terms:

> Equity fastens on the conscience of the person who receives from another property transferred for a specific purpose only and not therefore for the recipient's own purposes, so that such person will not be permitted to treat the property as his own or use it for other than the stated purpose ... if the common intention is that property is transferred for a specific purpose and not so as to become the property of the transferee, the transferee cannot keep the property if for any reason the purpose cannot be fulfilled.

[13.8] In *Australasian Conference Association Ltd v Mainline Constructions Pty Ltd (in liq)* (1978) 141 CLR 335, an argument based on *Quistclose* was raised claiming that moneys advanced by a bank under a guarantee given to a builder did not form part of the general assets of the builder. The builder took the guarantee instead of a retention fund. The bank unconditionally guaranteed to pay to the proprietor of the property the amount provided by the guarantee on demand. After the builder went into receivership the proprietor called on the guarantee. The bank paid the money to the proprietor who then proposed to use part of it to pay outstanding moneys owing by the builder to sub-contractors. The bank challenged this. The court held that the proprietor was entitled to use the money to pay the sub-contractors and that any surplus was to go to the builder and not the bank. Gibbs ACJ considered the argument based on *Quistclose* (at 353):

> That case is authority for the proposition that where money is advanced by A to B, with the mutual intention that it should not become part of the assets of B, but should be used exclusively for a specific purpose, there will be implied (at least in the absence of an indication of a contrary intention) a stipulation that if the purpose fails the money will be repaid, and the arrangement will give rise to a relationship of a fiduciary character, or trust.

[13.9] In *Re Australian Elizabethan Theatre Trust* (1991) 102 ALR 681, the Australian Elizabethan Theatre Trust (AETT) received gifts, which were allowable as tax deductions to the donors, on behalf of other bodies in the arts and theatre world which did not enjoy such exemptions. The Commissioner of Taxation ruled that he would only allow deductions where money was transferred voluntarily and that any such gift was unconditional. It was practice for anyone wishing to make a tax deductible donation to some artistic or theatrical purpose to give the money to the AETT, expressing a 'preference' for the manner in which it was to be applied. Donations of this sort in which a 'preference' was expressed were deductible, provided the AETT received them in its own right and had an unfettered discretion as to how the money would be applied. In March 1991 a provisional liquidator was appointed to conduct the affairs of the AETT. Prior to the appointment of the provisional liquidator the AETT had received various donations in which a 'preference' had been expressed in favour of three artistic organisations. Those three organisations sought declarations to the effect that the AETT held those moneys on trust for them respectively. Gummow J held that no trust arose in favour of any of the organisations. The gifts were 'unconditional' and words expressing any preference were merely precatory. On the same basis, there were no grounds upon which the AETT's bank could be held liable as a constructive trustee by reason of receiving such donated moneys. Having discussed the authorities and some commentary on the point Gummow J observed, at 694:

> To speak of a *Quistclose* trust as if it were a new legal institution, rather than an example of the particular operation of principle upon the facts as found, is to set the listener or reader off on a false path.

Gummow J also said, at 692, that while these cases talk of moneys paid for 'a purpose' the trusts which are recognised under the *Quistclose* principles are not some special species of non-charitable purpose trusts. To stand as valid private trusts they must satisfy the normal requirements for such trusts, which include an identifiable beneficiary or beneficiaries or class of objects, so there cannot be a trust for the purpose of buying equipment: *Re EVTR* [1987] BCLC 646. In *Re Northern Developments (Holdings) Ltd* (Chancery Division, 6 October 1978, unreported) a group of banks provided money to a company for the purpose of paying its unsecured creditors. Megarry VC held that a trust came into existence which was enforceable by the banks, the company and the unsecured creditors. In the case of the unsecured creditors, his Lordship said that they had an interest analogous with that of a beneficiary in an unadministered deceased estate; they could not compel distribution to them in *specie* but could enforce due administration of the trust and, presumably, restrain the 'trustee' from applying the funds for any other purpose.

[13.10] But what are the principles referred to by Gummow J in *Re Australian Elizabethan Theatre Trust*? There is nothing new in the proposition that a person receiving money from another, on terms that it held for the benefit of the payor, holds the moneys received on trust. As Lord Selborne LC put it in *Lyell v Kennedy* (1889) 14 App Cas 437 at 457:

> A man who receives the money of another on his behalf, and places it specifically to an account with a banker ear-marked and separate from his own moneys, though under his control, is in my opinion a trustee of the fund standing to the credit of that account. For the constitution of such a trust no express words are necessary; anything which may satisfy a Court of Equity that the money was received in a fiduciary character is enough. It is not requisite that any acknowledgement of such a trust should be made to the *cestui que trust* or his agent; to whomsoever made it is evidence against the trustee.

Quite clearly if A pays money to B to hold on trust for C a valid trust will be created in favour of C. If A pays money to B upon a primary trust to pay the money to C upon the happening of some event, the declaration of a dividend, the rendering of an account by C for certain work, C turning 21 or whatever, a trust in C's favour will be created but will only be enforceable by C upon the happening of the event. Subject to that, and any contrary intention on A's part, such as that B may treat the money as his own if the event does not happen, B may be required to hold the money on a secondary trust in favour of A, a resulting trust which will come into play in the event of the failure of the primary trust. Both the primary and the secondary trust in that example will be enforceable by A. Once the primary trust is fulfilled, that is, B pays C, both trusts will be discharged and a relationship of debtor and creditor will exist between B and A. If A pays money to B to be applied for some purpose, such as payment to C upon the happening of some event, with the intention that B gives an administrative and not a beneficial receipt for the money, so that the moneys never become B's beneficially, but A does not intend to create a trust for C, B will hold the money subject to a fiduciary power to pay it in accordance with A's wishes or, failing that, upon trust for A. In those circumstances, C will not have any standing to enforce the arrangement. Where the circumstances are otherwise neutral, that is, there are no special circumstances indicating that B in the examples above and similar cases receives money as trustee, where A pays money to B, or on B's behalf, the payment will give rise to a relationship of debtor and creditor in the absence of any mutual agreement that the moneys are held on trust. In *Ausintel Investments Pty Ltd v Lam* (1990) 19 NSWLR 637, a shareholder arranged for moneys to be paid from her bank account in reduction of the company's indebtedness to a third party under an arrangement whereby she was to receive an allotment of further shares. The shares were not issued. The shareholder sought to wind up the company. The company repaid the money but refused to pay interest. Meagher JA, with whom Gleeson CJ agreed, found there was no mutual agreement that the moneys deposited for the company's benefit should not become a part of its general assets and rejected the submission that a *Quistclose* trust arose.

Precatory trusts

[13.11] Whatever words are used by a settlor or testator, the court must consider whether they display the necessary intention to bind the alleged trustee or whether they simply confer a power which is not binding, or whether they are no more than words of mere request. Where words of request are used, the gift is sometimes called a 'precatory trust', from the latin *precari* — to pray. The issue to be decided then is whether, despite the use of words of request, or of prayer or entreaty, a binding trust is nonetheless intended. The answer to that question will depend very much on the facts of each case. The words 'it is my will and desire' that shares of a deceased estate be settled on the testator's daughters in a certain way were held to be binding on the trustee in *West v FCT* (1949) 79 CLR 319. In *Re Alston* [1955] VLR 281, a testatrix's words 'It is my express wish' that Newman Spielvogel be granted a lease of two properties for ten years at £2 per week, with a right to terminate, were held not to constitute a binding direction to the trustee to grant such a lease, although they clearly gave the trustee authority to do so[6] where a will is prepared by a solicitor it is less likely that words of request will be construed as any more than that.

Certainty of subject matter

[13.12] The subject matter of a trust, the trust property, must also be described with sufficient certainty. If the subject matter of a trust is not certain then the trust will fail. In *Mussoorie Bank v Raynor* (1882) 7 App Cas 321, a testator left property to his wife 'feeling confident that she will act justly to our children in dividing the same when no longer required by her'. The Privy Council held that no trust in favour of

---

6. See also *Dean v Coles* (1921) 30 CLR 1; cf *Re Atkinson* (1911) 103 LT 860.

the children was created. Apart from the precatory words, it was not clear what property was intended to be the subject of such a trust. This does not mean that a gift of the 'residue' of a deceased estate will fail for uncertainty, even where no express provision is made for the payment of debts ad liabilities: *Re Ferguson* [1957] VR 635.

Certainty of object

[13.13] The objects of a fixed private trust, that is, one in which the extent of the beneficial interest of each *cestui que trust* is fixed by the terms of the trust, must be identified with sufficient clarity to satisfy the list certainty rule, that is, in that the beneficiaries are 'ascertainable' in the sense that they could be listed when the trust comes into operation. The objects of a discretionary trust must be described with sufficient certainty to satisfy the criterion certainty test, that is, whether it can be said that a given individual is or is not a member of the range of objects: *McPhail v Doulton* [1971] AC 424. Charitable trusts are treated more leniently in this, as in other requirements, and will be upheld, if need be by the application of some scheme, provided that a general intention to benefit charity is shown. The advent of a more flexible test for the description of the objects of discretionary trusts is of recent origin and the complete ramifications of this development are yet to unfold. The traditional rule for certainty of object for trusts was laid down early last century in *Morice v The Bishop of Durham* (1804) 9 Ves 399; 32 ER 656:

> A testatrix bequeathed all her personal estate to the Bishop of Durham upon trust to pay her debts and legacies, and to apply the residue in favour of such objects of benevolence and liberality as the Bishop in his own discretion should approve of. The Bishop was appointed sole executor. Upon the application of the woman's next of kin this residuary bequest was held to be invalid. Sir William Grant MR stated the rule, for private trusts, at 9 Ves 404, 32 ER 658, 'There can be no trust over the exercise of which this Court will not assume a control: for an uncontrollable power of disposition would be ownership and not trust. If there be a clear trust but for uncertain objects, the property, that is the subject of the trust, is undisposed of and the benefit of such trust must result to those to whom the law gives the ownership in default of disposition by the former owner. But this doctrine does not hold good with respect to trusts for charity. Every other trust must have a definite object. There must be somebody in whose favour the court can decree performance'.

[13.14] *Morice v The Bishop of Durham* stands as authority for what is known as the 'beneficiary principle', that is, that for every non-charitable trust there must be an identifiable beneficiary, or identifiable beneficiaries, in whose favour the court can decree performance. It was cited as authority for the proposition that a trust 'to be valid must be for the benefit of individuals' by Lord Parker in *Bowman v Secular Society Ltd* [1917] AC 406 at 441.

> In *Re Astor's Settlement Trusts* [1952] Ch 534, property was settled on trust with an intermediate gift of income, for a period of certain lives in being plus 20 years, in favour of various non-charitable purposes, such as the promotion of international relations and the improvement of newspapers and other publications. Roxburgh J held the intermediate gift of income to be invalid on two grounds. In the first place, on the authority of *Morice v The Bishop of Durham*, because there was no person in whose favour the court could decree performance, and, second, on the same authority, because the subject and objects of a trust must be ascertained, upon principles familiar in other cases, and because in this gift there were many uncertain phrases in the enumeration of purposes, so that it was not possible for the court, if called upon to carry out the purposes declared, to do so without having to select from them by eliminating those which were

too uncertain. His Lordship also added that those two grounds had their origin in the a single principle: that a court of equity does not recognise as valid a trust which it cannot both enforce and control.

[13.15] In *McPhail v Doulton* [1971] AC 424 at 455–7, Lord Wilberforce rejected the notion that a court in enforcing a trust would necessarily divide the trust property equally between the objects and distribute it to them. Apart from the court assuming responsibility for the trust property and attempting to administer the trust itself, his Lordship said that, if called upon to execute a power of appointment in the nature of a trust, the court would do so in the manner best calculated to give effect to the settlor's or testator's intentions. It could do so by appointing new trustees or by authorising or directing representative persons of the class of beneficiaries to propose a scheme of arrangement, or even should the proper basis for distribution appear by itself, directing the trustees to so distribute. That view was echoed by Windeyer J in *Lutheran Church v Farmers' Co-operative* (1970) 121 CLR 628 at 652. This approach has narrowed the field covered by the rule in *Morice v The Bishop of Durham*. The beneficiary principle must now be seen as restricted to beneficiaries whose shares in the beneficial interest of the trust are fixed. In the case of discretionary trusts, or other trusts where it is clear that the party creating the trust did not necessarily intend that the objects should share the benefits equally, the requirements of certainty will be satisfied if it can be said with certainty whether a given individual is, or is not, a member of the range of objects. In that case the question cannot be whether there are persons in whose favour the court can decree performance. That would be an inappropriate way to deal with a discretionary trust. The only relevant question must be whether there is an identifiable range of objects who can enforce due administration of the trust.

13–2 Trusts for Unincorporated Associations

[13.16] Under the beneficiary principle a trust, to be validly created, must be for the benefit of individuals and not for some purpose, unless for a valid charitable purpose. A gift in favour of a corporation satisfies the test as it is a gift to an individual, and not a trust for the purposes of the corporation: *Bowman v Secular Society Ltd* [1917] AC 406. The application of the rule in *Morice v Bishop of Durham* to gifts on trust for unincorporated associations, clubs and such like bodies, has created some problems. Such associations have no legal personality separate from their members, and so cannot be 'beneficiaries' under this principle. The general rule was stated by the Privy Council in *Leahy v A-G (NSW)* [1959] AC 457; (1959) 101 CLR 611:

> A testator, by clause 3 of his will, made a gift of a grazing property upon trust 'for such order of nuns of the Catholic Church or the Christian Brothers as my executors and trustees shall select'. Because that expression included contemplative, or closed, orders of nuns, the gift could be only upheld as a valid charitable trust by the operation of s 37D of the Conveyancing Act 1919 (NSW), which would have restricted the gift to the possible charitable objects that is, active orders. The trustees wished to retain the right to select closed orders and argued that clause 3 was valid as an absolute gift to the order selected. The Judicial Committee advised that a gift on trust for an unincorporated association would, prima facie, be valid as a gift for the individual members. That presumption would be overturned, and the trust would fail, if on proper construction the gift was for present and future members, in which case it failed as a gift in perpetuity, or if it was a gift for the non-charitable purposes of the association, in which case it

would fail under the beneficiary principle. Accordingly, the gift in clause 3 of this will failed as a private trust because the subject matter, and the object, indicated that the testator did not intend to make an absolute gift to the individual members of any order selected.

[13.17] In giving their decision in *Leahy's* case the Judicial Committee expressed disapproval of a line of authority, including *Re Drummond* [1914] 2 Ch 90 and *Re Price* [1943] Ch 422, under which such 'purpose' trusts had been upheld where the society was able to spend the gift, both capital and income, at once. While safe on the ground of perpetuity such gifts still lacked the necessary element of a proper beneficiary. The rule stated in *Leahy's* case was adopted and applied by the High Court in *Bacon v Pianta* (1966) 114 CLR 634 to strike down a gift by a testator of the whole of his estate 'to the Communist Party of Australia for its sole use and benefit' on the grounds that it was both a bequest to present and future members of the Party and that it was for the non-charitable purposes of the party.

[13.18] The beneficiary principle was embellished in *Neville Estates Ltd v Madden* [1962] Ch 832 by Cross J who held that a gift to an unincorporated association could be upheld, not only where it was a gift to the individual members as joint tenants, so that any member could sever his share and claim it, but also where it could be construed as a gift to the members as tenants in common subject to their contractual rights and liabilities towards one another as members of the association. Cross J considered that such a gift would not fail for uncertainty or perpetuity unless there was something in the rules of the association which prevented the members from dividing the subject matter of the gift between themselves at any time. That approach has been followed in England in *Re Recher's Will Trusts* [1972] 1 Ch 526 and in Victoria in *Re Goodson* [1971] VR 801, in which it was applied to uphold a gift for 'the general purposes of the Loyal Orange Institution of Victoria'. This 'constitutional principle' might have some merit, in that it could save some gifts which would otherwise fall under the scythe of the beneficiary principle, but it contains some serious flaws. In *Cameron v Hogan* (1934) 51 CLR 358, the High Court held that members of a voluntary association did not enter into a contract *inter se*, while in *Wise v Perpetual Trustee Co Ltd* [1903] AC 139 at 149, the Privy Council, per Lindley LJ, held that, unless the rules provide to the contrary, members of a club are assumed to be under no personal liability to indemnify the trustees of club property or other members beyond their subscriptions. Apart from the questionable proposition that the members of a club or society necessarily enter into a contract *inter se* dealing with their rights to 'club property', those contractual rights and liabilities are seemingly given priority over the proprietary rights which the members, prima facie, have in that 'club property'. This so-called contract also seems capable of assigning beneficial interests in the 'club property' from departing and deceased members to present and future members, and from present members to new members without any regard for the Statute of Frauds or any Wills, Probate and Administration legislation. The constitutions of many clubs and societies contain no provisions dealing with the rights of members to 'club property'. Silence might be golden rule in this instance as it would indicate that the members could distribute the property by dissolving their association, but that is hardly a satisfactory way of resolving these rather complex questions.

[13.19] A better analysis of the relationship between property held or managed for the benefit of an unincorporated association, the rights of members and the duties of officers of the association with respect to that property can be found in the judgment of Helsham J in *Harrison v Hearn* [1972] 1 NSWLR 428:

The Executive Council of the Students' Council at Macquarie University resolved to give some of the Student's Council's money to La Trobe University Students Representative Council to assist that Council in paying legal costs incurred in what was called a struggle to retain control of that Society's funds. A student at Macquarie sought to restrain the Council from making the payments. Helsham J granted the injunction holding that the Students' Council was obliged to use the funds it received for the interests and welfare of students of Macquarie and that the members of the Executive Council owed a fiduciary duty to the people they represented in disposing of the funds. Even though individual students had no proprietary right in the property of the Council they had a sufficient interest to seek a declaration or to apply for injunctive relief to prevent improper use of the Council's funds.

[13.20] The relaxation of the beneficiary principle wrought by Re Baden's Will Trusts, McPhail v Doulton obviously applies to trusts for the benefit of unincorporated associations, just as it does to powers of appointment in the nature of a trust. It is thus no longer necessary to ascertain all the members of an association, nor to show that the gift is one to the individual members as joint tenants, provided the trust is 'administratively workable' and that it can be said with certainty whether a given individual is or is not a member of the group intended to benefit from the gift. In such a case the emphasis rests on the enforcement of the trust, and the standing of the party seeking to enforce it, rather than the persons in whose favour the court could decree performance.[7] Should a court be called upon to enforce a trust in favour of a club or society now, it is highly unlikely that it would do so by distributing the trust property among the members. It would be more likely to appoint new trustees or to order some scheme of arrangement. This aspect of enforceability was stressed in Re Denley's Trust Deed [1969] 1 Ch 373, in which Goff J said that the beneficiary principle was confined to purpose trusts which were abstract or impersonal, and that it did not apply to purpose trusts which provided benefits to individuals, albeit indirectly, who possessed standing to enforce the trust. On this view a trust will fall outside the mischief perceived by the beneficiary principle where, although expressed as a trust for a purpose, it is directly or indirectly a trust for the benefit of identifiable individuals who can approach the court to enforce the trust. In such a case it would be possible to say whether a given postulant is or is not a person entitled to enforce the trust. The enforcement approach proposed by Goff J in Re Denley was referred to with approval in Re Lipinski's Will Trusts [1976] Ch 235:

A testator bequeathed his residuary estate upon trust to the Hull Judeans (Maccabi) Association, an unincorporated body, to be used solely in constructing and improving new buildings for the association. As the association was primarily concerned with the promotion of sport among Anglo-Jewish youth it was not a charitable body. Oliver J held that the designation of the gift made it impossible to construe it as one for the individual members. However, as the specified purpose was for the benefit of ascertained beneficiaries, that is, the members of the association, the gift was valid as one for a purpose which benefitted ascertainable individuals. His Lordship also took note of the fact that the members could alter the constitution to allow for a division of the assets between themselves.

[13.21] The perpetuity problem has been eased, in New South Wales, by s 16 of the Perpetuities Act 1984 (NSW) which sets a perpetuity period of 80 years for a settle-

---

7. General support for this view can be found in WA Lee, 'Trusts and Trust-like Obligations with respect to Unincorporated Associations', by in PD Finn (ed), Essays in Equity, Law Book Co, Sydney, 1985, pp 179–95.

ment in favour of a non-charitable purpose and allows for such dispositions to be dealt with on a wait-and-see basis. This extends the indulgence which courts have allowed to purpose trusts in which the trust is limited for a period not in excess of the perpetuity period — usually 21 years where there is no reference to any lives in being — and allows them to run for 80 years. The Act also saves gifts for the present and future members of associations. Section 9(4) provides that where a gift in favour of a class would infringe the rule against perpetuities because some person might become a member outside the period, then, once it is apparent that such an infringement will take place, that person is treated as if he or she was not a member of the class in relation to the interest concerned. In Western Australia, s 106 of the Property Law Act 1969 (WA) provides that any limitation in favour of such a class shall be construed as one in favour only of those members of the class who attain a vested interest within the perpetuity period.[8] 'Wait and see' provisions also apply in Victoria, Queensland and the Australian Capital Territory.[9]

[13.22] The acceptability of trusts for the non-charitable purposes of unincorporated associations remains a matter of some controversy. A trust for a purpose and not for persons has been said to fail for lack of certainty of object, rather than just on the principle that a private trust to be valid must be in favour of a beneficiary or beneficiaries.[10] Where such a trust is contained in a will it could be argued that it ought to be considered a delegation of will-making power, although it is questionable whether that doctrine applies to trusts which are not void for uncertainty of object in any event.[11] The approach taken by Goff J in *Re Denley* is both sensible and desirable but difficult to adopt for any judge at first instance in Australia under the shadow cast by *Leahy's* case and *Bacon v Pianta*. *Re Denley* has not escaped academic criticism in Australia. The authors of the fifth edition of *Jacobs'* have dismissed it as contrary to the authorities and difficult to justify in principle.[12] However, if the principle to which they refer is that in *Morice v Bishop of Durham* then it must be acknowledged that *Re Baden, Mc Phail v Doulton* has wrought a fundamental change in that principle. Authorities based on the original, unchanged principle would not necessarily carry much weight. It is submitted that *McPhail v Doulton* offers justification for the approach taken in *Re Denley*. But it does not sanction pure purpose trusts, even where some benefit flowed to individuals from the fulfilment of that purpose. It also seems necessary that the gift, either expressly or by necessary implication, must show an intention that the purpose is to be carried out for the benefit of individuals.

[13.23] It is both unfortunate and unnecessary that the law in this area is so complicated. If trusts serve any useful social purpose it is as a vehicle for the management of the property of those lacking legal capacity to manage their affairs and for the management of property on behalf of groups too numerous to manage their common interests efficiently. To the person in the street the concept of 'club' funds or assets

---

8. In Queensland both the perpetuity problem and the structures of the beneficiary principle have been remedied, to some extent, by of the Succession Act 1981 (QLD) s 63 which provides that a legacy or devise to an unincorporated association for the purposes of the association or for the present and future members of the association shall take effect as a legacy or devise in augmentation of the general funds of the association.
9. Perpetuities and Accumulations Act 1968 (Vic), s 9; Property Law Act 1974 (Qld), s 210; Property Law Act 1969 (WA), s 103; Perpetuities and Accumulations Act 1985 (ACT), s 9.
10. *Morice v Bishop of Durham* (1804) 9 ves 399, per Sir William Grant MR at 404; 32 ER 656 at 658; and *Re Astor's Trusts* [1952] Ch 534.
11. See paras **[12.20]** and **[12.30]**-**[12.33]**.
12. *Jacobs'*, para [1104].

and the employment of those funds or assets for 'club' purposes is perfectly understandable and so is the idea of the enforcement of those obligations at the suit of any member. The idea that such funds be managed by way of a trust or that the persons responsible for their management be trustees is capable of being understood by the average club member. The employment of unduly technical and artificial rules divorced from the realities of accepted social organisation serves neither society nor the law.

13-3 Purpose Trusts

[13.24] Despite the apparent stringency of the beneficiary principle there is an odd little body of cases in which trusts for non-charitable purposes without any human beneficiary, sometimes called trusts of imperfect obligation, have been upheld. The most common of these have concerned gifts for the maintenance of graves and tombstones, and gifts for the upkeep of pets or other animals as well as trusts for the non-charitable purposes of unincorporated associations. Those categories are not exhaustive of these trusts. There have been other miscellaneous anomalies as well.

[13.25] In England trusts in favour of a variety of purposes have been upheld, some quite bizarre. In *Pettingall v Pettingall* (1842) 11 LJ Ch 176, a bequest of £50 per annum by a testator for the upkeep of his favourite black mare was upheld by Knight-Bruce VC, although it was noted that there were residuary beneficiaries who could apply to the court to ensure that the terms of the trust were carried out. Other purposes have included a gift to erect a sepulchral monument and to maintaining some horses: *Mitford v Reynolds* (1848) 16 Sim 105; 60 ER 812; an annuity of £750 per annum which was charged on certain land for the purpose of providing for the maintenance of the testator's horses and hounds for 50 years should any of them live so long: *Re Dean* (1889) 41 Ch D 552; and even a gift for the promotion and furthering of foxhunting: *Re Thompson* [1934] Ch 342. In *Re Endacott* [1960] Ch 232, the Court of Appeal refused to uphold a disposition to a parish council 'for the purpose of providing some useful memorial' to the testator. Lord Evershed MR said that the anomalous exceptions ought not to be extended while Harman LJ thought they were 'occasions when Homer has nodded'.

[13.26] Homer has not slept here and judges in Australia have not been so easily moved by the sentiments which seemed to sway North CJ and some of his brethren. In *Public Trustee v Nolan* (1943) 43 SR (NSW) 169, Roper J having held that a trust to erect a carillon on the shores of Sydney Harbour was not a trust for a charitable purpose, refused to uphold the same gift as a valid private trust on the ground that it was a trust for a purpose and not for any human beneficiary. *Leahy's* case also stands as a significant barrier against any local attempt to add to the odd menagerie of anomalous exceptions which can be found in the English cases.

[13.27] The beneficiary principle only applies to dispositions on trust. It does not apply to powers. So, in principle, a gift on trust for certain human or charitable objects which is subject to a power of appointment in favour of some non-charitable purpose will be a perfectly good disposition.[13] Such a power would have to be a mere power as a power in the nature of a trust would fall foul of the beneficiary principle.

---

13. *Jacobs'*, para [1108]; see also *Re Wootton* [1968] 1 WLR 681 at 688, per Pennycuick J.

It would be necessary for such a mere power to satisfy the criterion certainty test. But the power, unlike a trust, would not need to be for the benefit of a person.

13–4 The Constitution of a Voluntary Trust

[13.28] For a voluntary trust to be enforceable at the suit of the beneficiaries it must be completely constituted. Once that stage is reached it will not be open to the trustee to argue that the beneficiaries are volunteers: *Paul v Paul* (1882) 20 Ch D 742. An incompletely constituted trust can only amount to an agreement to create a trust which, of course, will not be enforceable without consideration. A trust may be constituted in a number of ways:

[13.29] **Transfer to trustees.** This may be effected either by settlement *inter vivos* or by will. The former would appear to contemplate completion of the transfer of title to the trust property at law, if it is legal property, however, the general view is that it will be sufficient if the settlor does all that he alone can do, thus satisfying the rule in *Milroy v Lord* (1862) 4 De GF & J 264 at 274, 45 ER 1185 at 1189, that is, that, 'In order to render a voluntary settlement valid and effectual, the settlor must have done everything which according to the nature of the property comprised in the settlement was necessary to be done to transfer the property and render the settlement binding upon him'.[14] The result is that a valid trust may be constituted in some cases where the legal title has not vested in the trustees but they have been put in a position in which they can complete that title unaided.[15] So that where X seeks to create a trust of Blackacre in favour of B by transferring Blackacre to T to hold on trust for B the trust will be complete when T receives an executed memorandum of transfer in registrable form and the certificate of title to Blackacre. While the complete constitution of the trust of Blackacre may be somewhat moot, there would clearly be a trust of the pieces of paper, the transfer and title deed, in favour of B. It would also appear to be essential that the trust be acknowledged by the intended trustee. Execution of a deed of trust will clearly suffice although a signature accepting a memorandum of transfer might not, of itself, signify acceptance of the specific trust intended. In the case of a trust created by will, where the intended trustee is also the executor of the will, it is not necessary for legal title to the trust property to be transferred into the executor's name. An executor has complete rights of property in the assets of the estate by virtue of the grant of probate.

[13.30] **Declaration of trust.** A voluntary trust created by way of declaration of trust will be fully constituted, and thus enforceable at the suit of the beneficiaries, even though they may be volunteers, once the settlor has made an express declaration of trust intended to be binding on him or herself, subject only to any statutory requirement that such a trust be in writing.

[13.31] **Direction to a trustee.** Where a beneficiary of an existing trust wishes to create a new trust in favour of a third party he or she may do so by directing the trustee to hold the property on trust for the new beneficiary thereafter. Such a direction, being a disposition of a subsisting equitable interest, must be in writing: *Grey v IRC* [1960] AC 1.

---

14. See *Corin v Patton* (1990) 169 CLR 540 and [312]–[320].
15. *Jacobs'*, paras [616Q]–[621]; Ford & Lee, pp 96–8.

[13.32] While these principles are fairly straightforward, some confusion, and a considerable amount of academic condemnation,[16] has been caused by the decision in *Re Pryce* [1917] 1 Ch 234: see **[1.15]**. The main thrust of the criticism of Eve J's judgment in that case rests on the principle that there can be a completely constituted trust of the benefit of a voluntary covenant: *Fletcher v Fletcher* (1844) 4 Hare 67; 67 ER 564 and that the trustees, rather than approaching the Chancery Division to ask whether they 'ought' to take proceedings for breach of the covenant to settle after-acquired property, should have commenced an action at common law for breach of covenant in accord with their duty to preserve the trust property. The difficulties created by *Re Pryce* have been compounded by later decisions which have followed it: *Re Kay's Settlement* [1939] Ch 329; *Re Cook's Settlement Trust* [1965] Ch 902; and *Perpetual Trustee Co Ltd v Willers* (1955) 72 WN (NSW) 244.

The requirement of writing for express trusts

[13.33] Under the Statute of Frauds legislation in each State,[17] *inter vivos* declarations of trust respecting any land or interest in land must be manifested and proved by some writing, while any disposition of a subsisting equitable interest must be in writing signed by the disponor or the disponor's agent. Under the relevant wills legislation in each State,[18] testamentary trusts must be in writing to be validly created. Despite these statutory injunctions, equity will not allow the words of these statutes to be used as an instrument of fraud. The effect of the Statute of Frauds on trusts created *inter vivos*, and the nature of exceptions to that rule on grounds of fraud are discussed in Chapter Three. Similar exceptions to wills and probate legislation have been made in cases involving so-called secret trusts.

Secret trusts

[13.34] As the name suggests, these are trusts not disclosed on the face of a will but which, in certain circumstances, will be upheld. Secret trusts fall into two categories: wholly secret trusts and partially secret trusts. Wholly secret trusts occur where a testator makes an apparently absolute gift, that is, 'I give Blackacre to X'. But X will not be able to take the property as his own if the testator, prior to his death, regardless of whether before or after the making of the will, told X that Blackacre must be held on trust for someone else, or some other object, and X has accepted that trust. X will then hold Blackacre as trustee under the terms of the arrangement reached with the testator. If the agreed purpose becomes impossible to perform, or is otherwise illegal, X will not be able to take the property as his own. He will hold it on trust for the testator's next of kin, or other takers on intestacy.[19] The essential elements for a wholly secret trust were: (i) the intention of the testator to subject the primary donee (the party actually named as recipient in the will) to an obligation in favour of the secondary donee (the party actually intended to benefit); (ii) communication of that inten-

---

16. *Jacobs'*, paras [605]–[615].
17. Conveyancing Act 1919 (NSW) s 23c; Property Law Act 1958 (Vic) s 53; Law of Property Act 1936 (SA) s 29; Property Law Act 1969 (WA) s 34; Conveyancing and Law of Property Act 1884 (Tas), s 60(2); Property Law Act 1974 (Qld) s 11.
18. Wills, Probate and Administration Act 1898 (NSW), s 7; Wills Act 1958 (Vic), s 7; Wills Act 1936 (SA), ss 8 & 9; Wills Act 1970 (WA), s 8; Wills Act 1840 (Tas), s 9; Succession Act 1867 (Qld), s 39.
19. See *Voges v Monaghan* (1955) 94 CLR 231.

tion to the primary donee; and (iii) acceptance of that obligation by the primary donee, either expressly or by acquiescence: *Ottaway v Norman* [1972] Ch 698.

[13.35] A partially secret trust occurs where the will shows that a trust is intended but the precise object of the trust is not indicated. In such a case the nominated trustee cannot take beneficially and the property will either be held on trust for the testator's next of kin or residuary beneficiaries or for the object of the secret trust, depending upon whether the nominated trustee is informed of the secret object before the execution of the will or codicil creating the trust: *Re Fleetwood, Sidgreaves v Brewer* (1880) 15 Ch D 594. This principle applies notwithstanding the parol evidence rule: *Blackwell v Blackwell* [1929] AC 318. The communication of the identity of the intended beneficiary to the nominated trustee does not need to be in writing. A trust created in this way will only extend to the property covered by the instructions given to the proposed trustee, it will not cover additional property left in the same bequest: *Re Cooper, Le Neve Foster v National Provincial Bank* [1939] Ch 811.

Mutual wills

[13.36] These involve an agreement usually between two people to make wills in favour of each other providing reciprocal benefits with some provision in each case that should the one predecease the other then the survivor will make provision for some third party or parties mutually agreed upon. It is the essence of such an agreement that the wills are not to be revoked, especially that of the survivor after the death of the first of the two. The survivor will then be bound not to revoke his or her will after the other's death provided the other died without revoking the agreed will. If the survivor revokes the agreed will, he or she will then become constructive trustee upon the terms of that agreed will: *Birmingham v Renfrew* (1937) 57 CLR 666.

13–5 Trusts Arising from Agreement or Common Intention

[13.37] An agreement to create a trust is a contract rather than a trust, and the existence and enforceability of any such trust will be determined by the law of contracts, rather than that of trusts. If consideration is provided for a promise to create a trust the court can overlook formal defects which would be fatal to a voluntary declaration. Where the parties to a purported agreement are dealing at arm's length any question of the validity of the contract and thus of the trust should not be difficult to determine under recognised principles governing the formation of contracts. Where the parties are not dealing at arm's length, as is the case with spouses and others living in close domestic circumstances, the normal evidence of a formed contract will usually be lacking. The growing prevalence of close domestic relationships outside marriage from the 1960s produced an increasing volume of property disputes between former de facto spouses, and others. The courts attempted to grapple with these problems in a number of different ways. One such device which was employed was the trust arising from an agreement between, or common intention shared by the parties.

[13.38] Despite the paucity of the evidence available in domestic property disputes, they must still be decided upon established principles, under which the courts declare the rights of the parties, rather than altering them, subject to any statutory power to do otherwise.[20] The first of these established principles, and the starting point for any sensible analysis of one of these problems, is that of implied or resulting trusts, discussed in more detail in Chapter 16. Under that general rule, where one person purchases property in the name of another the legal titleholder will be presumed to hold that title upon a resulting trust for the purchaser. That principle will apply where the purchase moneys are provided by two or more people. The legal titleholder or holders will be presumed to hold that title on trust for those contributing to the purchase price in proportions which reflect their respective contributions: *Calverley v Green* (1984) 155 CLR 242 at 247, per Gibbs CJ. That presumption can be rebutted by evidence of a contrary intention on the part of the purchaser, such as an intention to make a gift. An intention forming part of an agreement or common intention between the parties as to the manner in which the beneficial interest will be shared can constitute a contrary intention rebutting the presumption.

> In *Pettitt v Pettitt* [1970] AC 777, a husband claimed a share of the proceeds of sale of a house belonging to his wife, on the basis of minor improvements he had made to the house and garden, mostly pieces of carpentry. The house had been purchased with the wife's money. The House of Lords rejected the man's claim, holding that, in the absence of any agreement or common intention, or any question of estoppel, where one party performs work or expends money on the property of another he or she will have no claim on that property. Any such common intention must be an actual intention either expressed by the parties or one which could be inferred from the facts and not an intention imputed to them on the basis of what reasonable spouses would do in the circumstances.

[13.39] The decision in *Pettitt* was affirmed shortly thereafter in *Gissing v Gissing* [1971] AC 886, in which a wife claimed an interest in a house owned and paid for by her husband on the strength of expenditure on furniture and the laying out of a lawn. Like Mr Pettitt, she lost. The judgments in these cases cannot be commended for their clarity, nor for their precision. The type of trust arising on these principles was not specified, nor were the necessary elements of the agreement itself. Some of the outstanding issues have since been explored in later decisions,[21] while the Court of Appeal, led by Lord Denning turned them on their head by decreeing constructive trusts on the basis of an intention imputed to the parties,[22] or some general test of what was 'fair' in the circumstances.[23] In *Cowcher v Cowcher* [1972] 1 WLR 425, Bagnall J held that an agreement or common intention, to be recognised under these principles, had to represent a consensus shared by the parties as to the proportions of the purchase moneys which the parties would be deemed to have provided (the 'money consensus'). A trust created on that basis would be a resulting or implied trust in which the beneficial interests of the parties were determined by their actual, or deemed, contributions to the cost of acquisition of the property.[24] A different

---

20. Most notably, the Family Law Act 1975 (Cth) which created a separate regime for property disputes between the parties to a marriage upon the dissolution of that marriage, and the De Facto Relationships Act 1984 (NSW) which conferred wider powers on the courts dealing with property disputes between former de facto spouses in that State.

21. See *Richards v Dove* [1974] 1 All ER 888; *Bernard v Josephs* [1982] Ch 391; *Burns v Burns* [1984] 1 Ch 317.

22. *Falconer v Falconer* [1970] 3 All ER 449.

23. *Eves v Eves* [1975] 3 All ER 768.

24. Bagnall J's decision was warmly applauded by the authors of the 5th edition of *Jacobs' Law of Trusts in Australia*, paras [1214] and [1217] but has not been adopted by any other authority since and must be regarded as something of a hybrid. There is no doubt that such an agreement could be made. It is just highly unlikely that people would think about the matter in those terms.

approach was taken in *Re Densham* [1975] 1 WLR 1519 by Goff J who said that, if the parties thought about the matter at all, they would think about ownership and not some artificial monetary value which could be ascribed to their actual contributions (the 'interest consensus').

[13.40] This doctrine was applied in Australia by the New South Wales Court of Appeal in *Allen v Snyder* [1977] 2 NSWLR 685.

> Mr Snyder took proceedings seeking to evict Mrs Allen from a house, the legal title to which stood in his name, and in which they had lived together from 1966 to 1974. Mrs Allen claimed that the beneficial interest in the house was shared equally between the two. Glass JA, with whom Samuels JA agreed, said the court would uphold a trust arising from an agreement or common intention as to the division of the beneficial interest, provided the claimant contributed as contemplated. The agreement or common intention had to be actual. either expressed or capable of being inferred from the facts. The majority rejected a submission that an intention could be imputed to the parties. Glass JA also held that the trust enforced in such a case was an express trust arising from an agreement between the parties as to their respective interests, rather than the deemed value of their contributions. On the facts the court found that while there was a common intention that Mrs Allen should have a beneficial interest upon marriage, or in the event of Snyder's death, there was no intention that she should have such an interest while living with him as a de facto spouse.

[13.41] *Allen v Snyder* clarified some of the issues surrounding this doctrine, at least in New South Wales, but some questions remain. In identifying the trust enforced as an express trust, Glass JA properly excluded the resulting or implied trust. The respective shares of the parties in the beneficial interest of the property reflect the terms of the agreement, and not the level of their respective contributions to the purchase cost. Those contributions, which need not be direct contributions to the purchase price, act as consideration in the agreement and only have to be sufficient, and not necessarily adequate. However, in identifying the trust arising as an express trust, Glass JA cited *Rochefoucauld v Boustead* [1897] 1 Ch 196; *Bannister v Bannister* [1948] 2 All ER 133 and *Last v Rosenfeld* [1972] 2 NSWLR 923, all cases upholding the principle that the Statute of Frauds could not be used as an instrument of fraud.[25] That principle cannot be challenged; but the statutory exception to the requirement that dispositions of interests in land, or subsisting equitable interests, be in writing,[26] and that declarations of trust of interests in land be manifested and proved by writing,[27] is, in New South Wales, the Conveyancing Act 1919 (NSW), s 23c(2), which excepts only resulting and constructive trusts. The last two of the cases cited by Glass JA use the language of constructive trusts and, despite his Honour's careful exposition, it might be better to look at trusts arising in these cases, not as express trusts directly created by the parties, but rather as constructive trusts imposed by the court in the event of the unconscionable conduct of the defendant in failing to abide by the terms of the agreement and give effect to the express trust.

[13.42] This doctrine of trusts arising from agreement or common intention has also proved difficult to apply in practice. Proof of such an agreement can turn on one conversation held long ago and never reduced to writing, where the recollections of the parties are likely to be contradictory, making it very difficult to advise a client on his or her title. Furthermore, despite the blunt rejection of the 'imputed' trust on the

---

25. See paras **[3.49]** and **[3.50]**.
26. Section 23c (1)(a) and (c) of the Conveyancing Act 1919 (NSW) respectively.
27. Section 23c (1)(b) of the Conveyancing Act 1919 (NSW).

grounds of artificiality and judicial caprice, the power given to the court to 'infer' a common intention from the facts can produce results which seem just as contrived. In *Zaborskis v Zaborskis* (1982) 8 Fam LR 622, Kearney J found a common intention to share the beneficial interest in a house equally in a case where the parties had lived together for 36 years, during which time the woman had not made financial contributions but had produced five children. The only evidence presented of any statement of an intention as to the manner in which their interests were to be shared was a declaration by the man, when they went to one of the properties in which they had lived during the time, that 'This is your house; this is my house!' By contrast, in *Burns v Burns* [1984] 1 Ch 317, the English Court of Appeal found no common intention in a case where the parties had co-habited for 19 years in a relationship which had produced two children. The woman made no contribution to the initial purchase price, because she was pregnant at the time, but did earn income during the last five years of the relationship, and then at a greater rate than the man. In some cases a common intention has been found to be subject to a condition precedent, usually the marriage of the parties: *Allen v Snyder* [1977] 2 NSWLR 685; *Currie v Hamilton* [1984] 1 NSWLR 687. In *Muschinski v Dodds*, Waddell J, at first instance,[28] found a common intention that the beneficial interest in the property was to be shared equally between the parties, principally because of the actions of the woman in instructing solicitors that the purchase was to be effected in that way, despite the fact that the man's financial contribution came to less than 10 per cent of the cost of acquisition. On the other hand, in *Calverley v Green* (1984) 155 CLR 242, the High Court found no common intention to share the beneficial interest equally, even though the house there had been conveyed into joint names and the woman was a joint mortgagor. The courts have also taken a more stringent approach when considering the terms of any alleged 'agreement'. In *Delehunt v Carmody* (1986) 161 CLR 464, a contest arose between the former de facto spouse and the estranged wife of a man who had died. The man was the registered proprietor of the house in which he and the de facto had been living. The New South Wales Court of Appeal found that no enforceable agreement existed because there had been no agreement on the question of survivorship: see **[16.8]**. In England the House of Lords has confirmed its orthodox conservative approach in these matters in *Lloyds Bank v Rosset* [1991] AC 107.

Not every informal arrangement will give rise to a trust enforceable as one arising from agreement or common intention. On the current state of the law in Australia, there is no reliance or detriment based theory of contract. This notion was expressly rejected by the New South Wales Court of Appeal in *Beaton v McDivitt* (1985) 13 NSWLR 134, following the decision of the High Court in *Australian Woollen Mills v Commonwealth* (1954) 92 CLR 424. Accordingly, the 'bargain theory' of contract which requires consideration to move from the promisee to the promisor still holds sway in our legal system.

[13.43] The difficulties presented by the narrowness of rules concerning trusts arising from agreement or common intention have been ameliorated by the application of other equitable doctrines. The rule that co-owners are entitled to contribution, each from the other, or others, for outgoings and expenses incurred in respect of the mutually owned property provides scope for an account to be taken on what could be described as revenue matters between parties sharing the beneficial interest in some property pursuant to an agreement or common intention: *Bernard v Josephs* [1982] Ch 391. The employment of constructive trusts and other remedies such as

---

28. (1 July 1981, unreported); affirmed (1982) 8 Fam LR 622.

equitable charges to relieve against unconscionable retention of benefit has provided scope for a principled resolution of these disputes without undue recourse to artificial constructions: see generally *Muschinski v Dodds* (1985) 160 CLR 583, *Baumgartner v Baumgartner* (1987) 164 CLR 137 and *Hibberson v George* (1989) 12 Fam LR 723 for the employment of constructive trusts generally in these cases.[29]

---

29. See Chapter 17.

Chapter Fourteen

The Variation and Termination of Trusts

14-1 Variation of Trusts

[14.1] The court has no inherent power to vary the terms of a trust, even where such a variation may be agreed to by the current trustee and the beneficiaries: *Tickle v Tickle* (1987) 10 NSWLR 581. The court has inherent power to sanction deviations from the trust in circumstances of emergency: *Re New* [1901] 2 Ch 534, but that is not a power that can be invoked, for instance, to improve the tax position of the trust. In view of the duty of a trustee to adhere to and carry out the terms of the trust, a trustee who departs from the terms of the trust does so at his or her peril. To escape liability in such circumstances the trustee would need to show that any such variation was necessary and beneficial: *Harrison v Randall* (1851) 9 Hare 397; 68 ER 562. This situation prompted Lord Lindley to remark in *Perrins v Bellamy* [1899] 1 Ch 797 at 798 that it was the duty of a trustee 'to commit judicious breaches of trust'. That may have been so, especially in 1899 and may still be the case but it places the trustee in an invidious position. The circumstances in which a trust operates can change, creating difficulties not contemplated when the trust was settled and not provided for in the trust deed. Life estates, a common feature of trusts both in England and Australia, proved vulnerable when tax changes were introduced after World War II, in Australia particularly when cesser of interest provisions rendered life tenancies liable to death duties. A practice developed in England of obtaining the approval of the court for variations designed to reduce the impact of new tax laws. All that came to an end with *Chapman v Chapman* [1954] AC 429 in which the House of Lords stated that the court had no power to sanction variations to the beneficial interests in a trust settlement. According to their Lordships, the court's inherent powers were restricted to authorise variations of trusts in four situations:

(a) changes in the nature of investments on behalf of infants, such as, approving investments in realty instead of personalty;

(b) investments in business transactions not strictly authorised by the trust;

(c) payment of maintenance out of income directed to be accumulated; and

(d) compromises in favour of unborn infants.

In *Tickle v Tickle* (1987) 10 NSWLR 581, Young J, noting that *Chapman v Chapman* was not strictly binding on him, and that s 50 of the Minors (Property and Contracts) Act 1970 (NSW) empowered the court, if it considered it for the benefit of a minor, to authorise a person to enter into a contract or disposition of property on behalf of a minor, held that there was a fifth exception to the general rule that a court has no power to vary a trust. That exception arose where circumstances have occurred which have tended to thwart the intentions of the creator of the trust and the parties or their guardians consent to a course which will effect such intentions cy-près.

[14.2] One consequence of *Chapman v Chapman* was legislation adopted in Australian States giving the court power to authorize variations to trusts, including, in New South Wales, 'adjustment of the respective rights of the beneficiaries' as the court may think fit, in cases in which it was 'expedient".[1] In Victoria, Queensland, South Australia and Western Australia the court is given a power of 'varying or revoking all or any of the trusts', or enlarging the powers of the trustees of managing or administering' property subject to the trusts.[2] This does not mean that these statutory powers can be used to effect a variation of the beneficial interests under a trust where no other change is sought in the management or administration of the trust: *Ku-ring-gai Municipal Council v A-G* (1953) 19 LGR 105. In Tasmania the court may make orders enlarging the powers available to trustees for the management or administration of the trust,[3] but there is no power to alter the beneficial interests under the trust.

[14.3] In those States where the court has power to authorise variations to the beneficial interests under the trust it must still be satisfied that such variation is in the interests of the parties concerned. Such applications involve cost and some delay and will not be granted automatically.[4] Traditionally the courts have been reticent about expanding the powers conferred by any settlement or will and it has only been the relatively recent development of comprehensive trustee legislation that has enabled trustees to break out of the narrow confines of poorly drawn trusts. In all Australian States that legislation gives the court authority to confer a power on trustees, generally speaking, where it is expedient to do so in the opinion of the court.[5] The powers conferred by statute in this regard give particular scope for extending the powers of investments, either generally or with respect to particular transactions. The High Court has taken a broad view of this jurisdiction to confer powers on the ground of expediency. In *Riddle v Riddle* (1952) 85 CLR 202, Dixon J, for the majority, rejected the view that the trust would have to show itself to be a special case. In most States, with the notable exception of Queensland where most of the statutory powers are declared to be applicable whether or not any contrary intention is expressed in the trust instrument, statutory powers are subject to the words of the trust. That does not mean there must be an express exclusion. It is sufficient if such an application would be inconsistent with the purport of the instrument: *IRC v Bernstein* [1961] Ch 399. This power has been applied to vary a trust to allow investment in equities other than the shares of one particular company which were the only authorised equity investment allowed under the trusts of a will. In *Re Baker, dec'd; Rouse v A-G (Vic)* [1961] VR 641 the power to amend under s 63 of the Trustee Act 1958 (Vic) was used to give a trustee power to invest in a range of securities, including equities in listed stocks. The trustees had been restricted by the will to investments in first mortgages, government securities and shares in Kodak (Australasia) Pty Ltd, shares in which company made up the bulk of the estate until converted into cash by the trus-

---

1. Trustee Act 1925 (NSW), s 81.
2. Trustee Act 1958 (Vic), s 63A; Trusts Act 1973–81 (Qld), s 94; Trustee Act 1936–84 (SA), s 59c; Trustees Act 1962–78 (WA), s 90.
3. Trustee Act 1898 (Tas), s 47.
4. See for example *Palmer v McAllister* (1991) 4 WAR 206.
5. Trustee Act 1925 (NSW), s 81; Trustee Act 1958 (Vic), s 63; Trusts Act 1973 (Qid), s 94; Trustee Act 1936–74 (SA), s 59b; Trustees Act 1962–72 (WA), s 89; Trustee Act 1898 (Tas), s 47. See Ford & Lee, paras [1204]–[1205], pp 527–34.

tees in accordance with the terms of the will. Adam J followed *Riddle v Riddle* but said, at 646, he thought it proper for the court to err on the side of caution in sanctioning unauthorised investments. The trustees were given power to invest in other equities but only in established stocks, a more limited power than the trustees had sought.

[14.4] In most modern trust deeds it is almost standard practice to include a provision allowing for amendment of the deed, in whole or part. The extent of any such express power of amendment will depend largely upon its terms. In *Graham Australia Pty Ltd v Perpetual Trustees WA Ltd* (1989) 1 WAR 65, the Full Court of the Supreme Court of Western Australia upheld a variation of a unit trust by resolution of the unit holders, as was provided for in the deed. The variation allowed the trustee to redeem units at their current value rather than their value at least seven days prior to the request for redemption as provided in the original deed. The variation was made retrospective. Some members had requested repurchase of their units after the 1987 sharemarket crash, at pre-crash values. The court upheld the amendment as one made properly within the power. The court found that the amendment was made in good faith and for the benefit of the unitholders as a whole. The amendment was also held to be effective as against the unitholders who had requested repurchase, even though they had remained unitholders only because of the trustee's breach of contract in refusing their request for repurchase until after the meeting of all unitholders. Powers of variation are to be generously construed. In *Kearns v Hill* (1990) 21 NSWLR 107, the New South Wales Court of Appeal overturned a decision of Young J striking down a variation of a family trust whereby a new class of potential beneficiaries was added. The court acknowledged that in the case of modern discretionary trusts, the intention of the settlor was to provide for sufficient flexibility in the trust to cope with changes resulting from war, taxes and depression. In construing any such trust the court should not do so in any narrow or unreal way and should construe each provision according to its natural meaning, and in such a way to give it its most ample operation. According to Meagher JA, with whom Mahoney and Clarke JJA agreed, the power to 'vary or amend any of the provisions' in the Deed meant what it said and that included a power to amend the express list of beneficiaries.

Amendments to superannuation trust deeds

[14.5] Wide powers of variation are commonly included as part of the standard machinery of any modern trust. In superannuation trusts a power of variation is essential in view of the frequency of changes to regulations governing the tax treatment of superannuation funds since 1987, many of which have required amendment of the deeds of trust for such funds. Express powers of variation do not necessarily confer an absolute licence on trustees to rewrite their trusts. In *Wilson v MGM* (1980) 18 NSWLR 730, Kearney J considered a superannuation fund deed containing a clause empowering trustees of a superannuation fund and the employer company to alter or amend the deed 'in any respect which would in the opinion of the company not prejudice any benefit secured by contributions made on behalf of any member' did not confer an absolute discretion. The deed also provided that any surplus in the hands of the trustees was to be applied 'for the provision of such (further) benefits to such members as the Company may direct'. His Honour held that the reference to 'benefits' in the amendment clause included these possible further benefits. Accordingly, he was of the view that an amendment to the trust deed whereby, on the winding up of the trust, any surplus monies in excess of the amount payble to members for benefits secured by their contributions were to be paid to the company was not in conformity with the power of the amendment. Any amendment which prevented the surplus being applied for the provision of 'such (further) benefits' being prejudicial to benefits secured by contibutions made on behalf of members. Kearney J also considered that the fiduciary obligations imposed on the company prevented it from using its power of amendment to benefit itself. Presumably that issue would not arise where the power of amendment was vested in the trustee and the trustee was separate from the principal employer. In *UEB Industries Ltd v Brabant* [1992] 1 NZLR 294, there was a purported amendment to a superannuation trust deed which would have enabled the company to take the surplus of moneys in the fund over and above the amount required to pay benefits to members. The deed stipulated that no amendment could be made which would adversely affect a member's interest without the member's consent. The deed provided for distribution of any surplus on winding up among the members. It also stated that contributions made by the company ceased to be its property. The court held that the proposed amendment was clearly adverse to the interests of members. A different result was reached, although not a decision which is inconsistent in principle with the judgments in the *MGM* and *UEB* cases, in *Lock v Westpac Banking Corporation* (1991) 25 NSWLR 593.

A member of the Westpac Staff Superannuation Scheme challenged a resolution of the board of the Bank amending the deed to allow the repayment to the bank of the surplus in the fund over the amount required to meet the fund's liabilities, including benefits secured to members. The scheme was a defined benefit scheme. The rules specified the amount of benefits payable to members, the circumstances in which those benefits would be payable, and the contributions payable by members and by the bank to the fund. The variation clause gave the board of the bank, with the consent of the trustees of the fund, power to alter or replace the provisions of the deed and rules provided that the value of the rights of members and their dependants accrued at the date of alteration were not thereby reduced without the written consent of at least 75 per cent of the members. The extent of members' rights was certified by an actuary. The amount of the surplus available came to $300 million. Waddell CJ in Eq noted that courts take a different approach to the interpretation of pension and superannuation trusts to that applied to traditional trusts. Pension plans being based on a contract between employer and employees pursuant to which both contribute to the fund for the purpose of providing defined benefits in defined circumstances to employees are to be interpreted in a more practical way than traditional trusts. In this case, his Honour held that the bank was not precluded from exercising the power of amendment in the manner proposed. Even if, as was submitted, the deed provided that on dissolution of the fund the surplus should be distributed amongst the members, his Honour did not think that meant that the surplus should be held on an irrevocable trust to provide defined benefits and to await the possibility of a dissolution of the fund. Waddell J also rejected a submission that in a defined benefit scheme, once the defined benefits had been provided for, the company was precluded by some fiduciary obligation from acting in its own interests with respect to the surplus in the fund. In exercising powers with respect to a superannuation fund a company is under a duty to act in good faith, as it is in its other dealings with its employees, but is not subject to any fiduciary obligation, beyond securing the benefits defined by the scheme. His Honour also held that the trustees had not acted in breach of duty by consenting to the amendment. They were entitled to consider whether the amendment was in the interests of the members and the bank as a whole.

[14.6] As these cases demonstrate, it is important to consider the provisions of a superannuation trust or other similar deed when assessing the validity of any proposed amendment, particularly one designed to return any surplus to the employer.

In *Lock v Westpac*, Waddell J stressed that in construing such instruments the court should adopt a practical and purposive approach, having regard to the surrounding circumstances, consistent with the view stated by Warner J in *Mettoy Pension Trustees Ltd v Evans* [1990] 1 WLR 1587. Waddell J also cited *Hockin v Bank of British Columbia* (1990) 46 BCLR (2d) 382 with approval. In that case the deed provided that on termination of the scheme the entire fund was to be applied for the benefit of members, retired members and their families. The employer bank had been taken over. There were only two employee members left, and a substantial number of other claims for benefit. Both at first instance and on appeal the court held that the bank had not irreversibly alienated its contributions to the fund and that it was not contrary or inconsistent with the settlement of the trust for the provisions of the scheme to be partially revoked to restore the excess to the bank as settlor of the scheme. There is nothing very radical in that proposition. A trust had been established to provide defined retirement and associated benefits to employees of the bank who became members of the scheme. That purpose had been achieved. There was a surplus. It is consistent with the general principles of resulting trusts that those moneys should revert to the settlor: see Chapter 16. Parallels can also be drawn with the *Quistclose* trust line of cases: moneys being contributed to the fund subject to a primary trust to pay benefits under the scheme with a secondary trust in favour of the employer of any surplus after fulfilment of the primary trust: see **[13.4]**–**[13.10]**.

14–2 The Failure or Setting Aside of a Trust

[14.7] A fully constituted trust in which there is sufficient certainty as to subject matter, object and intention to create a trust will be valid and cannot be set aside unless found to be in breach of some statutory provision or principle of the general law. Under the Bankruptcy Act 1966 (Cth) voluntary settlements made within two years of the settlor's bankruptcy may be void under s 120 and other dispositions made with the intent to defraud creditors, or to confer a preference on one creditor at the expense of others, will be struck down under ss 121–122.

Illegality or immorality of purpose

[14.8] The courts will not lend their assistance to people seeking to carry out some purpose which is against the law, or the policy of the law. Illegality in this context has the same meaning in the law of trusts as it does in the law of contracts. The modern application to this principle can be traced to the judgment of Lord Mansfield in *Holman v Johnson* (1775) 1 Cowp 341 at 343; [1775–1802] All ER Rep 98 at 99, in a case concerning an illegal contract:

> The objection that a contract is immoral or illegal as between plaintiff and defendant, sounds at all times very ill in the mouth of the defendant. It is not for his sake, however, that the objection is ever allowed; but it is founded in general principles of policy, which the defendant has the advantage of, contrary to the real justice, as between him and the plaintiff, by accident, if I may say so. The principle of public policy is this: *ex dolo malo non oritur actio*. No court will lend its aid to a man who founds his cause of action upon an immoral or an illegal act. If from the plaintiff's own stating or otherwise, the cause of action appears to arise *ex turpi causa*, or the transgression of a positive law of this country, there the court says he has no right to be assisted.

Or, as Lord Eldon put it in *Muckleston v Brown* (1801) 6 Ves 52 at 68–9; [1775–1802] All ER Rep 501 at 506; 31 ER 934, where a plaintiff comes to equity seeking to be relieved against his or her own act, an act constituting a fraud upon the law, and the defence is also dishonest, as between the two species of dishonesty, 'the court would not act; but would say "Let the estate lie where it falls"'. This principle was applied by his Lordship in *Curtis v Perry* (1802) 6 Ves 739, a case in which Chiswell, a Member of Parliament, and Nantes acquired a number of ships in partnership. The ships were, however, registered in Nantes' name only so as to avoid a statutory prohibition against ships owned by MPs being used for government contracts. A dispute arose between partnership creditors and Nantes' private creditors. Lord Eldon held in favour of the latter, saying (at 746):

> The moment the purpose to defeat the policy of the law by fraudulently concealing that this was his property is admitted it is very clear he ought not to be heard in this court to say that it is his property.

It was not sufficient to show that the trust was set up for the purpose of attaining some illegal purpose if that purpose has not been, or cannot be achieved. The onus of showing that the illegal purpose has been achieved rests on the party seeking to deny the trust: *Perpetual Executors and Trustees of Australia Ltd v Wright* (1917) 23 CLR 185. A trust of leaseholds, which had been transferred to a third party by the plaintiff for the purpose of defeating his creditors, was held to be enforceable. By the time the claim to enforce the trust was brought, the plaintiff had been declared bankrupt and had entered into an arrangement with his creditors under which he agreed to recover the leaseholds on their behalf. The court accepted that the original, illegal purpose (that is, of defeating the creditors) had not been carried into effect: *Symes v Hughes* (1870) LR 9 Eq 475. The same indulgence was not extended to a man who paid £1,000 to a company to give a false impression of his credit worthiness to Berlin bankers. In the event, the bankers made no enquiry but the company went into liquidation before the man got his money back. The Court of Appeal held that he had left it too late: *Re Great Berlin Steamboat Company* (1884) 26 Ch D 616. In *Martin v Martin* (1959) 110 CLR 297, a man put land into his wife's name, supposedly to avoid federal land tax. The High Court held that the man's purposes were nebulous as there was no definite liability which would have been incurred if he had purchased the land in his own name and thus no illegal purpose had been achieved. As a result he was not precluded from claiming the beneficial interest in the land. Courts in England have not been so concerned about whether the unlawful purpose has been achieved and have refused to enforce trusts where an intention to achieve some illegal aim, such as defeating creditors, has been shown: *Gascoigne v Gascoigne* [1918] 1 KB 223, or avoiding tax: *Re Emery's Investment Trusts* [1959] Ch 410, regardless of whether that aim had been achieved. A party could not lead evidence of his or her own illegality to rebut the presumption of advancement: *Gascoigne v Gascoigne*. There is some doubt in the current law in England as to whether the strict policy stated by Lord Mansfield in *Holman v Johnson* still applies so that courts will not enforce any trust infected by illegality, or whether the courts will only intervene where the party seeking to enforce the trust must lead evidence of his or her own illegality to do so. In *Tinsley v Milligan* [1994] 1 AC 340, a house was purchased by two women but put in the name of one, the plaintiff, although their intention was that they would be joint owners. Their purpose in doing this was to falsely represent to the Department of Social Security that the defendant had no interest in the house nor in the business conducted by the two of them from the house. A claim by plaintiff for orders for possession was dismissed by the trial judge while the defendant succeeded in her counter-claim for a declaration that the plaintiff held the property on the trust for the two of them in equal shares. Appeals against that decision were dismissed, by majority, by both the Court of Appeal and the House of Lords. In the House of Lords the majority held that it was open to the defendant to prove what was the true position and claim her beneficial interest. Lord Browne-Wilkinson, for the majority, said at 376:

> In my judgment the time has come to decide clearly that the rule is the same whether a plaintiff founds himself on a legal or equitable title: he is entitled to recover if he is not forced to plead or rely on the illegality, even if it emerges that the title on which he relied was acquired in the course of carrying through an illegal transaction.

Applying that principle in the case before him, Lord Browne-Wilkinson said that the defendant could show that she had contributed to the purchase price of the house and that there was a common understanding between herself and the plaintiff that they owned the house equally. She had no need to prove why the house had been purchased in that way. Their Lordships said the result would have been otherwise if the presumption had applied; it would have been necessary to plead the illegal intention to rebut any presumption of advancement. The same approach has been applied in Canada where, in cases involving only a claim based on a presumption of resulting trust where it was not necessary for the plaintiff to rely on evidence of fraudulent intent to recover the property, trusts otherwise tainted by illegality have been upheld: *Marks v Marks* (1974) 18 RFL 323 (Ont CA); *Gorog v Kiss* (1977) 78 DLR (3d) 690 (CA). Lord Goff, in dissent in *Tinsley v Milligan*, referred to *Holman v Johnson* (1775) 1 Cowp 341 at 343; 98 ER 1120 at 1121, quoting Lord Mansfield, 'No court will lend its aid to a man who founds his cause of action upon an immoral or an illegal act'. Lord Goff noted, at 354, this is a principle of policy, not a principle of justice. The fact that it can produce harsh results may seem unfortunate, but that is the price of enforcing policy. The majority view in *Tinsley v Milligan* was applied by Hill J in *Weston v Beaufils* (1994) 122 ALR 240 to recognise trusts in favour of a man who had transferred properties to his solicitor to avoid tax penalties which he anticipated with the introduction of the tax file number system. Hill J drew a distinction between the actual illegal conduct, the original conspiracy between Weston and Beaufils, and the legal acts, such as the conveyances of property, carried out in furtherance of the illegal agreement. Hill J put it in these terms, at 265, 'To permit Mr Weston to recover property transferred is to put an end to the illegal purpose, not to enforce it. In permitting Mr Weston to recover, the court is merely giving effect to the resulting trust arising by virtue of the transfer having been made without consideration, it is not giving its aid to the unlawful agreement'. Hill J also noted, at 268, that there was much to be said for the view that on the facts the illegal purpose had not been carried out and that the restoration of the property to Weston restored the situation to where it was before the conspiracy was implemented.

[14.9] The approaches taken by both the majority and the minority in *Tinsley v Milligan* have been authoritatively rejected in Australia:

> In *Nelson v Nelson* (1995) 132 ALR 133, Mrs Nelson purchased a house in Petersham in the names of her son, Peter, and daughter, Elizabeth, with moneys provided by Mrs Nelson from her own resources and from her late husband's estate. Subsequently, Mrs Nelson purchased another property in Paddington in her own name, with the assistance of a War Service Home Loan. In applying for that loan she signed a declaration saying that she had no financial interest in any house or dwelling other than the one for which the subsidy was sought. On the sale of the Paddington property, Mrs Nelson, and her son sought declarations that the property and the proceeds of its sale were held on trust for Mrs Nelson. Elizabeth argued that the presumption of advancement applied in her favour or, alternatively, that the trust asserted was vitiated by illegality.

The New South Wales Court of Appeal held that the trust in favour of Mrs Nelson could not be upheld. This was a case in which the unlawful purpose of obtaining the War Service Home Loan by concealing Mrs Nelson's interest in Bent Street had been achieved. On appeal, the High Court reversed that decision and found a trust in Mrs Nelson's favour, on condition that she repay to the Commonwealth the difference between the subsidised rate of interest she had been paying under the Defence Service Homes mortgage and the rate she would have been paying without the subsidy over the term of the mortgage.

Deane and Gummow JJ acknowledged that the trust which Mrs Nelson sought to enforce was tainted by illegality but held that the trust created was, nonetheless, enforceable, but on terms which made good the concern of the Commonwealth, the party misled into granting subsidised interest by Mrs Nelson's fraudulent statement. They rejected the old policy approach of letting the loss lie where it might fall. Instead their Honours said that the question of illegality had to be considered in the light of the underlying policy of the legislation in question.

That view was reflected in the judgment of McHugh J who said, at 193, that courts should not refuse to enforce legal or equitable rights simply because they arose out of or were asociated with some unlawful purpose unless the statute concerned showed an intention that such rights should be unenforceable, or where the imposition of the sanction was either not disproportionate in the circumstances or otherwise necessary in the circumstances. Those latter two exceptions were themselves subject to an exception where the legislation displayed an intention that the penalties and sanctions contained in the statute were to be the only legal consequences of the particular illegality.

Dawson J also rejected the majority view in *Tinsley v Milligan*. He found that the trust was not vitiated by illegality and was prepared to uphold it without conditions. The Commonwealth having power to pursue its own remedies against Mrs Nelson.

Toohey J rejected both the majority and minority views in *Tinsley* and said that the relevant question was the purpose of the Act.

The question which remains open in Australia after *Nelson v Nelson* is whether any circumstances exist in which a trust will be held to be unenforceable on the grounds of illegality. In most cases, the wrongful act will be subject to some statutory sanction or penalty. In some instances, it may be desirable to enforce the trust in order to set in train other proceedings which may redress the wrongdoing. Thus, for example, if A transfers property to B for the purpose of hiding it from A's spouse in anticipated Family Court proceedings, equity may well uphold the trust so that the beneficial title to the property will vest in A and be available when proceedings are recommenced in the Family Court for a variation of the original property orders. The recognition of the trust for those purposes will not interfere with any prosecution of A for perjury and of A and B for conspiring to pervert the course of justice.

[14.10] Trusts tending to promote immorality or undermine the sanctity of marriage have been held to be void. Trusts in favour of future illegitimate children have traditionally been struck down, whether children of the settlor or someone else: *Re Ayles' Trusts* (1875) 1 Ch D 282. Where a gift is expressed to be in favour of 'children' it used to be presumed to be in favour of legitimate children unless the circumstances of the case dictate otherwise: *Hill v Crook* (1873) LR 6 HL 265. This application of the general prohibition of immoral trusts has been cut down by statute in some States,[6] and by changing social attitudes generally.[7] Cohabitation agreements are also

6. Children (Equality of Status) Act 1976 (NSW) which makes parents joint guardians of their ex-nuptial children: *Youngman v Lawson* [1981] 1 NSWLR 439, who also enjoy the status of being their legitimate children, although ex-nuptial: *Seidler v Schallhofer* [1982] 2 NSWLR 80 at 101, per Hutley JA; Status of Children Act 1974 (Vic), s 3.
7. See also *Andrews v Parker* [1973] Qd R 93; *Tanner v Tanner* [1975] 1 WLR 1346; *Horrocks v Forray* [1976] 1 WLR 230; *Nichols v Nichols* (SC(NSW), Needham J, 12 December 1986, unreported).

not contrary to public policy for similar reasons.[8] A trust in restraint of marriage, such as a trust for A and B but in case either should marry then his or her share to pass to the other, will be void as placing a general restraint upon marriage; although a trust for one's widow, or widower, which ceases upon their remarriage will be valid: *Lloyd v Lloyd* (1852) 2 Sim (NS) 255; 61 ER 338. Other particular restraints upon marriage, such as marriage to someone of a particular religion,[9] nationality,[10] or social class,[11] have been upheld. It is interesting to note that in the last example Bacon V-C explained that 'the law does not prohibit testators from indulging in bad feelings provided that no principle of public policy is contravened'.[12] In view of the present public policy against discrimination on various grounds it must be doubted whether the courts will lend their assistance to such displays of bad feeling. Trusts which would tend to threaten other valued social institutions, such as the relationship between parent and child,[13] will also be struck down on similar public policy grounds.

14–3 Restraints on Alienation

[14.11] If property is settled on trust for someone absolutely, any provision restraining the donee from alienating it or otherwise exercising the normal rights of ownership will be void. However, in this context an absolute gift must be distinguished from a determinable interest. A determinable interest is one which will automatically determine, that is, terminate, upon the happening of some specified event which might never occur. Often this will be a matter of drafting and construction. So, in a gift to X on condition that he does not mortgage or charge it and if he attempts to do so then to Z, the condition will be void for repugnancy and the gift will be construed as an absolute gift to X: *Re Machu* (1882) 21 Ch D 838. In some circumstances it is possible to impose a valid condition subsequent on a limitation which gives the grantor a right of re-entry if the condition is broken, such as a gift of Blackacre to X in fee simple on condition she never sells it out of the family: *Re Macleay* (1875) LR 20 Eq 186.[14] On the other hand, a gift to Y until he attempts to mortgage or charge it and then to Z will be valid as a properly created determinable interest: *Hatton v May* (1876) 3 Ch D 148; *Nixon v Verry* (1885) 29 Ch D 196. Similarly, where property is given absolutely but is subject to a proviso that it will not be available for the donee's creditors on bankruptcy, the proviso purporting to exclude the claims of the creditors will be void: *Snowdon v Dales* (1834) 6 Sim 524; 58 ER 690. However, a gift expressed to be determinable on bankruptcy will be valid: *Brandon v Robinson* (1811) 18 Ves 429;

8. *Seidler v Schallhofer* [1982] 2 NSWLR 80; De Facto Relationship Act 1984 (NSW).
9. *Duggan v Kelly* (1847) 10 Ir Eq R 295.
10. *Perrin v Lyon* (1807) 9 East 170; 103 ER 538 LC.
11. *Jenner v Turner* (1880) 16 Ch D 188.
12. Ibid, at 196.
13. *Re Boulter, Boulter v Boulter* [1922] 1 Ch 75.
14. *Jacobs'*, para [921] and para [949]. The learned authors of *Jacobs'* reconcile the apparent inconsistency between *In re Macleay* and the general principle against repugnancy by saying the principle does not preclude partial restraints on alienation. In *Macleay* the donee was only precluded from selling the property outside the family, which was quite extensive. Curiously, none of the early authorities on repugnancy cited in *Jacobs'* (p 133, n 82) were cited in *Macleay*. In that case Sir George Jessel MR relied mainly on principles stated in Coke on Littleton, that a feoffment on condition that the feoffee shall not alienate the land to anyone is void but a condition that he not alienate it to some particular person, or to the heirs of that person, is good. It must be doubted whether such a restriction would survive today.

34 ER 379, although there is some doubt as to whether this applies to a gift of fee simple.[15]

Protective trusts

[14.12] Income can be settled on 'protective trusts' under which the income is available for the maintenance, support and benefit of a named principal beneficiary for his or her life, or some shorter period, during which time the trust will be determined by any one of a number of events which, if done or suffered by the beneficiary, would have the effect of depriving him or her of the benefit of the income. These provisions are embodied in the trusts legislation of each State except South Australia and may be incorporated into a deed simply by directing that certain income is to be held on protective trusts.[16] The circumstances which lead to a forfeiture under protective trusts have been the subject of some debate. Generally any act which effects or which might bring about a charge on the income of the trust will lead to a forfeiture.[17]

14–4 The Rule against Perpetuities

[14.13] It has long been the policy of the courts to prevent property being tied up for inordinately long periods of time. This is not a policy against perpetual ownership. If it was, it would not be possible to settle property on trust for a corporation which is by its nature perpetual. The evils which are sought to be avoided are restrictions which mean that the property cannot be alienated, that is, transferred absolutely, for an unduly long time and remoteness of vesting. If property is settled upon successive life tenants for several generations there will not be anyone, until the expiry of all those generations, free to alienate the entire estate in the property subject to the gift. Not only that but, down the chain, interests will vest in favour of, say, the first grantee's grandson or great-grandson at some remote time in the future.

[14.14] The old rule against perpetuities developed from a rule against gifts which purported to create an infinite series of contingent remainders, in the form of successive and perpetual life estates. The rule prohibiting future interests of that kind is also known as the rule in *Whitby v Mitchell* (1890) 44 Ch D 85 and provided that where an interest in realty was given to an unborn person any remainder to the issue of such person was void, together with all subsequent limitations. Accordingly, a gift to X for life remainder to his unborn son for life with remainder to the children of that son and their heirs would vest a life estate in X with a contingent life estate in remainder in favour of his son, if he had one, but all subsequent interests in remainder would be void and, upon the death of the son, or on the death of X if he died without leaving a son to survive him, the land would revert to the original grantor or his heirs in fee simple. This old rule has been abolished in New South Wales, Victoria, Queensland and Western Australia,[18] leaving future interests at the mercy of the so-called modern

---

15. *Jacobs'*, para [922]; *Re Luck* [1912] 2 Ch 422 which held that a fee simple could be made determinable in this way, and criticism of that decision in (1917) 33 LQR 236.
16. Trustee Act 1925 (NSW), s 45; Trusts Act 1973 1981 (Qld), s 64; Trustee Act 1898 (Tas), s 30; Trustee Act 1958 (Vic), s 39; Trustees Act 1962–78 (WA), s 61.
17. *Jacobs'*, paras [925]–[929].
18. Conveyancing Act 1919 (NSW), s 23A; Property Law Act 1974 (Qld), s 216; Perpetuities and Accumulations Act 1968 (Vic), s 12; Property Law Act 1969 (WA), s 114.

rule against perpetuities. That rule emerged in the seventeenth century to strike down attempts to create future contingent interests where the contingency might not occur within a reasonable time. This made it a rule against remoteness of vesting, rather than a rule against the creation of interests in perpetuity. The aim of the modern rule was to ensure that at some reasonable time after its creation, property subject to a conveyance or settlement would vest in someone capable of dealing with it absolutely. The rule was established in *Cadell v Palmer* (1883) 1 Cl & Fin 372; 6 ER 956 and provided that any interest limited to arise at some time in the future as a vested interest would be void *ab initio* unless it would necessarily vest, if it was to vest at all, within the period of a life in being plus 21 years after the date on which the instrument creating the interest came into operation. Every interest which would not vest within that period, that is to say any interest which might not vest, however slim the possibility, was void and all and any interests limited subsequent to and dependent upon the void interest were likewise void. The rule applied to a wide range of interests, both real and personal, including equitable interests created by will or by trust *inter vivos*.

[14.15] Initial certainty. A limitation, that is, the form of words used to effect or state a conveyance or settlement of a future interest, was void if, at the time the instrument creating it came into operation, there was any possibility that the interest, or any of the interests, created by that limitation might vest outside the perpetuity period. The fact that the interest would probably vest inside the time could not save it, nor was it possible to wait and see whether the gift would infringe the rule. Accordingly, a gift to A for life remainder to any wife he might marry for life remainder in fee simple to such of A's children as are living at the death of the survivor of A and his wife would create a vested life estate in favour of A with a contingent life estate in remainder in favour of any wife he might marry. The contingency there being the woman's marriage to A, and her survival after his death. That life estate in remainder would not be defeated by the rule as it would vest in interest upon A's marriage, that is, during the course of a life in being, not having been named in the instrument, and in possession on A's death. However, the gift in remainder in fee simple to the children would be void because A's prospective wife would not be a life in being and might be born after the commencement date for the gift and might survive A by more than 21 years. Because the children who were to take could not be ascertained until the wife's death their interest could not vest, in interest or possession, until then.

[14.16] Vesting. In this context 'vest' means vest in interest and not necessarily in possession. If, in the example given above, the remainder in fee had been expressed to be in favour of such of A's children as are living at his death it would have been good as the gift in favour of the children would vest in interest upon A's death, even though vesting in possession would be postponed until the wife's death. A gift in favour of X for life and then for Y in fee simple would give X a life estate vested in possession while Y would have a vested interest in fee simple in remainder. That interpretation would hold so long as the gift could be construed as one under which Y, or his heirs should Y predecease X, was to take upon X's death. If the remainder to Y was expressed to be conditional upon him surviving X, that is, to X for life remainder to Y if he survives X then Y's interest would be contingent and could only vest if and when X died and Y was still alive. For any interest to vest in interest, the person or persons entitled to the interest must be ascertained; the interest must be ready to take effect in possession immediately upon termination of the prior interest; the gift must not be subject to any contingency; and, where the gift is in favour of a class, every member of the class must be ascertained, that is, identified, and the exact share of each must also be ascertained.

[14.17] A life in being and 21 years. The perpetuity period is calculated, in the case of each limitation considered under the rule, by reference to the life or lives in being referred to in the gift. So, in the case of a gift to D for life and thereafter to E for life with remainder in fee simple to such of the children of D as are living at the death of the survivor of D and E , the lives in being would be D and E, both living persons named in the gift. The lives in being in any limitation must be designated either expressly or by necessary implication. In the case of a gift in a will to 'my grandchildren' the children of the testator will be the lives in being. The same allowance could not be made for a gift to the grandchildren of Y, where Y was alive at the death of the testator, because he may have more children. It is not essential that the lives used as lives in being in any gift take any interest under the limitation: *Cadell v Palmer*. It became common practice to use 'royal lives' clauses under which gifts were limited to vest 21 years after the death of the survivor of the lineal descendants of Queen Victoria, or King George V, or, more commonly in recent times, Queen Elizabeth II, living at the date the instrument came into effect. Any lives in being referred to in a limitation, even though they need not be 'lives' who will take any interest under the gift, must be sufficiently ascertainable; a gift limited to vest 21 years from the death of the survivor of all persons living at the death of the settlor was held to be void for uncertainty in *Re Moore* [1901] 1 Ch 936.

[14.18] Where no lives in being are designated in the gift the perpetuity period under the general law test is 21 years. For instance, where a testator devised some gravel pits to trustees to work the pits until they were exhausted and then to sell them and divide the proceeds among the testator's issue then living, the gift was held to be void because it might have taken more than 21 years to exhaust the pits; even though they were in fact exhausted within six years: *Re Wood* [1894] 2 Ch 394.

[14.19] Subsequent gifts. A gift which is subsequent to and dependent upon a void gift will also be void. For instance, in the case of a gift to the first of X's daughters to marry but, if none do so, to Y, where X is alive at the testator's death but has no married daughters, the gift to Y will be void. X is the life in being. His daughters are not and he may have more daughters after the testator's death. As it is possible that no daughters might marry within 21 years of X's death, the gift to the first daughter to do so is void, and, because the gift to Y is dependent upon the gift to the daughter not taking effect, it also fails. It cannot be said for certain that the gift in favour of the daughters, if it was to fail, would fail within the perpetuity period. A later gift will still be valid, however, where the subsequent gift is not dependent upon a prior void limitation. For example, in a devise to A for life remainder to the first of A's children to be admitted as a barrister for life remainder to such of the children of B as attain the age of 21 the gift to the would-be barrister would fail, because it could not be said for certain that one of A's children would be admitted to the Bar, let alone that one would do so within 21 years of A's death. But the gift in remainder of the fee to B's children would be good as it is not dependent upon the void limitation to the possible barrister.

[14.20] Class closing. Where a gift is made to a class of people, such as to all the children of A who attain the age of 21, all members of the class must be ascertained or ascertainable within the perpetuity period. If any member of the class might possibly take a vested interest outside the period, the gift to the whole class will be void. Hence the requirement that, for a gift to a class to be valid under the rule, the class must be closed within the perpetuity period. So, a gift to A for life and thereafter to such of his children as attain adulthood and marry would give A a life estate but the remainder would fail as A may have more children and, while they would all attain adulthood within 21 years of A's death, they might not all marry within that time. This rule does not apply to gifts to a number of people where the share of each beneficiary is determined in advance, as each member of such a group takes a separate, and separable, vested interest.

[14.21] Powers of appointment. In the case of a general power of appointment, that is, a power under which the donee of the power can appoint to anyone including him or herself, the perpetuity period commences from the date on which the power is exercised. Before that, because the donee possesses power to appoint to him or herself, the property subject to the power is treated as belonging to the donee, and is thus vested in interest, if not necessarily in possession. The general power must, of course, vest in the donee within the perpetuity period under the instrument conferring the power. Where a gift arises from the exercise of a special power of appointment, that is, a power to appoint in favour of a group or class, the perpetuity period commences from the date on which the instrument conferring the special power comes into force. Under the Perpetuities Act 1984 (NSW), s 6(1), the difficulties surrounding the definition of the varieties of powers is resolved, for the purposes of the rule against perpetuities, by treating only powers under which the appointor has unconditional authority to appoint to him or herself as general powers. All other powers are treated as special under the amended rule. Section 8(2) applies a wait-and-see rule to any provision of a settlement which purports to confer a general power outside the period and which would otherwise be invalid. The wait-and-see rule is also applied to special powers under s 8(3) so that powers are only treated as infringing the rule to the extent that they are not fully exercised within the period, which, under the Act, is 80 years from the date the instrument creating the power comes into operation.

[14.22] Accumulations. Under the common law, a direction to accumulate income was valid if it was restricted to the perpetuity period. In *Thellusson v Woodford* (1799) 4 Ves Jr 227; 31 ER 117, a testator took advantage of that rule to leave his fortune upon trust to accumulate the income therefrom during the lives of his three sons, grandsons and great-grandchildren living at his death and to distribute it on the death of the survivor amongst the eldest lineal descendants of his three sons. This was altered by statute, the Accumulations Act 1800 (Imp), which was substantially adopted in New South Wales as ss 31 and 31A of the Conveyancing Act 1919 (NSW) which prohibit any settlement or disposition by any person of any property whereby the income of that property will be accumulated for any period longer than either:

(a) the life of the settlor;

(b) 21 years from the death of the settlor; or,

(c) the minority of any person living at the death of the settlor or of any person who would, if of full age, be entitled to the benefit of the income so accumulated.[19]

Those sections were repealed by s 19 of the Perpetuities Act 1984 (NSW) which, under s 18, allowed directions for the accumulation of income where the disposition

---

19. Similar legislation was enacted in Victoria, ss 164-166 Property law Act 1958, and South Australia, ss 60-62 Law of Property Act 1936. The English Act operated by paramount force in Queensland, Tasmania and Western Australia.

of the accumulated income is, or may be, otherwise valid; that is to say, where the disposition of that income satisfies the rule against perpetuities as amended by the 1984 Act. Accumulations of income, under both the old law and the present legislation, are subject to the rule in *Saunders v Vautier* (1841) 4 Beav 115; 49 ER 282 which allows a beneficiary or a class of beneficiaries, for whose sole benefit the accumulation is directed and who is or are of full age and absolutely entitled to a vested interest in the property concerned, to demand that the property be transferred to him or them thus putting an end to the accumulation: *Berry v Green* [1938] AC 575; *Maxwell v De Satge* (1921) 21 SR (NSW) 273.

[14.23] Reduction in age. Where a gift is limited to commence upon the recipient attaining a certain age, and, would thereby be void, because that limitation prevents the recipient taking a vested interest until some time later than 21 years after the death of a life or lives in being, as in the case of a gift to the first of A's children to attain the age of 25, statutory provision has been made for 'reading down' the offending age to the age of majority, provided that the limitation would be void if the original age requirement was retained, and would be void only for that reason, and could be saved by the application of the legislation.[20]

[14.24] The rule against perpetual trusts. The rule against perpetuities is not concerned with the duration of any interest; it seeks only to ensure that the interest concerned will vest in favour of some ascertainable beneficiary or beneficiaries within a reasonable time after the commencement of the instrument creating it. In the case of trusts for non-charitable purposes there is an additional rule that such a trust will be void if, by the terms of the trust, the capital is to be kept intact so that only the income can be used for a period exceeding the perpetuity period.[21] The objection to such gifts is not that they may vest outside the period but that they are of indefinite duration, thus rendering the property inalienable: *Re Cain* [1950] VLR 382 at 391, per Dean J. That rule is not without problems. A trust for non-charitable purposes offends the rule that for every trust there must be a human beneficiary in whose favour the court can decree performance: *Morice v The Bishop of Durham* (1804) 9 Ves 399; 32 ER 656, or, at least, one who possesses standing to enforce the trust. Despite that, courts have generally upheld such trusts where they have not infringed this rule against perpetuity.[22] In most cases, as no life in being is specified in the limitation, that has meant that the trust would be valid if limited for no more than 21 years from commencement date, although gifts on trust for 'so long as the law permits'[23] or to trustees 'so far as they legally can do'[24] have been held to be valid. Under the Perpetuities Act 1984 (NSW), s 16, the perpetuity period for such purpose trusts is now 80 years from the date on which the instrument creating the trust comes into effect and s 16(3) applies a wait-and-see provision to gifts which would, but for that section, infringe the rule by lasting more than 80 years and such trusts can be presumed to be valid until it is certain that they will exceed that time.

---

20. Conveyancing Act 1919 (NSW), s 36; Property Law Act 1974 (Qld), s 213; Perpetuities and Accumulations Act 1968 (Vic), s 9; Property Law Act 1969 (WA), ss 105 and 107.
21. DE Allen, 'The Rule Against Perpetuities Restated' (1964) UWALR 27 at 73.
22. *Jacobs'*, paras [1101]–[1108].
23. *Pirbright v Salwey* [1896] WN (Eng) 86.
24. *Re Hooper* [1932] 1 Ch 38.

Perpetuities Act 1984 (NSW)

[14.25] Statutory reform of this complex rule was introduced in New South Wales by this Act which received royal assent on 13 June 1984. The Act presupposes the common law rule and operates by amending elements of it, albeit quite dramatically in some respects, so that much of the law surrounding the old rule remains relevant.[25] The major changes are wrought by s 7, which fixes a perpetuity period of 80 years from the date on which a settlement takes effect, and s 8 which allows interests which would otherwise infringe the rule to be dealt with on a wait-and-see basis, so that they are to be treated as if they do not infringe the rule until it is certain that they will. This means, for instance, that interests created under a trust coming into effect now which are limited to commence within 21 years from the death of the survivor of the descendants of Queen Elizabeth II living at the date of the settlement will be valid, at least initially, even though the 21st year after the death of the survivor of the Queen's present descendants would in all probability fall outside the 80 year limit. Only those interests which would certainly vest later than 80 years will fail; and that might not be determined until the expiry of the full period.

Statutory reforms in other States

[14.26] Eighty year perpetuity periods have also been allowed in Victoria, Queensland, Western Australia and the Australian Capital Territory as a means of overcoming the complexity of the common law, although the common law period has also been retained as a valid alternative in the first three.[26] This legislation also provides for a 'wait-and-see' rule, thus alleviating the particular difficulties arising from the initial certainty rule.[27] Some of the harsher aspects of that rule have been ameliorated in these States by provisions dealing with presumptions and parenthood.[28]

14–5 Avoidance by the Settlor

[14.27] Once a trust has been fully constituted by a voluntary declaration, or by the settlement of property on third party trustees, the party creating the trust, that is, the settlor, will not be able to revoke it and recall the property, unless he or she can show evidence of misrepresentation, mistake or undue influence: *Allcard v Skinner* (1887) 36 Ch D 145 at 182–3, per Lindley LJ. The only way in which a settlor could exercise such a power would be if the power was expressly included in the deed under which the trust was established. Such a provision may be unwise for tax reasons. The reservation of such a power in the settlor may be deemed to effect a retention of the beneficial interest in the property settled.[29] Depending upon the wording of any such power of revocation, the power may also be exercisable by the settlor's trustee in bankruptcy.[30] Unless a settlor actually wishes to retain power to recall the property

---

25. See generally CM Sappideen and PJ Butt, *The Perpetuities Act 1984*, Sydney, 1986.
26. Perpetuities and Accumulations Act 1985 (ACT), s 8(1); Property Law Act 1974 (Qld), s 209; Perpetuities and Accumulations Act 1968 (Vic), s 5; Property Law Act 1969 (WA), s 101.
27. Perpetuities and Accumulations Act 1985 (ACT), s 9; Property Law Act 1974 (Qld), s 210; Perpetuities and Accumulations Act 1968 (Vic), s 6; Property Law Act 1969 (WA), s 103.
28. Property Law Act 1974 (Qld), ss 210–212; Perpetuities and Accumulations Act 1968 (Vic), ss 6–8; Property Law Act 1969 (WA), ss 102 and 108.
29. See s 102 of the Income Tax Assessment Act 1936 (Cth) as amended.
30. Ford & Lee, para [1604], p 678.

settled, the wiser course would be to consider whether a power of variation rather than revocation will suffice and whether to confer that power on the settlor, or on some other party, an appointor for want of a better title, with a proviso that the power cannot be exercised in any way which would have the effect of conferring a beneficial interest in the trust property on the settlor or the appointor or both, as the case may be.

14–6 Termination by the Beneficiaries

[14.28] Under the rule in *Saunders v Vautier* (1841) 4 Beav 115; 49 ER 282, a beneficiary who is of legal age, *sui juris* and absolutely entitled can call upon the trustee to transfer the property to him or her and thus terminate the trust. Where there is more than one beneficiary, provided they are all of age, legally capable and absolutely entitled, they can agree to terminate the trust by calling for a distribution: *Gosling v Gosling* (1859) Johns 265; 70 ER 423. In that case Wood VC stated the principle in clear terms:

> The principle of this court has always been to recognise the right of all persons who attain the age of twenty one to enter upon the absolute use and enjoyment of property given to them by a will, not withstanding any directions by the testator to the effect that they are not to enjoy until a later age:— unless during the interval the property is given for the benefit of another. If the property is once theirs, it is useless for the testator to attempt to impose any fetter upon their enjoyment of it in full so soon as they attain twenty one. And upon that principle, unless there is in the will, or in some codicil to it, a clear indication of an intention on the part of the testator not only that his devisees are not to have the enjoyment of the property he has devised to them until they attain twenty five, but that some other person is to have that enjoyment — or unless the property is so clearly taken away from the devisees up to the time of their attaining twenty five so as to induce the Court to hold that as to the previous rents and profits there has been intestacy — the Court does not hesitate to strike out of the will any direction that the devisees shall not enjoy it in full until they attain the age of twenty five.

The right of a beneficiary who is absolutely entitled to terminate the trust is rather blunt; it may be used to direct the trustee to transfer the trust property to third parties, whether those third parties are trustees of new trusts or not, but it cannot be used to impose a new co-trustee on the existing trustee, nor to otherwise interfere in the trustee's exercise of his or her powers in the management of the trust: *Re Brockbank* [1948] Ch 206.

[14.29] Where some beneficiaries are of age and some are not, no effective direction can be given to the trustee to make a distribution. If the trust property is divisible, any beneficiaries who are of age can each call for a distribution of their aliquot share: *Whatakane Paper Mills Ltd v Public Trustee* (1939) 39 SR (NSW) 426, provided that the interests of other beneficiaries will not be prejudiced by any such partial distribution: *Manfred v Maddell* (1950) 51 SR (NSW) 95. In *Lloyds Bank v Duker* [1987] 1 WLR 1324, the trust property consisted of 999 of 1,000 issued shares in a private company. A beneficiary entitled to 34/80ths of the estate sought to compel the trustees to transfer to her 574 shares representing her share in the estate. Those shares would have been worth far more to her than the remaining 425 shares would have been to the other five beneficiaries. The court refused to grant the orders she sought and ordered that all the shares be sold on the open market and the proceeds divided in the appropriate proportions. In making a distribution the trustee may, with the consent of the beneficiary concerned and provided no contrary intention appears in the trust instrument, appropriate any asset of the trust for the purpose and make the distribution *in specie*.[31] In any other case it will be necessary to approach the court to seek approval for any distribution; and that approval will not be granted automatically. The courts will not approve or allow a distribution which might detrimentally affect the interests of others, including persons unborn, or the settlor's next of kin who might take upon the happening of some contingency: *Teague v Trustees Executor & Agency Co Ltd* (1923) 32 CLR 252; *Berry v Green* [1938] AC 575. In the case of a discretionary trust, none of the beneficiaries will have a vested interest in any part of the trust property unless and until the trustee exercises his or her discretion in their favour. In those circumstances, it is difficult to say that all the beneficiaries have a single cumulative interest sufficient to invoke the rule in *Saunders v Vautier*. Their interests are competitive rather than complementary: *Re Weir's Settlement Trusts* [1971] Ch 145; *Sainsbury v IRC* [1970] Ch 712. Nonetheless, it has been held that the objects of a discretionary trust can combine to terminate the trust, at least where the class of objects is closed and the trustee is obliged to distribute all the income each year: *Sir Moses Montefore Jewish Home v Howell & Co (No 7) Pty Ltd* [1984] 2 NSWLR 406. Where the range of objects is described by reference to some common criterion it may be impossible to ascertain the whole class and it is difficult to see how this principle could be applied in such a case.

14–7 Termination by Distribution

[14.30] Distribution may also be effected at the instigation of the trustee, pursuant to express or implied powers of distribution. Distribution in this manner may be complete or partial. In the case of a complete distribution the trust will be brought to an end, there being no more trust property. In the case of a partial distribution, for instance in exercise of a power of advancement, the trust will continue. Where all the beneficiaries are of full age and capacity, and absolutely entitled, the trustee is under a duty to distribute: *Hawkesley v May* [1956] 1 QB 304 subject to any contrary intention in the trust instrument. In *Hawkesley v May* the trustees failed to advise the first of two beneficiaries entitled to a joint fund to come of age of his rights under the fund and, particularly of his right to sever the joint tenancy. They accumulated income arising from his share even after his sister, the other beneficiary, turned 21. Havers J held that the trustees were bound to pay the income of the eldest share to that beneficiary after he came of age without any demand being made of them.

This duty will not apply where a distribution to one beneficiary of his or her share would be detrimental to the other beneficiaries or otherwise contrary to the terms of the trust. It will obviously not apply to a discretionary trust, although the trustee there will usually have a discretion to make distributions of income and capital, including a final distribution of capital and any accumulated income.

---

31. Trustee Act 1925 (NSW), s 46; *Jacobs'*, paras [2059]–[2063], pp 575–9; Ford & Lee, paras [1620]–[1625], pp 689–93; similar statutory powers of appropriation exist in other States: Trustee Act 1958 (Vic), s 31; Trusts Act 1973–81 (Qld), s 33(1)(l), (m); Trustees Act 1962–78 (WA), s 30(1)(k), (l).

14–8 Winding up a Trust

[14.31] This really means the winding up or bankruptcy of the trustee, with appropriate disposition of the trust property thereafter. Prima facie, the assets of the trust will not be available to pay out the general creditors of the trustee and will not form part of the trustee's estate in bankruptcy. However, where the trustee is entitled to an indemnity out of the trust for debts or other liabilities properly incurred in the administration of the trust, his or her creditors are entitled to be subrogated to those rights and to claim against the trust estate to the extent of the trustee's indemnity: *Re Staff Benefits Pty Ltd* [1979] 1 NSWLR 207. In this respect, distributions by a trustee to beneficiaries prior to a winding up may constitute voidable preferences as against any liquidator subsequently appointed: *Octavo Investments Pty Ltd v Knight* (1979) 144 CLR 360 (see Chapter 19 generally).

14–9 Avoidance by Third Parties

[14.32] Bankruptcy. A voluntary settlement made within the two years before the settlor is declared bankrupt, or made within five years by a settlor who was insolvent at the time, is voidable at the suit of the trustee in bankruptcy, as is any covenant or contract to settle property on the settlor's husband, wife or children which has not been executed prior to the bankruptcy.[32] Similarly, any conveyance of property made with the intent to defraud creditors will be void against the trustee in bankruptcy.[33] Trusts created after an act of bankruptcy committed within six months of the presentation of the bankruptcy petition will also be caught by the doctrine of 'relation back' which vests all property belonging to the bankrupt at that time in the Official Trustee.[34]

[14.33] Family law. Under the Family Law Act 1975 (Cth), Pt VIII, the Family Court has power to make orders with respect to the property of the parties to a marriage, including power to make such orders as it thinks fit altering the rights of the parties to that property. By s 85 the court can set aside a disposition made by a party for the purpose of defeating an existing or anticipated order. In exercising these powers the Family Court is directed to have regard to the interests of third parties interested in the property. In exercise of this power the Family Court may also order that a disposition of property by a party to the marriage,[35] or, in certain circumstances, a third party,[36] be set aside if the transaction would defeat or hinder an existing or anticipated order under s 79. The power to set aside transactions under s 85 is to be distinguished from the power to issue injunctions under s 114. The most common circumstances in which the court will exercise its jurisdiction under s 85 is when a party to the marriage purports to dispose of real property, usually the matrimonial home. However, the disposition of funds through a trust may also be set aside under this section. For the court to exercise its jurisdiction under s 85, there must be some connection between the disposition and the defeat of the s 79 property order: *In the Marriage of Toohey* (1991) 14 Fam LR 843.

---

32. Bankruptcy Act 1966 (Cth), s 120.
33. *Ibid*, s 121.
34. *Ibid*, ss 58, 115, 116.
35. Family Law Act 1975 (Cth), s 85.
36. Family Law Act 1975 (Cth), s 85(3); see also *Re Keays* (1985) 10 Fam LR 610.

[14.34] The issue in many instances in proceedings for orders under s 85 is whether an entitlement to income as a beneficiary of a discretionary trust amounts to 'property' within the meaning of the Family Law Act, s 4(1).[37] In *Re Keays* (1985) 10 Fam LR 610, the Full Court of the Family Court, Asche, Pawley and Nygh JJ, held that the question of whether an amount held in a pension fund was the property of the husband was determined by the provisions of the trust deed governing the fund. The deed in question gave the trustees a discretion to forfeit the pension if it was not paid to the person to whom it was payable. In those circumstances the husband's 'interest' was held not to constitute property within the meaning of s 4(1) and consequently, any dealing by the Public Trustee was beyond the control of the court.

---

37. See *In the Marriage of Crapp* (1979) 5 Fam LR 47.

Chapter Fifteen

15–1 General Principles

[15.1] Charitable trusts are express trusts in favour of purposes recognised as 'charitable' at law and, once so recognised, are treated differently from private trusts in a number of ways. The principal difference is that trusts in favour of charity are trusts for purposes only. A charitable trust does not need to have any ascertainable human beneficiary. Charitable trusts are under the control of the court, which has the power to review their administration, and to execute any trust where the trustees fail to do so. The Attorney General, on behalf of the crown, as *parens patriae* of charities,[1] has the power and is under a duty to enforce proper performance of charitable trusts. The role of the crown and the courts in the administration of charitable trusts reflects their essentially 'public' nature. Charitable trusts are also treated differently under the rule against perpetuities and the so-called rule against perpetual trusts. A charitable trust will only fail under the rule against perpetuities if the trust itself is limited to commence upon the happening of some future and contingent event which might not occur within the perpetuity period: *Chamberlayne v Brockett* (1872) 8 Ch App 206; *A-G (SA) v Bray* (1964) 111 CLR 402. Notwithstanding that general rule, a gift over to a charitable purpose upon failure of a condition imposed upon a prior gift to charity will not render the second gift void under the rule against remoteness of vesting, even though failure of the condition might not occur within 21 years of the commencement of the first gift: *Re Tyler* [1891] 3 Ch 252. Both these rules are preserved in New South Wales by the Perpetuities Act 1984 (NSW) the only differences being that in the case of the general rule the perpetuity period becomes 80 years by virtue of s 7 of that Act, while s 8 applies a wait-and-see provision to any doubtful gift. The rule on gifts over from one charity to another is preserved by s 14(4). The common law rule that a trust in favour of a charitable purpose can be of indefinite duration is also preserved by s 16(4). Trusts for charitable purposes, like other gifts to charity, will usually be exempted from the operation of revenue statutes and the definition of 'charitable' in the revenue context is generally taken to be the same as that for the law of trusts. Under s 23(e) of the Income Tax Assessment Act 1936 (Cth) the income of any 'religious, scientific, charitable or public educational institution' is declared to be exempt from tax. Under s 23(j), the same exemption is applied to the income of any fund 'established by will or instrument of trust for public charitable purposes'. A 'charitable institution' under s 23(e) is not necessarily a trust. There may be no trust element involved: *Stratton v Simpson* (1970) 125 CLR 138.

---

1. The Attorney General acts on behalf of the crown as the *parens patriae* of charities. Some States of Australia have embodied this common law duty in statute for example, see Charitable Trusts Act 1962 (WA), Pt IV.

The word 'charitable' in s 23 is not defined in the Income Tax Assessment Act and carries the legal meaning which traces back to the Statute of Elizabeth 1601: *Adamson v Melbourne and Metropolitan Board of Works* [1929] AC 142; *Swinburne v FCT* (1920) 27 CLR 377.

[15.2] Aside from these specific distinctions between the treatment afforded to charitable trusts and that of private trusts, courts will also interpret charitable trusts more leniently. Unless the party creating the trust shows an intention to benefit a narrow and particular object, the court will not allow a trust for charity to fail simply because the designated object cannot be fulfilled or is uncertain in some respects. This will be the case as long as the gift displays a general intention to benefit charity, or an intention to benefit some particular charitable purpose which remains capable of fulfilment, even though the means by which the gift was to be implemented might be impracticable, or even non-existent. In *A-G (NSW) v Perpetual Trustee Co Ltd* (*McDonell's* case) (1940) 63 CLR 209, a testatrix left a farming property on trust as a training farm for Australian orphan lads. The farm was, in the event, unsuitable for that purpose because it would have run at a loss and lacked a sufficient variety of farming activities to provide good training. The next of kin argued that the gift had failed. The High Court, by a majority, held that a general charitable intention was shown and that the gift should be applied by way of a scheme. Dixon and Evatt JJ, in a joint judgment, discussed the distinction between charitable and private trusts, at 222:

> A charitable trust is a trust for a purpose, not for a person. The objects of ordinary trusts are individuals, either named or answering a description, whether presently or at some future time. To dispose of property for the fulfilment of ends considered beneficial to the community is an entirely different thing from creating equitable estates and interests and limiting them to beneficiaries. In this fundamental distinction sufficient reason may be found for many of the differences in treatment of charitable and ordinary trusts. As a matter of reason, if not of history, it explains the differences between the interpretation placed on declarations or statements of charitable purposes and the construction and effect given to limitations of estates and interests. Estates and interests are limited with a view to creating precise and definite proprietary rights, to the intent that property shall devolve according lo the form of the gift and not otherwise. Whatever conditions are expressed or implied in such limitations are therefore as a rule construed as essential to the the creation or vesting of the estate or interest unless an intention to the contrary appears. But to interpret charitable trusts in the same manner would be to ignore the conceptions upon which such trusts depend.

[15.3] The law of charity is concerned with gifts for charitable purposes, not gifts for charitable institutions. In practice this distinction is rarely crucial as a gift to a charitable institution will generally be construed as a gift to the charitable purposes of that body. A gift to an apparently charitable institution which pursues some purposes which are charitable and some which are not will fail as a charitable trust unless it can be saved by legislation which deems such gifts to be for the charitable purposes only: *Stratton v Simpson* (1970) 125 CLR 139,[2] or is otherwise confined by its own terms to the charitable purposes of the institution.

---

2. Such as Charatible Trust Act 1993 (NSW), s 23 formerly Conveyancing Act 1919 (NSW), s 37D.

The meaning of 'charitable' at law

[15.4] The legal meaning of charity is different from charity in the lay or eleemosynary sense (that is, relating to the giving of alms or other relief for the needy or destitute). In some respects the legal meaning of charity is narrower; a gift for benevolent or philanthropic purposes will not be charitable: *Morice v The Bishop of Durham* (1805)10 Ves 522; 32 ER 947, and in others, wider; the advancement of education and religion and the building and maintenance of public works, for example, fall within the definition of charitable purposes at law. The modern law of charities is derived from the Statute of Charitable Uses of 1601, 43 Eliz I c 4, which sought to reform the administration of charities at that time. The preamble to that statute set out a list of charitable purposes:

> ... for relief of aged, impotent and poor people ... the maintenance of sick and maimed soldiers and mariners, schools of learning, free schools, and scholars in universities: ... for repair of bridges, ports, havens, causeways, churches, seabanks and highways; ... for the education and preferment of orphans; ... the relief, stock or maintenance of houses of correction, ... for marriages of poor maids; ..y. for supportation, aid, and help of young tradesmen, handicraftsmen, and persons decayed; ... for relief or payment of fifteens, setting out of soldiers, and other taxes ...

In *Morice v The Bishop of Durham* (1804) 9 Ves 399; 32 ER 656 Sir William Grant MR held that the legal concept of charity was found in the various purposes listed in 43 Eliz I c 4, and any others which fell within the spirit and intendment of that statute, a view affirmed on appeal by Lord Eldon (1805) 10 Ves 522; 32 ER 947. Other purposes outside the 1601 list which were recognised as charitable then, particularly those concerned with the advancement of religion, were accommodated into this scheme by being treated as matters falling within the spirit and intendment of the statute.[3] That statement of the legal meaning of charity has gone unchallenged in the modern law of charity.[4]

[15.5] A major gloss on these principles governing the recognition of charitable purposes at law was effected by Lord Macnaghten in *Comm'rs for Special Purposes of Income Tax v Pemsel* [1891] AC 531, in which his Lordship categorised charity under four headings. Those four headings have been employed ever since in the law of charitable trusts as a preliminary classification to be applied when considering the validity of any gift as a trust for a charitable purpose. Lord Macnaghten, having discussed the meaning of the word 'charitable' at law in general terms, said, 'Charity in its legal sense comprises four principal divisions: trusts for the relief of poverty; trusts for the advancement of education; trusts for the advancement of religion; and trusts for other purposes beneficial to the community, not falling under any of the preceding heads'.

---

3. FM Bradshaw, *The Law of Charitable Trusts in Australia*, Butterworths, Sydney, 1983, p 3 [hereafter 'Bradshaw'].

4. In England the statute 43 Eliz I c 4 was repealed by the Mortmain and Charitable Uses Act 1888 which, however, preserved the preamble. That later Act was itself repealed by the Charities Act 1960, s 38 but that repeal has not affected the case law which has built up from the preamble to the Elizabethan statute. 43 Eliz I c 4 was repealed in New South Wales the Imperial Acts Application Act 1969–75 (NSW), s 8 and in Queensland by the Trusts Act 1973 (Qld), s 103. In each case the repeal was declared not to alter the established rules of law relating to charities. The Elizabethan statute is not in force in Victoria but has been regarded as being so in Western Australia and Tasmania: see Bradshaw, *op cit*, p 6.

In *Incorporated Council of Law Reporting v FCT* (1971) 125 CLR 659, the Council had as its sole purpose the production of law reports and was prevented by its articles of association from applying its income in any other way. The question arose as to whether its income was thus exempt from income tax as income of a charitable institution. The High Court held that the Council was a charitable institution. Barwick CJ, at 669 considered the concept of objects of public utility which would satisfy the quality of charity. He said that any notion that the concept was one of an eleemosynary nature was seen to be untenable by some of the instances cited in the preamble to the Elizabethan statute, such as the repair of bridges and so forth. Those instances suggested, in his view, that the provision of some of the indispensibles of a settled community was charitable in the eyes of the law. The production of law reports was, on those grounds, within the spirit and intendment of the Elizabethan statute and thus a charitable purpose at law.

Barwick CJ's formulation cannot be taken as a complete substitute for the traditional test. If some 'object of public utility' does not fall within the spirit and intendment of the Elizabethan statute it will fail as a charitable purpose.[5] That does not mean that the legal concept of charity is fixed. It is not. The law of charity is evolutionary in nature and purposes not recognised as charitable in one age may be treated as such in a later period. Lord McNaghten's categorisation of charitable trusts in *Pemsel's* case included reference to purposes which, by analogy, could be deemed within the spirit and intendment of 43 Eliz I c 4. The use of analogy for establishing whether a particular purpose is charitable has ensured that the boundaries of charitable trusts reflect contemporary attitudes. An obvious example is that of a gift in favour of the Roman Catholic Church. In 1601, Roman Catholicism was considered a superstitious use and such a gift would have been regarded as a criminal offence and subversive of national security. In *Re Bushnell* [1975] 1 All ER 721, a gift for the advancement and propagation of socialised medicine was held not to be a valid charitable gift as it could not be said, at the date of death of the testator in 1941, whether a system of socialised medicine would be for the benefit of the public. This case also illustrates the rule that the question of the validity of any gift as a charitable trust must be determined according to the law and conditions applying at the date the instrument creating the gift came into operation.

Public benefit in charitable trusts

[15.6] To be considered 'charitable' under these principles, a trust must be for the benefit of the public. This means that it must be for 'public' and not 'private' purposes and that the purpose must benefit an appropriate section of the public. Accordingly, a gift to an order of nuns of the Roman Catholic Church was held not to qualify as a valid charity where the order concerned was cloistered and the sisters devoted themselves to prayer, contemplation and penance within their convent and did not engage in any external works. Lord Simonds said that the intercessory prayer of the nuns and the edification allegedly provided by their piety were not of benefit to the public, being matters manifestly not susceptible of proof: *Gilmour v Coats* [1946] AC 426.[6] While the courts have been concerned to see that the public actually bene-

---

5. *Royal National Agricultural and Industrial Association v Chester* (1974) 48 ALJR 304.
6. Compare *Crowther v Brophy* [1992] 2 VR 97, where Gobbo J of the Supreme Court of Victoria doubted that *Gilmour v Coats* represented the law in Australia and held that the test in that case was not the appropriate test and that the enhancement of life, both religious and otherwise, for those who found comfort and peace of mind in their resort to intercessory prayer was a more appropriate test.

fits from any purportedly charitable gift, they have also had regard to any detriment to the public which might flow from the pursuit of the proposed purpose. In *National Anti-Vivisection Society v IRC* [1948] AC 31, Lord Simonds, again, held that the desirability of preventing cruelty to animals was more than overborne by the disadvantages which would flow from any ban on the use of animals in medical research. In doing so he rejected an argument that once a court had found that a given purpose was charitable it should look no further to consider the disadvantages which might flow from the implementation of that purpose. The requirement for public benefit does not apply to gifts for the relief of poverty: *Dingle v Turner* [1972] AC 601; and trusts for the advancement of education are seen as beneficial to the community generally, in the sense that the education of some is beneficial to the whole. This does not mean, however, that a trust for the education of certain private individuals will satisfy this test: *Caffoor Trustees v Comm'r of Income Tax* [1961] AC 584. Trusts for the advancement of religion are considered to be beneficial to the community because people attending religious services are likely to go back into the community inspired to do good for society and their fellow citizens.

[15.7] It is not necessary that the trust in question benefit the public as a whole in order to satisfy this requirement of public benefit. It will be sufficient if the gift benefits a section of the public, even a numerically small section, This will not apply where membership of the group to benefit is determined by blood relationship to certain named persons, such as a gift in perpetuity for the education of descendants of three named persons: *Re Compton; Powell v Compton* [1945] Ch 123. This rule was been applied to strike down a gift for the education of children of employees or former employees of a particular company or any of its subsidiaries: *Oppenheim v Tobacco Securities Trust Co Ltd* [1951] AC 297, on the ground that it lacked the necessary element of public benefit, even though the company employed over 110,000 people.

> In *Davies v Perpetual Trustee Co Ltd* [1959] AC 439, certain land was devised for the purpose of establishing a college for the Christian education of the children of Presbyterians descended from people in the colony of New South Wales hailing from or born in the north of Ireland. The Privy Council held that not to be a valid charitable trust as the selection of beneficiaries was dependent upon a purely personal element.[7]

[15.8] In Australia the definition of 'section of the public' is that set by the decision of Lowe J in *Re Income Tax Acts (No 1)* [1930] VLR 211 in which his Honour defined a section of the public as any group to which any member of the public could belong if he chose to, say, live in a particular area or adhere to a particular faith. Such groups were to be distinguished from others in which there was some bar which admitted some to membership and rejected others. That definition was adopted and affirmed by the High Court in *Thompson v FCT* (1959) 102 CLR 315 to disallow a gift in favour of children of members of the Masonic Order, as membership of that order was subject to a vote by existing members. The position in England is not as straightforward. In *IRC v Baddeley* [1955] AC 572, Viscount Simonds said that for trusts in favour of purposes of public utility within the fourth of Lord Macnaghten's categories the public benefit requirement could only be satisfied if the object pursued was for the benefit of the whole of the community, or at least as many members of the community as, according to the nature of the gift, could avail themselves of its benefit and that this requirement was not satisfied if the class of people entitled to benefit was restricted

---

7. Compare *Re Tree* [1945] Ch 325 in which a trust to assist people who had resided in a particular borough in or prior to 1880, or descendants of those people, to emigrate to any of the British Dominions was upheld.

by some artificial qualification such as adherence to a particular faith or residence within a certain geographical area.

[15.9] It is not essential that the gift take effect within the jurisdiction in order to benefit a 'section of the public'. The court will still be concerned to see that a benefit flows to a section of the Australian public, if only in the satisfaction of some moral duty to help those in 'need' in some foreign country: *Re Lowin* [1967] 2 NSWR 140. In *Kytherian Association of Queensland v Sklavos* (1958) 101 CLR 56, a gift to establish a sanitarium on a Greek island was upheld on these principles. In *Re Stone* (1970) 91 WN (NSW) 704, Helsham J, in upholding a gift to promote the interests of a company whose aims concerned the settling of Jewish migrants in Israel, took this to mean that the purpose would be considered to see if it was beneficial to the foreign community and not inimical to the legal concept of charity in our law, although that approach does seem to differ from that taken in *Re Lowin* (see [15.15]).

[15.10] The major exception to this public benefit requirement is that of gifts for the relief of poverty in which gifts for the benefit of particular poor persons have traditionally been upheld; an anomaly which has endured into the modern age, at least for poor persons fitting a particular description: *Dingle v Turner* [1972] AC 601. This anomaly can be explained by the importance afforded to the relief of poverty in late Elizabethan England and the added public benefit seen to flow then to any parish which would benefit from the reduced liability of its members to contribute to levies of the poor rate, which was fixed by reference to the number of paupers in the parish.

[15.11] If it is necessary to change the law in order to effect the designated purpose then that purpose cannot be considered charitable by a court of equity. The courts must uphold the law; they cannot support the view that it is for the benefit of the public that the law be changed. In *National Anti-Vivisection Society v IRC* [1948] AC 31, the society's purpose of suppressing vivisection was seen as political and one of its main objects the enactment of legislation prohibiting the practice. In *Re Shaw* [1957] 1 All ER 745 at 756, a gift in the will of George Bernard Shaw to establish a trust to reform the alphabet was held to be political, in the same way that gifts for the secularisation of education have been regarded as political.

15-2 Trusts for the Relief of Poverty

[15.12] This classification is taken directly from the preamble to 43 Eliz I c 4 which refers to gifts for the 'relief of aged, impotent and poor people' and for that reason trusts for the benefit of the aged and impotent, which are usually taken to mean the sick and disabled, have generally been considered in conjunction with trusts for the relief of poverty. The expression is not, however, conjunctive and must be read disjunctively otherwise a gift would not be good unless the objects were not only poor but old and sick as well: *Re Glyn's Will Trusts* [1950] 2 All ER 1150. Trusts for the benefit of the aged, regardless of whether the recipients might also be poor or not, have been accepted as valid charitable gifts in New South Wales: *Trustees of Church Property of the Diocese of Newcastle v Lake Macquarie Shire Council* [1975] 1 NSWLR 521.

> In *Le Cras v Perpetual Trustee Co Ltd* [1969] 1 AC 514, income from certain property was given on trust for the general purposes of St Vincent's Private Hospital. The Privy Council upheld this as a valid charitable trust on the ground that the provision of medical care for the sick was prima facie a charitable purpose being a matter of the relief of the 'impotent' within the preamble to 43 Eliz I c 4 and that, while not all hospitals

could be regarded as charitable institutions, as some are conducted principally for the purpose of making a profit for their proprietors, or their facilities may not be available to a sufficient section of the public, this did not apply to St Vincent's. The charging of fees for medical services was not enough, of itself, to disentitle a hospital from recognition as a charitable institution and, in this case, St Vincent's was operated as a non-profit venture. As the validity of providing relief to the sick as a charitable purpose was not dependent upon those sick people also being poor, the fact that the class of people likely to be treated in the hospital was restricted to those who could afford to pay the fees did not, of itself, rob this gift of the quality of charity.

[15.13] It is not necessary that the objects of any gift for the relief of poverty be actually destitute. A gift for the benefit of the widows and orphans of deceased officers and ex-officers of a bank who, in the opinion of the bank, were, by reason of their financial circumstances, deserving of assistance, was upheld as a charitable trust in *Re Coulthurst's Will Trusts* [1951] Ch 661. In *Re Glyn's Will Trusts* [1950] 2 All ER 1150, a gift for building free cottages for working class women aged 60 and over was held to be a valid charitable trust. Conversely gifts for 'working class' employees of a particular firm,[8] for ex-members of the forces who needed assistance to pay money owing on houses or farms,[9] and for the 'workpeople' of a particular firm, whose earnings averaged between 15s and £3 per week,[10] have been held not to be charitable. It is not necessary that the gift specify the relief of poverty as its purpose provided that intention is apparent from the wording of the gift,[11] or that the gift will have the effect of relieving poverty.[12]

[15.14] Gifts for the relief of poverty do not need to show the same element of public benefit as other charitable trusts. Traditionally gifts for the poor kinfolk of the testator, even for named poor persons, have been upheld.[13] Despite their similar treatment in other ways, this leniency does not extend to gifts for the relief of the aged or impotent. The poor relations cases may be anomalous, and have been criticised as such,[14] but they, and trusts for 'poor employees',[15] are still valid as charitable trusts. The distinction between public, or valid charitable trusts for the relief of poverty, and private trusts depends only upon whether the gift is for the relief of poverty amongst a particular description of poor people or is merely a gift to particular poor persons: *Dingle v Turner* [1972] AC 601.

---

8. *Re Sanders Will Trusts* [1954] Ch 265.
9. *Re Gillespie* [1965] VR 402.
10. *Re Drummond* [1914] 2 Ch 90.
11. As in *Downing v FCT* (1971) 125 CLR 185, in which a gift for the amelioration of the condition of the dependants of any member or ex-member of the armed forces was upheld as a valid charitable gift for the relief of poverty.
12. In *Re Niyazi's Will Trusts* [1978] 3 All ER 785, Megarry V-C held that a bequest for the construction of a working man's hostel carried a sufficient connotation of poverty.
13. *Isaac v Defriez* (1754) Amb 595; 27 ER 387; *A-G v Duke of Northumberland* (1877) Ch D 745.
14. *Re Compton* [1945] Ch 123.
15. *Re Gosling* (1900) 48 WR 300.

15-3 Trusts for the Advancement of Education

[15.15] Trusts for purposes which promote learning in a broad sense will be upheld as valid charitable gifts. Accordingly, gifts to found or support schools or other institutions of learning will fall within this category. In *A-G v Lady Downing* (1766) Amb 550; 27 ER 353, a gift to establish a university college at Cambridge was upheld notwithstanding the fact that it would be necessary for the trustees to obtain a Royal Charter. Gifts for school buildings,[16] scholarships,[17] professorships,[18] and prizes,[19] will all be valid under this heading. A wide variety of fields of study have been recognised as advancing education including practical legal training,[20] dramatic art,[21] study and training in any branch of aviation,[22] and natural history[23] to name only a few. But education in this context is not restricted to learning within the institutionalised education system. It has also been taken to include the Boy Scout movement,[24] chess playing,[25] the performance of choral works,[26] the publication of a work by a reputable author,[27] organ playing,[28] and the maintenance of the Archibald bequest for an annual prize for the painting of a portrait of some man or woman distinguished in Art, Letters, Science or Politics by an artist resident in Australasia.[29] Institutions, such as the Royal Society,[30] and, the Royal Literary Society,[31] not specifically involved in teaching have also been held to be appropriate objects of charitable gifts in this class because of their role in the dissemination of knowledge. Trusts to promote the training of members or potential members of political parties or the dissemination of political propaganda have been rejected consistently as gifts for the advancement of education.[32] However, the mere exclusion of adherents to a certain political philosophy from eligibility to apply for a scholarship has been held not to render a trust

---

16. *Wilkinson v Malin* (1832) 2 Cr & J 636.
17. *Re Leitch* [1965] VR 204.
18. *Yates v University College London* (1875) LR 7 HL 438.
19. *Chesterman v FCT* [1926] AC 128.
20. *College of Law (Properties) Pty Ltd v Willoughby MC* (1978) 38 LGRA 81.
21. *Associated Artists Ltd v IRC* [1965] 1 WLR 752.
22. *Re Lambert* [1967] SASR 19.
23. *Re Benham* [1939] SASR 450.
24. *Re Webber* [1954] 1 WLR 1500.
25. *Re Dupree's Deed Trusts* [1945] Ch 16.
26. *IRC v Royal Choral Society* [1943] 2 All ER 101.
27. *Re Hamilton-Grey* (1938) 38 SR (NSW) 262.
28. *Re Levien* [1955] 1 WLR 964.
29. *Perpetual Trustee v Groth* (1985) 2 NSWLR 278.
30. *Royal Society of London v Thompson* (1881) 17 Ch D 407.
31. *Thomas v Howell* (1874) LR 18 Eq 198.
32. *Bonar Law Memorial Trust v IRC* (1933) 49 TLR 220 — involving a gift for a college, to be run by the trust, for educating people in economics, political and social science and political history with special emphasis on the British constitution and Empire. The court considered those aims gave the governing body authority to promote lectures which would simply be propaganda for the conservative party. Similarly, a bequest to prominent members of the Labour Party, on trust for the purpose of adult education along lines set out in a party memorandum was struck down on the same grounds in *Re Hopkinson* [1949] 1 All ER 346.

invalid.[33] It is not essential for the validity of a trust for education that the education take place in Australia, nor that the recipients be Australians.

In *Re Lowin* [1967] 2 NSWR 140, a testator left a bequest for a competition for the best composition by a Viennese or Austrian composer of a song cycle to be conducted in Vienna. His next of kin challenged this bequest. Both the trust fund and the trustees were in Australia. The gift was held to be a valid charitable gift. While the 'public' to be benefited by any gift was that of New South Wales, or Australia, the implementation of a gift outside the jurisdiction could satisfy that requirement if there was a moral sense of obligation in the local community towards those in 'need' overseas. Some gifts, such as trusts for the relief of poverty or famine, were obviously good, while others, such as a trust for the military training of the army of a hostile state, were clearly bad. Because of universal interest of music its advancement in Austria was considered to have sufficient nexus with the benefit of a substantial section of the local public.

[15.16] Education in this sense has been generally taken to mean the dissemination of knowledge rather than simply the increase of knowledge and, thus, pure research is prima facie not seen as advancing education. Where the research is directed to increasing the store of communicable knowledge, however, it will be a valid object of charity and gifts for scientific research,[34] and research into the theory of education,[35] into consumption and cancer,[36] and into the alleged 'Bacon-Shakespeare Manuscripts', to show that a mere butcher could not have been the author of the greatest works of English literature,[37] have been held to be valid charitable trusts.

[15.17] The section of the public benefited by trusts for the advancement of education is the whole community which gains from any improvement of the general level of education in society, and from some fields of study, such as medicine, in particular. Nonetheless, trusts for the education of the members of the donor's family, or of the descendants of three named families in perpetuity, will be treated as private trusts: *Re Compton* [1945] Ch 123. In *Oppenheim v Tobacco Securities Trust Co Ltd* [1951] AC 297, a trust for the education of children of employees and ex-employees of a group of companies was also held to be a private trust — a harsh result considering that the companies employed over 110,000 people and that a trust for the education of the children of some particular village with a much smaller population would certainly be valid. Any attempt to mask a trust for the education of the members of a family group behind a gift for education generally, in which the trustees are directed to apply the benefits in favour of classes of beneficiaries, amongst whom the relatives of the donor rank in priority to the rest, will also be struck down as a private trust: *Caffoor Trustees v Comm'r of Income Tax* [1961] AC 584.

[15.18] The promotion of sport as part of the system of training in an educational institution has been held to be a valid charitable object, although the promotion of sport, per se, is outside the legal definition of charity: *Re Nottage* [1895] 2 Ch 649. In *Re Mariette* [1915] 2 Ch 284, a trust to build Eton five tennis courts and to provide prizes for athletics at a school was upheld as a valid trust for education, as was a gift to foster rugby union at Sydney University in *Kearins v Kearins* (1956) 57 SR (NSW)

---

33. *Equity v Trustees Executors & Agency Co v Attorney-General (Vic)* (SC(Vic), Nathan J, 12 February 1992, unreported). The gift purported to exclude from eligibility for the scholarship any person who was a 'communist', a 'communist sympathiser' or 'under communist domination and or control'.
34. *Taylor v Taylor* (1911) 10 CLR 218.
35. *Re Schulz* [1961] SASR 377.
36. *Re Travis* [1947] NZLR 382.
37. *Re Hopkins Will Trusts* [1965] Ch 669.

286. Ordinarily it has been necessary to show that the sporting activities promoted by any such gift are part of the general activities of the educational institution concerned. That view has certainly changed in England now and, with the general recognition of the benefits of exercise as a matter of public health, not to mention the fact that professional sport can provide a career at least as lucrative as any other calling, the provision of sporting facilities, particularly for the young, seems likely to be viewed more generously than it was last century.

> In *IRC v McMullen* [1981] AC 1, a gift to encourage students at schools and universities to play association football (that is, soccer) was upheld by the House of Lords notwithstanding the fact that the gift encompassed training in the sport outside any syllabus and beyond the grounds of any school. Lord Hailsham considered this to be a matter of the broader education of the young. In coming to that conclusion his Lordship referred to the provisions of the Education Act 1944 (UK) which laid down guidelines for a statutory system of education and, in particular, to s 7 of that Act which prescribed that it would be the duty of the local education authority for every area to contribute towards 'the spiritual, moral, mental and physical development of the community', and of s 53 which, when talking of the social and physical training elements of education, spoke of the establishment of facilities and organisational structures for those purposes. His Lordship noted that these principles had been applied to uphold as charitable gifts for annual treats for schoolchildren in a particular locality: *Re Mellody* [1918] 1 Ch 228; to playgrounds for children: *Re Chesters* (25 July 1934, unreported) (referred to in *IRC v Baddeley* [1955] AC 572 at 596); to a children's outing (*Re Ward's Estate* (1937) 81 SJ 397); to a prize for chess for boys and young men resident in Portsmouth: *Re Dupree's Deed Trusts* [1945] Ch 16; and for the furthering of the Boy Scout movement by helping to purchase sites for camping, outfits etc: *Re Webber* [1954] 1 WLR 1500.

15–4 Trusts for the Advancement of Religion

[15.19] Apart from 'the repair of churches' there is no reference to religion in 43 Eliz I c 4 but despite that the advancement of religion was clearly recognised as a charitable purpose long before 1601.[38] In this context, 'religion' in Australia now means all religions, including those which do not necessarily rest on any belief in a deity.

> In *Church of the New Faith v Comm'r for Payroll Tax for Victoria* (1983) 154 CLR 120; 49 ALR 65, the Church of Scientology sought exemption from payroll tax on the ground that it was a religious institution. Crockett J at first instance and the Full Court on appeal held that the religious pretensions of Scientology were a sham and that it had taken on the guise of a religious body to obtain taxation benefits. The High Court held Scientology to be a religion. Mason ACJ and Brennan J (at 154 CLR 136; 49 ALR 68) said that the question of whether scientology was a religion could not be answered by examining the truth or meaning of its writings, many of which were obscure. Instead the question turned on whether the beliefs, practices and observances accepted by Scientologists could be described as a religion. To establish that it was necessary to show whether the cult in question held some belief in a supernatural being, thing or principle, whether its beliefs and practices related to man's place in the universe and his relation to things supernatural, and whether the cult and particularly its adherents or members accepted certain canons of conduct to give effect to those beliefs. Murphy J took the view that religious freedom was a fundamental theme in our society and that the truth or falsity of religions was not the business of the courts. If religions had to

---

38. Bradshaw, *op cit*, p 22.

show their doctrines were true then all might fail. Only a body whose claim to be religious could be dismissed as a hoax could be denied recognition. Any body which claims to be religious and whose beliefs or practices are a revival of, or resemble, earlier cults, is religious.

Where donors nominate a particular religious denomination, the court may have to determine what church groups are included. For example, the term 'protestant' has been held to mean any christian except a member of the Roman Catholic, Orthodox or Old Catholic churches, and includes not only Presbyterians, Methodists, Lutherans and members of the Church of England, but Seventh Day Adventists and other relatively new protestant fundamentalist groups: *In the Matter of Umpherson* (1990) 53 SASR 293.

[15.20] The 'advancement' of religion means the promotion of the spiritual teaching of the religious body concerned and the maintenance of the spirit of its doctrine and observances: *Keren Kayemeth Le Jisroel Ltd v IRC* [1931] 2 KB 465 at 469, per Rowlatt J and embraces the maintenance and spread of religious doctrine, the provision of facilities for worship, and the support of persons who conduct or propagate religious teaching: *United Grand Lodge of Ancient Free and Accepted Masons of England v Holborn Borough Council* [1957] 1 WLR 1080 at 1090, per Donovan J. A wide variety of gifts has been upheld under this heading. Obviously a trust to provide for the fabric of the church: the building, restoration, maintenance, repair, decoration or furnishing of church buildings, including any tomb, vault or cemetery which is part of the fabric of a church,[39] will be a valid charitable trust,[40] provided the church is not a private chapel,[41] and the gift is not simply for the building or maintenance of a private monument.[42] Trusts to maintain the observances and rituals of the church will be upheld, but where a fundamental rule of the church is that the liturgy should be celebrated in a particular way and property is held on trust for that purpose, any substantial departure from the standard liturgy in a service celebrated on that property may amount to a breach of trust: *A-G (NSW) v Holy Apostolic and Catholic Church of the East (Assyrian)* (1989) 98 ALR 327. A trust for the saying of masses for the souls of named individuals where the service is open to the public will be valid: *Nelan v Downes* (1917) 23 CLR 546, even where the service includes intercessory prayer for named individuals: *Crowther v Brophy* [1992] 2 VR 97. Prayer alone, or a trust to achieve some object by that means will not be upheld as charitable; private prayer is not a purpose of public or general utility: *Re Joy* [1886–90] All ER 1110.

[15.21] For all the guidance provided by these general principles their application by the courts has been notably inconsistent. Gifts to the vicar, churchwardens, or minister of a parish simpliciter have been upheld as valid charitable gifts for an exclusively charitable purpose,[43] as has a gift to a Church of England bishop for 'diocesan purposes', which, unlike 'parish purposes' are considered restricted to the religious, and thus charitable work of the church concerned.[44] Gifts to ministers of religion, or other church officers, to be used at their discretion have been held to be valid charitable trusts, even when that discretion is unfettered,[45] while a gift to an archbishop to be used as he might judge most conducive to the good of religion in his diocese was

---

39. *Re Vaughan* (1886) 33 Ch D 187.
40. *Re King* [1923] 1 Ch 243.
41. *Hoare v Hoare* (1886) 56 LT 147.
42. *Pedulla v Nasli* (1990) 20 NSWLR 720.
43. *Re Flinn* [1948] Ch 241; Re Simpson [1946] Ch 299.
44. *Re Macgregor* (1932) 32 SR (NSW) 483.
45. *Re Garrard* [1907] 1 Ch 382: Re Moroney (1939) 39 SR (NSW) 249.

held not to be charitable as activity conducive to the good of religion might not constitute the advancement of religion within the meaning of that expression in the law of charity.[46] Similarly, a gift to the vicar and churchwarden of an English church for 'parish work' was held not to be charitable,[47] as was a gift to an archbishop for 'work connected with the Roman Catholic Church in the said archdiocese'.[48] In general terms it appears that a gift which is not exclusively for purposes recognised as advancing religion in the legal sense will fail, although that rule has been applied more leniently in some cases than in others.

[15.22] Trusts for the advancement of religion must also benefit the public. In *Neville Estates Ltd v Madden* [1962] Ch 832, Cross J explained that the public benefited by such gifts was not just the congregation at any service of worship but the community at large which benefited from the spiritual and moral improvement of the members of that congregation. For the public to enjoy that benefit it is necessary for the members of any such congregation, or holy order, to go out into the world. Accordingly, gifts in favour of closed religious communities, such as cloistered orders of nuns who devote themselves to a life of prayer and penance in isolation from society, have been consistently struck down as lacking demonstrable public benefit.[49] Where any such withdrawal from the world is merely temporary and in preparation for a return to the world to propagate the teachings of the church there will be sufficient public benefit: *Joyce v Ashfield Municipal Council* [1975] 1 NSWLR 744.

15–5 Trusts for Purposes Beneficial to the Community

[15.23] This category covers trusts for purposes outside the three headings discussed above which are nonetheless beneficial to the community. For a gift to be upheld as a valid charitable trust under this heading it must be beneficial to the community and must fall within the spirit and intendment of the preamble to the statute 43 Eliz I c 4: *Royal National Agricultural and Industrial Association v Chester* (1974) 48 ALJR 304. The range of purposes which satisfy those criteria is not fixed and can be seen to be evolutionary. In *Scottish Burial Reform and Cremation Society v Glasgow Corporation* [1968] AC 138, the purpose of promoting cremation was seen as a proper extension of the 'repair of churches' listed in the preamble, which had been extended to the repair of burial grounds attached to churchyards. As a matter of public utility, cremation was seen as a purpose consistent with such things as the 'repair of bridges, ports, havens, causeways, churches, sea banks and highways'.

In *Royal National Agricultural and Industrial Association v Chester* (1974) 48 ALJR 304, a retired poultry farmer and pigeon fancier left a will bequeathing the residue of his estate to the appellant association to apply the income 'in improving the breeding and racing of Homer Pigeons' [sic]. The validity of that gift was challenged by Mr Chester's next of kin. The High Court held that for such a gift to be charitable it must be both beneficial to the community and within the spirit and intendment of the preamble to the statute 43 Eliz I c 4. While the breeding of pigeons for racing might be described as

---

46. *Dunne v Byrne* [1912] AC 407.
47. *Re Ashton* [1938] Ch 482.
48. *Re Davies* (1932) 49 TLR 5.
49. *Cocks v Manners* (1871) LR 12 Eq 574; *Gilmour v Coats* [1949] AC 426; *Leahy v A-G (NSW)* [1959] AC 457; (1959) 101 CLR 611.

being beneficial to the community in a very general way there was no justification for deciding that it was a purpose instanced in the preamble to the statute of Elizabeth I.

[15.24] Because it is necessary for any purported gift to charity to satisfy both these requirements, inclusion in this category cannot be determined by a simple test of public benefit. The identification of a purpose as one falling within the spirit and intendment of the Elizabethan statute will depend upon whether the purpose in question can be fitted directly or by analogy into one of the purposes listed in the preamble to that statute or, otherwise, into a purpose since recognised as falling within the spirit and intendment of that list. That proposition inevitably leads to a list of single instance decisions from which the reader is expected to draw some general, if incomplete picture of the purposes which courts have been prepared to recognise as charitable under this heading. Gifts for public works clearly fall within the ambit of trusts for the 'repair of bridges, ports, havens, causeways', and the like. So gifts for the 'improvement of the City of Ballarat',[50] for 'the beautification and advancement of the township of Bunyip',[51] for the provision of a concert hall for the City of Launceston,[52] and for an agricultural showground in Brisbane, notwithstanding that the ground would be used for purposes other than agricultural shows most of the time,[53] have been upheld as valid charitable trusts; and yet, by the same token, a trust to erect a carillon on the shores of Sydney Harbour was held not to be charitable.[54]

[15.25] Trusts for the benefit of a section of the community, such as the inhabitants of a particular locality, even if very wide, or a gift 'to my country England',[55] or for the benefit of the community in Australia,[56] or quite narrow, such as a gift for the inhabitants of a borough,[57] town,[58] or parish,[59] or for some identifiable and deserving group within society, such as trusts for the benefit of aborigines,[60] returned soldiers,[61] the dependants of serving members of the armed forces,[62] Navy League Sea Cadets,[63] or the victims of Cyclone Tracy,[64] have been upheld as valid charitable trusts under this fourth head and similar gifts would be upheld provided they were not also impressed with some trust for a purpose which is not charitable, such as 'for providing some useful memorial to myself'.[65]

---

50. *Re Bones* [1930] VLR 346.
51. *Schellenberger v Trustees Executors Agency Co Ltd* (1952) 86 CLR 454.
52. *Monds v Stackhouse* (1948) 77 CLR 232.
53. *Brisbane City Council v A-G(Qld)* (1978) 52 ALJR 599.
54. *Public Trustee v Nolan* (1943) 43 SR (NSW) 169.
55. *Re Smith* [1932] 1 Ch 153. *CSD (NSW) v Way* (1951) 83 CLR 570.
56. *CSD (NSW) v Way* (1951) 83 CLR 570
57. *Re Norwich Town Close Estate Charity* (1889) 40 Ch D 298
58. *Re Baynes* [1944] 2 All ER 597.
59. *Re Mann* [1903] 1 Ch 232.
60. *Re Mathew* [1951] VLR 226; *Re Bryning* [1976] VR 100; *Aboriginal Hostels Ltd v Darwin City Council* (1985) 33 NTR 1.
61. *Verge v Somerville* [1924] AC 496.
62. *Downing v FCT* (1971) 125 CLR 185.
63. *Re Belcher* [1950] VLR 11.
64. *Re Darwin Cyclone Tracy Relief Trust Fund* (1979) 39 FLR 260.
65. *Re Endacott* [1960] Ch 232; *Pedulla v Nasti* (1990) 20 NSWLR 720.

[15.26] Trusts for other purposes which might be classified as matters in which the community recognises some moral responsibility will be upheld, provided the gift is not for a political purpose. Trusts for the care of homeless, stray and unwanted animals,[66] and for the prevention of cruelty to animals,[67] have been upheld as valid charitable gifts, although trusts to suppress vivisection have been consistently struck down because any moral benefit is outweighed by the detriment to medical science.[68] In *Re Grove-Grady* [1929] 1 Ch 557, a bequest to establish a refuge for animals in the wild free from interference by man, but not from their natural predators, was struck down as lacking any demonstrable public benefit. Similarly, a gift for the benefit of animals simpliciter has been held not to be charitable: *Murdoch v A-G (Tas)* [1992] ACLD 47, per Zeeman J. A gift for the purchase of an area of land for the establishment and preservation of native flora and fauna was struck down in *Re Green* [1970] VR 442 on the ground that no benefit to the community would necessarily result, as the public was not to be allowed access to the area. That decision can, perhaps, be isolated on its facts as it did not relate to the preservation of existing flora and fauna. In *A-G (NSW) v Sawtell* [1978] 2 NSWLR 200, a trust for the preservation of native wild life was upheld. Public access might also not be a crucial issue if it could be shown that the public would benefit generally from the protection afforded to the environment by any such gift. In *Re Verrall* [1916] 1 Ch 100, the purpose of 'promoting the permanent preservation for the benefit of the nation of lands and tenements (including buildings) of beauty or historic interest, and as regards lands for the preservation (so far as is practicable) of their natural aspect features and animal and plant life' was upheld as a valid charitable object. One can only assume that the protection of the environment would be recognised as a valid charitable purpose now, provided any gift on trust for that purpose was not rendered invalid as a political trust.

[15.27] While the relief of human suffering has long been recognised as a valid charitable purpose, the relief or redemption of prisoners and captives being actually mentioned in the statute of Elizabeth I, trusts for the purposes of Amnesty International, *viz*, the release of prisoners of conscience, were held to be trusts for political purposes, and thus not charitable: *McGovern v A-G* [1981] 3 All ER 493. This principle has also been applied to disallow trusts for the 'political restoration of the Jews to Jerusalem and to their own land' long before the creation of the State of Israel,[69] for the improvement of relations between the peoples of England and Sweden,[70] and for the formation of an informed public opinion and greater co-operation in Europe and the West in general.[71] This rule striking down trusts for political purposes has been applied in three types of case: trusts to change the law, trusts for a particular political party or doctrine, and trusts for what could be loosely termed 'propaganda' or social engineering.[72] This does not mean, however, that any matter which is the subject of legislation, or which is the subject of political debate, will be invalid as the object of a charitable trust. In *Royal North Shore Hospital v A-G (NSW)* (1938) 60 CLR 396, a trust to extend the teaching of technical education in state schools was upheld despite argument that the pursuit of such a purpose would necessarily involve political propaganda designed to change government policy on the question. Rich J: at 419, dis-

---

66. *A-G (SA) v Bray* (1964) 111 CLR 402.
67. *Re Inman* [1965] VR 238.
68. *National Anti-Vivisection Society v IRC* [1948] AC 31.
69. *Habershon v Vardon* (1851) 4 De G & Sm 467; 64 ER 916.
70. *Anglo-Swedish Society v IRC* (1931) 47 TLR 295.
71. *Re Koeppler's Will Trusts* [1984] 2 All ER 111.
72. *Re Shaw* [1957] 1 All ER 745

missed that submission saying, 'When it is said that a gift for political purposes is not charitable it cannot be meant that the advancement of every public object even if religious, eleemosynary or educational ceases to be charitable if the State is concerned or affected by the result'.

[15.28] Trusts for sporting purposes, other than those connected with education, do not qualify as gifts for charity under this heading,[73] although gifts for the provision of facilities for public recreation have been upheld.[74] In *Re Nottage* [1895] 2 Ch 649, a trust to provide a cup for yachting was held not to be a charitable gift. Considering the stress placed on the role of exercise in public health now, and the fact that the law of charity is evolutionary in nature, this may be an area ripe for change, although the courts may draw a distinction between sports in which the principal aim is exercise and other games involving serious risk of injury. In *Guild v IRC (Scotland)* (HL, 27 February 1992, unreported), the House of Lords upheld a gift for the provision of sporting facilities as a charitable trust on the grounds that it improved the conditions of the lives of people in the community generally and not just those suffering some social disadvantage. In some jurisdictions statutory provision has been made for the recognition of recreational charities, primarily to overcome any detrimental effect of the decision in *IRC v Baddeley* [1955] AC 572.[75]

15–6 Mixed Charitable and Non-charitable Gifts

[15.29] A trust displaying a general charitable intention cannot fail for uncertainty but a trust for some purposes which are charitable and some which are not is not in the same position. Such mixed gifts can be classified into three types: *Hunter v A-G* [1899] AC 309 at 323, per Lord Davey. These categories have less significance following the introduction of statutory schemes to save gifts displaying a general charitable intention, which otherwise might fail for uncertainty of objects.[76]

[15.30] **Compendious gifts.** These are gifts where the charitable purposes are so mixed with non-charitable objects that they cannot be separated by the court. This usually arises where gifts are made for broad purposes which are listed alternatively, such as, 'charitable or benevolent' purposes, or compendiously, such as, 'undertakings of public utility'. In such a case, because the trustee is not bound to apply the gift, or any part of it, for purely charitable purposes or the trustee has no discretion and is bound to apply it as directed by the terms of the trust, the trust will fail for uncertainty under the general law. These otherwise invalid trusts are saved, however, by legislation such as the Charitable Trust Act 1993 (NSW) s23 (formerly Conveyancing Act 1919 (NSW), s 37D[77]) which allows them to be construed as if no part of the trust fund could be applied for any non-charitable and invalid purpose. It is neces-

---

73. *Re Nottage* [1895] 2 Ch 649 (a cup for yachting); *Peterborough Royal Foxhound Show Society v IRC* [1936] 2 KB 497 (livestock breeding); *Re Patten* [1929] 2 Ch 276 (cricket).
74. *Re Hadden* [1932] 1 Ch 133; *Re Morgan* [1955] 1 WLR 738.
75. Recreational Charities Act 1958 (UK); Trusts Act 1973–81 (Qld), s 103; Trustee Act 1936–84 (SA), s 69c; Charitable Trusts Act 1962 (WA), s 5.
76. See [15.33] for discussion of this legislation and its effects on mixed charitable and non-charitable gifts.
77. For similar provisions in other States see also Trusts Act 1973 (Qld) s 104; Trustee Act 1936 (SA), s 69A; Property Law Act 1958 (Vic), s 131; Trustees Act 1962 (WA), s 102.

sary, of course, that the trust display a sufficiently certain intention to benefit charity. Where the objects of a trust include some charitable, as well as some non-charitable purposes, but those various objects are expressed conjunctively, so that the purposes can be seen to be cumulative, that is, a gift for 'charitable and benevolent', or for 'charitable and philanthropic' purposes, the trust will be a valid charitable gift.

[15.31] Gifts which can be apportioned. Where the trustee has a discretion to apportion the trust property between a number of purposes, some of which are charitable and some of which are not, in default of any apportionment by the trustee, the gift will be applied by being divided into equal portions for each of the potential objects, with the appropriate shares thus going to charity and the rest to the private objects, provided they satisfy the requirements for the validity of a private trust. If some or all of the non-charitable objects are invalid then the share of the fund which would have otherwise gone to those objects will pass to the testator's next of kin, or result to the settlor or his next of kin: *Re Clarke; Bracey v National Lifeboat Association* [1923] 2 Ch 407. These gifts are subject to the Charitable Trust Act 1993 (NSW) s 23 (formerly Conveyancing Act 1919 (NSW), s 37D) and its equivalents (see **[15.33]**).

[15.32] General gifts to charity. Where there is a general gift for charity or a named charitable organisation, but some of the purposes to which the fund might be applied are not strictly charitable, the trust will be upheld as a valid charitable trust and the trustee will be constrained from applying the gift in any manner not recognised as charitable at law. An obvious illustration of the application of this principle would occur in the case of a gift to a charitable organisation which carried out some activities which were not strictly charitable.[78]

[15.33] Statutory schemes. Statutory provisions operate in all States except Tasmania to offer a mechanism whereby the courts can give effect to gifts to charity, which might otherwise fail for uncertainty.[79] The relevant parts of s 23 of the Charitable Trusts Act 1993 (NSW), formally s 37D of the Conveyancing Act 1919 (NSW),[80] are:

> 23(1) A trust is not invalid merely because some non-charitable and invalid purpose as well as some charitable purpose is or could be taken to be included in any of the purposes to or for which an application of the trust property or of any part of it is directed or allowed by the trust.
>
> (2) Any such trust is to be construed and given effect to in the same manner in all respects as if no application of the trust property or of any part of it to or for any such non-charitable and invalid purpose had been or could be taken to have been so directed or allowed.

These provisions will not be used to save gifts which are too vague or indefinite to display any clear intention to benefit charity.[81] They will, however, be employed where severable and distinct objects are expressed and those which are not charitable can be omitted. In *Re Griffiths* [1926] VLR 212, a trust to be divided amongst 'other persons than my said near relatives and/or charitable institutions or organisations' was saved by excising the words 'other persons than my said near relatives'. Where a

---

78. *Congregational Union of New South Wales v Thistlethwayte* (1952) 87 CLR 375.
79. Charitable Trusts Act 1993 (NSW) formally Conveyancing Act 1919 (NSW), s 37D; Trusts Act 1973 (Qld), s 104; Trustee Act 1936 (SA), 569A; Property Law Act 1958 (Vic), s 131; Trustees Act 1962 (WA), s 102.
80. Formerly the Conveyancing Act 1919 (NSW), s 37D.
81. For example, a gift 'to my trustee and executor to be disposed of by him as he may deem best': *Re Hollole* [1945] VLR 295.

trust is expressed to be in favour of objects described compendiously, and some objects fitting that description are charitable, and some are not, s 23 can be applied to restrict the trust to those objects within the group which are charitable: *Union Trustee Co of Australia Ltd v Church of England Property Trust* (1946) 46 SR (NSW) 298; *Leahy v A-G (NSW)* [1959] AC 457. In the latter case the Privy Council was willing to apply Conveyancing Act 1919 (NSW), s 37D to read a gift in favour of any 'Order of Nuns of the Catholic Church or the Christian Brothers as the trustee might select' to exclude closed orders of nuns.

15–7 The Enforcement and Effectuation of Charitable Trusts

Enforcement

[15.34] It is the duty of the Crown, through the Attorney General as *parens patriae*, to protect and enforce charitable trusts. In this sense, the Crown acts on behalf of the 'beneficiary' of the trust. Where there is a particular charitable institution which is concerned with the charity in question, that institution will have standing to represent the charity and the Attorney General will not necessarily need to appear: *Ware v Cumberlege* (1855) 20 Beav 503 at 510, per Romilly MR; 52 ER 697 at 700–1. If a variation of a trust for charity is sought, the Attorney General will ordinarily need to appear, although that is not certain where there the charity can be represented by an institution.[82] The court also has a general power over charities which extends to making orders for their enforcement and for the necessary action to remedy any breach of trust. In *Smith v Kerr* [1902] 1 Ch 774, this power was invoked to restore a trust which had been established in favour of Clifford's Inn, one of the Inns of Chancery which had provided rooms for those training as advocates in the Inns of Court, over 300 years before. The Inn had ceased to exist and the parties holding the property had treated it as their own. Orders were made setting up a trust in favour of legal education. Where property is left on trust in favour of charity generally it is the duty of the Crown to dispose of the property, usually by the preparation of a scheme: *Re Pyne* [1903] 1 Ch 83. The Charities Procedure Act 1812 (Imp), which has been re-enacted in most Australian States,[83] enables persons interested in the charity to petition the court on questions concerning the administration of the trust or any alleged breach of trust.

Effectuation

[15.35] The administration of a gift in favour of charity will depend, in the first instance, upon the words of the particular gift. Where those words are deficient, or the gift cannot be implemented in its original form, the court will supply the necessary details to remedy any defect, if need be by the application of some suitable scheme. In some cases, where the settlor displays a particular charitable intention, a

---

82. *Sir Moses Montefiore Jewish Home v Howell & Co (No 7) Pty Ltd* [1984] 2 NSWLR 406 but cf Jacobs; para 1060.

83. Imperial Acts Application Act 1969 (NSW), s 17; Trusts Act 1973–81 (Qld), s 106; Trustee Act 1936–84 (SA), s 60; Religious Successory and Charitable Trusts Act 1958 (Vic), ss 61–62; Charitable Trusts Act 1962 (WA), s 21(1).

gift which cannot be implemented will fail. Such cases are rare. If the court finds a general charitable intention in the gift it will not be allowed to fail and will be given effect as a valid gift in favour of charity. A particular charitable intention is shown when the settlor or testator clearly intends to benefit the designated object and no other, and the language of the gift demonstrates an intention that the gift should fail if it cannot be implemented precisely in the manner expressed. A general charitable intention will be found in any case where a gift is expressed in such a way that it shows an intention that any impracticable direction is not to be regarded as indispensable to the implementation of the trust: *A-G (NSW) v Perpetual Trustee Co Ltd* (1940) 63 CLR 209 at 225, per Dixon and Evatt JJ. Obviously, the greater the detail given in the directions establishing the trust, the greater the likelihood that the gift would be construed as displaying a particular charitable intention.

> In *Re Lysaght* [1965] 2 All ER 888, a testatrix bequeathed moneys to the Royal College of Surgeons to provide student scholarships for British born students provided they were 'not of the Jewish or Roman Catholic faith'. The College refused to accept the gift on those terms. Buckley J found that the refusal of the College created an initial impossibility but that the testatrix had evinced a general charitable intention. His Lordship considered that the religious discrimination provision was not essential to the testatrix's intention and applied the gift by way of a scheme with the offending provision deleted.

General schemes

[15.36] Where a charitable purpose designated by a settlor or testator can be achieved but the gift lacks sufficient detail about the implementation and administration of the trust, the court can supply the necessary machinery to supplement the original directions by way of a general scheme of administration for the trust. In supplying directions in this way the court can have regard to a wide range of matters, including the background and interests of the donor, and, provided the gift displays the requisite charitable intention, the court's powers to settle details of the trust are quite wide and largely unfettered. Sir Samuel Romilly's Act 53 Geo III c 101, which has been adopted or re-enacted in every Australian jurisdiction,[84] gives the court power to make appropriate orders for the administration of charitable trusts, including the variation of such trusts.

Cy-près schemes

[15.37] If the designated purpose cannot be achieved for any reason but the donor has displayed a general charitable intention then the court can apply the gift for some other charitable purpose by way of a cy-près scheme; the aim being to settle a scheme making use of the gift in some manner 'as near as possible' to the expressed intentions of the donor. An interested person or charitable organisation or the Attorney General may submit proposals for application of the gift. For example, a gift for the benefit of homeless children displays a general charitable intent, but could be given to any number of charitable organisations such as Dr Barnardo's Homes, The Smith Family or the Salvation Army. The Attorney General, the trustees or any or all of

---

84. Imperial Acts Application Act 1969 (NSW), s 17; Trusts Act 1973 (Qld), s 106; Trustee Act 1936–74 (SA), ss 60–69; Supreme Court and Civil Procedure Act 1932 (Tas), s 57(2); Religious Successory and Charitable Trusts Act 1958 (Vic), ss 61–62; Charitable Trusts Act 1962 (WA), s 8; and in the Australian Capital Territory the Imperial Act applies by its own force.

these groups would have standing to submit a plan for a cy-près scheme for judicial consideration. The necessity for such a scheme may arise in a number of different ways. The designated purpose might be vitiated by some initial impossibility; such as uncertainty as to the precise object, illegality of the expressed purpose, or, possibly, the fact that that object may no longer exist: *A-G (NSW) v Barr* (CA(NSW), 11 October 1991, unreported). In such circumstances the court will select a purpose; an exercise which has produced odd results in some cases.

In *Da Costa v De Pas* (1754) Amb 228; 27 ER 150, a Jewish testator left funds on trust to establish a Jesuba for the instruction of people in the Jewish faith. Judaism was, at that time, regarded as a superstitious use under English law and thus the designated purpose was illegal. As the testator's intention was, nonetheless, charitable, the gift was applied cy-près to support a foundling hospital and the instruction of the children in that hospital in the Christian religion.

In *A-G v Ironmongers Co* (1841) Cr & Ph 208; 41 ER 469, a bequest on trust for the redemption of British slaves in Turkey or Barbary was applied cy-près for the support of charity schools as there were no British captives in either place at the time.

The results of such an exercise of judicial discretion continue to be unpredictable. Recent Australian authority suggests that where a charitable intention is clearly manifested, the courts are less likely to reflect their own political or cultural biases in accepting a scheme for the application of the gift.

In *Perpetual Trustee Co v Braithwaite* (SC(NSW), 29 May 1992, unreported), a testatrix directed that her estate be applied for the 'gratuitous reception, maintenance care and treatment of convalescents (other than mental cases)' including a direction that her home 'Camelot' be established as a convalescent home. Having first decided that the will manifested a charitable intention and second, that the substance of the gift was the establishment of a convalescent home, and that no practicable cy-près scheme could involve the use of 'Camelot', Brownie J held that the trustee be authorised to sell the home and hold the proceeds of $5.5 million on trust. The court accepted a submission from the Attorney General that the funds be applied for the construction of a Community Health Centre and Day Care Hospital, thereby achieving the objects of the testatrix in providing for the needy in perpetuity.

In New South Wales the Charitable Trusts Act 1993 (NSW) provides by Pt 3, a scheme for the application of the application of charitable property cy-près. Under s 9(1), the circumstances in which the original purposes of a charitable trust can be altered to allow the trust property or any part of it to be applied cy-près are said to include circumstances in which the original purposes, wholly or in part, have since they were laid down ceased to provide a suitable and effective method of using the trust property having regard to the spirit of the trust. It would appear, particularly from the use of the word 'include' in that section that s 9 is to be interpreted in light of the existing law of charity but may widen the powers of the court to apply property cy-près upon being satisfied that the original purposes no longer provide a suitable and effective method of using the trust property, even though those purposes might, in strict terms, still be capable of fulfilment. Under s 10(2), a general charitable intention is to be presumed unless there is evidence to the contrary in the instrument establishing the charitable trust. In view of the regularity in which courts have found general charitable intentions in construing charitable gifts this would appear to encapsulate the existing position, although the presumption of general charitable intention will make the process of deciding these matters in New South Wales slightly easier. Under s 12 the Attorney General is given power to order a scheme without a decision by the court provided the value of the trust property does not exceed

$500,000. The court may refer the matter to the Attorney General to establish a scheme if it is of the view that under s 13(2) one ought to be established. The Attorney General may, under 14(1) refer matter to the court if the subject matter is contentious or involves some special question of law or fact making it more fitting to be dealt with by the court. Where a scheme is ordered by the Attorney General, under s 18, an appeal may be brought from such an order by any trustee of the charitable trust concerned or, with the leave of the court, by any other person. Under s 6 proceedings concerning any alleged breach of a charitable trust or the administration of a charitable trust may not be commenced unless the Attorney General has authorised the bringing of such proceedings or otherwise if leave to bring such proceedings is obtained by the court. Under s 6(2) the court is not to give leave unless satisfied that the Attorney General has been given an opportunity to consider the matter and to consider whether to authorise proceedings.

[15.38] The need for a cy-près scheme might also arise in the event of some supervening impossibility or because the designated object has been fulfilled and there is a surplus. Cases of this type are more common in England, where there are many old and curious trusts for charity still in operation long after their creation. In such a case the cy-près doctrine can be invoked to apply the fund, or so much of it as remains, for some other purpose. Where the recipient organisation ceases to exist for some reason, a court can apply a cy-près scheme to distribute the fund to other appropriate organisations. For example, in *Perpetual Trustee Co Ltd v Minister for Health (NSW)* (SC(NSW), Cohen J, 13 December 1990, unreported), a gift of income and future corpus to the Crown Street Women's Hospital in Sydney became the subject of a cy-près scheme when the hospital was closed and its facilities divided among other women's hospitals in the region. In a similar situation, it was held that the Central Sydney Area Health Service was entitled to the benefit of a gift to the Sydney Homeopathic Hospital after that hospital had been transferred to the control of that health service: *Central Sydney Area Health Service v A-G (NSW)* (Rolfe J, 4 October 1990, unreported). In this respect those advising potential testators should note that most hospitals, certainly not public hospitals, do not possess separate legal personality. While the work of a particular hospital may be the charitable 'purpose' to be served by the gift, the legal entity which actually conducts that purpose will most likely be the relevant local area health service.

[15.39] In settling a cy-près scheme the court can have regard to a wide range of matters and can take evidence about the interests of the testator, and may even hear the opinions of people familiar with the donor as to his or her likely attitude to any proposed schemes. In those circumstances the court is exercising an administrative and not a judicial function and is not bound by the normal rules of evidence.

In *Phillips v Roberts* [1975] 2 NSWLR 207, a testatrix left property to improve biblical knowledge by establishing a new church. Helsham J held that purpose to be impracticable, although he did find that the woman had displayed a general charitable intention. The trustees prepared a scheme under which the fund was to be applied for the benefit of the Australian Institute of Archeology. The Attorney General proposed a division of the fund among six theological seminaries. Helsham J chose the first and, in doing so, heard evidence from a friend of the testatrix that the last thing she would have wanted was the use of her money to train priests. On appeal, Hutley JA said that in receiving evidence when carrying out its duties settling a scheme, the court was still bound to observe the rules as to the form in which evidence was presented but that, otherwise, the content of such evidence was not limited and could include direct evidence of the wishes or prejudices of the testatrix. When the directions of the testatrix are impracticable and consideration has to be given to the implementation of a scheme the court is no longer construing the will; it is engaged in an administrative task.

15–8 The Lapsing or Failure of Charitable Trusts

[15.40] Once a charitable trust has been established it will, ordinarily, continue indefinitely, unaffected by any rule against perpetuities. If the charitable organisation which initially receives the benefit of a charitable trust ceases to exist or is transformed in some way the gift will not lapse nor will it revert to the next of kin or other eligible beneficiaries under the will: *Perpetual Trustee Co v Minister for Health (NSW)* (SC(NSW), Cohen J, 13 December 1990, unreported). The remaining subject matter of the gift will remain bound by the trust for charity and, if need be, will be re-settled on some appropriate arrangement by way of a scheme. If a gift to charity is expressed to be subject to a condition subsequent, such as a conveyance to trustees for a home for orphan girls 'for ever' but upon a decision being made to discontinue the home, other trusts were to operate, the gift to charity will cease upon the happening of the condition: *Re Coopers' Conveyance Trusts* [1956] 1 WLR 1096. A charitable trust may be subject to a condition precedent, such as the testator's estate having sufficient funds to satisfy the gift, but, in that event, failure to satisfy the condition will prevent the trust from coming into existence. Failure of a condition subsequent, such as that in *Re Cooper*, will bring about a cesser of the charitable trust, provided, of course, that the condition occurs within the perpetuity period, after which time it will be void and the gift to charity will become absolute.

[15.41] Apart from failure occurring through the operation of some express condition, a gift to charity may also fail *ab initio* where the proposed trust is impracticable or impossible to effect. No failure on that ground can arise where the trust displays a general charitable intention — the property will simply be applied by way of a scheme. Where, however, the gift displays a particular charitable intention and that intention cannot be carried out, the gift will lapse. Where property is left to a particular charitable institution, and that institution is no longer in existence at the testator's death, but the gift can be construed as a gift to the charitable purposes of the institution, and those purposes can still be carried out, the gift will be upheld as a valid gift for those purposes. In this respect, despite statements to the contrary in English decisions,[85] no distinction should be drawn between incorporated and unincorporated institutions: *Sir Moses Montefiore Jewish Home v Howell & Co (No 7) Pty Ltd* [1984] 2 NSWLR 406. It is submitted that it would require special circumstances for a trust in favour of a particular charitable institution to be construed as a trust in favour of that institution, and not its purposes. If a bequest is made in favour of the purposes of a named institution and only those purposes, and those purposes cannot be carried out at the date of the testator's death, then the gift will lapse.[86] If the institution still exists at the testator's death the gift will not lapse, notwithstanding that the insti-

---

85. *Re Vernon's Will Trusts* [1972] Ch 300; *Re Finger's Will Trusts* [1972] Ch 286.
86. *Re Wilson* [1913] Ch 314, in which a testator left money to pay the salary of a schoolmaster at a school which was not in existence, but which the testator had believed would be built with funds raised by public subscription. Because the will referred to the school in considerable detail Parker J did not consider the gift open to the construction as a gift in favour of education in the district generally.

tution may have changed its constitution so that it carries out other purposes as well,[87] or even quite different purposes. In the latter case, despite the fact that the particular object cannot be pursued by the intended means, the gift will not fail. Provided the designated charitable purpose can be attained, the bequest to charity will be upheld, if need be by means of a cy-près scheme. The same will apply where a gift is made to a named charitable institution which does not, in fact, exist but the purposes supposedly pursued by the fictitious organisation can be identified and the gift applied in their favour by way of a scheme: *Re Songest* [1956] 2 All ER 765. Once property has been applied on trust for charitable purposes it cannot fail as a gift for charity, even if the original purposes fail. It cannot revert to private purposes: *Re Wright* [1954] 2 All ER 98. In New South Wales, the Dormant Funds Act 1942 (NSW) provides for the further application by the Commissioner of Dormant Funds of property which has been donated to charity but which has become a dormant fund within the meaning given to that expression in the Act.

---

87. *Re Watt* [1932] 2 Ch 243.

Chapter Sixteen

Resulting or Implied Trusts

16–1 Introduction

[16.1] A resulting trust, sometimes called an implied trust, is a trust which arises by operation of law in favour of the creator of some prior trust or other interest, or the creator's representatives, in certain circumstances. Those circumstances fall into two broad classifications: cases in which a settlor fails to completely dispose of the beneficial interest, or where a surplus arises after the original purpose of a trust has been satisfied or has ceased to exist; and cases in which someone purchases property in the name of another. In the first case the description of resulting trust seems particularly apt while the second is perhaps better described as an implied trust. Unfortunately both expressions have been used interchangeably and both trusts have been treated as the same in character for so long now that linguistic reform seems beyond hope. Megarry J tried to distinguish between the two in *Re Vandervell's Trusts* [1974] Ch 269 at 289, by describing the first as 'automatic' resulting trusts, because the settlor still retains that part of the beneficial interest undisposed of (although that does not exactly cover the 'surplus' cases) and the second as 'presumed' resulting trusts because the disposition is complete but a trust is presumed in favour of the party providing the purchase money, and that presumption is rebuttable by evidence of a contrary intention.

16–2 Incomplete Dispositions

[16.2] **Incomplete gifts.** A resulting trust will be found where an express trust is properly created but the trust as settled does not dispose completely of the beneficial interest in the property which is subject to the trust, or where an express trust fails in whole or in part for want of certainty or some other reason. For example, where A settles property on trust for B for life, with no further limitation, there will be a resulting trust in favour of A, or A's representatives, of an interest in remainder in fee simple on B's death. Similarly, a disposition to A on trust, with no further words of limitation, will give rise to a resulting trust in favour of the disponor. Failure to dispose of all the property subject to some settlement will have the same effect as a failure to dispose of the entire fee simple; so that where a testator makes a series of specific gifts by will and omits to dispose of some property, the executor will hold that property on a resulting trust for the testator's next of kin.

[16.3] **Failure of an express trust.** Where an express trust fails because of the death of a beneficiary before the testator, or for uncertainty of object, or through some other factor which renders the original trust unenforceable or impossible of fulfilment, the trustees will hold the subject matter of the trust on a resulting trust for the settlor, or the next of kin or residuary beneficiaries of the testator, depending upon the wording of the will. The apparent failure of a gift will not necessarily give rise to a resulting trust where the gift is expressed in absolute terms.

In *Hancock v Watson* [1902] AC 14, a testator gave his estate to trustees to pay the income to his widow during her life and, upon her death, to divide the estate into five equal portions. Two of those portions were to be held under a trust of income for Susan Drake and after her death on trust for any child or children that might survive her, and, in the case of sons, attain the age of 25, and in default of any such issue that share of the estate was to be distributed amongst such of the children of the testator's brother Charles as the testator's widow might appoint and, failing such appointment, to be equally divided among Charles' children and payable, in the case of sons, on their attaining 25. The testator's widow died without making any appointment. Susan Drake died without issue. The gift to Charles' children failed under the Rule against Remoteness of Vesting because the sons were not to take until they reached 25. There was then no legislative cure for such a fault. However, as the gift to Susan Drake was in absolute terms, failure of the trusts engrafted onto that gift did not give rise to a resulting trust in favour of the testator's next of kin: the property passed to Susan's heirs.

[16.4] Surplus after fulfilment of original purpose. Where property is settled on trust for certain purposes and, after those purposes have been fulfilled, there is a surplus, subject to a contrary intention being shown, the surplus will be held on a resulting trust for the settlor, or settlors. In *Smith v Cooke* [1891] AC 297, partners in an apparently insolvent firm conveyed the business to trustees for the benefit of creditors of the business. There proved to be a surplus but the House of Lords held that the deed establishing the trust had effected an absolute assignment in favour of the creditors in consideration of a release granted to the firm. In most cases, however, this question has arisen in the context of donations for some particular cause.

In *Re Abbott Fund Trusts* [1900] 2 Ch 326, a fund was raised by subscription for the help of two deaf and dumb ladies, whose inheritance had been misappropriated by a trustee of their father's estate. On the death of the survivor of the two ladies the question arose as to whether there was a resulting trust of the balance of the fund in favour of the subscribers. Stirling J held that there was no intention that the ladies were to become absolute owners of the fund and, accordingly, declared a resulting trust in favour of the subscribers.

In *Re British Red Cross Balkan Fund* [1914] 2 Ch 419, a fund totalling £28,682 was raised by public subscription for assisting the sick and wounded of the Balkan War. At the end of the war there was an unexpended balance of £12,655/19/6. The Red Cross circularised its subscribers asking whether the unexpended moneys could be retained for the general purposes of the society. Two thousand, three hundred and ten subscribers of £23,279 consented, 21 of £295 dissented and 923 of £5,108 did not reply. The question arose as to whether the rule in *Clayton's* case (that is, where an account is kept between parties it is presumed the first receipt into that account will be the first payment out) applied. If so, then the balance in hand was derived from donations received after 8 November 1912. Astbury J held that the rule did not apply. The balance of £12,655/19/6 belonged to all the subscribers rateably in proportion to their subscriptions. Those who wished their money returned should receive a pro rata rebate. This case was heard on 16 July 1914!

In *Re Gillingham Bus Disaster Fund* [1958] 1 Ch 300, a memorial fund was raised by donations given in response to an appeal by local mayors published in the newspapers following a bus crash which claimed the lives of a number of Royal Marine cadets and injured several others. The total raised came to nearly £9,000. After expenditure on funeral expenses and care for the disabled there was a surplus of over £6,000. Harman J held that the trust failed for uncertainty as a trust for charity and ought not to be applied as a gift to charity under a cy-près scheme. Instead his Lordship applied the general principle that where money was held upon trust, and the trusts declared did not exhaust the fund, the moneys reverted to the donor or settlor under a resulting trust. In doing so he rejected a submission that the moneys were *bona vacantia* even though some donors could not be found and directed an enquiry to ascertain their identity.

[16.5] A finding that such a surplus is *bona vacantia* (goods without apparent owner in which no one claims property except the crown) is not impossible. In *Cunnack v Edwards* [1896] 2 Ch 679, the balance of a fund raised by a friendly society formed for the purpose of providing for the widows of deceased members was held to be *bona vacantia* on the death of the last widow. Where donations made to some fund, such as a disaster relief fund, can be characterised as an out-and-out gift, any surplus will be treated as *bona vacantia*: *Re West Sussex Constabulary's Widows Children & Benevolent Fund Trusts* [1971] Ch 1, although it would seem reasonable to treat, say an anonymous gift to such a fund, as an out-and-out gift to charity and, in the event of a surplus, to apply it by way of scheme toward a fund for the relief of similar suffering.

In *Re Producers' Defence Fund* [1954] VLR 246, the Victorian Rural Producers Association, a voluntary Association, was dissolved. With the consent of the members, the funds of the association were disposed of by being settled on trustees who were to hold the funds, at their discretion, to foster and promote the industrial and commercial interests of rural producers. The trust was held to be invalid, being a trust for a non-charitable purpose. Smith J found that, in settling the funds on the trustees, the members had intended a final disposition. Accordingly, there was no resulting trust. The beneficial interest thus passed to the Crown as *bona vacantia*.

[16.6] Superannuation fund surpluses.
Surpluses can arise in both defined benefit and defined contribution schemes, although they are more easily identified in the former. Once all accrued benefits have been paid or accounted for, anything left in the fund is surplus. While the fund is a continuing fund the surplus will be more difficult to identify and is, at best, notional, as was recognised by Walton J in *Re Imperial Food Ltd's Pension Scheme* [1986] 2 All ER 802 at 812. Attempting to identify the surplus in a continuing scheme is an actuarial exercise and there are several approaches to the question.[1] Where a superannuation fund is wound up or otherwise terminated, the question arises whether there is a resulting trust of the surplus in favour of the employer (there could not be a resulting trust in favour of the employees/members; their contributions are specifically allocated to benefits in their favour under the scheme and could not form part of any undisposed residue). The fund may contain express provision for the disposal of any surplus, or, at least a power of variation enabling the trustee or the employer to amend the deed to make provision for disposal of the surplus (see **[14.5]–[14.6]**). The trustee or employer, whoever holds the power, will hold it as a fiduciary power and will be bound to exercise it in good faith, and subject to a duty to consider when and how to exercise it: *Mettoy Pension Trustees Ltd v Evans* [1990] 1 WLR 1587. If the deed is silent on the distribution of the surplus it may become *bona vacantia*. In *Rees v Dominion Insurance Co of Australia Ltd (in liq)* (1981) 6 ACLR 71, an employer company which operated an accumulation superan-

---

1. EA Slater, 'Superannuation Fund Surpluses', *Butterworths Superannuation and Retirement Benefits*, vol 2, p 12,401.

nuation fund (a defined contribution fund) went into voluntary liquidation. All employees were paid their accrued benefits leaving moneys in reserve in the fund. The rules of the fund precluded the company from having any interest in the fund except as provided for in the rules (which made no such provision). The deed did say that on winding up of the company the fund was to be terminated and any surplus distributed to the members in proportion to their accounts. Membership was defined by employment with the company. At the time the surplus was identified, all the 'members' had been terminated and were no longer employees of the company. The court held that the surplus passed to the Crown as *bona vacantia*. A similar result obtained in *Re ABC Television, Goodlatte v John* (Ch D, Foster J, 22 May 1973, unreported). The employer was wound up. The deed did not specifically provide for disposition of the surplus, although it did contain powers of amendment. The deed provided that on the winding up of the employer the trust was to be dissolved. Foster J took that to include any powers, including powers of amendment under the trust, and held that the surplus was thus undisposed of and passed to the Crown as *bona vacantia*. The surplus may also revert to the employer, as settlor of the fund, on a resulting trust, as happened in *Re Canada Trust Co and Cantol Ltd* (1979) 103 DLR (3d) 109. In *Davis v Richards & Wallington Industries Ltd* [1990] 1 WLR 1511, Scott J, considering a pension fund in which only an interim deed had been executed before the employer company was wound up, held that the surplus in the fund went on a resulting trust to the employer as settlor. His Lordship expressed the view that on the failure of a trust a resulting trust arises in favour of the settlor by presumption of law unless the settlor has clearly expressed an intention to the contrary. That must be the correct approach. Legoe J came to a different conclusion in *Simes & Martin Pty Ltd (in liq) v Dupree* (1990) 55 SASR 278, but took the view that as the employer was also the trustee it was in a position of conflict and was bound to distribute the surplus to the members. With respect, his Honour seems to have overlooked some of the matters which fall for consideration when determining the nature of the duty of a trustee or employer of a superannuation fund in dealing with the surplus in the fund. Once the benefits payable to members have been paid or provided for the employer will usually be entitled to have regard to its own interests with respect to any surplus. Unless the deed governing the fund makes it clear that the employer has irrevocably alienated all contributions it has made to the fund there is no objection in principle to the surplus, comprised of employer contributions, being repaid to the employer: see *Lock v Westpac Bank* (1991) 25 NSWLR 593, and **[14.5]–[14.6]**.

[16.7] Loans upon conditions. Where money is advanced upon a condition that it will be used for a certain purpose, and that purpose becomes impossible to fulfil, the money loaned will be held on a resulting trust for the lender and will not be treated as part of the general assets of the borrower: *Barclays Bank Ltd v Quistclose Investments Ltd* [1970] AC 567 (see **[13.4]–[13.10]**). The application of this doctrine in any given case will depend very much on the intentions of the parties to the transaction in question. Where money is deposited with a third party as security for the performance of a contract, and the contract is duly performed so that the security is no longer required, the moneys deposited will be held on a resulting trust for the depositor: *Theiss Watkins White Ltd v Equiticorp Australia Ltd* [1991] 1 Qd R 82. That result will, of course, be subject to any other agreement between the parties, such as that the deposited money should be put to some other use on completion of performance. If a secured creditor releases funds or releases part or the whole of a mortgage debt to enable payment of other debts of a bankrupt and there is a surplus which passes to the official receiver, there will be no resulting trust of those moneys in favour of the secured creditor: *Re Miles; National Australia Bank Ltd v Official Receiver* (1988) 85 ALR 216.

16–3 Purchase in the Name of Another

[16.8] Where one person purchases property in the name of another, and there is no evidence of any contrary intention, nor any question of a presumption of advancement, the titleholder will be presumed to hold the property on a resulting trust for the purchaser. If two or more people provide the purchase money the property will be held on a resulting trust for those purchasers in proportions representing their contributions to the whole price, regardless of the state of the legal title. That principle can be traced safely back to *Dyer v Dyer* (1788) 2 Cox 92 at 93; 30 ER 42 at 43, in which Eyre CB expressed the rule in these terms:

> The clear result of all the cases, without a single exception, is, that the trust of a legal estate, whether freehold, copyhold, or leasehold; whether taken in the names of the purchasers and others jointly, or in the name of others without that of the purchaser; whether in one name or several; whether joint or successive, results to the man who advances the purchase-money. This is a general proposition supported by all the cases, and there is nothing to contradict it; and it goes on a strict analogy to the rule of the common law, that where a feoffment is made without consideration, the use results to the feoffor. It is the established doctrine of a Court of equity, that this resulting trust may be rebutted by circumstances in evidence.

That principle was applied in *Napier v Public Trustee (WA)* (1980) 32 ALR 153; 55 ALJR 1 in which Aickin J, with whom Gibbs, Mason, Murphy and Wilson JJ agreed, expressed the rule in these terms: 'The law with respect to resulting trusts is not in doubt. Where property is transferred by one person into the name of another without consideration, and where a purchaser pays the vendor and directs him to transfer the property into the name of another person without consideration passing from that person, there is a presumption that the transferee holds the property upon trust for the transferor or the purchaser as the case may be'.

[16.9] Where two or more people contribute to the purchase price in other than equal shares equity will presume that the beneficial interest is held on trust for them in shares representing those contributions as tenants in common. Where the parties contribute equally, equity had followed the law and presumed that the beneficial interest was held for them as joint tenants. That presumption must however be viewed in the light of the common law as it stands. In New South Wales that means the Conveyancing Act 1919 (NSW), s 26.[2]

> In *Delehunt v Carmody* (1986) 68 ALR 253; 61 ALJR 54, a house was purchased through the equal contributions of two people but registered in the name of one. There had been an express oral agreement between the two that they would own the property in equal shares and that it would be put in their joint names in due course. After the death of the man, the woman claimed complete beneficial interest in the property by right of survivorship. The New South Wales Court of Appeal found that it was an essential part of any enforceable contract relating to co-ownership that there must be a term dealing with the question of survivorship and that without such a term there would be no concluded contract. Here no such term could be implied. As a result no express

---

2. s 26(1) In the construction of any instrument coming in to operation after the commencement of this Act a disposition of the beneficial interest in any property whether with or without the legal estate to two or more persons together beneficially shall be deemed to be made to or for them as tenants in common, and not as joint tenants.

(2) This section does not apply to persons who by the terms or by the tenor of the instrument are executors, administrators, trustees or mortgagees, nor in any case where the instrument expressly provides that persons are to take as joint tenants or tenants by entireties.

trust was found and a resulting trust was decreed in favour of the parties as tenants in common in equal shares by virtue of the Conveyancing Act 1919 (NSW), s 26. An appeal was allowed to the High Court on the limited ground that the Court of Appeal had erred in holding that s 26 displaced the equitable presumption that where two persons advance purchase money in equal shares they hold the beneficial interest as joint tenants. Generally equity preferred tenancies in common, on the principle that equity is equality, but where the parties advanced the purchase money in equal shares equity would follow the law and presume a joint tenancy. The High Court held that equity follows the rules of the law in their present state, which meant that in New South Wales it follows s 26 and a tenancy in common would be presumed. Gibbs CJ expressed his disagreement with the finding of the Court of Appeal that there was no express trust.

Delehunt v Carmody is an unsatisfactory decision in some respects. The finding of the Court of Appeal that some express provision governing survivorship was essential in an agreement such as that between this couple appears to undermine the authorities on trusts arising by agreement or common intention, both in the apparent refusal of the court to infer such a term from the facts and in its insistence that the terms of such an agreement be spelled out in so much detail. The narrow scope of the appeal meant that that issue did not come before the High Court and the man's de facto partner was left to share the title with his former wife as tenants in common in equal shares, a result which was clearly not intended by the man and woman when they bought the property.

[16.10] Contributions to the purchase price in this context mean direct contributions to the cost of acquisition of the property and not the payment of some outgoing charged on the property. Payment of instalments due on a mortgage is not a contribution toward the purchase price. It is a payment towards securing the release of a debt secured on the property.[3] A party who makes no cash contribution toward a purchase but is a joint mortgagor will be deemed to have contributed an aliquot share of the money borrowed on mortgage toward the acquisition: *Ingram v Ingram* [1941] VLR 95. Other costs of acquisition, such as legal fees, stamp duty, mortgagee's charges and the like, will count as contributions to the 'purchase price', being costs necessarily incurred in the acquisition of the property: *Currie v Hamilton* [1984] 1 NSWLR 687 at 691, while expenditure on furniture and interior fittings, other than items which come as fixtures with the property will not.[4] Money expended on, or improvements effected to, the property of another will not give rise to any beneficial interest in favour of the party paying the money or effecting the improvements unless there is some agreement or common intention between the parties or circumstances giving rise to an estoppel: *Pettitt v Pettitt* [1970] AC 777, or which provide grounds for a finding that it was unconscionable for one to retain the full beneficial interest in some benefit conferred by the other: *Muschinski v Dodds* (1985) 160 CLR 583.

In *Calverley v Green* (1984) 155 CLR 242 a man and a woman lived together in a de facto relationship from 1968 to 1978. Until late 1973 they had lived in a house owned by the man. In that year they purchased a house at Baulkham Hills in their two names as joint tenants. The purchase price was $27,250 of which the man provided $9,000 and $18,000 was borrowed on mortgage. Both were parties to the mortgage. The decision to add the woman to the title was made after the man experienced difficulty in obtaining finance in his name alone. The two then lived in the house until April 1978 when the woman left. She took proceedings seeking to have trustees for sale appointed

---

3. *Calverley v Green* (1984)155 CLR 242 at 257–8, per Mason and Brennan JJ.
4. In this respect, the decision in *Currie v Hamilton* must be preferred to that of Bryson J in *Little v Little* (1988) 15 NSWLR 43 in which his Honour held that legal fees, stamp duties, mortgagee's charges and such like expenses did not constitute contributions to the purchase price.

under the Conveyancing Act 1919 (NSW), s 66G and claimed a half share in the proceeds. The High Court held that when property is conveyed to several purchasers and they have contributed unequally to the purchase price, the presumption is that they hold the property on a resulting trust for themselves as tenants in common in shares proportionate to their contributions. In this case the woman's execution of the mortgage made her a contributor of half the money borrowed on mortgage. That presumption could be rebutted by a presumption of advancement or by evidence of a contrary intention on the part of the party supplying the greater part of the purchase moneys, including an intention held in common by the parties, but there was no evidence of any such intention in this case. No presumption of advancement can arise in favour of a de facto spouse.

[16.11] Rebutting the presumption. The presumption of resulting trust can be rebutted by evidence of a contrary intention, that is to say, evidence that no such trust is intended. Obviously, it will be the intention of the party supplying the purchase moneys, or the greater part of those moneys, which will determine this issue. Such a contrary intention might involve an intention to make a gift of the interest, or an intention forming part of some agreement or common intention between the parties as to the division of the beneficial interest. The presumption will also be rebutted if it can be shown that the purchase moneys were provided by way of loan to the title-holder. In this sense, it is the contributions which govern the matter, while intention plays a negative role.

> In *Bloch v Bloch* (1981) 37 ALR 55, a man and his parents purchased some flats in the man's name; the parents contributed 19/60ths of the purchase price. The parents later sought a declaration that they were entitled to 1/3 of the net proceeds of the sale of the flats. The son responded by claiming that the trust which arose in favour of the parents was an express trust which was rendered void by the Statute of Frauds. Wilson J, with whom Gibbs CJ, Murphy and Aickin JJ agreed, found that the circumstances in which the flats had been acquired, with the purchase effected by the father in the son's name while the son was in New Guinea pursuant to an earlier arrangement, did not possess the necessary certainty to establish an express trust. Wilson J found, nonetheless, that there was a resulting trust in favour of the parents of 1/3 of the proceeds. Even though the parents had actually contributed less than 1/3 to the purchase price, Wilson J took subsequent payments of mortgage instalments into account in reaching that figure. Brennan J preferred to treat the trust as one arising from a common intention that the respective interests of the parties should be in proportion to their contributions and that those contributions should include mortgage payments as what they sought to acquire was the unencumbered property.

[16.12] It is submitted that the view of Brennan J should be preferred, especially since the restatement of the orthodox approach to these matters in *Calverley v Green*. If a common intention can be found that mortgage instalments should be taken into account, it is better to treat any trust thus arising as a product of an agreement or common intention between the parties which in fact rebuts the presumption of resulting trust rather than as some sort of resulting trust of questionable ancestry. The fact that the agreement creating the express trust in such circumstances is not in writing should not prevent a court from upholding it. In *Bloch v Bloch*, the High Court referred to *Allen v Snyder* [1977] 2 NSWLR 685 without criticising Glass JA's finding in that case that trusts arising from agreement or common intention were express trusts which were enforced even though not in writing. Brennan J strengthened that contention when discussing the Statute of Frauds, at 64, 'Whatever be the classification of the trust which binds the person entrusted with the legal title to property, his repudiation of the terms upon which he was entrusted with that property "is fraudulent use of another's confidence, and the statute is not intended to cover fraud": per Isaacs J in *Cadd v Cadd* (1909) 9 CLR 171 at 187)'.

[16.13] Presumption of advancement. Where a man purchases property in the name of his wife, or of his child or some other person in relation to whom he stands in loco parentis it is a rebuttable presumption of law that the man has made a gift of that property for the advancement of the wife or child in question. This presumption has been criticised,[5] but was affirmed by the High Court in *Calverly v Green*. The presumption was extended to purchases by a man in the name of his fiancee: *Wirth v Wirth* (1956) 98 CLR 228, and to purchases by a mother in the name of her child or children: *Dullow v Dullow* (1985) 3 NSWLR 531. The presumption does not, however, apply in the case of a purchase by a man in the name of his de facto wife: *Calverley v Green*, nor to a purchase in the name of a step child: *Re Bulankoff* [1986] 1 Qd R 366. As with the presumption of resulting trust itself, this presumption can be rebutted by evidence of a contrary intention on the part of the party providing the purchase moneys: *Martin v Martin* (1959) 110 CLR 297.

[16.14] Joint bank accounts. The presumption of resulting trust, and that of advancement as well, will apply where one person opens a bank account in his or her name jointly with that of someone else. The question of whether the beneficial interest in any funds in the account will result to the party providing the money will depend upon the circumstances and, particularly, upon the intention of that party.

> In *Russell v Scott* (1936) 55 CLR 440, Katie Russell had held, at her death, a bank account in the joint names of herself and her nephew, Percy Russell. That account showed a balance of £1,395/12/4. Another £75/5 which Percy had drawn out of the joint account stood in an account in his name only. A beneficiary under Katie Russell's will sought a declaration that the moneys in both accounts formed part of the estate. All the moneys deposited in the joint account had come from the deceased. The defendant, Percy Russell, had looked after Mrs Russell, particularly in the last three years before her death in 1934. Mrs Russell opened the account in February 1932. Her stated purpose in doing so had been that 'Percy would look after her, pay her accounts and any money remaining in that bank would be Percy's'. Dixon and Evatt JJ held that the presumption of resulting trust applied to the transaction, and that there was no presumption of advancement in this case. As there was evidence of a contrary intention the presumption of resulting trust was rebutted and Percy, already constituted owner at law, was entitled to the beneficial interest.

16–4 Gratuitous Dispositions

[16.15] Before the Statute of Uses a conveyance of real property from A to B without consideration gave rise to a resulting use in favour of A. After the Statute, the use was executed and the grantor was considered to be seised of the land; in other words he retained the legal estate making the conveyance ineffectual. In order to effect a voluntary transfer of the legal estate to a third party it was necessary, after 1535, to express a use in favour of the transferee to overcome any implication of a use in favour of the grantor. So it became common for conveyances to be made 'unto and to the use of' the transferee. The revival of equitable interests following the advent of

---

5. *Pettitt v Pettitt* [1970] AC 777 at 811, per Lord Reid; at 811, per Lord Hodson; and at 824, per Lord Diplock; cf Lord Upjohn, at 817.

the modern trust raised the question of whether such a voluntary conveyance gave rise to a resulting trust. The issue was not satisfactorily resolved in England, with Lewin (for)[6] and Underhill (against)[7] at odds on the issue. In Australia, Cussen J, in *House v Caffyn* [1922] VLR 67, held that no presumption of resulting trust arose in the case of a voluntary conveyance of Torrens title land nor to a conveyance of land under common law (or 'old system') title to a stranger in whose favour a use was expressed. This principle has been said not to apply to a conveyance of old system title land where the conveyance was expressed to be for valuable consideration which was shown to be false: *Wirth v Wirth* (1956) 98 CLR 228 at 236–7, per Dixon CJ. If a voluntary conveyance was made by a father to his child, or by a man to his wife, or wife to be, the presumption of advancement would come into operation: *Wirth v Wirth*, above.

[16.16] In New South Wales the Conveyancing Act 1919 (NSW), s 44 provides that no use is to be held to result from the absence of consideration in a conveyance of land to which no uses or trusts have been declared and that every limitation which could be made by way of use under the Statute of Uses can be made by direct conveyance without the intervention of uses. Similar legislation has been enacted in Queensland and Western Australia.[8] In 1971 the Statute of Uses was repealed in New South Wales by the Imperial Acts Application Act 1969 (NSW), s 8. Even though that repeal has removed the need to express a use in a voluntary conveyance it is submitted that it has not changed the law on the implication of a resulting trust in the case of a voluntary conveyance, and that no resulting trust will be implied on a transfer of realty without consideration.[9] In Victoria the possibility of pre-1535 resulting uses being resurrected by the repeal of the Statute of Uses by ss 5 and 7 of the Imperial Acts Application Act 1980 was dealt with by the enactment of the Property Law Act 1958 (Vic), s 19A(3) which is in substantially similar terms to the Law of Property Act 1925 (UK), s 60(3) which provides:

> In a voluntary conveyance a resulting trust for the grantor shall not be implied merely by reason that the property is not expressed to be conveyed for the use or benefit of the grantee.

In Victoria those words are followed by a qualification saving the normal equitable rules concerning resulting trusts. The net effect of these various provisions appears to be that unless the transferor displays an intention that the transferee is not to take beneficially, a voluntary transfer of real property, whether Torrens title or not, will carry with it both the legal and equitable titles and will not give rise to a resulting trust in favour of the transferor.

[16.17] The possibility of a presumption of resulting trust in the case of a voluntary transfer of personalty is, if anything, more difficult to fathom. While the matter is not beyond question the better view seems to be that of the authors of *Jacobs'* that, if no presumption of resulting trust arises upon a voluntary transfer of land, it would be strange if it did arise on a voluntary transfer of personalty.[10]

---

6. *Lewin on Trusts*, 15th ed, p 131.
7. *Law of Trusts and Trustees*, 12th ed, p 190 ff.
8. Property Law Act 1974 (Qld), s 7; Property Law Act 1969 (WA), ss 38 and 39.
9. *Jacobs'*, para [1220]; Ford & Lee, para 2109.
10. *Jacobs'*, para [1220].

Chapter Seventeen

Constructive Trusts

17-1 General Principles

[17.1] A constructive trust is a trust imposed by operation of law, regardless of the intentions of the parties concerned, essentially as a remedial device whenever equity considers it unconscionable for the party holding title to the property in question to deny the interest claimed by another. In this sense the constructive trust operates as both a remedy and as an institution, giving effect to fundamental equitable principles. As Deane J put it in *Muschinski v Dodds* (1985) 160 CLR 583 at 613–14, having noted that the nature and function of the constructive trust have been the subject of considerable discussion throughout the common law world for several decades:[1]

> In a broad sense, the constructive trust is both an institution and a remedy of the law of equity. As a remedy, it can only properly be understood in the context of the history and the persisting distinctness of the principles of equity that enlighten and control the common law. The use or trust of equity, like equity itself, was essentially remedial in its origins. In its basic form it was imposed as a personal obligation attaching to property, to enforce the equitable principle that a legal owner should not be permitted to use his common law rights as owner to abuse or subvert the intention which underlay his acquisition and possession of those rights. This was consistent with the traditional concern of equity with substance rather than form. In time, the relationships in which the trust was recognised and enforced to protect actual or presumed intention became standardised and were accepted into conveyancing practice (particularly in relation to settlements) and property law as the equitable institutions of the express and implied (including resulting) trust. Like express and implied trusts, the constructive trust developed as a remedial relationship superimposed upon common law rights by order of the Chancery Court. It differs from those other forms of trust, however, in that it arises regardless of intention ... Viewed in its modern context, the constructive trust can properly be described as a remedial institution which equity imposes regardless of actual or presumed agreement or intention (and subsequently protects) to preclude the retention or assertion of beneficial ownership of property to the extent that such retention or assertion would be contrary to equitable principle.

Once imposed by order of a court a constructive trust possesses all the qualities of a trust: a trustee, trust property, personal obligations attached to that property and an

---

1. Pound, 'Equitable Remedies' (1919–20) 33 Harv L Rev at 420–3; Scott, 'Constructive Trusts' (1955) 71 LQR at 39; Maudsley, 'Proprietary Remedies for the Recovery of Money' (1959) 75 LQR at 234; Waters, *The Constructive Trust*, 1964; Goff & Jones, *The Law of Restitution*, 3rd edition, 1986, esp chs 1 and 2; Oakley, *Constructive Trusts*, 1978; J Wade, 'Trusts, the Matrimonial Home and De Facto Spouses' (1978–80) 6 U Tas L Rev at 97; JD Davies, 'Informal Arrangements Affecting Land' (1976–79) 8 Syd L Rev at 578; JL Dewar, 'The Development of the Remedial Constructive Trust' (1982) 60 Can Bar Rev at 265.

object or objects, and in that sense can be seen as an equitable institution in the same way as other trusts.[2] The existence of a constructive trust is, however, dependent upon the order of the court, even though that order may operate retrospectively by dating the origin of the trust from some earlier wrongful act. The constructive trust then acts as a remedy employed to prevent unconscionable insistence on strict legal or equitable rights. These two categorisations of the constructive trust, as an institution and as a remedy, are not mutually exclusive. One is concerned with the nature of the trust once decreed, while the other concentrates on the purpose of any such decree.[3] Constructive trusts can also be imposed for temporary purposes to facilitate some result desired by the court, but they rely upon an order of the court for their existence. Even though a party may later show grounds upon which a constructive trust would have been ordered, if no such decree has been made, and other rights or interests have intervened, the matter cannot be dealt with as if a constructive trust had been decreed.

[17.2] The remedial nature of the constructive trust does not mean, however, that it is a remedy available in any circumstances in which the imposition of such a trust might seem fair or appropriate. In *Muschinski v Dodds* (1985) 160 CLR 583, Deane J discussed the use of the constructive trust as a remedy, saying, at 615:

> The fact that the constructive trust remains predominantly remedial does not, however, mean that it represents a medium for the indulgence of idiosyncratic notions of fairness and justice. As an equitable remedy, it is available only when warranted by established equitable principles or by legitimate processes of legal reasoning, by analogy, induction and deduction, from the starting point of a proper understanding of the conceptual foundation of such principles.

In the process Deane J said that there was no place in Australia for the so-called 'constructive trust of a new model ... imposed by law whenever justice and good conscience require it', thereby dismissing the arbitrary invention put forward by Lord Denning in the English Court of Appeal in the early 1970s.[4] Deane J rejected any suggestion that proprietary rights should be governed by some mix of judicial discretion saying, at 616:

> Long before Lord Seldon's (sic) anachronism identifying the Chancellor's foot as the measure of equitable relief, undefined notions of 'justice' and what was 'fair' had given way in the law of equity to the rule of ordered principle which is of the essence of any coherent system of rational law. The mere fact that it would be unjust or unfair in a situation of discord for the owner of a legal estate to assert his ownership against another provides, of itself, no mandate for a judicial declaration that the ownership in whole or in part lies, in equity, in that other: cf *Hepworth v Hepworth*.

Without using the words, Deane J issued a stern warning about what has been described elsewhere as 'palm tree justice'[5] or 'rough justice'.[6] That proposition did not, however, in Deane J's analysis, mean that general notions of fairness were excluded from any consideration of the principles of constructive trusts. As he said, at 616:

> That is not to say that general notions of fairness and justice have become irrelevant to the content and application of equity. They remain relevant to the traditional equitable

---

2. *Muschinski v Dodds* (1985) 160 CLR 583 at 613–14, per Deane J.
3. *Muschinski v Dodds* (1985) 160 CLR 583 at 614, per Deane J.
4. See **[17.22]**.
5. *Bryson v Bryant* (1992) 29 NSWLR 188 at 196, per Kirby P.
6. *Hepworth v Hepworth* (1963) 110 CLR 309 at 318, per Windeyer J.

notion of unconscionable conduct which persists as an operative component of some fundamental principles of modern equity.[7]

Deane J's formulation sets out two bases upon which the court can decree a constructive trust: those recognised by established equitable principles and others where the application of the remedy can be extended by proper analogy. Deane J noted that the doctrine of unjust enrichment, which operates as the fundamental basis in principle for the imposition of constructive trusts in the United States,[8] and in Canada,[9] does not apply as a general principle in Australian law and that, while unjust enrichment can be identified as the notion underlying disparate cases in our law in which one party is called upon to account to another for some benefit derived at that other's expense, the imposition of a constructive trust in any given case depends upon the application of one of a number of the recognised heads of liability or some principle beyond those heads which can be recognised as providing proper grounds for the imposition of a constructive trust by way of analogy drawn from the established categories. On the present state of the law in Australia, unjust enrichment is not a ground for a deceree of a constructive trust. However, the test which has emerged from *Muschinski v Dodds* to determine whether constructive trust should be decreed in any given case is whether it is inequitable, or unconscionable, in the circumstances, for the defendant to retain the benefit of the relevant property.

[17.3] The remedial nature of the constructive trust was emphasised by Gummow J in *Re Stephenson Nominees Pty Ltd* (1987) 76 ALR 485 at 502:

> ... a constructive trust may be imposed upon a particular asset or assets not because pre-existing property of the plaintiff has been followed in equity into those assets but because, quite independently of such considerations, it is, within accepted principle, unconscionable for the defendant to assert a beneficial title thereto to the denial of the plaintiff.

and, at 503:

> Whilst the constructive trust may readily be seen as a restitutionary remedy for unjust enrichment at the expense of the plaintiff, this by no means will always be the case. The constructive trust may be imposed as a cautionary or deterrent remedy even where there has been no unjust enrichment at the expense of the plaintiff. For example, leading cases have made it plain that it is no answer to the application to company directors of the rule forbidding fiduciaries placing their interest in conflict with their duty, that the profits they have made are of a kind the company itself could not have obtained or that no loss to the company is caused by their gain: *Furs Ltd v Tomkies* (1936) 54 CLR 583 at 592; *Regal (Hastings) Ltd v Gulliver* [1967] 2 AC 134(n). Relief by way of constructive trust may be available in these cases even though the profit or benefit obtained by the fiduciary was not one the obtaining of which was an incident of his duty to the plaintiff: *Hospital Products Ltd v United States Surgical Corporation* (1984) 156

7. See, for example, *Legione v Hateley* (1983) 152 CLR 406 at 444; *Commercial Bank of Australia v Amadio* (1983) 151 CLR 447 at 461–4, 474–5.
8. Scott, *The Law of Trusts*, 3rd ed, vol V, 1967, para 461; GT Bogert, *Trusts*, 6th ed, West Publishing Co, St Paul, Minnesota, 1987, sections 77 and 84; 'A constructive trust is the formula through which the conscience of equity finds expression. When property has been acquired in such circumstances that the holder of the legal title may not in good conscience retain the beneficial interest, equity converts him into a trustee ... A court of equity in decreeing a constructive trust is bound by no unyielding formula': *Beatty v Guggenheim Exploration Co* 225 NY 380 at 386, 389; 122 NE 378. Dean Pound referred to constructive trusts as 'specific restitution of a received benefit in order to prevent unjust enrichment': 33 Harv LR 420 at 421.
9. *Pettkus v Becker* (1980) 117 DLR (3d) 257.

CLR 41 at 107–9. In such situations the constructive trust operates not to restore to the company that of which it was deprived by the conduct complained of, but to enforce observance of the fiduciary duty not to prefer personal interest to duty to the plaintiff.

However, this explanation of the constructive trust fails to place proper emphasis on the growing jurisdiction in equity to award equitable compensation, a more apt description of the cautionary or deterrent remedy referred to by Gummow J. In the past, in cases in which a breach of duty by a fiduciary was the cause of a loss suffered by the principal, which loss did not result in any corresponding gain to the delinquent fiduciary, the remedy imposed has been described as a 'constructive trust'. Whatever the label, that relief is essentially compensatory. The fiduciary is called upon to make good the loss out of his own resources, that is, moneys that were never property of any trust in favour of the principal. In view of the new frankness about equity's juris-diction to grant relief by way of equitable compensation in appropriate cases (see Chapter 25) it seems preferable, as a matter of logic as much as law, to describe these deterrent and compensatory remedies by that label rather than straining the defini-tion of constructive trusts. If this view is accepted, the constructive trust becomes more readily identifiable as a restitutionary remedy. The recognition of some greater flexibility in this area, and particularly of the option of equitable compensation as an available remedy, may produce better results. One difficulty with the constructive trust as a remedy is that it tends to give all or nothing to the plaintiff, although it can be awarded subject to conditions. Equitable compensation provides a mechanism for giving a more measured relief in appropriate cases.

17–2 Breach of Fiduciary Duty

[17.4] Liability under this head principally depends upon identification of a fiduciary duty and then proof of a breach of that duty. Those matters were canvassed in Chap-ter 5. Assuming the duty and the breach, either in the form of the making of an improper gain by exploiting a fiduciary position, or by entry into some engagement in which there was a possibility of a conflict between interest and duty,[10] the question then becomes one of whether a constructive trust will be imposed (and, if so, what will then be the subject matter of such a trust) or whether some other remedy, such as account of profits, equitable charge or equitable lien will be applied. In *Industrial Development Consultants v Cooley* [1972] 1 WLR 443, the defendant was held to be trus-tee of the benefit of contracts which he had taken up in his own name with a Gas Board, having been sent originally to negotiate for those contracts on behalf of his then employer, the plaintiff (see **[5.14]**).

In *Timber Engineering Co Pty Ltd v Anderson & Ors* [1980] 2 NSWLR 488, the plaintiff company manufactured and sold timber connecting and framing devices for use in building work. The defendants were employees of the plaintiff and two of them, hav-ing fraudulently sold the plaintiff's products on their own account, joined together with others to set up a company, Mallory Trading Pty Ltd, to which they diverted part of the plaintiff's business. Kearney J found that the business and goodwill of Mallory Trading represented a benefit received by the defendants in breach of their duty and that both the genesis and subsequent growth of that business were derived from the resources and facilities of Timber Engineering which were available to the two princi-

---

10. *Chan v Zacharia* (1984) 154 CLR 178 at 198–9, per Deane J.

pal defendants and that the business of Mallory Trading should be treated as being held on trust for Timber Engineering from the time it was set up. His Honour held further that that trust continued thereafter, notwithstanding further developments in Mallory Trading's business through the exertions of the defendants. Those endeavours were matters which could be taken into account by making the necessary allowances if appropriate. In ordering the defendants to account for the profits they had made from their fraudulent venture Kearney J held that the two principals who had been employees of the plaintiff should account without any allowance for their own industry, while the other defendants were given such an allowance.

[17.5] The decision in Timber Enginering should be considered alongside that of the High Court in *Hospital Products Ltd v USSC* (1984) 156 CLR 41 in which the majority of the High Court were of the view that the business of Hospital Products Ltd was not held on trust for USSC, and that the only liability of the defendant there was in damages for breach of contract: see **[5.11]**. In *Hospital Products* the contract between Mr Blackman and USSC was one between manufacturer and distributor while that in Timber Engineering was between employer and employee. In *Hospital Products* only Mason J was prepared to find a breach of fiduciary duty, and that was a limited fiduciary duty in respect of USSC's product goodwill. In Mason J's view the manufacturing of copies of USSC's products and the promotion and sale of HPI packaged and labelled goods constituted breaches of that duty. The appropriate remedy for that breach, according to Mason J, was not a constructive trust of the whole of HPI's business but restoration of the order for account of profits made at first instance. Such fine distinctions did not trouble the majority of the House of Lords in *Boardman v Phipps* [1967] 2 AC 46 who upheld the order that Mr Boardman was constructive trustee of his shares in Lester & Harris Ltd (see **[5.7]**).

[17.6] The extent of any property fixed by a constructive trust will depend upon the circumstances of the case, and the matters to be taken into account will include the degree of the defendant's perfidy. In *Birtchnell v Equity Trustees Executors & Agency Co Ltd* (1929) 42 CLR 384, one of three partners in a real estate business made a private deal to share profits with a person who had purchased land through the firm, and who was then to subdivide and sell the land, again through the firm. The High Court held that the land speculation deal fell within the scope of the partnership business and awarded an account of the profits made by the then deceased partner. One anomaly in this area is the decision in *Lister v Stubbs* (1890) 45 Ch D 1 and the cases which follow it (see **[5.33]–[5.34]**), although the constructive trust might not be impossible to obtain in such cases.[11]

The Keech v Sandford principle

[17.7] Under the principle laid down in *Keech v Sandford* (1726) Sel Cas T King 61; 25 ER 223 a trustee of a tenancy who obtains a renewal of a lease for itself must hold that lease as part of the trust estate. In *Chan v Zacharia* (1984) 154 CLR 178, Deane J expressed the view that this rule should be seen as an illustration of the general principle holding fiduciaries liable to account for improper gains, and as one of the cases which established that principle, rather than as a separate doctrine. He did add, however, that the rule in *Keech v Sandford* gave rise to an irrebuttable presumption that

---

11. RP Austin, 'Constructive Trusts', in PD Finn (ed), *Essays in Equity*, Law Book Co, Sydney, 1985, p 198.

where a trustee renewed a lease in his own name there was a breach of duty (see **[5.18]** and **[5.19]**).

17–3 Other Sources of Principal Liability

Unconscionable conduct or undue influence

[17.8] In most of these cases, once the unconscionable conduct has been identified, the property which will be the subject of any constructive trust will be readily identifiable as the property or benefit acquired by the defendant through the unconscionable dealing: see Chapter 6. A contract obtained by fraudulent misrepresentation or unconscionable conduct is voidable in equity. The party to whom the representation is made or has suffered from the unconscionable dealing may elect to set the contract aside, but until that action is taken the other party is not a constructive trustee of the property transferred pursuant to the contract, and no fiduciary relationship exists between the two: *Lonrho plc v Fahed* [1991] 4 All ER 961 at 971, per Millett J; *Daly v Sydney Stock Exchange Ltd* (1986) 160 CLR 371 at 387–90, per Brennan J.

> In *Lonrho v Fahed*, Lonrho sought a declaration that the defendants held certain shares which they had acquired in a public company on trust for Lonrho. Lonrho had held 29.9 per cent of the shares in that company but had given an undertaking to the Secretary of State for Trade and Industry that it would not acquire more than 30 per cent. Lonrho sold its shares to the defendants who then proceeded to buy further shares in the public company. After being released from its undertaking by the Secretary of State, Lonrho brought a claim seeking rescission of the share sale agreement and a declaration that the defendants held the extra shares they had acquired in the public company on trust for Lonrho. Lonrho failed. Millett J noted that the extra shares had been acquired by the defendants from third parties and had never been Lonrho's property. He stated that equity would intervene by way of constructive trust, 'not only to compel the defendant to restore the plaintiff's property to him, but also to require the defendant to disgorge property which he should have acquired, if at all, for the plaintiff. In the latter category of case, the defendant's wrong lies not in the acquisition of the property, which may or may not have been lawful, but in his subsequent denial of the plaintiff's beneficial interest. For such to be the case, however, the defendant must have either acquired property which but for his wrongdoing would have belonged to the plaintiff, or he must have acquired the property in circumstances in which he cannot conscientiously retain it as against the plaintiff'.

Breach of confidence

[17.9] The obvious difficulty in this area arises from the fact that confidential information is not property. As a result, the subject matter of any decree of a constructive trust will be difficult to identify. Obviously, if the information has been wrongfully patented the confider will be entitled to a constructive trust of the patent but, in most cases, the appropriate relief will come from account of profits, injunction, restitution and delivery up: see Chapter 8. While the duty of confidence has grown sufficiently to be recognised as a separate doctrine of equity in its own right,[12] it is an obvious and appropriate field in which the doctrine of constructive trusts can be extended by analogy in the manner suggested by Deane J in *Muschinski v Dodds*: see **[17.3]**. A

---

12. MG&L., para [4107].

decree of constructive trust was the remedy imposed by the majority of the Supreme Court of Canada in *Lac Minerals Ltd v International Corona Resources Ltd* (1989) 61 DLR (4th) 14 for breach of confidence: see **[5.4]**.

Equitable estoppel

[17.10] Under this doctrine the appropriate relief is the minimum equity required to do justice which, in many cases, will require the imposition of a constructive trust: see Chapter 4.

Frustration of an express trust

[17.11] Where an express trust is established, by agreement or common intention, or, perhaps by express declaration, for some particular purpose, and that purpose, and thus the trust itself, becomes impossible to fulfil equity can fashion a trust to resolve the situation. A trust arising in these circumstances may not be a constructive trust. In some cases the better terminology would be that of a resulting trust. However, that was not the terminology adopted by Needham J in *Malsbury v Malsbury* [1982] 1 NSWLR 226. In that case a man provided money for the purchase of a house in the names of his son and daughter-in-law for the purpose of providing a home for the man, his wife and the son and daughter-in-law. The man's wife died and the marriage of the younger couple broke down. Needham J found that an express trust arose from the common intention of the parties that the younger couple would hold the property on trust for the four of them as a home. The changed circumstances had rendered that trust impossible to perform. In the circumstances the son and daughter-in-law could not hold the property for their own benefit and a constructive trust was decreed in favour of the father in proportion to his contribution to the original purchase price. His Honour could have used the language of resulting trusts just as easily in the circumstances.

Unconscionable retention of benefit

[17.12] The most positive step in recent times to extend the availability of the constructive trust was that taken by the High Court in *Muschinski v Dodds* (1985) 160 CLR 583:

> A de facto couple decided to purchase a property at Picton and restore a cottage standing on it for use as an arts and craft centre. They planned to erect a pre-fabricated house on the property as a residence. Mrs Muschinski provided the purchase price of $20,000 from the sale of her home while Dodds was expected to pay the construction and improvement costs from $9,000 which he anticipated from the settlement of his divorce, and from bank loans. He also expected to be able to contribute more once he got a job. Upon legal advice, and in accordance with their instructions, particularly those of Mrs Muschinski, the property was conveyed to them as tenants in common in equal shares. In the event, they failed to obtain council approval to build the house; Dodds only received $3,500 from his divorce settlement, most of which was spent on holidays for the pair; Dodds did not find work and their personal relationship broke down. In July 1980 Mrs Muschinski commenced proceedings seeking a declaration that she was beneficial owner of the whole of the land. Apart from labour, their respective contributions to the purchase and improvement of the property were, roughly, $25,000 to $2,500, or, about 9:1. No mortgage was obtained to finance the purchase although borrowings were contemplated in some of the later stages of the overall plan.

Both at first instance, before Waddell J, and in the Court of Appeal, Mrs Muschinski failed. Despite the heavy proportion of her contributions it was held, at both levels, that the presumption of resulting trust, which would otherwise have afforded her a beneficial interest commensurate with those contributions, was rebutted by her intention to transfer one half of the beneficial interest in the property to Dodds as a sign of her faith in him.

All the members of the High Court agreed with that analysis. Brennan and Dawson JJ considered it unnecessary to take the matter any further other than to say that the conveyance had been made on terms of the assurances by Dodds and that, on the partial non-fulfilment of those assurances, Mrs Muschinski might have made a claim in equity for compensation, but she had not done so, insisting on bringing a proprietary claim only. Gibbs CJ found that because the parties had contracted jointly and severally to pay the purchase price for the Picton property, the appellant was entitled to contribution for the excess she had paid over and above her proper share, on the principle of contribution between joint and several debtors. Deane J disagreed with the line of reasoning followed by the Chief Justice. In his view, it was Mrs Muschinski's intention to make the initial payments of purchase moneys and other costs and therefore she had no right to claim reimbursement of any of those moneys by virtue of any doctrine of contribution between joint and several debtors. Instead Deane J applied by analogy the principles applicable to the rights and duties of the members of a partnership or joint venture upon the failure of that joint endeavour in the absence of express contractual provisions dealing with such circumstances, and in the absence of any attributable blame, under which the partners or joint venturers were entitled to proportionate repayment of their capital contributions to the failed venture. The fundamental rule employed by Deane J, on the authority of *Atwood v Maude* (1868) 3 Ch App 369, was that where a payment has been made on the basis and for the purposes of a planned joint venture and the substratum of that joint endeavour is removed without attributable blame, there being no intention that assets and liabilities should remain where they happen to lie at the time of such failure, then the various parties to the venture will be precluded from retaining assets or asserting other rights to the extent that it would be unconscionable for them to do so. The failure of the parties to provide in their agreement or understanding for such a contingency will not exclude the operation of these principles. Mason J, in a short judgment, agreed with the orders proposed by Deane J. He said that in the circumstances, because of the common intention of the parties that Mr Dodds take an immediate and unconditional interest in the property, it was not inequitable that he retain that share. However, Mason J considered that it would be unconscionable for Dodds to retain his share without crediting Mrs Muschinski with the contributions which she made to acquisition and improvement of the property.

[17.13] The practical difference between the approach taken by Deane J and that taken by the Chief Justice is perhaps that one doctrine is concerned with a right to contribution while the other is more in the nature of a duty to account. In some circumstances the party who has made the greater capital contribution will be entitled to a proportionately greater share of any surplus after the parties have been repaid their initial contributions but, on the facts of *Muschinski v Dodds*, Deane J thought it was not inequitable for Dodds to retain one half of the surplus from the proceeds of sale of the Picton property, that is to say the moneys representing the improvement in value of the property over and above the initial purchase price. Dodds had made a contribution to that improvement in the form of labour and Deane J did not think unconscionable of Dodds to retain one half of that element of the property. The principles stated by Deane J in *Muschinski* have since been endorsed and applied by the rest of the High Court in *Baumgartner v Baumgartner* (1987) 164 CLR 137.

A couple had lived as de facto man and wife for four years, with interruptions. At first they lived in a home unit owned by the man but, after the birth of a child, they moved into a house built on land at Leumeah and which was purchased in the man's name only. Funds for the purchase of the land and the building of the house came from the balance of the proceeds from the sale of the man's home unit and a loan from a building society. That loan was taken out in the man's name only as the society would not lend to unmarried couples. Otherwise the two pooled their salaries to pay living expenses and fixed commitments in approximate proportions of 55 per cent by the man and 45 per cent by the woman. After their separation the woman sought orders declaring that the man held his interest in the property on trust for her or, in the alternative, that he held the property subject to a charge in her favour. The High Court, per Mason CJ, Wilson and Deane JJ, in a joint judgment with which Toohey and Gaudron JJ in separate judgments generally agreed, applied the principles stated by Deane J in *Muschinski v Dodds* and found that the parties' arrangement in pooling their funds to provide for their various expenses was sufficient to establish a joint relationship, one of the purposes of which was to secure accommodation for themselves and their child. In those circumstances the man's assertion that the property was his alone amounted to unconscionable conduct justifying equitable intervention and the imposition of a constructive trust. That trust was not however, one in favour of the parties in equal shares but rather in proportions of 55 per cent /45 per cent with an allowance in favour of the man for his initial contribution of $12,883 from the proceeds from the sale of his unit, less the amount paid by way of instalments on the mortgage secured on that unit from the pooled funds during the period of cohabitation, and for instalments he had paid on the mortgage secured on the Leumeah property after the termination of the relationship, subject to an offset to reflect any benefit to him from sole use and occupation of the property during that period, and, again in favour of the man, for the value of furniture taken by the woman which had been purchased with pooled funds.

Mason CJ, Wilson and Deane JJ stated the essential principle, at 149:

> Where parties have pooled their resources for the purposes of their joint relationship and, in doing so have made contributions, financial and otherwise, to the acquisition of land, the building of a house on that land, the purchase of furniture and other fittings and the making of their home, and there is no evidence of any agreement between the parties to the contrary, then it would be inequitable of one to deny that the other was entitled to a beneficial interest in the property acquired and improved by their joint efforts.

Cohen J has since applied that approach to a case involving a pooling of labour where the parties' efforts were directed toward providing a home for themselves and to improving the value of the property in *Miller v Sutherland* (1990) 14 Fam LR 416.

[17.14] *Muschinski v Dodds* was applied in *Nichols v Nichols* (SC(NSW), 12 December 1986, unreported) which involved a dispute between a man and his former mistress over a house on Lord Howe Island which the man had paid for, as a home for the two of them and their twin sons, but which was purchased in the woman's name because she was a resident of the island. Needham J found that there was no agreement or common intention and considered that the real question was whether it would be inequitable in the circumstances for the woman to retain the benefit of the man's expenditure, relying on the principles stated by Deane J in *Muschinski v Dodds*, at 615. Having taken into account the man's clear intention to provide a home for the woman and their children, and the fact that the house which had been built was the finest house on the island, his Honour found that it would be unconscionable for the woman to retain such a grand house if the man's rights to use it were removed but that it would not be unconscionable for her to retain so much of the proceeds of sale of the house as would provide her and the children with a house on the island adequate to meet their needs and decreed a constructive trust of the house for the purpose of its sale and the division of the proceeds in that manner. The principles stated in *Muschinski v Dodds* are not limited to domestic property disputes. They are of general application as is illustrated by the decision of the New South Wales Court of Appeal in the case of *Carson v Wood* (1994) 34 NSWLR 9. The Carsons and the Woods had been involved in a manufacturing business together for over 30 years. In 1986 they entered into a new arrangement. Under that agreement certain trade marks which had been under the control of the Woods were to be transferred to a joint venture company in which both had interests. Other aspects of the reorganisation went ahead but the trade marks were not transferred. It was held at first instance by McLelland J, and on appeal by the Court of Appeal, that it was unconscionable for the Woods to deny the interest then claimed by the Carsons in the trade marks. In coming to that decision Sheller JA said, at 26:

> In the present case the matters which, in my opinion, introduce the necessary element of unconscionable conduct by the Wood family in denying to the Carson family any interest in the Australian trade marks and combine to entitle the Carson family to relief are the purchase from the Wood family by the Carson family of a one-half share of the Australian trade marks for valuable consideration in 1983, the common intention that the Carsons would continue to retain that share after the 1986 agreement came into effect and the retention by the Carson family of that share as an essential pre-condition to the transfer to the Wood family of the Carsons' interests in the trade mark proprietor Woodson (Sales). In this case the appropriate relief would be a declaration that Woodson (Sales) has since the transfer by the Carson family of their shares held the Australian trade marks in trust as to a one-half interest therein for such company as the Carson family may nominate.

Unjust enrichment

[17.15] In *Muschinski v Dodds*, Deane J rejected the notion that constructive trusts can be awarded in Australia under a general doctrine to prevent unjust enrichment. The doctrine of unjust enrichment met with the approval of a majority of the Supreme Court of Canada as the basis for decreeing a constructive trust in *Rathwell v Rathwell* (1978) 83 DLR (3d) 289. In that case Dickson J spelt out the terms of this rule, at 306:

> As a matter of principle, the Court will not allow any man to appropriate to himself the value earned by the labours of another ... but, for that principle to succeed, the facts must display an enrichment, a corresponding deprivation, and the absence of any juristic reason — such as contract or disposition of law — for the enrichment.

That principle was accepted unanimously by the Supreme Court of Canada and applied as the determinative factor in *Pettkus v Becker* (1980) 117 DLR (3d) 257. It is a principle which has received support from some commentators,[13] and sharp criticism from others.[14] It has since been applied in Canada as the means of resolving domestic property disputes. In *Sorochan v Sorochan* [1986] 2 SCR 39 (SC), it was employed to decree a constructive trust in favour of a farmer's wife of half the farm property, title to which stood in the husband's name. The woman had lived and worked on the farm for forty two years. The Supreme Court decreed the constructive

---

13. Goff & Jones, pp 11ff.
14. MG&L, para [1349].

trust on the basis of unjust enrichment notwithstanding the fact that the husband had owned the property before cohabitation commenced.

[17.16] The High Court has recognised unjust enrichment as the true basis of the common law doctrines of quantum meruit in *Pavey & Matthews Pty Ltd v Paul* (1987) 162 CLR 221 and recovery of money paid under mistake in *ANZ Banking Group Ltd v Westpac Banking Corp* (1988) 164 CLR 662; *David Securities Pty Ltd v Commonwealth Bank* (1992) 109 ALR 57. Whether unjust enrichment will be recognised as the principle underlying any of the doctrines of equity must remain a matter of conjecture at this stage. It is significant to note, however, Deane J's injunction in *Muschinski v Dodds* (1986) 160 CLR 583 at 615, that the constructive trust will be available 'only when warranted by established equitable principles or by legitimate processes of legal reasoning, by analogy, induction and deduction, from the starting point of a proper understanding of the conceptual foundation of such principles'. In *Pavey & Matthews v Paul*, he said, at 604, that unjust enrichment 'constitutes a unifying legal concept which explains why the law recognises, in a variety of distinct categories of case, an obligation on the part of a defendant to make fair and just restitution for a benefit derived at the expense of a plaintiff and which assists in the determination, by the ordinary processes of legal reasoning, of the question whether the law should, in justice, recognize an obligation in a new or developing category of case'.

[17.17] In *Re Stephenson Nominees Pty Ltd* (1987) 76 ALR 485, Gummow J went to some lengths to rebut the proposition that a constructive trust could be imposed in Australian law on the grounds of unjust enrichment. His two principal arguments, as stated, at 502, were: (a) that there is no general principle in Australian law requiring restitution in cases of unjust enrichment; and (b) even if there were it would not necessarily follow that the constructive trust was the appropriate remedy. He then stressed, in the passage quoted in [17.3], that the constructive trust is not necessarily seen as a restitutionary remedy. However, as discussed in [17.3], the cases in which 'constructive trusts' have been imposed as a cautionary or deterrent remedy might be better characterised as cases of equitable compensation. If these 'compensatory' or 'deterrent' constructive trusts are recognised as orders more in the nature of equitable compensation there would be scope for the recognition of the constructive trust as purely restitutionary relief. That would leave open the question of whether unjust enrichment and unconscionable retention of benefit were expressions of the same principle or whether there was some fundamental difference between the two. This question exercised the mind of Toohey J in *Baumgartner*, at 152–5, without requiring any decision on the point. Unjust enrichment along the lines of the Canadian model has met with approval in the New Zealand Court of appeal in *Gillies v Keogh* [1989] 2 NZLR 327 at 332, per Cooke P and at 347 per Richardson J. An illuminating discussion of unjust enrichment in Australia can be found in the judgment of Kirby P in *Bryson v Bryant* (1992) 29 NSWLR 188. The learned President was prepared to adopt unjust enrichment as an appropriate legal principle in the circumstances of that case (see [17.28]), but was not able to persuade the other two members of the Court of Appeal. Deane J referred to unjust enrichment in *Foran v Wight* (1989) 168 CLR 385 expressing the view that it provided the rationale for a purchaser's right to recover its deposit following repudiation by the vendor, at 438:

Upon rescission the purchasers were entitled to obtain restitution of the deposit which they had paid. Their claim for the return of the deposit was not founded on the rescinded contract. Nor did it represent a claim for damages for the vendors' breach of its terms. It was a claim founded in the equitable notions of fair dealing and good conscience which require restitution of a benefit received as, or as part of, the *quid pro quo* for a consideration which has failed (cf per Lord Wright, *Fibrosa Spolka Akcyjna v Fairbairn, Lawson, Combe, Barbour Ltd* ([1943] AC 32 at 64–66); *Muschinski v Dodds* (1985) 160 CLR 583 at 618–620). If it be necessary to clothe that claim in a nomenclature, the appropriate one in a modern context is "restitution" for, or of, "unjust enrichment". The benefit whose receipt falls into one of the categories of case which the law characterises as unjust enrichment may be actual. Alternatively, it may be constructive as, for example, where it involves full or partial performance of something requested to be done. The benefit constituting the unjust enrichment in the present case was actual in that it would seem to be common ground that the deposit which the purchasers seek to recover was actually received by or on behalf of the vendors.

While unjust enrichment may not be recognised as a principle underlying the jurisdiction of Australian courts of equity to grant decrees of constructive trust, there may be one geographical exception: Parramatta. In *In the Marriage of Toohey* (1991) 14 Fam LR 843 at 856, McCall J cited Toohey J in *Baumgartner*, at 152, as authority for the proposition that, 'the declaration of a constructive trust is the remedy available once unconscionable conduct or unjust enrichment has been established by the principles of equity'. A better approach can be found in the judgment of Prior J in *Marriott Industries Pty Ltd v Mercantile Credits Ltd* (1990) 55 SASR 228. The judicial confusion evident in the judgment of McCall J in *Toohey* indicates a real possibility that unjust enrichment may emerge as a doctrine of equity in Australian law by a process of judicial mistake, which seems to fall somewhat short of the processes of judicial reasoning preferred by Deane J in *Muschinski v Dodds*.

Other possible sources of liability: by analogy, by induction and deduction

[17.18] In *Hospital Products Ltd v USSC* (1984) 55 ALR 417, Deane J agreed with the majority that there was no fiduciary duty owed by the Hospital Products companies to USSC, either generally or in respect of any local product goodwill, however, he was still prepared to impose a constructive trust to enforce an account of profits against HPL as equitable relief appropriate to the circumstances of the case. Deane J's ground for imposing a constructive trust was HPL's appropriation to itself of the local goodwill of USSC products by a course of conduct which involved a calculated breach of contract and that USSC was thus 'entitled to a declaration that HPL was liable to account as a constructive trustee for the profits of that Australian business in accordance with the principles under which a constructive trust may be imposed as the appropriate form of equitable relief in circumstances where a person could not in good conscience retain for himself a benefit, or the proceeds of a benefit, which he has appropriated to himself in breach of his contractual or other legal or equitable obligations to another'. As that matter had not been argued, Deane J deferred further exploration of the point until another time. The idea of awarding a constructive trust for breach of contract may seem heresy to some. But, provided Deane J's qualification that it be employed in cases involving a calculated breach, it appears a sensible and justifiable extension of this equitable jurisdiction. In such a case, damages would be inappropriate and, just as equity has traditionally provided relief by way of specific performance where damages are inadequate, so it appears a proper development that the remedial device of constructive trust be employed as a discretionary remedy on the same grounds. The arguments raised by Gummow J in *Re Stephenson Nominees Pty Ltd* (1987) 76 ALR 485 at 502–3 against the recognition of unjust enrichment as the basis for the jurisdiction to decree constructive trusts, as set out in **[17.3]**, present a barrier to this development. However, if the non-restitutionary applications of the 'constructive trust' are categorised as equitable compensation then the principal objection put forward by Gummow J would disappear. The debate would then turn on whether the unjust enrichment formula on the Canadian model is more appropriate, with the necessary proof of enrichment of the defendant at the plaintiff's expense, or whether the doctrine of unconscionable retention of benefit developed in the High Court in *Muschinski v Dodds* and *Baumgartner* is, in fact, a more sophisticated device in any event. It is interesting to note in this context that Deane and Dawson JJ recognised unjust enrichment as the basis for equitable relief against forfeiture in *Stern v Macarthur* (1988) 165 CLR 489 at 526–7 (see **[17.15]**). The difference between the two doctrines is that unjust enrichment is concerned more with the enrichment of the defendant, the benefits conferred in the circumstances and then with whether it is 'unjust' that those benefits be retained. Unconscionable retention of benefit focuses attention on the conduct of the defendant and whether, in the circumstances, it is unconscionable for the defendant to deny the plaintiff's claim or to retain the benefits conferred in the circumstances without recognising, either in whole or in part, the claims advanced by the plaintiff. In this sense the unconscionability can arise on the steps of the court. The unconscionable conduct being the defendant's denial of the plaintiff's claim in the proceedings.

Other constructive trusts

[17.19] These include the 'constructive trust' imposed on the vendor of land, the trust imposed on the balance of the proceeds of a sale by a mortgagee, and trusts arising from other arrangements, such as mutual wills and secret trusts.

17–4 Domestic Property Disputes

[17.20] Following the decision of the High court in *Muschinski v Dodds*, the constructive trust was widely used as a remedial device in domestic property disputes, particularly between former de facto spouses. In addition to the constructive trust, other equitable principles, such as resulting trusts, express trusts arising from agreement or common intention and equitable charges have also featured in recent years as the legal machinery for the resolution of domestic property disputes. The employment of this shopping basket of equitable niceties warrants specialised discussion, if only to dispel the confusion this multiplicity of doctrines can cause. There has also been considerable statutory involvement in this area, most notably the Family Law Act 1975 (Cth), under which the Family Court is given power to deal with property disputes between parties to a marriage, including power, if the court considers it appropriate, to alter the property rights of the parties.[15] In New South Wales there is the De Facto Relationships Act 1984 (NSW), which confers special powers on the Supreme Court in dealing with property disputes between heterosexual de facto spouses, including power to adjust their property interests.[16] Equitable principles

---

15. Family Law Act 1975 (Cth), s 79.
16. Section 20(1)(a) gives the Supreme Court power to make such order adjusting the interests of de facto partners with respect to property as seems just and equitable having regard to the financial and non-financial contributions made directly or indirectly by or on behalf of the de facto partners to the acquisition, conservation or improvement of any property of the partners or either of them or to the financial resources of the partners or either of them. By s 20(1)(b), contributions, in the context of s 20(1)(a) are taken to include contributions made in the capacity of homemaker or parent to the welfare of the other or to the family comprised of the de facto partners and any children of theirs or accepted by them as members of a family unit.

remain relevant in both areas. They are relevant in any assessment of the actual property rights of the parties before any adjustment or alteration in those rights is effected by judicial fiat, although the judges of the Family Court have exercised their discretion to alter people's property rights without attempting to state what those rights were in the first place relying on the unfettered discretion conferred by s 79: *Mallett v Mallett* (1984) 156 CLR 605. Equitable principles have intruded into matrimonial property questions in other ways, particularly at the interface between family law and bankruptcy. Where one spouse faces bankruptcy the other will be keen to establish his or her rights in equity to property to which the other has title so as to isolate those assets from the clutches of the other spouse's creditors.[17] The power to adjust property rights as between former de facto spouses under the De Facto Relationships Act 1984 (NSW) has been generously interpreted in some cases of late by the New South Wales Court of Appeal in *Black v Black* (1991) 15 Fam LR 109 and *Dwyer v Kaljo* (1992) 15 Fam LR 645, although the tide of generosity seems to have ebbed with the decision of the Court of Appeal in *Wallace v Stanford* (CA(NSW), 29 June 1995, unreported). In that case, Mahoney JA, with whom Sheller JA agreed, said that the court, in assessing the contributions of the parties could not consider, and reward, the contributions of one in isolation from the contributions of the other. The power to 'adjust' property rights under de facto property legislation is a power which is only available in cases which fall within the ambit of that legislation. Not all cases do. Many of these disputes arise between parent and child, or the members of an extended family. Same sex couples are not covered by the Act. De facto property legislation has been enacted in Victoria, by the Property Law Amendment Act 1987 (Vic) which substantially re-enacts the property provisions of the New South Wales Act, and in the Northern Territory, in the De Facto Relationships Act 1991 (NT), which sets up a regime for dealing with property questions similar to that in New South Wales. In other States and the Australian Capital Territory de facto couples must rely on general equitable principles.

[17.21] In the past the problem which faced parties to a de facto relationship, or, indeed to a marriage before the advent of modern family law legislation, in obtaining some just determination on the disposition of their assets through the courts was the limited power available to the courts to recognise the contributions made during the course of any such relationship, let alone make any orders altering the respective rights of the parties in any property. The court's power was essentially declarative. It could only recognise the property rights of the parties as they stood according to law. Before *Muschinski v Dodds*, there was little if any scope to prevent unconscionable retention by one partner of benefits conferred by the other if the matter was not covered by some express agreement or common intention. The position as it stood then was put by Windeyer J in *Hepworth v Hepworth* (1963) 110 CLR 309 at 317–18:

> Community of property arising from marriage has no place in the common law. We have nothing that corresponds with the various regimes relating to matrimonial property that exist in countries that have the civil law. Since the abolition of dower and curtesy and the enactment of Married Women's Property Acts, questions arising between husband and wife as to the ownership in law of property that they have enjoyed, or are enjoying, in common thus fall to be decided according to the same scheme of legal titles and equitable principles as govern the rights of any two persons who are not spouses.

---

17. JM Housego, 'Bankruptcy and Family Law — Is There an Equitable Solution?' (1991) 5 AJFamL 57.

Windeyer J then discussed the operation of the presumptions of resulting trust and advancement in property questions arising between spouses. The starting point for the development of the modern law governing domestic property disputes can be found in the decisions of the House of Lords in *Pettitt v Pettitt* [1970] AC 777 and *Gissing v Gissing* [1971] AC 886: see **[13.38]–[13.39]**. Those cases stand as authority for the principle that a person who performs work or expends money on the property of another will have no claim on that property unless he or she can show some agreement or common intention, or otherwise establish a case in estoppel. The common intention had to be an actual intention either expressed by the parties or one which could be inferred from the facts and not an intention imputed to them on the basis of what reasonable spouses would do in the circumstances. This approach was adopted in Australia in *Allen v Snyder* [1977] 2 NSWLR 685. In that case Glass JA said that the agreement to which the court gave effect was one concerning the parties' respective interests in the property rather than some convoluted understanding whereby the parties agreed that indirect contributions would be deemed to be direct contributions: see **[13.39]–[13.42]**. These decisions gave the courts a very narrow field within which to work in attempting to resolve property disputes between parties living in close domestic circumstances. Proof of an agreement was paramount despite Lord Hodson's dictum in *Pettitt*, at 810, that the 'conception of a normal married couple spending the long winter evenings hammering out agreements about their possessions appears grotesque'. The retreat into a laager of strict legal form was not conceived in a vacuum. The House of Lords' decisions in *Pettitt* and *Gissing* were very much a reaction to decisions of Lord Denning MR in cases such as *Fribance v Fribance (No 2)* [1957] 1 WLR 384; *Hine v Hine* [1962] 1 WLR 1124 and *Appleton v Appleton* [1965] 1 WLR 25 in which the learned Master of the Rolls had asserted that the courts had an almost unfettered discretion in disposing of family assets.

[17.22] Lord Denning was not easily put off. Despite the clear rejection of an imputed common intention, let alone any notion that the court could do what it thought 'fair' in the circumstances, he proceeded to hand down a series of decisions in the Court of Appeal during the 1970s in which constructive trusts were applied on all sorts of odd grounds. In *Falconer v Falconer* [1970] 3 All ER 449 he spoke of an intention imputed to the parties to create a trust. In *Hussey v Palmer* [1972] 3 All ER 744 at 747, he said, '... it is a trust imposed by law whenever equity and good conscience require it. It is a liberal process, founded on large principles of equity, to be applied in cases where the defendant cannot conscientiously keep the property for himself alone ...'. In *Cooke v Head* [1972] 2 All ER 38, language similar to that of the law of partnerships, or joint ventures was used. This line of cases reached its peak, or nadir as some would have it, in *Eves v Eves* [1975] 3 All ER 768 in which Lord Denning said that the woman in that case was entitled to such a share in the house 'as was fair in view of all she had done and was doing for (the man) and the children and would thereafter do'. The trust imposed was, according to Lord Denning a constructive trust of 'a new model'.

[17.23] This line of authority prompted Deane J in *Muschinski v Dodds* (1985) 160 CLR 583 at 615, to say, that the constructive trust could not be used as 'a medium for the indulgence of idiosyncratic notions of fairness and justice', and that it will be available only when 'warranted by established equitable principles or by legitimate processes of legal reasoning'. The tide also seems to have ebbed in England since Lord Denning's retirement, as can be seen in *Burns v Burns* [1984] 1 Ch 317. In *Lloyds Bank plc v Rosset* [1991] AC 107, the House of Lords held that a wife who claimed an equitable interest by way of constructive trust in a house in her husband's name could only succeed if she could show that there was prior to acquisition, 'or exceptionally at some later date', an agreement, arrangement or understanding reached between the parties that the property was to be shared beneficially. The finding of such an agreement could only be based on evidence of express discussions between the parties 'however imperfectly remembered and however imprecise their terms might have been'. Once a finding to that effect was made it would be necessary for the spouse asserting a claim to show that he or she has acted to his or her detriment or significantly altered his or her position in reliance on the agreement in order to give rise to a constructive trust or proprietary estoppel. Failing evidence of such an agreement, and subsequent detriment, only direct contributions to the purchase price, either initially or by paying mortgage instalments could readily justify the inference necessary to create a constructive trust. On this authority, despite the use of the expression 'constructive trust', there is only room in England for express trusts arising from actual agreement or common intention, or resulting trusts arising from contributions to the purchase price. The payment of mortgage instalments may be seen as more of a contribution to the purchase price in England than is the case in Australia because of English conveyancing practice. English decisions on this area of the law must be read with great circumspection. *Muschinski v Dodds* has not happened there yet. In view of the paternalism redolent in the speeches in *Lloyds Bank v Rosset* it may never happen. Australian jurisprudence can gain much by consideration of developments in Canada and New Zealand in this area of the law, but not the United Kingdom where judges continue to show a peculiar reluctance to recognise property rights in favour of women and others of lowly caste.

[17.24] Discomfort with the structures of the agreement or common intention model led to the development in Australia of the general principle of unconscionable retention of benefit in *Muschinski v Dodds* and *Baumgartner v Baumgartner*: see **[17.12]– [17.14]**. On those principles, where the substratum of a joint relationship or joint endeavour is removed without attributable blame and where the benefit of money or other property contributed by one party on the basis and for the purposes of the relationship or endeavour would otherwise be retained by the recipient in circumstances in which it was unconscionable for that party to retain that benefit, in whole or in part, equity can intervene to insist that the recipient surrender the relevant property or its value to the extent that conscience dictates: per Deane J, at 620). As has been discussed above, these cases have also been taken to stand as authority for a wider principle prohibiting unconscionable retention of benefit beyond situations which might be described as failed joint endeavours: see *Nichols v Nichols*; *Carson v Wood* in **[17.14]**.

[17.25] In the same period the High Court restated the orthodox principles of resulting trusts in *Calverley v Green* (1985) 155 CLR 242: see **[16.10]**. Using the methodology imposed by that regime one can begin by looking at the direct contributions of the parties to the cost of acquisition of any property in question to establish the presumed division of beneficial interests under the doctrine of resulting trusts, and any presumption of advancement which might apply. Once the presumptions have been employed to establish that base point, the next step in an ordered analysis of the application of these various doctrines to any given facts is to consider whether there is evidence of any contrary intention, such as an intention to make a gift, or an intention forming part of an agreement or common intention between the parties which could rebut the presumption of resulting trust, or advancement if that presumption has come into play. The next step calls for an enquiry as to whether there are any grounds upon which a constructive trust might be imposed to disturb the pattern of beneficial ownership worked out through the first two stages. The issue then is, in broad terms, whether it is unconscionable in the circumstances for one or other party to retain a benefit conferred on them in the circumstances, applying *Muschinski* and *Baumgartner*. McHugh JA applied *Baumgartner* in *Hibberson v George* (1989) 12 Fam LR 723, holding, at 742, that there need not be a physical pooling of money. The emphasis placed on contributions in the Australian model, including non-financial contributions as a homemaker and parent, provides the courts here with a power to dispense justice in these disputes on the basis of matters which are susceptible to proof by reliable objective means. The English approach can send the court hounding after the false scent of 'the intentions of the parties', of which the only evidence may be the contradictory recollections or reconstructions of conversations from years gone by.

[17.26] The English approach has been applied in at least one case in Australia, *Green v Green* (1989) 17 NSWLR 343. A man, who already had one de jure and one de facto wife, induced the plaintiff, then aged 14, to come to Australia from Thailand saying he would look after her, pay her expenses and arrange for her education. He maintained a relationship with her, as he did with his other spouses, and she bore two children by him. After the birth of the first child he bought a house, saying to the girl that he had bought it 'for her'. She moved in and lived there for six years, when she moved to live in another house provided by the man, swapping with one of his sons. She made no financial contribution to either property nor had she contributed to any pooling of resources. After the man's death there was a contest over the second house between the plaintiff and his executors. The Court of Appeal, by majority, Gleeson CJ and Priestley JA, Mahoney JA dissenting, held that she was entitled to a constructive trust over the house on the basis that it had been the common intention of the parties that she should have some form of proprietary interest in that property and that she had acted to her detriment in relation to their joint lives on the faith of the mann's promises or representations.

[17.27] One can sympathise with the plaintiff in *Green v Green*, and even agree with the result. But the reasoning in the majority judgments is quite odd.[18] In coming to his decision in *Green*, Gleeson CJ cited *Muschinski v Dodds* and *Baumgartner* as authority for the proposition that equity will intervene to declare the existence of a proprietary rights where it would be unconscionable on the part of the person against whom the claim is set up or deny the equitable interest claimed. But then, from 354, referred to the passage in Lord Diplock's judgment in *Gissing v Gissing* [1971] AC 886 at 905 quoted above: see **[17.22]**. Having discussed these authorities, Gleeson CJ cited with approval the decision of the English Court of Appeal in *Grant v Edwards* [1986] Ch 638 and that of the Privy Council, in an appeal from Fiji, in *Maharaj v Jai Chand* [1986] AC 898. He cited *Grant v Edwards* as authority for the test to be applied in the case. On that authority, two elements were necessary to establish a constructive trust based on actual intention: first, that there was a common intention that both should have a beneficial interest; and second, that the claimant acted to his or her detriment on the basis of that common intention. That proposition appears to turn the principle of trusts arising from agreement or common intention on its head, requiring not that a party contribute as contemplated, that is, provide consideration, but that that party act to his or her detriment. It also appears to confuse the elements of equitable estoppel, as it is now, with those of trusts arising from agreement or common intention. On the contract point, the view expressed by Gleeson CJ also appears to be

---

18. For an example of the current approach to these matters in England, see *Hammond v Mitchell* [1992] 2 All ER 109.

contrary to the earlier view of the Court of Appeal upholding the supremacy of the bargain theory of contract in *Beaton v McDivitt* (1987) 13 NSWLR 162 (see **[13.42]**) which expressly overruled a judgment of Young J at first instance asserting an alternative detriment theory of contract. *Grant v Edwards* is dubious authority on other grounds. In coming to their decision in that case the members of the English Court of Appeal relied on *Pettitt v Pettitt*, *Gissing v Gissing*, and *Burns v Burns* [1984] Ch 317 as well as *Eves v Eves* [1975] 1 WLR 1398. *Eves v Eves* appears to be quite contrary to the two earlier House of Lords decisions and, in view of the stern injunction issued by Deane J in *Muschinski v Dodds* against using constructive trusts to satisfy idiosyncratic notions of justice and fairness, it must be regarded as a decision which has been expressly and strongly disapproved of by the High Court. *Green v Green* need not have been decided in the way it was. Had it been argued, it would have been open to the court to come to the same result on the principles of unconscionable retention of benefit, as Needham J did in *Nichols v Nichols* (SC(NSW), 12 December 1986, unreported) (see **[17.14]**), or to employ equitable estoppel in much the same way as the English Court of Appeal employed proprietary estoppel in *Pascoe v Turner* [1979] 1 WLR 431.

[17.28] The extent of the effectiveness and operation of the principles laid down by the High Court in *Muschinski v Dodds*, at least to the extent to which they apply to contributions or benefits provided in the form of non-financial services particularly as a homemaker, has also been challenged by the New South Wales Court of Appeal in *Bryson v Bryant* (1992) 29 NSWLR 188:

> The executor and sole heir of Margaret Moate claimed a beneficial interest as tenant in common in one half share in a house in Sans Souci in which Margaret Moate had lived for over 50 years as wife to her husband George. George and Margaret were married in about 1930. In about 1932 they moved onto the land, which was then vacant land and camped there while a house was built. The block of land was purchased in George's name for a consideration of £70. The transfer was not registered until 1959 for reasons unknown. Margaret participated in the building work while the house went up particularly in keeping the site clean and cooking meals for herself and George. The house was built by George and his brothers. Margaret's younger brother, the appellant, also lent some help. The only utility was one cold water tap at the front of the property. George was an electrician but was out of work at the time and remained out of work until 1935 when he got a job with the Electricity Commission. Margaret later inherited a sum of about £75 which she spent that money on some items required for the house. Margaret and George lived together in the house until about 1987 when they both went into nursing homes. Throughout the marriage Margaret did all the cooking and all the housework as well as caring for George who suffered from tuberculosis. There were no children of the marriage. Margaret died in July 1988. George died the following February. By his will made in 1975 George left the property on trust for Margaret for her life and thereafter to the Red Cross and in the event that Margaret predeceased him, to the Red Cross absolutely. At first instance Young J dismissed the claim saying that all the things done by Margaret had been done out of love and affection and that they gave rise to no equitable claim. An appeal to the Court of Appeal was dismissed, by majority. For the majority, Sheller JA, after discussion of the authorities, came to the view that in the circumstances it was not unconscionable of George's executor to retain full beneficial ownership of the house to the exclusion of Margaret's estate, notwithstanding her contribution to the acquisition, maintenance and improvement of the property over those years because, in a sense, that possible unconscionability had been satisfied by Margaret's accommodation in the house for her life. Samuels A-JA was of the view that there was no unconscionability involved, saying, at 229: 'It seems to me to follow that the fact that one spouse discharged all domestic expenses and made a generous allowance to the other does not of itself entitle that spouse to a share in

property separately acquired by the other. Equally, the fact that one spouse was the houseperson and faithfully, to quote from counsel's submissions, performed "all the cleaning, all the washing, all the shopping, sewing and cooking all the meals for the two of them for sixty years" ... would of itself entitle that spouse to a share in the separately acquired property of the other ...'. Samuels A-JA affirmed what was said at first instance that these things were done out of love and affection. He found that there was no relevant contribution there being no evidence that Margaret had contributed to the acquisition of the land. Her performance of domestic duties did not change that in his Honour's view.

Kirby P, in dissent, said he was of the view that the remedy of constructive trust was appropriate in the case and that contributions of this kind could give rise to an equity recognisable if need be by the remedy of constructive trust — saying at 204: 'It is unconscionable that Mr Moate's estate should take the entirety of the value of the matrimonial home to be disposed of exclusively according to (George's) wishes and with complete disregard for (Margaret's) wishes as expressed in her will providing benefits to her brother. If she had an interest in the matrimonial home, both for financial contribution and domestic services therein (as I believe she did) it was an interest which would be protected by constructive trust, declared by the court'. In coming to that view Kirby P said that the contribution of a wife as a homemaker or parent should not be regarded as inferior, referring to *Mallett v Mallett* (1984) 156 CLR 605.

An application for special leave was refused by a bench comprising Dawson, Gaudron and McHugh JJ. In refusing leave their Honours said that, while they did not necessarily agree with the view of the majority of the Court of Appeal, the facts were too thin to justify a grant of leave.

[17.28] *Bryson v Bryant* leaves unanswered the question of the role and significance of non-financial contributions, particularly as homemaker, to the improvement and maintenance of property. The approach taken by Kirby P may yet prevail and be taken as the more correct statement of principle from *Bryson v Bryant*. The approach taken by the trial judge and the majority of the Court of Appeal in *Bryson v Bryant* must also be considered in the light of the approach taken in Canada, for example in *Peter v Beblow* (1993) 101 DLR (4th) 621 in which McLachlin J expressed his view of the role of non-financial contributions:

> [It] is no longer tenable in Canada, either from the point of view of logic or authority ... to distinguish domestic services from other contributions. The notion that household and child care services are not worthy of recognition by the court fails to recognize the fact that these services are of great value, not only to the family, but to the other spouse.

In the same case Cory J observed, at 633–4, that the granting of relief by way of a personal judgment or a property interest to the provider of domestic services should adequately reflect the fact that the income and earning capacity and the ability to acquire assets by one party has been enhanced by the unpaid domestic services of the other. Echoes of these views can be seen in the judgment of Kirby P in *Bryson v Bryant*, at 203–4, where his Honour discussed the treatment by the law of contributions by way of domestic assistance:

> It is important that the 'brave new world of unconscionability' should not lead the court back to family property law of twenty years ago by the back door of a pre-occupation with contributions, particularly financial contributions, made by claimants of beneficial interests and at the time of the acquisition of the property in question; ... nor should the 'brave new world' be confined to helping farmers' and bee-keepers' wives, leaving others, who have provided 'women's work' over their adult lifetime to be told condescendingly, by a mostly male judiciary, that their services must be regarded as

'freely given labour' or only or, catalogued as attributable solely to a rather one-way and quaintly described 'love and affection', when property interests come to be distributed: see *Van Gervan v Fenton* (1992) 109 ALR 283 at 298.

In the event, Kirby P based his decision in favour of Mrs Moate's executor on her contributions of a financial nature without seeing the need to decide the matter solely on the question of her contributions by way of domestic services. While the question of the value of non-financial contributions remains vexed after *Bryson v Bryant*, the case stands as authority for the proposition that equitable interests in the nature of a right to claim an interest by way of resulting or constructive trust are heritable. The right does not die with the person initially entitled to bring the claim. It survives the benefit of his or her estate: per Kirby P, at 211; *Scott v Pauly* (1917) 24 CLR 274; *Lempriere v Ware* (1871) 2 VR (E).

Capital accounts and revenue accounting in domestic property disputes

[17.29] The remedy of constructive trust in domestic property cases operates as a proprietary remedy in that it effectively declares that a party has some right or interest in particular property. It is, in a sense, a capital remedy. A finding of such a trust will not preclude the taking of accounts between the parties on what might be called revenue items, such as mortgage instalments and other outgoings on the property, repair costs (as opposed to capital expenditure on renovations), rent received, and any notional revenue benefits, such as the benefit of occupation to the party who remains in the house, and, if warranted, rent paid elsewhere by the party excluded. These revenue accounts are adjusted in accordance with the general principles governing accounts between co-tenants: *Bernard v Josephs* [1982] Ch 391. Co-owners are entitled to the equitable remedy of account for rents and profits received against their fellows both under the general law: *Strelly v Winsor* (1685) 1 Vern 297; 23 ER 480, and by statute,[19] with an allowance made for expenditure on improvements: *Squire v Rogers* (1979) 27 ALR 330. The allowance for expenditure on improvements is limited. Where one co-tenant has paid for improvements which have enhanced the value of the property the other tenant will not be entitled to a proportionate share in that increase in value without making an allowance for the other co-tenant's expenditure, but the improver can get no more than the cost of the improvements: *Watson v Gas* (1881) 51 LJ (Ch) 480; *Brickwood v Young* (1905) 2 CLR 387, although he or she may be entitled to all the rents and profits derived from the improvements depending upon the circumstances of the case: *Squire v Rogers*. It is not clear whether a co-tenant would also be entitled to claim an account for outgoings other than mortgage payments, such as rates and body corporate levies, although that would seem a natural corollary of the obligation to account for rents and profits received. Where the mortgage payments relate to moneys borrowed for improvements, the improver may not be entitled to claim the full proportion of those outgoings from a non-improver who will not share equally in the profits flowing from that expenditure. A claim for rent saved by occupation of the jointly owned property would appear to be on weaker ground, especially where both (or all) the co-tenants occupy the premises under intimate domestic circumstances.[20] Where capital contributions consist of payments towards the purchase price of the property as well as the cost of improvements it may be nec-

---

19. (1705) 4 & 5 Anne c 3 s 27 (a provision repealed in New South Wales by the Imperial Acts Application Act 1969 (NSW), s 5).
20. MG&L, para [2512].

essary to separate the two figures in view of the way in which contributions towards improvements are treated under the general rules governing accounts between co-tenants. The normal rule in such cases is that the improver can only get the lesser of his or her costs or the enhanced value due to the improvements: *Squire v Rogers*. The right of the major contributor to claim a share in the residue of the proceeds of the property proportionate to his or her contribution will depend upon the equities of the particular case. In *Muschinski v Dodds*, Deane J did not think it appropriate to make such an order in favour of Mrs Muschinski. When discussing the rights of the parties to the residue of the proceeds, the profit on their joint investment, Deane J drew no distinction between contributions towards the purchase price and payments for improvements.

[17.30] Where a claim is brought on the basis of moneys spent on improvements to another person's property, the principles in *Squire v Rogers* will not apply. The claimant will not be a co-tenant, simply an improver. In such a case the court may consider it appropriate to give the improver the cost of the improvements, that is, the value of the money spent, or the increase in value of the property arising from the improvement, depending upon the circumstances of the case. Any such order, which is essentially a personal remedy against the titleholder, will usually be secured by the granting of an equitable charge over the property in question: see, for example, *Hibberson v George* (1989) 12 Fam LR 725. Some of the issues arising from this accounting process are illustrated in *Breen v Plumb* (CA(NSW), 3 March 1992, unreported):

> A man who owned a house at Bateman's Bay allowed his daughter and her de facto husband to live with him in the house under an arrangement whereby an extra storey was added to the house. The addition was paid for by the young couple by a loan secured on the property. Sometime later, after a clash between the plaintiff and the de facto, the plaintiff left the house. In subsequent proceedings Young J held that the plaintiff was obliged to compensate the defendants for the value of the improvement while they had to pay him an occupation fee for their exclusive occupation of the house after his enforced departure and compensate him for rent he had to pay elsewhere while excluded from the house. That decision was upheld on appeal, although there were some adjustments to the figures, most notably reduction of the sum payable to the defendants for the value of the improvement on the basis that the property was saddled with an $8,000 mortgage. On the final analysis the plaintiff was owed more by the defendants than he was obliged to pay them and he was awarded costs.

17–5 Third Parties as Constructive Trustees

[17.31] Ordinarily liability as a constructive trustee can only be incurred by someone directly connected with the plaintiff, either as trustee, fiduciary or through some other relationship. A decree of constructive trust will not be awarded against some third party or stranger to the trust or fiduciary relationship unless the stranger can be shown to have engaged in conduct justifying such a grave step. Such conduct has been categorised as conduct falling within one of the three cases recognised by Lord Selborne LC in *Barnes v Addy* (1874) 9 Ch App 244. In that case decree of constructive trust was sought against solicitors who advised a trustee who entrusted funds to an agent. The funds were lost and a claim was brought against the solicitors. It was held they were not liable. Lord Selborne stated the principle, at 251:

That responsibility (that is, of the trustee) may no doubt in equity be extended to others who are not properly trustees, if they are found either making themselves trustees de son tort, or actually participating in any fraudulent conduct on the part of the trustee to the injury of the cestui que trust. But, on the other hand, strangers are not to be made constructive trustees merely because they act as agents of trustees in transactions within their legal powers, transactions, perhaps, of which a Court of Equity may disapprove, unless those agents receive and become chargeable with some part of the trust property, or unless they assist with knowledge in a dishonest and fraudulent design on the part of the trustees.

Under that formulation three categories of third party constructive trustees are recognised: (a) trustees de son tort; (b) third parties who receive and become chargeable with trust property; and (c) third parties who assist with knowledge in a dishonest and fraudulent design. The remedy of constructive trust applied on these principles differs from tracing. The constructive trust is employed essentially as a personal remedy against the third party held liable. Tracing is a remedy based on rights of property. In *Re Montagu's Settlement Trusts* (1985) [1987] Ch 264 [1992] 4 All ER 308, [1992] 4 All ER at 329–30, Sir Robert Megarry V-C said that tracing is primarily a means of determining rights to property, whereas the imposition of a constructive trust against a third party in receipt of trust property creates personal obligations that go beyond mere property rights. Apart from the claim against an alleged trustee de son tort, where the claim is essentially one for compensation, the intermeddling by the supposed trustee having caused some loss to the trust, these cases are concerned with personal claims against the parties where the trust property itself can no longer be traced. In cases involving knowing receipt of trust property by a third party a claim based on the principle in *Barnes v Addy* is a personal claim against the alleged receiver and not a tracing claim against the property in that person's hands. In a claim against a person who has provided knowing assistance in a breach of trust or fiduciary duty the action is founded in the necessary assumption that the third party has never had possession of trust property and could only be liable on a personal basis. In a claim brought against a party for knowing receipt the plaintiff may well have both a proprietary claim by way of tracing as well as a personal claim under *Barnes v Addy*. In most of the cases in which the principle has been invoked the property is no longer traceable having either passed from the hands of the third party receiver or otherwise been inextricably mixed with other property so that the remedy of tracing is no longer available.

Trustees de son tort

[17.32] This means a trustee of his or her own wrong: one who intermeddles with trust property without proper authority and is held liable to account for any loss which results. Where someone assumes control of the trust property and purports to act as trustee without appointment that person will be considered in law a trustee de son tort: a trustee of his or her own wrong. In *Re Barney* [1892] 2 Ch 276, a widow who was trustee of her deceased husband's estate continued to carry on the business run by her husband without authority to do so under the will. Two friends of the husband agreed to assist her by looking after accounts and expenditure to maintain relations with the bank. The business failed and the children, the other beneficiaries under the will, sought to have the friends made liable as constructive trustees. Kekewich J dismissed the claim on the basis that the two friends did not have sufficient control of the trust property, in the sense that they did not have power to pay money away at their discretion. While they had assisted the trustee in the commission of a breach of trust they had not done so with knowledge that the breach was dishonest. In coming to this decision Kekewich J stated the principle in these terms: 'I apprehend that when the law says that a man is responsible as a trustee for the money under his control, it means money which he can, if he will, put into his own pocket or pay away as he pleases to someone else'. It is not necessary to prove dishonesty on the part of the intermeddler: even someone who intervenes with the best of intentions but without authority will be liable. A person who presumes to act as a trustee 'could not be heard to say, for his own benefit, that he had no right to act as a trustee': *Lyell v Kennedy* (1889) App Cas 437 at 459 per Lord Selborne citing Turner LJ in *Life Association of Scotland v Siddall* (1861) 3 De GF & J 58: 45 ER 800. This category differs from that of third parties who receive and become chargeable because the intermeddler claims not to act on his or her own behalf but on behalf of the beneficiaries and because the obligation to account is different, with the trustee de son tort only liable for any losses incurred through his or her interference. Persons falling within this category are not protected from liability by any statute of limitations: *Taylor v Davies* [1920] AC 636.[21]

[17.33] A person employed as an agent by a trustee will not be liable as a trustee de son tort so long as the agent's activities are confined to acts that fall within the agency: *Morgan v Stephens* (1861) 3 Griff 226 at 236, per Stewart V-C; 66 ER 392 at 397. In *Mara v Browne* [1896] 1 Ch 199, a solicitor who acted for two trustees in respect of mortgage investments made by them which were found to be in breach of trust was held not to be liable as constructive trustee for a loss incurred as a result of the investments. The solicitor escaped liability even though the investments were made on his advice; he took some of the funds invested into his own bank account before they were on lent and advanced a portion of the sum lent out of his own money. The investments were found to be improperly speculative and inadequately secured.[22] A person who does not necessarily receive trust property but is in a position to exercise control over it can be held liable as a trustee de son tort, as in *Re Barney*. Where the alleged constructive trustee is a solicitor or other agent it will be relevant whether that agent acts in accordance with the instructions of a principal and whether the activities of the agent fall within the normal course of conduct of business expected of such an agent.[23] A banker who rolled over invested moneys in the absence of instructions otherwise was held not to be a trustee de son tort in *DFC New Zealand Ltd v Goddard* [1992] 2 NZLR 445. The relationship between the investor and the bank was that of debtor and creditor, not one of trust. The bank lacked sufficient control to become a trustee of its own wrong.

'Knowing receipt' and 'knowing assistance' cases

[17.34] Modern consideration of the application of the principles stated in *Barnes v Addy* has been much influenced by the decision of Peter Gibson J in *Baden, Delvaux and Lecuit and others v Société Générale pour favoriser le Développement du Commerce et de l'Industrie en France SA* [1983] BCLC ChD 325 and [1992] 4 All ER 161; on appeal [1992] 4 All ER 279 (*Baden Delvaux*). In that case a claim on these grounds was brought against Société Générale (SG) for paying out moneys deposited with it by the Bahamas Commonwealth Bank Ltd (BCB), those moneys having been first deposited with BCB by entities controled by the notorious fraudster Robert Lee

---

21. RP Austin, 'Constructive Trusts' in PD Finn (ed), *op cit*, at pp 205–6.
22. See also *Williams-Ashman v Price* [1942] 1 Ch 219.
23. RP Austin, 'Constructive Trusts' in PD Finn, *op cit*, at 209–10.

Vesco. SG paid the moneys out on instructions from BCB. In the circumstances, SG was held not to be liable as a constructive trustee to those whose money was lost as a result. Peter Gibson J held that to be liable as a constructive trustee because of 'knowing assistance' in a breach of trust four requirements had to be satisfied: (a) a trust or fiduciary relationship had to be shown to exist; (b) there had to be a dishonest or fraudulent design on the part of a trustee or fiduciary involving more that misfeasance; (c) the third party had to be shown to have assisted in the dishonest design. This was a matter of fact and while the assistance had to be of more than minimal importance, there was no requirement that the assistance be shown to have actually caused the loss; and, (d) the stranger or the third party had to possess the requisite knowledge. To satisfy the requirement of knowledge it had to be shown that the third party knew that a trust existed, although it was not necessary to show knowledge of all its details; and that a fraudulent design existed, but not necessary the whole design. Peter Gibson J considered submissions based on five different levels of knowledge [1983] BCLC at 436 those levels are:

(i) actual knowledge;

(ii) a wilful shutting of one's eyes to the obvious;

(iii) a wilful and reckless failure to make enquiries that an honest and reasonable man would have made;

(iv) knowledge of circumstances which would have indicated the facts to an honest and reasonable man; or,

(v) knowledge of circumstances which would have put an honest and reasonable man on inquiry.

As far as the last two levels of knowledge were concerned Peter Gibson J was of the view that where a stranger was put on inquiry, and inquiry was made and answered, the only relevant question was whether the answer provided actual knowledge or would have put an honest and reasonable person on further inquiry. Where a stranger put on inquiry made no inquiries, the court had to determine on the balance of probabilities what answers would have been elicited by proper inquiries and whether they would have put a person on further inquiry.

[17.35] The application of these principles and the operation of the five levels of knowledge considered by Peter Gibson J in the *Baden Delvaux* case were reviewed by the English Court of Appeal in *Belmont Finance Corp Ltd v Williams Furniture Ltd (No 1)* [1979] 1 All ER 118 at 130, 136: [1979] ChD 250 at 267. On the question of knowledge, Buckley LJ said, at 267, that a stranger could be made liable for knowing assistance if possessed of knowledge in the first three categories identified in *Baden Delvaux* but not for merely possessing constructive notice. Goff LJ expressed a similar view, at 275, at least in cases involving knowing assistance in a dishonest and fraudulent design. *Belmont Finance* was a case involving knowing assistance. In *Re Montagu's Settlement Trusts* [1987] Ch 264 [1992] 4 All ER 308, Sir Robert Megarry V-C, considered these principles in the context of a knowing receipt case. The 10th Duke of Manchester had received and held heirlooms which had previously been settled on a trust from which they were not to be released to the Duke beneficially. The trustees, in breach of the trust, had released items covered by the settlement to the Duke and some had been lost. The question in Sir Robert Megarry's view as to whether a third party could be held liable on these grounds turned essentially on whether the conscience of the recipient was sufficiently effected to justify the imposition of a trust. That question turned in large part on the knowledge of the recipient and not on notice to that person. The levels of knowledge which could render a person liable as a third party receiving were in his view, categories (i), (ii) and (iii) of the categories

331

identified in *Baden Delvaux*. The Vice-Chancellor was not convinced that knowledge of types (iv) and (v) in the *Baden* list would suffice to establish liability for knowing receipt. He referred with approval to the judgments of Sachs and Edmund Davies LJJ in *Carl Zeiss Stiftung v Herbert Smith & Co (No 2)* [1969] 2 Ch 276. In that case Sachs LJ expressed the view, at 298, that mere notice was not enough. A further element had to be proved: that of dishonesty or of consciously acting improperly, so that an innocent, even if negligent, failure to enquire is not enough. Edmund-Davies LJ spoke of a 'want of probity', at 301, and said that nothing short of it will do, not even gross negligence. The *Carl Zeiss* case involved an action brought by the East German Carl Zeiss company, which claimed to be the original and genuine Carl Zeiss business, against the London solicitors for the West German Carl Zeiss, seeking orders that the solicitors held certain moneys which they had received from their client on a constructive trust. The Court of Appeal dismissed the claim holding that notice of a claim against a solicitor's client was not sufficient to amount to notice of a trust or of a misapplication of trust moneys sufficient to make the solicitors liable as constructive trustees especially where unsolved and difficult questions of law and fact remained to be settled. In *Re Montagu*, Megarry V-C thought the carelessness involved in such circumstances would not normally amount to a want of probity (that is, uprightness, or honesty) on the part of the recipient and therefore a third party who received trust property ought not be held liable as constructive trustee in such circumstances.

Third parties who receive and become chargeable with trust property

[17.36] To be held liable as a constructive trustee on this basis it is not enough that the third party merely receive trust property. That person must also 'become chargeable' with the trust property, in the sense that the third party must give a 'beneficial' receipt for the property, and not merely an 'administrative' receipt.[24] Accordingly, a bank will not be liable as a party who knowingly receives trust property under this heading unless the bank in some way appropriates moneys deposited with it to its own account. There has not been clear discussion of this principle in Australia but the question of knowing receipt, and in particular, the level of knowledge required to hold a recipient liable has been the subject of discussion in a number of cases in England and New Zealand.

[17.37] In *Lipkin Gorman v Karpnale Ltd* (1986) [1992] 4 All ER 331, claims were brought against a gambling club and a bank in respect of losses arising from a solicitor's gambling addiction. Alliott J, having discussed the authorities cited above held, at 349, that a person would be liable as a constructive trustee as the knowing recipient of trust property if, with want of probity on his or her part, he or she had actual or constructive knowledge that the money or other property being received was being paid out in breach of trust. In this sense Alliott J held that all five levels of knowledge identified in *Baden Delvaux* were relevant in a case involving knowing receipt, but added the requirement stated by Megarry V-C in *Re Montagu* that the third party also be shown to have acted without probity. In *Eagle Trust plc v SPC Securities Ltd* (1991) [1992] 4 All ER 488, Vinelott J held that a third party would only be liable as a constructive trustee of money which that person received in payment of a commercial liability and which had already passed through his hands if it was possible to show

24. See *Westpac Banking Corporation v Savin* [1985] 2 NZLR 41 at 69, per Richmond J.

that that third party knew that the money was misapplied trust money, in the sense that he or she had knowledge within one of the first three categories from the *Baden Delvaux* list. Conversely a person would not be liable merely because he or she had reason to suspect that there had been a breach of trust disentitling the trustee to make the payment. Beyond those three levels of knowledge Vinelott J considered that a third party could be liable if, in the absence of any evidence or explanation by the defendant, the circumstances were such that knowledge could be inferred. Such knowledge could be inferred, in his view, if the circumstances were such that an honest and reasonable man would have inferred that the monies were probably trust monies and were being misapplied, and either would not have accepted them or would have kept them separate until he had satisfied himself that the payer was entitled to use them in discharge of the liability. These questions came before the English Court of Appeal, albeit on an application for a *Mareva* injunction, in *Polly Peck International plc v Nadir* [1992] 4 All ER 769. In that case Scott, LJ, with whom Lord Donaldson MR and Stocker LJ agreed, said, at 777, that liability as a constructive trustee in a 'knowing receipt case' did not require that the misapplication of the trust funds be fraudulent, it did, however, require that the defendant should have knowledge that the funds were trust funds and that they were being misapplied. As far as the tests of knowledge were concerned Scott LJ was of the view that actual knowledge and wilful and reckless failure to make such inquiries as an honest and reasonable man would have made (categories (i) and (iii) of the *Baden Delvaux* list) would suffice. He expressed some doubt as to whether liability could arise where the defendant was shown to have no more than knowledge of facts which would have put an honest and reasonable man on inquiry (*Baden Delvaux* (v)) but said that he did not consider the case before him, being an appeal on an order for a *Mareva* injunction, as the right occasion for settling the issue. He did say, however, that the various categories of mental state identified in *Baden Delvaux* are not rigid categories with clear and precise boundaries. One category, he said, may merge into another.

[17.38] In New Zealand in the Court of Appeal in *Westpac Banking Corporation v Savin* [1985] 2 NZLR 41, Richardson and McMullin JJ expressed the opinion, *obiter*, that in knowing receipt cases liability could arise where it was shown that the defendant had knowledge within any of the five categories identified in *Baden Delvaux*. Richmond J, *obiter*, also expressed preference for the views stated in the English Court of Appeal in the *Belmont Finance* cases and, in particular, for the proposition that an agent cannot be held liable as a recipient of trust property unless it can also be shown that the agent acted dishonestly. It would not be enough, in that formulation, merely to prove that the recipient had acted negligently. The approach taken by Richmond J was followed in *Equiticorp Industries Group Ltd v Hawkins* [1991] 3 NZLR 700 at 728 were Wylie J held that the five types of knowledge identified in *Baden Delvaux* applied to 'knowing receipt' cases. He said that in knowing assistance cases only types (i) to (iii) would apply unless a lack of probity could be shown. In coming to that conclusion he also said, at 728: 'I adhere to the concept of want of probity. In my opinion mere carelessness, neglect or oversight which is not wilful or reckless, is not unconscionable, if it were we must all stand condemned. Who would cast the first stone? I prefer the more conservative approach taken by so many judges in England since *Baden Delvaux*, by Sir Clifford Richmond in *Westpac v Savin* and by Tompkins J in *Marr v Arabco* [*Marr v Arabco Traders Ltd* (1987) 1 NZBLC 102, 732]'. In *Marshall Futures Ltd v Marshall* [1992] 1 NZLR 316, Tipping J also expressed a preference for liability in knowing receipt cases be limited to circumstances where it could be shown that the recipient had knowledge within any of the five categories in *Baden Delvaux* although he noted, at 326, the state of the law at this point had not been settled by the Court of

Appeal in a binding way. Both Tipping J in *Marshall Futures* and Wylie J in *Equiticorp v Hawkins* rejected the earlier decision of *Powell v Thompson* [1991] 1 NZLR 597 in which Thomas J had approached a knowing receipt case on the basis of underlying unconscionability or unjust enrichment, an approach which appears to have been misconceived. The division of opinion in New Zealand was noted by Henry J in *Springfield Acres Ltd (in liq) v Abacus (Hong Kong) Ltd* [1994] 3 NZLR 502. Henry J expressed a preference for the approach taken by Wylie J in *Equiticorp v Hawkins* that in knowing receipt and dealing cases a third party would be liable if shown to possess knowledge within any of the five categories identified in *Baden Delvaux* while in knowing assistance cases only categories (i), (ii) and (iii) could suffice. These questions were considered by the Supreme Court of Western Australia in *Ninety Five Pty Ltd (liq) v Banque Nationalè de Paris* [1988] WAR 132. In that case a company's own money had been used in purchasing its own shares, in breach of the then s 67 of the Companies Act 1961 (WA), after completing a circle involving a number of share transactions. In the process those moneys had come into the hands of the defendant bank. Smith J found the bank liable as a third party receiving trust property. In coming to that decision he said he did not think it essential to prove want of probity on the part of a third party who receives trust property.

[17.39] People falling into this category of third party receivers have sometimes been lumped together with trustees de son tort but on the limitations question alone it seems important to distinguish between the two. That limitation question is by no means clear. In *Soar v Ashwell* [1893] 2 QB 390 at 405, Kay LJ was prepared to exempt from the protection of any limitation 'the stranger who has concurred with the trustee in committing a breach of trust, and has taken possession of the trust property, knowing that it was trust property, and has not duly discharged himself of it by handing it over to the proper trustees or to the persons absolutely entitled to it'. A person fitting into this category must have given a beneficial receipt for the trust property, as opposed to a merely administrative one. A bank would not therefore not fall into this category automatically. Once it can be shown that a third party has received trust property, purportedly as beneficial owner of that property, but not as a bona fide purchaser without notice, the third party will hold the property on the original trusts, subject to any defence of change of position. The operation of these principles in practice can be seen in two New Zealand decisions with similar facts but different results. In *Lankshear v ANZ Banking Group (New Zealand) Ltd* [1993] 1 NZLR 481, a bank was held liable for knowing receipt where it had received money from a customer, a cheque for NZ$80,000, made out to the customer, which were moneys invested in a property development venture by a woman who was entering into a joint venture with the customer. The money was paid into an account already $53,000 overdrawn. Shortly after receiving the money the bank terminated the customer's overdraft facility and called up his loans, purporting to appropriate the money in the process. The bank's diary notes showed that the manager of the bank knew that the customer had a partner who was to inject $100,000 into a particular development and specified that as the purpose for which the money was to be used. *Lankshear* is useful in distinguishing the two types of case. In taking the money required to pay out the overdraft, the bank was giving a beneficial receipt. In allowing the customer to draw on the balance of the moneys for purposes other than those for which the money was paid, the bank gave only an administrative receipt and could only be said to have provided 'knowing assistance'. In *Nimmo v Westpac Banking Corporation* [1993] 3 NZLR 218, moneys placed with an investment company were banked by that company with Westpac in New Zealand and subsequently transferred to an account with Westpac in Sydney operated by the company. A director of the investment company embezzled most of the money in that account. Westpac was held not to be liable as a constructive trustee. It had not 'received' the moneys in any relevant sense and lacked sufficient knowledge to be liable for 'knowing assistance'.

Assisting with knowledge in a dishonest and fraudulent design by a trustee

[17.40] To establish liability under this principle it is necessary to show, first, a trust or other fiduciary relationship involving trust, second, a dishonest and fraudulent design on the part of the 'trustee', third, assistance by a stranger in that design, and, fourth and finally, sufficient 'knowledge' on the part of the stranger.[25] In Australia the first requirement will be satisfied by showing an existing trust or fiduciary relationship.[26] The second element begs at least one question: is 'fraud' used in the common law sense, that is, involving conscious dishonesty, or in the equitable sense, that is, breach of an equitable obligation. The fact that the words are used conjunctively appears to suggest the former, although the context suggests the latter. In *Consul Developments Pty Ltd v DPC Estates Pty Ltd* (1975) 132 CLR 373 at 396, Gibbs J said that dishonesty and fraud included dealing with trust property by a trustee in a manner which he knew to be inconsistent with the trusts. In *Belmont Finance Corp Ltd v Williams Furniture Ltd* [1979] Ch 250 at 267, Buckley J said that 'dishonest' and 'fraudulent' meant just that and the words should be given no other meaning. Goff LJ, in the same case agreed saying, at 274, that it would be necessary to plead and prove dishonesty. There is no clear view from other commentators.[27] Lord Selborne's use of the word 'dishonest' suggests that, at the least, the 'design' must involve a conscious breach of trust. 'Assistance' will be largely a matter of fact. This element is tied to the fourth point of knowledge; it is difficult to see how a third party could be held liable as a constructive trustee without that party knowing that his efforts were 'assisting' in a breach of trust. In *Royal Brunei Airlines Sdn Bhd v Tan* [1995] 3 WLR 64, Lord Nicholls, in giving the advice of the Privy Council in an appeal from Brunei, criticised what he described as a tendency to cite and apply Lord Selborne's formulation as though it were a statute rather than examining the underlying principle behind holding a third party liable for some breach of trust. On the question of the meaning of 'dishonest and fraudulent design' his Lordship said:

> Drawing the threads together, their Lordships' overall conclusion is that dishonesty is a necessary ingredient of accessory liability. It is also a sufficient ingredient. A liability in equity to make good resulting loss attaches to a person who dishonestly procures or assists in a breach of trust or fiduciary obligation. It is not necessary that, in addition, the trustee or fiduciary was acting dishonestly, although this will usually be so where the third party who is assisting him is acting dishonestly.

[17.41] The level of 'knowledge' required to render a stranger assisting in a breach of trust liable for that breach has been a matter of some controversy, although more so in England than Australia. Unlike a third party who receives and becomes chargeable with trust property, in which case the normal rules as to actual or constructive notice of the trust will suffice to fix the recipient with liability, a stranger who merely assists has a fair claim to be treated more leniently.

---

25. *Baden Delvaux & Lecuit v Société Générale pour favoriser le Développement du Commerce et de l'Industrie en France SA* ('*Baden Delvaux*') [1983] BCLC 325.
26. *Consul Developments Pty Ltd v DPC Estates Pty Ltd* (1975) 132 CLR 373 at 397, per Gibbs J.
27. *Jacobs'*, para [1338]; Ford & Lee, para 2222.

In *Consul Development Pty Ltd v DPC Estates Pty Ltd* (1975) 132 CLR 373, the respondent company, DPC Estates, which was owned and controlled by a solicitor named Walton, carried on a property development business. Robert Grey was employed as manager of DPC Estates and was also a director. Grey's tasks included selecting suitable sites for development. Grey told Clowes, an articled clerk employed by Walton, about a number of properties which would make good investments. Grey said that DPC Estates was in financial difficulties and could not afford to invest in them. Clowes confirmed from other sources that DPC was in some difficulty. Consul Developments Pty Ltd, Clowes' family company, purchased the properties. DPC Estates later claimed that both Grey and Consul Developments held their interests in the properties on constructive trust for it. Both claims were dismissed by Hope J at first instance but were upheld by the Court of Appeal. Consul appealed successfully against that decision to the High Court. Stephen J, with whom Barwick CJ agreed, held that 'knowledge' within the second leg of *Barnes v Addy* did not extend to constructive knowledge and that apart from actual knowledge of the breach of trust, or a wilful shutting of the eyes to the obvious,[28] a stranger to the trust would only be liable as a constructive trustee if he had knowledge of circumstances telling of a breach of fiduciary duty. Gibbs J said that the principle in *Barnes v Addy* applied equally to a third party assisting a fiduciary in breach of his fiduciary duty, and that 'dishonest and fraudulent design' encompassed any breach of trust or fiduciary obligation. Gibbs J also considered that it would be going too far to hold a third party liable for an innocent failure to make enquiry when the circumstances would have put an honest man on inquiry and that apart from actual knowledge of the breach, or a wilful shutting of the eyes to the obvious, a stranger participating in a breach of trust or fiduciary duty would only be liable if he had knowledge of all the facts, in which case he could not escape liability by his own moral obtuseness. McTiernan J dissented on the ground that he considered Clowes to have had actual knowledge of the breach.

[17.42] In England, in *Selangor United Rubber Estates Ltd v Cradock (No 3)* [1968] 1 WLR 1555 and *Karak Rubber Co Ltd v Burden* [1972] 1 All ER 1210 claims were brought against banks on these grounds where the bank in each case had been used as a conduit in part of a chain of transactions whereby a company's moneys had been used to purchase shares in that company. In *Selangor Rubber*, Ungoed-Thomas J held the bank could be liable as a constructive trustee if it knowingly assisted in a fraudulent and dishonest disposition of the trust property. The knowledge required in such a case was knowledge of circumstances which would indicate to an honest, reasonable man that a dishonest and fraudulent design was being committed. In *Karak*, Brightman J held that knowledge in this context meant actual or constructive knowledge of circumstances indicating to a reasonable banker that such a design was being committed. In *Carl Zeiss Stiftung v Herbert Smith & Co (No 2)* [1969] 2 Ch 276, the Court of Appeal took a different approach, as mentioned above, saying that a third party had to be shown to have acted dishonestly or with a want of probity to be held liable on this count. The approach taken in the rubber cases to the required knowledge in knowing assistance cases, to the extent that it suggests that knowledge of facts which would put a reasonable person on enquiry would be sufficient, must be regarded as having been rejected by the High Court in *Consul Developments*. Most of the other English and New Zealand authority on these issues has been handed down since *Consul Develpoments* and the effect of those discussions on the law in Australia remains to be seen.

---

28. *Carl Zeiss Stiftung v Herbert Smith & Co (No 2)* [1969] 2 Ch 276 at 298, per Sachs LJ, quoted with approval by Stephen J at 409–10.

[17.43] The English courts have had some opportunity to review these matters since the rubber cases. In *Lipkin Gorman v Karpnale Ltd* (1986) [1992] 4 All ER 331, Alliott J held that a stranger would not become liable for knowing assistance in a breach of trust unless the stranger could be proved subjectively to have known of the trustee's fraudulent scheme when rendering assistance or had shut his or her eyes to the obvious or had wilfully and recklessly failed to make such inquiries as an honest and reasonable man would have made. In other words, Alliott J held that liability for knowing assistance required a case that fell within the first three levels of knowledge in *Baden Delvaux*. In *Lipkin Gorman*, while the gambling club was held not liable as a stranger assisting, the bank was held to have knowledge in the third category, that is to say it was found to have wilfully and recklessly to have failed to make such inquiries as an honest and reasonable banker would have made. In *Agip (Africa) Ltd v Jackson* (1990) [1992] 4 All ER 451, the English Court of Appeal, Fox LJ with whom Butler-Sloss and Beldam LJJ agreed, indicated acceptance of the *Baden Delvaux* formulation but noted it was only an explanation of the general principle and was not necessarily comprehensive. The relevant enquiry, in their Lordships' view, was what the defendant actually knew. In that case an oil company was defrauded by its accountants who diverted money through other entities. The defendants were held liable. Their knowledge included knowledge that a large amount of money was involved: over US $10 million in under two years; it had all come along the same path; the money originated with Agip, an oil company with operations in Tunisia and the destination for the money was a firm of jewellers in France. In the circumstances the defendants must have known that they were laundering money, and that they were helping their clients to make arrangements to conceal dispositions of money which had a degree of impropriety which neither they nor their clients could afford to have disclosed. Despite that knowledge they made no inquiries at all. In *Eagle Trust plc v SPC Securities Ltd* (1991) [1992] 4 All ER 489 at 497, Vinelott J restated the proposition that there had to be something amounting to dishonesty or want of probity on the part of the stranger before liability could be found in a knowing assistance case. Constructive notice of the fraudulent design was not enough, although knowledge might be inferred in the absence of evidence by the alleged trustee if such knowledge would have been imputed to an honest and reasonable man. In making that finding Vinelott J applied *Agip (Africa) Ltd v Jackson* saying that knowledge might be inferred, at least in civil cases, if knowledge falling within categories (iv) and (v) of the *Baden Delvaux* classification were established and the trustee failed to give evidence or offer any explanation of his or her conduct. If the circumstances were such that an honest and reasonable man would have appreciated that he was assisting in a dishonest breach of trust, the court may infer from the defendant's silence that he either appreciated the fact or that he wilfully shut his eyes to the obvious or wilfully and recklessly failed to may inquiries from fear of what he might learn. In giving his reasons in *Eagle Trust plc*, Vinelott J referred to the judgment of Fox LJ in *Agip (Africa) Ltd v Jackson*, and noted that Fox LJ did not address the question of whether dishonesty or want of probity had to be shown in order to render the defendant stranger liable for knowing assistance. Vinelott J said, however, that these matters were implicit in Fox LJ's judgment, in that he accepted the conclusion of the trial judge, Millet J, that in a 'knowing assistance' case something amounting to dishonesty or want of probity on the part of the defendant must be shown.

[17.44] In Vinelott J's view, in order to make a defendant liable as constructive trustee on the basis of knowing assistance the plaintiff had to show that the defendant knew, in one of the senses set out in categories (i), (ii) or (iii) of the *Baden Delvaux* categorisation that the moneys were trust moneys being misapplied; or that the circumstances were such that, in the absence of any evidence or explanation by the defendant, that knowledge could be inferred. That inference might be drawn if the circumstances were such that an honest and reasonable man would have inferred that the moneys were properly trust moneys and were being misapplied and would either have not accepted them or would have kept them separate until he had satisfied himself that the payment was proper. In *Polly Peck International plc v Nadir (No 2)* [1992] 4 All ER 769, the English Court of Appeal said that before a defendant could be held liable as a constructive trustee for knowing assistance in the misapplication of trust property something amounting to dishonesty or want of probity had to shown. A stranger could not be held liable for knowing assistance in a fraudulent breach of trust unless knowledge of the fraudulent design could be imputed to him or her. Where liability was sought to be imposed on the basis that the defendant had received and dealt with the trust property in some way, the misapplication of funds did not have to be fraudulent but it did have to be shown that the defendant had had knowledge, whether actual or constructive, that the funds were trust funds and that they were being misapplied.

[17.45] This plethora of authority makes it slightly difficult to identify the relevant principle. In view of the High Court's decision in *Consul Developments v DPC Estates*, to reject the knowledge tests proposed in the Rubber cases for knowing assistance, the approach taken in New Zealand by Wylie J in *Equiticorp Industries Group Ltd v Hawkins* [1991] 3 NZLR 700 and Tipping J in *Marshall Futures Ltd v Marshall* [1992] 1 NZLR 31 appear to state the preferable position. On those authorities the appropriate tests are: (a) for knowing receipt cases: knowledge amounting to knowledge within one of the five types of knowledge identified in *Baden Delvaux*; while in (b) knowing assistance cases, only types (i) to (iii) would apply, unless knowledge in categories (iv) and (v) could be shown coupled with a lack of probity. On the authority of Smith J's judgment in *Ninety Five Pty Ltd (liq) v Banque Nationale de Paris* [1988] WAR 132 want of probity would not be required in knowing receipt cases. In applying these tests one should note the words of Scott LJ in *Polly Peck International plc v Nadir* that these levels of knowledge are not rigid and one can merge easily into another. Furthermore, it should be noted that these tests require proof of 'knowledge' not 'notice'. While knowledge can be imputed to a party, as was done in *Agip (Africa) Ltd v Jackson*, it must be on the basis that, in view of what the third party actually knew, the court can impute to that party knowledge of what those facts mean in a legal sense. Knowledge of the facts without an appreciation of their legal meaning will not be a defence: *Ninety Five Pty Ltd (liq) v Banque National de Paris* [1988] WAR 132.

[17.46] These issues were canvassed again by the Privy Council in *Royal Brunei Airlines Sdn Bhd v Tan* [1995] 3 WLR 64.

Royal Brunei airlines brought proceedings against the defendant, the principal director and shareholder of Borneo Leisure Travel (BLT), a company which had carried on a business as a travel agency. BLT had received moneys for the sale of tickets on the airline which it was conceded were held on trust for the airline. Those moneys had been paid into the ordinary trading account of BLT and not into a special trust account and had been spent on ordinary business expenses of BLT. The Privy Council held the defendant liable on the basis of the reasoning quoted from Lord Nicholls above: see **[17.40]**. In the process his Lordship also rejected the *Baden Delvaux* categories of knowledge saying that, 'knowingly' is better avoided as a defining ingredient of the principle, and in the context of this principle the Baden scale of knowledge is best forgotten. Tan was found liable because: (a) BLT committed a breach of trust by using money instead of simply deducting its commission and holding the money intact for the airline; (b) Tan knowingly participated in that he caused or permitted the company to apply the money in a way he knew was not authorised by the trust; (c) in that sense, Tan could be said to have acted dishonestly, and so could the company, because his state of mind could be attributed to the company.

It remains to be seen whether the Privy Council's expressed preference for the treatment of these matters under broad principles of equity without slavish regard to the minutiae of the various proposed categories of knowledge will be widely adopted. The *Royal Brunei* case was not one in which knowledge was really an issue. On a virtually identical set of facts the Ontario Court of Appeal held the directors of a travel agency liable but on quite a different basis. They were held liable on the ground that, as directors of a corporate trustee, they were liable to beneficiaries of the trust for breaches of trust committed by that corporation: *Air Canada v M&L Travel Ltd* (1991) 77 DLR (4th) 536 (see [1915]). PD Finn has argued in favour of a search for unifying principle in these matters and urged a test involving three elements:[29]

1. Has a fiduciary committed a breach of fiduciary duty or breach of trust?

2. Has the third party participated in the matter in which the breach occurred?

3. In so doing, did that party know or have reason to know that a wrong was being committed by the fiduciary on his or her beneficiaries?

[17.47] It remains to be seen what effect, in any, the lengthy discussion of these questions in England and New Zealand will have in Australia. The courts at first instance and even for intermediate appellate courts, the High Court's decision in *Consul Developments* must remain the principal guide, although that case says little about 'knowing receipt' cases. These issues were discussed by Finn J in the Federal Court in *Australian Securities Commission v AS Nominees Ltd* (1995) 133 ALR 1 at 19 in which he noted that the various controversies which have beset the 'knowing assistance' limb of *Barnes v Addy* cannot be said to have been stilled in Australian law, particularly the 'knowledge' requirement.[30] He noted, however, that accessorial liability on these grounds was a particularly useful device to employ against directors of a corporate trustee who cause their company to commit a breach of trust.

---

29. PD Finn, 'The Liability of Third Parties for Knowing Receipt or Assistance' in Waters (ed), *Equity, Fiduciaries and Trusts*, Carswell, 1993.
30. See Lodge, 'Barnes v Addy: The Requirements of Knowledge' (1995) 23 *Aust Bus L Rev* 25.

Chapter Eighteen

The Duties and Powers of Trustees

18-1 Appointment and Removal of Trustees

Capacity to be a trustee

[18.1] Any person or persons, including a corporation, capable of holding property in their own name can act as a trustee. A number of people can act as trustees of the same trust, as a committee or unincorporated association. Under the general law there was no restriction on the number of persons who might be appointed trustees. For private trusts there is a statutory limit of four as the maximum number of persons who can be appointed trustees of the one trust in all States, except South Australia and Tasmania.[1] In New South Wales if an infant is appointed trustee, the appointment will be void but without prejudice to any power to appoint a new trustee under the terms of the trust. Upon coming of age the infant trustee will not be entitled to apply to be restored to the trusteeship.[2] A statutory power to appoint a substitute trustee instead of the infant, or any other trustee who refuses or is unfit to act or incapable of acting, exercisable by either the appointor nominated in the instrument or by a continuing trustee or by the personal representative of the last surviving trustee, is provided by the Trustee Act 1925 (NSW), s 6(2)(e). Elsewhere in Australia the appointment of an infant trustee is not automatically void. The infant cannot exercise any powers or discretions and can be replaced by the court but is entitled to apply for reinstatement upon coming of age. Corporations can act as trustees but not as executors and trustees of deceased estates unless the corporation is a trustee company authorised to do so by statute.[3]

Appointment of trustees

[18.2] A person may be appointed as a trustee either in the instrument creating the trust or by the exercise of any power of appointment contained in that instrument or

---

1. Trustee Act 1925 (NSW), s 6(5)(b); Trusts Act 1973–81 (Qld), s 11 (In Queensland the Attorney-General may approve the appointment of more trustees); Trustee Act 1958 (Vic), s 40; Trustees Act 1962–78 (WA), s 7(2)(n).
2. Conveyancing Act 1919 (NSW), s 151A.
3. Trustee Companies (Amendment) Act 1964 (NSW); Trustee Companies Act 1968–75 (Qld); Trustee Companies Act 1953–75 (Tas); Trustee Companies Act 1984 (Vic). South Australia and Western Australia do not have general trustee company legislation. Both States have passed several individual statutes dealing with particular trustee companies: *Jacobs'*, paras [1405–10].

by exercise of a statutory power conferred on some other person or the court. In most cases people or corporations acting as trustees of trusts created *inter vivos* are appointed by the settlors of those trusts in the original trust deed at the time of creation of the trust. In the case of deceased estates the trustee will either be the person or persons named as executor and trustee in the will or the person or persons to whom letters of administration have been granted. No one is obliged to act as a trustee and if the original trustee refuses to accept the office, or if that person, having accepted the office, dies or otherwise becomes incapable of exercising it, the appointment of a new trustee will be necessary. Equity will not allow a trust to fail for want of a trustee. If the original trustee disclaims the office so that the property revests in the settlor, the settlor will be bound to hold the property as trustee under the trusts declared: *Mallot v Wilson* [1903] 2 Ch 494,[4] subject only to the question of whether the trust was completely constituted in the first place. It is possible for a settlor to reserve to him or herself a power to revoke the trusts he or she is creating and to add to or to vary such trusts. If the power of revocation includes a power to create new trusts those new trusts will be irrevocable unless a power to revoke them is reserved in the original instrument. Beneficiaries of such a revocable trust will have vested interests which are liable to be divested. In Australia it is rare for a settlor to reserve any such power of revocation, or to reserve any power under which he or she might be able to acquire a beneficial interest under the trust. Under s 102 of the Income Tax Assessment Act 1936 (Cth), the Commissioner of Taxation can assess a trust for tax at the rate payable by the settlor if the settlor retains a power of revocation; the income of the trust will then be deemed to be added to the settlor's personal income.

[18.3] It is usual to include a power of appointment in an express trust so that any vacancy in the office of trustee can be filled easily. The power of appointment is sometimes conferred on the original trustees and sometimes on third parties. The circumstances in which such a power of appointment can be exercised will depend upon the terms of the trust. Trustee legislation throughout Australia contains statutory powers of appointment which are exercisable by those named as appointors in the trust deed, by the continuing or surviving trustees where there are no nominated appointors, and by the personal representatives of the last surviving trustee. In all States except New South Wales, which requires a registered deed, any appointment under this power can be made by an instrument in writing.[5] These various provisions allow for the appointment of a new trustee, or new trustees where the previous trustee has died, or is otherwise unwilling or incapable. Absence from the jurisdiction for more than a year will also justify a trustee's replacement under this statutory power although the exact grounds differ from State to State.[6] The statutory power of appointment also includes a power to appoint separate sets of trustees who can be appointed to hold separate portions of the trust property.[7] Any person holding or exercising a power of appointment is bound to do so in good faith.

---

4. Note: This involved a common law conveyance which is capable of passing title without assent. Quaere whether the same would apply in the case of a Torrens title transfer which will not be in registrable form unless 'accepted' by the transferee.
5. Trustee Act 1925 (NSW), s 6(4); Trusts Act 1973–81 (Qld), s 12(1); Trustee Act 1936–84 (SA), s 14(1); Trustee Act 1898 (Tas), s 13(1); Trustee Act 1958 (Vic), s 41(1); Trustees Act 1962–78 (WA) s 7(1).
6. *Jacobs'*, para [1511].
7. Trustee Act 1925 (NSW), s 6(5); Trusts Act 1973–81 (Qld), s 12(2)(b); Trustee Act 1936–84 (SA), s 14a(1); Trustee Act 1898 (Tas), s 13(2)(b); Trustee Act 1958 (Vic), s 42(1); Trustees Act 1962–78 (WA), s 7(2)(b).

In *Andco Nominees Pty Ltd v Lestato Pty Ltd* (1995) 17 ACSR 239, one of the objects of a discretionary trust, the MAVK trust, challenged the appointment of a particular company as trustee of the trust. The company had been appointed by a Mr Smith, an accountant selected as appointor of the trust pursuant to orders of the Family Court by a Registrar of that court. Mr Smith was a member of a firm of accountants associated with the solicitors for the wife in bitterly contested Family Court proceedings and the company appointed by him as the new trustee was controlled by partners of that firm. Santow J dismissed the Summons. In coming to that decision, he noted the principle that an appointor under a power of appointment should, in exercising the power, act with good faith and sincerity, with the entire and single view to the real purpose and object of the power and not for the purpose of carrying into effect any bye (ie, collateral) or sinister (that is, beyond the scope or intent of the power) purpose. However, he considered that any indirect benefit derived by Mr Smith, through his position as a partner in the firm of accountants and that firm's role as accountants to the nominated trustee, Andco, would not infringe the trust deed; there being no basis for concluding that the Trustee, either directly or through the accountants, would charge more than permitted by the Trust Deed. In the circumstances of the case Santow J found that there was no evidence that Smith and Andco had any prior agreement that Andco would exercise its powers as trustee simply to benefit the wife and without regard to proper consideration of the claims of all beneficiaries, and therefore the appointment by Mr Smith of Andco was not a corrupt appointment nor a fraud on the power.

In slightly different circumstances, in *Re Burton; Wily v Burton* (1994) 126 ALR 557, the Official Trustee of a bankrupt sought orders to the effect that the bankrupt's position and rights as appointor of a family trust constituted 'property of the bankrupt' under the Bankruptcy Act 1966 (Cth), s 116. Davies J rejected that application holding that the power of removal and appointment was not 'property' within the meaning of that word in s 116.

[18.4] The court has an inherent power to make orders appointing new trustees, either in substitution for or in addition to the existing trustees, where it is inexpedient, difficult or impracticable for a new trustee to be appointed without the assistance of the court. That power has been enshrined in statutory form in all States.[8] This statutory jurisdiction does not replace the court's inherent jurisdiction and, while it will usually not act where the person having power to appoint a new trustee is willing to do so, the court may still make such an appointment in those circumstances where, for instance, proceedings concerning the trust are before it and it is appropriate for the court to make orders which include the appointment of new trustees. When considering the appointment of new trustees, the court will take into account the wishes of the creator of the trust, as far as they can be discerned from the trust instrument, the principle that no appointment should be made which might favour the interests of some beneficiaries over those of others, and whether the appointment would promote or impede the execution of the trust: *Re Tempest* [1866] LR 1 Ch App 485.[9]

Appointment on the death of a sole trustee

[18.5] Where an individual acts as sole trustee, and that individual dies, and there is no express machinery in the trust instrument to provide for such an occurrence, such as an appointor with power to appoint a new trustee, the trust has a problem. Even

---

8. Trustee Act 1925 (NSW), s 70; Trusts Act 1973–81 (Qld), s 80; Trustee Act 1936–84 (SA), s 36; Trustee Act 1898 (Tas), s 32(1); Trustee Act 1958 (Vic), s 48; Trustees Act 1962–78 (WA), s 77.
9. See *Jacobs'*, paras [1529]–[1538]; Ford & Lee, paras [826]–[827].

where a power to appoint a new trustee exists there can be administrative difficulties in the transition period before the trust assets are vested in the new trustee. In the absence of any express provision, the personal representative of the deceased trustee will take over control of the assets of the trust; in New South Wales and South Australia as bare trustee only without any of the rights and powers conferred by the instrument of trust; in Victoria, Western Australia and Tasmania, with those powers, by virtue of statute, until appointment of a new trustee.[10] In Queensland, the Public Trustee assumes control of the trust pending appointment of a new trustee.[11] Once new trustees are appointed they take over from these interim appointees: *Re Routledge's Trusts* [1909] 1 Ch 280. Where there is no other machinery under the trust to deal with such circumstances, the personal representative of the last surviving trustee has a statutory power to appoint new trustees.[12] These complications provide a good reason for the employment of a corporate trustee.

Disclaimer by a trustee

[18.6] No person is bound to accept the obligations of a trustee and any nominated trustee can disclaim the trust. If, however, the nominated trustee accepts the trust, he or she cannot then disclaim it nor retire from the trust except by the proper procedure. A disclaimer can, and should best be in writing but one can also be inferred from conduct, particularly inaction: *Re Clout and Frewer's Contract* [1924] Ch 230. This does not mean that a trust will not take effect until it is clear that the trustee has not disclaimed it. The better view appears to be that the trust property will vest in the trustee at once but that the trustee may repudiate the trust by disclaiming it when he or she is informed of it: *Standing v Bowring* (1885) 31 Ch D 282.

Retirement of trustees

[18.7] The retirement of a trustee will usually be allowed for under the trust instrument but, in any case, is provided for by statute.[13] Where retirement is provided for in the trust deed itself, some procedure will also be laid down for the appointment of a new trustee, either by the retiring trustee, the continuing trustees or by some third party appointor and for the transfer of any trust property vested in the outgoing trustee. The statutory regimes allow for retirement by an instrument in writing, except in New South Wales and Tasmania which require a registered deed, provided that there are at least two continuing trustees left to manage the trust, and that those continuing trustees consent to the retirement, and that all things necessary to vest the trust property in the continuing trustees have been done. Where a trustee retires from a trust knowing or suspecting that the continuing trustees will commit a breach of trust after his or her retirement he or she will be equally liable with them for any loss arising to the trust estate from the contemplated breach: *Head v Gould* [1898] 2 Ch 250. These statutory regimes may be varied by the terms of the trust; so it is prudent in New South Wales and Tasmania to include a power to retire by instrument in writing.

---

10. Conveyancing and Law of Property Act 1884 (Tas), s 34(1); Trustee Act 1958 (Vic), s 22; Trustees Act 1962–78 (WA), s 45(2).

11. Trusts Act 1973–81 (Qld), s 16(2).

12. Trustee Act 1925 (NSW), s 6(4); Trusts Act 1973–81 (Qld), s 12(1); Trustee Act 1936–84 (SA), s 14(1); Trustee Act 1898 (Tas), s 13(1); Trustee Act 1958 (Vic), s 41(1); Trustees Act 1962–78 (WA), s 7(1).

13. Trustee Act 1925 (NSW), s 8; Trusts Act 1973–81 (Qld), s 14; Trustee Act 1936–84 (SA), s 15; Trustee Act 1898 (Tas), s 14; Trustee Act 1958 (Vic), s 44; Trustees Act 1962–78 (WA), s 9.

Removal of trustees

[18.8] Apart from any express power to remove a trustee which may be included in the trust instrument, and the statutory power to appoint new trustees in place of those who may have died, been declared bankrupt or convicted of a felony, remained out of the state for over a year or otherwise become unfit or incapable of acting, the power to remove a trustee who otherwise desires to remain in office rests firmly on the court's inherent jurisdiction over trusts. Where the trustee has been guilty of some positive misconduct there will not be any problem but not every mistake or neglect of duty will induce the courts to remove a trustee. The acts or omissions complained of must be 'such as to endanger the trust property or to show a want of honesty, or a want of proper capacity to execute the duties, or a want of reasonable fidelity': *Letterstedt v Broers* (1884) 9 App Cas 371. The court will not remove a duly appointed trustee, particularly one appointed by the original settlor, unless there are good grounds for doing so. Mere conflict with the beneficiaries will not suffice: *Re Henderson* [1940] Ch 764. A trustee will not be removed simply because some beneficiaries desire it: *Guazzini v Patterson* (1918) 18 SR (NSW) 275, nor even if they all require it: *Re Brockbank* [1948] Ch 206. The court will have regard to the best interests of the trust estate as a whole. The fact that a trustee is a beneficiary will not be grounds for removal, even where the trust is a discretionary trust, although a trustee in that position was removed by the court in *Hobkirk v Ritchie* (1933) 29 Tas LR 14, not because he was also a beneficiary but because he was in serious financial difficulty. Like much of the inherent jurisdiction of courts of equity, the power of removing a trustee is a matter for the court's discretion and the grounds upon which it will be exercised will only be expressed in broad terms so that the court can deal with any given case on its merits.

> In *Princess Anne of Hesse v Field* [1963] NSWR 998, the executors and trustees of a deceased estate were appointed liquidators of a company in which the estate held a majority shareholding. They received a commission for acting as liquidators. Jacobs J held that they had placed themselves in a position of conflict and should pay to the trust a proportion of their commission equal to the proportion of the company's shares owned by the estate. His Honour refused to remove them as trustees, however. In all the circumstances he considered them the best people to deal with the administration of the trust and the company.

18-2 Vesting of Trust Property

[18.9] At the creation of any trust the trust property must be vested in the trustee. Where the trust is created by express declaration the property must, by necessary implication, be vested in the trustee. If it is not the declaration will be ineffective. Where a trust is created *inter vivos* by transferring property to trustees, for the trust to be completely constituted, the trust property must be vested in the trustees at the time the trust is expressed to come into operation. It is common practice for a trust to be established by the settlement of a nominal sum, say $100, on the trustee at the outset while the other assets of the trust are transferred thereafter by way of purchase, with the necessary funds being lent to the trust for the purpose, or by way of voluntary transfer. The method chosen will usually be determined by the stamp duty and any other transfer tax implications at the time. Where new trustees are appointed, whether by a nominated or statutory appointor or by the court, and for whatever reason, it will be necessary to vest the trust property in the incoming trustee or trustees. This matter is provided for in legislation which is substantially the same in the various States, the only difference being that in Victoria, Queensland and Western Australia there is no provision for vesting upon the retirement of a trustee because those States require the necessary conveyances to be effected before retirement.[14] In Queensland, an instrument appointing a new trustee will vest the trust property in the incoming trustee without any further conveyance or transfer, subject to the provisions of any other Act. Where some form of transfer is prescribed by another Act, such as the Real Property Act 1900 (NSW), an instrument of appointment will not vest title to any property under such an Act in the trustee by itself. It will be necessary to transfer the property in accordance with the requirements of the Act. In the case of property which does not require formalities such as registration or notification to be validly transferred at law, the deed of appointment of a new trustee may also act as the conveyance of the legal title in those assets. However, where registration or some other procedure is required by law it will be necessary to complete those steps before the trust property can vest in the incoming trustee. The court also has the power to make vesting orders in appropriate cases such as where the person in whom the trust property is presently vested is incapable of making a valid assignment. There are a number of grounds specified in the trustee legislation of the various States for making such an order.[15]

In *Andco Nominees Pty Ltd v Lestato Pty Ltd* (1995) 17 ACSR 239 (see [18.3]), Andco, having been appointed as trustee of the MAVK trust pursuant to steps taken on the basis of orders of the Family Court, demanded that Lestato Pty Ltd, the previous trustee, transfer to it the shares in Thurlstane (Aust) Pty Ltd which were the major asset of the trust. On 29 August 1994 Young J made an order, pursuant to s 71 of the Trustee Act 1925 (NSW) vesting in Andco the 13,247 shares in Thurlstane standing in the name of Lestato. Andco wrote to Thurlstane seeking alteration of the company register to show Andco as owner of the shares. Thurlstane sought to rely on a provision in its Articles giving existing members pre-emptive rights to purchase any shares up for transfer. Andco sought orders, in effect, that the transfer or transmission of the 13,247 shares in Thurlstane vested in Andco be registered pursuant to s 1094 of the Corporations Law. Santow J held that Andco Nominees was entitled to be registered as shareholder of the shares in Thurlstane pursuant to s 1094 of the Corporations Law without the necessity to submit those shares for sale to other shareholders under the pre-emptive rights clause and without the directors of Thurlstane having any discretion to refuse to register the transfer. In doing so he held that a vesting order, under s 78(1) and (2) of the Trustee Act, vests ownership by operation of law and that therefore a vesting order operates as a transmission and not a transfer. The fact that Andco was not registered did not prevent it from having legal title.

18-3 Duties of a Trustee

[18.10] The duties cast on trustees are the essence of the equitable institution known as the trust. Unlike contractual obligations at common law, a trustee's duties do not

---

14. Trustee Act 1925 (NSW), s 9; Trusts Act 1973–81 (Qld), s 15; Trustee Act 1936–84 (SA), s 16; Trustee Act 1898 (Tas), s 15; Trustee Act 1958 (Vic), s 45; Trustees Act 1962–78 (WA), s 10.
15. Trustee Act 1925 (NSW), s 71; Trusts Act 1973–1981 (Qld), ss 82–3; Trustee Act 1936–84 (SA), ss 36–7, 41; Trustee Act 1898 (Tas), ss 33–4; Trustee Act 1958 (Vic), ss 51–2; Trustees Act 1962–78 (WA), ss 78–9 (*Jacobs'*, paras [2505]–[2510]; Ford & Lee, paras [840]–[852]).

necessarily arise from the fact that consideration has been provided by another party. Most trusts arise from express declarations, and not from agreements to create a trust. Most trustees accept their duties voluntarily. Yet they are policed more strictly in the performance of their duties than parties to a contract. A trustee in breach of duty will not be required simply to make good any loss suffered by the trust which was reasonably foreseeable as likely to flow from the breach. A trustee in breach will be obliged to restore the trust to the position in which it would have stood had the breach not been committed.[16] But the duties cast on trustees are not all the same. Where a trust is established by some written instrument the duties of the trustee will be determined largely by the terms of that instrument. Most of the duties discussed below can be, and often are, varied or even abrogated entirely by the provisions of particular trusts. That does not reduce their value. The general principles governing the duties, and the powers, rights and liabilities of trustees must be properly understood if one is to comprehend the nature of any trust and the duties imposed upon any trustee. If they are to be varied or abrogated by the terms of some deed of trust the person drafting the document must appreciate the nature and purpose of what is being done. That said, it must also be acknowledged that the duties, and the powers, rights and liabilities of a trustee under any given trust instrument will, inevitably, depend upon the terms of the trust, and thus upon the skill and intent of the person drafting the instrument creating that trust.

Duties upon accepting the trust

[18.11] Upon accepting a trust, new trustees must 'inquire of what the property consists that is proposed to be handed over to them and what are the trusts'.[17] They should examine all the relevant documents in doing so to ascertain that everything is in order.[18] Thereafter their basic duties are fairly straightforward: 'the duty of a trustee is properly to preserve the trust fund, to pay the income and the corpus to those who are entitled to them respectively, and to give all his cestuis que trust, on demand, information with respect to the mode in which the trust fund has been dealt with, and where it is'.[19] In doing so the trustees are bound to adhere to the terms of the trust, to act personally, and, above all, to carry out all their duties and exercise all their powers as fiduciaries under a general duty to act always in good faith in their dealings with and on behalf of the trust. New trustees are also obliged to take possession of any trust property not given to them at the time of their appointment. Where the trust assets consist of property such as land, shares in companies, debentures, moneys on deposit and the like, the trustee will be obliged to secure possession of the indicia of title to those assets and to see that those documents are lodged safely away from theft or the possibility of fraudulent dealing. If legal title is not vested in the trustee at the outset, he or she will be obliged to ensure that the property is duly transferred to him or her: *Westmoreland v Holland* (1871) 23 LT 797. If the trust is owed outstanding debts, other than, of course, moneys invested for the purpose of obtaining income in the form of interest, the trustee will be obliged to collect those debts, or, at least, obtain an acknowledgement from the debtor to prevent time running against the trust: *Partridge v Equity Trustees Executors and Agency Co Ltd* (1947) 75 CLR 149. The trustee's duty in getting in the trust assets requires the trustee to take

---

16. *Re Dawson (dec'd)* [1966] 2 NSWR 211; *Hagan v Waterhouse* (1992) 34 NSWLR 308.
17. *Hallows v Lloyd* (1888) 39 Ch D 686 at 691, per Kekewich J.
18. Pettit, p 319.
19. *Low v Bouverie* [1891] 3 Ch 82 at 99, per Lindley LJ.

such steps in doing so as may be necessary and reasonable. If that means taking proceedings in the courts, then that is what the trustee must do. In such a case, however, considering the costs, and sometimes the uncertainty involved in major litigation the prudent trustee may be advised to seek the advice and directions of the court under the court's inherent powers or under the Trustee Act 1925 (NSW), s 63 or its equivalent in some other States before embarking on costly proceedings where the outcome is uncertain.[20]

Duty to preserve trust property

[18.12] This duty encompasses a number of matters which some writers have treated separately when considering the question of the duties of trustees. It clearly includes the trustee's obligation to get in the trust property and preserve it, as well as the duty to properly invest the trust fund. In making those investments and managing them thereafter the trustee must act with reasonable care, diligence and prudence, so as to avoid any loss or damage arising from a want of such care, diligence or prudence. Those are all positive duties. There is also the negative obligation of not conniving or knowingly assisting in any act or conduct which would involve a breach of trust, or which could result in some loss or damage to the trust property.

The duty to insure trust property

[18.13] Trustees are given a statutory power to insure in each State with slight differences as to the source from which premiums may be paid and the status of any moneys received by way of the proceeds of any policy.[21] It had been the view of some that, unless the trust instrument gave some express or implied direction concerning insurance of the trust property, the trustee was not under a duty to insure.[22] Although others disagreed with that view.[23] Thus a trustee would not be liable for any loss arising from a failure to insure: *Re McEacharn* (1911) 103 LT 900. That traditional view was open to question depending upon the nature of the trust property and whether some duty to insure might be implied as part of the settlor's intention: *Davjoyda Estates Pty Ltd v National Insurance Co of NZ Ltd* [1965] NSWR 1257. However, at least in New South Wales, the question appears to have been settled.

In *Pateman v Heyen* (1993) 33 NSWLR 188, a claim was brought against the trustee of a deceased estate seeking compensation for the loss resulting from a fire which destroyed the house which was the major asset of the estate. The deceased was a fisherman living on the North Coast of New South Wales. He appointed the defendant as his executor. The sole beneficiary was the plaintiff who was aged 13 at the death of the deceased. After giving consideration to selling the house, the defendant leased it for the purpose of preserving the assets while waiting for the plaintff to come of age. The defendant insured the property initially but later overlooked a renewal of the insurance with the result that the insurance lapsed on 1 September 1985. The property was not insured when it was destroyed by a fire in July 1987. Cohen J reviewed the authorities

---

20. Trustee Act 1925 (NSW), s 63; Trusts Act 1973 (Qld), s 96; Trustee Act 1936–68 (SA), s 91; Rules of the Supreme Court O 55 r 3 (Vic); Trustee Act 1962–1978 (WA), s 92.
21. Trustee Act 1925 (NSW), s 41; Trusts Act 1973 (Qld), s 47; Trustee Act 1936–74 (SA), s 25; Trustee Act 1958 (Vic), s 23; Trustees Act 1962–72 (WA), s 30(1)(g); Trustee Act 1898 (Tas), s 21 (see Ford & Lee, paras [1124] and [1244]).
22. *Jacobs'*, para [2030]; PH Pettitt, *Equity and the Law of Trusts*, 6th ed, Butterworths, London, 1989 at 394; Riddall, *The Law of Trusts*, 3rd ed, 1987, p 317.
23. Ford & Lee, para [1244].

and the views of the commentators on the point, including two decisions of the Supreme Court of Connecticut: *Willis v Hendry* 20 A (2d) 375 (1941) and *Merchants Bank & Trust Co v New Canaan Historical Soc* 54 A (2d) 696 (1947) which held that a trustee was under a general duty to insure in such a way and in such an amount as would an ordinarily prudent person. On the authority of the Superior Court of Pennsylvania that duty did not extend to a duty to insure buildings for their full replacement cost as new: *Re Estate of Lychos* 470 A (2d) 136 (1983). Cohen J said that in his opinion those American authorities were correct, saying, at 197–8, that he could not see why a trustee should not be required to act in respect of insurance in the same way as a prudent person would be expected to act in respect of his or her own property. That duty extended, in his Honour's view, in appropriate cases to insuring the property for its full replacement value, while in other cases it may be sufficient to insure for the present value of the property. Cohen J postulated that there may be circumstances in which it would not be reasonable to expect a trustee to insure, for instance where there was no income available to pay premiums. In the instant case, Cohen J considered that the trustee was under a duty to insure but only for present value and thus liable to compensate the estate for the value of the house as it was at the date of the fire, the difference between the improved and the unimproved value of the property.

The duty to properly invest the trust fund

[18.14] In carrying out the duty to properly invest the trust fund a trustee is obliged to exercise reasonable care and diligence and to act as a prudent man of business would, having regard to the range of investments authorised by the trust. The courts have shown a flexible attitude in dealing with questions about the performance of these duties. While keen to see that trustees do not foolishly waste the property entrusted to them, the courts have shown some reluctance to punish an honest trustee for an error in judgement. In *Re Speight; Speight v Gaunt* (1883) 22 Ch D 727, a trustee employed a stockbroker to make some investments for him. The broker fraudulently misappropriated the funds and the beneficiaries sought to hold the trustee personally liable for the loss thus arising. The Court of Appeal held that the trustee was not liable for breach of trust. In coming to that decision, Sir George Jessel MR said of the obligations of a trustee conducting a business, that, 'a trustee ought to conduct the business of the trust in the same manner that an ordinary prudent man of business would conduct his own, and that beyond that there is no liability or obligation on the trustee'. And, of the attitude of the court: 'where you have an honest trustee fairly anxious to perform his duty and to do as he thinks best for the estate, you are not to strain the law against him to make him liable for doing that which he has done and which he believes is right in the execution of his duty, unless you have a plain case made against him … I think it is the duty of the court in these cases where there is a question of nicety as to construction or otherwise to lean to the side of the honest trustee, and not be anxious to find fine and extraordinary reasons for fixing him with any liability upon the contract'.

[18.15] Where the trust deed authorises investment in a wide range of activities, including investments of a speculative nature, a trustee is still under a duty to act prudently and in good faith in exercising those express powers. A trustee may commit a breach of this duty to properly invest the trust fund even though all investments fall within the range authorised by the trust instrument.

In *Re Whiteley; Whiteley v Learoyd* (1886) 33 Ch D 347, trustees were authorised under a will to invest in 'real securities in England or Wales'. They invested £3,000 on mortgage over a freehold brickpit, on which a brickmaking business was being conducted, and over four freehold houses. The owners of all five properties were subsequently liquidated and the proceeds of sale were insufficient to repay the money advanced by the trustees. Beneficiaries of the estate sought restitution from the trustees. The Court of Appeal held that even though the investments were investments in real securities, the trustees were not therefore free from liability. It was open to the court to consider whether this was a proper investment in the circumstances. Cotton LJ said trustees must take such care in conducting the business of the trust as a reasonably cautious man would use, having regard not only to the interests of those entitled to the income but also to the interests of those who will take in the future. In this case, as the value of the brickpit depended upon it being sold as a going concern, and the value of the land was otherwise less than the amount advanced, the prudent man would not have lent so much on it. The trustees were not, however, liable for the loss on the residential properties. Lindley LJ said the duty of a trustee is not to take such care as a prudent man of business would take if he had only himself to consider; the duty is rather to take such care as an ordinary prudent man would take if he were minded to make such an investment for the benefit of other people for whom he felt morally obliged to provide. His Lordship also added that while the court ought not to encourage laxity and want of care it should not convert honest trustees into insurers of the moneys committed to their care.

[18.16] The duty to preserve the trust property can cast positive obligations on a trustee:

In *Elder's Trustee and Executor Co Ltd v Higgins* (1963) 113 CLR 426, a testator had carried on a grazing business on two adjoining properties: 'The Brook, which was in his name and 'Burnt Oak', which stood in the names of the testator and his two sisters as tenants-in-common in equal shares. The testator had a lease from his sisters of their shares in 'Burnt Oak', which lease contained an option to purchase the sisters' interests for £4,278 at any time during the currency of the lease. After the testator's death his trustee continued the grazing business. The trustee renewed the tenancy agreement upon its expiry, including the option to purchase, with a variation under which the land was divided into several parcels and the trustee was given the option to purchase those parcels individually as and when it thought fit. The business lacked the capital to take up the option but the trustee had the power to mortgage and the necessary money could have been raised. Upon the expiry of the second agreement the sisters refused to renew the option to purchase. The testator's widow purchased one lot which was essential for carrying on the business, but the others were all sold to strangers at prices far greater than the price fixed in the option. The High Court held the trustee to have breached its trust by failing to exercise the option. In doing so, their Honours rejected an argument that the trustee had acted in good faith in deciding not to exercise a discretion and could not therefore be held liable. This was not a case of the exercise of a particular discretion but of the general duty of a trustee holding property for persons in succession and carrying on a business. The question was not whether the trust could afford to buy a new asset but whether it could afford not to buy something which was needed to preserve the value of the main asset of the estate. Considering the value of the option by itself, it was not the act of a prudent trustee to let it go.

The court will have regard to the whole of the circumstances surrounding the trust and the conduct of the trustee in determining whether a trustee has committed a breach of duty and, if so, the extent and nature of the breach.

In *Re Lucking's Will Trusts* [1968] 1 WLR 866; [1967] 3 All ER 726, Peter Lucking was trustee of his mother's estate, which included 6,980 shares in a company in which Lucking and his wife held the balance of the 10,000 issued shares in the company. The company ran a small factory in Chester employing about 20 people. Lucking lived in London and entrusted the affairs of the company to a manager, even to the point of giving the manager signed blank cheques for an account of the company's in which they were joint signatories. The manager was paid a salary of £2,000 plus a bonus on profits over £6,000 per annum. The trustee received regular accounts from the manager but relied on the manager's explanation of those accounts, including a sum of £2,800 shown as 'loan to director'. By the time the manager was dismissed in 1961 that 'loan' had climbed to £15,890. The company's turnover had increased during the manager's time in office but the net profits had not and the balance between assets and liabilities had actually declined. After his dismissal, the manager was declared bankrupt and none of these moneys were repaid. In 1961 the plaintiff, the trustee's niece and a beneficiary of the estate, took proceedings against Lucking and Spencer Block claiming damages for breach of trust. Block had been appointed a co-trustee by Lucking in 1956 although Lucking had not told him about the manager's unauthorised loan account. Noting that this was an action against the trustees as holders of the shares for breach of trust, and not as directors for breach of their duty to the company, Cross J held that Peter Lucking had not acted as a prudent man of business would when the majority shareholder in a private company by accepting only such information as to the affairs of the company as he is entitled to as a shareholder. Lucking was not guilty of a breach of trust for the manager's undue business expenses. That may have constituted an unnecessary concession and an error of judgement but not a breach of trust. Lucking was, however, in breach in respect of the manager's overdrawings. He should not have signed cheques without seeing the amounts and the payees. This might have been justifiable while Lucking had no cause to doubt the manager's trustworthiness but all that changed in 1957 when Lucking became aware that the manager was overdrawing at a rate of over two-thirds of his agreed salary each year. Lucking was therefore liable for the loss suffered by the trust shareholding for his failure to supervise the manager's drawings adequately after 1957. Block was not liable. He was entitled to rely on what Lucking told him about the company and was therefore not in the position of a mere passive co-trustee who lets the other trustee decide matters on which they ought to have exercised a joint discretion.

[18.17] The standard of care expected of a trustee in managing the investment of the trust fund will be higher where the trustee is a professional trustee company, as opposed to a privately managed proprietary company which happens to be a trustee. A professional trustee company cannot expect to be allowed the benefit of the doubt which Sir George Jessel was prepared to allow an honest trustee in *Speight v Gaunt*.

In *Bartlett v Barclays Bank Trust Co Ltd (No 1)* [1980] Ch 515, Barclays Bank was trustee of 99 per cent of the shares in Bartlett Trust Limited (BTL), a property management company, pursuant to a settlement made in 1920 by Sir Herbert Bartlett. The beneficiaries of the trust were Bartlett's children, as life tenants, and thereafter their appointees subject to an accrual in the event of a failure of issue. By 1960 there were no Bartlett family members, nor any representatives of the bank on the board of BTL. From that time the company engaged in a policy of speculative property development, which included an ambitious project opposite the Old Bailey. The purpose behind that project was, in part, the promotion of the sale of shares in BTL to the public, a plan which was later shelved, although the Old Bailey project was kept going. The directors did not keep the bank's trustee department fully informed of these activities, although BTL did borrow £1 million from the finance department of the Bank which told the trust department about the loan. £1 million was equal to half the asset value of the trust. In the end, planning permission was refused for the Old Bailey project and the collapse of the property boom in 1974 saw the other plans founder as well. Bartlett Trust Holdings (which had been floated to take over from BTL) was left with a heavy loss. Seven Bartlett grandchildren took proceedings against Barclays for breach of trust. Brightman J held that the bank was liable. His Lordship said that had the trust existed without the incorporation of BTL, so that the bank held the properties directly on the trusts of the settlement, there would have been a clear breach of trust to hazard the trust's money on such projects. The fact that the bank had the power to prevent the loss, if need be by calling a general meeting of BTL and replacing the directors, did not mean that it was therefore liable for that loss. As shareholder in BTL the bank was bound to act as a prudent man of business would. If facts came to its knowledge which told that the company's affairs were not being conducted as they should be, or which put it on inquiry, it should have taken appropriate action — either by consulting with the directors, or replacing them if need be. A trustee in that position should not content itself with receipt of the sort of information which a company gives to its shareholders at an Annual General Meeting. Where the trustee is a trust corporation which has held itself out as having the skill and expertise to carry on the specialised business of trust management, the standard of care imposed is higher than that expected of the ordinary prudent man of business.

[18.18] The duty to properly invest the trust fund involves balancing of a number of competing factors. The duty to preserve the trust fund is principally concerned with the protection of the capital of the trust. The trustee will thus be concerned to ensure that the capital value of the trust is maintained and protected against inflation where possible. The trustee will also be concerned to secure the best income return from the trust assets, provided that the capital is not put at risk in the process. In considering all these matters, the trustee must also have regard to the range of investments authorised by the trust deed itself, or, if the trust instrument is silent on the point, to the range of trust investments authorised by statute.[24] In taking all these matters into account, the trustee must balance the need to provide the maximum appropriate income for the income beneficiaries or any life tenant against the obligation to protect the value of the capital against inflation for the benefit of any remainderman or capital beneficiaries. Other obligations imposed on the trustee may also impact upon decisions made about the preservation of the fund. The available powers of investment may restrict the nature of investments the trustee can make to preserve the capital value. The need to provide for annuities or other incidental gifts as part of the trust may also reduce the trustee's flexibility in dealing with inflation and other factors which impinge upon the maintenance of the capital value of the trust. The nature of a trustee's duty in this respect is best illustrated by the case of *Nestle v National Westminster Bank* (Hoffman J, 29 June 1988, unreported); [1994] 1 All ER 118 (CA).

William Nestle died in 1922 leaving a will under which he established certain trusts. Nestle's wife was 43, his sons George and John were 18 and 9 respectively. Nestle left an annuity of £1,500 per annum in favour of his wife. The upkeep of the family home and the children's education expenses were met partly by the annuity and partly by advancements of capital by the trustee. The two sons were entitled to the income of the residue in two stages: annuities of £250 per annum when they turned 21 and half the income each for life once they turned 25. The National Westminster Bank (NWB) was trustee. Under the will it had a discretion to make advancements of capital to either son. The bank also had power to retain existing investments even though they may be 'wasting, speculative or revisionary'. The trustee was authorised to invest in securities or investments which were the same or of a similar nature to those held by Nestle at his death: government guaranteed stocks or securities, railway or municipal stock, bonds or debentures or by way of mortgage on real property. Georgina Nestle was the remainder beneficiary under these trusts. In November 1986, on the death of her father, John Nestle, the last life tenant, Miss Nestle became absolutely entitled to the fund. Shortly thereafter she commenced proceedings against NWB claiming that it was in breach of its duty to preserve the trust fund. In 1922 the Nestle estate had been

---

24. Trustee Act 1925 (NSW), s 14; Trusts Act 1973 (Qld), s 21; Trustee Act 1936–74 (SA), s 5; Trustee Act 1898 (Tas), s 5; Trustee Act 1958 (Vic), s 4; Trustees Act 1962–72 (WA), s 16.

worth £50,000. With adjustments for the retail prices index, that sum was equivalent to £1 million in 1988. In 1988 the capital of the fund amounted to only £269,203. The index of ordinary shares which stood at 119.8 in 1922 had, by November 1986 reached 6,352.2. On those figures, had the trust been invested in ordinary shares in 1922, it would have been worth £1.8 million in 1988. Miss Nestle relied on those figures as the basis of her claim. The bank argued that a trustee exercising investment powers is not under a duty to achieve results but to exercise reasonable skill and care, and to balance the interests of life tenant and remainderman. The bank also argued that any complaint of breach of trust must relate to particular acts or omissions which constitute breaches of trust and each of those acts or omissions must be judged by the circumstances as they existed at the time. Both at first instance, per Hoffman J, and in the Court of Appeal, Miss Nestle's claim was rejected.

Hoffman J considered the principle governing the duty of a trustee in investing the trust fund. Citing the judgement of Lindley LJ in *Re Whiteley* (1886) 33 Ch D 347 at 355: see **[18.15]**. In commenting on that rule, Hoffman J said:

> This is an extremely flexible standard capable of adaption to current economic conditions and contemporary understanding of markets and investments. For example, investments which were imprudent in the days of the gold standard may be sound and sensible in times of high inflation. Modern trustees acting within their investment powers are entitled to be judged by the standards of current portfolio theory, which emphasize the risk level of the entire portfolio rather than the risk attaching to each investment taken in isolation. This is not to say that losses on investments made in breach of trust can be set off against gains in the rest of the portfolio but only that an investment which in isolation is too risky and therefore in breach of trust may be justified when held in conjunction with other investments ... But in reviewing the conduct of trustees over a period of more than 60 years, one must be careful not to endow the prudent trustee with prophetic vision or expect him to have ignored the received wisdom of his time.

Hoffman J rejected a submission that the duty to preserve the capital value of the fund for the benefit of the remainderman meant preserving the real value of the fund as opposed to its monetary value. Considering that question in the context of the duty of the trustee to act impartially between life tenant and remainderman he sad:

> The preservation of monetary value of the capital requires no skill or luck. The trustees can discharge their duties, as they often did until 1961, by investing the whole fund in gilt-edged securities. Preservation of real values can be not more than an aspiration which some trustees may have the good fortune to achieve. Plainly they must have regard to the interests of those entitled in the future to capital and such regard will require them to take into consideration the potential effects of inflation, but a rule that real capital values must be maintained would be unfair to both income beneficiaries and trustees.

Hoffman J preferred to assess the matter on the basis of whether the trustee had acted fairly in making investment decisions rather than considering whether the trustee had held the scales equally between life tenant and remainderman. The image of the scales suggested a weighing of known quantities whereas investment decisions are concerned with predictions of the future. Investments will carry current expectations of their future income yield and capital appreciation and these expectations will be reflected in their current market price, but there is always a greater or lesser risk that the outcome will deviate from those expectation. He considered trustees to have a wide discretion. They were entitled to take into account the income needs of the life tenant and the fact that the life tenant was known to the settlor and a primary object of the trust whereas the remainderman was a remoter relative or a stranger. It would be an inhuman law which required trustees to adhere to some mechanical rule preserving the real value of the capital when the tenant for life was the testator's widow who had fallen upon hard times and the remainderman was young and well off. Hoffman J rejected that test as one requiring a gift of prophesy rather than ordinary skill and care. He rejected the evidence of the plaintiff's expert who said the trustee should have invested in equities, noting that that same expert had written a book some years before advocating investment in fixed interest deposits. Instead, he preferred the opinion of the bank's expert on trust administration and quoted from that expert's report:

> The difficulty ... perhaps sheer impossibility ... of satisfying both [life tenant and remainderman] is reflected in the fact that there is no such thing as an authentic 'proper balance'; although it will be easy enough to say that a fund is unbalanced in extreme cases there must be a wide band in the middle, so to speak, where there is room for a genuine difference of opinion. An opinion on this subject will reflect the view taken of the present state of the market, the prospects for both fixed interest stocks and equities in the future and the present and future circumstances of the beneficiaries. Clearly an equation containing so many variables is not going to resolve itself into an inevitable solution.

Hoffman J then conducted an extensive review of the history of the investments of the trust fund, including the matters taken into account in setting aside an appropriate fund to pay the annuity due to the widower. Had that annuity been paid out of gilt-edged securities it would have been necessary to invest most of the fund in those securities leaving an insufficient capital sum to pay the annuities due to the sons when they turned 21. Hoffman J concluded that the bank had acted properly in accordance with correct principles of prudence and fairness. The Court of Appeal upheld Hoffman J's decision but was not as kind in its comments about the bank. It did not endorse his opinion that the bank had acted 'conscientiously, fairly and carefully'. Instead it found that the bank had failed in its duty to appreciate the scope of its powers of investment and had not reviewed the investments regularly. For example, some moneys had been invested in railway stock in companies with railway interests in China. In the 1920s that was a reasonable investment. In the 1930s it looked less than wise. In the 1940s and 1950s it was hopeless. However, the Court of Appeal considered that those matters were not sufficient to render the bank liable to the plaintiff. Miss Nestle had not proved that the bank's failure to diversify the equities between 1922 and 1960 had caused her loss. Although the bank had not been an effective manager of the trust investments under its control, it had not been shown to have committed any breach of trust resulting in loss.

[18.19] As well as the positive duty to invest the trust fund properly, the trustee is also under a negative duty not to participate in any activity which might occasion a loss to the trust. This includes a duty not to deal with the trust property for his own benefit, or otherwise to profit from the trust. Much of this has been canvassed in Chapters 5 and 17, in the discussions of fiduciary obligations, and the imposition of constructive trusts for breach of those obligations. The duty not to profit from his office also obliges a trustee to act gratuitously. The position of trustee is considered to be an honorary office, and not one which should be taken up for mercenary reasons.[25] The rationale behind this rule is that a trustee should not be put in a position in which there might be a conflict between duty and interest. Despite that, in many cases trustees do receive remuneration for their services, but certain conditions must

---

25. *Ayliffe v Murray* (1740) 2 Atk 58; 26 ER 433.

be satisfied before they can do so. The right to receive remuneration must be expressly or impliedly conferred by the instrument creating the trust, or there must be some special agreement between the trustee and the beneficiaries, all of whom must be sui juris. The courts are very wary of such agreements and will strike them down if there is any suggestion of undue influence or pressure.[26] The court has an inherent jurisdiction to award remuneration in proper cases. In doing so it can have regard to the time spent by the trustee in carrying out the trust, the difficulty of that work and the benefits conferred on the trust. In exercising this power the court may award future remuneration for anticipated efforts. This jurisdiction includes a power to vary previously agreed rates of remuneration: *Re Duke of Norfolk's Settlement Trusts* [1982] Ch 61. A solicitor who acts as a trustee will only be allowed to charge for his or her professional costs if expressly authorised to do so in the trust instrument. Otherwise he or she is restricted to claiming out of pocket expenses only. The only exception to this is the rule in *Cradock v Piper* (1850) 1 Mac & G 664; 41 ER 1422 which allows a solicitor-trustee to charge costs for his or her firm when acting on behalf of him or herself and a co-trustee, or him or herself as trustee and a beneficiary, in litigation where the cost of acting for him or herself as well as the other has not added to the total costs of the action.

The duty not to participate in any activity which might cause the trust to suffer a loss is not confined to matters of conscious and positive wrongdoing. It also covers matters which can be regarded as technical wrongs, even though the trustee has acted in good faith. For example, a trustee cannot purchase trust property unless expressly authorised to do so by the trust instrument or, if there is no such power, by the court. It does not matter whether such a sale is for a proper value. The only other exception is that a trustee may purchase from the trust with the informed consent of all the beneficiaries (who must, of course, all be of age and *sui juris*) for a fair price. The basis of this duty is that a trustee must not put him or herself in a position in which his or her interest and duty might conflict. When exercising a power of sale over trust property the trustee's duty will be to obtain the best price. As a purchaser his or her interest will lie in securing the lowest price.[27] In *Holder v Holder* [1968] Ch 353, a man named as executor in a will, but who had renounced his executorship, purchased two farms from the estate. He had intermeddled in the estate, which, according to the authorities, meant his renunciation was ineffective.[28] Despite that, the Court of Appeal reversed an order setting aside the sale on the basis that it had a discretion not to set aside a sale to a trustee where the transaction in question seemed fair in all the circumstances. This decision has since been described as one which 'must be regarded as wrongly decided',[29] and as likely to be distinguished because of its highly particular facts.[30]

Duty of loyalty

[18.20] A trustee is under a duty to acquaint him or herself with the terms of the trust and, having done so, is bound to adhere to and to carry out those terms. A trustee may only depart from the words of the trust with the approval of the court. The

---

26. *Jacobs'*, para [1733].
27. *Ex parte James* (1803) 8 Ves 337; 32 ER 385; *Aberdeen Railway Co v Blaikie Bros* (1854) 1 Macq 461; [1843–60] All ER Rep 249.
28. *Mordaunt v Clarke* (1868) LR 1 P & D 592; *Re Lord and Fullerton's Contract* [1896] 1 Ch 228.
29. *Jacobs'*, para [1738].
30. Ford & Lee, para [918].

trustee is also under a duty not to impeach the trust. The trustee cannot challenge any of its provisions; although he or she is entitled to approach the court on any question concerning the construction of the trust instrument. If anyone else challenges the instrument, the trustee is bound to defend it. The duty of loyalty also takes in the duty incumbent on a trustee not to place him or herself in a position in which his or her interest and duty might conflict. Loyalty to the trust involves more than just a negative duty of not doing anything contrary to the interests of the trust. A trustee must also act with entire good faith when carrying out the trust and must not seek to achieve any extraneous object in exercising discretions and powers conferred by the trust. In the past, when trusts were fairly narrowly drawn, the courts tended to take a generous view of this duty in cases where a trustee might have to stretch the powers expressed in by the trust in order to best serve the other duties of preserving the trust assets and protecting and providing for the welfare of the beneficiaries; or, as Lindley LJ put it, in quoting a comment which he attributed to Selwyn LJ, who died in 1869, 'The great use of a trustee is to commit judicious breaches of trust'.[31] These difficulties have been alleviated to a considerable extent by statutory powers to vary trusts and the common practice of including wide powers of variation in modern trusts: see Chapter 14. The duty of loyalty also extends to a duty to place the interests of the beneficiaries ahead of any other concerns which might appeal to the personal views of the trustees.

In *Cowan v Scargill* [1985] 3 WLR 501, the trustees of a mineworkers' pension trust refused to approve an annual investment plan of £200m unless the investments were restricted to exclude foreign investment and investments in energy sources which competed with coal. The beneficiaries of the trust were retired coal miners and the widows and children of ex-miners. The trustees were held to be in breach of their fiduciary duty for failing to put the best interests of their beneficiaries first. Those best interests would usually be the financial interests of the beneficiaries.

Where the beneficiaries can be seen as a particular group with particular concerns, their financial interests may be overridden by other considerations: *Harries v Church Commissioners for England* [1992] 1 WLR 1241.

[18.21] The duty to adhere to the terms of the trust includes the duty to pay the correct beneficiaries and to distribute the income and capital of the trust in accordance with the settlor's, or testator's, intentions. If a trustee overpays a beneficiary under a mistake of fact or law he or she is entitled to recoup the overpayment out of other moneys due to that beneficiary from the trust: *Merriman v Perpetual Trustee Co Ltd* (1895)17 LR (NSW) Eq 325. If there are no further funds to set off against any such overpayment the trustee could sue to recover money paid under mistake where the beneficiary can be shown to have been unjustly enriched: *David Securities Ltd v Commonwealth Bank*: see [6.11]. In addition to any action by the trustee other beneficiaries may be entitled to recover the overpayment through the medium of tracing: see [20.9]–[20.20]. There is now a considerable breastwork of statutory defences to protect the honest trustee against personal liability for mistakes made when distributing trust property.[32]

---

31. *National Trustees Co of Australasia Ltd v General Finance Co of Australasia Ltd* [1905] AC 373 at 375–6.

32. See *Jacobs'*, paras [1729]–[1732].

Duty to keep accounts and supply information

[18.22] A trustee must keep full and proper accounts of the trust property and must render accounts when required by the beneficiaries, subject to the trustee's right to be paid the cost of producing such accounts. In complying with this duty the trustee may employ professional accountants. Where the accounts are at all complicated or otherwise beyond his or her capabilities, the trustee is virtually bound to seek such assistance. The trustee is also obliged to provide the beneficiaries with full details of the trust investments, including evidence verifying those investments, and full information about any other trust property. When a beneficiary comes of age and, thereby, becomes entitled to a share of the fund, the trustee is obliged to inform the beneficiary of any rights he or she may have under the trust instrument: *Hawkesley v May* [1956] 1 QB 304.[33]

> In *Re Londonderry's Settlement* [1965] Ch 918, trustees of a discretionary trust decided to exercise their discretion and distribute the entire fund, thus bringing the trust to an end. One beneficiary, who was a member of the class of income and capital beneficiaries under the discretionary power, and who was also entitled to the income in default of appointment, objected to this decision and sought copies of certain documents including the minutes of meetings of the trustees, the agenda and other papers prepared for the meetings and correspondence between the trustees relating to those meetings. The trustees objected to that demand. The Court of Appeal held that the beneficiary was not entitled to access to those documents relating to the trustees' deliberations. So long as the trustees exercise their power, that is, their absolute discretion to appoint, bona fide with no improper motive, their exercise of that power cannot be challenged in the courts — and their reasons for acting as they decide are, accordingly, immaterial. Trustees exercising a discretion are not obliged to disclose their reasons. The mere fact that those reasons are reduced to writing does not change that. Salmon LJ ventured a definition of trust documents, saying, at 926, that they:
>
> (i) are documents in the possession of the trustees as trustees;
>
> (ii) contain information about the trust which the beneficiaries are entitled to know; and,
>
> (iii) the beneficiaries have a proprietary interest in the documents and, accordingly, are entitled to see them.

[18.23] The list given by Salmon LJ is of some help although his Lordship's third element appears to beg the same question he was attempting to answer. The better interpretation of this list might be that a document could only be described as a trust document if it satisfied the first two elements, in which case it then fell under the rule set out in the third. The beneficiary's rights are restricted to rights of inspection of the books and records of the trust, but title to those records, like other trust property,

---

33. The extent of this duty is a matter of some debate. Ford & Lee argue, at para [934], that it may go so far as to require the trustee to advise the beneficiary of his or her rights under the general law, presumably of trusts, although the learned authors note that it is not the trustee's duty to act as the beneficiary's legal adviser. Meagher & Gummow, *Jacobs'*, para [1715n], dismiss this suggestion as fanciful on the ground that most trustees are 'at best only accountants — and beneficiaries "gaping rustics"' and that 'If the duty did exist it would presumably extend to presenting every beneficiary with a copy of this [ie, their] book' (not, presumably, Ford & Lee). While it would be obviously inappropriate for a trustee to attempt to lecture the newly matured beneficiary on the intricacies of, say, the rule in *Howe v Lord Dartmouth*, there could well be circumstances when a mere statement of the rights of that beneficiary in that trust will not suffice and a more general survey is called for. If the position is complex the trustee may be obliged to advise the beneficiary to obtain independent legal advice. It is not a duty that can be disclaimed on the ground of difficulty or incomprehensibility.

is vested in the trustee and the beneficiary cannot claim possession of that material: *Re Simersall* (1992) 108 ALR 375.

Duty to act personally

[18.24] A trustee must act personally, and if there is more than one trustee they must also act unanimously. It is part of this rule that a trustee must not act under dictation when executing the trust. A trustee cannot delegate his or her powers unless:

(a) the delegation is specifically permitted by the trust instrument;

(b) the delegation is specifically permitted by statute; or,

(c) in cases not covered by (a) or (b), the trustee, as a matter of necessity, is bound to employ an agent. In this case, provided the trustee acts prudently in doing so, and the business delegated to the agent falls within the scope of that agent's ordinary business, the trustee will be allowed to delegate.

In considering this duty a distinction should be drawn between matters involving the execution of the trust, including the exercise of any powers and discretions conferred on the trustee, in which the trustee must act personally, or appoint a true delegate under a power conferred by the trust or by statute, and other matters concerning the business of the trust, including the implementation of decisions taken in execution of the trust, in which the trustee may properly appoint an agent. In the latter case the issue is not one of delegation but of agency. The trustee's duty then is to appoint an appropriate agent and to ensure, as far as is reasonable and practicable, that the agent is doing his or her job. In *Ex parte Belchier* (1754) Amb 218; 27 ER 144, an assignee of a bankrupt (that is, trustee of the bankrupt's estate) who employed a broker to sell a quantity of tobacco was held not liable for the loss suffered by the trust when the broker went into liquidation after receiving the proceeds of sale. A similar result was obtained in *Speight v Gaunt* (1883) 22 Ch D 727: see **[18.14]**. On the other hand, in *Wyman v Paterson* [1900] AC 271, trustees who allowed a solicitor to receive trust moneys and to hold them thereafter for over six months were held liable when the solicitor was declared bankrupt and the trust moneys were lost. The liability of the trustees in that case, however, arose from the fact that they had left the money with the solicitor for such a long time, without investing it elsewhere, rather than their action in allowing the solicitor to receive the money in the first place.

[18.25] Statutory powers of delegation are contained in the trustee legislation of every State.[34] In New South Wales the power to delegate under the Trustee Act 1925 (NSW), s 53, while wide in some respects, only allows a trustee to delegate the power to receive and hold trust money to a bank. Anyone drafting a trust in New South Wales would need to ensure that an express power to delegate the right to receive and hold trust moneys was included in the deed, unless the settlor wished to restrict the trustee to the statutory power.

Duty to consider

[18.26] A trustee who is invested with powers and discretions is under a duty to consider how best to exercise them, and, depending upon the nature of any given discre-

---

34. Trustee Act 1925 (NSW), s 53; Trusts Act 1973 (Qld), s 54; Trustee Act 1936–74 (SA), s 24; Trustee Act 1898 (Tas), s 20; Trustee Act 1958 (Vic), s 28; Trustees Act 1962–72 (WA), s 53. These various provisions are set out and discussed in detail in *Jacobs'*, paras [1724]–[1728].

tion, whether to exercise it at all. In a discretionary trust the power to which this duty will most commonly apply is the power or discretion to appoint — the power to distribute the income and/or capital of the trust. The matters which the trustee will have to take into account in fulfilling this duty will depend upon the type of trust and the state of the trust fund. Where the trust is, say, an employees' benefit fund, or superannuation fund, the trustee will have to consider such things as the number of employees, the likelihood of future payments from the fund, the level of contributions, if any, to the fund by the employee concerned. In a family trust different considerations will apply. If a trustee seeks the approval of the court to an exercise of his or her fiduciary duties and discretions, the trustee thereby surrenders the discretion to the court and must put before the court all the material necessary for the discretion to be exercised: *Marley v Mutual Security Merchant Bank* [1991] 3 All ER 198.

[18.27] Where the trustee is under an obligation to exercise a given power, the authorities say the court may compel him or her to do so, although a failure or refusal to exercise such a power may be rectified by some other decree, such as the appointment of new trustees or the institution of a scheme of arrangement.[35] Determining when a trustee has 'failed' to exercise the power to appoint in a discretionary trust may be difficult. It is clear, subject to any contrary intention being shown in the instrument creating the trust, that no requirement that the power be exercised within a 'reasonable time' can be implied in such a power: *Neill v Public Trustee* [1978] 2 NSWLR 65. In that case Hope JA expressed the view that it would be 'somewhat astonishing' if provisions creating special powers of appointment under which beneficial interests in property can be created should be subject to the same rules as to the time of their exercise as those applicable to administrative powers, such as powers of sale. In the latter, the trustees cannot exercise their powers so as to vary the relative rights of the beneficiaries while powers of appointment authorise the creation of beneficial interests. While an instrument creating a discretionary trust to appoint, as opposed to a discretionary power to appoint, might be more likely, as a matter of construction, to contain an implication that the appointment be made within some time, the principles expressed in *Neill v Public Trustee* mut apply to trusts to appoint just as much as to powers to appoint.

[18.28] In exercising powers of appointment, whether trust powers or mere powers, the trustee's duty to consider will be concerned, primarily, with the manner and time for the exercise of the power. Where the power in question is a mere power, the trustee will also have to consider whether to exercise the power at all. That does not, however, relieve the trustee from the duty to consider. In *Re Hay's Settlement Trusts* [1982] 1 WLR 202, Megarry V-C stated his opinion of the duties of a trustee holding a discretionary, or mere, power of appointment, at 210, while noting that he did not consider his list to be exhaustive:

> Apart from the obvious duty of obeying the trust instrument, and in particular making no appointment that is not authorised by it, the trustee must, first, consider periodically whether or not he should exercise the power; second, consider the range of objects of the power; and, third, consider the appropriateness of individual appointments.

Lord Wilberforce considered the duties of a trustee holding a mere power in *McPhail v Doulton* [1971] AC 424 at 449:

---

35. *McPhail v Doulton* [1971] AC 424 at 455, per Lord Wilberforce.

A trustee of an employees' benefit fund, whether given a power or a trust power, is still a trustee and he would surely consider in either case that he has a fiduciary duty ... It would be a complete misdescription of his position to say that, if he has a power unaccompanied by an imperative trust to distribute, he cannot be controlled by the court unless he exercised it capriciously, or outside the field permitted by the trust.

[18.29] It is probably unwise to attempt a comprehensive definition of what might constitute a 'capricious' exercise of a power. A trustee must act seriously when executing the trust, and would be clearly in breach of this duty if the income was allocated by some random method such as cutting a deck of cards or drawing names out of a hat. By the same token, this does not mean that the trustee must seek out all possible options before deciding on the exercise of a particular power. An exercise of a power outside the permitted field, often called a fraud on the power, will be determined by the limits set by the trust for the exercise of the power. In the case of powers of appointment this means the range of objects in favour of whom the trustee may exercise the power of appointment. The question of whether any particular appointee falls outside the field specified by the trust will be determined by construction of the trust itself. A fraud on the power is a technical fault and, if it can be shown that an appointment has been made in favour of an invalid object, it will not matter that the trustee acted in good faith in making the selection. If in doubt on such a question a trustee can only protect him or herself by seeking the direction of the court.

[18.30] Beyond those two cases there is a third: failure to exercise the power in good faith. The courts have traditionally been reluctant to interfere in the exercise of any discretion vested in a trustee. As trustees are not obliged to disclose their reasons for exercising their discretions it is difficult to show that any particular decision has not been made in good faith. Despite that evidentiary difficulty, the principles are reasonably clear. A trustee exercising a power of appointment must 'act with good faith and sincerity, and with an entire and single view to the real purpose and object of the power, and not for the purpose of accomplishing or carrying into effect any bye or sinister object': *Duke of Portland v Lady Topham* (1864) XI HLC 54 at 55, per Lord Westbury LC. Any attempt by a trustee to exercise a power so as to secure a benefit for him or herself, or some other person not an object of the power, will clearly breach this rule.[36] In *Gisborne v Gisborne* (1877) 2 App Cas 300, the House of Lords refused to interfere with the exercise by a trustee of a discretion to appoint in which the trustee held 'uncontrollable authority', to appoint or not to appoint, saying that such a power would be without check by any tribunal provided there were no *mala fides* in its execution. In that case the trustee was also a residuary legatee and stood to gain by preserving the property subject to the power but, as the testator had created that situation, the trustee's decision not to appoint could not be described as an improper exercise of his discretion. In determining the purpose and intention of the appointor/trustee the court will be concerned to establish those things as matters of substance, rather than simply being satisfied with their form.[37] The onus of proof rests on the party alleging the fraud on the power.[38] In identifying the test to be applied to determine whether a power has been exercised for ulterior or improper motive the court might be guided by the test proposed by Mason, Deane and Dawson JJ in *Whitehouse v Carlton Hotel* (1987) 162 CLR 285 at 294 , where their Honours

36. *Vatcher v Paull* [1915] AC 372 at 378, per Lord Parker.
37. *Re Burton's Settlements* [1955] 1 Ch 82 at 100, per Upjohn J; cf *Re Nicholson* [1939] Ch 11.
38. *Gordon v Australia & New Zealand Theatres Ltd* (1940) 40 SR (NSW) 512 at 517, per Jordan CJ.

stated the appropriate test for determining whether a power of allotment of shares available to the directors or majority of the company had been exercised for some impermissible purpose:

> As a matter of logic and principle, the preferable view would seem to be that regardless of whether the impermissible purpose was the dominant one or but one of a number of such objects or causes, the allotment will be invalidated if the impermissible purpose was causative in the sense that, but for its presence, 'the power would not have been exercised': per Dixon J, *Mills v Mills* (1938) 60 CLR at 186.

Duty to act impartially between beneficiaries — capital and income — The rule in Howe v Lord Dartmouth

[18.31] A trustee must act impartially between beneficiaries, particularly in matters concerning the distribution of the income and capital of the trust, unless otherwise authorised by the trust. In a discretionary trust the trustee will obviously be authorised to act otherwise. The duty of impartiality is most commonly applied in the context of trusts for the benefit of a life tenant and remainderman in which the trustee is bound to secure the best income for one while preserving the capital value of the trust property for the other. In fulfilling the duty to balance those two interests the trustee must sell any wasting or reversionary property held by the trust. Wasting property means property which is depreciating in value, such as an interest in a mine or quarry which will be eventually worked out. Reversionary property means assets which are not presently producing income but which will or may do so in the future, such as a mortgage in which instalments will not be received for some years, or a collection of antique clocks, which produce no income but which will appreciate as capital assets.

[18.32] Aside from those applications of the duty of impartiality, the most commonly cited example is the operation of the rule in *Howe v Lord Dartmouth* (1802) 7 Ves 137; 32 ER 56; in the administration of deceased estates where the will has made provision for estates in succession, that is, a life estate followed by estates in remainder in fee simple. Where a testator settles residuary personal property in succession and the will contains no direction to convert the property, there is, in the absence of any contrary intention, a presumption that the beneficiaries are intended to enjoy the property in succession and the trustees are thus required to convert any property presently consisting of wasting or reversionary assets into investments authorised by the general law, or by the will. This avoids benefiting one, usually the life tenant, at the expense of the other. There is a second leg to this rule whereby property which should have been converted but which has not been converted will be treated, for the purposes of determining the rights of the life tenant and remainderman *inter se*, as though it had been converted at the appropriate time, on the basis of the maxim that equity regards as done that which ought to be done. This rule is limited in its application. It only applies to gifts by will of property, which must be settled in succession, and then only to general gifts of personalty, that is, specific legacies of personalty and devises of realty do not fall under it.

[18.33] The practical effect of the rule in *Howe v Lord Dartmouth* is that the trustee of a deceased estate, under a will in which personalty has been settled in succession, has a duty to sell any assets or investments of the estate which are not in a form authorised by the general law, or by the will if it contains any such provision, and to invest the proceeds in authorised securities.[39] Pending that actual conversion the rights of

---

39. Trustee Act 1925 (NSW), s 14; see *Jacobs'*, paras [1807]–[1816].

the life tenant and remainderman to the capital and income of the estate are governed by a complex set of rules.[40] The unauthorised investments are treated as having been notionally converted and the life tenant is entitled to interest on those
investments, or, actually, on their notionally converted value, at a judicial rate of interest appropriate for authorised investments, or consols, as they are sometimes
called.[41] Where the will contains no power to postpone conversion, that notional
conversion is deemed to take place one year after the testator's death: *Re Fawcett*
[1940] Ch 402. Where there is a power to postpone conversion, the assets are deemed
to have been converted at the date of death: *Re Parry* [1947] 1 Ch 23. If the trustees
are given power to postpone conversion indefinitely the rule in *Howe v Lord Dartmouth* will be displaced. The testator's intention in such a case being to make a specific
gift of the property concerned to the remainderman and, by necessary implication, of
its actual income to the life tenant. In *Brown v Gellatly* (1867) 2 Ch App 751, a testator
directed his executors to operate several ships which he owned for the benefit of the
estate until they could be sold. It was held that there was no indefinite power to postpone conversion and that the life tenant was only entitled to interest on the value of
the ships at the judicial rate and not to their actual profits. In *Wentworth v Wentworth*
[1903] AC 163, a testator devised his residue upon trust to convert with a power to
postpone conversion for 21 years. He also directed that the surplus income should be
accumulated over those 21 years and go to augmenting the capital. The Privy Council
held that while rents and royalties received over the first 21 years should be accumulated and form part of the capital, the estate was to be deemed to have been converted at the end of the 21 years. In the case of a reversionary asset, such as moneys
due under a mortgage which are not payable until some time after the testator's
death, the net amount received will be apportioned between life tenant and remainderman by calculating the amount which, if invested at the judicial rate of interest for
authorised investments at the date of the testator's death, accumulating compound
interest at that rate thereafter until the date of realisation, would, at that date, produce
the amount actually received. The sum so calculated is then treated as capital and the
balance as accumulated interest: *Re Chesterfield* (1883) 24 Ch D 643.

[18.34] Any surplus of actual income over the notional interest payable to the life
tenant pending actual conversion is treated as capital and re-invested. The life tenant
then receives interest on that additional capital as well. The life tenant can only be
paid out of actual income, whatever his or her notional entitlement may be. If the
actual income is not sufficient to pay him or her the full amount of judicial interest he
or she will be entitled to a charge on the capital for that shortfall which must be paid
from the proceeds upon conversion. If the executors fail to convert the property
when they should, and the trust suffers a loss, of either income or capital, they will be
personally liable for that loss. In making up any such loss, the duty of the executors
will be to put both life tenant and remainderman in the position each would have
enjoyed respectively had the executors done their duty: *Bate v Hooper* (1855) 5 De GM
& G 338; 43 ER 901.

[18.35] Where advancements have been made by the testator during his or her lifetime to beneficiaries named in his or her will, and the will directs that those advancements be taken into account in determining shares of the residuary estate, deemed

---

40. See *Jacobs'*, ch 19 on this and other questions of capital and income generally.
41. For a long time the rate applied was 4%. In *Re Lewin* [1961] VR 528, 5% was the rate set. The
authors of *Jacobs'* suggest that the rate may now be much higher. In their 4th edition they give a figure of 8%, but, in their 5th edition, para [1914] they give no figure, simply saying that it may be much
higher. Ford & Lee simply adopt 8% from the 4th edition of *Jacobs'*. See also [19.14].

income on those advancements is to be included in calculating the shares of income payable to life tenants under this rule: *Re Poyser* [1908] 1 Ch 828.[42]

Capital and income — apportionment generally

[18.36] Apart from the special requirements of the rule in *Howe v Lord Dartmouth*, trustees administering estates for the benefit of life tenants and remaindermen must distinguish between capital and income for the purposes of properly apportioning the trust fund while complying with the duty of impartiality. In most cases the distinction between what is capital and what is income is not difficult to draw. In some situations, however, the question is not so easy. Where there is a capital profit on the sale of some asset in the estate, for instance, the profit will be treated as an augmentation of the capital of the trust, and not income, so that there will not be any apportionment between life tenant and remainderman. This will even apply to a sale of shares pregnant with dividend: *Scholefield v Redfern* (1862) 2 Dr & Sm 173; 62 ER 587, subject to the existence of any unusual circumstances which might unduly prejudice the life tenant, in which case the courts may make an exception.[43] Where the trust holds shares in a company, any dividends paid in cash on those shares will clearly be income. The position is less certain where the company distributes its profits by issuing bonus shares, or by giving its shareholders the option of taking cash or shares. If the company decides to capitalise its profits any bonus shares thus issued will be held by the trustee as capital. If the company declares a dividend and gives the shareholder the option of re-investing that dividend by purchasing further shares, that dividend will belong to the life tenant, as will any shares purchased with it by the trustee: *Re Kennan* [1924] VLR 356. On the other hand, if the company offers bonus shares in lieu of dividend, on such advantageous terms that it is clear that the company's purpose is to capitalise its profits, the bonus shares thus acquired will be treated as capital: *Bouch v Sproule* (1887) 12 App Cas 385. If the shares held by the trust give the trustee sufficient voting power to determine the question of whether profits are capitalised or distributed as dividends, the rule is that the trustee must exercise those voting rights so as best to maintain strict impartiality between life tenant and remainderman: *Re Campbell* [1973] 2 NSWLR 146. Where a trust holds shares, the shares will represent the capital of the trust while dividends will be income. In this sense, an election by the company to capitalise profits rather than paying them out as dividend will transform them into capital. In *Hill v Permanent Trustee Co of NSW Ltd* (1933) 33 SR (NSW) 527; [1930] AC 720 (PC) the Privy Council held that where a company makes a payment to its shareholders, except by way of an authorised reduction of capital or a distribution of assets on winding up, that money will belong to the life tenant unless there is some provision in the trust deed to alter that outcome. Conversely, where a company elects to keep its profits and increase its capital. The fully paid shares issued as a result are capital.

[18.37] Where the trust conducts a business, either on its own account or as one of a number of partners in some concern, there will often be difficulties in deciding whether some particular receipt is capital or income. The decision in any given case

---

42. The method of calculating intermediate income in *Re Poyser* was approved of by the High Court in *Re Tennant* (1941) 65 CLR 473. But, note that there is another approach: *Re Hargreaves* [1900–03] All ER Rep 80. See *Jacobs'*, paras [1916]–[1919].
43. *Londesborough v Somerville* (1854) 19 Beav 295; 52 ER 363; *Bulkeley v Stephens* [1896] 2 Ch 241 and *Re Winterstroke's Will Trusts* [1938] Ch 158; but cf *Re Firth 's Estate* [1938] Ch 517. See *Jacobs'*, paras [1933]–[1934].

will usually be determined by the nature of the business involved. In *McBride v Hudson* (1962) 107 CLR 604, a pastoral property was left to the testator's widow and son in common during the life of the widow and thereafter to the son and the testator's daughter. During the widow's lifetime the number of sheep on the property rose from 1859 to 4346, by natural increase. The son later claimed that the additional sheep represented income of the estate and not capital. The High Court held that all 4,346 were capital. Taylor J observed that the meaning of the word 'profits' in any case will depend upon the nature of the business concerned and the manner in which it is customarily carried on and, if in carrying on a business trustees adopt a conventional and appropriate method of accounting to determine the profit for any period, no exception can be taken. In *McBride*, there was nothing in the terms of the will, nor in the nature of the business, which could justify a claim by the life tenant to unrealised book profits. In *Kelly v Perpetual Trustee Co Ltd* (1963) 109 CLR 258, a different result obtained. The estate carried on a tin smelting business from 1917 until 1950 when the business was sold. The sale included a quantity of surplus tin which had never been brought into the profit and loss account of the company and which was sold for over £184,000. The High Court held that the surplus tin recovered each year was a profit of the business to which the life tenant was entitled. The fact that the tin had not been entered in the accounts of the company as profit was irrelevant. In coming to that decision the High Court rejected an argument there was a difference between a gain made in the ordinary course of business and the proceeds of realisation on the closing down of the business, saying that an item of profit does not lose its character merely because it is sold otherwise than in the course of business. In coming to that conclusion the court distinguished *McBride v Hudson* by saying there was no analogy between lasting and barren stocks of surplus tin and flocks or herds of live animals which produce a natural increase.

[18.38] In *Re Richards* [1974] 2 NZLR 60, the New Zealand Supreme Court considered facts very similar to those of *McBride* and held that the life tenant was entitled to so much of the livestock as could be described as surplus stock, that is, the surplus above the optimum number for the property. In that case the trustees had engaged in a deliberate policy of building up the stock numbers. While such a policy might be part of the prudent management of any farming operation, it should not be conducted at the expense of the life tenant. Ford and Lee suggest that this approach may not be entirely appropriate for Australia where extremes of climate require that trustees managing a farming business be given very broad discretions in stock management.[44] So that, while a life tenant may not be able to claim 'surplus' stock built up during good years, a loss of stock from drought, flood or fire should be treated as primarily a capital loss and not something to be made up by the life tenant alone: *Thomas v Thomas* [1939] St R Qd 301.

18–4 Powers of a Trustee

[18.39] Duties are what a trustee must do in carrying out the trust. Powers are what the trustee may do in the administration of that trust. While that gives the trustee a discretion not to exercise any given power he or she will still hold that power as a fiduciary and must observe the duty to consider when making any decision about the exercise of any of the powers conferred by the trust instrument or by law. The pow-

---

44. Ford & Lee, para [1127.3].

ers exercisable by a trustee are derived from three sources: the trust instrument, statutory powers available to the trustee and any power conferred on the trustee by the court. For powers conferred by the court, see Chapter 14.

Powers of sale

[18.40] A trustee will not be entitled to sell any trust property unless powers of sale are expressly or impliedly conferred by the trust instrument, by statute or by order of the court. A power of sale will be implied where the beneficial interests in the trust property are willed in succession, in favour of a life tenant and remainderman, so that the trustee is under a duty to convert the property. It has been held that a direction to distribute also confers an implied power of sale.[45] While there is a general statutory power to postpone sales,[46] there is no general statutory power of sale, although powers of sale are provided by statute in some circumstances, that is, where the trustee has to pay or apply capital money for any purpose, or where the trustee must pay rates and charges due on trust property and lacks the funds to do so otherwise.[47]

Powers of management

[18.41] In modern times trusts have been used for a variety of purposes, including as the vehicle for the conduct of a business. In such a case the intention of the settlor will be to provide the trustee with adequate powers to manage the business of the trust as a flexible source of continuing benefit, rather than simply overseeing its conversion and the distribution of the proceeds among those intended to benefit. Subject to any express powers in the trust, a trustee with active duties in the management of trust property has a duty to maintain the property in a good state of repair, and thus is bound to attend to its repair and any necessary maintenance work.[48] A trustee without active duties to perform has no power to effect repairs, let alone make any improvements, without the authority of the court. That duty, and its corresponding power, does not, however, extend to the improvement of the trust property without express authorisation in the trust deed.[49] Clearly, the careful draftsperson will give the trustee power to effect such repair and improvement as the trustee deems expedient. Statutory powers of management are provided in the trustee legislation of all States except Victoria and Tasmania.[50] Under the general law a trustee cannot carry on a business unless expressly authorised by the trust instrument or by the court. In Queensland and Western Australia the power to conduct a business is conferred by statute.[51]

---

45. *Altson v Equity Trustees, Executors and Agency Ltd* (1912) 14 CLR 341; *Pagels v MacDonald* (1936) 54 CLR 519.
46. Trustee Act 1925 (NSW), s 27B with corresponding powers of management during any postponement under Conveyancing Act 1919 (NSW), ss 66D and 151C. There are sections similar to s 27B in the Trustee Acts in Victoria (s 13), Queensland (s 32) and Western Australia (s 27), but not in South Australia or Tasmania.
47. Trustee Act 1925 (NSW), s 38 (see *Jacobs'*, paras [2004]–[2007]).
48. *Amos v Fraser* (1906) 4 CLR 78 at 84, per Griffith CJ.
49. *Harkness v Harkness* (1903) 20 WN (NSW) 216.
50. Trustee Act 1925 (NSW), ss 82 and 82A; Trusts Act 1973 (Qld), s 33 Trustee Act 1936–74 (SA), s 25a; Trustees Act 1962–72 (WA), s 30 (see Ford & Lee, paras [1243.1]–[1243.6].
51. Trusts Act 1973 (Qld), s 57; Trustees Act 1962 1972 (WA), s 55.

Powers of maintenance and advancement

[18.42] Where a trust is settled so that interests under it are vested but not presently payable, or are contingent upon the happening of some event, the question may arise as to whether the trustee has the authority to make payments out of the income for the maintenance, or out of capital for the advancement of beneficiaries in anticipation of their rights under the trust. No such power was available to trustees under the general law unless by express provision in the trust instrument. Statutory powers of maintenance and advancement are provided in all States.[52] A power to make advancements of capital are construed liberally. Such a power is recognised as one which is, 'frequently conferred on trustees under settlements of personalty ... to enable them in a proper case to anticipate the vesting in possession of an intended beneficiary's contingent or reversionary interest by raising money on account of his interest and paying or applying it immediately for his benefit': *Pilkington v IRC* [1964] AC 612. In that case, the Court of Appeal recognised that while the exercise of such a power might result in a shrinkage of the capital of the fund, that possibility was recognised and accepted as an incidental risk in the exercise of such a power, and it was felt on the whole to be advantageous to have such a power in a system in which the possession of capital might be deferred for some time.

[18.43] Under the statutory power to make payments for the maintenance, education and benefit of an infant a trustee may apply income for the benefit of an infant beneficiary even though the infant's interest is contingent and gives no right to intermediate income, that is, income received pending the happening of the contingency, provided that income is not expressly disposed of otherwise by the trust instrument.[53]

---

52. Trustee Act 1925 (NSW), ss 43–44; Trusts Act 1973 (Qld), s 61–63; Trustee Act 1936–74 (SA), ss 33, 33a; Trustee Act 1898 (Tas), s 29; Trustee Act 1958 (Vic), ss 37–8; Trustees Act 1962–72 (WA), ss 58–60.
53. Note the effect of Convayancing Act 1919 (NSW), 536B on the disposition of intermediate income (see *Jacobs'*, para [2051]).

Chapter Nineteen

The Rights and Liabilities of Trustees

19-1 Rights of a Trustee

The right of reimbursement and indemnity

[19.1] A trustee who has expended money or incurred debts on behalf of the trust is entitled to reimbursement from the trust funds for the moneys expended and to an indemnity for debts and other obligations incurred. This right extends to all expenses and obligations properly incurred in the administration of the trust. If the loss arises from some activity which is ultra vires the trust, the trustee will have no right to recoupment from the trust.[1] The right to indemnity is a general law right,[2] and has been confirmed by statute.[3] In *Re Raybould* [1900] 1 Ch 199, a judgment was obtained by a third party against the trustee of a deceased estate, the assets of which included certain collieries, for damages arising from subsidence at one of the collieries. It was held, provided the damage had not been caused by any reckless or improper working of the business by the trustee, that the trustee was entitled to be indemnified out of the trust estate for any damages and costs awarded against him. A trustee is also entitled to recover costs incurred in any proceedings conducted on behalf of the trust, on a solicitor and client or trustee basis.[4] In addition to the right of reimbursement the trustee is also entitled to use the trust property in the first instance to discharge a liability incurred for the purposes of the trust.

[19.2] The amount of trust property available for recoupment of expenses by the trustee can be limited by the will, with the result that excluded trust assets will not be available to creditors after the death of the testator: *Ex parte Garland* (1803) 10 Ves 110; 32 ER 786. A trustee in default will lose this right of indemnity, at least until the breach or default has been made good.[5] In *Re Staff Benefits Pty Ltd* [1979] 1 NSWLR 207 (see [9.14]), Needham J expressed the view, *obiter*, that this might not apply to breaches which did not relate to the subject matter of the indemnity, and it could certainly be argued that it should not apply to breaches which cause no loss to the trust.[6]

---

1. HAJ Ford, 'Trading Trusts and Creditors' Rights' (1981) 13 Melb ULR 1 at 16.
2. *Worrall v Harford* (1802) 8 Ves 4 at 8, per Lord Eldon; 32 ER 250 at 252.
3. Trustee Act 1925 (NSW), s 59(4); Trusts Act 1973 (Qld), s 72; Trustee Act 1936–68 (SA), s 35(2); Trustee Act 1898 (Tas), s 27(2); Trustee Act 1958 (Vic), s 36(2); Trustee Act 1962–78 (WA), s 71.
4. *National Trustees Executors and Agency Co of Australasia Ltd v Barnes* (1941) 64 CLR 268.
5. *Re Staff Benefits Pty Ltd* [1979] 1 NSWLR 207 at 215.
6. Ford, 'Trading Trusts and Creditors' Rights', *op cit*, at 14.

The estate of an executor of a deceased estate who committed a breach of trust by agreeing to sell the major asset of the trust, a house, at an undervalue ($50,000 as opposed to an estimated real value at the time of $100,000) was held not to be entitled to an indemnity out of the trust for the late executor's personal liability on the contract except to the extent of her own interest as a beneficiary of the estate and to the extent of the interest of another beneficiary who instigated or facilitated the sale: *Stokes v Churchill* (1994) NSW Conv R 55–694, per Santow J.

Right to reimbursement from beneficiaries

[19.3] In *Hardoon v Belilios* [1901] AC 118, the Privy Council held that the trustee's right to indemnity included a right in personam against the beneficiary as well as a right in rem against the assets of the trust, at least where the beneficiary is *sui juris* and absolutely entitled. It was also suggested that this would extend to multiple beneficiaries, provided all were *sui juris*. This right of indemnity against the beneficiary was said to be based, not on any consent or request by the beneficiary, express or implied, but on 'the plainest principles of justice (that) require that the *cestui que trust* who gets all the benefit of the property should bear the burden', per Lord Lindley, at 125. This right will not apply in the case of a discretionary trust where the 'beneficiaries' are simply objects of the trustee's discretion. Such objects have no right to call on the trustee to give them any benefits from the trust. They could hardly be called upon to meet its liabilities.[7] The same conclusion must apply to a trust in favour of an unincorporated association: *Wise v Perpetual Trustee Co Ltd* [1903] AC 139 at 149, per Lord Lindley. Where a beneficiary assigns his or her interest in the trust, the assignor remains liable to indemnify the trustee for any liability, including liabilities incurred after the assignment, unless the assignor secures a release from the trustee. As between the assignor and the assignee there would be an implied undertaking that the assignee would indemnify the assignor in respect of any liability, although that would not affect the trustee's right to demand an indemnity from either of them: *Matthews v Ruggles-Brise* [1911] 1 Ch 194.

[19.4] In *JW Broomhead (Vic) Pty Ltd (in liq) v J W Broomhead Pty Ltd & Ors* [1985] VR 891, McGarvie J held that the principle in *Hardoon v Belilios* applied to a unit trust and that unit holders who were *sui juris* and who had not disclaimed the trust were bound to indemnify the trustee in respect of a liability incurred by the trustee in the course of carrying out the trust, to the extent of each unit holder's proportion of the beneficial interest in the trust. The liability to indemnify the trustee attached to unit holders who were themselves trustees of other trusts, as some were of discretionary trusts. Those unit holders were, presumably, entitled to be indemnified out of the assets of the trusts for which the units were held and thus the trustee of the unit trust had access to the assets of those discretionary trusts by way of subrogation to the rights of the unitholder/trustee. A unit holder who disclaimed the trust when she became aware that units had been issued to her and other infant unit holders were held not to be liable to indemnify the trustee. That meant that the trustee was not indemnified for the whole of the loss by the unit holders. It was only reimbursed for a proportion of the loss representing the proportion of unit holders liable and able to pay. Where a unit holder was insolvent that unit holder's proportion remained unpaid; it was not spread among the solvent unit holders. The liability of beneficiaries under the principle in *Hardoon v Belilios* may be excluded by express provision in the instrument of

---

7. *Ibid*, at 8.

trust. In *McLean v Burns Philp Trustee Co Pty Ltd* (1985) 2 NSWLR 632, Young J held that a clause in a public unit trust purporting to exclude the unit holders from personal liability to indemnify the trustee against liabilities incurred in the course of carrying out the trusts operated to exclude the unit holders from liability. In *Countryside (No 3) Pty Ltd v Bayside Brunswick Pty Ltd* (SC(NSW), Brownie J, 20 April,13 May 1994, unreported), Brownie J held that Countryside (No 3) Pty Ltd, as a creditor of the trustee was entitled to succeed against the unit holders of a unit trust in a claim for damages arising from a breach of contract alleged against the trustee for failure to complete a contract for the purchase of land from the plaintiff. There was no provision in the trust excluding the beneficiaries from any liability to indemnify the trustee. Some unit holders pleaded in their defence that they had not taken up their units at the time the trustee entered into the contract and ought not to be held liable to indemnify the trustee for liabilities incurred before they became unit holders. Brownie J dismissed that argument on the basis that there was a clear inference that the unit holders took up their units knowing of the obligations of the trustee and that they had done so intending to benefit from the development of the land being purchased. In addition to the units taken up by the first unit holders in the Bayside Brunswick Unit Trust, a substantial number of further units had been issued at a discount to some unit holders. The trust deed provided that all units were of equal value. Brownie J held that the unit holders were liable to indemnify the trustee in proportions reflecting their actual unit holdings, regardless of the subscription price paid for any particular units.[8]

Right to reimbursement and indemnity from the assets of the trust

[19.5] A trustee who carries on a business on behalf of the trust, with authority to do so under the deed, will still be personally liable for any debts incurred, but will be entitled to reimbursement for all expenses properly incurred in the conduct of that business. In general, a trustee who carries on a business without authority will not be entitled to reimbursement, although that will not necessarily debar a creditor from claiming against the trust estate, at least to the extent of any benefit that creditor has conferred on the trust. In *Devaynes v Robinson* (1857) 24 Beav 86; 53 ER 289, executors directed by the will to sell real estate mortgaged it instead. Lord Romilly MR declared that the mortgage was not binding and directed that the properties be sold. The mortgagee was held to be entitled, however, to stand as a creditor against the purchase money. In Queensland and Western Australia personal representatives are empowered by statute to carry on the deceased's business for a minimum of two years, and, in doing so, may employ any part of the estate which is subject to the same trusts.[9] In the case of a deceased estate the picture may be complicated by the claims of creditors of the estate, both in respect of debts incurred by the testator before his or her death and debts subsequently incurred by the executor.

In *Vacuum Oil Co Pty Ltd v Wiltshire* (1945) 72 CLR 319, an executor carried on a service station business, despite a lack of power to do so in the will. Prior to his death in 1932, the testator had built up a debt of £575 with Vacuum Oil. In December 1933 the executor obtained an order from the court authorising him to carry on the business for another three months. In the event, he carried it on until October 1936. By that time the £575 had been reduced to £431 but a further debt of £36 had been incurred. Vacuum disputed the trustee's decision to postpone its claim to that of other trade credi-

---

8. An appeal against this decision was heard on 14 August 1996.
9. Trusts Act 1973 (Qld), s 57; Trustees Act 1962–68 (WA), s 55.

tors of the estate on the ground that Vacuum had assented to the executor's continued trading after the expiry of the court order in 1934. The High Court held that Vacuum's conduct did not amount to assent to the postponement of its claim pending the outcome of the attempt to trade out of difficulties and that its claim should not, therefore, be postponed to that of other trade creditors. Latham CJ laid down certain principles governing the rights of a trustee in such circumstances:

1. An executor is entitled to carry on a business, subject to any express power in the will, for the purpose of realising that business, and only for that purpose. If he incurs debts in doing so, they are his debts, not the debts of the testator. But, as against both creditors of the business and beneficiaries of the estate, he is entitled to an indemnity out of the assets of the estate.

2. If an executor is authorised to carry on a business he will still be personally liable for any debts incurred, although, as against the beneficiaries, he will be entitled to an indemnity out of the estate, and from any assets acquired in carrying on the business, for those debts.

3. If an executor, without express power to do so, carries on a business otherwise than for the purpose of realisation, the debts are his debts and he has no rights, as against either the creditors or the beneficiaries, to meet them out of the trust assets.

4. If a beneficiary, or a creditor, authorises him to carry on the business, the executor will be entitled to an indemnity as against that beneficiary or creditor.

5. Such an authorisation can be construed from the assent of the beneficiary or creditor concerned, although it is not easy to determine what conduct amounts to such assent.

6. Mere knowledge that the business is being carried on otherwise than for the purposes of realisation, and subsequent inaction, will not amount to assent.

7. This principle is not an example of the equitable doctrine of acquiescence. A person acting in infringement of the rights of another under that doctrine should be acting under a mistake as to his own rights.

8. Assets acquired by the executor in carrying on the business are assets of the estate and will be available to estate creditors on the same basis as assets held by the testator at the date of his death.

9. Where an estate is administered in bankruptcy no distinction will be drawn between assets acquired before and after death.

10. While creditors whose debts are owed by the executor personally are not, strictly speaking, creditors of the estate, they will still be allowed to prove in the bankruptcy of the estate because the executor may be entitled to an indemnity from the estate, and those creditors will then be entitled to access to the estate through the executor.

[19.6] A trust has no separate legal existence and creditors of the trustee have no direct access to the assets of the trust. Their only recourse is to take action against the trustee and their only means of access to the assets of the trust is by subrogation to the trustee's right to be indemnified out of those assets for debts properly incurred in execution of the trust. Creditors need only show that proceedings against the trustee have been or are likely to be fruitless before they will be able to proceed directly against the trust assets,[10] or against the beneficiaries, provided there is no express exclusion of their liability: *Countryside (No 3) Pty Ltd v Bayside Brunswick Pty Ltd* (SC (NSW), Brownie J, 20 April 1994, unreported). The trustee's right of indemnity from the assets gives rise to a lien in his or her favour over the trust assets, and that is the right to which creditors would seek to be subrogated as they could not levy execution

---

10. *Owen v Delamere* (1872) LR 15 Eq 134 at 139–40. Note: *Octavo Investments Pty Ltd v Knight* (1979) 144 CLR 360 at 367; DR Williams, 'Winding Up Trading Trusts: Rights of Creditors and Beneficiaries' (1983) 57 ALJ 273 at 275.

on a common law judgment against the trust assets themselves.[11] The trustee's right of indemnity has been described as a first charge on the assets of the trust[12] and is transmissible in bankruptcy to the trustee in bankruptcy of the bankrupt trustee's estate. In *Octavo Investments Pty Ltd v Knight* (1979) 144 CLR 360, Coastline Distributors Pty Ltd (Coastline), a company which had acted as a trustee, was wound up. In the six months prior to presentation of a winding up petition, Coastline had made repayments of $49,750 in borrowed moneys to Octavo Investments Pty Ltd (Octavo), a company with common directors. When the liquidator claimed those moneys back from Octavo as a preferential payment, Octavo argued that they were trust moneys in Coastline's hands. The High Court held that the payment to Octavo was a voidable preference. The trustee's right to be indemnified out of the trust assets for trading liabilities, and the consequential right to retain possession of the trust property as against the beneficiaries for that purpose, gave it an interest in the trust property which amounted to a proprietary interest which passed to the trustee in bankruptcy for the benefit of the creditors of the trading trust.

[19.7] Professor Ford has criticised the description of the trustee's right of indemnity, or exoneration as he puts it (in the sense that the trustee could apply trust property directly to meet obligations of the trust, rather than paying them him or herself and then seeking recoupment) as a proprietary interest.[13] Ford argues that, rather than a proprietary interest, the trustee's rights over the trust property are more in the nature of a fiduciary power, a power which is subject to other considerations, particularly whether the trustee is in breach and thereby barred from access to the assets. Despite that criticism, he acknowledges that it would be obviously unsatisfactory if an insolvent trustee-debtor could prefer a creditor.[14] It should be noted, in this context, that the definition of 'property of a bankrupt' under the Bankruptcy Act 1966 (Cth), s 5, includes 'property divisible amongst the creditors of the bankrupt and includes any rights and powers in relation to that property that would have been exercisable by the bankrupt if he had not become bankrupt'. In view of that it is difficult to argue with the contention that a bankrupt trustee's right of indemnity against the trust assets, at least in the sense of a right of recoupment for moneys laid out, is a right of 'property', for the purposes of the Bankruptcy Act.

[19.8] The extent to which trust property will be available on the bankruptcy of the trustee is a matter of some controversy. *Octavo* decided that a payment to one creditor of the trust's trading operation by the trustee out of the trust assets was voidable as a preference, but beyond that there are many difficult questions. Can assets available to the trustee by virtue of the right of indemnity be used to meet the trustee's private debts? Can the assets of the trust be used to meet the expenses of the liquidation of a corporate trustee? In *Re Byrne Australia Pty Ltd* [1981] 1 NSWLR 394, Needham J answered the first question in the negative, holding that trust assets could only be applied to meet trust liabilities. In *Re Enhill Pty Ltd* (1982) 7 ACLR 8, the Victorian Full Court came to the opposite view and held that where a bankrupt trustee was entitled to an indemnity from the trust, the trust assets would be available to the liquidator to cover the costs of the liquidation and to pay out private creditors of the trustee, to the extent of the value of the indemnity. The authors of *Jacobs'* dismiss that decision as 'obviously wrong' saying it is based on the fallacy that trust property

---

11. *Jennings v Mather* [1902] 1 KB 1; *Stevens v Hince* (1914) 110 LT 935; *Re Johnson* (1880) 15 Ch D 548 at 552.
12. *Re Pumfrey* (1882) 22 Ch D 255 at 262.
13. Ford, 'Trading Trusts and Creditors' Rights', *op cit*, at 26–7.
14. *Ibid*, at 27.

transferred to a trustee to meet a trust liability somehow ceases to be trust property.[15] In *Re Suco Gold Pty Ltd* (1983) 7 ACLR 873, the South Australian Full Court expressed a similar opinion. That view must be correct where the trustee is exercising the right which Ford describes as a right of 'exoneration', that is, where the trust assets are applied immediately by the trustee to meet trust liabilities. But where the trustee's right is in the nature of a right of recoupment, that is, where a trust liability has been paid for by the trustee out of his or her own pocket and the trustee is, in effect and in fact, owed that money out of the trust, trust moneys, to the extent of that right of recoupment, will be available to pay the trustee's general creditors. There is no conflict with the fundamental principles of trusts if that valuable right is made available to the private creditors of the trustee. Both *Re Enhill Pty Ltd* and *Re Suco Cold Pty Ltd* answered the second question in the affirmative while Needham J was of a different opinion. The latter view is supported by the authors of Jacobs' on the ground that trust assets can only be applied to meet expenses of the trust, and the costs of the liquidation are not such an expense.[16] Once again, it is submitted that the position would be different if the trustee's right was one of recoupment rather than exoneration. In *Grime Carter & Co Pty Ltd v Whytes Furniture Pty Ltd* [1983] 1 NSWLR 158 and also in *Re ADM Franchise Pty Ltd* (1983) 1 ACLC 987, McLelland J chose not to follow *Re Byrne* and applied the reasoning of *Re Suco Gold* instead. Despite the views of the authors of Jacobs' and the judgment of Needham J, whose views on any point of equity cannot be dismissed lightly, the principles stated in *Re Suco Gold* must be preferred. As a practical matter, no one would undertake the unfortunately necessary work of acting as liquidator of a corporate trustee if the costs of liquidation could not be recouped out of trust moneys. Furthermore, the expenses of a liquidator when incurred in the winding up of a trust when things have gone badly must be viewed in the same light as fees and charges paid by the trust to accountants, brokers and solicitors when the going is good.

The right of contribution

[19.9] Where there is more than one trustee all the trustees will be jointly and severally liable to the beneficiaries for any loss arising from a breach of trust. If such a loss occurs and one trustee makes restitution to the trust, that trustee will be entitled to contribution from the others: *Bahin v Hughes* (1886) 31 Ch D 390. In that case, a passive trustee was held not to be entitled to be fully indemnified by the active trustee for a loss incurred when the active one made an honest mistake in investing trust moneys in breach of trust. All the trustees were held to be equally liable to indemnify the beneficiaries. In *Bacon v Camphausen* (1888) 58 LT 851, a passive trustee who resided in Paris, was held to be liable to contribution for a loss caused by his active co-trustees in England. There had been an arrangement between the trustees that the absent one would not be troubled about the affairs of the trust. When the trust suffered a loss upon the failure of a mortgage security, and the loss was made good by one trustee, the absent one was held liable to contribute. A trustee who is also a beneficiary and who concurs in a breach of trust will not be entitled to contribution from his or her fellow trustee, except to the extent to which the loss exceeds his beneficial interest: *Chillingworth v Chambers* [1896] 1 Ch 685. That arises from the combined effect of the rule that trustees are equally liable to make good any loss arising from a breach of trust and the rule that a *cestui que trust* who acquiesces in a breach of trust

---

15. *Jacobs'*, para [2114].
16. *Ibid*.

will not be entitled to an indemnity from the trustee. A trustee who has obtained a benefit in breach of trust will not be entitled to contribution in making restitution, nor would a trustee whose breach is intentional, even though that trustee does not profit from the wrong. In such a case, the other trustees will be entitled, and indeed would be obliged, to take proceedings for restitution on behalf of the trust against the miscreant: *Powlet v Herbert* (1791) 1 Ves Jun 297; 30 ER 352. If the trustees place particular reliance on the professional or business skills of one of their number, and that trustee discharges those responsibilities negligently so that the trust suffers a loss, the negligent trustee may be liable to indemnify the others for the whole loss: *Lockhart v Reilly* (1856) 25 LJ Ch 697; although that will not relieve a passive trustee who has encouraged the impropriety from being held liable to contribute in making good the loss: *Head v Gould* [1898] 2 Ch 250.

Right to impound a beneficiary's interest

[19.10] A trustee who commits a breach of trust at the request of, or at the instigation of, a beneficiary will be entitled to impound that beneficiary's share of the trust assets to secure an indemnity from that beneficiary for liability imposed on the trustee to make good any loss arising from the breach.[17] In *Fletcher v Collis* [1905] 2 Ch 24, a beneficiary entitled to a life interest consented to the sale of certain trust property and the distribution of the proceeds to his wife, who spent the money. The trustee was later ordered to make good the loss and paid the money into court. A claim by the life tenant for the interest received from the money paid into court was dismissed.

[19.11] If a beneficiary instigates, requests or authorises an investment which is outside the powers conferred on the trustee, the trustee will be entitled to the protection of this rule. However, if the investment is within its powers, the trustee will not be allowed the benefit of the section if the investment fails and it can be shown that the trustee failed to exercise reasonable care in investing the trust fund: *Re Somerset* [1894] 1 Ch 231.

Right to obtain the opinion, advice and direction of the court

[19.12] If in doubt about the powers available or the duties imposed by the trust, a trustee may seek the opinion, advice and direction of the court under a statutory right conferred in all States except Tasmania.[18] A trustee making application for such advice must put before the court all material and relevant facts. A trustee who follows this procedure, and complies with the requirements of full disclosure, will be protected thereafter in acting on the advice given: *Re Grose* [1949] SASR 55. A trustee who acts on other advice even that of the most senior counsel will not be protected if it is found that there has, in fact, been a breach of trust. The trustee, may, nonetheless, be relieved from liability if it can be shown that it has acted honestly and reasonably and ought fairly to be excused: see **[19.16]**.

---

17. Trustee Act 1925 (NSW), s 86(1); Trusts Act 1973 (Qld), s 77; Trustee Act 1936–68 (SA), s 57; Trustee Act 1898 (Tas), s 53; Trustee Act 1958 (Vic), s 68; Trustee Act 1962–78 (WA), s 76.
18. Trustee Act 1925 (NSW), s 63; Trusts Act 1973 (Qld), s 96; Trustee Act 1936–68 (SA), s 91; Rules of the Supreme Court O 55 r 3 (Vic); Trustee Act 1962–78 (WA), s 92.

19-2 Liability of a Trustee

[19.13] A trustee in breach of trust will be liable to make good any loss suffered by the trust, regardless of whether the breach is the result of intentional dishonesty or merely a technical wrong, an error of judgment, and even though the trustee acted honestly and in good faith. For instance, where trustees are under a duty to sell unauthorised investments, and fail to do so promptly, they are liable for the difference between the price at which the investments would have been sold and the actual sale price: *Grayburn v Clarkson* (1868) 3 Ch App 605. Where trustees make an unauthorised investment they are liable for any loss incurred when it is realised: *Knott v Cotte* (1852) 16 Beav 77; 51 ER 588. Where more than one breach of trust has been committed the trustees will not be able to set-off a profit arising from one breach against a loss suffered on another: *Wiles v Gresham* (1854) 2 Drew 258 at 271; 61 ER 718 at 723, unless the gain and loss arise from the same transaction or related dealings: *Fletcher v Green* (1864) 33 Beav 426; 55 ER 433; *Bartlett v Barclays Bank Trust Co Ltd (No 1)* [1980] Ch 515. The court has power to excuse a trustee who has acted honestly and reasonably and who ought fairly to be excused. A trustee may also be excused from liability by the terms of the instrument although, it is submitted, no form of words could excuse someone who was properly a trustee from liability for any act committed mala fide.

[19.14] The obligation of a trustee in breach is to put the trust estate into the same position it would have enjoyed had the breach not occurred.

> In *Re Dawson (dec'd)* [1966] 2 NSWR 211, the trustee of a deceased estate improperly paid £NZ4,700 to an agent who misappropriated the money. By the time action was taken to recoup the loss the Australian currency, which had been at par with the New Zealand pound when the payment was made, had been revalued and the sum required in Australian currency to make good the loss was £A5,829 8s 3d. It was submitted on behalf of Dawson's executors that the trustee's liability to restore the money to the trust should be measured at the date of default. Street J held that the obligation of a defaulting trustee was one of effecting restitution to the estate and was not limited by common law principles governing remoteness of damage. His duty was to put the trust estate in the same position as it would have been in if there had been no default. Monetary compensation is assessed by reference to the value of the assets at the date of restoration.

In that case, Street J said at 218, 'the general principle is that where a trustee has, through his breach of trust, occasioned loss to the trust's estate then he is liable to make good that loss together with interest'. The interest rate referred to there by Street J was the 'trustee rate' said to be the rate obtainable in government stock at the time: *Pallette Shoes Pty Ltd (in liq) v Krohn* [1937] VLR 314. This rate is distinguished from the 'mercantile' or commercial rate applied as a means of recovering profit received or presumed to have been received by a trustee as a result of misapplication of trust funds: *Hagan v Waterhouse* (1991) 34 NSWLR 308 at 392. Until recent times the trustee rate was 4 per cent as a matter of policy: *Re Tennant Mortlock v Hawker* (1942) 65 CLR 473 at 507, per Dixon J. In 1966, Street J applied 4 per cent as the relevant rate in *Re Dawson*. In 1979, Powell J applied the rate of 8 per cent in *AE Goodwin v AG Healing* (1979) 7 ACR 481 at 493. Fluctuations in interest rates were given as the explanation by Dixon J in *Re Tennant: Mortlock v Hawker* (1942) 65 CLR at 473 at 507–8 for the policy of the court in fixing a rate which over a long period represents a fair or mean rate of return for money. Kearney J disagreed with that view in *Hagan v Waterhouse* questioning whether it was appropriate that it should continue to apply in a period of high and fluctuating interest rates. In view of the fundamental change which has resulted in our financial system following deregulation, Kearney J was of the view, at 393, that it was no longer appropriate to apply a policy fixing a settled mean rate of interest but rather that the mercantile rate should apply, suggesting that bank overdraft rates provide the appropriate scale, and that that would reflect the reality of the marketplace as it exists under a regime not in contemplation in 1942 or 1966. In *Hagan v Waterhouse*, Kearney J applied a rate of 5 per cent up to 1970 for an estate in which probate had been granted to the executors in December 1954, 7 per cent thereafter up to 1974 and thereafter at the rate specified from time to time in the practice notes in the Supreme Court Rules for the judicial rate of interest. In *Pateman v Heyen* (1993) 33 NSWLR 188 at 200, Cohen J noted the trustees are liable to pay interest in respect of a lost suffered by the trusts through their breach but would not be required to pay interest at the mercantile rate if the breach arose out of mere negligence or inadvertence. In that case the trust had suffered a loss through the negligence of the trustee in failing to renew insurance on the major property which was the subject of the trust. In the circumstances, Cohen J applied a rate of interest of 8 per cent from the date of the loss to the date of judgment as the appropriate measure of interest on the loss suffered. He declined to make an order for compensation for rent lost following the destruction of a house property by fire. The breach by the defendant trustee was in not having appropriate fire insurance policy in place. Had that breach not occurred the insurer would have paid a sum of the money to the trustee which would then have been invested at interest. There was no relevant loss to the trust of rent arising from the breach.

The liability of directors of corporate trustees

[19.15] Where a corporation which is a trustee commits a breach of trust the traditional view has been that the directors of that company would not be held personally liable: *Wilson v Lord Bury* (1880) 5 QBD 518, except in a case where trust property could be followed into the hands of a director: *Bath v Standard Land Co Ltd* [1911] 1 Ch 618. The rationale behind those decisions was that directors were no more than agents of the company, and were accountable to the company rather than to the beneficiaries of the trust. In *Wilson v Lord Bury*, Baggallay LJ dissented strongly, urging that a distinction should be drawn between a corporate trustee which must necessarily act through its directors and an individual trustee who, when acting through an agent, can exercise control over the actions of that agent. In *Bath v Standard Land*, Fletcher-Moulton LJ also dissented and argued that the majority view was based on a fallacy that a fiduciary obligation can be prevented simply by the person in question becoming an agent of the trustee. This protection has not been afforded to directors in Canada.[19] In *Air Canada v M & L Travel Ltd* (1991) 77 DLR (4th) 536, in a judgment of the Ontario Court of Appeal, the directors of a company which operated a travel agency were held personally liable for losses arising from the misuse of trust moneys, being moneys received for tickets supplied by the airline. Griffiths JA, who delivered the judgment of the court, said, at 554, that 'where the breach of trust by the corporation is expressly induced by a director, that director should bear personal liability for the breach'. The directors in that case were 'the sole owners and operating minds of the corporation'; and they 'directed and authorised the deposit of funds

---

19. *Scott & Scott v Riehl & Schumak* (1958) 15 DLR (2d) 67; *Wowanesa Mutual Ins Co v JA (Fred) Chalmers & Co Ltd* (1969) 7 DLR (3d) 283; *Andrea Schmidt Construction Ltd v Clatt* (1979) 104 DLR (3d) 130; *Henry Electric Ltd v Farwell* (1986) 29 DLR (4th) 481.

from Air Canada sales in the general account without in any way designating (those) funds as trust funds'. In Scotland a distinction has been drawn between the directors of an ordinary limited public company, who could not be expected to know every detail of the company's affairs, and the directors of a private company who would know everything that was done in the company.[20] In *Sinclair v Brougham* [1914] AC 398, the House of Lords held that there was a fiduciary relationship between the directors of the building society and *ultra vires* depositors: see **[5.14]**. In New South Wales, Powell J expressed his view of the law on this point in *Mulkana Corp NL (in liq) v Bank of NSW* (1983) 8 ACLR 278:

> I believe that the true position is that, while directors are not, properly speaking, trustees, but fiduciary agents, the range of duties and obligations to which they are subject, or which are imposed on them, include duties or obligations which place them, in relation to moneys or property which are in their possession, or over which they have control, in a position analogous to, although not identical with, that of trustees.

The South Australian Supreme Court discussed this question in *Hurley v BGH Nominees Pty Ltd (No 2)* (1982) 1 ACLC 387; (1984) 37 SASR 499; 2 ACLC 497, Walters J expressing the view, *obiter*, that directors of a corporate trustee must not disregard the interests of beneficiaries. In *ASC v AS Nominees Ltd* (1995) 133 ALR 1 at 18, Finn J, while noting that in certain factual circumstances directors of corporate trustees will be held to owe fiduciary duties to the beneficiaries of the trust, questioned whether it would be desirable for such directors to be considered fiduciaries in all respects *vis-a-vis* the beneficiaries of their company's trust. The better approach, in his view, is to consider such directors might be liable as knowing accessories to a breach of trust under the second leg of *Barnes v Addy* (see **[17.40]–[17.47]**).

[19.16] This issue has been dealt with in part by the Corporations Law, s 233 (formerly s 229A of the Code) the relevant provisions of which provide that where a corporation which acts as a trustee incurs a liability for which it is not entitled to be fully indemnified out of the assets of the trust, the directors of the corporation at the time the liability is incurred will be jointly and severally liable to discharge the liability. Under s 233(2) no such liability is incurred where the corporation's inability to be indemnified out of the assets of the trust arises merely from the absence or insufficiency of those assets. In other words, liability under s 233 is sheeted home to directors when the corporate trustee forfeits its right to indemnity, as it will do when the liability is incurred in breach of trust. Directors who are 'innocent' are exempted under s 233(1). 'Innocence' is defined under s 233(3) as a director who, had the directors been trustees at the time, would have been entitled to be fully indemnified by the other 'trustees' for the subject liability. 'Liability' is defined as meaning a debt, liability or other obligation. Subject to being able to attach liability to a director under any other provision of the Corporations Law, such as s 592, s 233(2) effectively bars any claim which the creditors of a trust might wish to bring against the directors of an insolvent corporate trustee which cannot meet its debts out of the assets of the trust. Directors will be held personally liable, however, where the liability is incurred from some activity which falls outside the scope of the trust, and the trustee is thereby not entitled to an indemnity. It will not matter then whether the trust has sufficient assets to meet the liability or not — the trustee could not apply them to meet the debt, nor seek reimbursement from the trust if it first paid them from its own general funds. A creditor seeking to take advantage of this provision might have to suffer a judgment against it on a claim to be subrogated to the trustee's right of indemnity from the

---

20. *Brenes & Co v Downie & M'Dougall* [1914] SC 97.

trust first, on the ground that the trustee's rights in that regard were barred because the transaction constituted a breach of trust, before it could safely proceed under Corporations Law, s 233. The definition of 'liability' includes liability of the trustee to make good any loss arising from a breach of trust. If the trustee is a $2 company, obviously, it will not be able to make good any such loss from its own resources. Because the liability arises from a breach of trust, the trustee would not be entitled to an indemnity from the assets of the trust. The beneficiaries could then invoke s 233 in seeking to recover from the directors personally.

[19.17] It remains to be seen what effect s 233 has and, in particular, whether it will have the effect of equating the position of directors of a corporate trustee with that of trustees for all purposes. In this respect the saving provision in s 233(3) is rather curious. Does it purport, for instance, to import all the principles governing trustees' duties, and the rights of trustee *inter se* into any situation involving a corporate trustee? It is not clear, for example, whether a director who was not 'innocent' under s 233 could argue that his or her liability should be reduced on the ground that the loss suffered by the trust had been incurred at the request or instigation of a beneficiary. Can directors sued under s 233 claim the benefit of s 85 of the Trustee Act 1925 (NSW), and its equivalents elsewhere,[21] and argue that they have acted honestly and reasonably and ought fairly to be excused? Is an 'innocent director' under s 233 the same as a trustee not liable to make contribution under the principles in *Bahin v Hughes* (1886) 31 Ch D 390? (See [19.9].) The answer for the present must be 'perhaps'. There are some fundamental differences between the position of company directors and trustees which make it difficult to simply equate one with the other. Trustees must act unanimously. The board of a company can act by a simple majority. Can a director who votes against a decision which proves to be a breach of trust claim the benefit of s 233(3) as an 'innocent director'? The answer again has to be 'perhaps'. But there is no precedent in the law of trusts which provides an answer. Section 233 is not a marvellous piece of drafting. The better course for attaching personal liability to directors of corporate trustees, at least in favour of the beneficiaries of the trust, would be the adoption of the dissenting judgments in *Wilson v Lord Bury* and *Bath v Standard Land* in unequivocal terms.

Relief of trustees from liability

[19.18] Where a trustee has acted honestly and reasonably, and ought fairly to be excused for some breach of trust, the court has statutory power to relieve the trustee in whole or in part from personal liability for the breach.[22] All three elements must be satisfied. It is not enough to show that the trustee has acted honestly and reasonably; grounds must also be advanced to show that the trustee ought fairly to be excused: *National Trustee Co v General Finance Co* [1905] AC 373. This is a matter for the court's discretion and, while some guidance can be obtained from cases in which this power has been considered,[23] the court will not lay down any list of conditions under which a trustee will be relieved from liability under this section: *Holland v Administrator of German Property* [1937] 1 All ER 807.

---

21. Trusts Act 1973 (Qld), s 76; Trustee Act 1936–68 (SA), s 56 ; Trustee Act 1898 (Tas), s 50; Trustee Act 1958 (Vic), s 67; Trustee Act 1962–78 (WA), s 75.
22. Trustee Act 1925 (NSW), s 85; Trustee Act 1958 (Vic), s 67; Trusts Act 1973 (Qld), s 76; Trustee Act 1936–68 (SA), s 56; Trustee Act 1898 (Tas), s 50; Trustee Act 1962–78 (WA), s 75.
23. See *Jacobs'*, paras [2215]–[2218].

Lapse of time

[19.19] Under the general law there was no limitation period in respect of any action brought by a beneficiary against a trustee for breach of an express trust: *Beckford v Wade* (1805) 17 Ves Jun 87 at 97; 34 ER 34 at 38, per Sir William Grant MR. An express trust in this context means a trust expressed by the parties, whether in writing or orally, but does not include any trusts arising from the actions of the parties or by operation of law: *Sands v Thompson* (1883) 22 Ch D 614. This rule has been amended by statute, with slight variations from State to State,[24] so that a limitation period of six years now applies to actions for breach of trust except where the claim is founded on fraud or a fraudulent breach of trust to which the trustee was a party, or was privy; or, where the claim is one to recover trust property, or the proceeds of trust property, still retained by the trustee; or, to recover trust property received by the trustee and converted to his or her own use. In New South Wales the limitation period is 12 years in these cases, even where the trust is a constructive trust, with time running from the date of discovery, or receipt of notice, including constructive notice, of the facts giving rise to the cause of action. Time only begins to run against a beneficiary once his or her interest has vested in possession. So, a trustee in breach against whom action has not been taken for more than six years, or twelve as the case may be, by a life tenant will be safe from proceedings by the life tenant but will still be liable to the remainderman after the death of the life tenant: *Re Somerset* [1894] 1 Ch 231.

Release and acquiescence

[19.20] Just as a beneficiary may forfeit rights against a trustee in breach by instigating, or consenting to a breach of trust, so the beneficiary might also lose those rights by acquiescing in the breach after the event, or by releasing the trustee from liability for any wrongdoing. In the case of a release the beneficiary must be *sui juris*, must know all the relevant facts and the legal effect of his or her actions, and must not be subject to any undue influence on the part of the trustee: *Farrant v Blanchard* (1863) 1 De GJ & SM 107; 46 ER 42; *Holder v Holder* [1968] Ch 353 at 369–70, per Cross J. The onus of proving the release will rest on the trustee. Acquiescence is more difficult to identify. It may consist of the adoption by the beneficiaries of a transaction effected by the trustee. It can also arise simply from a failure to act on the part of the beneficiaries over some years.[25] But delay itself will not necessarily be a bar. The length of time taken by the beneficiary must also act as evidence of his acquiescence or assent: see Chapter 21.[26]

---

24. Limitation Act 1969 (NSW), ss 47–50; Limitation Act 1960 (Qld), s 25; Limitation of Actions Act 1936 (SA), ss 31–32; Trustee Act 1898 (Tas), s 56; Limitation of Actions Act 1958 (Vic), s 21; Limitation Act 1935 (WA), s 47.

25. *Hourigan v Trustees Executors & Agency Co Ltd* (1934) 51 CLR 619.

26. *Life Association of Scotland v Siddal* (1861) 3 De GF & J 58; 45 ER 800; *Story v Gape* (1856) 2 Jur NS 706.

Chapter Twenty

20-1 Rights of Beneficiaries

Right to extinguish the trust

[20.1] A beneficiary who is *sui juris* and absolutely entitled to a vested interest can direct the trustee to transfer the legal title and thereby extinguish the trust: *Saunders v Vautier* (1841) 4 Beav 115; 49 ER 282 (see **[14.28]**–**[14.29]**).

Right to compel performance of the trust

[20.2] The beneficiaries, or any one of them, make take proceedings to compel performance of the trust, or otherwise to protect their beneficial interests, whether vested or contingent. If need be, those proceedings may extend to an order removing the trustee and appointing a new trustee in his place: *Miller v Cameron* (1936) 54 CLR 572. Such a serious step will not be taken lightly and discord between trustee and beneficiaries will not, by itself, provide sufficient ground: *Re Henderson* [1940] Ch 764. In principle at least, the acts or omissions complained of 'must be such as to endanger the trust property or show a want of honesty or a want of proper capacity to execute the duties, or a want of reasonable fidelity': *Letterstedt v Broers* (1884) 9 App Cas 371.[1] If the trustee has failed to take proceedings to recover some property of the trust the beneficiary may commence the necessary action in his or her own name if the relief sought lies in equity. If it is a common law matter, the beneficiary must sue the trustee for execution of the trust and then apply for the appointment of a receiver and for leave to sue in the names of the trustee and the receiver.[2]

Right to restrain a breach of trust

[20.3] A beneficiary can obtain an injunction to prevent a trustee from taking any intended action which would constitute a breach of trust: *Howden v Yorkshire Miners Assoc* [1905] AC 256. This right can be exercised by any beneficiary, regardless of whether his or her interest is vested or contingent. It has been used to restrain a bishop of the Anglican Church from using church property for forms of services contrary to those prescribed by the Book of Common Prayer: *Wylde v A-G* (1948) 78 CLR 224. This is a matter which falls within the exclusive jurisdiction of equity. Only equitable defences, such as laches or acquiescence, may be raised. It is not necessary

---

1. *Jacobs'*, para [1546].
2. *Ibid*, para [2303].

to show that irreparable harm would flow to the trust from the breach: *Heavener v Loomes* (1923) 34 CLR 306.

Right to possession of the trust property

[20.4] Where a beneficiary is *sui juris* and absolutely entitled the beneficiary can call for possession of the trust property unless the trustee has active duties to perform in respect of it, although, in such a case, provided the beneficiary's interest is not limited, the beneficiary may still obtain possession of the property by extinguishing the trust. A beneficiary whose interest is of a limited nature, ie, a life interest, will not be allowed into possession unless the trust instrument authorises such an allowance or appropriate undertakings are given to protect the property for the interests of those subsequently entitled. Otherwise, the trustee has title to and possession of the property of the trust, including its books and records. A beneficiary is entitled to inspect the records of the trust but cannot demand possession of them: *Re Simersall* (1992) 108 ALR 375.

Right to approach the court on questions of construction

[20.5] Beneficiaries have a statutory right to approach the court by way of summons for determination of any question concerning the construction or administration of the trust.[3]

Right to information

[20.6] The beneficiaries of a trust, including the objects of a discretionary trust, are entitled to information about the trust: *Spellson v George* (1987) 11 NSWLR 300; *Tierney v King* [1983] 2 Qd R 580. A beneficiary cannot require the trustee to give reasons for the exercise of any discretion: *Re Londonderry's Settlement* [1965] 918. On the same authority, while the beneficiaries are entitled to have access to what can be called 'trust' documents, they do not have the same right to access to confidential documents of the trustees, particularly where such documents may relate to the trustees' considerations in the exercise of their discretions. A beneficiary is entitled to inspect the books and records of the trust, but title to those records, like other trust property, is vested in the trustee and the beneficiary cannot claim possession of that material: *Re Simersall* (1992) 108 ALR 375.

20–2 Rights of Discretionary Beneficiaries

[20.7] The objects of a discretionary trust are in a different position from that of the beneficiaries of a normal fixed trust. The rights of any of the objects of a discretionary trust to either the income or capital of the trust are subject to the exercise of the trustee's discretion to select from the range of objects and to determine the quantum of the benefit to be conferred on any object so selected. Put at its highest, the interest of any one beneficiary, or object, of a discretionary trust in the property of the trust is contingent upon the exercise by the trustee of this discretion. That discretion will

---

3. Trustee Act 1925 (NSW), s 63; Trusts Act 1973–81 (Qld), s 96; Trustees Act 1962–78 (WA), s 92; SA RSC O 55 r 1; Tas, 0 65 r 1; Vic RSC O 55 r 3.

normally authorise the trustee to appoint to any one object to the exclusion of all the others, with the result that the collective rights of the whole class of objects could add up to more than the entire beneficial interest in the trust property. Those interests are competitive rather than cumulative. The interest of any one of the objects of a discretionary trust is also not a valuable right for the same reason. An object of a discretionary trust of income does not have any proprietary interest in the subject matter of the trust. The only right of an object of a discretionary trust of income is a right to require the trustees to consider whether to exercise their discretion: *Gartside v IRC* [1968] AC 553. In that case Lord Reid, at 606, expressed the view that where a trustee held a trust power of appointment and was bound to distribute, with a discretion only as to the proportions in which the income was distributed, then the individual rights of the beneficiaries, when taken together, would extend to the whole income. However, in *Sainsbury v IRC* [1970] 1 Ch 712, Ungoed-Thomas J held that under an exhaustive discretionary trust where the trustees were required to distribute the whole of the income, the only right which any object had was to have the trustees exercise their discretion properly and to be protected in that right. Accordingly, an object of a discretionary trust did not have possession of a quantifiable interest and the totality of the separate unquantifiable interests of the objects did not constitute one quantifiable interest. This approach was taken to its logical conclusion in *Re Weir's Settlement Trusts* [1971] 1 Ch 145. The Inland Revenue claimed estate duty on the death of the second last member of a class of objects of a discretionary trust on the basis that the trust fund then became property in which the deceased had an interest, ceasing on the death of the deceased, to the extent that a benefit accrued or arose in favour of another by virtue of that cesser of interest. The Court of Appeal held that where the penultimate member of a discretionary class died no such interest passed and the survivor was entitled to receive the income under the same continuing trust, and not as a tenant for life or under any new trust.

[20.8] In *Moses Montefiore Jewish Home v Howell & Co (No 7) Pty Ltd* [1984] 2 NSWLR 406, Kearney J came to a different view, although not in the context of a claim for death or estate duty. He considered that in the case of an exhaustive discretionary trust, ie, one in which the trustee had a trust power rather than a mere power, the objects of that power could be said to possess, collectively, the entire beneficial interest in the trust fund. On that view the objects of a discretionary trust could combine and, if unanimous, could call upon the trustee to distribute the fund and terminate the trust. Presumably the trustee would retain its discretion to apportion the capital and any undistributed income in the event of such a termination. Of course, this proposition presumes a discretionary trust in which all the objects can be ascertained. In view of the fact that a discretionary trust need only satisfy the criterion certainty test to be valid, it might not be possible to identify all of the objects for the purpose of this exercise. In the great majority of cases that will not be possible. As it is only necessary that the range of objects for a discretionary trust, even an exhaustive trust, be described with sufficient certainty that it can be said whether a given individual is or is not an object of the trust, or power,[4] only in rare cases will it be possible to say that the class of objects is closed. While the interest of a beneficiary under a discretionary trust is most accurately described as a right to be considered that is not the end of the matter. The objects of a discretionary trust, like the beneficiaries of a deceased estate still in the course of administration, have a right to secure proper administration of the trust, which includes both proper management of the trust fund and proper exercise of the trustee's powers and discretions.

---

4. *Re Baden's Will Trusts; McPhail v Doulton* [1971] AC 424; *Horan v James* [1982] 2 NSWLR 376.

20–3 Tracing

[20.9] Tracing is available as a remedy both at common law and in equity. Tracing at common law is available where it can be shown that a defendant has received the plaintiff's money and the extent of the defendant's liability will be determined by the amount received. Liability under this count at common law depends upon receipt of the money rather than its retention. As a result, dishonesty or lack of inquiry on the part of the recipient are irrelevant. Because identification of the receipt is the crucial element at common law the remedy is of limited utility where the plaintiff's monies are mixed with that of others.[5] In *Banque Belge Pour l'Etranger v Hanbrock* [1921] 1 KB 321 a fraudster, a cashier, diverted money by means of endorsed cheques into an account in his name and then later paid money from that account to his lover, Mlle Spanoghe. No other monies were deposited in her account during the relevant period and the plaintiff was held to be entitled to trace those monies at common law. In *Agip (Africa) Ltd v Jackson* (1990) [1992] 4 All ER 451 a claim for tracing at common law failed because the money had been mixed twice before it reached the defendants' account. The point was stated by Lord Haldane LC in *Sinclair v Brougham* [1914] AC 398 419 that the relevant test for tracing at common law was that of ascertainment and, for instance, where money was paid into a bank account, provided it could be identified as the product of the original money then the plaintiff would have a common law right to claim it. Equity, unlike the common law, allows money to be followed into a mixed fund and then charges the fund. In equity, tracing is a right or claim available to a beneficiary of a trust, or to anyone to whom a fiduciary obligation is owed, and, possibly, to others, whereby the claimant may follow property into the hands of third parties who have received it, or trace it into whatever different form it has taken by way of exchange or otherwise. The basic principle of tracing in equity was stated in *Frith v Cartland* (1865) 2 H & M 417; 71 ER 525 at 526, per Page-Wood VC:

> A trustee cannot assert a title of his own to trust property. If he destroys a trust fund by dissipating it altogether, there remains nothing to be the subject of a trust. But so long as the trust property can be traced and followed into other property into which it has been converted, that remains subject to the trust. A second principle is that if a man mixes trust funds with his own, the whole will be treated as trust property, except so far as he may be able to distinguish what is his own.

[20.10] Tracing generally arises when a trustee converts trust property to his own use but can also apply to misappropriations by fiduciaries and to other cases in which courts have held tracing to be appropriate in the circumstances. Where the trustee or fiduciary concerned has sufficient funds to make good the loss, tracing will be of marginal value. Proper restitution can be secured by a personal claim against the delinquent trustee. However, where the wrongdoer is insolvent, or the claim is blocked by some other difficulty, such as a statute of limitations, the proprietary relief afforded by tracing will be singularly attractive.

[20.11] Limitations on the doctrine of tracing. There is a view that tracing can only be obtained where some pre-existing fiduciary relationship can be shown. That restriction did not, however, restrain the court from allowing the plaintiff to trace a sum of over $US2 million paid by clerical error in *Chase Manhattan Bank NA v Israel-*

---

5. *Agip (Africa) Ltd v Jackson* (1990) [1992] 4 All ER 451 at 463–4, per Fox LJ with whom Butler-Sloss and Beldam LJJ agreed.

British Bank (London) [1979] 3 All ER 1025. In coming to that decision Goulding J applied a broad principle that money received under a mistake of fact cannot, in conscience, be retained by the payee. In support of that view his Lordship cited *Sinclair v Brougham* [1914] AC 398.

> A building society conducted an *ultra vires* banking business for a number of years. During that time it received moneys from both *intra vires* contributors to the building society and *ultra vires* depositors. Upon the winding up of the society, after payment out of general creditors, the question remained of the competing rights of these two groups — the *intra vires* customers and the *ultra vires* depositors. There was not enough money to pay out both groups in full. The House of Lords held that the liquidator should distribute the funds among the contributors and the depositors *pari passu* in proportion to the amounts credited to them in the books of the society. Lord Parker held that a fiduciary relationship had existed between the directors of the building society and the depositors. Lord Haldane LC also spoke of a fiduciary relationship but said that the loans made by the depositors were not accepted in breach of that duty. His Lordship, however, spoke of the availability of tracing in the auxiliary jurisdiction of equity, 'wherever money was held in equity to belong to the plaintiff ... The property was never converted into a debt, in equity at all events, and there has been throughout a resulting trust, not of an active character but sufficient, in my opinion, to bring the transaction within the general principle.'

[20.12] This decision has been the subject of considerable criticism, in part because of the lack of any clear ratio decidendi.[6] In *Re Diplock's Estate* [1948] 1 Ch 465 the Court of Appeal took Lord Parker's view of a fiduciary relationship between the directors and the depositors as the ratio, but that view is not without difficulties. If there was such a relationship, the directors and not the society would be liable to the *ultra vires* depositors for any shortfall while the *intra vires* contributors would have first call on the assets of the society itself. It is conceivable that there could have been a fiduciary relationship between the society and the depositors, but that was not what his Lordship said. The authors of the fifth edition of Jacobs' are particularly critical of Lord Haldane's suggestion that tracing is available in the auxiliary jurisdiction of equity. As they point out, traditionally tracing has been confined to the exclusive jurisdiction. Despite this apparent departure from tradition, *Sinclair v Brougham* has not led to any revolution in equity jurisprudence, perhaps as much as anything because of the uncertainty surrounding the actual grounds of the decision in the case. A case involving similar facts today would be examined in the light of the decision in *Barclays Bank v Quistclose Investments* [1970] AC 567, which would necessitate a much closer examination of the intentions of the parties than that made in *Sinclair v Brougham*. Messrs Goff and Jones have argued that the true purpose of tracing is as a remedy to prevent unjust enrichment and that the crucial issue is the identification of the property as that of the plaintiff rather than proof of any fiduciary relationship between the parties. Tacit support, at least, can be found for that view in *Black v Freedman* (1910) 12 CLR 105 in which the High Court allowed an employer to trace moneys stolen by an employee and paid into an account in the name of the thief's wife. Where tracing is allowed in such a case against a third party who is a volunteer it might be possible to construct a case for a fiduciary relationship arising, at least when the third party becomes aware of the source of the funds, but that is slightly artificial and a claim based on the proprietary rights of the plaintiff and the unjust enrichment otherwise of the defendant deals better with the realities of the situation. The prospects for clarification of this question in Australia must now be considered in the

---

6. Jacobs', paras [2711]–[2712].

light of the decision of the High Court in *Pavey & Matthews Pty Ltd v Paul* (1987) 69 ALR 577 in which that court recognised unjust enrichment as the principle underlying the common law claim of *quantum meruit*, and the cases which have since followed this theme: see Chapter 17.

[20.13] Tracing into a mixed fund. Where a trustee mixes trust property with his own the remedy of tracing is not excluded.

In *Re Hallett's Estate* (1880) 13 Ch D 696, a solicitor, to whom two parcels of bonds had been entrusted by different parties, sold the bonds and deposited the proceeds in his own account. The solicitor died insolvent and the two parties sought to trace into the account. The Court of Appeal allowed both claimants a charge over the account for the proceeds of sale of the bonds. Sir George Jessel MR stated certain principles which apply in such cases (at 709): Where a fiduciary wrongfully invests monies entrusted to him in some purchase the beneficial owner has the right to elect to take either the property purchased or to hold that property as security for the amount of trust money paid out;

Where a trustee has mixed money with his own there is a distinction—the *cestui que trust* cannot elect to take the property because it was not purchased with trust money purely and simply but with a mixed fund. However, the beneficiary is entitled to a charge on the property purchased for the amount of the trust money laid out on the purchase; Where the trust moneys are paid into a mixed fund and the trustee makes withdrawals from that fund he will be presumed to be acting honestly and withdrawing his own money first, thus displacing the general rule, that in Clayton's case,[7] that the first money paid into an account is presumed to be the first withdrawn.

In *Brady v Stapleton* (1952) 88 CLR 322 a bankrupt, prior to his bankruptcy, transferred 32,000 fully paid shares in a company to Brady, who already held 1300 shares in the same company. Brady knew the transfer had been made to him with the intent of defrauding creditors. After receiving the shares Brady transferred 17,000 of them to the bankrupt's wife. The court found that Brady held the shares on trust for the bankrupt. The question then arose as to which of the shares held by Brady and the bankrupt's wife were subject to the trust. The High Court, per Dixon CJ and Fullagar J (at 337), held that it did not matter into what other form the trust property had been changed so long as it could be ascertained as such, and the right to trace only ceases when the means of ascertainment fail. Where the trust property, whether it is money or some other form of property, is mixed with other property of the same type equity would impose a charge on the indistinguishable mass to satisfy the claim.

[20.14] The right to trace into a mixed fund is not limited to a claim for money which has been misappropriated. It can apply to chattels, provided that the chattels in question can be identified and can be separated from the mixed asset or assets.

In *Borden (UK) Ltd v Scottish Timber Products Ltd* [1981] Ch 25 the plaintiff supplied resin to the defendant for use in the manufacture of chipboard. The contract provided that 'property' in the resin would pass when it was paid for but it was contemplated that the resin would be used in manufacture in the meantime. After the defendant went into receivership the plaintiff claimed a charge over chipboard manufactured with resin supplied but unpaid for. The Court of Appeal refused to grant any such charge. Once mixed with the other products used to make the chipboard the resin could not be recovered. Bridge LJ was of the view that the plaintiff's 'title' to the resin under the contract simply disappeared with the resin once it was used in the manufacturing process at which point it ceased to exist as resin.

---

7.   (1816) 1 Mer 572; 35 ER 781.

In *Borden v Scottish Timber* Bridge LJ distinguished *Aluminium Industrie Vaassen BV v Romalpa Aluminium Ltd* [1976] 1 WLR 676 in which a similar contractual provision had allowed a claim *in rem* on the bases that the defendants in *Romalpa* were bailees of the goods concerned, aluminium foil strips, that there had been no admixture of those goods with any others through any process of manufacture and that the foil was being held by the defendants as agents of the plaintiffs for the purposes of selling it, not to use it in any process of manufacture or construction.

[20.15] The right to trace into a mixed fund will depend upon what happens to that fund after the trust moneys are paid into it. If the trustee continues to draw on the account and exhausts it the trust funds will be gone. It will not matter that the trustee later pays in further funds. There is no presumption that the trustee, in paying money into the account, is repairing the breach of trust: *James Roscoe (Bolton) Ltd v Winder* [1915] 1 Ch 62. Sarjant J in that case held (at 69) that *Re Hallett* only applied 'to such an amount of the balance ultimately standing to the credit of the trustee as did not exceed the lowest balance of the account during the intervening period'. This 'lowest intermediate balance' rule applies to the period from receipt of the money by the trustee, in whatever form, including cheques, and not from the date of clearance of any cheque whereby the moneys were paid to the trustee: *Lofts v MacDonald* (1974) 3 ALR 404. If, however, the trustee purchases something of value with money withdrawn from the mixed account the beneficiary will be allowed to claim that property. In *Re Oatway* [1903] 2 Ch 356 a trustee paid £3,000 of trust funds into his own account. He then purchased £2,000 worth of shares with that fund and dissipated the rest. The shares were treated as trust property even though purchased with an early withdrawal. Where a trustee mixes assets with his own in such a way that they cannot be sufficiently distinguished, the onus lies on the trustee to distinguish the separate assets: *Re Tilley's Will Trusts* [1967] 1 Ch 1179. In that case a widow, executrix of her late husband's estate, thoroughly confused the trust property with her own, using trust moneys to pay off her bank overdraft of £23,000. It was held that, in that case, there was no property against which a tracing order could be made.

[20.16] Where property is purchased with trust funds and the trustee's own money the beneficiary will be entitled to a charge over the property to secure restitution of the trust moneys, including a proportionate share of any increase in value of the property so purchased.

In *Scott v Scott* (1962) 109 CLR 649 a trustee of a deceased estate used trust moneys together with some of his own to purchase a property in which he lived until his death. Shortly before his death he repaid to the trust the moneys he had used for the purchase. The property purchased had increased substantially in value in the meantime. The High Court held that the trust was entitled to a share in the increase in value in proportion to the amount of trust funds applied for the original purchase.

[20.17] Ordinarily in such a case the beneficiary's rights will be restricted to a charge over the property. The beneficiary will not be able to claim the property itself. That restriction may, however, be lifted if the circumstances are such as to justify awarding the property to the beneficiary. In *Paul A Davies (Australia) Pty Ltd v Davies* [1983] 1 NSWLR 440 a fiduciary used trust moneys as a deposit for the purchase of a property. The rest of the purchase money was obtained by way of a mortgage loan secured on the property. The Court of Appeal held that this was not an appropriate case in which to award the beneficiary only a proportionate part of the value of the property purchased, in part, with trust moneys as no part of the purchase price had been paid for by the trustee with his own money. In *Australian Postal Corporation v Lutak* (1991)

21 NSWLR 584 an employee of Australia Post used $20,000 obtained from a fraudulent sale of stamps to purchase a house in the joint names of his wife and himself for $90,000. The balance of the purchase money was borrowed on mortgage from the State Bank of NSW. Bryson J applied *Paul A Davies (Australia) Pty Ltd v Davies* in a roundabout way to hold that Australia Post was entitled to its $20,000 back from the sale proceeds, the State Bank was to receive back its $70,000 while Australia Post received the balance of the proceeds of sale, a sum of about $31,000. Bryson J considered that Australia Post had an election: it could treat the matter as a purchase by the Lutaks effectively on its behalf, in which case Australia Post would be equitable owner of the property, or it could trace the $20,000.

[20.18] Mixing of one lot of trust money with another.

Where a trustee mixes trust moneys from more than one source there are two views as to the approach to be taken when seeking to trace into that mixed fund. One is that the rule in *Clayton's* case (*Devaynes v Noble; Clayton's case* (1816) 1 Mer 572 at 608; 35 ER 781 at 793) should apply to the trust moneys, so that the first money paid is deemed to be the first money drawn out. That was the approach taken in *Re Stenning* [1895] 2 Ch 433:

A solicitor operated a bank account into which he paid his own moneys and his clients' trust moneys. At the date of his death that account had a credit balance of £4443. One client, a Mrs Smith, claimed a sum of £448 from that account, being moneys held on trust for her which the solicitor had paid into the account. After paying Mrs Smith's money into the account the solicitor had deposited, in sequence, sums of £999, £1094, and £500, which he held on behalf of three other clients respectively. Thereafter the balance of the account always exceeded £448 but did drop as low as £1088, that is, less than the sum of the trust moneys paid in, at one point. Mrs Smith was held not to be entitled to any of the money standing in the account at the solicitor's death. The rule in *Hallett's* case applies only between trustee and beneficiary. Where a trustee mixes the money of more than one beneficiary the rule in *Clayton's* case applies as between the *cestuis que* trust, so that the first trust money paid in will be deemed to be the first trust money paid out. Further moneys paid into the account by the trustee could not be said to create a new trust.

That approach might work with a small estate and relatively uncomplicated facts, as was the case in *Re Stenning*. But where the accounts are complex and moneys have been received from a considerable number of beneficiaries and the delinquent trustee has paid the money into a number of different accounts, applying the rule in *Clayton's* case becomes difficult, if not practicably impossible, and likely to produce an inherently unfair result. The better view must be to adopt the alternate approach. The effective contributors to the pool of mixed funds should be paid *pari passu* in proportions reflecting their respective contributions to the mixed fund. That was the approach taken by the House of Lords in *Sinclair v Brougham* [1914] AC 398. The issues to be taken into account by a court in considering whether to apply the rule in *Clayton's* case or the approach taken in *Sinclair v Brougham* was discussed at some length by the English Court of Appeal in *Barlow Clothes International Ltd (in liq) v Vaughan* [1992] 4 All ER 22 (CA). It was also the view apparently preferred by Hope JA in *Stephens Travel Service Pty Ltd v Qantas Airways Ltd* (1988) 13 NSWLR 331 at 348. Considering the case where a trustee mixes the moneys of two or more trusts and there is insufficient money to meet all claims, Hope J said:

There, possibly depending in the case of a particular beneficiary upon the application of the rule in [*Clayton's* case], the beneficiaries may be able to claim and recover only a part of the moneys to which they are entitled; that is, their claims on the fund may have to abate because of the trustee's default. In such a case it may be that the appropriate remedy is a charge. It may be argued that otherwise the result would be that two or more beneficiaries would have overlapping titles to the same money. My tentative view is that the entitlements of beneficiaries with charges over a fund can and must abate if the fund is insufficient to meet all claims, there is no reason why the entitlements to take *in specie* should not be abatable.

Hope JA did not expressly say the entitlements of the beneficiaries should abate proportionately but that can be the only sensible interpretation of his comments. If the rule in *Clayton's* case were applied the beneficiary whose funds were the last in would probably be paid out in full without any abatement. If all entitlements are to be subject to abatement, proportional abatement would be the only fair method.

In *Barlow Clowes International Ltd (in liq) v Vaughan* [1992] 4 All ER 22 (CA) an investment company registered in Gibraltar and associated English companies went into liquidation and receivers were appointed. The companies had managed certain investment portfolios and at the time of the collapse owed over £115m to approximately 11,000 investors. The amount available for distribution to investors was far less than the total of their claims. The case turned on an argument as to whether it was more appropriate to apply a first in first out process of accounting or whether the investors ought to be repaid *pari passu*. The court held that the rule in *Clayton's* case, that is to say first in first out, would be applied where monies from two or more investors were paid into the one account if the rule provided a convenient method of determining competing claims where several beneficiaries' monies had been blended in one account and there was a deficiency (per Dillon LJ at 33) or where there had been a wrongful mixing of different sums of trust money in a single account (per Leggatt LJ at 45). However, where the application of the rule would be impractical or would result in injustice between the investors or beneficiaries because a relatively small number of investors would get most of the fund, and some would get none, the rule would not be applied if a preferable alternative method of distribution was available (per Woolf LJ at 42). The rule would also not be applied where it was contrary to the intention, express or implied, of the investors or beneficiaries. Such an intention would be displayed where the investments were paid into a common pool indicating that the investors intended their monies would be combined together, and therefore mixed in one or more bank accounts with the result that each would have an equitable charge on the fund for the amount of his or her investment and thus, an aliquot share of the investment pool (per Leggatt LJ at 45–6 and Woolf LJ at 42).

Each case will depend on its facts. The judgments in *Barlow Clowes* suggest strongly that where monies are misappropriated and paid into more than one account it is inappropriate to apply *Clayton's* case. In *Re Winsor v Bajaj* (1990) 75 DLR (4th) 198 McKeown J in the Ontario Court of Appeal came to a similar conclusion holding that when tracing was ordered out of a mixed fund distribution should be on a pro rata basis if that can be done fairly. The first in first out method was only to be used, in his view, if pro rata distribution was not possible and a daily or hourly accounting was required over some period of time. These principles will not prevent an individual who can trace misappropriated funds to a particular asset or fund from obtaining an order charging the traceable asset or fund with the whole of the monies lost.

In *El Ajou v Dollar Land Holdings plc (No 2)* [1995] 2 All ER 213 a Saudi businessman who had been one of the victims of a massive fraud was able to trace monies lost to him in the order of £3.25m into the assets of an English property company. There were many other defrauded investors who might have had a similar claim. Robert Walker J was prepared to give the plaintiff a charge over the assets of the land holding company to the full extent of his loss. In coming to that decision his Lordship noted that tracing in equity depended not on the actual imposition of an equitable charge but on equity's capacity to impose such a charge: the charge itself was notional. The rights of third parties, identified or otherwise, could not be raised as a defence to a tracing claim because each case depended on its individual circumstances. In this case none of the other victims who might have had the right to seek to trace into the monies held by Dollar Land Holdings had done so and, accordingly, that company was ordered to pay the whole sum of £3.25 million plus interest.

[20.19] Tracing property into the hands of third parties. A *bona fide* purchaser of the legal estate without notice of any trust will take any trust property so purchased free from the claims of the beneficiaries. Where third parties receive trust property in any circumstances short of a *bona fide* purchase they may be liable as constructive trustees. Problems can arise, however, if those third parties are innocent volunteers and then mix the trust funds with their own property.

In *Re Diplock's Estate* [1948] 1 Ch 465 a testator who died in 1936 left his residuary estate 'for such charitable institutions or other charitable or benevolent object or objects in England' as his executors should in their absolute discretion think fit. The bequest was eventually held to be invalid as a charitable trust because of the inclusion of 'benevolent' objects. By that time the executors had distributed over £200,000 to 139 charitable institutions. The next of kin sought to trace the funds paid to these various institutions while also seeking orders *in personam* against the institutions themselves. The Court of Appeal upheld the claims *in personam* and, in doing so, rejected an argument by the institutions that a third party volunteer receiving trust property paid in breach of trust was only liable to account for it if he or she could be shown to have acted unconscientiously. The institutions were not ordered to pay interest on the moneys they had received except for those which had invested the money in interest bearing accounts. All the institutions were solvent and substantial and the claim *in personam* would have disposed of the matter but the Court also considered the claims in rem and laid down some general principles:

1. Where trust property is transferred to a volunteer who takes without notice, and there is no question of mixing, then the volunteer will hold the property on trust for the rightful beneficiaries.

2. Tracing will be available against a third party receiving trust property even though there was no pre-existing fiduciary relationship between the third party and the claimant.

3. Moneys spent by the charities on altering or improving buildings could not be traced.

4. Money used to pay off unsecured debts owed by the charities was gone and could not be traced. Nor could the next of kin be subrogated to the rights of the creditors whose claims had thereby been satisfied.

5. A claim to be subrogated to the rights of a secured creditor who was repaid by one of the charities was also rejected.

6. Where the trust moneys had been paid into a mixed bank account the rule in *Clayton's* case was applied so that the first money paid into those accounts would be considered to be the first withdrawn.

7. Where the third party took money out of a mixed account and paid it into a special account it could, thereby, 'unmix' the funds.

8. Where a charity had purchased war stock with the trust money, and with other moneys as well, the trust was allowed a rateable proportion of the war stock held by the charity.

9. If the volunteer purchased property with a mixed fund including trust moneys then the beneficiary will be allowed a charge over the asset thus acquired to secure repayment of the trust moneys used for the purchase.

10. If such a 'mixed asset' increases in value the beneficiary will not be entitled to any proportionate share in that increase in value.

[20.20] The reluctance of the court to come down harshly on the charities which had acted in good faith in receiving and disbursing this money is understandable but, considering that the claim *in personam* was upheld making them liable to disgorge the full amount anyway, some of the points decided by the Court of Appeal are difficult to sustain as a matter of logic as much as law. The refusal to give a charge over property improved with the beneficiary's money, or to allow subrogation to the rights of unsecured and secured creditors paid off with the beneficiary's money seems illogical when placed alongside the general principle that a third party volunteer receiving trust property holds it as trustee for the true beneficiary. It would be reasonable to bar the right to trace moneys wrongfully paid to a third party if the third party has changed its position, in the belief that the original payment was lawful, in such a way that it would be inequitable to allow tracing. The better view may be that expenditure on improvements to buildings can constitute a sufficient change of position. Where the trust property, in the form of money, has been merged with the fabric of an existing building it must be said that the trust property has disappeared. That alone, however, would not prevent a court of equity from granting a charge over the improved property to secure an order for equitable compensation, a personal as opposed to a propriety remedy, for the repayment of the trust moneys thus spent. Of course, the money spent on improvements was spent on buildings such as hospitals and churches, hardly commercial properties of which it could be said that the improvements had enhanced their resale value.

[20.21] Tracing against bankers. While a beneficiary or other party entitled to trace moneys can follow those moneys into the trustee's bank account, that right is subject to that of the bank as *bona fide* holder. The bank will forfeit that protection if it allows the defaulter to transfer money from a trust or agency account into his personal account: *Pannell v Hurley* (1845) 2 Coll 241; 63 ER 716; *British American Elevator Co v Bank of British North America* [1919] AC 658. In such a case the bank might itself be held to be a constructive trustee; for example, if a bank allowed a cheque bearing only one signature to be drawn on a joint signatory partnership account in favour of the personal or family account of the partner who had signed the cheque. Otherwise, where a trustee pays trust funds into an overdrawn account, and the banker has no notice that they are trust funds, the bank will have first call on all such moneys: *Thomson v Clydesdale Bank Ltd* [1893] AC 282.

20–4 The Rights of a Beneficiary of a Gift Subject to Engrafted Trusts

[20.22] Under the so-called rule in *Lassence v Tierney* (1849) 1 Mac & G 551 41 ER 1379, where there is an absolute gift to a legatee in the first instance and trusts are engrafted or imposed on that absolute interest which fail, either from lapse or invalidity or any other reason, then the absolute gift takes effect so far as the trusts have failed to the exclusion of the residuary legatee or next of kin as the case may be. In *Russell v Perpetual Trustee Co Ltd* (1956) 95 CLR 389 the High Court applied this rule in considering certain gifts made in exercise of a power of appointment to three named persons as tenants in common in equal shares, subject to a trust to pay the income of each one's share to him or her during his or her lifetime, and upon the death of any one, the capital of his or her share to be on trust for the children then living of that deceased beneficiary. The purported gift to the children was outside the terms of the power and was void. The High Court, per Dixon CJ and Williams J at 397, held that the gift to the three named beneficiaries was absolute in its terms and that, in the circumstances, they took absolutely, not as life tenants. Similarly, in *Duncan v Cathels* (1957) 98 CLR 625 the High Court applied the rule in *Lassence v Tierney* to held that certain gifts, each on trust to a named beneficiary for life, and thereafter for such of the children of that beneficiary as the beneficiary might appoint, with provisions in default of appointment, were absolute gifts to each of the named beneficiaries. In *Duncan v Equity Trustees Executors and Agency Co Ltd* (1957) 99 CLR 513 it was held that the rule in *Lassence v Tierney* (1849) 1 Mac & G 551; 41 ER 379 did not apply to a similar gift but one in which provision was made that, in the event that the gift lapsed, the interest should accrue to other shares in the estate. The court said that the rule in *Lassence v Tierney* is no more than a rule of construction and can always be excluded by a settlor or testator. One of the ways in which it can be excluded is by making express provision for what is to happen in the event of the failure of an engrafted trust. Had the other provisions stood alone, the court said that the rule in *Lassence v Tierney* would have governed the case.

[20.23] A similar rule of construction operates where there is an absolute gift in perpetuity of a specific proportion of the income of a trust. Such a gift will operate, subject to any contrary intention being shown on the proper construction of the instrument, as an absolute gift of that proportion of the capital of the trust: *Congregational Union of NSW v Thistlethwayte* (1952) 87 CLR 375. This principle will also apply where the trustee holds under a discretionary trust, provided it is properly described as such, ie, the trustee is obliged to pay out the whole of the fund, even though it has a discretion as to the manner and the proportions of that payment, and not where the trustee has a discretionary power, that is, where it is not obliged to make a distribution in favour of any object: *Re Smith* (1928) Ch 915.

Chapter Twenty One

Equitable Defences

21-1 Laches and Acquiescence

[21.1] Equity assists the diligent and not the tardy. So the maxim goes, but mere delay or indolence will not necessarily be fatal to a plaintiff's rights in equity. In order to rely on the plaintiff's delay as a defence, the defendant must show that the plaintiff's actions constitute acquiescence in the defendant's conduct or that, in response to the plaintiff's inaction, the defendant has changed its position in such a manner that it would be unjust in the circumstances to grant the relief sought. 'Acquiescence' in this context means refraining from exercising or enforcing a right to which the plaintiff is entitled and of which the plaintiff knows, thereby accepting the contrary right asserted by the defendant. This form of acquiescence must be distinguished from acquiescence as it applies in the doctrine of equitable estoppel. In estoppel, acquiescence occurs when someone sees an act about to be done which will impinge upon his or her rights and stands by while those rights are invaded. The quiescent party may thereby be denied the remedy to which he or she would otherwise have been entitled for the wrong done. In the context of the defence of laches, acquiescence occurs when a person who is entitled to equitable relief under some existing state of affairs, and who is aware of his rights, does nothing to enforce them and assents to the continuation of that state of affairs: *Cashman v 7 North Golden Gate Gold Mining Co* (1897) 7 QLJ 152; *Glasson v Fuller* [1922] SASR 148.

[21.2] 'Acquiescence' can be used in two senses. A person who sees some right or interest of his being violated or infringed and does nothing can be said to have acquiesced in that infringement. It can also happen where the infringement takes place in circumstances in which the rightful owner does not know or appreciate that his or her rights are being infringed. In that case, when the rightful owner later comes to know that he or she has rights which have been infringed and makes no protest about a continuation of that state of affairs, that failure to protest can amount to acquiescence: *Glasson v Fuller* [1992] SASR 148. Acquiescence, as an element in the defence of laches and acquiescence, means standing by with knowledge of one's rights both in fact and law: *Clark v Clark* (1882) 8 VLR (E) 303; *Re Howlett* [1949] Ch 767; and with knowledge that there is a remedy for the wrong: *Robinson v Abbott* (1894) 20 VLR 346. Knowledge of the relevant facts gives rise to a presumption of knowledge of the rights available on those facts: *Stafford v Stafford* (1857) 1 De G & J 193; 44 ER 697, and access to the means of knowledge is as good as knowledge: *Allcard v Skinner* (1887) 36 Ch D 145. Without the requisite knowledge there can be no acquiescence. In *Brand v Chris Building Co Pty Ltd* [1957] VR 625, a builder who built a house on the wrong block of land by mistake failed in an attempt to rely on acquiesence as defence when the plaintiff, the owner of the block, sought an injunction to restrain him from going onto the land to demolish the house. It was found as a fact that the plaintiff had no knowledge that the house was being built.

[21.3] Deane J discussed the loose usage of the word 'acquiescence', and its equally loose pairing with the word 'laches', in *Orr v Ford* (1989) 167 CLR 316 at 337–9. Strictly used, he said, acquiescence indicates a contemporaneous and informed, or knowing, acceptance or standing by which is treated by equity as assent, that is, consent, to what would otherwise be an infringement of rights. Deane J identified three principal variants of acquiescence: (i) a representation by silence of a type which may found an estoppel by conduct; or (ii) acceptance of a past wrongful act in circumstances which give rise to an active waiver of rights or a release of liability; or (iii) an election to abandon or not enforce rights. Deane J also recognised the existence of what he described as 'an inferior species of acquiescence' not involving estoppel, waiver or election but which involved the use of acquiescence as a defence in equity. This lesser species of acquiescence is also used in three variants: (i) as an indefinite overlapping component of a catchall phrase also incorporating 'laches' or 'gross laches' and/or 'delay'; (ii) in the same context as laches to indicate either mere delay or delay with knowledge of the acts of another person, which encourages that other person reasonably to believe that his acts are accepted (if past) or not opposed (if contemporaneous); and (iii) as an alternative to 'laches' to dividing the field between inaction in the face of an assertion of adverse rights' (acquiescence) and inaction in prosecuting rights (laches). Dean J noted that laches, an old French word for slackness or negligence or not doing, comprehends silence or inaction in the face of an unwarranted assertion of adverse rights by another as well as inaction or delay in prosecuting one's own rights. Deane J contrasted the use of laches in the wide sense, that is, acquiescence which encompasses 'all the rules under which lapse of time before a suit is brought can operate as a defence' including the rules defining more particular independent defences such as assent, waiver, release and estoppel by representation and the use of laches in the 'narrow sense' meaning a mere lapse of time.

[21.4] Laches will be easier to employ in some cases than others. In a claim for interlocutory relief delay by itself may be a bar: *Legg v Inner London Education Authority* [1972] 3 All ER 177; *Texaco Ltd v Mulberry Filling Station Ltd* [1972] 1 All ER 513.[1] In a suit for equitable relief in aid of a legal right, other than a claim for specific performance or interlocutory relief, equity will be slow to refuse relief on the ground of laches unless the legal right is statute barred: *Fullwood v Fullwood* (1878) 9 Ch 176. That approach will not, of course, preclude a claim based on estoppel by acquiescence under the principle laid down in *Ramsden v Dyson* (1866) LR 1 HL 129 or equitable estoppel on the authority of *Waltons Stores (Interstate) Pty Ltd v Maher* (1988) 164 CLR 387. In suits for specific performance, despite statements in some cases that the plaintiff must be ready, willing, and even prompt and eager, to pursue his or her claim,[2] there have been some notable and authoritative exceptions.[3] It has been argued that laches cannot apply to defeat a party seeking to enforce an express trust but this was clearly not accepted by the High Court in *Orr v Ford*. It was also a view rejected earlier in *Hourigan v Trustees Executors and Agency Co Ltd* (1934) 51 CLR 619 in which the appellant brought proceedings in 1932 challenging the title of the trustees

---

1. MG&L, paras [2173] and [3606].
2. *Eads v Williams* (1854) 4 De G M & G 674 at 691; 43 ER 671 at 678; *Oriental Inland Steam Co Ltd v Briggs* (1861) 4 De GF & J 191; 45 ER 1157; MG&L, para [3606].
3. *Fitzgerald v Masters* (1956) 95 CLR 420; *Mehmet v Benson* (1965) 113 CLR 295.

of his late mother's estate to two shops which had formed part of the residue of his father's estate. The father had died in 1873. Under his will the father vested the residue in his wife 'to be used by her at "discretion' in educating and providing for my two sons'. In 1895 the appellant, who had been admitted as a solicitor, prepared a conveyance of the two shops from the father's executor to his mother. The conveyance recited the devise in the will in favour of the wife. The widow died in 1917. The court held that the claim was not statute barred but that, per Rich and Dixon JJ, Starke J dissenting, having regard to the lapse of time, the circumstances of the case, the nature of the relief claimed and the necessity of taking an account, the appellant's rights, if any such rights had existed, were barred by laches, acquiescence and delay. Rich J discussed the principles, at 629–30:

> After 37 years have elapsed from his decision to concede that the property was his mother's he now seeks to subvert all these arrangements. To do this he resorts to a Court of equity. This inequitable claim he supports upon the ground that no laches and acquiescence can answer an express trust and although he did not think so himself, he says he has now discovered that his mother is an express trustee. His contention overlooks some important qualifications of the generality upon which he relies. If a party in a position to claim an equitable right which is not undisputed lies by and acts in such a way as to lead to a belief that he has no such claim, or will not set it up, and thus encourages the party in possession to so deal with his own affairs that it would be unfair to him and to others claiming under him to tear up the transactions and go back to the position which might originally have obtained, the Court of equity will not, even where the claim is that an express trust is created, disregard the election of the party not to institute his claim and treat as unimportant the length of time during which he has slept upon his rights and induced the common assumption that he does not possess any.

[21.5] The subject matter of the claim will also be important. If it concerns a mining venture, whether in the form of shares in a mining company or some other interest, or, indeed, any other business or enterprise which is by its nature speculative or hazardous, equity will require the plaintiff to pursue his or her rights promptly rather than standing by to see whether the venture will succeed: *Boyns v Lackey* (1958) 58 SR (NSW) 395.

> In *Re Jarvis* [1958] 1 WLR 815; [1958] 2 All ER 336, one sister stood by while the other ran a tobacconist business which had been bequeathed to both of them, for her own benefit. The quiescent one was held to be disentitled on these grounds. The plaintiff brought her claim in 1951. Their father had died in 1941 and the defendant had reopened the business in 1944, having paid off its debts and then turned it into a profitable operation. While the plaintiff's delay was held to be sufficient to deny her claim to a share of the profits of the business, it did not preclude her rights to one half share of the trust estate.

Action to set aside allegedly wrongful allotments of shares must be commenced promptly, as otherwise third party rights might arise on the faith of the apparently valid shareholding: *Haas Timber & Trading Co Pty Ltd v Wade* (1955) 94 CLR 593. On the other hand, actions to set aside some transaction on the grounds of undue influence or unconscionability have been allowed many years after the wrongful act, that is, 20 years in *Bester v Perpetual Trustee Co Ltd* [1970] 3 NSWR 30 and 13 years in *Bullock v Lloyds Bank Ltd* [1955] 1 Ch 317 (see [6.34] and [6.31] respectively). In the latter case the plaintiff became aware of her right to apply to have a deed set aside nine years after its execution but then spent the next four years making fruitless requests to the trustee of the settlement to exercise a power of revocation available to him. In

Allcard v Skinner (1887) 36 Ch D 145, the plaintiff, who had made generous gifts to an Anglican convent under the influence of head of that convent, delayed six years before bringing her claim. During that time she consulted with her brother, who was a solicitor, about her affairs generally, and also converted to Roman Catholicism. Two members of the Court of Appeal accepted that the defence of laches had been made out. Lindley LJ remarked that this was more than a matter of a lapse of time; her conduct had amounted to a confirmation of the gift. In *Latec Investments Ltd v Hotel Terrigal Pty Ltd* (1965) 113 CLR 265, the respondent/mortgagor delayed five years before taking action to set aside a wrongful sale by the mortgagee. By that time the interest of a third party trustee for debenture holders had intervened and the case was eventually decided on the question of priorities between the equity of the respondent to set aside the wrongful sale and the equitable interest of the third party (see [2.11]). Laches was raised in argument against the defrauded mortgagor but was not mentioned by any member of the court in the reasons given for the decision. The respondent's problems in *Latec Investments* obviously began with its own insolvency but it should be noted that want of means is no excuse for delay in equity: *Greig v South New Zealand Gold Mining Co* (1884) 1 QLJ 189. However, if the plaintiff's impecuniosity has been caused by the defendant's actions, particularly in the facts giving rise to the claim, the defence of laches should not be so readily afforded to the defendant.

[21.6] Laches in the second sense, that is, delay which has led to circumstances rendering it unjust to allow the plaintiff's claim because it would prejudice the rights of those who had acted on the assumption that the existing state of affairs would continue, relies less on the question of knowledge and looks more at the position of the defendant or of third parties. Laches has been allowed as a defence on these grounds where property has passed through several pairs of hands and money has been spent on it so that it would be unjust to undo the original wrong, even though that might have been a wrongful sale by a trustee: *Bonney v Ridgard* (1784) 1 Cox Eq Cas 145; 29 ER 1101. Similarly, where the defendant or some third party acts to his or her detriment in reliance on the plaintiff's failure to act, the court may hold that the plaintiff is thereby disentitled to relief: *Lamshed v Lamshed* (1963) 109 CLR 440. Such changed circumstances can include the loss of evidence, even by the fading of personal memory: *Hughes v Schofield* [1975] 1 NSWLR 8.

In *Orr v Ford* (1989) 167 CLR 316; 84 ALR 146, a Dr Stone purchased a leasehold selection, 'Cockatoo' under the Land Act 1962 (Qld) in 1968. He agreed with Orr that on payment by Orr of $30,000 towards the purchase price of the selection, Orr would become entitled to a half interest in the property. Orr paid the $30,000. After Dr Stone's death his executors denied that the selection was held on trust. They argued that Orr's claim was defeated by laches, acquiescence and delay and/or in the alternative, any such alleged trust was illegal and unenforceable by reason of ss 91 and 296 of the Act. Section 91 provided that any person who applied for land under the Act as trustee, or who acquired land as trustee, 'shall be deemed ... to have acquired or to hold the land by a fraud' on the Act. Under s 296 the right or title of any person acquired or held by fraud by the Act was liable to forfeiture. Section 235 provided power for permission to be given for trusts in favour of children and other descendants. Wilson, Toohey and Gaudron JJ held that while ss 91 and 296 had the effect of making an interest acquired under the Act liable to forfeiture, they did not prevent the trust taking effect upon acquisition. The laches claim was based on the fact that Dr Stone had purported to exclude Orr and his wife from the property in December 1977. No claim was made by Orr to the property until 1982. Dr Stone made a specific devise of Cockatoo. No estoppel arose because Stone had not been led into a false belief that Cockatoo was his entirely by Orr's inactivity. Dr Stone had asserted that belief as early as 1977. The respondents argued they were prejudiced in presenting their case by reason of Orr's delay, largely because of the death of important witnesses, especially Dr Stone, in the interim. Wilson, Toohey and Gaudron JJ conceded that prejudice of that sort could be a relevant factor but did not consider it to be so on these facts. The case against Orr was simply that he had stood by. There was no claim of any release or waiver of his rights. Their Honours upheld the appeal and granted Orr a 50 per cent beneficial interest in Cockatoo, subject to an allowance in favour of Dr Stone's estate of $125,000 for half the cost of improvements effected to the property by Dr Stone. Deane J, with whom Mason CJ agreed, came to a similar but not identical view. He noted that the disability created by ss 91 and 296 related to the holding by the trustee. Those sections did not speak of the unenforceability of the equitable interest of the beneficiary in such a situation. Deane J, in considering the defence of laches, noted that this was a case concerning a claim of laches, and not one of acquiescence or a combination of the two. Deane J thought it difficult to envisage circumstances falling short of waiver, release, election or estoppel, in which laches would defeat the claim of a beneficiary to an interest in an express trust. The only possible cases he could identify were those where there had been some mistake about the identity or existence or extent of the trust property or where there might be some prejudice to third parties. He concluded that Orr's conduct in standing by for eight years in the knowledge of Dr Stone's unequivocal assertion of complete beneficial title constituted 'gross laches' sufficient to deny Orr's claim to a 50 per cent interest in Cockatoo on the basis of his arrangement with Dr Stone, but not sufficient to deny a claim to 30/156ths of the property on the basis of Orr's contribution to the original purchase price.

21-2 Set-off

[21.7] A set-off exists when a defendant has some claim which can be raised against the plaintiff to 'set-off', in whole or in part, the plaintiff's claim. Unlike a counterclaim, a set-off can only be used as a defence to reduce or completely negative any verdict in the plaintiff's favour. It is not a matter for separate proceedings against the plaintiff; if it were it would be raised by way of counterclaim and not as a set-off. The distinction between set-off and counterclaim is best illustrated in the case of a company winding up. If a company raises a set-off in defence to a winding up petition, there will be a genuine dispute over the debt. If, however, the company seeks to rely on a counterclaim, it cannot really argue that the petitioner's claim is in dispute: *Dow Securities Pty Ltd v Manufacturing Investments Ltd* (1981) 5 ACLR 501 .

[21.8] There was no right of set-off at common law until its introduction by the so-called Statutes of Set-off, 1 Geo II c 22 (1728) and 8 Geo II c 24 (1734), which allowed mutual debts to be set-off, even where one party was the executor or administrator of the estate of the party suing or being sued, and even though the debts were deemed in law to be different in nature. Bankruptcy statutes as far back as 4 & 5 Anne c 4 (1705) allowed set-off in all cases where there were 'mutual credits, mutual debts or other mutual dealings'. Where the nature of the dealings between the two parties involves the keeping of an account, with various items of debit and credit, receipt and payment, no question of set-off can arise from the mere process of accounting. Only when a balance in favour of one party shows after an account is taken can it be used as a set-off.[4] Equitable set-off is not a creature of statute, although authority for it prior to 1728 is rather thin.[5]

---

4. Halsbury 4th ed, vol 42, para 1465, p 989.
5. MG&L, para [3706]; Halsbury, *ibid*, para 1466 n 1, pp 989–90.

[21.9] Whatever the true genesis of equitable set-off, and despite the fact that it was different in some ways from set-off at law, equity followed the law in this matter and the equitable doctrine was extended by analogy with the statutory creation in several respects. Equity would recognise a common law set-off, for instance, unless it was inequitable for the defendant to rely on it in the circumstances.[6] Equity also recognised rights of set-off by analogy with the law in circumstances where a cross-demand was of a type that would have been allowed as a set-off at law if it had been a common law claim. So an equitable debt, which could not, of course, be raised at common law, would be allowed as a set-off in equity against a common law debt. An example of this can be seen in *Clark v Cort* (1840) Cr & Ph 154; 41 ER 449 in which moneys owing to a bank on a bankrupt builder's overdrawn account were allowed as a set-off against a claim against a firm of bankers for building work done by the bankrupt builder even though the bankers concerned had only acquired an interest in the overdrawn account by taking over the business of the builder's previous banker.

[21.10] The basic principles of purely equitable set-off, that is, that part of the doctrine of set-off developed by equity free from the influence of common law set-off, were stated in *Rawson v Samuel* (1841) Cr & Ph 161 at 178–9; 41 ER 451 at 458, by Lord Cottenham LC, in which his Lordship said that equitable set-off 'exists in cases where the party seeking the benefit of it can shew some equitable ground for being protected against the adversary's demand. The mere existence of cross-demands is not sufficient'. In that case the court refused an application for an injunction to restrain an action at common law for damages for breach of contract. The plaintiff in equity, the defendant at common law, had sought the injunction on the ground that no proper account had been taken of the dealings between the parties and that the right to have such an account taken should be set-off against any damages awarded at common law. Lord Cottenham held that it was not even a case of cross-demands because any damages awarded for breach of contract would not form part of the accounts between the parties and because it was not even clear that the taking of an account would show a balance in favour of the defendant at common law. The right to an account was allowed as a set-off in *O'Connor v Spaight* (1804) 1 Sch & Lef 304 in response to a landlord's claim for arrears of rent. But there the rent formed part of the dealings which were the subject of the accounts and the amount of rent owing could not be ascertained without a proper accounting.[7] A right to set-off can be excluded by contract, either expressly or by necessary implication: *Grant v NZMC Ltd* [1989] 1 NZLR 8.

[21.11] For a claim to be used as a set-off in equity it has been said that it must impeach the claim against which it is raised; it must go to the basis of the plaintiff's right to relief. The mere existence of some other demand which the defendant might be able to make against the plaintiff will not suffice, despite some authorities which have ignored this distinction: *Aries Tanker Corp v Total Transport Ltd* [1977] 1 All ER 398 at 404–5, 406–7; *James v Commonwealth Bank of Australia* (1992) 37 FCR 445 at 458 (*sub nom Re Just Juice Corporation Ltd* 109 ALR 334 at 348; 8 ACSR 444 at 460).[8] In *General Credits (Finance) Pty Ltd v Stoyakovich* [1975] Qd R 352, mortgagors being sued for the balance owing to the mortgagee after the sale of the mortgaged property were allowed to set-off a claim in account against the mortgagee for selling the property at

---

6. *Re Whitehouse & Co* (1878) 8 Ch D 595 at 597; MG&L, para [3707].
7. MG&L, para [3708] (which also lists other examples of purely equitable set-off).
8. MG&L, para [3710].

an undervalue as it was a matter which went to heart of the mortgagee's right to demand the balance.

In *Lord v Direct Acceptance Corporation Ltd (in liq)* (1993) 32 NSWLR 362, Direct Acceptance lent money to Bonnie Breck Pty Ltd secured by a fixed and floating charge given by Bonnie Breck Pty Ltd and a guarantee given by Raymond Lord. The loan was repayable on 1 April 1992. The money was not repaid and Direct Acceptance claimed $9 million plus interest from Lord under the guarantee. Lord claimed that there should be a further reduction of $6.5 million plus interest representing a sum placed on deposit with Direct Acceptance as part of the loan arrangement by another company, Me and Angus Pty Ltd, a company controlled by Lord. The money deposited by Me & Angus was lodged by way of security for the repayment of the loan by Direct Acceptance to Bonnie Breck and was not repayable by Direct Acceptance unless and until all money owed to it by Bonnie Breck had been repaid in full. That argument was put on three grounds, contract, equitable set-off and s 86 of the Bankruptcy Act 1966 (Cth). Giles J rejected all three grounds at first instance and that view was upheld unanimously by the Court of Appeal. Sheller JA, with whom Kirby P and Meagher JA agreed, approved of the statement of principle set out in Meagher, Gummow & Lehane para 3709, that it is an indispensible requirement of equitable set-off that the set-off actually go to the root of, be essentially bound up with, 'impeach' the title of the plaintiff. If available on these facts, the set-off would operate on judgment or perhaps earlier to diminish or extinguish Direct Acceptance's claim. On the facts, Sheller JA did not think the debt owed by Lord to Direct Acceptance was impeached by the fact that Direct Acceptance owed money to a third party, albeit a third party that was a company controlled by the plaintiff, saying (at 369), '... I see no reason why the availability to a surety of a set-off which reduces or extinguishes the principal debt, payment of which the surety guarantees, supports the proposition that the liability of the principal debtor should be reduced or extinguished by taking account of a sum due by the creditor to the guarantor. The consequence is that the creditor is obliged first to have recourse to a chose in action which belongs to the surety and is entitled, only to the extent that that [chose in action] is insufficient, to recover any balance from the principal debtor'. That, in his Honour's view, would make the surety primarily liable to discharge the debt, a result in which he saw no equity.

In coming to his decision Sheller JA distinguished *Bank of New Zealand v Harry M Miller* (1992) 26 NSWLR 48 on the ground that in that case the depositors had also been the guarantors and, arguably, the deposits could have been set-off against any claim by the creditor against them. In view of the fact that the moneys deposited by Me and Angus Pty Ltd in *Lord v Direct Acceptance* were deposited as part of whole transaction, ie, as a necessary pre-condition to the money being advanced by Direct Acceptance in the first place, and that Lord had obviously been the one who caused Me and Angus Pty Ltd to deposit the money, it seems odd that the Lord, as guarantor, was not entitled to employ the money deposited by way of set-off in proceedings seeking to recover the full amount of the debt from him. In view of the proviso that Me and Angus Pty Ltd could not recover the deposit until the principal debt was paid out in full, and that Direct Acceptance argued that the deposit of $6.5 million was not available to Lord by way of set-off, the deposit could sit in limbo for eternity in the event that Direct Acceptance obtained a judgment against Bonnie Breck and Lord for $9 million plus interest which remained unsatisfied, both having gone into liquidation or bankruptcy in the meantime. Surely the better view must be that Lord be allowed to set off the $6.5 million, perhaps subject to preliminary directions that Me and Angus Pty Ltd be represented and be given the opportunity to voice any objection. The end result would be that Direct Acceptance would have access to the $6.5 million deposit and would obtain a judgment against Lord for $2.5 million.

[21.12] Common law set-off, as created by the Statutes of Set-off, is a more restricted doctrine than equitable set-off. Because the statutes talk of 'mutual debts' between the plaintiff and the defendant, common law set-off is only available as a defence to a claim for a liquidated sum, and then requires another liquidated sum as the set-off. Both sums must also arise from common law claims. Mutuality is essential in common law set-off; the two claims must arise between the same parties and concern the same subject matter. The element of mutuality also means that a joint debt cannot be setoff against a several debt. Common law set-off is subject to some odd restrictions. For instance, set-off is not available at common law against a claim by a landlord for arrears of rent. Before the Judicature Act 1873 (Imp) a defendant at common law who sought to rely on a set-off based on equitable principles had to commence separate proceedings in Chancery for a common injunction to restrain his opponent at common law. The introduction of the judicature system overcame that problem as it allowed a set-off on equitable grounds to be raised in an action at law without the necessity for separate proceedings. The result has led to some blurring of the distinction between common law and equitable set-off.

> In *D Galambos & Son Pty Ltd v McIntyre* (1975) 5 ACTR 10, the plaintiff claimed the balance of $1,053 due under a building contract. The defendants did not dispute the amount, but counter-claimed seeking $5,000 for faulty and incorrect work. Woodward J held that the matters raised by the defendants should have been pleaded in the alternative as giving rise to a defence either directly against the action at law, that is, as a failure in part to perform a contract, or as defective performance of that contract directly reducing the value of the work done or the goods supplied on the grounds stated by Baron Parke in *Mondel v Steele* (1841) 8 M & W 858 at 871; [1835–42] All ER Rep 511 at 515–16, or by way of set-off, on the ground that claims of money due under a contract and damages for breach of the same contract may be set-off against each other where the equity of the case requires that it should be so: *Newfoundland Government v Newfoundland Railway Co* (1888) 13 App Cas 199. In coming to that decision his Honour discussed the question of whether the defendants could rely on the plaintiff's various breaches of contract as providing a defence by way of set-off to an action for moneys owing under the contract. He noted that since the Judicature Acts there has been no doubt about the right of a defendant to counterclaim in such a case. In regard to equitable set-off, having referred in particular to *Rawson v Samuel*, he said that the prerequisites of such a set-off were:
>
> (i) Clear cross-claims (or cross demands) for debts or damages, which,
>
> (ii) Were so closely related as to subject matter that the claim sought to be set-off impeached the other, in the sense that it made it unjust to allow recovery without deduction.

At common law the Statutes of Set-off permitted the setting off of opposing claims for liquidated sums. A claim for unliquidated damages could only be used defensively at common law by way of a counterclaim, and costs of the claim and counterclaim would be dealt with separately: *Stooke v Taylor* (1880) 5 QBD 569 at 573–5 and 581–2, per Cockburn CJ. After the Judicature Acts unliquidated damages could be pleaded as a set-off in an action at law in the same circumstances in which there could previously have been an equitable set-off of such damages, that is, where those damages would previously have entitled the defendant to file a bill in Chancery to restrain the plaintiff from proceeding with his action at law.

[21.13] In coming to his decision in *D Galambos & Son Pty Ltd v McIntyre*, Woodward J declined to follow the apparent authority of *McDonnell & East Ltd v McGregor* (1936) 56 CLR 50 in which Dixon J, citing *Newfoundland v Newfoundland Railway* as his authority, had said that unliquidated damages could not be the subject of set-off, neglecting, as Woodward J noted, to include the qualification 'by law' in the passage borrowed from the Privy Council in *Newfoundland Railway*.

[21.14] In New South Wales there is some controversy over the survival of common law set-off following the repeal of the Statutes of Set-off by the Imperial Acts Application Act 1969 (NSW), s 8. Those provisions were not re-enacted and the only source of any authority for the courts in that State to recognise a set-off, other than one based on purely equitable grounds, is the Supreme Court Act 1970 (NSW), s 78 which empowers the court to grant to the defendant in any proceedings 'all such relief against any person as the Court might grant against that person if he were a defendant in separate proceedings commenced by the defendant for that purpose'; and the relief which the court may grant in such a case includes, 'relief in respect of any equitable estate or right, or other matter of equity, or in respect of any legal estate, right or title claimed or asserted by the defendant'. Part 15, r 25 of the Supreme Court Rules also provides that where a claim by a defendant to a sum of money, whether ascertained or not, is relied on as a defence, in whole or in part, to a claim made by a plaintiff, it may be included in the defence and set-off against the plaintiff's claim, whether or not the defendant also crossclaims for that sum. In *Dillingham Constructions Pty Ltd v Steel Mains Pty Ltd* (1975) 132 CLR 323, the High Court held s 78 to be purely procedural. The question arose again for consideration in *Stehar Knitting Mills Pty Ltd v Southern Textile Converters Pty Ltd* [1980] 2 NSWLR 514. In that case Glass JA held that, although the procedure which formerly existed under the Statutes of Set-off was abrogated in 1969, a more sophisticated procedure came into force under the Supreme Court Act 1970 (NSW). That procedure, he thought, allowed a defendant to raise claims which were formerly known as pleas of set-off, pleas of cross-action and pleas on equitable grounds. Hutley JA said that the Statutes of Set-off were truly procedural and thus, with the possible exception that the authority to plead in bar had gone, s 78 and Pt 15, r 25 preserved the statutory right to set-off one claim against another, possibly through a more flexible set of devices. The correctness of the decision in *Stehar Knitting Mills* has been questioned, but even those who criticise it concede that rights of set-off can be safely categorised as substantive rights only in so far as they are pleas in bar, that is, pleas which show a substantial defence to the action.[9] The rights of set-off conferred on defendants by s 78 and Pt 15, r 25, if those provisions can be taken as literally as Glass JA suggests, appear to be wider than those which operated before, both at law and in equity. In the event *Stehar Knitting* has been accepted and Australian courts have shown a willingness to exercise this useful and flexible procedure for pleading of matters by way of set-off: see *Sydmar Pty Ltd v Statewise Developments Pty Ltd* (1987) 73 ALR 289; *Tooth & Co Ltd v Smith* (Clarke J, 5 September 1984, unreported). In the latter case, Clarke J observed that a determination as to whether an equitable set-off exists in any particular case requires an examination of the closeness of respective claims and that no general rule can be laid down except by stating that such a set-off will arise where the circumstances of the case are such that it would be unjust or inequitable for the plaintiff to proceed with his or her claim. This approach was applied by Giles J in *AWA Ltd v Exicom Australia Pty Ltd* (1990) 19 NSWLR 705:

> AWA agreed to sell Exicom a certain business and assets as defined by a deed dated 30 September 1988 embodying the agreement between the two. The transaction gave rise to two proceedings: in No 50271 of 1989, in which Exicom claimed from (*inter alia*) AWA, damages for breach of contract and for contravention of the Trade Practices Act 1974 (Cth), s 52, and, No 50057 of 1990 in which AWA claimed from Exicom

---

9.   MG&L, para [3713].

$887,623 plus interest as money payable pursuant to certain clauses of the deed. Exicom's defence to AWA's claim was in the following terms:

> In answer to the whole of the summons of the plaintiff the defendant says that it is entitled to a set off against the claim of the plaintiff for such part of the amount due to it pursuant to its claim in proceedings No 5027 [sic] of 1989 as is equal to the plaintiff's claim herein.

AWA moved to strike out the defence, contending that Exicom's claims were not claims which could be pleaded as a defence. Exicom contended that it was entitled to plead its claims as a defence by way of equitable set-off. Giles J came to the view that the respective claims, as pleaded, and as fleshed out by reference to the deed, were so closely related that it would have been unjust and inequitable to permit AWA to proceed with its claim without Exicom being able to prosecute its claim as an equitable defence. Both claims arose under the deed. While each party claimed for breaches of different clauses of the deed, both claims were 'by way of working out the bargain between the parties in relation to the sale of the business and the assets'.

AWA v Exicom was followed by Rogers J in *AMP Society v Specialist Funding Consultants Pty Ltd* (1991) 24 NSWLR 326 at 328–9.

[21.15] The Statutes of Set-Off have been repealed in Queensland by the Imperial Acts Application Act 1969 (Qld). In Queensland, O 22 r 3 of the Supreme Court Rules allows a defendant to plead by way of set-off or set up by way of counterclaim against the plaintiff any right or claim, whether such set-off or counterclaim sounds in damages or not. However, O 22, r 3 is only procedural and does not determine whether there is a right of set-off in any given case. In that respect regard must be had to the established principles of set-off: *Knockholt Pty Ltd v Graff* [1975] Qd R 88; *General Credits (Finance) Pty Ltd v Stoyakovich* [1975] Qd R 352; *Eversure Textiles Manufacturing Co Ltd v Webb* [1978] Qd R 347 at 348. In Victoria the Statutes of Set-off were repealed by the Imperial Acts Application Act 1922 (Vic), s 7 although that legislation had a saving provision to the effect that the section shall not affect '... Any established principle or rule of law or equity or established jurisdiction ... Notwithstanding that the same respectively may have been in any manner affirmed recognised or derived by in or from any enactment hereby repealed'. A similar saving provision appeared in the Imperial Acts Application Act 1980 (Vic), s 5.

[21.16] In *Bank of Boston Connecticut v European Grain and Shipping Ltd* [1989] AC 1056 at 1101–3, the House of Lords, appeared to distinguish between the concept of a cross-demand which 'impeached the title to the legal demand' found in *Rawson v Samuel* and the test of a cross-demand 'flowing out of and inseparably connected with the dealings and transactions which also give rise to the claim' found in *Newfoundland Government v Newfoundland Railway Co* (1888) 13 App Cas 199 at 1106, and to prefer the latter. Those comments were *obiter*. Their Lordships upheld established authority, especially *Aries Tanker Corporation v Total Transport Ltd* [1977] 1 WLR 185, that there was no defence by way of set-off available to a charterer to a claim for freight under a charterparty, even where the right upon which the set-off is claimed impeached the shipowner's claim for freight. The requirement that the defendant's claim 'impeach' that of the plaintiff has not been applied strictly in some recent decisions. In *AWA v Exicom* Giles J held that set-off was available where the two claims were so closely related that it would be inequitable to allow the plaintiff to proceed with its claim without the defendant's claim also being dealt with. The line of authority of which *AWA v Exicom* is an example has been criticised by Gummow J as contrary to established principle, that principle being, the test laid down in *Ramson v Samuel* that equitable set-off will only be available when the defendant's claim impeaches the plaintiff's demand, in *James v Commonwealth Bank of Australia* (1992) 37 FCR 445 at 457–60 (*sub nom Re Just Juice Corporation Ltd* 109 ALR 334 at 347–52; 8 ACSR 444 at 460–2).[10] Gummow J argues, at 109 ALR 350–1, that the Judicature system has only introduced procedural changes and does not alter substantive rights. The decision of the New South Wales Court of Appeal in *Lord v Direct Acceptance Corporation Ltd (in liq)* (1993) 32 NSWLR 362 (see [21.11]) appears to re-assert the orthodox view preferred by Gummow J.[11] The availability of a right of set-off to a party to an agreement will only be excluded by clear and unequivocal words. A lease which provided that rent and other moneys payable under the lease were to be paid free of deductions has been held not to exclude a right of set-off: *Re Partnership Pacific Securities Limited* [1994] 1 Qd R 410.

The rule in Cherry v Boultbee

[21.17] This is a rule which is similar to the equitable doctrine of set-off but not so alike that it can accurately be described by the term 'set-off'. It applies in cases in which a debtor is left a pecuniary legacy by his or her creditor and allows the estate to deduct the amount of the debt from the legacy. The rule takes its name from *Cherry v Boultbee* (1839) 4 My & Cr 442; 41 ER 171 in which a brother owed money to his sister. The brother became bankrupt and the sister later died leaving the brother a legacy greater than the debt. The brother's assignee in bankruptcy sued the sister's executors for the legacy. They sought to set-off the amount of the debt against the legacy. Lord Cottenham said that the executor's right to retain a sum equal to the debt was not a right of set-off so much as a right to pay out of the fund in hand. As that right could only arise when there was a right to receive the debt, his Lordship held the rule could not apply because the sister's estate was never entitled to receive more than dividends on the debt, the brother having been declared bankrupt before his sister's death. The rule was more precisely stated in *Re Peruvian Railway Construction Co* [1915] 2 Ch 144 at 150, by Sargant J, 'Where a person entitled to participate in a fund is also bound to make a contribution in aid of that fund, he cannot be allowed to participate unless and until he has fulfilled his duty to contribute'. In essence, the debtor, being possessed of assets of the fund against which he or she has a claim, is obliged to pay him or herself *pro tanto* out of the assets in hand first before coming against the fund: *Turner v Turner* [1911] 1 Ch 716 at 719, per Cozens-Hardy MR; *Courtenay v Williams* (1844) 3 Hare 539 at 553–4, per Wigram V-C; 67 ER 494 at 500.

[21.18] If a creditor elects to pursue the debt by other means, such as proving in the debtor's bankruptcy, he or she will forfeit rights under this rule: *Stammers v Elliott* (1867) LR 3 Ch 195. The rule in *Cherry v Boultbee* is not limited to debts and legacies. It applies in all cases where one party is under a liability to contribute to some fund and is also a beneficiary to that fund. In such circumstances the debtor can be obliged to look to him or herself first to satisfy the claim, that is, where a *cestui que* trust is indebted to the trust: *Priddy v Rose* (1817) 3 Mer 86; 36 ER 33, or where a debenture-holder is indebted to the company.

---

10. See also MG&L, para [3710].
11. See generally: R Derham, 'Recent Issues in Relation to Set-off' (1994) 68 ALJ 331. See also *Walker v Department of Social Security* (1995) 129 ALR 198.

21–3 Release and Waiver

[21.19] Equity will recognise as a valid defence, whether against a legal or an equitable claim, an assertion that the plaintiff has released the defendant from his or her obligations or, otherwise, has waived his or her rights against the defendant. Waiver is a difficult expression to use with certainty in this, or indeed any context, because it is not a term of any fixed meaning and has been used to signify a number of different things.[12] While there are some old cases in which voluntary releases of legal debts were upheld,[13] the better view is that equity will not recognise any purported release of a legal right unless it is supported by consideration or has otherwise been effective as a release at law, that is, if an obligation under a deed is released by an instrument under seal: *Reeves v Brymer* (1801) 6 Ves 516; 31 ER 1172; *Commissioner of Stamp Duties v Bone* (1976) 135 CLR 223; [1977] AC 511 . A release may be effected by way of gift. In *Re Ward* (1984) 55 ALR 395, a written acknowledgement of a gift of a debt by the creditor to the debtor was held to be effective to discharge the debt, although set aside on other grounds as a settlement void under Bankruptcy Act 1966 (Cth), s 120, either as a valid assignment or because it gave rise to a promissory estoppel.

[21.20] In the case of equitable rights the position is more straightforward. Equity will recognise a voluntary release, which may be effected in writing, orally, or by conduct, so long as it provides 'proof of a fixed, deliberate and unbiased determination that the transaction should not be impeached … [which] … may be proved either by the lapse of time during which the transaction has been allowed to stand, or by other circumstances': *Wright v Vanderplank* (1856) 8 De GM & G 133 at 147, per Turner LJ; 44 ER 340 at 345–6. To avail him or herself of this defence a defendant must show that the plaintiff was aware of both the nature and circumstances of the transaction giving rise to the right in equity and of his right to relief in equity, even if only in the sense that he or she knew the transaction was questionable: *Allcard v Skinner* (1887) 36 Ch D 145.

[21.21] In *The Commonwealth v Verwayen* (1990) 170 CLR 394 at 427, Brennan J said of waiver, that 'a right is waived only when the time comes for its exercise and the party for whose sole benefit it has been introduced knowingly abstains from exercising it, a mere intention not to exercise a right is not immediately effective to divest or sterilise it'. Toohey J, at 474, was of a different view. He thought a party who had renounced a right could not withdraw the waiver. Gaudron J, at 485, saw waiver as a principle separate from estoppel and took the expression to signify 'deliberate action or inaction which has resulted in a changed relationship to which the parties will be held whether or not detriment is actually established'. Mason CJ, at 406, did not think waiver could destroy a legal right unless it was supported by consideration or the act of waiver could also be categorised as falling under estoppel or the doctrine of election. Deane J, at 449–50, reiterated the view he had expressed in *Foran v Wright* (1989) 168 CLR 385 at 433–5 that the arbitrary doctrine of waiver is being increasingly absorbed and rationalised by the more flexible doctrine of estoppel by conduct. Despite the understandable but gallant efforts of Toohey and Gaudron JJ, the majority view which appears to flow from *Verwayen* is that waiver will only operate to defeat a party's rights in the circumstances proposed by Brennan J, that is to say only if it is supported by consideration or can otherwise be characterised as a matter giving rise to an estoppel or a binding election.

---

12. See MG&L, para [1723].
13. MG&L, para [3502].

21–4 Limitation Defences in Equity by Analogy with Statutes of Limitations

[21.22] Equity acts on the analogy of statutes of limitation. In certain cases the statutes of limitation apply expressly to equitable claims. In these cases a court of equity acts in obedience to the statutes and applies their express bar. When claims are made in equity by way of equitable proceedings which are not the subject of any express statutory bar, but the equitable proceedings correspond to a remedy at law in respect of the same matter which is subject to a statutory bar, a court of equity, in the absence of fraud or other special circumstances, adopts, by way of analogy, the same limitation for the equitable claim: *Motor Terms Co Pty Ltd v Liberty Insurance Ltd* (1967) 116 CLR 177 at 184, per Kitto J. But the principle applies only in equitable suits, not statute-based actions.[14] This rule depends on some correspondence between equitable and legal remedies. When there is no common law counterpart to the equitable remedy, that is, specific performance, a court of equity does not apply the statute of limitation by analogy: *Fitzgerald v Masters* (1922) 95 CLR 420.[15] Where one party receives the proceeds of sale of furniture and insurance moneys as trustee for another, under a duty to pay those moneys to the second party and not merely other money to the same amount, there is no scope for applying the statute of limitation by analogy since there is no legal rule with which an analogy can be drawn: *Cohen v Cohen* (1929) 42 CLR 91 at 100, per Dixon J. The receiver of the money in such a case does so as an express trustee.

[21.23] The statute of limitation is applied by analogy where a debt is owed: *Cohen v Cohen* (1929) 42 CLR 91 at 102. A winding up petition may properly form the basis of an order for the liquidation of a company even if the debt on which it is based becomes statute-barred after the date of the petition and before the date of the order: *Motor Terms Co Pty Ltd v Liberty Insurance Ltd* (1967)116 CLR 177.[16] Where a plaintiff can proceed either in equity or at law, for example, for an account, a court of equity will adopt the same limitation period as at law: *Urquhart v McPherson* (1880) 6 VR (E) 17. Equity, in applying statutes of limitation by analogy, will not do so in cases of 'concealed fraud'. That is, it will not do so in such a way as to permit time to run until the discovery of the fraud. Nor will it do so where the defendant fraudulently conceals the existence of a cause of action from the plaintiff. In *R v McNeill* (1922) 31 CLR 76 at 100, Isaacs J put the proposition in these terms:

> [Equity] usually applies, from a sense of fitness, its own equitable doctrine of laches and adopts the measure of time which Parliament has indicated in analogous cases, but, when a greater equity caused by fraud arises, it modifies the practice it has itself created and gives play to the greater equity.[17]

It has been said that in equity where fraud is involved time runs, not from the discovery of fraud, but from the time when the plaintiff might with due diligence have

---

14. *Motor Terms Co Pty Ltd v Liberty Insurance Ltd* (1967) 116 CLR 177 at 184.

15. Compare *R v McNeil* (1922) 31 CLR 76 at 100, per Isaacs J.

16. At 195, per Menzies J: 'By analogy with the Statute of Limitations, it could hardly happen that a petitioning creditor loses his right to proceed while waiting for the court to hear and to determine his petition'. But he added: 'The problem as I see it, however, is not so much the application of the Statute of Limitations by analogy; it is rather a problem of the construction of the Companies Act ...'.

17. In *Montgomerie's Brewery Co Ltd v Blyth* (1901) 27 VLR 175 at 203, Holroyd J said: 'It is fraud in itself not to disclose a fraud which the fiduciary duty of the person who knows it binds him to disclose'.

discovered it: *Urquhart v McPherson* (1880) 6 VR (E) 17 at 23. This doctrine of concealed fraud is an answer only to equitable claims; it cannot be used to prevent the defendant pleading the Statute of Limitations in a common law action.[18] A secret profit made by an agent from the use of his principal's property or from the use of information gained the course of the principal's business is not merely an equitable debt, but is subject to a constructive trust.[19] The statute of limitation is applied by analogy in cases of constructive trusts, where an equity is fastened on the alleged trustee not because he or she intended to become trustee of the property but because of the character of his or her dealings with it and in spite of his or her intention to take the property for him or herself; but it is not applied by analogy where a person, intending to act in a fiduciary capacity, has received property for another, for such a person is either an express trustee or stands in the same position: *Cohen v Cohen* (1929) 42 CLR 91 at 100, per Dixon J.

---

18. *R v McNeill* (1922) 31 CLR 76 at 99–100, per Isaacs J; *Metacel Pty Ltd v Ralph Symonds Ltd* (1969) 90 WN (Pt 1) (NSW) 449 (it is not applicable to actions for damages for negligence and breach of contract).

19. *DPC Estates Pty Ltd v Grey and Consul Development Pty Ltd* [1974] 1 NSWLR 443 at 462 and 470–1, per Hardie and Hutley JJA, limiting *Lister & Co v Stubbs* (1890) 45 Ch D 1 to its own facts.

Chapter Twenty Two

22-1 The Nature of Specific Performance

[22.1] Specific performance is an order of the court directing a party to a contract to perform obligations due by that party under the contract. There are two schools of thought on the precise meaning of 'specific performance'. Under the first it applies only to executory contracts. In that view, as put by Meagher, Gummow and Lehane, a distinction must be drawn between specific performance in the 'proper sense' or 'true sense' in which it means an order compelling a party to an executory contract to execute some document or do some act in the law, such as delivery of some chattel, which will put the parties 'in the position relative to each other in which by the preliminary agreement they were intended to be placed',[1] and specific relief analogous to specific performance, under which a party to an executed contract is ordered to perform obligations due under that contract according to its terms.[2] The second school led by Messrs Heydon, Gummow and Austin, with support from the Privy Council, argues that this distinction is no longer necessary.[3] The first set of learned authors advance three major reasons for maintaining the distinction:

(a) To obtain specific performance in the 'proper sense' a party must prove that he has performed, or is ready, willing and able to perform his obligations under the contract, while this may not be necessary in the case of relief in the nature of specific performance: *Sydney Consumers' Milk and Ice Co Ltd v Hawkeshury Dairy & Ice Society Ltd* (1931) 31 SR (NSW) 458 at 462–3. In practical terms this difference is unlikely to be of any consequence. The maxim that he who seeks equity must do equity applies to both and a plaintiff in breach of its obligations under an executed contract would receive little help from an argument that this rule only applied to a suit for specific performance in the proper sense.

(b) Without the distinction specific performance will be confused with suits for mandatory injunctions and matters such as whether the order sought effects enforcement of part only of the contract, and not the whole, may be taken into account when they are, strictly speaking, relevant only to claims for specific performance in the 'true sense'. It is difficult to see any practical difficulty which might arise from this. As the learned authors acknowledge, matters such as ade-

---

1. MG&L, paras [2001]–[2002]; *Wolverhampton and Walsall Railway Co v London and North Western Railway Co* (1873) LR 16 Eq 433 at 439, per Lord Selborne; *Packenham Upper Fruit Co v Crosby* (1924) 35 CLR 386 at 394, per Isaacs and Rich JJ; and *JC Williamson Ltd v Lukey and Mulholland* (1931) 45 CLR 282 at 297, per Dixon J.
2. *Packenham Upper Fruit Co v Crosby, supra,* and *JC Williamson Ltd v Lukey and Mulholland, supra.*
3. HG&A, para [3801]; *Australian Hardwoods Pty Ltd v Commissioner for Railways* [1961] 1 All ER 737 (Mr Gummow, as he then was, presumably being of two minds on the point).

quacy of damages, hardship and other discretionary defences are relevant to both specific performance and claims to relief in the nature of specific performance.[4] In this sense mandatory injunctions are also indistinguishable from specific performance: *Burns Philp Trust Co Ltd v Kwikasair Freightlines Ltd* [1964] NSWR 63.[5]

(c) An order of true specific performance is an order that the whole contract be carried out, not specific obligations under it, unless they are severable, while specific relief can be given in respect of separate obligations under an executed contract. Heydon, Gummow and Austin argue that this point is open to criticism, and has been criticised; that the authorities cited in support of it are not that strong, and that the issue is too minor to justify the rigid division between the two very similar forms of relief. In both the intervention of equity is based upon the inadequacy of damages at common law.[6]

The distinction seems to be of little practical effect but it should be noted that Deane J referred to it, without demur, in *Hewett v Court* (1983) 149 CLR 639 at 665. In many other instances courts have not drawn this distinction and, thus, many cases frequently cited as authorities on aspects of specific performance actually concern claims for specific relief of executed contracts rather than specific performance in the 'true' sense of an executory contract.

22-2 Inadequacy of Relief at Common Law

[22.2] Equity follows the law and will not provide a remedy for breach of contract where there is an adequate remedy at law, that is, where common law damages will provide adequate relief. In general this means that specific performance will not be decreed for breach of a contract to supply something which the plaintiff could simply replace by purchasing it in the market place with the damages received for the breach. Some property is considered unique and irreplaceable in that way. Land, despite the similarity between blocks in many suburban sub-divisions, has always been regarded as unique in this sense, so a contract for the sale, mortgage or lease of land will always be considered appropriate for relief by way of specific performance: *Adderley v Dixon* (1824) 1 Sims & St 607; 57 ER 239, even though the purchaser is buying the land for the purposes of development and profit: *Pianta v National Finance & Trustees Ltd* (1964) 38 ALJR 232. The obligation to convey or transfer must have arisen before specific performance can be decreed. That will not be the case, for instance, where the consent of the Minister of Lands under Closer Settlement legislation is required for the transfer: *Brown v Heffer* (1967) 116 CLR 344 at 350. A contract for the sale of shares, stock or other securities will also be specifically enforceable where the shares or securities cannot be readily obtained in the market: *ANZ Executors and Trustees Ltd v Humes Ltd* [1990] VR 615, unless the securities are readily obtainable on the market in which case damages will be adequate: *Re Schwabacher* (1907) 98 LT 127. In *Dougan v Ley* (1946) 71 CLR 147, specific performance was decreed of a contract to sell a taxicab together with its licence and registration because the registration and licence of a taxicab was then very difficult to obtain. That does not mean that mere shortage of supply of some particular goods will render them appropriate subjects for decrees of

---

4. MG&L, para [2003].
5. HG&A, para [3801].
6. *Ibid.*

specific performance: *Cook v Rodgers* (1946) 46 SR (NSW) 229, although each case must turn on its own facts. Rare or unique chattels, such as works of art, breeding stock, particular items of jewellery and even china jars of unusual beauty, will also be appropriate subjects for decrees of specific performance: *Falcke v Gray* (1859) 4 Drew 651, even though the peculiarity of the chattel in question arises from its special commercial or sentimental value to the plaintiff: *Doulton Potteries Ltd v Bronotte* [1971] 1 NSWLR 591. The essential question, however, is the adequacy of damages at law, rather than the nature of the subject matter of the contract: *Aristoc Industries Pty Ltd v RA Wenham (Builders) Pty Ltd* [1965] NSWR 581, although the special treatment afforded to land indicates that with some types of property inadequacy of damages will always be presumed. A contract for the sale of a special chattel will usually attract the remedy of specific performance. However, the plaintiff may forfeit the right to specific performance if by the terms of the agreement between the parties and by the pleading of the case the plaintiff puts a fixed price on the article sought to be recovered, as happened in *Dowling v Betjemann* (1862) 2 John & H 544; 70 ER 1157, in which an artist sought restitution of a picture painted by himself. A contract for the sale of animals or stock on a farm will not be specifically enforceable: *Perne v Lisle* (1749) Amb 76; 27 ER 47 in which Lord Hardwicke declined to grant specific performance of a contract to provide African slaves. The same cannot be said of a contract to sell a particular animal.

In *Borg v Howlett* (SC(NSW), Young J, 24 May 1996, unreported), the plaintiff sought specific performance of a contract for the sale of a thoroughbred horse. The defendant, a horse breeder, entered four horses in yearling sales, intending to sell three, including one identified as Lot 109, and to keep one, identified as Lot 101. Both colts were by the same sire, Southern Gentleman but out of different dams, Lot 109 from National Chimes and Lot 101 from Max's Desire. The plaintiff's agent was the successful bidder on Lot 109. By mistake, the defendant delivered Lot 101 to the plaintiff. The sale took place in March 1994. The defendant discovered the mistake in February 1995 and offered to refund the purchase price. The plaintiff had a poor opinion of horses bred from Max's Desire and did not wish to keep the horse. The plaintiff sought specific performance of the contract to sell him Lot 109. Young J rejected a defence based on mistake as the plaintiff had not contributed to the mistake in any way and there was no plea of hardship which might sway the court's discretion otherwise (see *Tamplin v James* (1880) 15 Ch D 215 at 221 per James LJ; *Slee v Warke* (1949) 86 CLR 271 at 278). While noting that, perhaps surprisingly, there were no authorities directly on point, Young J decreed specific performance of the contract to sell the horse identified as Lot 109.

In coming to his decision in *Borg v Howlett*, Young J referred to a number of cases in which specific performance had been decreed in contracts for special chattels, for example: *Duke of Somerset v Cookson* (1735) 3 P Wms 391; 24 ER 1114 (silver altar piece); *Doulton Potteries Ltd v Bronotte* [1971] 1 NSWLR 591 (a die used in the manufacture of pipes) and *McKeown v Cavalier Yachts* (1988) 13 NSWLR 303 (a yacht). Young J noted a submission that damages would be difficult to assess in this case, the plaintiff having lost the 'chance' that the horse in Lot 109 would be a winner. However, he held that such matters can only be taken into account as a factor in deciding whether damages would be an adequate remedy, the matter being one of fact to be decided on the facts of each case.[7] One of the facts which could be taken into account, in Young J's view, was the special or unique value of the chattel to the plaintiff, as might be the case where the plaintiff requires the chattel to complete a set. The categories of cases in which specific performance might be decreed are not closed. Each case

---

7. Spry, *Equitable Remedies*, 4th ed, Law Book Co, 1990, p 62.

depends on its own facts and the circumstances, including the state of the market which prevails at the time: *Timmerman v Nervina Industries (International) Pty Ltd* [1983] 1 Qd R 1. A contract for the sale of unascertained goods was made the subject of a decree in the nature of specific performance in *Sky Petroleum Ltd v VIP Petroleum Ltd* [1974] 1 All ER 954. Goulding J granted an interlocutory injunction to restrain the defendant from withholding supplies of petrol under an exclusive contract for the supply of such products for 10 years from 1970 in circumstances in which, because of the state of the market, the plaintiff was unlikely to be able to obtain supplies from elsewhere.

[22.3] Specific performance may be decreed of a contract to pay money where the party seeking that remedy is a vendor under a contract for sale under which the purchaser would have been entitled to specific performance.

In *Turner v Bladin* (1951) 82 CLR 463, an oral agreement was made for the sale of the plant, fittings, effects and goodwill of a quarry business for £7,500. The defendant purchaser paid a deposit of £2,100 and was allowed in to commence operations. The balance of the purchase money was payable by instalments of £500 at intervals of six months thereafter. No further moneys were paid and the plaintiff took proceedings to recover the balance. The defendant submitted, inter alia, that the agreement, as an agreement which was not to be performed for a year, was unenforceable by virtue of s 128 of the Instruments Act 1928–36 (Vic). He also argued that, because the balance was not immediately payable under the agreement, specific performance could not be ordered. The High Court found that this was also a contract for the sale of an interest in land, the right to work the quarry being a profit à prendre. The court ordered specific performance of the agreement, so far as it had not been performed. Proceedings for specific performance of a contract which is of such a kind that can be specifically enforced can be commenced as soon as one party threatens to refuse to perform the contract or any part thereof or actually refuses to perform any promise for which the time for performance has arrived. The court distinguished the statement made by Dixon J in *JC Williamson Ltd v Lukey and Mulholland* (1931) 45 CLR 282 at 297, that specific performance is not available unless complete relief can be given and the contract carried into full and final execution so that the parties are put in the relation contemplated by their agreement, by saying that his Honour was there discussing the kind of contract which is capable of specific performance and not the time at which a suit for specific performance may be instituted. Where a contract is of such a kind that a purchaser can sue for specific performance, the vendor can also sue for specific performance, even though the claim is merely one to recover a sum of money. Where a vendor seeks specific performance of a contract to pay purchase money by instalments he can obtain an order for payment of the instalments which are overdue with liberty to apply in respect of future instalments as they become payable.

[22.4] A contract to lend money will not be specifically enforced, although specific performance in the 'true' sense may be granted of an agreement to grant a mortgage. An indemnity agreement will be specifically enforced at the suit of the debtor where it obliges the party giving the indemnity to pay the creditor first, rather than simply reimbursing the debtor: *McIntosh v Dalwood (No 4)* (1930) 30 SR (NSW) 415. Similarly, an agreement to grant an annuity, and an instrument creating an annuity, will be specifically enforced, as the alternative of a separate action at common law upon each default would be inadequate: *Keenan v Handley* (1864) 2 De GJ & S 283; 46 ER 384. A contract between A and B under which A promises B to provide some benefit to C will be specifically enforceable at the suit of B where B would, otherwise, only be entitled to nominal damages at law, which would, obviously, be inadequate: *Coulls v Bagot's Executor & Trustee Co Ltd* (1967) 119 CLR 460; *Beswick v Beswick* [1968] AC 58.

[22.5] Specific performance will also be decreed under the doctrine of part performance in cases where no relief is available at law because the contract in question is unenforceable in that jurisdiction for want of compliance with some statutory form and yet, on the equities which have arisen in the circumstances from acts of part performance, particularly those of the plaintiff, the defendant would be guilty of fraud in equity if he or she sought to rely on the statute: see **[3.22]–[3.28]**.

[22.6] It is also open to question whether damages at law can be considered adequate where the defendant is insolvent, so that any order for damages would be worthless in practical terms. Doubt as to the solvency of the defendant has been accepted by some authorities as a matter to be taken into account when assessing the adequacy of damages: *Hodgson v Duce* (1856) 2 Jur NS 1014; *Aristoc Industries Pty Ltd v RA Wenham (Builders) Pty Ltd* [1965] NSWR 581. Difficulty in enforcing an order for damages, as might be the case where the defendant has no assets in the jurisdiction, might be another factor in determining the adequacy of damages in a given case. The appropriateness of specific performance of a contract to build a prefabricated house was considered by some members of the High Court in *Hewett v Court* (1983) 149 CLR 639. In the event it proved unnecessary to decide the issue as the majority held that the purchaser was entitled to an equitable lien over the partially completed structure to secure the deposit and progress payments made, and that therefore his acquisition of that structure did not constitute a preference. Wilson and Dawson JJ were of the view that specific performance was not appropriate, although they seemed more persuaded by the fact that the builder did not have possession of the site, and thus did not satisfy the criteria for specific performance of building contracts laid down by Romer LJ in *Wolverhampton Corp v Emmons* [1901] 1 KB 515, than by the adequacy of any award of damages which might have been made.[8] It also seems open to question whether damages can be adequate where they are impossible or very difficult to calculate. For instance, in, say, a stud breeding contract, or a contract giving right of entry in some contest, the plaintiff's loss, in the event of repudiation by the other party, is the loss of a chance. Calculating the value of such a lost chance has been described as 'incapable of being carried out with certainty or precision': *Howe v Teefy* (1927) 27 SR (NSW) 301 at 307, per Street CJ, and even as 'a matter of guesswork': *Chaplin v Hicks* [1911] 2 KB 786 at 792, per Vaughan Williams LJ. In such a case an award of nominal damages would seem to be at least as precise as any other figure,[9] and it is therefore submitted that a court faced with such a dilemma, where specific performance is possible in the circumstances, should make a decree accordingly as the only means of providing an adequate remedy.[10] The same can be said of the prospects of success of a thoroughbred horse on the track or at stud: *Borg v Howlett* (SC(NSW), Young J, 24 May 1996, unreported).

---

8. ICF Spry, 'Some Recent Problems in Regard to Specific Performance' in PD Finn (ed), *Essays on Equity*, Law Book Co, Sydney, 1984, pp 131–41 at p 136 ff.
9. *Sapwell v Bass* [1910] 2 KB 486.
10. See Kearney J in *Wight v Haberdan Pty Ltd* [1984] 2 NSWLR 280.

22-3 Contracts for Personal Services and Contracts Requiring Constant Supervision

[22.7] Equity will not decree specific performance of contracts to provide personal services nor of contracts which would require constant supervision. Contracts which would involve the continuation of a personal relationship are included under this prohibition. The rationale behind equity's reluctance in contracts for personal services stems, in part, from an aversion to making orders which would smack of slavery, and, also in part, from common sense. The proper policing of any order of this nature, particularly as to the quality of the service provided under such compulsion, would be impossible. By the same token, specific performance will not be decreed of a contract, such as one for the sale of a farm, where the consideration provided for that promise includes the provision of personal services, such as those of managing the farm: *Maiden v Maiden* (1909) 7 CLR 727. An order compelling the performance of services must be distinguished from an order for specific performance in the 'true' sense compelling a party to enter into a service agreement: *Giles v Morris* [1972] 1 All ER 960. Of course, equity would not thereafter be concerned to police the services provided under that agreement. The plaintiff would be left to pursue the appropriate remedy at law for any breach of the agreement entered into pursuant to such a decree.

In *JC Williamson Ltd v Lukey and Mulholland* (1931) 45 CLR 282, the lessees of a theatre made an oral agreement with confectioners to give the confectioners an exclusive right to sell ice cream, confectionery and soft drinks in the theatre and its precincts, under certain terms, during the continuance of a lease of a shop which the confectioners had taken from the owner of the theatre for a term of five years. The confectioners exercised their rights for some time, but the lessees of the theatre later repudiated the agreement and revoked the licence. The confectioners took proceedings seeking an injunction and damages in addition to or in lieu thereof. As the agreement was not to be performed within the space of a year it was unenforceable at common law, because it was not in writing, under the Instruments Act 1928 (Vic), s 128. The confectioners argued that they were entitled to an injunction under the doctrine of part performance. The High Court held that no injunction could be granted on the ground of part performance and that therefore no damages could be awarded in lieu of any such injunction. Dixon J, with whom Gavan Duffy CJ agreed, said that specific performance in the proper sense was not available because the agreement between the parties was the final statement of their mutual obligations and not an agreement to execute some formal contract which would define and govern their respective rights. Specific performance was otherwise unavailable because the continued supervision of the court would have been necessary to ensure the fulfilment of the contract. As the right of the confectioners and their servants to enter the theatre under this contract depended upon such things as the character of the goods supplied and the dress and behaviour of their servants, this was not a contract of which equity would decree specific performance. Dixon J also said, at 299–300, that it would be inappropriate to grant an injunction restraining the lessees from breaking their part of the agreement when specific performance could not be awarded against the confectioners because to do so would involve constant supervision. However, as the contract was unenforceable at law, an injunction could only be granted on equitable grounds and not in aid of a legal right. The only equitable ground was part performance. Dixon J did not rule out the possibility that an injunction may be grounded upon the equities arising from acts of part performance but said that any negative stipulation sought to be enforced in that way must be one to which the acts of part performance directly relate. Here there were no acts which directly related to the existence of a duty not to revoke the licence, nor any duty not to allow a stranger to sell sweets in the theatre. Starke J also held that the agreement could not be specifically enforced because such an order would involve constant supervision. He considered that no injunction could be granted either to enforce the negative stipulations imposed on the lessees because to do that would be to enforce one stipulation of the contract while all the others remained unenforceable both at law and in equity. Evatt J, at 308, said that the doctrine of part performance does not apply to cases where the only equitable remedy available is that of injunction. McTiernan J criticised the argument that relief by way of an injunction, or damages in lieu thereof, might be granted under the doctrine of part performance on these facts, but held that the acts of the confectioners were not sufficient to amount to part performance in any case.

[22.8] The court's reluctance to attempt to enforce contracts which would require constant supervision stems from a desire to avoid constant and protracted litigation as the plaintiff returns to the court to complain of every breach of the order: *Wolverhampton and Walsall Railway Co v London and NW Railway Co* (1873) LR 16 Eq 433 at 439. A major exception to that general rule is the specific enforcement of building contracts, provided certain requirements are satisfied. In the first place the work to be done must be defined by the contract so that the court will know the exact nature of what is to be performed. Second, the plaintiff must have a substantial interest in having the work completed, so that damages at law would be inadequate; and, third, the defendant must have obtained possession of the land under the contract, so that he or she can proceed with the work: *Wolverhampton Corp v Emmons* [1901] 1 QB 515 at 525, per Romer LJ; *York House Pty Ltd v FCT* (1930) 43 CLR 427 at 437.

22–4 Mutuality

[22.9] Specific performance will not be ordered unless the court can secure performance of the obligations owed to the defendant by the plaintiff and any other parties to the contest, the obligations which the defendant is being called upon to perform being dependent on the performance of other obligations owed to the defendant by those other parties. In essence this rule requires that justice be done to the defendant as well as to the plaintiff. The element of mutuality must exist at the date of the hearing, regardless of whether or not it existed at some earlier time.[11] Accordingly, an infant will not be entitled to obtain specific performance of a contract as no similar decree could be made against him or her: *Flight v Bolland* [1824–34] All ER Rep 372, although a plaintiff who, after coming of age, ratifies a contract entered into by him or her when an infant, will be able to have it specifically performed: *Kell v Harris* (1915) 15 SR (NSW) 473. Mutuality may also be found to be lacking where the plaintiff's obligations under the contract involve personal service or would require constant supervision: *Thomas v Harper* (1935) 36 SR (NSW) 142. This defence of mutuality will not be available to the defendant if, at the date of hearing, the plaintiff has performed all that is required by the contract, or, if the plaintiff's performance is less than complete, the defendant has accepted that lesser degree of performance and thereby waived mutuality: *Price v Strange* [1977] 3 All ER 371.

---

11. MG&L, para [2031].

22–5 Defences to a Suit for Specific Performance

[22.10] Specific performance is a discretionary remedy. In any suit for specific performance the court will consider the conduct of the plaintiff and the circumstances of the defendant before making any decree. Where a contract is unenforceable for want of writing, contrary to some statutory provision such as the Conveyancing Act 1919 (NSW), s 54A(1), specific performance will not be decreed unless the plaintiff can show that to do otherwise would be to allow the defendant to use the statute as an instrument of fraud. In this respect the doctrine of part performance can provide grounds for a decree: see Chapter 3. Standard grounds of defence in equity, such as laches and acquiescence, will provide a defence to a claim for specific performance, just as they will for other suits for equitable relief: see Chapter 21. Matters to which the court will have particular regard in the context of suits for specific performance include:

- mistake or misrepresentation;
- unfair conduct of the plaintiff;
- hardship;
- breach of contract by the plaintiff;
- where specific performance is sought of only part of a contract;
- performance is impossible or would be futile.

[22.11] Mistake or misrepresentation. If a party to a contract is entitled to have the contract rescinded on the grounds of misrepresentation or mistake then, clearly, no decree of specific performance will be made against him or her. Mistake may also be a defence to a suit for specific performance in some cases where it is not sufficient grounds for rescission. Where the defendant's mistaken belief is induced, in whole or in part, by the plaintiff, the court may consider that sufficient grounds for denying a decree: *Neild v Davidson* (1890) 11 LR (NSW) Eq 209. In most cases where the defendant has operated under a mistake of his or her own making, for which the plaintiff carries no blame, the court will not refuse a decree: *Tamblin v James* (1879) 15 Ch D 215; to do so 'would open the door to fraud': per James LJ, at 221. The defendant can only raise his or her own mistake as a defence to an action for specific performance where he or she can also show that he or she would suffer undue hardship: *Fragomeni v Fogliani* (1968) 42 ALJR 263. But the remedy remains discretionary and each case must be decided on its own facts: *Slee v Warke* (1952) 86 CLR 271. A defendant who pleads mistake, but not hardship and who cannot demonstrate that the plaintiff has contributed to the mistake will not be entitled to rely on this doctrine: *Borg v Howlett* (SC(NSW), Young J, 24 May 1996, unreported).

[22.12] Unfair conduct of the plaintiff. This refers to unconscionable conduct, usually in the sense of procedural unfairness relating to the manner in which the contract was procured, rather than simply to any alleged 'unfairness' of the terms of the contract. It is not enough to simply point to some disparity in the consideration provided by both parties: *Axelsen v O'Brien* (1949) 80 CLR 219. The defendant would need to point to some unfair or unconscionable conduct on the part of the plaintiff which caused the defendant to accept those terms in the first place.

[22.13] Hardship. Equity will not decree specific performance where to do so would 'impose great hardship on either of the parties': *Dowsett v Reid* (1912) 15 CLR 695 at 705, per Griffith CJ. While easy to state, this defence is difficult to make out in practice. *Dowsett v Reid* is unusual in that the hardship there arose from the particular terms of the contract itself, a lease of certain rural land, including a hotel, which required the defendant, the lessor, to perform a number of onerous and, in some cases expensive, tasks while the lessee was not obliged to pay rent for some months. It has been upheld where a decree of specific performance would have been likely to cause the defendant to commence other proceedings: *Dowsett v Reid* (1912) 15 CLR 695; it was applied to refuse a decree which would have defeated the defendant's equitable lien over the purchase moneys, leaving him with only an action for damages: *Langen and Wind Ltd v Bell* [1972] 1 All ER 296, and where it would have obliged the defendant to pursue difficult and uncertain litigation to recover land so that it could then be conveyed: *Wroth v Tyler* [1974] 1 Ch 30 at 50–1. Specific performance will also not be decreed where it would have the effect of compelling a trustee, or other fiduciary, to commit a breach of trust: *Colyton Investments Pty Ltd v McSorley* (1962) 107 CLR1 77, that is, by selling at an under value.[12] Nor will specific performance be ordered where it would cause hardship to third parties interested in the property which is the subject of the contract in question: *Thomas v Dering* (1837) 1 Keen 729; 48 ER 488, and possibly any third parties.[13]

[22.14] Breach of contract by the plaintiff. He who seeks equity must do equity and must also come to equity with clean hands. A plaintiff seeking specific performance must not be in breach of the obligations imposed on him or her by the contract and, at the commencement of the action, must be ready and willing to perform any outstanding obligations due under the contract: *Green v Sommerville* (1979) 54 ALJR 50 at 56–7, per Mason J; *King v Poggioli* (1923) 32 CLR 222 (see **[1.11]**). The onus rests on the plaintiff to prove readiness and willingness: *Bahr v Nicolay (No 2)* (1988) 164 CLR 604. This rule will not, however, defeat a plaintiff in breach of 'inessential terms' of the contract: *Mehmet v Benson* (1964-5) 113 CLR 295 at 307–8, per Barwick CJ. In that case the plaintiff was a purchaser of land under a contract of sale which provided for payment of the purchase price on terms. He was substantially in arrears on those payments and yet was still awarded specific performance.[14]

[22.15] Where specific performance is sought of only part of a contract. The general rule is that if the court 'cannot compel specific performance of the contract as whole it will not interfere to compel specific performance of part of a contract': *Ryan v Mutual Tontine Westminster Chambers Association* [1893] 1 Ch 116 at 123, per Lord Esher MR. This principle was supported by the High Court in *JC Williamson v Lukey and Mulholland*. It will not necessarily apply where the agreement contains independent and severable stipulations, so that it might be said that there are several different contracts. Nor will it not apply where the plaintiff has entirely performed his or her part of the bargain and the only part of the contract remaining to be performed calls for performance by the defendant. This rule does not apply where the plaintiff seeks relief in the nature of specific performance of an executed contract.

[22.16] Performance is impossible or would be futile. Equity will not make an order which the court knows cannot be performed. It will not order A to specifically perform a contract to sell Blackacre to B if A has already conveyed that property to C. Similarly, equity will not order specific performance where the outcome would be futile — as would be the case in an action for specific performance of an agreement

---

12. See, for example, *Stokes v Churchill* (1994) NSW Conv Rep 55-694.
13. MG&L, para [2020].
14. See also *Australian Hardwoods Pty Ltd v Commr for Railways* [1961] 1 All ER 737 at 742, *Fullers' Theatres Ltd v Musgrove* (1923) 31 CLR 524 at 550; and *Axelsen v O 'Brien* (1949) 80 CLR 219 at 226.

for lease in which the term had expired before the hearing — unless the decree was of some tangible benefit to the plaintiff, as might be case if it revived rights which could be employed to obtain some other relief: *Mundy v Joliffe* (1839) 9 LJ Ch 95.

Chapter Twenty Three

23-1 General Principles

[23.1] An injunction is an order of the court compelling a party to refrain from doing something (a negative or prohibitory injunction) or to perform some positive act (a mandatory injunction). An injunction may be decreed as a final remedy, either alone or as an ancillary order to some other principal relief, or as interlocutory relief to protect the rights of a party pending the final outcome of litigation. *Quia timet* injunctions are used to restrain apprehended wrongs, rather than wrongs which have occurred and which are continuing. Traditionally injunctions were only available in equity, either in its exclusive jurisdiction as a means of enforcing equitable obligations or protecting equitable rights, or in the auxiliary jurisdiction where injunctions were employed to protect and enforce legal rights in cases where damages at common law were inadequate. Prior to the introduction of the judicature system the common injunction was used to restrain plaintiffs at common law from proceeding with their actions in cases where the defendant had a defence on equitable grounds which could not be pleaded at common law. The need for the common injunction was obviated, in part, by the reforms of the 1850s which gave defendants at common law the right to plead equitable defences, and, in whole, by the judicature system itself. Before the introduction of cross-vesting legislation across Australia in July 1988 competition between the jurisdictions of Federal and State courts in Australia led to the use of injunctions very much like the common injunction to enjoin the plaintiff in the State court from proceeding with his action: *Denpro Pty Ltd v Centrepoint Freeholds Pty Ltd* [1983] ATPR 40–363.

[23.2] The power to grant injunctions in equity stemmed from the inherent jurisdiction of the Court of Chancery to provide equitable relief. The courts of common law possessed no such inherent power. The power to cross vest provides a more civilised means of resolving jurisdictional contests and has been readily embraced by the courts.[1] In the event of a dispute between a Federal and a State court, the judicial power of the Commonwealth must prevail.[2] A power to grant injunctions was conferred on the common law courts in England in 1854,[3] and in New South Wales in 1857.[4] That power enabled the courts of common law to enjoin a party from contin-

---

1. *Seymour-Smith v Electricity Trust of South Australia* (1989) 17 NSWLR 648; *Mansell & Anor v Cumming* (1989) 86 ALR 637; *Deputy Commissioner of Taxation (NSW) v Chamberlain* (1990) 93 ALR 729; *Baffsky v John Fairfax & Sons Ltd* (1990) 97 ACTR 1.
2. MG&L, para [2104].
3. Common Law Procedure Act 1854 (Imp), ss 79–81.
4. Common Law Procedure Act 1857 (NSW), ss 44–47; later re-enacted as the Common Law Procedure Act 1899 (NSW), ss 176–179.

uing with or repeating some legal wrong. Unlike equitable injunctions issued in the auxiliary jurisdiction, access to an injunction at common law did not depend upon proof that the plaintiff was seeking to protect a proprietary right. The statutory power to grant injunctions at common law was limited, however, to cases involving claims on common law causes of action in which the plaintiff had a right to damages at common law, with the result that it could not be used to grant *quia timet* injunctions to restrain apprehended wrongs.[5] After the introduction of the judicature system, under which all divisions of the court have power to grant all remedies previously available in either common law or equity, equity's inherent power to grant injunctions and the statutory power conferred on the courts of common law have been harnessed together in the one court. There is also power conferred on courts exercising jurisdiction under the Trade Practices Act 1974 (Cth) to grant injunctions on grounds laid out in that Act under s 80: see generally *Trade Practices Commission v Gold Coast Property Sales* (1994) 126 ALR 139; *ICI Australia Operations Pty Ltd v Trade Practices Commission* (1992) 38 FCR 248; 110 ALR 47.

23-2 Injunctions in the Exclusive Jurisdiction

[23.3] Injunctions are awarded in the exclusive jurisdiction to restrain any breach of an equitable obligation, whether anticipated or continuing, as well as being decreed as an ancillary order to some other principal relief. Accordingly, an injunction will be available at the suit of a *cestui que trust*, or any other person entitled to enforce due administration of a trust, to restrain a trustee from committing an apprehended breach of trust or from continuing to commit an actual breach: *Fox v Fox* (1870) LR 11 Eq 142; *Park v Dawson* [1965] NSWR 298. A trustee may also enjoin his or her co-trustee from similar breaches: *Baynard v Woolley* (1855) 20 Beav 583; 52 ER 729. It is not necessary to show that the trustee has acted, or intends to act, in bad faith, so long as the trustee's actions would constitute a technical breach of the terms of the trust. An injunction may also be used in the mandatory or positive sense to compel a trustee to perform his or her duty, provided of course, that the matter is one in which the trustee is obliged to act, rather than one in which it has a discretion to act, or not to act. Injunctions are also available to protect other equitable rights. They can issue against third parties dealing with trust property: *Ackerley v Palmer* [1910] VLR 339, against other fiduciaries to restrain anticipated or continuing breaches of duty, and to restrain a party who has received confidential information from making unauthorised use of that information. It is not necessary in this jurisdiction to show that a proprietary right is sought to be protected. It is sufficient to show that the plaintiff has an equitable right: *Duchess of Argyll v Duke of Argyll* [1967] Ch 302. It has also been suggested that the employment of injunctions to protect a person's 'right to work', for which no damages at common law are available, constitutes recognition of a 'new equity' and thus falls within the exclusive jurisdiction rather than the auxiliary jurisdiction.[6] Injunctions were used to protect such a right in *Buckley v Tutty* (1971) 125 CLR 353.

Tutty was a contracted player with Balmain Rugby League Club. Under the rules of the NSW Rugby League clubs could retain players and demand a transfer fee if any player wished to move to another club. Balmain placed Tutty on a retain list. He took pro-

---

5. MG&L, para [2111].
6. MG&L, para [2131].

ceedings seeking a declaration that the transfer and retention rules were an unreasonable restraint on trade, and other orders. The NSW Supreme Court granted that declaration and also granted injunctions restraining the NSW Rugby League and Balmain from enforcing the rules against Tutty, despite the fact that there was no contractual relationship between Tutty and the League. The Rugby League appealed. The High Court held that the transfer and retention rules imposed an unreasonable restraint on trade and that the declaration and injunctions were properly decreed. Tutty had a sufficient interest to obtain the relief sought, including injunctions to restrain the League and Balmain from enforcing the rules against him. His right to work was affected and the two appellants had clearly demonstrated their intention to maintain the existing transfer and retention system if it was lawfully possible.

[23.4] Where an injunction is sought in the exclusive jurisdiction there can never be any question as to whether damages would be an adequate remedy if the injunction is refused. As the wrong complained of would be an equitable wrong, damages at common law would not be available. Damages under Lord Cairns' Act may, at the discretion of the court, be available in lieu of an injunction in such a case, even though the wrong complained of comprises a breach of a purely equitable obligation. In *Wentworth v Woollahra Municipal Council* (1982) 42 ALR 69 at 72, the High Court said that it was an incidental object of Lord Cairns' Act to enable the court to award damages in lieu of an injunction even where the 'wrong' complained of was a breach of an equitable obligation. This view has been strongly criticised but now appears to be firmly entrenched with the rapid growth of equitable compensation.[7] The development of the remedy of equitable compensation has had an impact on the award of injunctions in the exclusive jurisdiction. While it is unlikely that a plaintiff will ever be required to show that equitable compensation would be inadequate, a defendant may argue that compensation would provide a more appropriate remedy than the award of an injunction: see Chapter 25.

23-3 Injunctions in the Auxiliary Jurisdiction

[23.5] Injunctions are granted in the auxiliary jurisdiction principally to protect against infringements of legal rights, either apprehended or continuing, where damages would be an inadequate remedy. Injunctions are also awarded in the auxiliary jurisdiction to prevent multiplicity of litigation. In the first category of cases the plaintiff must first show that he or she has a legal right which equity will protect with an injunction. A legal right rendered unenforceable by statute will not be protected unless the circumstances of the case are such as to give rise to a right recognised in equity: *JC Williamson v Lukey & Mulholland* (1931) 45 CLR 282 at 297, per Dixon J, such as a right to specific performance pursuant to the doctrine of part performance: *Regent v Millett* (1976) 133 CLR 679; or an equitable licence coupled with a profit à prendre justifying orders on the basis of equitable estoppel: *Silovi v Barbaro* (1988) 13 NSWLR 466. The plaintiff's legal right must be threatened by some legal wrong. A claim by one trader that his or her goods were superior to those of a competitor gave the competitor no right to an injunction when the first trader had not committed an injurious falsehood in *White v Mellin* [1895] AC 154. The owner of a racetrack was refused an injunction when it sought to prevent the broadcasting of races at that track by someone who could observe them without trespassing in *Victoria Park Racing*

---

7. See paras [25.13] and [25.14] and also MG&L, para [2320].

and Recreation Grounds Co Ltd v Taylor (1937) 58 CLR 479. The illegitimate child of a mulatto slave woman and a member of an aristocratic French West Indian family could not be prevented from using the family name: *Du Boulay v Du Boulay* (1869) LR 2 PC 430. An injunction will also be refused where damages would be an adequate remedy. Consequently, an injunction will not lie to prevent trespass to goods, detinue or conversion. In practical terms, however, the question is not so much that of the adequacy of damages but, rather, whether it is just in the circumstances that the plaintiff should be confined to his or her remedy in damages.[8] Equity will, in an appropriate case, grant an injunction to restrain a party in the jurisdiction from prosecuting proceedings in another jurisdiction. The remedy of anti-suit injunction in relation to proceedings in a foreign court is an extraordinary remedy, and will only be granted in the most exceptional cases and after the exercise of great judicial restraint.

In *CSR Ltd v New Zealand Insurance Co Ltd* (1994) 36 NSWLR 138, the defendant (NZI) sought an injunction to restrain CSR from taking any further step in proceedings against NZI in New Jersey on the ground that the proceedings instituted in New Jersey were, in the circumstances, vexatious and oppressive, and amounted to unconscionable conduct or an abuse of the process of the New South Wales Supreme Court and were brought with an improper motive. The proceedings in New Jersey were commenced after those in New South Wales. NZI asserted that it would be oppressive to have to litigate essentially the same issues in New Jersey. The discovery material in the case ran to some 600,000 documents. The proceedings concerned indemnity claims by CSR under pubic risk liability and other insurances for claims against CSR for asbestos related injuries. A substantial number of claims had been brought against CSR as a defendant in various states in the United States. CSR commenced proceedings on 1 May 1992. While there were some later amendments, pleadings were closed in August 1992. For convenience the proceedings were divided into four sets of issues and proceedings concerning the first set of issues were heard in June/July 1993. Proceedings in the superior court of New Jersey were commenced by CSR on 6 June 1994. Rolfe J noted the residence of the parties in Australia, the fact that the contracts had been made in Australia and that the evidence on those matters was also situated in Australia, and found the effect of the commencement of the New Jersey proceedings was to bring pressure to bear on NZI with the consequence that the hearing date for the second raft of the issues would be aborted. Rolfe J found the proceedings in New Jersey to be vexatious and oppressive to NZI and granted the injunction sought. The mere inconvenience of conducting proceedings in two courts will not, of itself, be sufficient to establish an equity justifying the grant of such an injunction. An exception arises however, if the evidence shows that proceedings in the foreign court have been instituted for no reason other than to harass, vex or inconvenience the other parties.

[23.6] Equity will not grant an injunction where damages or some other remedy at law would provide adequate relief: *London and Blackwell Railway Co v Cross* (1886) 31 Ch D 354 at 369, per Lindley LJ. This proviso is sometimes described as a requirement that the plaintiff would suffer 'irreparable injury' or some similar expression. As a matter of logic as much as tradition wrongful dealing with chattels, such as conversion and detinue, has not been regarded as an appropriate ground for injunctive relief: *Penfolds Wines Pty Ltd v Elliott* (1946) 74 CLR 204, unless the goods concerned have special or unique value: *Aristoc Industries Pty Ltd v R A Wenham (Builders) Pty Ltd* [1965] NSWR 581. Similarly, the court will only interfere in the publication of alleg-

---

8. *Evans Marshall & Co Ltd v Eertola SA* [1973] 1 All ER 992 at 1005, per Sachs LJ; *State Transit Authority v Apex Quarries Ltd* [1988] VR 187; *Mott v Mount EdonGoldmines (Aust) Ltd* (1994) 12 ACSR 658; *Belgrave Nominees Pty Ltd v Barlin-Scot tAirconditioning (Aust) Pty Ltd* [1984] VR 947 and *Sanderson Motors (Sales) Pty Ltd v Yorkstar Motors Pty Ltd* (1983) 1 NSWLR 513.

edly defamatory material in the very clearest of cases: *Canada Metal Co Ltd v Canadian Broadcasting Corporation* (1974) 44 DLR (3d) 329, and usually only in cases where the alleged defamation might damage the plaintiff's business: *Crescent Sales Pty Ltd v British Products Pty Ltd* [1936] VLR 336, or where there is a threat of a repetition of publication of defamatory material: *Church of Scientology of British Columbia v Radio North West Ltd* (1974) 46 DLR (3d) 459, although, even then the court would still need to be satisfied that it would be unreasonable for a jury not to find the material defamatory: *Royal Automobile Club of Victoria v Paterson* [1968] VR 508. The court's reluctance to restrain the publication of allegedly defamatory material by interlocutory injunction is not only founded on the notion that damages would provide an adequate remedy. It is also based on the court's bias in favour of free speech and the difficulties of reaching a final judgment on all aspects of the case in defamation at an interlocutory hearing: *Edelsten v John Fairfax & Sons Ltd* [1978] 1 NSWLR 685; *Swimsure (Laboratories) Pty Ltd v McDonald* [1979] 2 NSWLR 796, particularly where the defendant raises the defence of justification and can produce material to support that defence: *National Mutual Life Association of Australia Pty Ltd v GTV* [1989] VR 747; *Chappell v TCN Channel Nine Pty Ltd* [1988] 4 NSWLR 153.

[23.7] Equity will not grant an injunction to restrain a defendant in possession of land from trespassing on the land. The plaintiff's proper remedy at law is an action for ejectment or recovery of possession of land: *Pedler v Washband* [1949] QSR 116. Injunctions will not be granted where appropriate relief is available under industrial law: *David Jones Ltd v Federal Storemen and Packers Union* (1985) 14 IR 75. The fact that the conduct sought to be restrained could render the defendant liable to prosecution under the Summary Offences Act 1970 (NSW) will not provide grounds for refusing an injunction: *Vincent v Peacock* [1973] 1 NSWLR 466. Equity will not grant an injunction where it would be futile to do so: *Death v Railway Commissioners for NSW* (1927) 27 SR(NSW) 187; nor will an injunction be granted where no useful purpose would be served by it: *Hughes v WACA* [1986] ATPR 48 at 134.

23-4 Injunctions at Common Law

[23.8] Courts of common law had no power to grant injunctions until the Common Law Procedure Act 1854 (Imp) conferred such a power on the courts of common law in England. The colonial legislatures in Australia followed suit, New South Wales, for example, with the Common Law Procedure Act 1857 (NSW), ss 44–47. The English legislation, as copied in Australia, conferred a jurisdiction to grant an injunction against a repetition or continuation of a breach of contract or other injury. The court was also given power to award damages in addition to or in lieu of the injunction. Under judicature legislation no separate power to award injunctive relief was conferred on the Common Law Division of the court. The power to grant injunctive relief was contained, in New South Wales in the Supreme Court Act 1970, s 66. Similar provisions operate in all other jurisdictions.[9]

[23.9] The introduction of legislation conferring a power to grant injunctions, or to appoint receivers[10] whenever it appears to the court to be just and convenient to do

---

9. Judiciary Act 1970 (Cth), s 39B; Supreme Court Act 1979 (NT), s 69(1); Supreme Court Act 1867 (Qld), s 22, SC Rules Ord 57; Supreme Court Act 1935 (SA), s 29(1); Supreme Court Civil Procedure Act 1932 (Tas), s 10(2); Supreme Court Act 1986 (Vic), s 37(1); Supreme Court Act 1935 (WA), s 24.
10. Note that not all of the relevant legislation refers to the appointment of receivers; see the Supreme Court Acts of Queensland, Tasmania and Western Australia.

so immediately raises the question of whether the court's power to grant injunctive relief has been widened and now rests solely on the literal words of the legislation, or whether the words 'just and convenient' are confined in their meaning by precedent to the established grounds for awarding injunctions. Section 66 of the Supreme Court Act 1970 (NSW) confers power to grant an interlocutory or a final injunction to restrain any threatened or apprehended breach of contract or other injury. The court is also given power to grant an interlocutory injunction in any case in which it appears just or convenient to do so. In *North London Railway Co & Great Northern Railway Co* (1883) 11 QBD 30, the Court of Appeal held that the English Judicature Act gave the court no power to issue an injunction in a case where no injunction would have been issued before the Act. That view was adopted in Victoria in *Attorney-General (Vic) v Shire of Huntley* (1887) 13 VLR 66 and by the High Court, at least by Dixon CJ, at 454, in *Mayfair Trading Company Pty Ltd v Dreyer* (1958) 101 CLR 428. In *Bremer Vulkan Schiffbau und Machinefabrik v South India Shipping Corporation* [1981] AC 909 at 980ff, the House of Lords affirmed the position taken by the Court of Appeal in *North London Railway Co*, saying, per Lord Diplock, at 980, that the court had jurisdiction to grant an injunction for the enforcement or protection of a legal or equitable right when it was just and convenient to do so. In the context of that case that meant the court could not intervene by injunction to control the conduct of an arbitrator appointed except under a power conferred by the arbitration clause in the ship-building agreement between the parties. Their Lordships rejected the proposition advanced in the Court of Appeal below that the court had some inherent jurisdiction over the conduct of the arbitrations.

[23.10] All this does not mean that the law of injunctions remains permanently frozen in its pre-1873 state. One immediate effect of the Judicature Acts must be that all divisions of the court have power to grant both equitable and common law injunctions. The emergence in modern times of the *Mareva* injunction has shown that this area of the law remains fecund, even though some have been unkind enough to cast doubt on on the legitimacy of this progeny.[11] The great utility and the versatility of injunctive relief suggests that matters will not rest there and that the *Mareva* injunction is likely to grow under the pressure of those two great engines of legal change: innovation and error.

23–5 Injunctions to Enforce Negative Covenants

[23.11] In granting injunctions in aid of legal rights courts of equity have not limited their concern to rights in property. Equity has actively intervened to enforce contractual obligations even though no proprietary right is threatened. Decrees of specific performance and to some extent mandatory injunctions (see **[23.22]–[23.25]**) are granted to enforce positive contractual obligations. Injunctions are also granted to enforce negative contractual stipulations. This jurisdiction to restrain breaches of negative covenants and negative contractual terms was outlined by Lord Cairns LC in *Doherty v Allman* (1878) 3 Ap Cas 709 at 719–20:

> My Lords, if there had been a negative covenant, I apprehend, according to well settled practice, a Court of Equity would have had no discretion to exercise. If parties, for val-

---

11. MG&L, paras [2185]–[2190].

uable consideration, with their eyes open, contract that a particular thing shall not be done, all that a Court of Equity has to do is to say, by way of injunction, that which the parties have already said by way of covenant, that the thing shall not be done; and in such a case the injunction does nothing more than give the sanction of the process of the Court to that which already is the contract between the parties. It is not then a question of the balance of convenience or inconvenience, or of the amount of damage or of injury — it is the specific performance, by the Court of that negative bargain which the parties have made; with their eyes open, between themselves.

That principle is applicable even though the contract itself is not specifically enforceable and damages may be an adequate remedy.[12] Lord Cairns' dictum has been cited and applied in many cases since. In *Ampol Petroleum Ltd v Mutton* (1952) 53 SR (NSW) 1, an injunction was granted to prevent a service station proprietor from selling the station without consent, in breach of a term in his contract with Ampol, under which that company agreed to supply him with petrol on certain terms, including a covenant by the proprietor not to assign the service station except to a purchaser approved of by Ampol. Despite Lord Cairns' statement that the court has no discretion in these cases, the granting of any injunction clearly remains a matter for the court's discretion. In *Dalgety Wine Estates Pty Ltd v Rizzon* (1979) 53 ALJR 647 at 655, Mason J said that the attitude of the courts to enforcing negative contractual terms varies with the nature of the contract, the character of the injunction and its effect upon the parties. In *Harrigan v Brown* [1967] 1 NSWR 342, the discretion was refused because the plaintiff was herself in breach of the contract and thus did not come to equity with clean hands.

[23.12] The jurisdiction to grant an injunction restraining breach of a negative stipulation may be exercised at the court's discretion, even though the orders made may amount to a decree of specific performance of a contract involving continuing obligations. In *Sanderson Motors (Sales) Pty Ltd v Yorkstar Motors Pty Ltd* (1983) 1 NSWLR 513, Yeldham J came to this conclusion in granting an injunction restraining a Mercedes-Benz distributor from terminating a dealership agreement with the plaintiff dealer contrary to the terms of the agreement. In *Kurt Keller Pty Ltd v BMW Australia Ltd* [1984] 1 NSWLR 353, a case also involving the attempted termination of a car dealership agreement, Powell J refused to exercise this discretion to grant an injunction restraining termination of the dealership. His Honour distinguished *Sanderson Motors* mainly on the grounds that the obligations of the dealer were far more extensive in *Kurt Keller* and the agreement would not be specifically enforced at the suit of either party. In doing so Powell J relied on comments by Long Innes J in *Wood v Corrigan* (1928) 28 SR(NSW) 492 at 500, that even an express negative stipulation will not found an injunction to restrain a breach of the contract if the contract as a whole is not the subject matter of equitable jurisdiction, and the breach can be remedied by damages. It has been said that this proposition could not possibly be correct, and that if it were a number of leading authorities, including *Lumley v Wagner*, have been wrongly decided.[13] Of course, in a judicature system, the court exercises not only the inherent power of courts of equity to grant injunctions but also the power conferred on common law courts to restrain, inter alia, repetitions or continuations of breaches of contract. It cannot matter in such a case that damages may provide an adequate remedy, nor that the contract could not be specifically enforced, nor that the contract is not 'the subject matter of equitable jurisdiction'.

---

12. MG&L, para [2138].
13. MG&L, para [2144].

[23.13] The jurisdiction to restrain breaches of negative stipulations applies to both express and implied contractual terms provided that the stipulation is negative in substance, regardless of its form: *Wolverhampton and Walsall Railway Co v London and North Western Railway Co* (1873) LR 16 Eq 433 at 440, per Lord Selborne. In *O'Keefe v Williams* (1910) 11 CLR 171, Isaacs J said that every exclusive right carried with it an implied negative undertaking not to do anything to contravene it;[14] while in *ACOA v Commonwealth* (1979) 53 ALJR 588, Mason J refused to grant an injunction sought by the appellant trade union to restrain the Commonwealth from ceasing to deduct union dues from the wages of its employees and pay those dues to the appellant, allegedly in breach of a contract with the union, on the grounds that the union was really trying to enforce a positive covenant. In doing so his Honour said, at 590, 'The stipulation is not negative in substance because mere inactivity on the part of the Commonwealth would not constitute performance. Performance requires deduction and payment to the plaintiffs'.

[23.14] Not all negative contractual stipulations attract this jurisdiction. Equity will not grant an injunction to enforce a negative stipulation in a contract for the sale of chattels: *Aristoc Industries Pty Ltd v RA Wenham (Builders) Pty Ltd* [1965] NSWR 581; unless it could be shown that damages would not be an adequate remedy, as in *Sky Petroleum Ltd v VIP Petroleum Ltd* [1974] 1 All ER 954 where the owner of a chain of service stations obtained an injunction restraining its distributor from withholding supplies because it had shown that it had little prospect of obtaining supplies from elsewhere. Similarly, an injunction will not be granted where it would have the effect of compelling performance of a contract for personal services or, otherwise, of enforcing a contract requiring constant supervision. In *JC Williamson Ltd v Lukey and Mulholland* (1931) 45 CLR 282 at 308, Evatt J said, 'In an injunction suit it is not suffi- cient to prove that a contract involves a substantial negative, where damages would be a complete remedy for the threatened breach and where the contract is of such a nature that it cannot be specifically enforced'. Whether enforcing a particular nega- tive stipulation would have any such undesired effect will depend on the facts of each case. In *Lumley v Wagner* (1852) 1 De GM & G 604; 42 ER 687; [1843–60] All ER Rep 368, a contract provided that a singer would not use her talents at any other theatre during the three months of the contract. The court awarded an injunction to restrain her from singing elsewhere in breach of that stipulation. Although such an order might have encouraged her to carry out her contract with the plaintiff the court acknowledged that it could not order her to sing. In *Page One Records Ltd v Britton* [1967] 3 All ER 822, the pop group 'The Troggs' appointed a sole manager for five years and a sole publisher for three. When they tried to terminate those contracts early the manager and publisher sought injunctions restraining the group from appointing anyone else. Stamp J refused the injunction distinguishing *Lumley v Wagner* on the ground that the plaintiff there was only obliged to pay the singer money in return for her services, an obligation which she could easily enforce. The duties of the manager and publisher were not of the type which could be specifically enforced at the suit of The Troggs. In *Warner Bros Pictures Inc v Nelson* [1937] KB 209, an order similar to that in *Lumley v Wagner* was sought against the actress Bette Davis to pre- vent her from working for another studio. Branson J said that where the enforcement of the negative covenants in a contract of personal service would amount to a decree

---

14. In *Atlas Steels (Australia) Pty Ltd v Atlas Steels Ltd* (1948) 49 SR (NSW) 157, Sugarman J refused to grant an injunction to enforce a negative covenant in an exclusive trading agreement. In doing so he held that only express negative stipulations could be enforced by way of injunction. That decision has been criticised by MG&L, para [2139], and is difficult to justify in law or logic.

of specific performance of the positive covenants in the contract, or to the giving of a decree under which the defendant had no choice other than to perform the services or remain idle, the court would not enforce those negative covenants. In Miss Davis' case the injunction was granted as she had the capacity and the means to earn a living outside the movies and her choices were not restricted to starvation or slave labour in the studios of the brothers Warner. In *Hill v CA Parsons & Co Ltd* [1972] Ch 305, the English Court of Appeal, by a majority, granted an injunction restraining an employer from dismissing an employee without sufficient notice even though that order had the effect of keeping a contract for services on foot. Lord Denning said that if the company did not want the man to work, the court would not order it to give him work, even though the company would still be obliged to provide the employee with benefits under the contract. That is an odd decision. Clearly an employer would not be entitled to a reciprocal injunction restraining an employee from stopping work and, if the court was mainly concerned with securing the benefits to which the employee would have been entitled during the proper period of notice, it is difficult to see why damages would not have been adequate.

[23.15] There have been some suggestions, such as in *Atlas Steels (Aust) Pty Ltd v Atlas Steels Ltd* (1948) 49 SR(NSW) 419, that these principles extend to contracts of agency in which the agent is contracted as 'exclusive' agent for a particular area. That view has been criticised,[15] and seems an unwarranted extension of this jurisdiction: see [23.11].

23-6 Injunctions to Protect Licences

[23.16] Where one person enters the land of another under a licence, and the licence is not coupled with a grant of any interest in the land, such as a right to quarry stone, the licence is revocable by the proprietor of the land at will, even if such a revocation is wrongful, in which case the licensee will be restricted to a remedy in damages: *Wood v Leadbitter* (1845) 13 M & W 838; 153 ER 351. If the licence is granted for valuable consideration, that is, it is a contractual licence, there is an active debate as to whether the licensee is entitled to obtain an injunction to restrain the licensor from revoking the licence, on the ground that the contract carries with it an implied negative stipulation not to revoke the licence, or whether the licensee is confined to a remedy in damages. In *Hurst v Picture Theatres Ltd* [1915] 1 KB 1, the English Court of Appeal held that *Wood v Leadbitter* was no longer good law after the Judicature Act and that a licence, in that case a ticket to see a film, could not be revoked and the licensee evicted from the cinema, at least not until the licence had been validly determined. That decision, by a majority, was based on three grounds:

(a) a contractual licence to enter land for some limited purpose, such as a ticket to see a film, was a licence coupled with a grant of a legal proprietary interest;

(b) the contractual right in *Wood v Leadbitter* was not recognised as a proprietary right in that case because such a right could only have been created by a deed before the Judicature Act, after which an interest in land could be created otherwise than by deed; and,

(c) that every contractual licence carried with it an implied negative stipulation not to wrongfully revoke the licence.

---

15. MG&L, para [2143].

The first proposition seems somewhat bizarre: that one could have a legal proprietary interest in a seat at the movies for the duration of the film. It may be that their Lordships did not frequent the cinema and, perhaps, took a dim view of the proprietors of such places. The second is only slightly less bizarre. Their Lordships no doubt considered the matter in the days when tickets to the cinema were sold as tickets for specific numbered seats, and the audience stood to attention as *God Save the Queen* was played before the curtain, and there were intermissions. But the fact that an interest in land could be created otherwise than by deed does not necessarily mean that a ticket to the movies will suffice. The absurdity is heightened if *Hurst* is applied, say, to a ticket for a seat on a train.[16] In *Cowell v Rosehill Racecourse Co Ltd* (1937) 56 CLR 605, the High Court declined to follow *Hurst's* case. Cowell had been ejected from the racecourse, on the basis that he was a trespasser, his right to remain having been terminated. Cowell claimed that he had a contractual right to be present. Latham CJ, Starke, Dixon and McTiernan JJ held that a licence to see a spectacle did not create a proprietary interest. The majority were of the view that a contractual licence, at least one in which the contractual rights were so transient, did not give rise to an equity to restrain revocation of the licence. Beyond that, the court did not reject the third leg of the decision in *Hurst's* case.

[23.17] *Cowell's* case is difficult to reconcile happily with *Doherty v Allman* (1878) 3 App Cas 709 and the chain of authority on negative stipulations. The transient nature of the licence afforded to a racegoer or theatre-goer can, perhaps, explain the difference, although that was not the deciding factor in *Cowell's* case. In the case of such short term licences it is obviously absurd to expect that an injunction could be obtained at the time the licence is purportedly revoked, even if it is a ticket to a double feature. The licensee's only remedy would be retrospective, and damages are a far more appropriate remedy in retrospect than an injunction after the event. In other licence cases, where the licence is of longer duration, equitable intervention by way of an injunction to restrain the wrongful revocation of a licence in line with *Doherty v Allman* would be both feasible and appropriate in some cases. That does not mean that short and long term licences are different in the eyes of equity. Refusal to grant an injunction in the case of a short term licence would rest on the principle that equity will not grant an injunction where it would be futile or impossible to do so. The distinction between short and long term licences was used by Myers J to justify the grant of an injunction to restrain the licensor from treating the plaintiff as a trespasser, on condition that the plaintiff observed the terms of the licence, in *Playgoers' Co-operative Theatres Ltd v Workers Educational Ass'n (NSW)* (1955) 72 WN (NSW) 374, but that decision has been criticised for disregarding the actual reasoning of the High Court in *Cowell*, in which Dixon J, while noting the transient nature of the licence, said that the shortness of time of the licence was not the reason for the plaintiff's failure.[17] These questions have been brought more sharply into focus in building cases, where the owner of the site has attempted to revoke the builder's licence to enter.

In *Hounslow London Borough Council v Twickenham Garden Developments Ltd* [1971] Ch 233 a local council sought an injunction to restrain the defendant builder from continuing to trespass by remaining on Council property, a building site, after the Council had purported to terminate its contract with the defendant. The contract was for the construction of one thousand Council dwelling units on a site of 27 acres. Progress on the work had been stalled by a strike from November 1968 until 30 June 1969 and thereaf-

---

16. Although evicting the ticketholder during the course of the journey may render the rail authority liable on a variety of common law grounds.
17. MG&L, para [2152].

ter, in the opinion of the Council's architect, the work had failed to proceed 'regularly and diligently'. On 19 January 1970 the Council purported to terminate the contract. The defendant refused to accept the notice and remained on the site. Megarry J refused the injunction sought by the Council, leaving it with a builder in occupation of Council property and a major housing development stalled. His Lordship thought that to grant the injunction might involve the Court in assisting in a breach of contract, because the question of the validity of the Council's purported termination depended on disputed facts. Megarry J held that there was an implied stipulation against revocation before completion of the work or determination of the contract in accordance with its terms. In coming to that decision he said that a licensee under a contractual licence which either expressly or by implication was subject to a negative obligation on the licensor not to revoke it was entitled in equity to an injunction restraining the licensor from revoking the licence or, if the licenior purported to revoke it, to restrain him from acting on that revocation. Where the contract provided for termination on specified events there was an implied negative stipulation that the licensor would not revoke the licence otherwise than in accordance with the contract. Megarry J thought it did not matter whether the contract was specifically enforceable where the grant of an injunction might assist in a breach of contract.

[23.18] The reasoning and the outcome in *Hounslow London Borough Council v Twickenham Garden Developments Ltd* seem absurd. Megarry J's punctilious concern with the possibility that the council might not have been entitled to terminate its contract with the builder, and that the court might thereby be assisting in a breach of contract if it were to grant the injunction sought by the council, seems to have blinded him completely to the possibility that by refusing the injunction he might be aiding and abetting a delinquent builder in continuing its own breach of the contract. The proposition that a builder's licence could not be revoked until completion of the work could leave a very bad builder on site forever. The council's concern to proceed as speedily as it could in the conditions that existed in England in 1970 with the construction of public housing does not seem to have been shared by his Lordship. The 2000 or so public tenants who might have been housed in the units had to make do elsewhere for one winter while the union blockaded the site and another while the court dithered. Fortunately, this nonsense has not been adopted in Australia. On very similar facts Helsham J came to a different decision in *Graham H Roberts v Maurbeth Investments Pty Ltd* [1974] 1 NSWLR 93, although there the builder also sought an injunction to protect its licence. Helsham J assumed that the licence had been revoked in breach of contract but still granted the relief sought by the owner and refused the injunction sought by the builder. He upheld the continuing validity of *Wood v Leadbitter* by holding that the owner's revocation of the licence was effective, even though in breach of contract, and that the builder was thus a trespasser. He held that the builder had no 'interest' in the land which could attract the protection of equity and that, as the contract was not one of which equity would decree specific performance, no injunction could be granted. In addition Helsham J also said that, even if there was an implied negative stipulation against wrongful revocation, the court should, in its discretion, refuse the relief sought by the builder. Helsham J's decision has received the support of commentators,[18] and, subject to some remaining doubts about the true effect of *Cowell's* case, provides a much more coherent statement of these principles than the confusion which appears to prevail in England.

[23.19] The confusion which seems to have plagued judicial minds, with the notable exception of Helsham J, on this question is hard to fathom. *Hurst's* case can perhaps

---

18. MG&L, para [2153].

be explained away as judicial unfamiliarity with some forms of popular entertainment. But these cases scream out for the injection of some basic common sense. There is no reason why a negative stipulation in a contract conferring a licence cannot be the subject of injunctive relief on the same basis as any other negative stipulation. There should be no need to show any additional element — such as the coupling of the licence with an interest in land. The grant of an injunction in aid of a licence is, like all injunctions, a matter for the court's discretion. If the injunction sought would require constant supervision, or was otherwise futile, the court would properly refuse it. If *Wood v Leadbitter* is good authority for the proposition that a contractual licence can be effectively revoked, even though in breach of the contract, and the licensee thereby converted into a trespasser, equity can still intervene to protect the licensee by, for instance, restraining the licensor from treating the licensee as a trespasser until the license has been validly revoked in accordance with the contract. But, in any case, a builder wrongfully dismissed from a job will have the same rights as anyone else who suffers from the wrongful repudiation of a contract — damages at common law. If a builder who is carrying out work on someone's land under a contract with the owner could restrain the owner from terminating the licence, in effect evicting the builder from site, then the builder could, in effect, obtain a decree of specific performance against the owner by holding the owner's property to ransom. An owner cannot obtain a decree of specific performance of the building contact against a builder. Equity will not decree specific performance for contracts for personal services and contracts requiring constant supervision: see **[22.7]** and **[22.8]**. Under the principle of mutuality the builder ought not to be entitled to a decree of specific performance against the owner: see **[22.9]**. If the owner does not wish to employ the builder any further, whether the owner's termination of building contract is wrongful or not, the continued occupation of the site by the builder can only operate to allow the builder to obtain unlawfully what he could not obtain lawfully, that is to say specific performance of the contract by the owner.

23–7 Injunctions against Unincorporated Associations

[23.20] Equity has traditionally been reluctant to intervene in the affairs of private clubs and associations, even when the affairs of such organisations have been conducted unfairly and to the prejudice of a member. Equity would only provide injunctive relief at the suit of members of a club claiming they had been wrongfully expelled where the purported expulsion was either: (a) contrary to natural justice; or, (b) contrary to the rules of the club; or (c) was effected maliciously or otherwise in bad faith: *Dawkins v Antrobus* (1881) 17 Ch D 615, and where the member could show that he or she had thereby been unjustly deprived of some proprietary right: *Rigby v Connol* (1880) 14 Ch D 482, which had to be substantial. An interest in a balance of subscriptions is not enough: *Amos v Brunton* (1897)18 NSWLR (Eq) 184. These rules apply even though the plaintiff's employment or trade is dependent upon membership of the association: *Graham v Sinclair* (1918) 18 SR (NSW) 75. This principle was given the imprimatur of the High Court in *Cameron v Hogan* (1934) 51 CLR 358, where the court refused a Premier of Victoria relief against his allegedly wrongful expulsion from the Australian Labor Party.

[23.21] Attempts have been made to escape from this doctrine by extending the meaning of proprietary interest in this context to include such things as a right to hold ecclesiastical office: *Macqueen v Frackleton* (1909) 8 CLR 673; and membership of a trade union: *Makin v Gallagher* [1974] 2 NSWLR 559; and by treating the purported expulsion as a breach of a negative stipulation: *Lee v Showman's Guild* [1952] 2 QB 329, even where the expulsion was wrongful only in the sense that it resulted from an honest misapplication of the rules. The contractual approach is sound in principle and accords with the general rules on the granting of injunctions. Its scope is limited, however, by the fact that in many of these cases no contract between the members can be implied, although such a contact is more likely to be found in the trade association cases. A partial solution to this problem lies in the equity recognised in *Buckley v Tutty* (1971) 125 CLR 353: see **[23.3]**. The exercise of that jurisdiction would allow the court to intervene in the affairs of trade associations to protect a person's right to work or to earn a livelihood while staying out of the affairs of purely social clubs.

23–8 Injunctions to Enforce Statutory Rights

[23.22] Where a statute confers a right to a civil remedy on an individual, equity will grant an injunction to protect and enforce that right, whether it be a right in the nature of property, such as that of the holder of a registered patent, or simply a private right conferred under statute which is capable of being protected by order of the court, such as a right to use the postal and telephonic services provided by the Commonwealth under the Post and Telegraph Act 1901 (Cth): *Bradley v Commonwealth* (1973) 128 CLR 557. It is submitted that it is not necessary to show a proprietary right to obtain an injunction under these circumstances provided that the statute clearly confers a private right on the plaintiff,[19] although in *King v Goussetis* [1986] 5 NSWLR 89 the New South Wales Court of Appeal suggest the question involves a wider review of the statute and the circumstances of the case.

[23.23] Where a public right is threatened, the Attorney General is the proper plaintiff in any proceedings for a injunction. A private individual cannot sue, although the Attorney General may sue at the relation of a private individual. In *Attorney-General v Gill* [1927] VLR 22, Dixon AJ held that this jurisdiction only applied to protect public rights that were proprietary in nature and did not extend to all statutory prohibitions. This view was overruled by the High Court in *Cooney v Ku-ring-gai Council* (1963) 114 CLR 582:

> The Council's building code prohibited the use of any building within a certain area 'for the purposes of any trade, industry, manufacture, shop or place of amusement'. Cooney used a house for social functions at which food, drink and entertainment were supplied for reward. The Council sought an injunction to prevent that use. Section 587 of the Local Government Act 1919 (NSW) provided that in any case in which the Attorney-General might take proceedings on the relation of or on behalf of the Council to secure the observance of any provision of the Act, the Council was deemed to represent the interests of the public sufficiently to take proceedings in its own name. The High Court upheld the decision of the Full Court of the New South Wales Supreme Court granting the injunction. Menzies J held that a proper case (for an injunction) is made out when it appears that some person bound by what may be described as a municipal law imposing a restriction or prohibition upon the use of land

---

19. MG&L, para [2133].

in a municipal area for the public benefit or advantage, has broken and will continue to break that law for his or her own advantage and to the possible disadvantage of members of the public living in the locality. He thought the wide discretion of the court to refuse relief was an adequate safeguard against abuse of this procedure. As far as *Gill's* case was concerned, Menzies J, having quoted a tide of authority contrary to *Gill* in the years since 1927, said, at 605, 'Prohibitions and restrictions such as those under consideration are directed towards public health and comfort and the orderly arrangement of municipal areas and are imposed, not for the benefit of particular individuals, but for the benefit of the public or at least a section of the public, viz, those living in the municipal area'.

[23.24] The decision in *Cooney* must be correct, provided the court considers in each case that it has a discretion and not a duty to grant such an injunction. What is being protected is the public interest, as determined by the Parliament, rather than some proprietary right. The jurisdiction to refuse an injunction to enforce a public right created by statute on discretionary grounds was exercised in *A-G (NSW) v Greenfield* (1962) 62 SR (NSW) 393 and *A-G (NSW) v British Petroleum Ltd* [1964–65] NSWR 2055. Damage does not need to be proved in such a public injunction; it is presumed to flow from the infringement of the public right. Equity has no criminal jurisdiction and will not issue an injunction to restrain the commission of a crime. As the commission of an act prohibited by statute is usually a criminal offence the scope for the application of injunctive relief to enforce public rights is necessarily restricted. Equity may intervene, however, if the act complained of is both an infringement of a public right and a crime. This rule was applied by Hogarth J in *A-G v Huber* [1971] 2 SASR 142 to grant an injunction preventing the staging of a performance of 'Oh! Calcutta!' in a relator action brought by a group of moral watchdogs. The Full Court, with Bray CJ in dissent, upheld that ruling. The majority judgment has been criticised as misconceived.[20] The rights of the public were not threatened; as Bray CJ said, they could protect themselves by staying away. A penalty was provided under the Police Offences Act (SA) for indecent behaviour in a public place so, if the players were guilty of such behaviour, the public might be vindicated if, by some chance, they were unable to keep away from the show. The granting of an injunction to prevent possible criminal behaviour also pre-empts the right of the supposed criminal to establish his or her innocence before a jury and, in effect, condemns the alleged wrongdoer without a proper trial.

In *Commonwealth v John Fairfax & Sons Ltd* (1980) 147 CLR 39 at 49 50, the Commonwealth obtained ex parte injunctions restraining the defendant from publishing material containing defence and foreign policy secrets in breach of s 79 of the Crimes Act 1914 (Cth) (the official secrets provision). After a contested hearing on the question of whether the injunction should be continued Mason J refused to grant an injunction to enforce s 79 but allowed the Commonwealth its injunction on other grounds, ie, breach of copyright. On the question of injunctions to restrain breaches of s 79 he said, 'The issue of an injunction to restrain an actual or threatened breach of criminal law is exceptional. The right, usually regarded as that of the Attorney-General, to invoke the aid of the civil courts in enforcing the criminal law has been described as of 'comparatively modern use', one which 'is confined, in practice to cases where an offence is frequently repeated in disregard of a, usually, inadequate penalty ... or to cases of emergency': *Gouriet v Union of Post Office Workers* [1978] AC 435 at 481, per Lord Wilberforce. It may be that in some circumstances a statutory provision which prohibits and penalises the disclosure of confidential government information or official secrets will be enforceable by injunction. This is more likely to be the case when it

---

20. MG&L, para [2135].

appears that the statute, in addition to creating a criminal offence, is designed to provide a civil remedy to protect the government's right to confidential information.

This right is only available to protect the interests of Australian governments. Foreign governments, even those with a common sovereign, cannot protect their 'public interest' in Australian courts: *A-G (UK) v Heinemann Publishers Australia Pty Ltd* (1988) 78 ALR 449.

[23.25] There is one general law exception to the rule that the Attorney General is the proper plaintiff in any action to restrain a public wrong. A private individual may obtain an injunction to restrain a breach of statute if the defendant has, by committing the statutory breach, infringed a private right of the plaintiff's or has caused special damage peculiar to the plaintiff: *Boyce v Paddington Borough Council* [1903] 1 Ch 109. The meaning of both 'a private right' and 'special damage' in this rule have been the subject of some debate. Mere financial loss has been held not to suffice for either: *California Theatres Pty Ltd v Hoyts Country Theatres Ltd* (1959) 59 SR (NSW) 188; *Helicopter Utilities Pty Ltd v Australian National Airlines Commission* [1962] NSWR 747. And yet, other commercial interests or considerations, which, in essence, are matters of concern to the plaintiff because of the financial consequences involved, may satisfy one or both of these elements, such as a fish authority charging fishmongers parking fees in breach of both the relevant fisheries legislation and a local government ordinance: *Phillips v NSW Fish Authority* [1968] 3 NSWR 784 (Helsham J); [1970] 1 NSWR 725 (CA).

In *Australian Conservation Foundation Inc v Commonwealth* (1980) 28 ALR 257; 54 ALJR 176, the appellant sought an injunction compelling the Commonwealth to comply with the Environmental Protection (Impact of Proposals) Act 1974 (Cth). The Foundation, although not threatened with any damage nor the infringement of any private right, sought to uphold the public law, on its own application, as part of its objects and values. Gibbs J stated the rule that a private citizen, who has no interest other than that which any member of the public has in upholding the law, has no standing to sue to prevent the violation of a public right or to enforce a public duty; and that, in this respect, there is no difference between the making of a declaration and the grant of an injunction. He was, however, prepared to treat the words 'special damage peculiar to the plaintiff' as equivalent to 'having a special interest in the subject matter of the action'. But a mere intellectual interest or emotional concern was not a sufficient interest for that purpose, nor was a belief, however strongly felt, that a particular law should be observed.

In *Wentworth v Woollahra Municipal Council* (1982) 42 ALR 69, the appellant sought a mandatory injunction requiring demolition of a neighbouring house, which the appellant alleged had been built in breach of the Council's planning ordinance. By the time the matter reached the High Court the appellant's house had been sold and she was seeking damages in lieu of an injunction under Lord Cairns' Act. The High Court confirmed Gibbs J's interpretation of 'special damage' in the Conservation Foundation case but held that s 68 of the Supreme Court Act 1970 (NSW) did not allow damages to be awarded in lieu of an injunction in a suit to enforce a public rather than a private right.

The decision in the *Conservation Foundation* case has not resolved the difficulties that arise in trying to apply *Boyce's* case to any given set of facts. Members of an Aboriginal community have been held to have a 'special interest' in the preservation of certain tribal relics sufficient to give them standing to enforce the Archaeological and Aboriginal Relics Preservation Act 1972 (Vic): *Onus v Alcoa of Australia Ltd* (1981) 149 CLR 27. An egg marketing authority has been held to have standing to restrain a producer from continuing to commit breaches of the Egg Industry Act 1983 (NSW): *Peck v NSW Egg Corporation* (1986) 6 NSWLR 1. A tenant of a building had standing to seek a mandatory injunction requiring the owner to comply with a notice under the Local Government Act 1919 (NSW) concerning fire safety: *King v Goussetis* (1986) 5 NSWLR 89. On these authorities Boyce's case is alive and well and thriving in Australia. In view of the lack of resolve sometimes shown by governments in maintaining a rule of law, and a lack of means to do so, it is not inappropriate that those with a special interest in the matter be allowed to approach the court. By the same token, the courts must be wary not to become the tools of zealous overseers of the public good.

23–9 Mandatory Injunctions

[23.26] A mandatory injunction is a positive injunction, that is, an order of the court compelling a party to perform some positive act, rather than simply an order compelling a party not to do something. Mandatory injunctions may take two general forms. The first are orders akin to specific performance, but not orders for specific performance in the 'proper' sense.[21] These are orders for the enforcement of executed contracts, or certain positive obligations in such contracts. The second are restorative in nature, usually compelling a person to undo the effects of some wrongful act committed in breach of statute or some contractual obligation. In seeking such a restorative mandatory injunction the plaintiff must show that, had the wrong not occurred, he or she would have been entitled to a *quia timet* injunction to prevent it. In the auxiliary jurisdiction the plaintiff must also show that damages would not be an adequate remedy.[22]

In *Redland Bricks Ltd v Morris* [1970] AC 652, excavations by the defendants on their land led to slippages on the plaintiffs' adjacent farming property because of lack of support. Future slippage was likely and would render the plaintiffs' land unusable for farming. The value of the land damaged was £1,500 and the cost of rectifying the slippage £30,000. A county court judge ordered the defendants to pay £325 for damage already suffered and granted a negative injunction restraining the defendants from withdrawing support and a mandatory injunction requiring them to take all necessary steps to restore support to the plaintiffs' land within six months. The House of Lords upheld an appeal against the mandatory injunction. They held that a mandatory injunction would only be granted when the plaintiff showed a very strong probability on the facts that grave damage would occur to him in the future, and that damages would be inadequate. In the case of a mandatory injunction, the question of the cost to the defendant of work required must be balanced against the anticipated possible damage to be suffered by the plaintiff. The conduct of the defendant will be relevant in any such deliberation If the defendant has acted wantonly and without regard for the plaintiff's rights, or has tried to evade the jurisdiction of the court, he may be ordered to repair even if the cost of repair is out of all proportion to the damage done. If, on the other hand, the defendant has acted reasonably, even though, in the event, wrongly, the cost of rectification must be balanced against the damage done. In this case, their Lordships considered that the trial judge should have gone no further than ordering the defendant, who had not acted unreasonably, to carry out some remedial works which would not have been too expensive and which might have had a chance of preventing further damage.

---

21. See [22.1].
22. MG&L, para [2190].

It seems unlikely that a plaintiff would need to prove a risk of 'grave damage', as *Redland Bricks* suggests. Any conduct which infringes the plaintiff's rights ought to be a proper subject for injunctive relief, subject only to consideration of the conduct of the defendant and any undue hardship which might flow from compliance with any orders sought. The cost to the defendant of complying with an order of the court, as opposed to the damage suffered by the plaintiff, would seem to be an appropriate matter for consideration in the granting of any discretionary relief, whether by way of a negative injunction or decree of specific performance, and not simply a question limited to suits for mandatory injunctions.

[23.27] A mandatory injunction will not lie against a public authority, or any other person or body for that matter, to compel performance of some positive duty created by statute. The proper remedy there is the common law writ of mandamus: *Glossop v Heston and Isleworth Local Board* (1879) 12 Ch D 102. A prohibitory injunction will, however, be appropriate to restrain such a body from doing any act which would be *ultra vires* any such positive statutory duty: *Blanch v Stroud Shire Council* (1947) 48 SR (NSW) 37.

23–10 Interlocutory Injunctions

[23.28] An interlocutory injunction is used, as its name suggests, as an interim measure to preserve the status quo pending the final decision in a case. The final relief sought may be a final injunction in terms similar to those of the interlocutory order; or it may be some other remedy or a combination of remedies. By definition, an interlocutory injunction is an order sought before all the evidence has been presented and before the matters in issue have been fully argued. Accordingly, the grounds upon which such interlocutory relief will be decreed and the matters which the court can take into account are different from those which apply to final injunctions. In the auxiliary jurisdiction it is necessary to show that irreparable damage would result if interlocutory relief is not granted, although in practical terms that simply means showing that the matter is one in which damages would not be an adequate remedy. In the exclusive jurisdiction, of course, there is no such requirement.

[23.29] The question of the grounds upon which an interlocutory injunction can be awarded has been the subject of some debate in recent years. In *Beecham Group Ltd v Bristol Laboratories Pty Ltd* (1968) 118 CLR 618, the High Court, Kitto, Taylor, Menzies and Owen JJ said the court addressed itself to two main inquiries: (i) whether the plaintiff has made out a prima facie case, in the sense that if the evidence remains as it is there is a probability that at the trial of the action the plaintiff will be held to be entitled to the relief sought; and (ii) whether the balance of convenience favours the grant of an injunction, that is, whether the inconvenience or injury which the plaintiff would be likely to suffer if an injunction were refused outweighs or is outweighed by the injury which the defendant would suffer if an injunction were granted. In addition, the plaintiff must give an undertaking that, in the event he or she is unsuccessful in the action, he or she will meet any damages suffered by the defendant for any injury caused by the injunction. A different approach was taken by the House of Lords in *American Cyanamid Co v Ethicon Ltd* [1975] AC 396. Lord Diplock, with whom the other law lords agreed, rejected the notion that the court should find a prima facie case, or a strong prima facie case before deciding to grant an interlocutory injunction. Instead his Lordship held that the court should award an interlocutory injunction where the plaintiff could show: (i) damages would not be an adequate remedy; (ii) that there is a serious question to be tried; and, (iii) interim relief is justified on the balance of convenience. Lord Diplock affirmed *American Cyanamid* in *NWL Ltd v Woods* [1979] 3 All ER 614 and stressed the necessity for the judge to consider the balance of convenience once he or she had reached the conclusion that there was a serious issue to be tried. That balance must be determined by contrasting the damage which the plaintiff is likely to suffer pending the final hearing of the matter if the injunction is not granted with the damage to the defendant if it is.

[23.30] There have been decisions since *American Cyanamid* which have attempted to reconcile these two positions by saying that they are consistent: *Shercliff v Engadine Acceptance Corp Pty Ltd* [1978] 1 NSWLR 729; or that there is 'little practical difference' between them: *TWU v Leon Laidley Pty Ltd* (1980) 28 ALR 589 at 600, per Deane J. Some commentators have argued that they are not inconsistent as the High Court, when talking of a 'probability of success' in the *Beecham* case did not mean a better than 50 per cent chance but only 'a sufficient likelihood of success to justify in the circumstances the preservation of the property' so that, under the *Beecham* test, a plaintiff need only show a strong possibility of success.[23] Despite that, Sir Anthony Mason has said that the two are as different as black and white although he did concede that whatever judges might say, the test they impose in practice is the serious question test principally because, in a case of any complexity, it is too much to expect the plaintiff to show a probability of success at the trial.[24] Notwithstanding the difference between the High Court's ruling in *Beecham* and the serious question to be tried test, Australian courts have readily embraced the latter approach. The *American Cyanamid* test was applied by Gibbs CJ, sitting alone, in *Australian Coarse Grain Pool Pty Ltd v Barley Marketing Board of Qld* (1982) 46 ALR 398 and likewise by Brennan J in *Tableland Peanuts Pty Ltd v Peanut Marketing Board* (1984) 52 ALR 651. It is now applied without comment on its heritage: *CBS Records Australia Ltd v Telmak Teleproducts (Aust) Pty Ltd* (1987) 72 ALR 270 at 283 per Bowen CJ, and by the Full Bench of the High Court: *Murphy v Lush* (1986) 65 ALR 651. In *CBS v Telmak*, Bowen CJ postulated that the cases which raise an issue whether there is a serious issue to be tried fall into three classes: one involving a question of fact; a second involving questions of mixed fact and law; and a third involving questions of law only. In the third class of case he considered that it may be appropriate for the court hearing the application for interlocutory relief to decide the question of law there and then, subject to whether such a course is practical in the circumstances.

[23.31] In some cases interlocutory injunctions are difficult to obtain. Interlocutory mandatory injunctions are rare: *Isenberg v East India House Estate Co Ltd* (1863) 3 De G J & Sm 263 at 272: 46 ER 637 at 641. The grant of an interlocutory mandatory injunction requires a higher degree of assurance that the granting of the injunction is right than that required for prohibitory injunctions: *State of Queensland v Telecom* (1985) 59 ALR 243 at 245 per Gibbs CJ. Although a different view was expressed by Gummow J in *Businessworld Computers Pty Ltd v Australian Telecommunications Commission* (1988) 82 ALR 499 in which his Honour declined to follow *Queensland v Telecom* as did Heden J in *Franconi Holdings Pty Ltd v Gunning* [1979–81] 1 SR (WA) 341. It had been the case that an interlocutory injunction would not be granted to restrain infringement of a patent where the alleged infringer proposed to challenge the patent or

---

23. MG&L, paras [2168] and [2172].
24. 'Declarations, Injunctions and Constructive Trusts; Divergent Developments in England and Australia' (1980) 11 Uni QLJ 121 at 128.

rather the validity of the patent (*Beecham Group v Bristol Laboratories Pty Ltd* (1968) 118 CLR 618 at 624), on the basis that such challenges often succeed: *Tefex v Bowler* (1981) 40 ALR 326 at 331–2.[25] This principle also applied to injunctions for the protection of registered designs: *Smith v Grigg* [1924] 1 KB 655. However, the applicability of this approach to registered patents under modern patent legislation has been questioned on the basis that the examination system under the modern legislation makes it much less likely that a challenge to validity will succeed: *Martin Engineering Co v Trison Holdings Pty Ltd* (1988) 81 ALR 543 at 549–50, per Gummow J . The traditional reluctance to grant interlocutory injunctive relief against infringement would, however, still apply to petty patent: *Peter Pan Electrics Pty Ltd v Newton Grace Pty Ltd* (1985) 8 FCR 557 at 566–7: 70 ALR 731 at 740–2. An interlocutory injunction will not be granted to restrain publication of a defamation unless the plaintiff can show that the matter complained of is so defamatory that no reasonable jury properly instructed could find otherwise: *Stocker v McEhinney (No 2)* [1961] NSWR 1043. In refusing such relief the court gives effect to the bias to the court in favour of free speech while noting the difficulties of establishing the various defences to defamation, such as justification or privilege, at an interlocutory stage: *Edelsten v John Fairfax & Sons Ltd* [1978] 1 NSWLR 685; *Gabrielle v Lobban* [1976] VR 689; *Harper v Whitby* [1978] 1 NSWLR 35; *Swimsure (Laboratories) Pty Ltd v McDonald* [1972] 2 NSWLR 796.

[23.32] An interlocutory injunction will not be granted unless the plaintiff undertakes to meet any damages found to have been suffered by the defendant as a result of the injunction if it proves later that the injunction should not have been granted: *Ansett Transport Industries (Operations) Pty Ltd v Halton* (1979) 25 ALR 639 at 649–50, per Aickin J ; affirmed on appeal *Air Express Ltd v Ansett Transport Industries (Operations) Pty Ltd* (1981) 33 ALR 578. The right to damages consequent upon this undertaking extends to compensation for injuries sustained by the defendants from the granting of the injunction: *Griffith v Blake* (1884) 27 Ch 474. The right to recover damages on this basis may be lost where there is delay on the part of the defendant: *Newcomen v Coulson* (1878) 7 Ch 764; *Ex Parte Hall; Re Wood* (1883) 23 Ch 644 at 651, per Baggallay LJ, at 652 per Cotton LJ and at 653 per Bowen LJ; *Ansett Transport Industries (Operations) Pty Ltd v Halton* (1979) 25 ALR 639 at 650.

23–11 'Mareva' Injunctions

[23.33] This is a special type of interlocutory injunction which takes its name from the decision of the English Court of Appeal in *Mareva Compania Naviera SA v International Bulk Carriers SA* [1975] 2 Lloyd's Rep 509. In that case an ex parte injunction was decreed in favour of the plaintiff shipowner against the defendant, a foreign company, which had funds in certain bank accounts in the United Kingdom, restraining the defendant from dealing with the funds in those accounts pending the outcome of the proceedings. At first *Mareva* injunctions were limited to commercial cases of debt involving a foreign defendant where there was some risk that the assets would be removed from the jurisdiction, but those limitations have been swept away under the pressure of demand for this very useful interlocutory remedy. Subsequently *Mareva* injunctions have been granted in a variety of matters involving many different claims against both domestic and foreign defendants: *Barclay-Johnson v Yuill* [1980] 3 All ER 190; *Rahman (Prince Abdul) bin Turki al Sudairy v Abu-Taha* [1980] 3 All ER 409;

---

25. MG&L, para [2173].

and to prevent dissipation of the assets within the jurisdiction as well as their removal from it: *Australian Iron & Steel v Buck* [1982] 2 NSWLR 889. This jurisdiction has also been held to encompass a power to make orders requiring a defendant to disclose its assets: *TDK Tape Distributor v Video Choice Ltd* [1986] 1 WLR 141; [1985] 3 All ER 345; for the delivery up of designated assets not specifically in issue in proceedings: *CBS United Kingdom Ltd v Lambert* [1983] Ch 37; and to restrain a defendant from dealing with assets outside the jurisdiction, at least where they had been inside the jurisdiction at the commencement of proceedings: *Ballabil Holdings Pty Ltd v Hospital Products* (1985) 1 NSWLR 155. The *Mareva* injunction is otherwise restricted to assets within the jurisdiction and cannot be employed to compel a defendant to deal in any particular way with assets outside the jurisdiction: *Ashtiani v Kashi* [1987] 1 QB 888 at 899, per Dillon LJ and at 904, per Neill LJ . In that case Neill LJ explained this limitation on the *Mareva* jurisdiction in the following terms:

> This jurisdiction to protect a plaintiff against the risk that the judgment of the court will be rendered ineffective because in the meantime the defendant will have disposed of or dissapated his assets is a jurisdiction which is exercised in personam. It may be said, therefore, that in principle there is not reason why a court could not make an order restraining a party over whom it has jurisdiction from dealing with his assets wherever such assets may be situated ... but it is quite clear from the way in which this jurisdiction has been exercised in the 11 years since the decision in the *Mareva* case in June 1975 that *Mareva* injunctions, as they are generally called, are limited to restraining the dealing by the defendant with assets of his which are within the jurisdiction.

In *Barclay Johnson v Yuill*, Megarry VC suggested that the *Mareva* injunction was available whenever there was a danger that the plaintiff might be deprived of the fruits of any prospective judgment by the removal of the defendant's assets from the jurisdiction or, presumably, from the reach of execution.

[23.34] The jurisdiction to grant *Mareva* injunctions has been strongly criticised by Meagher, Gummow and Lehane.[26] Those criticisms are, in essence, that there is no jurisdiction to grant a *Mareva* injunction, that it places the defendant at too great a disadvantage and gives the plaintiff too much of an advantage and that it can severely prejudice the rights of third parties dealing with the defendant. In *The Eleftherios* [1982] 1 All ER 798, a cargo of coal belonging to the defendant, which was on board a ship owned by a third party was enjoined until the third party obtained a variation of the order, even though there has been recognition of the fact that a *Mareva* injunction cannot be used to give the plaintiff preference over other creditors of the defendant, nor to freeze the defendant's assets pending resolution of the claim: *Iraqi Ministry of Defence v Arcepey Shipping Co SA ('The Angel Bell')* [1981] QB 65. Despite the strength of those criticisms the *Mareva* injunction has been accepted by the New South Wales Court of Appeal in *Riley McKay Ltd v McKay* [1982] 1 NSWLR 264, as a matter 'necessary for the administration of justice' in that State under the Supreme Court Act 1970 (NSW), s 23 and as arising from the inherent powers of the court. This jurisdiction has also been accepted in Victoria: *Praznovsky v Sablyack* [1977] VR 114; in Queensland: *Bank of New Zealand v Jones* [1982] Qd R 466; in Western Australia: *Sanko Steamship Co Ltd v DC Commodities (A'Asia) Pty Ltd* [1980] WAR 51 and the Australian Capital Territory: *Barisic v Topic* (1981) 37 ACTR 1. The Family Court has adopted the *Mareva* injunction as a useful device to employ against those who might attempt to defeat its orders: *In the Marriage of Mazur* (1992) 15 FamLR 574. *Mareva* injunctions have been accepted by the High Court, at least in the jurisdiction

---

26. MG&L, paras [2182]–[2187].

of the Federal Court under the Federal Court of Australia Act 1976 (Cth), s 23, which gives that court power, in relation to matters in which it has jurisdiction, to make, among other things, such interlocutory orders as the court thinks appropriate.

In *Jackson v Sterling Industries Ltd* (1987) 71 ALR 457, the respondent claimed against the appellant and others over the sale of a business alleging misleading or deceptive conduct under s 52 of the Trade Practices Act 1974 (Cth) and other wrongs. At first instance the appellant was ordered to provide security in the sum of $3 million in such manner as the parties might agree and, failing such agreement, as the court or its registrar may approve. An order was subsequently made requiring the appellant to pay $3 million to the Registrar of the Federal Court or to provide some other adequate security. The appellant appealed to the High Court. Deane J, with whom Mason CJ, Wilson, Dawson and Brennan JJ agreed, held that, despite its relative novelty, the *Mareva* injunction had become an accepted incident of the jurisdiction of superior courts throughout the common law world and that, as a general proposition, such an injunction can be granted '... if the circumstances are such that there is a danger of [the defendant] absconding, or a danger of the assets being removed out of the jurisdiction or disposed of within the jurisdiction, or otherwise dealt with so that there is a danger that the plaintiff, if he gets judgment, will not be able to get it satisfied': per Lord Denning in *Rahman (Prince Abdul) v Abu-Taha* [1980] 3 All ER 409 at 412. In this case, however, Deane J held that the orders made went beyond any order which could be properly made by the court. He identified three grounds upon which the order to pay $3 million by way of security was susceptible to attack: first, because the defendant was required to pay money into court, regardless of the source of that money, which was not identified as money in his possession; secondly, the payment of money into court as 'security' went beyond a mere order for the preservation of assets pending judgment or execution; and, thirdly, the order to pay money to the registrar failed to identify what the money was intended to secure or what was the entitlement of the appellant, or anyone else, to it after it had been so paid. He stressed that the purpose of a *Mareva* injunction was not to create security for the plaintiff or to require a defendant to provide security as a condition of being allowed to defend the action against him, nor was it intended to introduce, in effect, a new vulnerability to imprisonment for debt. Instead the *Mareva* injunction is designed to prevent a defendant from disposing of his actual assets so as to frustrate the process of the court by depriving the plaintiff of the fruits of any judgment obtained in the action.[27] Toohey and Gaudron JJ dissented, but not on the general question of the jurisdiction to award *Mareva* injunctions.

[23.35] The question of the required standard of proof and the test to be applied in granting a *Mareva* injunction was considered by the New South Wales Court of Appeal in *Patterson v BTR Engineering (Aust) Ltd* (1989) 18 NSWLR 319. In that case Meagher JA, having noted that after the decision of the High Court in *Jackson v Sterling Industries Ltd* the jurisdiction to grant *Mareva* injunctions must now be accepted, said that to obtain such an injunction the plaintiff must prove two ingredients: 'first, that he has a prima facie case against the defendant, and secondly, that there is some risk of a dispersal by the defendant of his assets so as to defeat the value of the plaintiff's victory if he ultimately wins'. He then said that proof of the second element could not be inferred upon proof of the first. He also rejected the submission, as did Gleeson CJ, that the plaintiff need to do no more than prove a 'more than the usual likelihood' of dissipation. The test proposed by Meagher JA was that a plaintiff be required to prove, on a balance of probabilities, that there is a real risk of the dissipation of assets. Rogers AJA approached the matter with more circumspection and

27. At this point Deane J referred to the discussion of that point in the judgment of Street CJ in *Balabill Holdings Pty Ltd v Hospital Products Ltd* (1985) 1 NSWLR 155 at 159ff.

refused to adopt the tests proposed by Meagher JA on the grounds that the *Mareva* injunction was still the subject of development on a case by case basis and that it would be undesirable to undertake the formulation of general tests or boundary lines at this stage. Gleeson CJ said that as a general rule the plaintiff would need to establish, first, a prima facie cause of action against the defendant, and second, a danger that, by reason of the defendant absconding or of assets being removed out of the jurisdiction or disposed of within the jurisdiction or otherwise dealt with in some fashion, the plaintiff, if he or she succeeds, will not be able to have the judgment satisfied. Beyond that the Chief Justice agreed with the view that it was undesirable for courts to attempt to be more precise in defining the standard of proof required to establish the existence of a danger that assets would be removed or dissipated. In the process he rejected the test that the court would only intervene if there is a more than usual likelihood of such a danger. Various formulations have been attempted by the courts, see *Ninemia Maritime Corporation v Trave Schiffahrtsgesellschaft & Co KG (The Niedersachsen)* [1983] 1 WLR 1412 at 1422–3; [1984] 1 All ER 413 at 419–20. In that case the Court of Appeal expressed the view that the test is whether the refusal of a *Mareva* injunction would involve a real risk that a judgment or award in favour of the plaintiffs remain unsatisfied. In support of that formulation they cited a number of other attempts at stating the appropriate principle. Those included:

(a) 'danger of the money being taken out of the jurisdiction so that if the plaintiffs succeed they are not likely to get their money': *Etablissment Esefka International Anstalt v Central Bank of Nigeria* [1979] 1 Lloyd's Rep 445 at 448, per Lord Denning MR;

(b) 'facts from which the commercial court, like a prudent, sensible commercial man, can properly infer a danger of default if assets are removed from the jurisdiction ... These facts should enable a commerical judge to infer whether there is likely to be any real risk of default': *Third Chandris Shipping Corporation v Unimarine SA* [1979] QB 645 at 671–2, per Laughton LJ;

(c) 'It must appear there is a danger of default if the assets are removed from the jurisdiction even if the risk of removal is great, no *Mareva* injunction should be granted unless there is also a danger of default': *Barclay-Johnson v Yuill* [1980] 1 WLR 1259 at 1265, per Sir Robert Megarry V-C; and

(d) 'a *Mareva* injunction can be granted against a man even if he is based in this country if the circumstances are such that there is a danger of him absconding, or a danger of the assets being removed out of the jurisdiction or being disposed of within the jurisdiction, or otherwise dealt with so there is a danger that the plaintiff, if he gets judgment, will not be able to get it satisfied': *Prince Abdul Rahman bin Turki al Sundairy v Abu-Taha* [1980] 1 WLR 1268 at 1273, per Lord Denning MR. It was perhaps sensible of the majority of the Court of Appeal not to attempt to draw any hard and fast rules for the requirements of proof of a risk or danger that assets would be removed or disposed of to defeat a judgment in favour of a plaintiff.

Like other instances of the exercise of an equitable jurisdiction, the granting of a *Mareva* injunction is discretionary and must depend largely on the circumstances of each case. The purpose of a *Mareva* injunction, as Deane J said in *Jackson v Stirling Industries Ltd*, at 625, is not to create a security for the plaintiff nor to require the defendant to provide security as a condition of being allowed to defend the action against him. Nor is it to introduce a risk of imprisonment for debt, where the defendant may face imprisonment for contempt of court for breach of the *Mareva* order. The purpose of a *Mareva* injunction is to prevent the defendant from disposing of his or her actual assets so as to frustrate the process of the court by depriving the plaintiff of the fruits of any judgment obtained in the action. A consideration of that question, once the initial hurdle of proof of a prima facie case or cause of action by the plaintiff has been established, will depend on a number of things. The character and conduct of the defendant will play a large part in the court's consideration. The court must consider not only whether the defendant has assets which are capable of being removed or disposed of prior to judgment but whether the defendant is a person who is likely to do so such a thing. Unless there is evidence of steps taken by the defendant to effect such a purpose, the court must consider whether, on other facts, the defendant is likely to behave in that manner. To establish the nature and extent of the defendant's assets in the process of considering whether to grant a *Mareva* injunction, the court can require the defendant to file an affidavit setting out his or her financial affairs. The defendant can be cross examined on that affidavit evidence, on limited grounds: *House of Spring Gardens Ltd v Waite* (1984) 11 FSR 173 at 182, per Slade J. Extreme cases can call for extreme measures. In *Kodak (Australasia) Pty Ltd v Cochran* (SC(NSW), Brownie J, 4 April 1996, unreported), Brownie J granted an injunction to restrain the defendant from leaving Australia, in addition to other *Mareva* orders. Just as courts of equity consistently refrain from attempting all embracing definitions of such concepts as unconscionability, so they should be wary of rushing in to settle hard and fast rules on the availability of discretionary remedies.

[23.36] A *Mareva* injunction does not give the plaintiff any proprietary rights in the assets subject to the injunction: *PCW (Underwriting Agency) Ltd v Dixon* [1983] 2 All ER 158, nor can a *Mareva* injunction be used to give the plaintiff preference over other creditors of the defendant: *Iraqi Ministry of Defence v Arcepey Shipping Co SA* ('The Angel Bell') [1981] QB 65. The *Mareva* injunction is also, almost certainly, an order *in personam*, against the conscience of the defendant, rather than an order *in rem* attaching the assets, although the practical consequences of the injunction will be to attach the assets pending further order of the court.[28]

[23.37] The jurisdiction to make orders in the nature of *Mareva* injunctions against third parties was considered by the New South Wales Court of Appeal in *Winter v Marac Australia Ltd* (1986) 7 NSWLR 11. Rogers J had made orders at first instance against the mother and sister of the defendant, Winter, restraining them from dealing with shares they held in two proprietary companies, in which they were the sole shareholders and directors, and which companies held shares in another company in which the defendant had an interest. Rogers J based that order on evidence that the defendant could persuade his mother and sister to accede to any request he might make in relation to those shares. In the Court of Appeal, Hope JA, with whom Samuels and Mahoney JJA agreed, held that Rogers J had erred and the grounds he had relied upon were not proper grounds for granting such an order. Before a court can make orders restraining the removal or disposal of assets held by third parties it must be shown that the person against whom the judgment may be obtained has some right in respect of or control over or other access, direct or indirect, to the relevant assets so that they or the proceeds of their sale or other disposition could be required to be applied in discharge of the judgment debt. That leaves the innocent third party whose business with the defendant may be prejudiced by a *Mareva* order at risk. A third party so affected may make application to the court for variation of the *Mareva* injunction, a costly exercise for a party who will be, in most cases, innocent of any involvement in any wrongdoing by the defendant.

---

28. MG&L, para [2189].

23-12 'Anton Piller' Orders

[23.38] This is another recent innovation in this area of the law, made possible largely by the technological innovation of the mobile phone. An *Anton Piller* order consists of an ex parte interlocutory mandatory injunction compelling the defendant to allow the plaintiff or its agents to inspect the property and premises of the defendant. Orders of this sort were first employed in cases involving bootleg copies of musical records and tapes for the purpose of discovering any material which had been copied in breach of the plaintiff's copyright. The order took its name from the decision of the English Court of Appeal in *Anton Piller KG v Manufacturing Processes Ltd* [1976] 1 Ch 55 which gave this type of order recognition at appellate level for the first time. It has since been adopted in Australia: *EMI (Australia) Ltd v Bay Imports Pty Ltd* [1980] FSR 328; *Chrysalis Records v Vere* (1982) 43 ALR 440. *Anton Piller* orders have been awarded outside the area of copyright to assist in tracing the proceeds of misappropriated bank accounts: *A v C* [1980] 2 All ER 347; *Bankers Trust Co v Shapira* [1980] 3 All ER 353, and to secure and preserve documentary evidence before a hearing: *Yousif v Salama* [1980] 3 All ER 405. The Family Court has also indicated a willingness to employ this remedy, although, unlike *Mareva* injunctions, it is difficult to see how it is appropriate to that jurisdiction.[29] Before an *Anton Piller* order can be granted the plaintiff must satisfy three essential pre-conditions: (a) there must be an extremely strong prima facie case; (b) the damage, actual or potential, which the plaintiff has suffered or will suffer must be very serious; (c) there must be clear evidence that the defendant has in its possession incriminating or damaging evidence or documents or other material and that there is a real possibility that material might be destroyed before any application interpartes could be brought: *Anton Piller KG v Manufacturing Processes Ltd* [1976] 1 Ch 55 at 62; [1976] 1 All ER 779 at 784; *Chrysalis Records v Vere* (1982) 43 ALR 440 at 447. *Anton Piller* orders give judicial licence to serious acts of trespass and carry the risk of grave abuse of defendant's rights. Such an abuse occurred in *Columbia Picture Industries Inc v Robinson* [1986] 3 WLR 542:

> Thirty five plaintiffs took proceedings against the defendant whom they alleged was a video pirate. At the commencement of the proceedings the plaintiffs obtained an *Anton Piller* order for the purpose of entering the defendant's premises and taking into the custody of the plaintiffs' solicitors any tapes infringing the copyright of any of the plaintiffs and a *Mareva* injunction freezing the defendant's deposits and bank accounts with the exception of drawings for living expenses. The defendant subsequently sought to have the plaintiffs' action set aside on the ground that they had failed to disclose material information to the court when applying for the ex parte orders and that the *Anton Piller* order had been oppressively and excessively executed. An *Anton Piller* order is granted on the basis that evidence otherwise essential to the plaintiffs case may be destroyed. Scott J stated certain criteria which he thought ought to be followed in implementing any such order:
>
> (a) Documentary material should not be retained any longer than is necessary to identify it and photocopy it.
>
> (b) A detailed record of all material taken should be made before the material is removed.
>
> (c) No material should be taken unless it is clearly covered by the order.
>
> (d) Seized material, the ownership of which is in dispute, should not be held by the solicitors for the plaintiff pending hearing but by the court, if that is possible, or, if it is not, by the solicitors for the defendant upon their undertaking as to its safe custody and and production, if required.

---

29. *In the Marriage of Mazur* (1992) 15 FamLR 574.

(e) Any plaintiff seeking an *Anton Piller* order must place before the court all the information which it has relating to the circumstances of the defendant which it can suggest points to the probability that in the absence of the *Anton Piller* order material which should be available will disappear.

When making an ex parte application for an *Anton Piller* order, the applicant must make full disclosure to the court of all matters relevant to the application of which the applicant has knowledge. Failure to comply with this requirement although not deliberate and arising from an error of judgment will lead to the order being discharged without any investigation of its merits: *Thermax Ltd v Shott Industrial Glass Ltd* [1981] FSR 289.

In that case the plaintiffs, alleging that the defendants were infringing their registered design for a circuit for a heated glass panel and that evidence of that infringment would be suppressed, obtained an *Anton Piller* order. The evidence in support of that application indicated that the defendant company was controlled by three former directors of the plaintiffs against whom the plaintifs had already commenced proceedings for breach of confidence. The defendant was in fact a member of the group of companies controlled by Carl Ziess Foundation. It was also the case that there had been correspondance between the plaintiffs and the defendant's solicitors relating to the earlier action in which the plaintiffs had sought and been refused inspection of the defendant's premises. Neither of those two matters were put before the judge. The defendant succeeded in an application to have the *Anton Piller* order set aside.

It is submitted that Australian courts should have regard to these guidelines when considering whether to make an *Anton Piller* order and should be satisfied that all conditions have been met before letting loose any posse comitatus which a plaintiff may wish to form. *Anton Piller* orders are often granted in conjunction with *Mareva* injunctions. As the first shot in litigation between the parties they can amount to a broadside which effectively blows the defendant out of the water before proceedings have really begun. The combined effect of these orders can destroy a healthy business. The adversary system is fundamental to our system of justice. Unless we are to go back to the days of the Norman kings when the first man to get the king's ear got the writ to suit his purpose, our courts will have to be vigilant in scrutinising applications for these draconian injunctions. Obtaining an *Anton Piller* order or *Mareva* injunction improperly, particularly where there has been failure to demonstrate sufficient candour in the application, may be an actionable contempt or, otherwise, provide grounds for an action for damages on the basis of a collateral abuse of process, not to mention the possibility of action for professional misconduct against any lawyers who are knowing participants in any such deception.[30]

---

30. See *Spautz v Gibbs* (1990) 21 NSWLR 230 at 270ff, per Priestley JA.

Chapter Twenty Four

24–1 Introduction

[24.1] A declaration is an authoritative statement by the court of the law or of the rights of a party in some matter, or the rights of certain parties *inter se*. Declaratory relief is also final relief, there can be no such thing as an interlocutory declaration. Traditionally equity had no power to grant declarations except by way of ancillary relief in support of some other principal relief, such as a declaration that one party was a trustee, before granting an injunction to restrain a breach of trust. An attempt was made in the Chancery Act 1850 (13 & 14 Vict c 35) to confer a power to give merely declaratory relief on Chancery but the Act was narrowly worded, being limited to a certain number of matters and requiring the parties to concur in stating a case for a declaration, and narrowly construed. Another attempt was made in s 50 of the Chancery Procedure Act 1852 which provided:

> No suit in the said court shall be open to Objection on the Ground that a merely declaratory Decree or Order is sought thereby, and it shall be lawful for the Court to make binding Declarations of Right without granting consequential Relief.

That was interpreted as meaning that declaratory relief was only available where some other principal equitable relief could have been granted, even though it was not sought: *Rooke v Lord Kensington* (1856) 2 K & J 753; 69 ER 986. It was not until the introduction of the Judicature Acts that courts in England, and subsequently in Australia in the jurisdictions which adopted that system, including the High Court,[1] were given power to entertain proceedings for declaratory relief whether or not any consequential relief is, or could be, claimed.

[24.2] In New South Wales the English Chancery Procedure Act 1850 was adopted in the Equity Act 1880 (NSW), s 50 and was re-enacted in the same words as s 10 of the Equity Act 1901. The same restrictive interpretation was placed on that section as had been placed on its English forebear. The Fourth Schedule to the Equity Act 1901 listed a range of matters in which declaratory relief could be given, and in those matters declarations were granted whether any consequential relief could be obtained and whether or not it was sought. That power was, however, restricted to the matters listed in the Fourth Schedule and would only be exercised by the court in cases in which there was no dispute as to the facts, as otherwise the court considered that the matter could only be dealt with in proceedings commenced by statement of claim. Section 10 was amended in 1924 to provide that 'No suit shall be open to objection on the ground that a merely declaratory decree is sought ...' and allowed the court to

---

1. High Court Rules, O 26 r 19.

grant declarations 'whether any consequential relief is or could be claimed or not'.[2] That was taken to apply only to 'suits' for purely equitable relief, however, and not to proceedings concerning common law rights, where a right to consequential relief still had to be shown': *Tooth & Co Ltd v Coombs* (1925) 42 WN (NSW) 93; *David Jones Ltd v Leventhal* (1927) 40 CLR 357. In 1965, s 10 of the Equity Act 1901 was replaced with a new s 10 which conferred a power to award declaratory relief essentially the same as that exercised in other jurisdictions under the judicature system.[3] That power was interpreted narrowly by some judges, particularly Myers J who, in *Salmar Holdings Pty Ltd v Hornsby Shire Council* (1970) 91 WN (NSW) 234, refused to grant a declaration that a proposed building would not be in breach of a residential district proclamation on the grounds that a Board of Appeal existed to deal with such matters under the Local Government Act 1919 (NSW) and that the Supreme Court's power to make declarations on matters falling within the jurisdiction of that Board was, by implication, excluded. Street J took the opposite view in *Sutherland Shire Council v Leyendekkers* [1970] 1 NSWR 356 and was supported by the Court of Appeal which reversed the decision in *Salmar Holdings* (in [1971] 1 NSWLR 192). The Court of Appeal held that the existence of an alternative remedy was not, in itself, sufficient ground for refusing a declaration and that the only limitation on the court's power to award declaratory relief was its discretion not to exercise its power in any case where the granting of a declaration was inappropriate or unjustified in the circumstances.

[24.3] The power to award declaratory relief in New South Wales now rests on s 75 of the Supreme Court Act 1970 (NSW) which provides:

> No proceedings shall be open to objection on the ground that a merely declaratory judgment or order is sought thereby and the Court may make binding declarations of right whether any consequential ruling is or could be claimed or not.

It is submitted that the introduction of s 75 has not changed the power to make declaratory orders conferred by the 1965 reforms. The description of the court's power to make such orders under that legislation is limited only by the court's discretion not to grant relief in inappropriate cases: *Salmar Holdings Pty Ltd v Hornsby Shire Council* [1971] 1 NSWLR 192 at 201, per Mason JA. That remains true of the court's power under the 1970 Act as well. Despite that seemingly boundless description of the jurisdiction to make declarations courts have shown some reluctance to intervene by way of declaratory relief in some circumstances.

[24.4] Limitation by statute. One such limitation occurs where the court's declaratory power is excluded by statute, either expressly or by necessary implication. However, any such exclusion must be an express ouster of this jurisdiction. The mere existence of some other remedy under a statute by recourse to another tribunal will not suffice: *Forster v Jododex Australia Pty Ltd* (1972) 127 CLR 421. In that case the court upheld the decision of Street J at first instance that the respondent was entitled to a declaration that the appellant could not obtain an authority to enter the respondent's land to carry out mining exploration, despite the fact that the mining warden had power to deal with such a dispute and despite the special nature of the matters in issue. For a statute to exclude this jurisdiction it would appear to be necessary, at least, that it create some novel right and an exclusive mode of enforcing the right in issue: *Salmar Holdings Pty Ltd v Hornsby Shire Council* [1971] 1 NSWLR 192 at 203, per Mason JA. In *Liverpool & London & Globe Insurance Co Ltd v JW Deaves Pty Ltd* [1971]

---

2. Administration of Justice Act 1924 (NSW), s 18.
3. Law Reform (Miscellaneous Provisions) Act 1965 (NSW).

2 NSWR 131, Else-Mitchell J held the court had no power to make declarations concerning the rights of a worker under the Workers' Compensation Act 1926 (NSW) which, by s 36, gave exclusive jurisdiction in such matters to the Workers' Compensation Commission. Similarly, in *Young v Public Service Board* (1982) 3 IR (NSW) 50, Lee J refused to grant a declaration construing an industrial award, holding that it was more appropriate that the matter be dealt with by the Industrial Commission of New South Wales, while in *Loftus v McDonald* (1974) 3 ALR 404 it was held that the provisions of the Bankruptcy Act 1966 (Cth) excluded the jurisdiction of the Queensland Supreme Court to make declarations as to beneficial entitlements in the funds of a bankrupt.[4] By contrast, in *Vowell v Shire of Hastings* [1970] VR 764 and *Marks v Swan Hill Shire* [1974] VR 896, declaratory relief was allowed challenging the validity of decisions of local councils, notwithstanding the availability of alternative relief by way of judicial review and *certiorari*.

[24.5] Criminal law. The power of the court to grant declaratory relief clearly extends to the criminal law and its procedure: *Sankey v Whitlam* (1978) 142 CLR 1; *Imperial Tobacco v A-G* [1980] AC 718, however, the courts have shown a distinct reluctance to exercise this power in such cases and will only do so in exceptional circumstances: *Conwell v Tapfield* [1981] 1 NSWLR 595, particularly when criminal proceedings have been commenced.[5] 'Ordinarily a declaration is not made that the defendant has committed a crime. There is no doubt at all that there is jurisdiction to make such a declaration in a proper case': *CAC v Transphere Pty Ltd* (1988) 15 NSWLR 597 at 603, per Young J. A commonly expressed view in cases of this type is that this jurisdiction will only be exercised where a failure to do so will result in some injustice: *Bourke v Hamilton* [1977] 1 NSWLR 470 at 493, per Needham J; *Imperial Tobacco Ltd v A- G* [1980] AC 718. In the latter case the House of Lords, in refusing a declaration that a charge of conducting an unlawful lottery had been improperly brought, held that where criminal proceedings were properly brought and were not vexatious or an abuse of the process of the court, it was not a proper exercise of judicial discretion for a judge in a civil court to grant a defendant in a criminal matter a declaration that the facts alleged by the prosecution did not amount to the offence with which the accused was charged, because to do so would be to usurp the function of the criminal court and prejudice the criminal trial. The different standard of proof in civil and criminal cases and the fact that issues of fact, including guilt or innocence, are decided in trials for indictable offences by a jury rather than the judge alone as is the case in any proceedings for a declaration, add weight to the caution shown by the courts to intervene in criminal matters. In principle, there is no distinction drawn between criminal charges involving moral turpitude, matters which are *mala in se*, that is, wrong in themselves, and cases involving a breach of some statute or regulation, matters which are *mala in prohibitia*, that is, acts merely prohibited by law,[6] but most of the cases in which courts have intervened by way of declaration have been of the latter type,[7] including a growing number of cases in which declarations have been sought as to whether certain conduct constitutes an offence under the Corporations

---

4. For other examples see MG&L, para [1919]; PW Young, *Declaratory Orders*, 2nd ed, Butterworths, 1984, paras 501–7, pp 41–5.

5. Young, *op cit*, paras 1701–2, p 152.

6. *Sankey v Whitlam* (1978) 142 CLR 1 at 21, Per Gibbs CJ.

7. Young, *op cit*, para 1704, pp 154–5.

Law.[8] It seems unlikely, however, that such a declaration will be made after a prosecution has been commenced: *Csidei v Anderson* [1977] 1 NSWLR 747.

[24.6] Academic or hypothetical questions. It has been a long-standing policy of the courts in these matters not to become involved in the determination of academic or hypothetical questions: *Salmar Holdings v Hornsby SC* [1971] 1 NSWLR 192 at 201, per Mason JA; *University of NSW v Moorehouse* (1975) 133 CLR 1. That means that the court may refuse a claim for a declaration on the ground that the issue is purely theoretical, or that there is no real dispute involved. In *Re Clay* [1919] 1 Ch 66, a declaration that the plaintiff was not liable under a certain deed of guarantee was refused on these grounds as no claim had been made against him. The courts also refuse to exercise this power where the declaration would serve no useful purpose: *A-G v Scott* (1904) 20 TLR 630; *The Dairy Farmers Co-operative Milk Co Ltd v Commonwealth* (1946) 73 CLR 381. In *Rivers v Bondi Junction-Waverley RSL Sub-Branch Ltd* (1986) 5 NSWLR 362, the New South Wales Court of Appeal refused to declare that breaches had occurred at the annual general meeting of the respondent at which directors were elected. No impropriety or oppression was alleged and, while voting was close, the matters raised did not appear to have affected the outcome. This is, however, a discretionary rule. There is no complete bar against the making of declarations on theoretical issues. The court may exercise its discretion in favour of granting a declaration on such an issue if it considers it appropriate to do so. In *Sterling Nicholas Duty Free Pty Ltd v Commonwealth* (1972) 126 CLR 297, the plaintiff sought declarations that certain proposals it had for the delivery of pre-sold duty free goods would not be in breach of legislation governing airport concessions. Even though those proposals had never been put into operation the High Court held that it was an apt case for the exercise of the declaratory jurisdiction. The courts' distaste for theoretical issues does not mean that declarations of future rights will not be granted, even though those future rights may depend upon the occurrence of events which may not happen, provided that it can be shown that there is some present reason for dealing with the question in advance rather than waiting on the contingencies: *Curtis v Sheffield* (1882) 21 Ch D 1 at 4, per Jessel MR; *The Trustees of Church Property of the Diocese of Newcastle v Ebbeck* (1960) 104 CLR 394 at 400–1, per Dixon CJ. A declaration usually will not be granted in proceedings in which there is no proper contradictor, a person with a true interest to oppose the declaration sought: *Russian Commercial & Industrial Bank v British Bank for Foreign Trade Ltd* [1921] 2 AC 438 at 448. This is a matter for the court's discretion rather than an absolute rule: *Territory Insurance Office v Kerin* (1986) 84 FLR 1. Although where a defendant ought to come forward, his or her silence should not defeat a declaration of the plaintiff's proper claims.[9] In *CAC v Transphere Pty Ltd* (1988) 15 NSWLR 597, Young J made declarations that certain conduct constituted offers to the public within s 169 of the Companies (NSW) Code. The defendants appeared in person, but presented no argument. Having noted the authorities on the need for a proper contradictor, His Honour considered it appropriate to make the declarations sought.

[24.7] Failure to resolve issues. Declaratory relief may also be refused where it would fail to resolve the issues between the parties. A declaration, for instance, that a contract is specifically performable without any further prayer for an order for specific performance would leave the matter hanging, generating further litigation: *Lucas*

---

8. *Ibid*, para 1706, pp 156–7, (now the Corporations Law), see the discussion of some of these issues in the judgment of Young J in *CAC v Transphere* (1988) 15 NSWLR 597.
9. Borchard, *Declaratory Judgments*, 2nd ed, 1941, p 48.

and Tait Investments Pty Ltd v Victoria Securities Ltd [1975] 1 NSWLR 170. In *Neeta (Epping) Pty Ltd v Phillips* (1974) 131 CLR 286, Barwick CJ and Jacobs J drew attention to the fact that the statutory power to provide declaratory relief, s 75 of the Supreme Court Act 1970 (NSW) in that case, must be read in conjunction with the standard provision in judicature legislation, s 63 in the New South Wales Act, requiring the court to finally determine all matters in controversy between parties. It was generally undesirable, in their view, to make such a declaration without orders for consequential relief unless the parties were agreed on the consequences which would flow from a declaration, such as that a contract had been validly rescinded. Parties cannot select issues from a dispute and bowl them up to a court to get a ruling if that will not resolve their litigation. This does not mean that no application for purely declaratory relief can be entertained unless a raft of ancillary orders is tied to it. The courts may adopt a common sense approach. A declaration on a pivotal issue at an early stage, such as the validity of a notice to complete (*Winchcombe Carson Trustee Pty Ltd v Ball Rand Pty Ltd* [1974] 1 NSWLR 477) will often remove the need or possibility of further protracted litigation. This is particularly so in vendor-purchaser cases where a declaration on the validity of a notice, or the effect of a condition concerning time, might be resolved after a short hearing within days of filing a summons. A full blown suit for rescission or specific performance might have to wait months or years in the list. In commercial cases the court must also consider whether the declaration sought might break a logjam between the parties which, while not providing a final determination of all outstanding legal issues between them, provides an appropriate basis for a commercial resolution of the matter. Modern judicature systems all contain rules allowing trial of separate issues where such a procedure is warranted.

[24.8] Standing. The plaintiff must also have sufficient standing to ask for the declaration sought. This question occurs most commonly in cases in which some individual or group seeks a declaration of some public right. As is the case with injunctions to protect public rights, the issue has revolved around whether the principles laid down in *Boyce v Paddington Borough Council* [1903] 1 Ch 109 apply to claims for declaratory relief in public law matters. A plaintiff who seeks to rely on *Boyce's* case must show that the public role also produces some interference with a private right available to the plaintiff or that the plaintiff has otherwise suffered some special damage in order to establish standing to injunct the commission or continuation of the public wrong. In England, in *Gouriet v A-G* [1978] AC 435, the House of Lords said that *Boyce's* case applied to suits for both injunctive and declaratory relief. In *Australian Conservation Foundation Inc v Commonwealth* (1980) 146 CLR 493, the High Court adopted a more flexible test and said that a plaintiff need only show that it had a special interest in the subject matter of the action, which meant more than an intellectual or emotional concern or a strongly held belief that a certain law should be observed. In that case the plaintiff society sought a declaration, in effect, that decisions allowing a proposed tourist development in Queensland were invalid. The declaration was refused on the grounds that the foundation had no more than an intellectual and emotional concern in the matter. Merely righting a wrong, upholding a principle or winning a contest was not enough. However, in *Onus v Alcoa of Australia Ltd* (1981) 149 CLR 27, the High Court held that representatives of a particular Aboriginal tribe had standing, as custodians for their people of certain relics, to restrain work on land with which they had traditional ties where the work in question threatened sacred sites on that land. The court was careful to note that the fact that the plaintiffs also had an emotional or intellectual interest did not preclude them from seeking a declaration in a matter in which they had standing. In *Robinson v Western Australian Museums* (1977) 138 CLR 283, the High Court held that a diver who had found a wreck off the

Western Australian coast had a sufficient interest to be able to challenge the validity of State legislation purporting to vest property in 'historic wrecks' in the Crown in right of Western Australia, but there the plaintiff stood to gain from salvage rights if he succeeded. In *Greaves v Commissioner of Police* [1984] ACLD 067, the secretary of the Police Association sought declarations concerning the power of the Minister for Police to give directions to the Commissioner after the Minister had directed the Commissioner to return a painting which a policeman had seized in the belief that it was obscene. Lee J refused declaratory relief as the claim would have required the court to pronounce on abstract questions as to the extent of executive control of the Commissioner of Police and there was no existing dispute between the Minister and the Commissioner nor between any officer and the Commissioner.

[24.9] Traditional equitable defences. Because the power to award bare declaratory relief is a creature of statute, and not a product of the inherent jurisdiction of equity, the traditional equitable defences, particularly those of clean hands and willingness to do equity, do not apply in the context of declaratory orders. The English Court of Appeal came to that view in *Chapman v Michaelson* [1909] 1 Ch 238, as did the High Court in *Mayfair Trading Co Pty Ltd v Dreyer* (1958) 101 CLR 428 at 450–6. The power to grant declarations is, nonetheless, a matter for the court's discretion, and relief will be refused where a declaration is sought in furtherance of wrongful acts, such as a declaration of the validity of a marriage contracted to circumvent immigration or extradition laws: *Puttick v A-G* [1979] 3 All ER 463.

[24.10] Administrative law. Declarations have also been widely used in proceedings against the Crown. Because it lacks any coercive element, the declaration has been described as the traditional remedy for the subject against the crown: *FAI Insurances Ltd v Winneke* (1982) 41 ALR 1 at 22. The employment of declarations in this way has been particularly useful in Australia where the federal system of government provides endless scope for challenging the validity of federal or state legislation and of delegated legislation under both systems.[10] The declaratory powers of the court have also been employed as a means of securing judicial review of administrative decisions. For example, in *NSW Fish Authority v Phillips* [1970] 1 NSWR 725 the plaintiffs succeeded in obtaining a declaration that the Authority's scheme of parking charges at its fish market was invalid; in *Thames Launches Ltd v Trinity House Corporation (Deptford Stroud) (No 2)* [1962] Ch 153 the plaintiffs obtained a declaration that they were entitled to operate their passenger boats without a licensed pilot, despite a ruling to the contrary by the defendants; in *Bawn Pty Ltd v Metropolitan Meat Industry Board* [1971] 1 NSWLR 47 the plaintiff obtained a declaration that the defendant was in error in determining the appropriate rate of compensation for condemned meat; in *Donnelly v Marrickville Municipal Council* [1973] 2 NSWLR 390 a declaration that a council decision to approve a development application was void was granted because the council had failed to notify the plaintiff who would have been entitled to object to the proposal.[11] Declarations are also used in public law to test the validity of federal and state laws: *A-G (Vic) v Commonwealth* (1945) 71 CLR 237; *Hughes & Vale Pty Ltd v NSW* (1954) 93 CLR 1; and to challenge the jurisdiction of tribunals: *Government of Gibraltar v Kenney* [1956] 2 QB 410; *Abbott v Sullivan* [1952] 1 KB 189. Apart from reviewing administrative actions which have already taken place, declarations can be used to test the validity of proposed administrative acts. Councils have been able to obtain declarations as to the validity of their rates: *Sutherland Shire Council v Ley-*

---

10. See Young, *op cit*, paras 1201–9, pp 109–14.
11. *Ibid*, paras 1301–16, pp 15–26.

endekkers [1970] 1 NSWR 356, just as ratepayers have been able to obtain declarations that proposed council expenditure is unlawful: *Prescott v Birmingham Corp* [1955] Ch 210. In the sphere of actions under federal administrative law the role of the normal declaratory jurisdiction of the courts has been largely supplanted by the Administrative Decisions (Judicial Review) Act 1977 (Cth) which sets up a separate regime for the judicial review of administrative decisions in that arena.

[24.11] Advantages and examples. While there are some discretionary limitations on the court's power to award declaratory relief it remains a broad and extremely useful jurisdiction, not least because of the speed with which declarations can be obtained and their capacity for pre-empting what would otherwise be expensive and protracted litigation. Declarations have been employed in a wide range of matters, including, that a solicitor has been guilty of professional misconduct: *Law Society of NSW v Weaver* [1974] 1 NSWLR 271; whether people are eligible for membership of, or have been wrongfully expelled from professional associations: *Draper v British Optical Association* [1938] 1 All ER 115; *Weinberger v Inglis (No 2)* [1918] 1 Ch 517; whether a person is a member of a club: *Young v Ladies Imperial Club* [1920] 2 KB 523; or other organisation: *Law v Chartered Institute of Patent Agents* [1919] 2 Ch 276; whether a plaintiff was under any contractual obligation to the defendant: *Ku-ring-gai Municipal Council v Suburban Centres Pty Ltd* [1971] 2 NSWLR 335; that a person has performed his or her obligations under a contract: *Mitchell-Henry v Norwich Union Life Insurance Society* [1918] 2 KB 67; that a contract has been discharged by frustration: *Johnson v Sargant* [1918] 1 KB 101; that a term of a contract is an unreasonable restraint on trade: *Dickson v Pharmaceutical Society of Great Britain* [1970] AC 403; that the defendant is in breach of contract: *Waldron v Rostrevor Estate Ltd* (1926) 38 CLR 280; whether or not a person is a member of a partnership: *Re Pinto Leite & Nephews* [1929] 1 Ch 221; whether a guarantor is exonerated from liability: *Ascherson v Tredegar Dry Dock and Wharf Co Ltd* [1909] 2 Ch 401; whether the plaintiff has a valid mining exploration licence: *Forster v Jododex Australia Pty Ltd* (1972) 127 CLR 421; whether a notice to complete a contract for sale of land and a subsequent purported rescission were valid: *Kadner v Brune* [1973] 1 NSWLR 498; whether a vendor has validly forfeited a deposit: *Shuttleworth v Clews* [1910] 1 Ch 176; whether a breach of a covenant in a lease is sufficient to work a forfeiture: *Puhi Maihi v McLeod* [1920] NZLR 372; whether a sum payable under a contract constitutes a penalty: *Premier Metal & Gravel v Smith's Concrete* [1968] 3 NSWR 775; as to the true construction of a company's articles of association: *McKinnon v Grogan* [1974] 1 NSWLR 295; and as to the validity of an allotment of shares: *Howard Smith Ltd v Ampol Petroleum Ltd* (1974) 48 ALJR 5; That list is but a sample. The range of circumstances in which declarations may be granted defies concise description. It seems sufficient to say that declaratory relief will be allowed in aid of any right recognised by the law where the court considers the matter an appropriate one in which to exercise this broad and utilitarian remedy.

Chapter Twenty Five

25-1 The Sources of Power to Award 'Damages' in Equity

[25.1] Traditionally equity had no power to award damages in the sense that they are known in the common law. It could award monetary remedies in the form of an account of profits, restitution or equitable compensation for breaches of equitable obligations, but not damages as they are known at law. Equity still possesses those powers and has shown some willingness to use them, particularly in recent years by developing the remedy of equitable compensation. Courts of equity also exercise a statutory jurisdiction to award damages in lieu of, or in addition to, equitable relief in certain cases. This power to award damages was conferred on the Court of Chancery by Lord Cairns' Act in 1858. That Act adopted in New South Wales as s 32 of the Equity Act 1880 and later as s 9 of the Equity Act 1901. That provision was re-enacted in New South Wales as s 68 of the Supreme Court Act 1970 provides that where the court has power to grant an injunction or to award specific performance it may award damages either in addition to, or in substitution for, the injunction or specific performance.[1]

25-2 Equitable Compensation

[25.2] Where restitution is ordered for breach of a purely equitable obligation, such as a misappropriation by a trustee, the monetary compensation is assessed on the basis of the principles stated by Street J in *Re Dawson (dec'd)* [1962] 2 NSWR 211:

> The obligation of a defaulting trustee is essentially one of effecting a restitution to the estate. The obligation is of a personal character and its extent is not to be limited by common law principles governing remoteness of damage ... if a breach has been committed then the trustee is liable to place the trust estate in the same position as it would have been in if no breach had been committed. Considerations of causation, foreseeability and remoteness do not readily enter into the matter ... The principles involved in this approach do not appear to involve any inquiry as to whether the loss was caused by or flowed from the breach. Rather the inquiry in each instance would appear to be whether the loss would have happened if there had been no breach ... The obligation

---

1. Corresponding provisions are: Supreme Court Act 1958 (Vic), s 62; Judicature Act 1876 (Qld), s 4; Supreme Court Act 1935 (SA), s 30; Supreme Court Act 1935 (WA), s 25; and Supreme Court Civil Procedure Act 1932 (Tas), s 11. In England Lord Cairns' Act has been repealed, as, it appears, have its successors. The courts behave as though it is still in force (see MG&L, para [2306] and n4).

to make restitution ... is of a more absolute nature than the common law obligation to pay damages for tort or breach of contract ... In equity this relief is couched in terms appropriate to require the defaulting trustee to restore to the estate the assets of which it has been deprived by his default. Increases in market values between the date of the breach and the date of recoupment are for the trustee's account ... This obligation means that where monetary compensation is to be paid by reference to the value of assets it is the value at the date of restoration, not the date of deprivation.

That case involved a deceased estate which included assets in New Zealand. One of the executors improperly paid away in £NZ4700 of the trust moneys which were lost to the trust estate. That payment was made in mid 1939 at which time there was parity between the Australian pound and the New Zealand pound. By the time the trustee was called upon to make restoration the £A had been devalued and to match the sum of £NZ4700 in Australian currency required a sum of £A5,829/8s/3d. It was held that the defaulting trustee ought to repay the estate at the rate of exchange prevailing at the time when restitution took place and not at the time of the breach.

[25.3] Equity's inherent jurisdiction to award monetary compensation for breaches of equitable obligations separate from the power to award damages under Lord Cairns' Act style legislation was recognised by McLelland J in *United States Surgical Corp v Hospital Products Ltd* [1982] 2 NSWLR 766 at 816. In *Markwell Bros Pty Ltd v CPN Diesels Qld Pty Ltd* [1983] 2 Qd R 508, Thomas J awarded damages by way of equitable compensation for breaches of various equitable obligations including breach of fiduciary duties and breach of confidence. Likewise, in *Fraser Edmiston Pty Ltd v AGT (Qld) Pty Ltd* [1988] 2 Qd R 1, Williams J awarded damages by way of equitable compensation for unlawful use of trust property in lieu of ordering an inquiry for the purpose of an account of profits. The defendants had not kept proper books of account and their evidence as to the financial affairs of the business was so unreliable that it was impracticable to order an inquiry in the normal way. In *Mordecai v Mordecai* (1987) 12 NSWLR 58, 'damages' were awarded for breach of trust in a case in which two brothers effectively transferred a business away from a company in which they had worked in partnership with a third brother. The third brother had died, after separating from his wife, and the purpose in transferring the business was to defeat claims by his wife and young child against the deceased brother's estate. The jurisdiction to award damages was not challenged. Damages were assessed on the value of the business removed.

[25.4] Equitable compensation awarded in exercise of this jurisdiction is a creature of equity. Like other equitable relief, equitable compensation is subject to the considerations which touch on the imposition of equitable remedies rather than matters which apply to an award of damages at common law. That is not to say that some matters which may be relevant to assessment of damages at common law cannot be taken into account in determining appropriate equitable compensation. Like other forms of equitable relief, equitable compensation is discretionary. That must mean it is a more flexible remedy than its common law cousin; and that flexibility must also mean that in appropriate cases equity may borrow from the law in determining the proper measure of compensation. That said, there are some features of equitable compensation which should be noted:

1. While the usual measure of equitable compensation will be the improper gain made by the defaulting trustee or fiduciary, equitable compensation can embrace the loss suffered by the trust estate or the plaintiff: *Nocton v Lord Ashburton* [1914] AC 932; *McKenzie v McDonald* [1927] VLR 134; *Catt v Marac Australia Ltd* (1986) 9 NSWLR 639.

2. Because compensation is awarded for breach of an equitable obligation more absolute in character than a common law duty of care or contractual obligation, it is not limited or influenced by such matters as remoteness of damage, forseeability or causation: *Gemstone Corporation of Australia Ltd v Grasso* (1994) 13 ACSR 695; *Hill v Rose* [1990] VLR 129.

3. Contributory negligence, in the sense in which it is used in the common law, cannot be relevant in any determination of equitable compensation, a matter which the New Zealand Court of Appeal failed to properly appreciate in *Day v Mead* [1987] 2 NZLR 443. However, matters which might constitute contributory negligence, or conduct very much akin to it, could be taken into account in the court's discretion in deciding the actual amount of compensation payable and the terms upon which it should be paid. In *Lipkin Gorman v Karpnale Ltd* [1992] 4 All ER 331 a claim was brought against a bank as a third party assisting in a dishonest and fraudulent design by the partners of a solicitor who had misapplied clients' moneys in servicing his gambling addiction. Alliott J found the bank liable, but, in view of the failure on the part of the partners to withdraw the signatory rights of their gambling colleague from the firm's accounts once they became aware of the misapplication of clients' moneys, he thought it would be inequitable to grant them any relief for losses incurred beyond that date.

4. The conduct of the plaintiff will not be irrelevant to any assessment of equitable compensation. If it is to be taken into account, however, it must be on equitable grounds — such as acquiescence, laches or collusion in a breach of trust, for example. A beneficiary, knowing that his or her trustee was investing trust money in the stock market in breach of trust, could not stand by and do nothing waiting to see if the investment proved profitable, relying on his or her rights to seek restitution from the trustee if it failed.

5. The conduct of the defaulting trustee or fiduciary may also be relevant. The court may grant a trustee or fiduciary guilty of some technical breach of duty which has led to some loss but who has otherwise acted in good faith some allowance for his or her efforts, as the House of Lords did in *Boardman v Phipps* [1967] 2 AC 46.

6. There is no concept of exemplary or punitive damages in equity. Interest may be charged on a sum awarded by way of compensation, but only as an element in a proper measure of restitution, not by way of penalty: *Bailey v Namol Pty Ltd* (1994) 53 FCR 102 at 113. A court of equity is not a court of penal jurisdiction. Restitution when awarded in equity is intended to give full compensation; not as a means of punishing anyone: *Vyse v Foster* (1872) 8 Ch App 309 at 333. Interest when so charged applies at the relevant trustee rate or the appropriate commercial rate, depending upon the circumstances of the case: *Hagan v Waterhouse* (1992) 34 NSWLR 308 at 391–2; *Pateman v Heyen* (1993) 33 NSWLR 188 at 200. The 'trustee' rate is the rate of interest obtainable on government stock at the time: *Palette Shoes Pty Ltd (in liq) v Krohn* [1937] VLR 314. A higher rate will apply if the transaction can be characterised as commercial rather than a trustee situation: *Re Hatton Developments (Aust) Pty Ltd* (1978) 3 ACLR 484. The New Zealand Court of Appeal's decision to award exemplary damages for a breach of confidence in *Aquaculture Corporation v NZ Mussel Co Ltd* [1990] 3 NZLR 299 must be wrong as a matter of principle as much as logic.

7. Equitable compensation may be sought against third parties, strangers to the trust or fiduciary relationship, where those third parties assist with knowledge in a dishonest and fraudulent design on the part of a trustee or fiduciary on the

basis of the principle in *Barnes v Addy* (1874) LR 9 Ch App 244. The burgeoning jurisdiction in equitable compensation provides a more rational basis for awarding relief against such third parties. It has always been somewhat artificial to describe a stranger to the trust as a constructive trustee when, by definition, that person has not received and is not holding any trust property. The better interpretation must be that the liability imposed on a stranger to a trust under the rule in *Barnes v Addy* is in the nature of an obligation to provide equitable compensation, rather than a decree that the stranger holds some asset or fund on 'constructive trust' for the benefit of the plaintiff.

8. Equitable compensation need not be limited to an award of a monetary sum. There seems no good reason why compensation could not take the form of an order compelling transfer of some asset to the plaintiff, rather than payment of a sum of money.

9. Like other equitable relief, equitable compensation may be decreed on conditions.

[25.5] Equitable compensation, in a case involving breach of fiduciary duties and its relationship with the equitable remedy of account of profits, was discussed at some length by the High Court in *Warman International Ltd v Dwyer* (1995) 128 ALR 201 (see detailed summary at **[5.32]**). In a joint judgment (at 208), Mason CJ, Brennan, Deane, Dawson and Gaudron JJ, cited Viscount Haldane LC in *Nocton v Lord Ashburton* [1914] AC 932 at 957–8: 'Courts of Equity had jurisdiction to direct accounts to be taken, and in proper cases to order the solicitor to replace property improperly acquired from the client, or to make compensation if he had lost it by acting in breach of a duty which arose out of his confidential relationship to the man who had trusted him'. In *Warman v Dwyer*, the High Court ordered Dwyer to account to Warman for the profit made by him, or by corporate entities under his control from the business conducted with the Bonfiglioli group for the four years after Dwyer had taken that business from Warman, with some allowance for Dwyer's skill and expertise.

The judgment in *Warman v Dwyer* poses more questions than it answers. On one view it can be seen as simply another application of the strict policy which prohibits a fiduciary from retaining a profit acquired in breach of duty, particularly in a situation in which the fiduciary has placed him or herself in a position of conflict between duty and personal interest. However, the case does little to address the commercial realities of such situations. It is clear that in Warman's hands the Bonfilglioli agency was being run down. It was also clear that Bonfilglioli was dissatisfied with Warman's performance. Dwyer deceived his employer in conducting secret negotiations with the Italians. He also failed to take up Warman's offer to buy the business. On the authority of *Hospital Products v USSC*, Warman, as a distributor, did not owe any fiduciary duty to Bonfiglioli. It is also clear that Dwyer's own position, both in terms of job satisfaction and, possibly, future employment security, was threatened by Warman's indifference to the agency business. But employers do not owe duties of a fiduciary nature to their employees. It is also clear on the facts that under the joint management of Dwyer and the Bonfiglioli interests, the agencies business enjoyed great success in the four years after breaking away from Warman, and that much of that success was derived from the pursuit of policies rejected by Warman, such as the local assembly of Bonfiglioli products. Much of the success was also attributable to Dwyer's efforts and skill in pursuing strategies which his superiors at Warman had rejected. And yet Warman was allowed to take, effectively, Dwyer's half share of the profits reaped from those labours. In return, the High Court was only prepared to give Dwyer an 'allowance' for his skill and expertise rather than a set proportion of the profits. The relevant principle was discussed by their Honours in their joint judgment, having noted the comments of Upjohn J in *Re Jarvis (dec'd)* [1958] 1 WLR 815 that the principles under which a fiduciary will be required to account will be different where the fiduciary acquires a business or part thereof from cases in which the fiduciary misappropriates some specific asset, said at 128 ALR 211–12:

> In the case of a business it may well be inappropriate and inequitable to compel the errant fiduciary to account for the whole of the profit of his conduct of the business or his exploitation of the principal's goodwill over an indefinite period of time. In such a case, it may be appropriate to allow the fiduciary a proportion of the profits, depending upon the particular circumstances. That may well be the case when it appears that a significant proportion of an increase in profits has been generated by the skill, efforts, property and resources of the fiduciary, the capital which he has introduced and the risks he has taken, so long as they are not risks to which the principal's property has been exposed. Then it may be said that the relevant proportion of the increased profits is not the product or consequence of the plaintiff's property but the product of the fiduciary's skill, efforts, property and resources. This is not to say that the liability of a fiduciary to account should be governed by the doctrine of unjust enrichment, though that doctrine may well have a useful part to play; it is simply to say that the stringent rule requiring a fiduciary to account for profits can be carried to extremes and that in cases outside the realm of specific assets, the liability of the fiduciary should not be transformed into a vehicle for the unjust enrichment of the plaintiff.

But, having said that, their Honours then said that it was for the defendant to establish that the plaintiff might be unjustly enriched and that, as a general rule, 'in conformity with the principle that a fiduciary must not profit from a breach of fiduciary duty', a court would not apportion profits unless there was some antecedent profit-sharing agreement. If the principle quoted above from *Vyse v Foster* (1872) 8 Ch App 309 at 333 that equity is not a court which imposes penalties is correct, and it must be, the remedy imposed on a defaulting fiduciary ought to be the actual gain attributable to his or her breach, and not a cent more nor a cent less. It is difficult to see in *Warman v Dwyer*, in view of Warman's rigid policy in dealing with the Bonfiglioli agency business, how it could possibly claim, let alone be awarded, any more by way of account of profits than a sum equal to its actual net profits from the agency for one year prior to the termination of the business, perhaps with some allowance for inflation. If the business in Dwyer's hands did better than that then the difference had to be attributable to his efforts and the risks he had taken, along with the input provided by the Bonfiglioli interests. It is certainly the case that Dwyer could not have called on Warman to indemnify him if the venture had failed. And what if Dwyer had simply resigned from Warman and gone to work for Bonfiglioli, or some wholly owned, Australian based Bonfiglioli subsidiary, on a salary with bonuses, which might have included shares in the company issued over time? On the authority of cases like *Buckley v Tutty* (1971)125 CLR 353 Dwyer had a right to work which is protected by the law. Also, as an employee, he could not be prevented from using skills and knowledge acquired during his working career: *Herbert Morris Ltd v Saxelby* [1916] AC 688. While it might be disloyal, and possibly even a breach of fiduciary duty for an employee to enter into discussions with some prospective new employer while still employed by his or her original employer, particularly where the new employer is a rival of the old or, as would have been the case with Bonfiglioli, a company with a trading association with the old employer which might be severed if the right employees came over, it is a common place event in the commercial world. And why should it be so different that Dwyer, instead of simply moving from one situation of employment to another, set up a business and ventured capital in the enterprise? There is a bias in Australian cultural attitudes and in our laws in favour of those who work in employment over those who set up in business. The unspoken assumption is that people will gain an income and a means of livelihood from getting a job and being paid a wage or salary; not from setting up a business and making profits. The making of profits in business is the sphere of those already established in business, whether they run their businesses efficiently or not. One is left with the feeling that Warman did far better out of litigating this matter than it ever would have done by simply running its business. The proposition stated by Tipping J in *Estate Realities Ltd v Wignall* [1992] 2 NZLR 615 at 631 must be a better statement of the principles to be applied in such cases in determining the appropriate remedy against a defaulting fiduciary:

> In deciding what profits or gains have been made the Court must consider all the circumstances of the case. There is no absolute bar or rule against allowing costs, expenses and other deductions and allowances in favour of a fraudulent or morally blameworthy fiduciary. The exercise is to define fairly the profit made or the gains derived from the transaction impugned. The nature of the breach of duty and the circumstances in which it occurred are relevant, as are the circumstances in which the gains or profits were derived and the amount of personal input from the fiduciary which was necessary to enable the gains or profits to be achieved. The jurisdiction is not penal. The fiduciary must not be robbed but, if guilty of improper conduct, cannot claim as of right to be rewarded, let alone liberally rewarded for discretionary elements such as skill, labour, expertise and personal exertion.

25-3 Damages under Lord Cairns' Act

[25.6] In the concurrent and auxiliary jurisdictions, where equitable remedies were applied in support of legal rights, monetary relief was not available except in some narrow cases where damages could be and were awarded in addition to a decree of specific performance: *Cleaton v Gower* (1674) Rep TF 164; 23 ER 90.[2] This created a major problem for a suitor in Chancery prior to 1858. If a plaintiff took proceedings in equity seeking specific performance or injunctive relief, but failed to obtain that relief, for instance, because the court considered damages an adequate remedy, the disappointed plaintiff could not simply amend the claim to ask Chancery to award those damages. A fresh action would have to be commenced at law. It was with this defect in mind that the Parliament sought to widen Chancery's power to award damages by introducing Lord Cairns' Act in 1858: see **[25.1]**. The power to award damages under the Act is linked to the equitable relief of either injunction or specific performance. Lord Cairns' Act was not taken to have widened equity's jurisdiction to the point where it could entertain any action for damages. The preferred view was that equity could only entertain suits for relief under the Act where, prior to 1858, the matter was one in which a court of equity could have ordered an injunction or specific performance: *Boyns v Lackey* (1958) 58 SR (NSW) 395 at 405. A party seeking damages under Lord Cairns' Act had to show an entitlement to one of those decrees before damages could be awarded.

In *King v Poggioli* (1923) 32 CLR 222, the purchaser of a rural property sought specific performance against the vendor and damages for the vendor's failure to complete on a specified day as stipulated. However, the purchaser refused to tender the full purchase

---

2. MG&L, para [2304].

price. He had retained a sum sufficient to cover the cost of stock lost through lack of grazing. It was held that specific performance was not available because the purchaser could not show that he was ready and willing to fulfil his part of the contract and, as he was not entitled to specific performance, so he could not get damages under s 9 of the Equity Act 1901 (NSW).

That decision raises the question of whether a plaintiff will be denied damages if a claim for specific performance or injunction fails for any reason, including the raising of some defence by the defendant. In *Goldsborough Mort v Quinn* (1910) 11 CLR 674, where specific performance of an option to purchase certain lands was decreed, the vendor argued that there was an ambiguity in the contract as to the method of calculating the purchase price. In the event the court held that the contract was not ambiguous but said, per Isaacs J, at 701, that had specific performance been refused on the grounds of a non-essential mistake, damages could have been awarded under s 9 of the Equity Act 1901 (NSW). On that view, if a plaintiff can establish a right to specific performance on the original pleadings, once the facts are established, damages under s 68 could be awarded notwithstanding defeat of the claim for the principal relief by the raising of some discretionary defence, a view seemingly accepted by the High Court in *Wentworth v Woollahra Municipal Council* (1982) 149 CLR 672 at 676. That is a reasonable interpretation. Lord Cairns' Act is commonly invoked where a vendor has sold some property to a third party after contracting to sell it to the plaintiff. If the sale to the third party has been completed, without the third party purchaser receiving notice of the plaintiff's interest, specific performance of the original contract will be impossible. In those circumstances, an award of damages is not only just and appropriate, it is the only possible remedy for the plaintiff.

25-4 Grounds on which Lord Cairns' Act Damages may be Awarded

[25.7] The grounds upon which damages can be awarded in lieu of injunction or specific performance have been the subject of some debate. In *Shelfer v City of London Electric Lighting Co* [1895] 1 Ch 287, Lindley LJ pointed out that the Court of Chancery had always protested against the idea that Lord Cairns' Act should be used to allow wrongful acts to continue just because the wrongdoer was prepared to pay for the injury he or she might inflict. In the same case AL Smith LJ laid down what he described as 'a good working rule', the notion that damages could be awarded in lieu of an injunction where the injury to the plaintiff's rights was small, the injury was capable of being estimated in money, and was one which could be adequately compensated by a small money payment, and that it would be oppressive to grant an injunction against the defendant. That decision has been criticised as tending to confine the jurisdiction of the court unnecessarily and the suggestion has been made that specific relief should be awarded unless the court considers it unreasonable to do so in the circumstances of the case.[3] Nonetheless, the 'good working rule' was accepted in *Morris v Redland Bricks* [1970] AC 652 in which a brick company excavated on their land and thereby withdrew support from a neighbouring market garden leading to slippage on the latter. The cost of restoring the support safely was more than £30,000 while an acre of land in the district cost £1,500. The majority of the English Court of Appeal found that only the final part of the rule was satisfied and granted a manda-

---

3. MG&L, para [2311].

tory injunction. The House of Lords allowed an appeal against that injunction on the ground that the appellants had not acted unreasonably and that the injunction had not specified what work they were to do. In the process their Lordships also held that Lord Cairns' Act had nothing to do with the case and left the unfortunate plaintiff with £325 damages for slippage which had already occurred, costs, and the prospect of further trips to court as and when further slippage took place.

[25.8] Lord Cairns' Act gave courts of equity a power to award damages in cases in which damages at common law were not available, such as actions to restrain threatened or apprehended wrongs and cases involving contracts which are only enforceable through the operation of the doctrine of part performance: *Leeds Industrial Cooperative Society Ltd v Slack* [1924] AC 851.

25–5 The Measure of Equitable Damages

[25.9] The measure of damages available under Lord Cairns' Act and its modern equivalents is a question of some controversy. While described as damages the remedy available under Lord Cairns' Act is still an equitable remedy and is subject to the same powers of discretion in the court as other forms of equitable relief. That discretion applies both to the issue of whether damages will be granted at all and to their quantum in the event that they are. The width of that discretion, at least on the question of assessment of damages, has been placed under some constraint recently by a rather conservative decision of the House of Lords in *Johnson v Agnew* [1980] AC 367: see [25.11]. A more liberal approach was taken by Megarry J in the earlier case of *Wroth v Tyler* [1974] 1 Ch 30:

> A vendor was prevented from completing a contract for the sale of a house for £6,000 when his wife registered a notice under the Matrimonial Homes Act 1967 (UK) on the title. The purchasers sought specific performance and other relief. It was agreed that the house was worth £7,500 at the date fixed for completion and £11,500 at the date of hearing. The purchasers, by then, could no longer afford a house of that type in that locality. Megarry J held that the measure of damages, unlike damages at common law which would usually be the difference between the purchase price and the market value at the date of completion, should operate so as to provide a remedy which was a proper substitute for specific performance. Accordingly he held that the court could award such damages as would put the purchasers into as a good a position as they would have enjoyed had the contract been performed, even if that meant assessing those damages at the date of hearing.

[25.10] The principle applied by Megarry J has since been adopted by the Court of Appeal in *Malhotra v Choudhoury* [1979] 1 All ER 186 and by the Supreme Court of New Zealand: *Souster v Epsom Plumbing Contractors Ltd* [1974] 2 NZLR 515. In Victoria, in *Bosaid v Andry* [1963] VR 465, Scholl J placed a different interpretation on the section, holding that damages should be assessed at the time the contract is brought to an end, which would not necessarily place a purchaser in the same position as might otherwise obtain had specific performance been awarded. In New South Wales *Wroth v Tyler* has been approved of in principle, although with some qualification, in *ASA Constructions Pty Ltd v Iwanov* [1975] 1 NSWLR 512:

> The Iwanovs entered into successive contracts to sell the same land to two different purchasers. Both purchasers subsequently brought proceedings seeking specific performance. At the hearing the second purchaser accepted the priority of the first and

restricted his claim to damages. As it was not clear at the time the second purchaser commenced proceedings that completion of his contract was impossible because of the prior contract, damages under s 68 were held to be available. Needham J declined to hold that the second man was entitled to damages assessed at the date of judgment as he had been aware of the existence of another purchaser from an early date and could have acted to mitigate his loss. While conceding the force of the reasoning of Megarry J in *Wroth v Tyler*, Needham J held that the appropriate time to assess damages in this case was the date of repudiation of the second contract by the vendor.

[25.11] On those authorities the power of a court of equity to award damages can be seen to be reasonably well founded and sufficiently flexible to fit Lord Cairns' Act into the general arsenal of equitable remedies. However, the House of Lords appeared to cut that interpretation down without making it completely inflexible in *Johnson v Agnew* [1980] AC 367. In that case their Lordships said that, apart from some cases in which damages could not be recovered at common law, such as an award of damages in lieu of a *quia timet* injunction, there was no warrant under Lord Cairns' Act to award damages differently from common law damages and that, while the date of breach would be the normal time at which they were assessed, the court had power to fix such other date as may be appropriate in the circumstances. The relevant date was the date the contract was 'lost', which might be as late as the date of judgment. *Johnson v Agnew* has met with some criticism and must only be of persuasive authority in Australia.[4]

[25.12] *Johnson v Agnew* was cited with approval by Aickin J in *Ansett Transport Industries v Halton, Interstate Parcel Express* (1979) 146 CLR 249 at 267–8; 25 ALR 639 at 655, where he referred to a passage which cited *Leeds Industrial Co-op Society v Slack* [1924] AC 851 as authority for the proposition that Lord Cairns' Act conferred a jurisdiction to award damages in some cases where damages were not available at law, such as damages in lieu of a *quia timet* injunction but that, otherwise, the Act did not provide for the assessment of damages on any new basis. The logic of that seems a bit thin. The words of the Act do not confer separate heads of power to award damages, those in line with the common law and others in matters foreign to the law. As damages can be awarded in lieu of an injunction to restrain some apprehended wrong, on the authority of *Leeds Industrial Co-op Society v Slack*, the Act clearly envisages the assessment of damages by a method different from that applied in the common law. It would seem an odd result if the Act was to be read as prescribing one system, an equitable system, for assessing damages awarded in lieu of or in addition to injunctions and another system, one parallel to the common law, for damages awarded in lieu of or in addition to a decree of specific performance.

[25.13] The shackles apparently placed on courts assessing damages under Lord Cairns' Act by *Johnson v Agnew* and *Ansett Transport Industries* proved no hindrance to Helsham CJ in Eq in *Madden v Kevereski* [1983] 1 NSWLR 305 where His Honour held that *Johnson v Agnew* and other cases provided authority for the court to fix the date for assessment of damages as any date that may be appropriate in the circumstances, including the date when, without default on the part of the plaintiff, the contract is lost. In *Madden v Kevereski*, Helsham CJ in Eq held the date on which the contract was lost to be the date of judgment as the court had exercised its discretion and decided not to award specific performance, although all the elements were present for the granting of such a decree. He also expressed the view that damages under s 68 were quite different from damages at law, which the court in its Equity Division could

---

4. MG&L, para [2314].

award anyway, because the plaintiff was required to make out a case for relief by way of injunction or specific performance before the section could apply. The approach taken by Helsham CJ in Eq must be preferred to that of the House of Lords. As a matter of logic as much as law it makes no sense to suggest that the power to award damages under Lord Cairns' Act is not a matter of discretion when that power is exercised in lieu of other remedies which are, and always have been, discretionary. In any case, the power to award damages in tort is sufficiently flexible to allow damages to be assessed at the date of hearing in appropriate cases: *Rentokil v Channon* (1990) 19 NSWLR 417. It would seem strange if equity's power was more restricted.

[25.14] In some cases compensation will be sought for loss of expenditure. In that sort of case the plaintiff will be asking to be restored to the position he or she would have enjoyed had the contract not been entered into, rather than what he or she would have enjoyed if it had been carried out. These two approaches are mutually exclusive so a plaintiff seeking equitable damages must elect for one or the other.

[25.15] It has been argued that substantial damages ought to be obtainable under Lord Cairns' Act, at the suit of the second party, the party to the contract, where the contract is for the benefit of a third party. At common law, substantial damages would not be available to the second party, but that party could obtain a decree of specific performance in equity. In those circumstances, it is appropriate that any damages awarded in lieu of such a decree must be of the same value as specific performance.[5]

25–6 Equitable Damages and Equitable Obligations

[25.16] The power to award damages in lieu of or in addition to injunction or specific performance is clearly available in the auxiliary jurisdiction where injunctions and specific performance are sought in aid of legal rights. There is also a school of thought which argues that damages under Lord Cairns' Act are available in the exclusive jurisdiction for breaches of equitable obligations. In *Re Leeds & Hanley Theatre of Varieties* [1902] 2 Ch 809, the Court of Appeal held that damages could be awarded against promoters of a company for breach of fiduciary duties. In *Seager v Copydex (No 2)* [1969] 1 WLR 809, damages were awarded for breach of confidence, although no mention was made of whether those were damages at common law, damages under Lord Cairns' Act, or 'damages' by way of equitable compensation. In *Talbot v GTV* [1980] VR 224, the Full Court of the Victorian Supreme Court employed the Victorian equivalent of Lord Cairns' Act to award damages for wrongful use of confidential information. The High Court has since expressed approval for the employment of Lord Cairns' Act in the exclusive jurisdiction of equity to award damages for breach of a purely equitable obligation.

In *Wentworth v Woollahra Municipal Council* (1982) 149 CLR 672; 42 ALR 69, the appellant sought a mandatory injunction requiring demolition of a house on property adjacent to her own on the grounds that the structure did not comply with the local council's planning ordinance. At first instance the appellant failed because the non-compliance was not considered to be sufficiently substantial. At the appellate stage the council was joined and the appellant amended her statement of claim to seek damages

---

5. MG&L, para [2316].

under Supreme Court Act 1970 (NSW), s 68 as well as an injunction. In discussing the history and role of s 68 the court, Gibbs CJ, Mason, Murphy and Brennan JJ said, at 72, 'The main object of the Act was to enable the Court of Chancery to do 'complete justice' between parties by awarding damages in those cases in which it had formerly refused equitable relief in respect of a legal right and left the plaintiff to sue for damages at common law. An incidental object of the Act was to enable the court to award damages in lieu of an injunction or specific performance, even in the case of a purely equitable claim'.[6] Their Honours then went on to hold that, as the Act had historically been concerned with private rights, it did not authorise an award of damages in favour of someone seeking to restrain breach of a public duty in a case where an injunction has been sought but not awarded.

[25.17] The finding that Supreme Court Act 1970 (NSW), s 68, and thus the other re-enactments of Lord Cairns' Act, allows damages to be awarded on a purely equitable claim has been strongly criticised. Meagher, Gummow and Lehane argue that the proposition that damages under Lord Cairns' Act can be awarded for breach of a purely equitable obligation is simply incorrect. They give four reasons in support of this claim:

1. That interpretation, ie, that damages under the Act can be awarded for breach of an equitable obligation, is contrary to the intention of the framers of the Act.

2. The word 'wrongs' in Lord Cairns' Act is synonymous with 'torts' because of the use of the term 'wrongful acts' in s 83 of the Common Law Procedure Act 1854 (Imp).

3. The notion of a purely equitable claim being specifically performed is a logical monstrosity because all claims for specific performance arise out of the purely common law notion of contract.

4. There is no need to award 'damages' for breach of a purely equitable obligation because equity has always had a power to award monetary relief by way of restitution.

The learned authors conclude by urging that this *dicta* should be best treated as having been uttered *per incuriam*.[7] In response to the first two objections one must ask to what extent matters of interpretation of a statute passed by the New South Wales parliament in 1970 should be governed by reports prepared for the parliamentary draftsman in England in the 1850s. In view of the fact that Lord Cairns' Act now applies throughout Australia by virtue of its re-enactment in judicature legislation, it would seem more appropriate to interpret its words in the context and spirit of that legislation rather than the inadequate and piecemeal reforms of a bygone era. One must also have regard to the normal rules of statutory interpretation and to the actual wording of the section. The third objection would carry more weight if Lord Cairns' Act only referred to specific performance. As it also refers to injunctions this claim loses some of its force. Mandatory injunctions are readily available to obtain positive enforcement of equitable obligations and, of course, the equitable doctrine of part performance provides for decrees of specific performance of contracts not recognised at law. In view of the growing use of equitable compensation the interpretation placed on s 68 by the High Court in *Wentworth v Woollahra MC* does not seem such a dire threat to the purity of equitable principle. The question which seems more pertinent is that of the distinction, if any, which should be drawn between 'damages' awarded by way of equitable compensation in the inherent jurisdiction and damages

---

6. The authorities cited in support of that principle were: *Leeds Industrial Co-operative Society Ltd v Slack* [1924] AC 851 at 857, per Viscount Finlay; *Landau v Curton* (1962) The Estates Gazette 369 at 374–5, per Cross J; *Ferguson v Wilson* (1866) 2 Ch App 77 at 88, per Turner LJ and at 91, per Cairns LJ; *Elmore v Pirrie* (1887) 57 LT (NS) 333 at 335, per Kay J.

7. MG&L, para [2321].

awarded under the modern equivalents of Lord Cairns' Act, and the consequences which would flow from employing one rather than the other. Equitable compensation is clearly a creature of the exclusive jurisdiction and is restitutionary in essence although not purely so. Lord Cairns' Act damages are mainly, but not exclusively, available in the auxiliary jurisdiction and can be said to be compensatory, although the discretionary nature of this jurisdiction provides scope for restitutionary relief as well.

Chapter Twenty Six

26-1 Rescission

[26.1] The equitable remedy of rescission enables a party to a contract to disaffirm the contract and return to his or her original position, so that the contract is set aside *ab initio*. In equity this right arises in a number of circumstances: when the contract is vitiated by mistake; where it is induced by a misrepresentation, whether fraudulent or innocent; and where it has been brought about through the exercise of undue influence or some other unconscionable conduct. Rescission in equity applies to all dispositions and transactions, and not merely to formal contracts.[1] Where a contract has been brought about by duress or fraudulent misrepresentation it will be voidable at common law as well as in the concurrent jurisdiction of equity. Rescission is not in itself a remedy ordered by the court. The function of the court is merely to adjudicate on the validity of the acts of the party disaffirming the contract. That may mean that ancillary orders will be necessary to compel the reconveyance of property transferred under the voidable transaction. The aim of rescission is to return the parties to their original positions, so that must be possible. In other words, restitutio in integrum must be possible in any case where rescission is sought. Not only that, but the party seeking rescission must be prepared to do equity and make any necessary restitution to the other.

In *Alati v Kruger* (1955) 94 CLR 216, the appellant sold a fruit business to the respondent, which sale included an assignment of the lease of the premises from which the business was conducted. The respondent later sought to rescind the sale on the ground that the appellant had fraudulently misrepresented the takings of the business. Rescission was granted at first instance. At the time of the trial the landlord had been willing to take a re-assignment of the lease but, by the time of judgment, the landlord had taken possession. The High Court dismissed the appeal against the order allowing rescission. In doing so Dixon CJ, Webb, Kitto and Taylor JJ said that, in equity, precise restitutio was not necessary if the court, by the exercise of its powers, including the taking of accounts and directing enquiries as to allowances for deterioration, can do what is practically just between the parties and restore them substantially to the status quo. In this case the respondent had not forfeited his right to rescind by leaving the premises and abandoning the business as he had given the appellant adequate notice of his claim to rescind and the appellant had had a reasonable opportunity to take the property back or to apply for the appointment of a receiver.

The court's attitude to *restitutio* may also be influenced by the conduct of the defendant. Where the defendant is innocent, in the sense that the misrepresentation inducing the contract was not made with conscious dishonesty, the court may be

---

1. MG&L, para [2404].

more reluctant to pull a transaction to pieces: *Spence v Crawford* [1939] 3 All ER 271 at 288–9, per Lord Wright. But, it should be noted that unless he or she is entitled to relief under some statutory provision dealing with misrepresentation (see Chapter 6), the plaintiff may have no remedy other than rescission in equity for an innocent misrepresentation. In making allowances for deterioration or improvements to property transferred under a voidable contract, allowances will not be made for matters of personal taste, nor for improvements made after the improver has reasonable notice of the alleged defect in his or her title. Nor will any allowance be made for losses sustained in carrying on a business transferred under a voidable contract; the court is only concerned with such compensation as will restore the status quo in relation to the subject matter of the contract: *Brown v Smitt* (1924) 34 CLR 160 at 165–6, per Knox CJ, Gavan Duffy and Starke JJ.

[26.2] Rescission is also used in a less precise sense to describe the rights of an innocent party confronted by a breach of contract by the other party in which case the innocent one has three choices he or she can either:

(a) ignore the breach entirely;

(b) elect to affirm the contract seeking a decree of specific performance, if the contract is susceptible to such an order; or

(c) treat the other's breach as a repudiation which relieves the innocent party from further performance under the contract.

That third choice can be described as rescinding the contract: *Harold Wood Brick Co Ltd v Ferris* [1935] 2 KB 199. Rescission in this sense, while relieving the wronged party from further obligation under the contract, is not rescission *ab initio*; there is no question of *restitutio*, and the wronged party is entitled to sue for damages for the breach: *McDonald v Dennys Lascelles Ltd* (1933) 48 CLR 457; *Photo Production Ltd v Securicor Transport Ltd* [1980] AC 827. Rescission may also be apt to describe rights expressly created by contractual stipulation allowing either or both parties to 'rescind' the contract upon the happening of certain events or the failure of certain conditions. Rights in the nature of, although not necessarily identical to, rescission have been created by statute in some instances, such as Trade Practices Act 1974 (Cth), s 75A; s 7 and the First Schedule of the Contracts Review Act 1980 (NSW).

[26.3] The right to rescind may be lost in a number of circumstances, for instance if the wronged party affirms the transaction with knowledge of the facts, or, perhaps, has unclean hands. An equity to rescind a contract or some other transaction will also be defeated by the interests of a bona fide purchaser of the legal estate, and even by one who takes an equitable estate for value and without notice: *Latec Investments Ltd v Hotel Terrigal Pty Ltd* (1965) 113 CLR 265. There is some doubt as to whether a person who affirms a contract must have knowledge both of the availability of the right to rescind as well as knowledge of the facts giving rise to that right. In *Sargent v ASL Developments Ltd* (1974) 131 CLR 634, Stephen J was of the view that it was only necessary that the party know of the facts giving rise to the inconsistent legal rights for the doctrine of election to operate. Mason J expressed the proposition in these terms, at 658:

> If a party to contract, aware of a breach going to the root of the contract, or of other circumstances entitling him to terminate the contract, though unaware of the existence of the right to terminate the contract, exercises rights under the contract he must be held to have made a binding election to affirm. Such conduct is justifiable only on the footing that an election has been made to affirm the contract; the conduct is adverse to the other party and may therefore be considered unequivocal in its effect. The justifica-

tion for imputing to the affirming party a binding election in these circumstances, though he be unaware of his alternative right, is that, having a knowledge of the facts sufficient to alert him to the possibility of the existence of his alternative right, he has acted adversely to the other party and that, by doing so he has induced the other party to believe that performance of the contract is insisted upon. It is with these considerations in mind that the law attributes to the party the making of a choice, though he be ignorant of his alternative right ... the affirming party can not be permitted to change his position once he has elected.

26-2 Restitution

[26.4] Equity will order specific restitution of chattels in any case in which damages at law would be an inadequate remedy. This jurisdiction has most often been invoked in cases concerning the recovery of heirlooms: *Pusey v Pusey* (1684) 1 Vern 273; 23 ER 465, and similarly valued or otherwise unique pieces.[2] The plaintiff must show title to the chattels, by ownership or possession, before any order for restitution can be made: *Gamba Holdings UK Ltd v Minories Finance Ltd* [1989] 1 All ER 261. When specific restitution is sought of chattels which can, conceivably, be given a monetary value, the court will not necessarily be satisfied with that as proof that damages would be an adequate remedy.

In *Aristoc Industries Pty Ltd v R A Wenham (Builders) Pty Ltd* [1965] NSWR 581, the plaintiff delivered 301 specially made chairs to a contractor who was building a hall at Royal Prince Alfred Hospital. After delivery it was found that the hall was not sufficiently completed to instal the chairs and the contractor refused to pay for them until they were installed. The contractor, who was in financial difficulty, then assigned its contract, including all materials on site, to the defendant. The plaintiff sought to recover the chairs and also sought an interlocutory injunction restraining the defendant from dealing with them in the meantime. Jacobs J rejected the defendant's argument that damages would be an adequate remedy. Once the chairs were installed they would be attached to the freehold and the plaintiff would fail in a common law claim in detinue. Because of the special nature of the chairs, the defendant could only secure a proper price for them from the defendant or the Crown, the owner of the hospital, so damages in conversion would not be a true measure of the plaintiff's loss. Jacobs J granted the injunction subject to the Crown having the opportunity to purchase the chairs at the original contract price in the interests of public welfare.

In *Doulton Potteries Pty Ltd v Bronotte* [1971] 1 NSWLR 591, Hope J awarded delivery up of a dye, used by the plaintiff in the manufacture of angled pipes, which had been given to the defendant to repair, overruling the defendant's assertion of a possessory lien to secure payment of the charges for that repair, which the plaintiff claimed were excessive.

The power of the New South Wales Supreme Court to make orders for the recovery of possession of chattels is now contained in s 74 of the Supreme Court Act 1970 which allows for the party seeking to recover the goods to pay money into court to cover any debt in respect of which a lien is claimed over the goods. As *Aristoc Industries v Wenham* demonstrates, specific restitution is like other equitable remedies, discretionary and capable of being imposed subject to conditions.

---

2. MG&L, para [2202].

26–3 Rectification

[26.5] Where parties set out the terms of an agreement or any other transaction in a written instrument which, by mistake, does not embody the true agreement between the parties, equity will allow rectification of the document. This jurisdiction covers virtually all documents including a conveyance of land,[3] policies of insurance,[4] and bills of exchange,[5] but not a will,[6] unless there is fraud, nor the articles of association of a company.[7] This jurisdiction is solely concerned with the rectification of documents, not the variation of contracts. It is not necessary, however, to show some prior concluded agreement which has been incorrectly set out in writing; it will suffice if it can be shown that the written instrument does not properly reflect the common continuing intentions of the parties at the time of execution of the document: *Joscelyne v Nissen* [1970] 2 QB 86.

In *Slee v Warke* (1952) 86 CLR 271, the owners of a hotel gave a lease to the respondent. It had been agreed that the lessee was to be entitled to an option, exercisable within the first year of the lease, to purchase the hotel, provided the purchase was not completed within that first year. A draft lease was prepared by the solicitors for the lessors which included an option exercisable at any time after the expiry of the first year of the lease. The lessee noticed the change but presumed that the lessors had changed their minds. The formal lease, including the error, was executed without the lessors becoming aware of the change. The lessee subsequently purported to exercise the option in the terms set out in the lease. The lessors refused to convey. The lessee obtained a declaration that they were bound to sell the pub to her. The High Court, per Rich, Dixon and Williams JJ held that the power of the court to rectify documents is not confined to cases in which there is an actual concluded contract antecedent to the instrument sought to be rectified. It can extend to the rectification of a document which does not give effect to the concurrent intention of the parties at the time of its execution. In this case there was no concurrent intention held by the parties at the date of execution that the option would only be exercisable in the first year. At most that was only the intention of the lessors; the lessee's intention was in accordance with the contract.

In *Maralinga Pty Ltd v Major Enterprises Pty Ltd* (1973) 128 CLR 336, at an auction sale of land the auctioneer announced that the vendor wanted $75,000 on completion and would accept a three year mortgage for the balance of the purchase price. The draft contract required cash on completion. The purchaser's agent was aware of that term and eventually signed the contract in that form. The property was knocked down to a purchaser for $155,000. The purchaser was refused rectification of the contract to include the mortgage. Where parties sign a written instrument which differs from the terms of an antecedent bargain, knowing that it is different, the instrument cannot be taken to have been executed under any mistaken belief as to its contents. Mason J said, at 350, that the purpose of the remedy is to make the instrument conform to the true agreement of the parties where the writing by common mistake fails to express that agreement accurately. An antecedent agreement is not essential to the grant of relief by way of rectification. It may be granted in cases in which the instrument sought to be rectified constitutes the only agreement between the parties, but does not reflect their common intention.

---

3. *White v White* (1872) LR 15 Eq 247.
4. *Collett v Morrison* (1851) 9 Hare 162; 68 E R 458; *Motteaux v London Assurance Co* (1739) 1 Atk 545; 26 ER 343.
5. *Druiff v Parker* (1868) LR 5 Eq 131.
6. *Harter v Harter* (1873) LR 3 P & D 11. Power to rectify a will in the Probate jurisdiction is now contained in statute in New South Wales, s 29A of the Wills Probate and Administration Act 1898. A similar although possibly more limited power is also found in the Succession Act 1981 (Qld), s 31.
7. *Scott v Frank F Scott* (London) Ltd [1940] Ch 794.

[26.6] Rectification will not be ordered if the written agreement contains the form of words intended by the parties, even if they took those words to have a different meaning or effect: *Bacchus Marsh Concentrated Milk Co Ltd (in liq) v Joseph Nathan & Co Ltd* (1919) 26 CLR 410. In *Frederick E Rose (London) Ltd v William H Pim Jnr & Co Ltd* [1953] 2 QB 450, rectification was refused where the parties used the word 'feveroles' under the mistaken belief that it described 'horsebeans'. Despite some *dicta* to the contrary, rectification will be allowed for a mistake as to the legal effect of some term, where both parties were under a common misapprehension on the point. So in a string of cases involving annuities described as payable 'free of tax', which were thereby void under the income tax legislation, the fatal words were replaced by words such as 'net sum payable after the payment of tax at the standard rate'.[8] Nor will rectification be available in cases of unilateral mistake except in cases of fraud or where the party seeking restitution believed that some provision was to be included but the other party omitted that provision knowing that the first party believed it would be in: *A Roberts & Co Ltd v Leicestershire County Council* [1961] Ch 555.

[26.7] Rectification may be allowed of a voluntary settlement, at the suit of the settlor: *Re Butlin's Settlement* [1976] Ch 251, or even the beneficiary: *Thompson v Whitmore* (1860) 1 J & H 268; 70 ER 748, provided the change sought is not contrary to the wishes of the settlor *Lister v Hodgkinson* (1867) LR 4 Eq 30, although any volunteer seeking rectification of a settlement in his or her favour will face a very difficult task. If the settlement is the product of a bargain between the settlor and trustees it will usually be necessary to show a mutual mistake shared by all parties, rather than a unilateral mistake on the part of the settlor alone: *Re Butlin's Settlement, supra.*

[26.8] Rectification is inappropriate if the mistake in the document is one which can be dealt with as a matter of construction, as will be the case, for instance, with obvious typographical errors and other deletions or insertions which, from the whole of the document, can be corrected simply as a matter of interpretation: *Fitzgerald v Masters* (1956) 95 CLR 420; *Watson v Phipps* (1985) 60 ALJR 1. The standard of proof required in proceedings for rectification is high. Mere suspicion of a mistake is not enough. The proof of the mutual mistake must be convincing: *Chamberlain v Thorton* (1892) 18 VLR 192 at 195. The evidence, whether parol or documentary, must be clear and unambiguous, and the court must be satisfied of the nature and extent as well as of the existence, of the mistake before rectification can be allowed: *Soloman v Soloman* (1878) 4 VLR (E) 40 at 49.

[26.9] Rectification will be allowed in circumstances where the issue is whether there is a contract at all. In *Sindel v Georgiou* (1984) 154 CLR 661, a contract for sale of land was rectified. After exchange the vendor's copy of the contract did not correspond with the purchaser's in that a number of details, including the name of the purchaser, the purchase price and the amount of the deposit were left blank. It was the clear intention of the parties to create a binding contract on exchange of parts notwithstanding the lack of correspondence of those parts, provided the lack of correspondence could be remedied by rectification. It would be different if their intention was only to be bound by an exchange of corresponding parts.

---

8. Pettit, p 509.

26–4 Account

[26.10] There was an action of account in the medieval common law, however, that action fell into disuse, partly because it only applied to certain relationships,[9] and largely because of the horrifically cumbersome nature of its procedure.[10] But disuse is not abolition, and even though the common law action was said to have been superseded by its more convenient equitable counterpart,[11] it remained available, at least in theory, to bedevil Chancery's power to order account in the auxiliary jurisdiction. In the exclusive jurisdiction there was no such problem and equity would order an account where it was necessary to protect or enforce some equitable right, such as that of a *cestui que* trust against a trustee, or between partners, or some other duty of confidence, such as that by a mortgagee in possession to his or her mortgagor.

[26.11] Prior to the introduction of the Judicature Acts any statement of the circumstances in which equity would decree an account in support of a legal claim necessitated a long and complex list which rested on the broad principle that the equitable jurisdiction would not be exercised where the matter could be as fully and conveniently dealt with at common law: *Shephard v Brown* (1862) 4 Giff 208; 66 ER 681; *Southampton Dock Co v Southampton Harbour & Pier Board* (1870) LR 11 Eq 254. However, there is no record of any common law action of account ever being brought in New South Wales.[12] Under the Supreme Court Act 1970 (NSW), all divisions of the court have power to order accounts. Parts 48 and 49 of the Rules, which deal with the ordering of accounts, appear to set different rules for accounts taken in the Equity Division from accounts ordered in other divisions of the court,[13] but these two parts are not mutually exclusive: *Hagan v Waterhouse* [1983] 2 NSWLR 395 at 398, per McLelland J. This uniformity of procedure has overcome the jurisdictional and procedural jigsaw which characterised prejudicature accounts, but many of the principles applied in those days remain valid, for example, those governing the respective rights of joint creditors and several creditors upon the dissolution of a partnership: *Anmi Pty Ltd v Williams* [1981] 2 NSWLR 138. Accounts between co-owners are discussed at **[17.15]**.

Wilful default

[26.12] In addition to ordering a party to account for moneys or other property actually received, the court may, where the defendant is in legal or physical possession of the property, order a party to account also for receipts or payments which, but for his or her wilful default, he or she ought to have received. Such an order will apply to a mortgagee in possession as a matter of course: *White v City of London Brewery* (1889) 42 Ch D 237. In other cases it will be necessary for the plaintiff to prove at least one act of wilful default in order to obtain an accounting on this basis: *Sleight v Lawson*

---

9. Guardian in socage, bailiff and receiver: *The Earl of Devonshire's* case (1607) 11 Co Rep 89a, although it was extended by statute to co-owners: (1705) 4 & 5 Anne c 16 s 27 (repealed in New South Wales by s 5 of the Imperial Acts Application Act 1969, see **[17.15]**).
10. A hearing to determine whether there was a relationship of accounting in the first place; then the taking of accounts before court appointed auditors; and, finally, an action in debt to recover the balance, if any, shown to be owed to the plaintiff (CHS Fifoot, *History and Sources of the Common Law*, London, 1949, pp 268–8; SFC Milsom, *Historical Foundations of the Common Law*, London, 1981).
11. *A-C v Dublin Corp* (1827) 1 Bli NS PC 312 at 337; 4 ER 888 at 898, per Lord Redesdale.
12. MG&L, para [2505].
13. Part 49 (Equity) and Part 48 (other divisions).

(1857) 3 K & J 292; 69 ER 1119; and this may be ordered where such wilful breaches are revealed during the course of a trial, in which case wilful default may be added as an amendment to the pleadings: *Re Youngs* (1885) 30 Ch D 421; although in an action for active breaches of trust relief can only be granted in respect of breaches alleged in the pleadings and established at the trial: *Re Wrightson* [1908] 1 Ch 789.

Settled accounts

[26.13] A plea of settled accounts may be raised as a defence to a suit for account in equity where there are mutual accounts, in the sense that there are debts on both sides, and the parties have agreed to strike a balance, and that balance represents the final balance of all their transactions: *Anglo-American Asphalt Co v Crowley Russell & Co* [1945] 2 All ER 324 at 331, per Romer J, even though that final balance might remain unpaid.[14] Such an agreement need not be in writing, although there will be obvious evidentiary problems if it is not. Settled accounts in equity should be distinguished from an account stated at common law, although there are many points of similarity between the two. Account stated is usually a cause of action used to recover the balance struck, rather than a defence. It can be used as a defence but, unlike its equitable counterpart, requires then that the balance be paid. Also, again unlike settled accounts, an account stated cannot be re-opened by the court on the ground that it was brought about by fraud.[15]

26–5 Delivery-up and Cancellation of Documents

[26.14] Where a document is void for actual fraud or voidable for constructive fraud, such as the exercise of undue influence, or unconscionable conduct inducing a contract, equity will order its delivery-up for cancellation: *Duncan v Worrall* (1822) 10 Price 31; 147 ER 232; *Hoare v Bremridge* (1872) 8 Ch App 22, to remove the risk of further mischief. Where, however, a document is void at law, or the invalidity appears on its face, delivery-up will not be ordered: *Gray v Mathias* (1800) 5 Ves 286; 31 ER 591; nor will it be ordered if the document is only partially void, that is, if it is only void as against creditors: *Ideal Bedding Co Ltd v Holland* [1907] 2 Ch 157.

[26.15] The right to delivery-up may be lost through laches and acquiescence, or where a plaintiff comes to equity with unclean hands: *St John v St John* (1805) 11 Ves 526; 32 ER 1192, or where the plaintiff is unwilling to do equity, as in *Lodge v National Union Investment Co* [1907] 1 Ch 300 where a borrower gave certain securities to the lender under a moneylending contract rendered unenforceable for breaching the provisions of the Act governing such contracts,[16] and sought delivery-up and cancellation of the securities. The court refused to order delivery-up without repayment of the moneys then outstanding on the contract. This case is slender authority as the plaintiff could have achieved the same result by seeking a declaration that the contract was unenforceable without being required to do equity, as another did in similar

---

14. MG&L, para [2507].
15. MG&L, paras [2508]–[2509].
16. Money Lenders Act 1902 (UK), s 2. (Note: This may not apply to more recent moneylending legislation.)

circumstances in *Chapman v Michaelson* [1909] 1 Ch 238. In *Kasumu v Baba-Egbe* [1956] AC 539, the Privy Council suggested that the court could not impose such terms where a contract was rendered unenforceable, and not void, as to do so would be to enforce the contract by another means. Although it seems odd to say that a contract may be indirectly enforced if it is void but not if it is merely unenforceable.[17] Delivery-up is also a very useful remedy in the area of industrial and intellectual property.[18] Under the Copyright Act 1968 (Cth), s 116 the owner of the copyright is deemed to be the owner of any infringing copy or plate from the time it was made, thus giving the owner of the copyright access to the actions of detinue and conversion to enforce rights against that material, although the courts also assume a jurisdiction to order delivery-up in such cases: *Lady Anne Tennant v Associated Newspapers* [1979] FSR 298.

26–6 Appointment of Receivers and Managers

[26.16] A receiver is someone appointed by the court, or outside the court pursuant to some express power created by a mortgage or other security, to take possession of or recover the property of another, usually on behalf of a creditor or beneficiary of that other party. Strictly speaking, a receiver is simply someone who receives the income, gets in the debts and other moneys due and pays the outgoings ascertained at the time of his or her appointment on the property or undertaking subject to the receivership. A receiver does not manage the property or undertaking in the sense that it is not the receiver's job to maintain it as a going concern, unless he or she is also appointed as a manager. If it were necessary to continue a business for the purpose of selling it as a going concern, a manager would have to be appointed, or a receiver and manager as they are generally called: *Re Manchester & Milford Railway Co* (1880) 14 Ch 645 at 653, per Jessel MR. The jurisdiction to appoint a receiver is one of the oldest remedies in Chancery: *Hopkins v Worcester & Birmingham Canal Co* (1868) LR 6 Eq 437 at 447, per Giffard V-C. The present jurisdiction to appoint a receiver in New South Wales rests upon the Supreme Court Act 1970, s 67 which provides that the court may, 'at any stage of the proceedings, on terms, appoint a receiver by interlocutory order in any case in which it appears to the Court to be just and convenient so to do'.[19] The jurisdiction to appoint a manager is not as ancient as that of receivers,[20] and the manager's commission is not as limited as that of a receiver, although normally the same person will be appointed as both.[21] The manager's role is essentially to conduct the business for a short time for the purpose of selling it as a going concern, or to wind it up; it is not the court's function to assume the management of a business or undertaking except for those purposes: *Gardner v London Chatham and Dover Railway* (1867) 2 Ch App 201 at 212, per Cairns LJ. The function of a court appointed receiver and manager is different in this sense from that of a privately appointed receiver. The latter may, and usually will, attempt to restore the fortunes of the business while the court appointed receiver will merely be concerned with preserving the profitability of the assets for those who will ultimately take them: *Duffy v*

---

17. MG&L, para [2709].
18. See MG&L, para [2710].
19. See also Judicature Act 1925 (UK) s 45(1) which is in similar terms.
20. *Re Newdigate Colliery Ltd* [1912] 1 Ch 468.
21. *Re Manchester & Milford Railway Co* (1880) 14 Ch D 645 at 653.

Super Centre Development Corp Ltd [1967] 1 NSWR 382 at 383–4, per Street J. Ordinarily an interested party will not be appointed as receiver: *Re Lloyd* (1879) 12 Ch D 447, however, an exception will be made to this rule where the parties consent or where it is in the best interests of the parties that someone connected with the business, such as a partner who is solvent and not guilty of improper behaviour, be appointed: *Collins v Barker* [1893] 1 Ch 578. A better approach may be that taken in *Lamerand v Lamerand (No 1)* [1962] NSWR 246 where a disinterested party was appointed as receiver and given leave to employ one of the partners in the management of the business. In *Boyle v Bettws Llantwit Colliery Co* (1876) 2 Ch D 726, the unpaid vendors of the colliery were appointed receivers as they were 'really the owners of the colliery' and were prepared to inject funds into the business.

[26.17] Apart from the appointment of a receiver to enforce an equitable mortgage or charge, the principal ground upon which a receiver will be appointed is the protection and preservation of property for the benefit of those who are, or who at the conclusion of litigation will be held to be, beneficially interested in it. In the case of a partnership, a receiver will be appointed where the partners cannot agree on the terms of dissolution, or where a partner has become insane, or been declared bankrupt: *Re Wilson* (1936) 9 ABC 192. The court may refuse to appoint a receiver where it is claimed that the partnership is not at an end, where the appointment of a receiver could destroy the business: *Tate v Barry* (1928) 28 SR (NSW) 380. It has been argued, notwithstanding that view, that the court should reserve the right to appoint a receiver in such circumstances, pending resolution of the dispute between the partners.[22] A receiver will be appointed at the suit of an equitable mortgagee or chargee upon default, although usually the creditor will be entitled to appoint a receiver out of court as most company securities include such a provision. Receivers have also been appointed of the assets and undertaking of a company at the suit of a debenture holder: *Moss Steamship Co v Whinney* [1912] AC 254; to resolve a dispute between shareholders: *Duffy v Super Centre Development Corp Ltd* [1967] 1 NSWR 382; in cases involving deceased estates and the property of other trusts where the trustee's insolvency[23] or misconduct,[24] has justified removal of the assets from his control; and of property, usually a business, which is the subject of a suit for specific performance: *Gibbs v David* (1875) LR 20 Eq 373; as well as to manage assets subject to litigation pending in a foreign court: *Transatlantic Co v Pietroni* (1860) Johns 604; 70 ER 561. Receivers have also been appointed at the suit of unsecured creditors in aid of a *Mareva* injunction to prevent dissipation of assets to frustrate the plaintiffs: *Ballabil Holdings Pty Ltd v Hospital Products Ltd* (1985) 1 NSWLR 155. The categories are not closed and, in view of the wording of the Supreme Court Act 1970 (NSW), s 67 and its equivalent in other jurisdictions, this remedy may be available whenever a case can be made out that the appointment of a receiver is 'just and convenient', bearing in mind the general ground cited at the head of this paragraph.

[26.18] A receiver appointed by the court is an officer of the court and interference in the conduct of the receivership without leave of the court will constitute a contempt: *Angel v Smith* (1804) 9 Ves 335; 32 ER 632. However, proceedings for contempt must be brought by a party to the action in which the receiver was appointed, rather than the receiver: *CAC v Smithson* [1984] 3 NSWLR 547. A receiver is neither an agent of any of the parties nor a trustee. A reciever will only be responsible to the

---

22. MG&L, para [2812].
23. *Smith v Smith* (1836) 2 Y & C Ex 353; 160 ER 433.
24. *Alliance Bank (Ltd) v Irving* (1865) 4 SCR (NSW) Eq 17.

court for his or her receivership: *Corp of Bacup v Smith* (1890) 44 Ch D 395. The receiver has possession of, but not property in the assets subject to the receivership: *Bolton v Darling Downs Building Society* [1935] St R Qd 37, and, if he or she enters into any contracts does so in his or her own name as principal: *Moss Steamship Co Ltd v Whinney* [1912] AC 254. On the same authority, a receiver appointed by the court acquires no rights of action and must seek leave of the court to bring an action in the name of the party in whose name the action must be brought. While neither an agent nor a trustee, a receiver appointed by the court is under duties of a fiduciary nature in carrying out his or her functions and may not profit from this office, beyond the remuneration allowed by the court: *Watkins v Lestrange* (1863) 2 SCR (NSW) Eq 85.

[26.19] The position of a receiver appointed out of court is quite different from that of one appointed by the court. The powers and duties of a receiver appointed out of court will depend, largely, upon the terms of the instrument under which the reciever is appointed, especially the security entitling the creditor concerned to appoint a receiver. A receiver appointed out of court is not an officer of the court and it will not be contempt to interfere in such a receivership, although any such interference may be restrained by injunction. A receiver appointed out of court acts as the agent of the debtor or mortgagor, and not the creditor or mortgagee, so that the acts of the receiver are those of the mortgagor, even though the receiver's primary concern will be to protect the interests of the party who appointed him or her: *Re B Johnson & Co (Builders) Pty Ltd* [1955] Ch 634. As an agent, a receiver appointed out of court incurs no personal liability for acts properly done by him or her as receiver: *Owen & Co v Cronk* [1895] 1 QB 265. The receiver's agency cannot be revoked by the mortgagor, although, if the mortgagor is a corporation, the receivership will be terminated by the making of a winding-up order against the company and the appointment of a liquidator: *Gosling v Gaskell* [1897] AC 573. A receiver appointed out of court is also not a fiduciary. Provided he or she is not guilty of fraud or *mala fides* a receiver who acts within the scope of the powers conferred by the receivership will not be liable for any breach of duty: *Re B Johnson & Co.* The obligations imposed on such a receiver have been said to be no more onerous than those incumbent upon a mortgagee exercising a power of sale.[25] Unlike a liquidator, a receiver appointed out of court does not entirely supplant the organs of a company over whose assets he or she has been appointed receiver. The receiver's powers of receivership and management oust those of the board and no acts on the part of the board or the company in general meeting which are inconsistent with the receivership will be allowed. Those organs of the company are still free to act in matters which do not affect the receiver and may even prosecute a claim which the receiver refuses to pursue, provided the directors offer adequate indemnity for any costs incurred: *Newhart Developments Ltd v Co-operative Commercial Bank Ltd* [1978] 1 QB 814. Situations in which there is much scope for independent action on the part of directors of a company in receivership will be rare. Usually the receiver will be given control over all the assets of the company. The directors could not employ company funds for any action without the consent of the receiver. Often receivers will be appointed pursuant to a floating charge. Invariably such charges will include a provision that upon default the charge will crystallise and the chargee will be entitled to appoint a receiver. Usually the provision dealing with crystallisation will also provide that crystallisation upon default effects an equitable assignment of the assets subject to the charge, usually all the assets and undertaking of the company both present and future: *Ferrier v Bottomer* (1972) 126 CLR 597.

---

25. MG&L, para [2847].

Appointment of receivers under the Corporations Law

[26.20] The power to appoint a receiver of the assets of a corporation is the same power to appoint receivers generally, that is, in New South Wales, the Supreme Court Act (NSW), s 67. The Corporations Law, by ss 416–434, provides a regime, including wide powers conferred by s 420, under which the receiver can operate. A further source of power to appoint a receiver is contained in the Corporations Law, s 1323, to protect the interests of persons and preserve the property of corporations where an investigation, prosecution or civil proceedings is being conducted into or brought against a person, including a corporation, and the court considers it necessary and desirable to appoint a receiver. There is also power, under the Corporations Law, s 260(2)(h), to appoint a receiver of a company as a remedy for oppression, although receivership is generally considered to be inappropriate in such cases: *Re Enterprise Gold Mines NL* (1991) 3 ACSR 531.